SOCIOLOGY
AND HISTORY

Werner J. Cahnman   Alvin Boskoff   EDITORS

SOCIOLOGY AND HISTORY

Theory

and

Research

The Free Press, New York

Collier-Macmillan Limited, London

Fp

To our teachers

Preface

THE READER may want to know how this book came about. Apart from being a book, it is the document of a movement. Its origins date back to 1954, when the American Sociological Society (not yet Association) assembled for its Forty-ninth Annual Meeting on the Urbana campus of the University of Illinois, under the Presidency of Professor Florian Znaniecki. In the preceding weeks, Werner Cahnman had exchanged views with the late Professor R. Richard Wohl, but because Wohl could not be present at Urbana, and also because he expressed the opinion that "the desire to use historical method in sociological investigation is a rather lonely and isolated enthusiasm," Cahnman decided to take the initiative in inviting a number of colleagues to meet with him during the convention for the purpose of discussing the creation of a "Committee for the Sociological Study of Historical Documents." The most encouraging reply came from Professor Howard Becker, of the University of Wisconsin, who wrote that he would try to change his schedule so that he could be present at the proposed meeting.

Howard Becker was indeed present, and so were Robert Bierstedt, Howard Jensen, Nicholas S. Timasheff, and Adolph S. Tomars. In addition, if memory serves, Reinhard Bendix and William Kolb dropped in for a short time. Florian Znaniecki wrote that he would very much like to attend so challenging a meeting as this one, but that he was prevented from doing so by his duties as President.

Others, like Milton Albrecht, Paul H. Furfey, Feliks Gross, Rudolf Heberle, Everett C. Hughes, Bela Kovrig, Marion J. Levy, Jr., Clement C. Mihanovich, Rudolph E. Morris, Edgar T. Thompson, Kurt H. Wolff, and John Zadrozny, who could not be present, expressed their interest in various ways; still others, among them Stanley Bigman, Alvin Boskoff, Sigmund Diamond, E. K. Francis, Ruby J. R. Kennedy, Ernest Manheim, and Robert A. Nisbet joined later. All in all, about 80 colleagues (sociologists) associated themselves with the Committee. Howard Becker became the chairman, Werner J. Cahnman the acting chairman. In the following year (1955), at another luncheon meeting in Washington, D.C., it was decided formally to ask the American Sociological Society to organize sessions on "Sociology and History" at future Annual Meetings. The petition was granted in the Presidency of Herbert Blumer. The first session was organized at Detroit (1956), with Professors Robert Bierstedt and Sylvia L. Thrupp as speakers, and Professor Rupert B. Vance as discussant. Subsequent sessions were organized at Washington, D.C. (1957), Seattle (1958), Chicago (1959), New York (1960), and Los Angeles (1963). They were chaired by Professor Ernest Manheim, Werner J. Cahnman, Robert A. Nisbet, Robert K. Merton, and S. D. Clark, respectively. The gap in the years 1961 and 1962 reflects the crisis brought about by the unexpected death of Professor Howard Becker in the summer of 1960.

By 1959, Cahnman had discussed with Professor Becker and a number of friends the desirability of constructing a book which would document the historically oriented work which sociologists had been doing, and negotiations to that end were initiated with The Free Press. Professors Everett C. Hughes and Robert A. Nisbet were especially helpful at that stage. A little later, in 1960, Professor Alvin Boskoff, who had previously edited a symposium in collaboration with the late Professor Becker, was designated as co-editor.

Many problems arose as the work proceeded in earnest. Whatever they were, the editors have worked together in developing as good a book as they were able to. As is generally true in scholarly cooperation, this was not always easy. We belong to different backgrounds, different generations, different scholarly traditions. Our association was chosen and freely entered into with full awareness of these differences, but also in the conviction that this would insure the broadest possible coverage and the inclusion of a wide variety of viewpoints. Every scholar must strive for objectivity in the face of his subjective inclinations, and the system of checks and balances which is inherent in cooperative endeavor would therefore seem desirable even if it might inhibit the expression of the more pronounced opinions of a given author or editor. A more secure anchorage and the prospect of a wider appeal are gained thereby, and these must compensate for the liveliness which may be lost.

At any rate, we want to assure our readers that we have worked together as smoothly as could have been expected and that we have learned a great deal from the give and take in which we were engaged. We accept full and equal responsibility for the selection of the participating authors and the pieces which are included in the anthology. Three sections of the book which are not signed individually are the result of our common effort. Some differences, however, ought to be noted. The linkage texts to Parts One and Two were drafted by Cahnman and, with some alterations, were accepted by Boskoff. The introductory and concluding chapters were drafted by Boskoff and enlarged by Cahnman. These chapters were reworked several times before they were considered adequate. Indeed, the last chapter worried us particularly because lack of space did not permit the construction of a formal bibliography, and consequently this chapter had to serve as a substitute. Hopefully the concluding chapter (together with authors and works quoted elsewhere in the book) should enable scholars to familiarize themselves with the range of literature which ought to be considered in any future work to be undertaken along the lines indicated in our book. Furthermore, we have organized the index in such a way as to facilitate quick and easy reference.

The historical character of a work can be defined in a variety of ways. We did not attempt to be overly selective in this regard. We have quoted chiefly works of a more or less historical character written by sociologists and those works written by others which appeared to have sociological relevance. By and large, we have restricted ourselves to works written in the English language or translated into English, but we have added those works in other languages which have come to our knowledge and which in our opinion constitute the indispensable minimum in reaching for a broadly based scholarship. It would be gratifying to learn that we have misjudged the readiness of American scholars to go to foreign sources beyond this minimum, at least in one of the west-European languages. This would be testimony to the emergence of a humanistic sociology.

One thing is certain, however. This book, which sails in largely uncharted seas, could not have been written without the generous encouragement the editors received from a great many friends and colleagues. We cannot mention all those who sustained us with their good wishes. Among those who went farther than that, we must first of all mention men who are no longer with us, especially Professors Howard Becker, Paul Honigsheim, and Bela Kovrig. In addition, we are most obliged for valuable advice and assistance to our colleagues Robert A. Nisbet, Robert K. Merton, Everett C. Hughes, Sigmund Diamond, Norman Birnbaum, Alex Inkeles, Joseph Maier, Kurt H. Wolff, Harry Bash, Adolph Tomars, Hellmuth Plessner, and Alessandro Pizzorno. Linda Handler, a student at Rutgers University, has helped with compiling the index and other work of a technical nature. Finally, our wives, Gisella L. Cahnman and Priscilla Boskoff, have shown unbelievable patience while we worked many hours late at night and on week ends. We hope they feel that their sacrifice was worth while.

We dedicate this book to our teachers because we realize that we could not have composed it without the guidance they have given us in former years. We have in mind especially Professor Otto von Zwiedineck-Suedenhorst, the successor of Max Weber at the University of Munich, whose thinking was derived in equal parts from the historical and the marginal utility schools in economics; Professor Jacob Strieder, the diligent historian of early capitalistic development; Professor Everett C. Hughes, the most Parkian among the students of the late Professor Robert E. Park at the University of Chicago; Professor Herbert Blumer, the leading theoretician in the field of collective behavior and social movements; Professor Robert K. Merton, who combines superior structural-functional theorizing with a sense of the historical quality of social phenomena; and Professor Rupert B. Vance, the knowledgeable interpreter of the most historical region in America, the American South. We could wish nothing better for ourselves than to have continued in the ways which they have taught us.

WERNER J. CAHNMAN
ALVIN BOSKOFF

Contributors

E. DIGBY BALTZELL is Professor of Sociology at the University of Pennsylvania. His major interests have been in social stratification and industrial sociology. His major work, *Philadelphia Gentlemen,* has recently been reissued as a paperback.

ROBERT N. BELLAH is Associate Professor of Sociology and Regional Studies, and a former Research Associate in the Center for Middle Eastern Studies at Harvard University. He is a specialist on Far Eastern and Middle Eastern societies and the author of *Tokugawa Religion,* as well as of various articles in sociological journals.

JOSEPH BEN-DAVID is a member of the Department of Sociology at the Hebrew University in Jerusalem. He is the author of *Agricultural Planning and Village Community in Israel* and of several articles on the sociology of professions and of science.

REINHARD BENDIX, Professor of Sociology at the University of California, Berkeley, is the author of many works, including *Max Weber: An Intellectual Portrait; Work and Authority in Industry; Class, Status, and Power* (with S. M. Lipset); and *Social Mobility in Industrial Society* (with S. M. Lipset).

LEE BENSON is Professor of History at the University of Pennsylvania, with a predominant interest in social factors connected with nineteenth-century politics in the United States. He is the author of *Turner and Beard; The Concept of Jacksonian Democracy;* and *Merchants, Farmers, and Railroads.*

NORMAN BIRNBAUM is a Fellow of Nuffield College, Oxford University, England. He has written widely on the sociology of knowledge and religion; one of his recent publications is "The Sociological Study of Ideology, 1940–1960," in *Current Sociology.* Vol. 9, No. 2, 1960.

MARC BLOCH, a student of Henri Pirenne, was Professor of Economic History at the Sorbonne, Paris. An outstanding scholar of medieval history, he was the author of *La société féodale; Les caractères originaux de l'histoire rurale française; La France sous les derniers capétiens 1223–1328; Les rois thaumaturges; Apologie pour l'histoire et métier d'historien* (posthumous); and other works. Bloch was a member of the French resistance in World War II. He was shot by the Nazis on June 16, 1944.

KENNETH E. BOCK is Associate Professor of Sociology at the University of California, Berkeley. He is the author of *The Acceptance of Histories* and various articles on the relation among history, sociology, and social change.

ALVIN BOSKOFF is Professor of Sociology at Emory University. His concentration on the relations between sociology and history derives from particular interest in the development of sociological theory, the urban community, and processes of social change. He is the author of *Modern Sociological Theory* (with Howard Becker); *The Sociology of Urban Regions;* and *Voting Patterns in a Local Election* (with Harmon Zeigler).

HAROLD BOWEN is a former Reader in Near Eastern History at the University of London. His major book is *The Life and Times of Ali ibn Isa.*

WERNER J. CAHNMAN is Associate Professor of Sociology at the Newark College of Arts and Sciences, Rutgers University, and member of the faculty at the New School for Social Research. Trained in economics and economic history as well as in sociology, he is the author and co-author of *How Cities Grew* (with Jean Comhaire), *Intermarriage and Jewish Life,* and numerous scholarly papers on race and intercultural relations and sociological theory.

STEPHEN C. CAPPANNARI, an anthropologist, is Chairman, Division of Human Behavior, School of Medicine, Vanderbilt University. He is a specialist in the field of culture and personality. Singly and jointly with Leonard W. Moss, he has published numerous papers on the culture and behavior patterns of southern Italian peasants.

AMÉRICO CASTRO is Professor Emeritus of Spanish at Princeton University. He is the author of *El Pensamiento de Cervantes; España en su Historia (The Structure of Spanish History); La Realidad Historica de España; De la Edad Conflictiva: El Drama de la Honra en España y en su Literatura,* and other books on the history of Spanish thought.

TUNG-TSU CH'U. Born in the province of Hunnan, China, and educated at Yenching University, he is Associate Professor of Chinese History at the University of British Columbia and Research Fellow at the East Asian Research Center, Harvard University. He is the author of *Chinese Feudal Society* (in Chinese); *Chinese Law and Chinese Society* (in Chinese); *Law and Society in Traditional China,* and *Local Government in China Under the Ch'ing.*

ROBERT V. DANIELS is Professor of History at the University of Vermont. His primary interest in Soviet history is reflected in such works as *The Nature of Communism; A Documentary History of Communism;* and *The Conscience of the Revolution: Communist Opposition in Soviet Russia.*

SIGMUND DIAMOND is Associate Professor of Historical Sociology at Columbia University. His published works include *The Reputation of the American Businessman; The Nation Transformed; A Casual View of America: The Home Letters of Salomon de Rothschild 1859–1861*, and various scholarly papers on aspects of social organization in seventeenth- and eighteenth-century North America.

WALTER FIREY is Professor of Sociology at the University of Texas and a specialist in human ecology and regional planning. In addition to many articles on ecology and land-use planning, his published works include *Land Use in Central Boston* and *Man, Mind, and Land*.

HAMILTON A. R. GIBB is Professor of Arabic and Director of the Center for Middle Eastern Studies at Harvard University. He is the author of *Islamic Society and the West; Modern Trends in Islam; Mohammedanism: An Historical Survey;* and *Studies on the Civilization of Islam*.

HARLAN W. GILMORE was Professor of Sociology at Tulane University. His interest in urban ecology and demography was reflected in numerous papers, in *The Beggar,* and in *Transportation and the Growth of Cities*.

RUDOLF HEBERLE is Professor Emeritus of Sociology at Louisiana State University, with special interests in demography, social theory, and political sociology. He is the author of *From Democracy to Nazism; Social Movements;* and many scholarly articles.

SERGE HUGHES is Associate Professor of Romance Languages at Hunter College, New York, and an expert on the writings of Benedetto Croce. He is the author of *The Marxist-Liberal Web in Italy, 1896–1925*.

NORMAN JACOBS is Professor of Sociology at the University of Illinois and the author of *The Origins of Modern Capitalism in Eastern Asia* and other works on social and economic aspects of East Asia.

JOSEPH MAIER is Professor and Chairman of the Department of Sociology and Anthropology at the Newark College of Arts and Sciences, Rutgers University. He is the author of *Sociology: The Science of Society* (with Jay Rumney) and *On Hegel's Critique of Kant*.

ERNEST MANHEIM is Professor of Sociology at the University of Kansas City and author of many articles on public opinion and sociological theory.

ROBERT M. MARSH is Professor of Sociology at Duke University. He is the author of *The Mandarins* and several papers on stratification in medieval China.

WILLIAM MILLER is a leading historian of the American businessman. His major works include *The Age of Enterprise* (with Thomas Cochran) and *Men in Business*.

HERBERT MOLLER is Professor of History at Boston University. His analysis of troubadour poetry is found in various scholarly papers, especially in "The Meaning of Courtly Love," *Journal of American Folklore* (1960).

WILBERT E. MOORE is Research Sociologist at the Russell Sage Foundation. He is interested in the theory of social change and is the author of many books on industrial sociology, including *Industrial Relations and the Social Order; Labor Commitment and Social Change;* and *The Conduct of the Corporation.*

LEONARD W. MOSS is Chairman, Department of Sociology and Anthropology, Wayne State University. He is a specialist on social organization and cultural change in peasant societies. Singly, and jointly with Stephen C. Cappannari, he has published numerous research papers on the culture and folklore of southern Italy.

ROBERT A. NISBET is Professor of Sociology and Dean, University of California, Riverside. His works include *The Quest for Community; Contemporary Social Problems* (with Robert K. Merton); and numerous scholarly papers.

THOMAS F. O'DEA is Professor of Comparative Religion at Columbia University. He is the author of *The Mormons* and *The American Catholic Dilemma.*

WILLIAM PETERSEN is Professor of Sociology at the University of California, Berkeley, and a specialist in demography. He is the author of *Planned Migration* and *Population* and editor of *American Social Patterns and Social Controversy.*

BRYCE RYAN is Professor and Chairman, Department of Sociology, University of Miami. He is the author of *Caste in Modern Ceylon* and various articles on rural communities and social change.

SYLVIA L. THRUPP is a historian who has specialized in the study of medieval English trade. She is widely known for her *The Merchant Class of Medieval London.* She is currently Editor of the pioneering periodical for social historians and historically oriented sociologists, *Comparative Studies in Society and History.*

ADOLPH S. TOMARS is Professor of Sociology at City College, New York. He is the author of *The Sociology of Art, The Performing Arts in New York, 1800–1915,* and papers on methodological issues in contemporary sociology.

JOSHUA TRACHTENBERG was both a rabbi and a scholar in the field of Jewish history. His works include *Consider the Years; Jewish Magic and Superstition;* and the recently reprinted *The Devil and the Jews.*

RUPERT B. VANCE is Kenan Professor of Sociology at the University of North Carolina, and has been principally concerned with population dynamics and regional studies. His major works include *Human Factors in Cotton Culture; Human Geography of the South; All These People;* and *The Urban South* (with N. J. Demerath). He is a former president of the American Sociological Association.

IMMANUEL WALLERSTEIN is Associate Professor of Sociology at Columbia University and a specialist on societal and political development in modern Africa. He is the author of *Africa: The Politics of Independence* and *The Road to Independence: Guinea and the Ivory Coast.*

ROBIN M. WILLIAMS, JR., is Professor of Sociology at Cornell University and a former president of the American Sociological Association. His major works include *The Reduction of Intergroup Tensions; American Society; Schools in Transition;* and *Strangers Next Door.*

FLORIAN ZNANIECKI, a philosopher and sociologist, has taught at Columbia University and the University of Illinois and has served as president of the American Sociological Association. He is the author of *The Polish Peasant in Europe and America* (with W. I. Thomas); *Cultural Reality; Laws of Social Psychology; The Method of Sociology; Social Actions; Cultural Sciences; The Social Role of the Man of Knowledge;* and *Modern Nationalities.*

Contents

Werner J. Cahnman
and
Alvin Boskoff

SOCIOLOGY AND HISTORY: REUNION AND RAPPROCHEMENT

I

SOCIOLOGY AND HISTORY are different academic disciplines, unlike each other in origin and intention, but dealing with the same subject matter: human interaction. This makes them partners and competitors at the same time. From the recognition of this complex relationship arises the need to examine the actual or potential interdependence of sociology and history, while respecting the legitimate and distinguishing characteristics of each. We can ill afford the mordant humor that asserts: "Sociology is history with the hard work left out; history is sociology with the brains left out."[1]

There is, unfortunately, a grain of agonizing truth in this flippant epigram. Sociologists, all too often, have tended to generalize either on uncritically accepted evidence or on evidence diligently assembled, but restricted in time and place; while some historians have rested secure in their knowledge of unique configurations and sequences without benefit of comparison or of conscious conceptualization. Sociologists have not always avoided mistaking correlational links for adequate causes; and some historians have relied on dogmatically asserted intuitions where only the most cautious of inferences would have been in order.

It is not our intention, however, to compile and compare lists of sins of omission and commission on both sides.[2] Nor do we want to generalize too confidently about either history or sociology, because each field has developed with some freedom and with considerable divergence in techniques, subject matter, objectives, and perspectives among its practitioners. In history, for example, we may note the subtle lines between and among political, economic, social and art historians, the gulf between the chronicler and documentarian, the biographer, the moralist, and finally the historian who presents a "thesis" or expounds general explanatory principles, like Turner, Beard, or Toynbee.[3] The latter may even be said to employ a "sociological approach," although this is not the kind of sociological approach to history which we would advocate.

In sociology we have identifiable differences between social psychologists, who either deal with the microscopic level of social interaction or with the collective context of human behavior; specialists in social organization, who focus primarily on structure, that is, on the patterned relations between groups; and social ecologists and demographers, who specialize in the products of interaction on a mass or statistical level, with secondary concern for the cultural and psychological aspects of the processes by which regularities or trends are achieved. On the whole, however, one can say that the historian's interest is focused on sequences and concatenations of action and interaction, with the acting individual as the symbolic point of convergence. The sociologist, on the other hand, is concerned with the institutionalization and transformation of patterns of interaction, whereby society is visualized as consisting of individuals and the individual as the product of social forces.

A field of knowledge, then, is distinguished by its problems, not by the object of its study or by the methods which are employed in studying it; by the way questions are asked, not by the way solutions are found. All the social sciences, including history, study man in his association and confrontation with other men, and they pursue this objective by whatever set of methods is suitable for the purpose. These methods differ, however, according to whether one studies societies that are past and gone or societies in the midst of which we live and work. In the first case, we must rely on the mute testimony of art, artifact and written document. Accordingly, the critical faculty and trained imagination of the interpreter are needed to separate the wheat from the chaff and to grasp the meaning of events from their consequences. It should be added that trade, revenue, and vital statistics, election returns and census data are to be subsumed under "documents" and that they are historical in character: they fix in print irretrievable moments and processes. As data collection becomes more refined and the data themselves more readily available, future historians will have to join sociologists in the judicial use of quantitative data, along with other evidence.[4]

There are advantages in studying past events—the perspective is clearer and once virulent attitudes are attenuated, if not entirely absent. But it is also evident that the study of completed events is forever limited to recorded facts, which are likely to be a small remnant of a multitude of relevant aspects of these events. The student of contemporary society, on the other hand, suffers from an embarrassment of wealth; he must be able to select from a staggering mass of available facts those portions that bear directly on a specific problem. In other words, the sociologist creates his own sources, in line with hypotheses which he has formulated. He is a participant observer of one situation, but not of another, he applies open-end interviewing to individuals who otherwise would have remained silent, or else he interviews categories of individuals according to pre-established schedules and with the help of sampling techniques; and he uses sophisticated statistical procedures, such as correlation, analysis of variance and covariance, factor analysis, scaling and sociometric techniques in determining the reliability, interrelations, and significant variations of the selected data. Surely, these advantages carry with them their pitfalls, especially if data are selected to fit a methodological device rather than the other way round. In that case, what is statistically significant may be of little relevance theoretically or materially. It remains nonetheless true that sociology promises to open new dimensions for the understanding of human conduct.

Moreover, if this is so, historical research cannot remain unaffected. The researcher of the future, whether he be a historian *proprement dit* or a professional sociologist, may isolate or hold constant specific factors in election returns or subject literary production to quantitative as well as qualitative analysis. Still, the difference between historians and sociologists would be not in the methods employed but in the kinds of questions asked. There would be no need for the sociologist to turn historian, if the historians asked the questions that are crucial to the sociologist.[5] All he would then have to do would be to use the historian's findings. But facts must yield meaningful patterns and the results will differ according to the way data are approached. Sociologists do approach them differently, although not necessarily contrary to the spirit of historical investigation. In other words, historians consistently seek to provide some implicit or explicit explanation for sequences of human events in terms of a unique concatenation of personality and circumstances.[6] This is what Febvre expresses with classic simplicity when he says that the historian's function is *"faire comprendre."*[7] But the logical step to the sociologist's objective is likewise simple and hardly revolutionary: if it is desirable and possible to attain some measure of understanding of specific events and related periods, it is also desirable and possible to discover the extent to which explanations applicable to one situation may be extended to comparable situations from other times and places. We believe, then, that the genuine differences between sociologists and historians stem not from logical or practical obstacles, but from legitimate but somewhat arbitrarily selected aims.

"Genuine differences" are emphasized because it is becoming increasingly apparent that at least some previously asserted distinctions have been belied in practice, while others seem to be differences in degree rather than in kind.

Let us briefly review some of these distinctions and differences.

1. *Description and Analysis.* The dichotomy between description and analysis is helpful neither to sociologists nor to historians. Indeed, these processes necessarily are reciprocal in practice.[8] For those who give prominence to analysis and explanation, responsible description, including statistical evidence, is an indispensable base. But the selection of facts for descriptive purposes always presupposes some criteria of relevance which, in turn, are grounded in an explanatory scheme. The historian who searches through personal documents, tax rolls, or cartularies, the sociologist who pores over census data or obtains attitude items through interviews—both operate with the notion that these orders of fact are useful in clarifying some substantive problem.

If analysis requires description, can description stop short of analysis? Two kinds of replies have been received from historians and from philosophers of history. One, represented by Collingwood, asserts that adequate description of what happened produces the explanation of why it happened.[9] Of course, adequate description is the crucial term; adequacy presumably refers to sufficient causes and is likely to depend on implied or explicit hypotheses. The other position is best stated by Pirenne[10] who makes three points that are eminently sensible to every practicing historian and sociologist. First, fully adequate facts are never available in either past or present. Second, to bridge factual gaps the investigator develops assumptions and hypotheses which are basically provisional or "working" analyses, whether recognized as such or not; they may be verified, modified, or entirely disproved. Third, since facts cannot speak for themselves, both historians and sociologists must select and systematize their data in order to communicate them to a professional or general public. This ordering, be it sequential-locational or logical-categorical in nature,[11] rests on implied or presumed relationships that are first, if ever so subtly, "imposed" on the facts before they can be derived from them. Responsible description, then, is incipient analysis; both must be complemented by trained imagination, leading to interpretation.

2. *The Unique and the General.* A presumed incompatibility between the unique and the general, between "idiographic" and "nomothetic" objectives, is a major obstacle to any discipline that seeks to extract meaning from its subject matter. Part of the difficulty, it appears, stems from a misunderstanding, or distrust, of scientific procedures and objectives. We are not licensed to treat fears, but we believe that the central misconceptions can be exposed. In the first place, uniqueness and generality are not features given in facts; they are analytical modes of appraising facts.[12] We may focus upon the uniqueness of facts by segregating them from other facts or by ignoring the points of similarity among such facts. Or we may choose to emphasize similarities in facts while ignoring the obvious but operationally irrelevant differences. The objective of the investigator determines the relative value of such analytic aspects. However, overemphasis on any one aspect leads to disaster. If the *differentia* among facts are neglected, overly simplified generalizations are developed which explain everything and therefore nothing; but if similarities in facts are totally neglected, their existence becomes immune from explanation, unless there is recourse to the unifying expediency of the "hero" in history.

Leading historians have hesitated to accept the practical complementarity of the unique and the general. Ranke warned against the imposition of general categories upon unique configurations, which, however, as he saw it, moved according to tendencies inherent in their own nature.[13] A social scientist, the anthropologist A. L. Kroeber, seconds Ranke, saying that "all recorded history is a series of objective unique events whose significance lies in their organization into distinctive patterns and not in ill-defined formulas or generalized denominators."[14] In this sense, that is, in line with the requirement of the maintenance and development of patterns within a configuration, uniqueness in events does not stand in the way of generalization. Yet, as Malin suggests, facts must be examined in as many ways as possible[15] and hence traits present in one configuration can be compared to those in another configuration, establishing similarities and dissimilarities, as is demonstrated, for instance, in the papers by Bloch, Diamond, Castro, and others in the present volume. Without such interplay between the general and the unique no explanation would be possible. In short, if some historians see no generalities in their data, it is because they do not look for them.[16] In that case, historically trained sociologists, along with better-informed historians, must step into the breach.

If historiography is not clearly idiographic, sociology is by no means unequivocally nomothetic. Such titles as Hughes' *French Canada in Transition* or Whyte's *Street Corner Society* show varying instances of the interpenetration of the unique, or particular, and the general, whether general concepts are brought to bear on the particular case or the particular case is made to serve as an instance of a generally observable process or interrelationship. However, as Lipset frankly admits, while most sociologists, contrary to historians, attempt a generalizing analysis, they frequently go no further than a particularizing analysis. In *Union Democracy,* the International Typographical Union is penetratingly analyzed as an entity in its own right, although the aim of the study is to contrast the I.T.U. with previously observed regularities in large organizations.[17] Obviously, a single case can only suggest the basis for a general rule, but it is hoped that related cases will be reported and that the accumulated instances will confirm, not a law, but a tendency or, as Max Weber would have put it, a probability.

3. *Freedom and Necessity.* The concept of probability mediates between the historian whose attention is focused on the fate of the individual actor and the sociologist whose interest is directed toward a general theory of action. At any given moment the actor finds himself confronted with a great many possibilities for action and the presumption is that he is free to make his choice. However, in explaining why a particular course of action was chosen among available alternatives, the historian refers to a number of determining factors, among which the background and personality of the actor as well as his assessment of the field of societal forces within which he acts are said to be of decisive import.

At this point, the sociologist adds two further considerations. One refers to the model of rational social action, as developed by Max Weber and elaborated by Talcott Parsons; the other to the concept of role. Max Weber asserts that freedom has nothing to do with arbitrariness because it rests on an assessment of the situation.[18] If the assessment takes into proper consideration all the elements inherent in the situation, the resulting action will be rational in the sense that the means selected will be conducive to achieving the desired end. This introduces no "rationalistic bias" because rational action serves as a model, or ideal type, of action, not as the reality image of action itself. Theoretically, of course, model and reality may coincide and, in that case, there is nothing further to explain. The actor's choice is then both free and thoroughly understandable. It is the deviations that have to be explained on the basis of the nonrational elements which enter into the situation. An even greater latitude is introduced by the role concept. For instance, each and every President of the United States is free to act according to his best judgment, but the conception which each has of his duties is guided by role specifications, that is, the kind of action which is called forth by the office of the Presidency. Here, freedom takes on the meaning of free interpretation, but with the understanding that such interpretation remains within bounds, at the penalty of impeachment.

None of the foregoing qualifications negates freedom. Men may act irrationally, that is traditionally, emotionally, or ignorantly, or they may act contrary to role expectations, but they do so at a price. Yet another aspect of the principle of probability follows from the very subject matter of sociology, namely, the element of societal constraint which is inherent in human interaction. For instance, crime, mental disorder, and suicide have a tendency to increase when normlessness overwhelms a society, although we may choose— even if we frequently do not—to remain honest, to preserve our sanity, and to stay alive. More significantly, customs and morals impose themselves upon the individual's actions in a stable society as does collective contagion in the case of sudden panic or widespread unrest. The individual may rebel against tradition or remain calm in the midst of disaster and general commotion, but this is not a frequent or likely occurrence; it does not represent typical behavior. Individual deviation is always present, but it is relatively insignificant in the observation of mass phenomena. Consequently, what can be interpreted as freedom for the individual carries the connotation of high probability for the collectivity or the group.

4. *Law and Causation.* In speaking about causation in history, we must recognize that we do not have before us isolated and unambiguously ascertainable causes which, in turn, lead to equally unambiguously ascertainable consequences. The history of humanity does not resemble a laboratory in which one undertakes test-tube experiments. Rather, historical situations are distinguished by the fact that mutually dependent chains of causation, which may either reinforce or counteract each other, lead to likewise interdependent reinforcing or counteracting chains of effects; and these, again, grow into new causes, leading to new effects, and so forth. The multitude of cause-and-effect relations can hardly be reduced to a single general principle, but the continually changing objects of observation can be described, compared, and evaluated. This means that we may have before us unity in variation: situa-

tions change over time, but if essential elements remain identifiable, the result may be that one situation, while not the exact equivalent of another, nevertheless contains an element of comparison which can serve as a guide in explanation. Within limits, comparison allows a causal interpretation to be corroborated or denied.

In an earlier stage of sociological inquiry, when sociology had not yet become clearly distinguishable from the philosophy of history, the quest for a single causal principle, applicable to all times and places, was believed to be possible of fulfilment. A critical reaction set in and, as a result, a number of historians and philosophers remain skeptical about the desirability of causal generalization in historical studies.[19] Others, their minds still inexorably fixed on the past, continue to use the term "sociological" for an approach to history which is presumed to maintain that human action is reducible to socio-economically determined motivations as an ultimate cause. Actually, universal causal theories of this kind have long been repudiated and the majority of sociologists seem to be aiming at matching a manageable variety of situations and social structures with a similar variety of appropriate causal theories. Generally speaking, this involves the judicious use of the comparative method[20] and the construction of historically relevant typologies.[21] In fact, it is only through a comparative approach that useful causal explanations can be achieved, since it is impossible to assess the validity and reliability of any causal interpretation that is based on a single sequence. Whether they consciously formulate it or not, historians can hardly take a different stand.

II

After having cleared away some of the conceptual and methodological obstacles that obscure the relations between sociology and history, we must now explain what we think of the sociologist's approach to history and make clear the principles upon which we have selected the papers for this volume.

To be sure, we have not entirely restricted ourselves to papers written by sociologists. Those historians who use sociological concepts and perspectives in describing and analyzing specific periods or problems are justifiably included herein because their careful attention to facts is matched by their ability to see them in a total context and to transcend even configurative thinking by calling to mind related phenomena in other periods or settings. This group includes Bloch, Gibb, Ch'u, Thrupp, Benson, Moller, and Castro. These are historians who are aware of such sociological concepts as social organization and disorganization, class and caste, social mobility, and public opinion. Others who emphasize the importance of ideas and personalities at the expense of conceptualization, significant as their contributions may be, would not be as relevant for our purposes.

Concerning sociologists, two major approaches, and their subdivisions, would seem to be available. One employs sociological concepts for the purpose of describing and analyzing actual historical situations and problems although, on the whole, on a higher level of generality than ought to be expected of historians. This approach supplements the work of the professional historian and involves considerable familiarity with firsthand as well as secondary sources. The interpretation of these sources has reference to the probable role of pertinent social and cultural structural variables, such as stratification, demographic composition, characteristics of audiences and publics, and so forth. Good illustrations of this approach may be found in the papers by Baltzell, Ben-David, Bendix, Birnbaum, Cahnman, Diamond, Heberle, Nisbet, Petersen, Ryan, Tomars, and Znaniecki.

In this kind of procedure, various levels of abstraction dovetail, as in the sequence Quebec-feudalism-transformation of planned societies (Diamond), or Ottoman Empire-millet system-secondary growth of kinship groups (Cahnman). Consequently, particularizing and generalizing analyses appear as functions of one another, with variable emphasis. One might also say that the analysis of *origin* and development appears here combined with the analysis of the *persistence* of patterns of behavior,[22] but with the static element removed. The rigid dichotomy of "development" and "persistence" is thus supplemented with a third perspective, and persistence is itself viewed as a phase of development, transformation as an aspect of continuity. That this is consonant with the best historical procedure there can be no doubt; in adopting it, sociology is enabled to complement the analysis of stable systems with the consideration of systems in the process of transformation.

The second approach, in contrast to the first, uses historical data for the purpose of illustrating and, possibly, testing the validity of sociological concepts, constructs and theories. Among works which emphasize illustration, Howard Becker's "culture case study" would be an example;[23] another would be the selection of patterns of facts which lend greater substance to existing sociological concepts and theories and even permit appropriate revisions in them. In this category belong the papers by Boskoff, Manheim, Miller, Vance, O'Dea, and Wallerstein. Midway between illustration and testing might be placed the attempts of some sociologists, such as Firey, Gilmore, Jacobs, Marsh, Moore and Williams, to confront general theories with crucial historical data in order to gauge the applicability of theories, or as a means of developing a modification of theories.

A radical variant of this approach is presented by Norman Jacobs.[24] Following Marc Bloch and Max Weber, Jacobs proposes to transform history into a science by ascertaining agreement, disagreement, and concomitant variation through the comparative method, and by selecting and arranging historical data "for demonstrating a meaningful and coherent sociological argument." Empirical time would thus be used as a relative scale, with "the arbitrary present" as a basic reference point. While we agree that the procedure stated by Jacobs is capable of yielding results in terms of establishing causal relationships by means of what Max Weber would have called "mental experiments," it must not be overlooked that Max Weber's line of reasoning is cut in half at this point. A "coherent argument" is not an end in itself, but serves the purpose of understanding concrete reality. The reality in question may be a unique locational-historical configuration, like "Japan," or a category of considerable universality, such as "capitalistic development," but it can hardly be treated as mere source material. Otherwise, theory becomes *"l'art pour l'art"*—an intellectual approach that does not permit further increments in understanding.

Generally, we believe that theories are tools, to be fashioned in answer to substantive problems and to be refashioned when they no longer serve. If they are made into ends, models are likely to be mistaken for entities ("reified") and the tool that should have been a servant turns out to be a master. The analysis by Moore and Williams of the *ante-bellum* society of the American South is conceived as a test case for structural-functional theory, but it is saturated with such a wealth of pertinent detail as to make both the persistence and the indeterminacy of the slavery system thoroughly comprehensible. In this case, both theoretical and historical interests are satisfied. However, though we agree with Neil J. Smelser that "any model must be put to the test in the light of the best available experimental, statistical and comparative data,"[25] we must face the fact that the cards are thereby stacked and that reality, instead of being the object of investigation, may be reduced to that which tests the model.

The question whether structural-functional theory offers a convenient key to historical understanding opens up an area of considerable complexity. If, with A. L. Kroeber,[26] we consider the essence of the historian's approach to be "the endeavor to achieve a conceptual integration of phenomena while preserving the integrity of the phenomena," the "test" conducted by Moore and Williams must be judged not only as a success in itself, but also as compatible with the requirements of historical understanding. But is it not possible that Kroeber rationalizes here the peculiar dilemma of the anthropologist? The functionalism of anthropologists, such as Radcliffe-Brown and Malinowski,[27] finds its justification in the fact that preliterate societies are bereft of records and hence are best studied synchronically. In this instance, the neglect of the diachronic approach is a virtue born of necessity. In historical societies, however, the element of change and development would seem to be indispensable, in addition to an outlook which preserves the integrity of phenomena.

On the diachronic level, some authors have doubted the capacity of structural-functional theory to deal adequately with problems of social change while others have replied in the affirmative.[28] We cannot enter here into an evaluation of this dispute except to say that both functionalism and historicism have arisen in reaction to "unilinear" theories of progress and evolution. Historicism stresses the interconnectedness of phenomena through time while functionalism stresses their interdependence in the here and now. To say that both approaches are theoretically compatible does not imply, however, that they are analytically interchangeable. Functionalism further differs from historicism in that it aspires to statements which are strictly scientific in character. Such statements are welcome; but to designate elements within a social structure as either functional, dysfunctional or functionally neutral in their consequences does not direct the search to the sources of change. It may help us to locate points of major and minor resistance to change, but it neither enables us to explain why certain decisions had to be taken in preference to others nor does it permit us to conclude that a social system could not have survived if other counsel had prevailed. For instance, as Goldthorpe points out, the element of "inevitability" in the development of social policies in England in the nineteenth century was hardly discernible when these policies were contested; it is lacking even in retrospect.[29] Surely, "there will always be an England"—but what a different England it could be![30]

At any rate, the social system, like other concepts, cannot "survive" because it does not exist. It is an auxiliary construct, not a reality in the sense in which an organism is a reality. If this simple truth is disregarded, the model of the social system, impressive as it is as a thought-structure, will not prevent those who use it from falling into the trap in which the Marxian and Spencerian systems were caught. Before one knows it, one imposes the preconceived correctness of a generalized theory upon subservient data and accepts as confirmation the predictable result that the outcome is identical with the input. Viewed in this light, even a work of diligent scholarship, such as Robert N. Bellah's analysis of Tokugawa religion, fails to be convincing because it proceeds in terms of "categories already given" and "is based on the assumption that the central value system of a society will tend to give primary emphasis to *one* dimension of social structure," in this case the political rather than the religio-cultural, integrative, or economic dimensions.[31] Means and ends are thus confounded: if facts are marshaled to confirm the one and only theoretical assumption, the researcher is prevented from developing those theoretical propositions which may be suited to explain the facts. Obviously these propositions, by dint of their historical relevance, do not easily lend themselves to the formulation of a highly generalized theory of social action. It cannot be gainsaid that the concept of social action is basic in sociology, but history as the realm of concreteness is replete with actions, not action, and hence requires theories, not theory.

Monistic thought-patterns extend in yet another direction. Where American sociology is indeed "historical"—in the sense of being time-and-space-bound in character—the fiction of generality is maintained, either intentionally or by implication. As an example, we may use the theory of concentric circles of city growth, as developed by the Chicago ecological school.[32] Essentially, this theory is a construct of residential patterns in a city in the plains, with natural and man-made obstacles, such as rivers, lakes, mountains, and transportation lanes removed, in analogy to J. H. von Thuenen's theory of production zones in an "isolated state"[33] or Alfred Weber's theory of the location of industries.[34] But in contrast to Thuenen's and Weber's constructs, which are "purely" theoretical, historical reality intrudes into the circle theory inasmuch as the growth of an "area in transition" around a central business district is typical of midwestern American railroad towns in the nineteenth and twentieth centuries. It is not repeated elsewhere to any marked degree, or, where it is, the phenomenon of an industrial nucleus of city growth, as in a railroad town, is likewise present. Many of the theoretical constructs of the Chicago school—"urbanism," "marginality," the "race relations cycle" and so forth—would have been similarly acceptable, *if* they had been cast in the form of historical or ideal-typical statements.

Between the Scylla of rigid generalization and the Charybdis of sheer empiricism a new sociology has steered its course. Especially in the last two decades, the increasingly sophisticated use of comparative materials and typological devices has channeled a considerable amount of effort into work which is both sociologically oriented and historically relevant. Those engaged in research of this sort agree with Parsons that ideal-type theory is "the most difficult level on which to develop a coherent generalized system," but they are likely to supplement that statement by saying that the development of such a "system" is not the purpose for which ideal type theory is intended.[35] Turning the argument around, they would rather assert that a generalized system does not lend itself as readily to historical analysis as does typology, whatever its use may be in another context. Indeed, the totality of social phenomena can be gathered by a single theoretical scheme only at the expense of their specific identities.[36]

On the other hand, one must be aware of the objections of those who view, with Croce, the construction of types and classes of fact as "abstractions which are certainly not the end of thought, since thought dissolves them when confronted with them, in order to penetrate to concrete, universal-individual reality."[37] Surely, the researcher's thought, in applying types and classes to factual situations, modifies and even dissolves them, but the resulting recognition of reality, nevertheless, rests on the classificatory scaffold which has been erected. Types are meant to be conceptual images, not descriptions of the events themselves. Actual life situations are of a mixed and conglomerate nature, but we stand to gain little by enumerating the bewildering multitude of phenomena which we encounter. If we want to achieve clarity we are constrained to select predominant traits and to train our sights on them.

To summarize, types are not ends in themselves; they guide investigation by focusing attention on significant clusters and concatenations of fact and serve as a means of evaluating factual evidence as variations from typological patterns. Comparison offers indispensable support because without the search for variations typology would cease to be a means to an end and become a dogmatic entity in its own right. If used as an auxiliary construct, typology mediates between the general and the unique, so much so that Max Weber regarded the formation of typological concepts as the major contribution of sociology to history.[38] Max Weber's "ideal types"—both the widely generalizable and the historically specific variety—explicitly exaggerated and simplified the cluster of variables under investigation and simultaneously established the type as a measure of empirical deviation. For instance, the charismatic type of authority conceptually excludes the traditional and legal-rational types, but this does not deny the appearance in actual fact of charismatic leadership in the midst of traditionally or legal-rationally oriented social systems.

Going somewhat beyond Weber, Howard Becker's "constructed types" of social systems in terms of their characteristic attitude toward change primarily attempt to be faithful to the complexities of reality by derivation from comparative "culture case studies." In addition, constructed types aim at subsuming the greatest possible number of single phenomena under a general denominator. Arthur Spiethoff, on the other hand, reduces widely generalizable types to "real types," that is empirically based *Gestalt* types. Theorist *and* historian, he requires type-formation for each problem in its actual setting. A type, he suggests, should be "as close as possible a representation of some historical reality."[39] Thus, as an economist, he analyzes "typical" stages of business cycles in a capitalistic system, but does not claim universal applicability for the resulting theory. His is a theory of the "middle range," not in terms of the level of conceptualization, as with Merton,[40] but in terms of periodization.

Combinations and modifications of all these approaches are in evidence in the work which we have reviewed for this volume. Obviously, the data and deliberations found here do not lend themselves to a set of propositions which would point the way toward the formulation of a single sociological theory of history. Moreover, it may be said that a theory which is "historical" in nature ought to be designed for the purposes of a particular study or derived from the circumstances surrounding a particular set of data. One example is provided by the theory of the demographic transition. This theory, which for some time has been held applicable to all societies in the process of industrialization, may indeed be more in the nature of an ideal-typical construction, actually applicable chiefly to English society between 1850 and 1945.[41] Other historically oriented sociological theories are involved in Howard Becker's principle of "normative reaction to normlessness," Karl Mannheim's conceptualization of "ideology" and "utopia," Robert K. Merton's treatment of "social structure and anomie."[42] As Christopher Becker puts it, "the success of Nazism showed [Howard Becker] that the movement from sacred to secular could be reversed." Mannheim's dichotomy was devised in order to point to "the emergence of the multiplicity of thought-styles" as an "aspect of the intellectual restlessness which characterizes our age." Merton's essays were informed by the realization that "contemporary American culture appears to approximate the polar type in which great emphasis upon certain success-goals occurs without equivalent emphasis upon institutional means."[43] In each case, the pressure of the problem is there first, the construction of the theory which serves to unlock its secrets comes afterwards.

The term "historical theory," as used in this context, refers to a theory which is designed to assist in the analysis of phenomena that are restricted to a localized situation or a period in history. This does not exclude intersocietal comparison or the application of the theory in question to a variety of situations or periods, provided that it is done flexibly. Nor does it prevent consideration of social change, as, for instance, in the case of "normative reaction to normlessness." What remains dubious, however, is whether a simple "general" theory can structure the pertinent data for all times and places; the attempt may result in the superimposition of theory upon reality. This happened with regard to the great paradigm of social theory, namely, classical economic theory.[44] Two historically oriented scholars had to come forward to set the case right: Henry Sumner Maine demonstrated that the propositions of classical economic theory were applicable to one type of society,[45] but not to another, while Max Weber attempted to save the same propositions by interpreting them ideal-typically, as models of "rational social action."[46] In addition, and astonishingly more akin to Maine and Spiethoff in this respect than to Weber, a scholar using the Parsonian approach, Marion J. Levy, Jr., has pointed out that in the nineteenth and twentieth centuries a historically unique situation "has given to the economic aspect of social life an importance and precedence rarely, if ever, evidenced in any previous society and has tended to obscure the importance of other variables."[47] This amounts to saying that the economic interpretation of history may have explanatory value for one particular society or period without thereby attaining universal validity.

We must rest our case at this point, leaving the remainder of the argument to the more intensive review of the literature and the selected studies included in this volume. It is our hope that this will provide some of the ways and means by which historians and sociologists may learn to cooperate with each other more fruitfully. There is a widespread feeling on both sides that such interchange is vitally needed and that a common path should be surveyed and cut through the thickets of scholarship. We are inclined to rely on historians themselves for suggestions as to what their contribution to the common enterprise should be.[48] The requirement for a historically oriented sociology, however, could well be described as a combination of "brains" and "hard work," with "brains" standing for conceptualization and "hard work" for a willingness to go to the sources. We are confident that the contributions to this volume indicate progress in this direction.

Notes

1. Donald G. MacRae, "Some Sociological Prospects," *Transactions of the Third World Congress of Sociology* (London: International Sociological Association, 1956), Vol. 8, 302.
2. There is a considerable literature pertaining to the interaction between historians and sociologists. Compare especially Patrick Gardiner, ed., *Theories of History* (New York: The Free Press of Glencoe, 1959), Part 2; Patrick Gardiner, *The Nature of Historical Explanation* (London: Oxford University Press, 1952); Hans Meyerhoff, ed., *The Philosophy of History in Our Time* (Garden City: Doubleday Anchor Books, 1959), Parts I, IV; Fritz Stern, ed., *The Varieties of History* (New York: Meridian Books, 1960), Part II; Quentin Gibson, *The Logic of Social Enquiry* (London: Routledge and Kegan Paul, 1960), chap. 15; Philip Bagby, *Culture and History* (London: Longmans Green, 1958); F. M. Powicke, *Modern Historians and the Study of History* (London: Odhams Press, 1955); Folke Dovring, *History as a Social Science* (The Hague: Nijhoff, 1960); Kenneth Bock, *The Acceptance of Histories* (Berkeley: University of California Press, 1956); Edward H. Carr, *What is History?* (London: Macmillan, 1961); Ben Halpern, "History, Sociology and Contemporary Area Studies," *American Journal of Sociology*, Vol. LXIII (July 1957), No. 1, 1–10; Sylvia L. Thrupp, "History and Sociology: New Opportunities for Cooperation," *American Journal of Sociology*, Vol. LXIII (July 1957), No. 1, 11–16; Kurt H. Wolff, "Sociology and History: Theory and Practice," *American Journal of Sociology*, Vol. LXV (July 1959), No. 1, 32–38; Arthur Schlesinger, Jr., "The Humanist Looks at Empirical Social Research," *American Sociological Review*, Vol. 27 (Dec. 1962), No. 6, 768–771; Philip M. Hauser and George C. Homans, "Schlesinger on Humanism and Empirical Social Research," *American Sociological Review*, Vol. 28 (Feb. 1963), No. 1, 97–100.
3. Frederick J. Turner, *The Significance of the Frontier in American History* (Madison: State Historical Society of Wisconsin, 1894), and subsequent writings by the same author; Charles A. Beard, *An Economic Interpretation of the Constitution of the United States* (New York: Macmillan, 1940); Arnold J. Toynbee, *A Study of History*, 12 vols. (London: Oxford University Press, 1945–1961). For a recent appraisal, compare: Lee Benson, *Turner and Beard: American Historical Writing Reconsidered* (New York: The Free Press, 1960).
4. E.g., Lee Benson, *The Concept of Jacksonian Democracy* (Princeton: Princeton University Press, 1961); Margaret T. Hodgen, *Change and History: A Study of the Dated Distribution of Technological Innovations in England* (New York: Wenner-Gren Foundation, 1952); Robert A. Dahl, *Who Governs?* (New Haven: Yale University Press, 1962).
5. A similar position has been taken by S. D. Clark, "Sociology, History and the Problems of Social Change," *Journal of the Canadian Political Science Association*, XXV (Nov. 1959), 389–400; the same author's sharpened formulation is found in *History and the Sociological Method* (mimeographed), an address given before the International Sociological Association, Washington, D.C., 1962; cf. Richard Hofstadter's related position in "History and the Social Sciences," in Fritz Stern, *op. cit.*, 364.
6. Gardiner, *The Nature of Historical Explanation;* Louis Gottschalk "The

Historian's Use of Generalization," in Leonard D. White, ed., *The State of the Social Sciences* (Chicago: University of Chicago Press, 1956), 436–450; Marc Bloch, *The Historian's Craft* (New York: A. A. Knopf, 1953), chap. 5; William Dray, *Laws and Explanation in History* (London: Oxford University Press, 1951); Bagby, *op. cit.*, 38–50; Carr, *op. cit.*, 81; Gardiner, *Theories of History*, 344–515.

7. Lucien Febvre, *Le Problème de l'incroyance au XVIe siècle* (Paris: Editions Albin Michel, 1947), 10.

8. Bagby, *op. cit.*, 50, 156; S. D. Clark, "Sociology, History, and the Problem of Social Change," *op. cit.* (1959), 389–400.

9. Collingwood, *op. cit.*, 177; Gibson, *op. cit.*, 186.

10. "What are Historians Trying to Do?" in Meyerhoff, *op. cit.*, 87–99. See also Powicke, *op. cit.*, 236, where the following remark by Carl Becker is cited: "Hoping to find something without looking for it, expecting to obtain final answers to life's riddle by absolutely refusing to ask questions—it was surely the most romantic species of realism yet invented, the oddest attempt ever made to get something for nothing."

11. "We may classify our empirical knowledge in either of two ways: either according to conceptions, or according to time and space in which they are actually found. The classification of perceptions according to concepts is the logical classification, that according to time and space the physical classification. Through the former we obtain a system of nature, . . . through the latter a geographical [and historical] description of nature." (Immanuel Kant, *Physische Geographie*, edited by F. T. Rink as *Gesammelte Schriften*, Bd. 9, 1923, 151–436.)

12. Gardiner, *The Nature of Historical Explanation*, 31–41; Carr, *op. cit.*, 59.

13. Ranke viewed these tendencies as "moral forces" which would have to be comprehended functionally as well as sequentially (*"in ihrer Wechselwirkung und Aufeinanderfolge"*); cf. Leopold von Ranke, *Die Grossen Maechte* (Leipzig: Insel Verlag, 1916), 60. Concerning divergent interpretations of Ranke, compare George G. Iggers, "The Influence of Ranke in American and German Historical Thought," in *History and Theory*, Vol. II, No. 1 (1962), 17–40.

14. A. L. Kroeber, *The Nature of Culture* (Chicago: University of Chicago Press, 1952), 86.

15. Malin, *op. cit.*, 145.

16. Bock, *op. cit.*, 110.

17. Seymour M. Lipset, Martin A. Trow, James S. Coleman, *Union Democracy* (New York: The Free Press, 1956), Appendix I *et passim*.

18. Edward A. Shils and Henry A. Finch, *Max Weber and the Methodology of the Social Sciences* (New York: The Free Press, 1949).

19. Malin, *op cit.;* Hexter, *op. cit.;* Collingwood, *op. cit.*, Part 5; Isaiah Berlin, *Historical Inevitability* (New York: Oxford University Press, 1957); Karl Popper, *The Poverty of Historicism* (London: Routledge and Kegan Paul, 1957), chaps. 2, 4.

20. Marc Bloch, "Toward a Comparative History of European Societies," in Frederick C. Lane and Jelle C. Riemersma, *Enterprise and Secular Change* (Homewood, Ill.: Richard D. Irwin, 1953); 494–521; Bock, *op. cit.;* C. Wright Mills, *The Sociological Imagination* (New York: Oxford University Press, 1959), 150–151; Howard Becker, *Through Values to Social Interpretation* (Durham: Duke University Press, 1950), chap. 2; Rushton Coulborn, *The Origin of Civilized Societies* (Princeton: Princeton University Press,

1959); Rushton Coulborn, ed., *Feudalism in History* (Princeton: Princeton University Press, 1956).

21. *Max Weber and The Methodology of the Social Sciences, op. cit.,* 90–100; Arthur Spiethoff, "Pure Theory and Economic Gestalt Theory: Ideal Types and Real Types," in Lane and Riemersma, *op. cit.,* 444–463; Howard Becker, "Interpretive Sociology and Constructive Typology," in Georges Gurvitch and W. E. Moore, eds., *Twentieth Century Sociology* (New York: Philosophical Library, 1945), 70–95; Howard Becker, "Culture Case Study and Greek History," *American Sociological Review,* 23 (October 1958), 489–504.

22. Seymour M. Lipset, *op. cit.,* 17–18, 402–403.

23. Howard Becker, "Culture Case Study and Ideal-Typical Method, With Special Reference to Max Weber," *Social Forces,* 12 (March 1934), 511–526.

24. Norman Jacobs, *The Origin of Modern Capitalism in Eastern Asia* (Hongkong: Hongkong University Press, 1958), 10–13.

25. Neil J. Smelser, *Notes on Functionalism and Scientific Analysis* (mimeographed), an address given before the International Sociological Association, Washington, D.C., 1962.

26. A. L. Kroeber, *op. cit.,* 70.

27. A. R. Radcliffe-Brown, "On the Concept of Function in Social Science," *American Anthropologist,* Vol. 37 (1935), 394–402; *Structure and Function in Primitive Society* (New York: The Free Press, 1952); *The Andaman Islanders* (New York: The Free Press, 1948); B. Malinowski, "Anthropology," *Encyclopaedia Britannica,* First Suppl. Vol. (London and New York, 1926), 131–140; "Culture," *Encyclopedia of the Social Sciences* (New York: Macmillan, 1931), Vol. 4, 621–646; *Argonauts of The Western Pacific* (London: Routledge, 1922). It should be noted, however, that a contrary position is taken by other anthropologists, *e.g.,* Melville J. Herskovits in "The Historical Approach to Afro-American Studies," *American Anthropologist,* Vol. 62 (1960), 559–567; but Afro-American studies are not concerned with preliterate societies.

28. A large part of the extensive literature on both sides of the fence is mentioned in Francesca Cancian, "Functional Analysis and Change," *American Sociological Review,* Vol. 25, No. 6 (Dec. 1960), 818–827, and in Harold Fallding, "Functional Analysis in Sociology," *American Sociological Review,* Vol. 28, No. 1 (Feb. 1963), 5–13. Both authors are on the side of the defenders of the compatibility of structural-functional theory and the analysis of social change. See also Alvin Boskoff, "Functional Analysis as a Source of a Theoretical Repertory and Research Tasks in the Study of Social Change," in George K. Zollschan, et al., eds., *Explorations in Social Change* (Boston: Houghton Mifflin, 1964). On the side of the critics, apart from those quoted in the Cancian and Fallding papers, cf. Walter Buckley, "Structural-Functional Analysis in Modern Sociology," in Howard Becker and Alvin Boskoff, editors, *Modern Sociological Theory* (New York: Dryden, 1957), 236–259, and E. K. Francis, "Prolegomena to a Theory of Social Change," *Kyklos,* Vol. XIV, Fasc. 2 (1961), 213–233. For balanced statements cf. Wilbert Moore, "A Reconsideration of Theories of Social Change," *American Sociological Review,* Vol. 25, No. 6 (Dec. 1960), 811–818; Robert A. Nisbet, "Social Structure and Social Change," *Research Studies of the State College of Washington,* Vol. XX, No. 2 (June 1952), 70–76; and Kenneth E. Bock, "Evolution, Function and Change," *Ameri-*

can *Sociological Review,* 28, No. 2 (April 1963), 229–236. Kingsley Davis, "The Myth of Functional Analysis," *American Sociological Review,* Vol. 24, No. 6 (Dec. 1959), 757–772, professes to see no difference of method or theory between those who wear the functionalist label and those who do not, as far as concrete analyses of social change are concerned. This position, which fuses sociology with functionalism, is not widely shared, however, on either side of the controversy.

29. John H. Goldthorpe, *The Development of Social Policy in England, 1800–1914: Notes on a Sociological Approach to a Problem in Historical Explanation* (mimeographed), an address given before the International Sociological Association, Washington, D.C., 1962.

30. Cf. Carl Hempel, "The Logic of Functional Analysis," in L. Gross, ed., *Symposium on Sociological Theory* (Evanston, Ill.: Row, Peterson, 1959). "It remains true," Hempel says on p. 296, ". . . even for a properly revitalized version of functional analysis, that its explanatory form is rather limited; in particular, it does not provide an explanation of why a particular item *i* rather than some functional equivalent of it occurs in system *s.*"

31. Robert N. Bellah, *Tokugawa Religion—The Values of Pre-Industrial Japan* (New York: The Free Press, 1957), 12.

32. Ernest W. Burgess, "The Growth of the City," in Robert E. Park, et al., eds., *The City* (Chicago: University of Chicago Press, 1925), 47–62; cf. James A. Quinn, *Human Ecology* (Englewood Cliffs, N.J.: Prentice-Hall, 1950), chap. IV.

33. Johann Heinrich von Thuenen, *Der isolierte Staat in Beziehung auf Landwirtschaft und Nationaloekonomie* (Jena: Gustav Fischer, 1910; 1st ed., 1842–1850).

34. Alfred Weber, *Theory of the Location of Industries,* translated by Carl Joachim Friedrich (Chicago: University of Chicago Press, 1929).

35. Talcott Parsons, *Essays in Sociological Theory, Pure and Applied* (New York: The Free Press, 1949), 91.

36. A similar position is taken by Julian H. Steward, *Theory of Culture Change: The Methodology of Multilinear Evolution* (Urbana: University of Illinois Press, 1955), 18 *et passim,* with reference to V. Gordon Childe and Leslie White.

37. Benedetto Croce, Foreword ("An Evaluation of *Dallo Storicismo alla Sociologia*") to Carlo Antoni, *From History to Sociology—The Transition in German Historical Thinking,* translated by Haydon V. White (Detroit: Wayne State University Press, 1959), V. The Italian text was first published as a review in *La Critica, XXXVIII* (1940), 302–303.

38. Cf. Note 77 in Werner J. Cahnman, "Max Weber and the Methodological Controversy in the Social Sciences," in this volume.

39. Arthur Spiethoff in F. C. Lane and G. C. Riemersma, *op. cit.*

40. Robert K. Merton, *Social Theory and Social Structure* (New York: The Free Press, 1957), Introduction.

41. The theory of the demographic transition postulates successive stages of high fertility and high mortality, high fertility and falling mortality, and finally controlled fertility and low mortality. Cf. William Petersen, *Population* (New York: Macmillan, 1961), 11–14, 401–402, 457–458, and the literature mentioned there as well as the same author's "The Demographic Transition in the Netherlands," in this volume.

42. Howard Becker, "Normative Reactions to Normlessness," *American Socio-*

logical Review, 25 (Dec. 1960), 803–809; Karl Mannheim, *Ideology and Utopia* (New York: Harcourt, Brace, 1940); Robert K. Merton, *op. cit.*, chaps. IV, V.

43. Becker, *op. cit.*, 804; Mannheim, *op. cit.*, 30; Merton, *op. cit.*, 136.

44. Another case of the superimposition of theory upon reality is found in the recent attempt of Gideon Sjoberg to compress the totality of urban history in the dichotomy of pre-industrial versus industrial cities. As a result, the author blurs the distinction between tribal, feudal and patrimonial societies, and between the clan-dominated city of the Orient, the politically defined city of Greek and Roman antiquity, and the economically oriented city of the European middle ages. He emerges with the finding that pre-industrial cities in their "basic form" are all alike because they have no industry. Cf., Gideon Sjoberg, *The Preindustrial City: Past and Present* (New York: The Free Press, 1960). 5, 6, 321, 329, *et passim.*

45. Henry S. Maine, *Village Communities in East and West*. Six lectures delivered at Oxford (London: J. Murray, 1871).

46. A. M. Henderson and Talcott Parsons, *Max Weber: The Theory of Social and Economic Organization* (New York: Oxford University Press, 1947), 96; Edward A. Shils, *op. cit.*, 89.

47. Marion J. Levy, Jr., *The Family Revolution in Modern China* (Harvard University Press: Cambridge 1949), 158n. Levy's statement needs qualification, however, insofar as the "economic aspect" of social life is neither more nor less important in the nineteenth century than in any other; rather, what comes to the fore in the era of liberal capitalism is the dominance of economically oriented considerations in decision-making. The decisions of the entrepreneurial class, especially, are necessarily economically oriented; and the entrepreneurial class exercised more influence in this period of history than in previous periods.

48. Richard Hofstadter's statement in Fritz Stern, *op. cit.*, 363, is certainly welcome. Hofstadter anticipates that "the next generation may see the development of a somewhat new historical genre, which will be a mixture of traditional history and the social sciences."

One   EVALUATION OF
THEORIES

BEFORE WE PRESENT A REPRESENTATIVE ANTHOLOGY of research papers which are historical in nature and written by contemporary sociologists (or by historians writing in a sociological vein), we must be aware of the work of those who came before us. Otherwise, our procedure would not be historical. This procedure has two aspects: we become conscious of what we owe to our predecessors, and we realize how much we differ from them. It is with these considerations in mind that the following seven papers should be understood.

The review starts with theories of progress and evolution because it is with these theories that sociology entered upon the stage of modern thought. Comte and Spencer and their immediate disciples have made the word "sociology" a familiar term; they have outlined the scientific character of the field; and they have proclaimed sociology a "new history." However, in his opening paper, Kenneth E. Bock makes it abundantly clear that the dissociation of ephemeral events from lasting process and the identification of social change with organic growth, which marks the Comtean and Spencerian schools, fails to come to grips with historical reality. Rather than pursue the metaphysical chimera of a universal law of history, Bock postulates "the acceptance of histories" as specific phenomena in time and place. He thereby sounds the keynote of another sociology—the one which is represented in this book.

Theories of progress and evolution occupied the stage along with cyclical theories, although the latter did not initially present themselves as sociologies. Moreover, while theories of progress and evolution were unilinear and had an unquestioningly optimistic bent, cyclical theories were deeply pessimistic, even cataclsmic in character. Possibly, in this regard, they are nearer to the mood of new generations. But, as Joseph Maier shows, the fact that they reflect an organic view of history explains their affinity to biological analogies and reduces their sociological relevance. Cyclical and conflict theories share with theories of progress and evolution the illusion that a universal law of history, thought to be analogous to the law of all nature, is a demonstrable proposition.

If theories of progress are viewed as thesis, and cyclical theories as antithesis, Hegelian dialectics provides the synthesis; and if Hegelian dialectics, conceived as a philosophy of the unfolding of the *Spirit,* is turned around and applied to the workaday world of human relations, Marxian sociology is born. In addition, Ricardo and the labor theory of value enter into the equation along with Hegel; and the mechanistic determinism of the nineteenth century transforms all these ingredients into an "iron law" of historical development from which the last trace of *Spirit* is gone. In the analysis of Robert V. Daniels, still another element makes its appearance: the desire to change the world—the revolutionary impetus, the messianic *credo*. To be sure, the attempt is made to prove "scientifically" that the fervent faith in the redeeming power of the proletariat is justified and that the revolution which is to end all history is "inevitable." It is obvious that neither science nor history can lend themselves to such a chiliastic "forcing of the end."

With Émile Durkheim, Ferdinand Toennies, and Max Weber the paradise of large scale solutions is definitely left behind and the complex reality of actual historical situations enters into the formulations of the methods and theories of sociology. In his paper on "Durkheim and History," Robert N. Bellah points out that Durkheim accepted the historical record as the data of sociological investigation and that he considered a greater or lesser emphasis on the particular or the general not as constitutive of opposed disciplines, but as the expression of distinct yet complementary viewpoints. He maintained that currently operative variables can be understood only if they are derived from their antecedents; beyond that, he considered history central to sociology because comparison is an indispensable requirement of the sociological method. Through comparison, history yields types, that is, generalizations which are not imposed upon reality but derived from it.

As sociology becomes more genuinely sociological, it also assumes greater historical relevance. Durkheim's concept of "social constraint" introduces society (that is, the forces of history) as an independent variable. Conversely, Max Weber establishes social action as the basic unit within society and "rational social action" as its model. But social action *in vivo* expresses itself in a multitude of social actions which must be organized into type concepts in order to attain intelligibility and scientific validity. These types are *nomina,* or heuristic constructs, not *realia;* they are not the concrete stuff of history. Consequently, rather than replace history, sociology becomes an auxiliary historical discipline, albeit an indispensable one: without sociological conceptualization, historians might fail to account for sufficient causes and relapse into hero worship. It is at this point that the new sociology, which is to supersede the Comtean and Spencerian kind of sociology, becomes clearly visible. In a paper which marks the climax of the series, Werner J. Cahnman traces the emergence of Max Weber's idealistic-positivistic synthesis through the protracted methodological controversy in the social sciences.

The remaining two papers require only a few words of explanation. In order to assess sociology's image among the related disciplines of philosophy and history, the question is posed how Benedetto Croce, the leading modern philosopher of history, views the claims of sociologists to provide a key to historical analysis. After initial attraction, stemming from a common Hegelianism, Croce rejected the scientistic pretensions of Marxism, but also the, respectively, mechanistic and collectivistic bias in the systems of Pareto and Durkheim. Even Max Weber's typological approach, although it avoided the "fallacy of misplaced concreteness," was not considered satisfactory. History, for Croce, remains the realm of liberty. However, Serge Hughes concludes that a meaningful dialogue between the Crocean philosophy of history and modern sociology is most likely to be carried on in Weberian terms.

The closing chapter, written by Alvin Boskoff, serves a number of purposes. It provides a focus for the diffuse theories of history in the more sharply formulated theory of social change. It connects a variety of recent American theories of social change with antecedent and corresponding theories originating in Europe. And it links past and present, theory and research. Many of the authors whose contributions appear in Part II are the students, or the students' students, of the men whose work is analyzed in the final chapter of Part I. At the same time the keynote of the entire review of theories is sounded once more. The increasing reluctance on the part of theoreticians and researchers in recent decades "to search for ultimate causes or principles" is confirmed and the "corresponding concern for more immediate contexts of description and analysis" finds renewed expression.

Kenneth E. Bock   # THEORIES OF PROGRESS
                                      # AND EVOLUTION

NINETEENTH-CENTURY STUDENTS of society and culture were generally convinced that an historical approach to their subject was required if scientific objectives were to be reached. Pioneers in both sociology and anthropology agreed that their principal task lay in explaining a present condition of European society and sketching a future path of development by probing far back in the history of man to uncover original forms and to then connect such origins with the present by a series of intermediate steps or stages. The resulting picture of "progress" or "evolution" was presumed to offer the only solid basis for analyzing any given state of society or culture as well as for providing guides to what could and should be done in the future.

As Auguste Comte put it, the aim of sociology must be "to discover by what necessary chain of successive transformations the human race, starting from a condition barely superior to that of a society of great apes, has been gradually led up to the present stage of European civilization."[1] Herbert Spencer agreed that it was in the investigation of the *geneses* of social phenomena that a true understanding of them was to be found. Sociology could properly be called a natural history that dealt with societies as incorporated wholes in an attempt to "give an account of the ways in which each of them came to be what it is—to give a history of the transformations through which it has passed."[2]

In nineteenth-century anthropology the same orientation is evident. Bendyshe, in 1863, saw a science of history as the "highest and most peculiar" objective of anthropology.[3] Edward Burnett Tylor obviously concurred, noting in his first major work that the meaning of contemporary ideas and practices can elude us if an explanation is not sought "in the condition of rude and early tribes." Anthropology must, therefore, seek to construct a scientific history of culture—"of the condition of knowledge, religion, art, custom, and the like" among tribes or nations.[4]

John Stuart Mill stated the logic behind this approach. While our immediate interest might be fixed upon the uniformities of relationship that exist among various social phenomena at any point in time, it is important to recognize, he argued, that such uniformities and the laws governing them derive from the more fundamental laws "which regulate the succession between one state of society and another." Any state of society, in other words, is the result of a state of society immediately preceding it. Hence, the basic problem of social science is "to find the laws according to which any state of society produces the state which succeeds it and takes its place."[5] The problem is clearly an historical one. The present is, indeed, a specious present that contains its own secret, in a sense, but certainly cannot reveal it. A study of statics, of order, of organization is admittedly important; but it must depend upon and be preceded by a study of history. If this be the genetic fallacy, it was a fallacy deeply rooted in nineteenth-century thinking.

The task of scientific history was grandly conceived by such men as Comte and Spencer, and the way in which they conceived it is intimately related to the substantive theories of history that they adopted. They would have nothing to do with the histories of conventional historians. Such histories were, in their opinion, twisted accounts of trivia—accounts, more or less accurate, of battles, sieges, diplomatic farces, royal intrigues, and other events that had no real significance in explaining the given state of a society or culture. Traditional historians had erred not only in this concentration on military and political history but, more important, in taking the discrete event as their basic datum. Having done this it became impossible for them ever to arrive at generalizations about historical movements in the larger sense, for particular events are unique and, therefore, as Spencer put it, "ungeneralizable."[6]

If a search for scientific "laws" of history was to be conducted apart from a detailed, empirical examination of events, just where were the laws to be sought? How, confronted with a mass of unorganized evidence, was the scholar to get started on such a formidable project as demonstrating how one state of society produces the state which succeeds it—and this throughout the whole experience of mankind? This was the mammoth problem with which Comte and Spencer chose to cope. They "solved" the problem by adopting, without question, the idea of progress or evolution as a philosophy of history.

This philosophy has been depicted in histories of ideas in such piecemeal fashion that a preliminary broad presentation of it might prove serviceable at the outset.

1. The basic assumption in the idea of progress or evolution is that change is characteristic of human society and culture. Any condition of society that we observe in the present is presumed to be the result of change in past time. Laws of history, therefore, must be laws of change.

2. Change is inevitable. It is "natural" for societies to change; it is to be expected. Where there is evidence of apparent stagnation, the validity of such evidence must first of all be questioned. If absence of change is, in fact, discerned, then this calls for special explanation in terms of obstacles, accidents, or unusual conditions. Conversely, change itself calls for no explanation in the sense that it needs to be accounted for by reference to happenings.

3. Change in society or culture is a result, basically, of the operation of forces within society or culture. More specifically, change is an unfolding of potential within society or culture. This potential might be found in man himself (human nature), as a unit of society, or in institutions or culture traits. "External" influences, such as the physical environment or the effects that societies or cultures have on one another, do operate; but they do not affect the course or direction of change; they can alter the tempo of change. External influences make it difficult to discern the "true course" of evolution.

4. Change—or at least basic change, the change responsible for the general form of any present condition of society or culture—is continuous, slow, and gradual. "Nature never makes leaps." Events, therefore, are insignificant in the process of change; they are, at least, the products of forces operative within society; they are manifestations of change. A speeding up or slowing of change is possible, but, again, this is to be explained in terms of intrusive factors, and the explanation is not encompassed by the idea of progress or evolution.

5. Change in society or culture has a direction; it is a movement toward

something. This direction or goal is determined by the nature of society or culture, i.e., something within society or culture. This internal determining principle may be discovered in human nature.

6. The direction of social change is from the homogeneous to the heterogeneous, from the simple to the complex, from the undifferentiated to the differentiated in form and function. There is also a tendency toward increase in size, within limits of both population and territory. (In the case of the idea of progress proper, the added judgment is made that change involves improvement or betterment. The criteria of improvement vary widely from writer to writer, but the general notion is that a progressing society is one that is becoming like European society.)

7. The laws of change operate uniformly through time and space. Hence, all societies and cultures traverse the same path of change, and it is possible to conceive of Society or Culture as a whole undergoing a specified development. It follows from this principle of uniformitarianism that different societies and cultures must represent phases or stages in the history of the most highly developed people or in the history of Society or Culture as such. A method for recovering the pattern of history is thus suggested.

8. Change, in short, is strictly analogous to the growth of an organism. Where infinite improvement is posited the analogy still holds, but with the proviso that the organism has no declining old age.

When stated in these broad terms, it is clear that the idea of progress or evolution is not a mere quirk of nineteenth-century thought, much less a simple derivative from Darwinian biology. Thomas Huxley probably exaggerated when he spoke of the "oldest of all philosophies, that of Evolution."[7] But perusal of Aristotle's *Physics* and *Politics* reminds us that he, too, defined nature as encompassing a principle of change—change that was slow, gradual, and continuous, that was inherent in the thing changing, that moved toward a goal determined by in-dwelling qualities, and that worked for the perfect realization of all that was potential in a thing. Aristotle did not hesitate to apply these notions in his depiction of the process whereby the state "came to be."[8] Thucydides took it for granted that nations pass through a certain "growth," and, lacking actual historical evidence, he recovered the early history of Athens by using contemporary barbarians or "backward" Greeks to document stages in Athenian development.[9] In fact, it was common practice among both Greek and Roman writers to construct stages of cultural development by reference to contemporary primitives—a procedure made possible only on the assumption that change is gradual and uniform through time and space.[10]

The continuity of the evolutionary tradition in European thought is apparent even in St. Augustine's philosophy of history, which was to become a model for Bossuet's *Discours sur l'histoire universelle,* which, in turn, inspired eighteenth-century conjectural histories. Although in St. Augustine there is a shift from the classical idea of cycles to the idea of Providence, the *form* of change remains the same, and the practice of deriving a presumably historical account from an analysis of qualities, factors, or elements in or behind the thing changing is retained. As a matter of fact, an examination of St. Augustine's historical method can be instructive for an understanding of eighteenth- and nineteenth-century procedures in the writing of natural or theoretical histories. The obscure practice of deducing History from Nature in these later efforts can be seen more clearly in St. Augustine's reconstruction of history from an analysis of God's Will. More specifically, the idea that history is slow, gradual change moving through defined stages as a result of potential within the thing changing gives shape to the *City of God*.[11]

When this background of European thinking on historical process is kept in mind, the allegedly radical change of outlook that came with the replacement of both the idea of cycles and the idea of Providence by an idea of infinite progress[12] becomes less important from a theoretical point of view. Granting the sharp contrast between the heavy sense of fate that characterizes Greek historical thought, or the limited temporal outlook of the Christian philosophy of history, and the enthusiasm of the early modern vision of boundless progress, there persists throughout these three perspectives the common view that history is change more or less analogous to biological growth and that the compelling intellectual task is to depict the stages in this growth through an analysis of *what* it is that is changing.

From this point of view, there appears to be no good analytic reason for distinguishing between the ideas of progress and evolution in social theory. The elements that the two ideas have in common are not only more numerous than those that separate them, but the common features are the theoretically significant ones. Among the writers we shall consider here, many tried valiantly to point up a difference between progress and evolution, making the obvious point that progress implied improvement, which involved the investigator in value judgments; evolution, on the other hand, was represented merely as orderly change in a determinate direction. The attempted distinction, however, was unstable, for it is clear that when eighteenth- and nineteenth-century theorists spoke of either the progress or evolution of society they referred to a movement of society toward a condition exemplified by contemporary Europe. Whether European society was pictured as the best society—as it usually was—or merely as the most complex or differentiated society had no bearing on the historical generalization that was being presented. It is fairly evident, moreover, that evolutionists had small success in avoiding value judgments when it came to the actual arrangement of social or cultural items in a supposedly temporal series.

The notion that we have escaped the naive qualities of the idea of progress once we have discarded the belief that things are always getting better and better has been misleading. This faith in the inevitability of improvement was, theoretically, a minor facet of what has traditionally been called the idea of progress. The conviction that we avoid the far-reaching implications of that idea simply by adopting, for example, an air of pessimism does not do justice to its complex ramifications.

While the actual formulation of the modern idea of social progress or evolution took place notably in the famous "Quarrel between the Ancients and the Moderns," foundations for the notion had been laid by Descartes. In 1637, Descartes wrote that God had put certain laws into nature, and everything that existed or took place was in conformity with these laws. If one conceived of such laws operating through time, then there was nothing heretical in saying that the world was not "produced at once in a perfect and finished state," but that it was coming "gradually into existence" in a manner legislated by God. Moreover, since God was the author of these laws they were eternal, they operated uniformly through space and time, and they were discoverable through a careful exercise of the human reason.[13]

The Moderns during the seventeenth-century Quarrel drew freely on these principles. Their object was to demonstrate that men had advanced intellectually, morally, and materially throughout past time and that they would continue to advance into an infinite future. While the immediate aim was to show that modern European scientists and artists were superior to their classical Greek and Roman predecessors, the argument broadened in scope when the point was made that since nature had produced great men in ancient times she must—according to the Cartesian principle of uniformitarianism—produce great men in all ages. Mere accumulation of accomplishments would, then, assure unending advance.

In developing their case the Moderns did not use historical evidence to buttress their position. They clearly distrusted such evidence, feeling that appeals to piecemeal and unreliable data would never settle the issue.[14] The Cartesian judgment that history was a "poor little conjectural science" held firm; history could never yield demonstrable truths that possessed the certainty of mathematics.[15] They sought, instead, a direct apprehension of the laws that would account for what *must* have happened, and they found them in an elaborate analogy between the growth of an individual and the growth of mankind. Just as St. Augustine had drawn a parallel between the experience of the individual and the race in the achievement of salvation, now the Moderns argued that just as an individual advances from day to day in the knowledge he possesses, so mankind advanced from age to age. Progress was inevitable; no mere empirical-historical demonstration was needed to establish that certainty.

Working with this analogy, the Moderns were also supplied with the form of progress. The progress of man was slow, gradual, and continuous; it proceeded through stages; it resulted from inherent qualities of rational human nature. True, the movement was subject to variations in tempo, but this was to be attributed to unusual circumstances or particular events—wars, malevolent rulers, barbarian invasions, and the like. Such occurrences, however, were not regarded as a part of the natural provision made for progress; they were not comprehended by the law of progress. Progress, on the other hand, was *not* explained by occurrences of any kind; it was to be expected, given the nature of things. Progress, in other words, was a *natural,* not an historical, phenomenon.[16]

The theory that emerges from the Quarrel is concerned almost exclusively with a process of intellectual development and, substantively, it is limited to a comparison of the relative positions of Greece or Rome and seventeenth-century Europe in this process. It is not an exaggeration to say, however, that the basic theoretical postulates of the modern idea of social evolution are complete in this seventeenth-century discussion. It is this circumstance that makes the task of eighteenth- and nineteenth-century conjectural historians so easy; and it is this fact that explains the relative absence of searching theoretical speculation in the later literature. The magnificent eighteenth-century effort to found an historical science of man was made with a theory at hand.

The picture of progress envisaged by the Moderns, however, soon became enormously complicated. They had dealt seriously with only two items in a cultural series, and their object had been to show a transition from a known antiquity to a known present in terms of a gradual change. As the world of human societies, past and present, expanded before the awe-struck eyes of voyaging Europeans, the cultural "series" took on tremendous proportions, and there was a question whether the vast array of differences could be encompassed within so simple a notion as the idea of progress. Despite considerable difficulties and doubts,[17] Europeans managed the task.

If the men of classical antiquity could be understood as representatives of the childhood of a maturing Europe, it seemed reasonable to assume that the savages of America, Africa, or the South Seas could be regarded simply as still earlier examples of stages in the development of mankind. If, moreover, similarities could be discerned between the cultures of relatively advanced contemporary savages and the most remote people of antiquity— Homeric Greeks, for example—the continuity of an evolutionary series seemed to be assured. Thus Père Lafitau was able to see in the customs of American Indians vestiges of a very early but historically known Old World culture. Such likenesses so impressed William Robertson that he was led to observe that history must run the same course among all peoples; the American Indian could, therefore, be used to "fill up a considerable chasm in the history of the human species." For both Lafitau and Robertson, as for most of their eighteenth-century contemporaries, these remarkable similarities and the uniformity of social or cultural development resulted directly from the psychic unity of mankind.[18]

Eighteenth-century students of man were actually confronted with a problem of cultural differences. The pressing fact was that the earth was found to contain a broad array of different cultures, and how this had come to be in a world that was, according to Cartesian doctrine, ruled by uniformly operating laws, proved to be a distressing question. The problem was solved by denying that the differences were fundamental and by viewing them merely as representative of differences of degree of growth achieved. In present-day language, there were "developed" and "underdeveloped" societies or cultures; but Society or Culture was the same, basically, wherever and whenever found.

The possibilities inherent in this point of view for constructing an historical science of man or society were first presented systematically by Turgot. The great range of differences observable in the present represented for him "every shade of barbarism and civilization," every degree of advance,—in fact, the "history of all the ages." Candidly accepting Europe as the highest civilization to date, he was provided with a criterion for arranging all known societies roughly in a single developmental series, a unilinear progress of mankind through hunting, pastoral, and agricultural phases. Although Turgot was well aware that this process had gone on unevenly, that it had been subject, at certain times and in certain places, to both deceleration and acceleration, his attention was focused upon the "natural" progress that had taken place and his theory comprehended that process only.[19]

This neat formula had wide appeal. It solved the irritating problem of differences by assimilating the strange and unknown—non-European cultures —to the familiar—European culture. And it accomplished this in a way flattering to Europeans, for other cultures now merely became imperfect European culture. More important from a theoretical point of view, it provided a means for depicting universal history in "scientific" fashion, without resort to a scanty and unreliable record of unique events about which one could not generalize. "History" now became observable in the present.

Eighteenth-century scholars applied the formula with enthusiasm. Cornelius de Pauw recovered the early history of the human species by pointing to the customs of recently observed American Indians. Adam Ferguson combed the voyage literature, which revealed to him "almost every situation in which mankind is placed," and thus depicted the successive stages of social development marked by hunting, pastoral, and agricultural pursuits. Lord Kames (Henry Home) used similar materials to sketch the "history of mankind." Adam Smith, although depending less on ethnographic data and appealing more directly to human nature, described the historical process by which nations reached opulence. Perhaps the grandest of these eighteenth-century efforts was Condorcet's historical picture of the progress of the human mind. Making the usual assumption that Western Europe marked the high point of progress, Condorcet sketched ten great epochs in human history, which he documented with descriptions of different peoples in widely separated times and places. He felt secure in the now common conviction that these instances of society or culture, when properly arranged, formed an "uninterrupted chain" from savagery to civilization.[20]

In examining the details of this remarkable literature it is easy to miss the theory that underlies it, for by this time the theory had become what Dewey called "familiar furniture of the mind," and it went unstated. It should be noted at the outset that eighteenth-century conjectural historians rejected absolutely the procedures of ordinary historians. Their aim was to get "behind" the events of history, to approach the temporal process in "philosophic" terms, and to emerge with broad generalizations that would reveal the "spirit" of history.[21] Having disdained the meticulous chronology of historians, and having thus deprived themselves of the dating method of establishing *time-direction,* something else had to be substituted for determining what came first, what came second, and so on. The ethnographic materials that they used to document stages of development were, after all, drawn from recent or contemporary observations. Savages, therefore, became "primal" only on a basis of some preconception of what the general historical process had been. The preconception used was the idea that there had been a development from a non-literate, non-agricultural, non-commercial, non-European type of culture to a literate, agricultural, commercial, European type. The criteria employed became more detailed than this, of course; working again from European standards, it was generally assumed that there had been a movement from promiscuity or polygamy to monogamy, from communal to private property, from animism and pantheism to monotheism, and so on. To some extent this development was generalized as movement from the simple to the complex, but specifically it was seen as progress from the non-European to the European. It was only by virtue of judgments of this sort, in any event, that a mere array of types was converted into a supposedly historical succession.

The form of the process of change depicted by the eighteenth-century philosophers is closely related to this method of tracing progress. The particular historical event is unimportant. The range of cultural differences forms a qualitatively continuous series. Interruptions or irregularities in the process are inexplicable in the light of the principle of uniformitarianism. The only picture of change that can emerge from these propositions is one of slow, gradual, and continuous development, and this picture is repeatedly reinforced in the literature by recourse to an elaborate biological analogy. It is, furthermore, in keeping with this analogy between the growth of society and the growth of an individual organism that a major preoccupation with origins is evident: if society is like an organism, then what it comes to be and how it comes to be can be most easily revealed by an analysis of the potential in its germinal or original form. As Ferguson put the case:

Natural productions are generally formed by degrees. Vegetables are raised from a tender shoot, and animals from an infant state. . . . This progress in the case of man is continued to a greater extent than in that of any other animal. Not only the individual advances from infancy to manhood, but the species itself from rudeness to civilization. . . .

If, in advanced years, we would form a just notion of our progress from the cradle, we must have recourse to the nursery; and from the example of those who are still in the period of life we mean to describe, take our representation of past manners, that cannot, in any other way, be recalled.[22]

Human nature theory, in one sense, provided these eighteenth-century humanists with the very foundation of their systems. Social or cultural development was inevitable; it was something that *must* have happened. But if the question of *why* it must have happened was pressed, the answer was usually found in the nature of man. Just as Aristotle had found man to be a political animal by nature, a fact that made the state come to be "of necessity," so the eighteenth-century philosophers found the springs of human action in the human constitution itself, and they endeavored to trace the origins of institutions ultimately to this source.[23]

When, therefore, in the nineteenth century, the founders of the young disciplines of sociology and anthropology resolved that their studies must be fundamentally historical in orientation and that their basic objective was to trace a succession of social or cultural types, they approached their task with a rich background of theory and method. When Comte acknowledged Condorcet as his intellectual father he was not paying mere lip service to the eighteenth century. When he announced that he would adopt the idea of progress as his leading rational conception of history, he felt himself on secure ground since it was an idea shared by "all men who possess a certain knowledge of the leading facts of history."[24] Spencer, with his proudly announced aversion to reading, could not be so candid in acknowledging his indebtedness to the past, and he died believing that he had discovered the universal law of progress in a textbook on physiology;[25] but his law is the same as Comte's. Tylor, however, knew that he was depending on old doctrine when he undertook to show that "the savage state in some measure represents an early condition of mankind, out of which the higher culture has gradually been developed or evolved, by processes still in regular operation as of old, the result showing that, on the whole, progress has far prevailed over relapse."[26]

Herbert Spencer may be regarded as having given the most clearly didactic expression to the nineteenth-century idea of social evolution. Sociology, for Spencer, was an historical study insofar as it was concerned with questions of origins and coming-to-be. If the barren empiricism of ordinary historical writing was to be avoided, however, the course of change had to be depicted as a "natural history of society" derived from an analysis of the nature of society."[27]

Evolution, in Spencer's view, resulted from the nature of society, and the form of that evolution was to be discerned by recognizing society as a species of organism. In identifying society as an organism, he made it clear that he was not merely indulging in metaphor, not using biological language only to clarify a sociological concept. For Spencer, it was a "fact" that society *is* an organism.[28] It followed, therefore, that what was known about biological organisms could be applied directly to society. The observation of the embryologist von Baer, that animals and plants develop from the homogeneous to the heterogeneous proved completely acceptable to Spencer as a theory of social evolution—"the history of all organisms whatever." It is important to recognize that what Spencer is talking about here is the life development of the *individual* organism, not about the evolution of *species*. Writing in 1857—two years before the publication of Darwin's *Origin of Species*—Spencer considered the possibility that species had also changed through time from the homogeneous to the heterogeneous, and though he considered this likely he felt that "the evidence is so fragmentary, that every conclusion is open to dispute."[29]

In the case of man, however, there could be no doubt. A change from the homogeneous to the heterogeneous had occurred in the progress of civilization as a whole and in the progress of each nation. Homogeneity was evident in "existing barbarous tribes," and a gradual differentiation was demonstrated in the great variety of societies intervening between this "early" condition and modern complex European society.[30]

All this was, for Spencer, only an empirical, not a rational generalization. In seeking to raise the demonstration of progress to the status of a law that would establish the necessity of evolution, he found the cause of advance in the principle that "every active force produces more than one change—every cause produces more than one effect." This multiplication of effects leads inevitably to the corollary that there has been an evergrowing complication of things. It follows that "the increase of heterogeneity so brought about is still going on and must continue to go on; and that thus progress is not an accident, not a thing within human control, but a beneficent necessity."[31]

Despite the elaborate logic involved here, it is quite clear that all Spencer has done is to recover a traditional analogy between society and an organism and so arrive at the notion that society is always changing slowly, gradually, and continuously as a result of forces contained within it. The laborious collection of data that went into his *Descriptive Sociology* and the painstaking arrangement of social or cultural types that constitutes his *Principles of Sociology* merely illustrate the basic conception of evolution adopted earlier. Spencer's use of the comparative method was only a marshaling of what he regarded as simple and complex social types in an order dictated by criteria derived from a biological concept.

Spencer's naiveté should not, however, be exaggerated. He occasionally expressed grave doubts about the applicability of the biological analogy and claimed that his system did not depend upon it.[32] In a rare moment of candor he observed that if societies differed from one another only in their stages of growth, comparison would easily disclose the course of evolution. Again, he noted, if societies developed independently of one another and of other intrusive factors, the evolutionary path could be more easily discerned. But, he admitted, societies often differ in kind, and intrusive factors do operate. These considerations did not, however, persuade him to abandon his theory or the comparative method. He merely observed that, given these difficulties, we must be careful to distinguish between general and special conclusions; and he comforted himself with the conviction that the more important general propositions did admit of establishment by means of the comparative method.[33]

The pattern of unilinear social evolution is clear in Spencer, despite these occasional reservations. He classified societies into simple, compound, doubly compound, and trebly compound types. He represented these groups and their sub-groups with illustrations drawn from contemporary primitives—primitives as they existed upon first contact with Europeans—ancient extinct civilizations, earlier historical stages of existing modern civilizations, and modern civilizations as they exist today. The range ran from headless, nomadic societies such as the Fuegians or Bushmen to contemporary British or French. He noted that certain generalizations emerge from this classification:

The stages of compounding and re-compounding have to be passed through in succession. . . . In this order has social evolution gone on, and only in this order does it appear to be possible. Whatever imperfections and incongruities the above classification has, do not hide these general facts—that there are societies of these different grades of composition; that those of the same grade have general resemblances in their structures; and they arise in the order shown.[34]

While it may be argued that Spencer had a theory of biological growth rather than a theory of history, the case of Auguste Comte is more involved. Comte accepted the idea of progress as the key to a scientific study of history. He saw a close analogy between society and an organism and thus consciously patterned his analysis of social change on physiological principles. He had no doubt that Europe represented the highest stage of social development to date, and he made the standard assumption that different societies through time and space could be regarded as evidence of the stages through which Europe had passed in its history. He believed that progress was inherent in human nature. Finally, he made the usual judgment that positive conclusions about social development could not be reached through the empirical procedures of traditional historians and that a scientific history must be highly abstract, avoiding any consideration of particular persons and events.[35]

There is, however, a singular element in Comte's sociology that distinguishes him from Spencer and that has largely escaped the attention of his critics. Comte felt that there were three general sources of data for reconstructing the course of social development: human nature, the ethnographic record of different societies and cultures, and history in the proper sense of the term.

The laws of human nature were fundamental, for what man had done was to be regarded as an inexorable result of the human constitution. No law of history that contradicted basic laws of human nature could stand. At the same time, Comte insisted that history could not be derived from an analysis of human nature because successive generations of men influenced each other to such an extent that the relationship between what happened and what man is becomes obscure. While, then, historical laws must be checked against "laws of the human organization," the former must be ascertained more directly.[36]

The ethnographic record did contain, for Comte, representations of every stage in social development. But here he openly faced a problem that had so often gone unrecognized. The series divulged by the record—on whatever criteria it might be arranged—was, after all, a *coexistent* series. It did not in itself reveal the direction of evolution. If this coexistent series, constructed by means of the comparative method, was to be confirmed as a *consecutive* series, independent evidence of another sort was needed.

It is for this reason that Comte turned to his third source—history; and it is as a consequence of this line of reasoning that he designates the historical method as the sociological method proper. Biology could provide us with broad guide lines in what it had to tell us of human nature. The comparative method, borrowed again from biology, could yield a classification that suggested a possible temporal sequence. But the actual course of social development had to be sought, ultimately, in an examination of historical evidence.[37]

It can hardly be said that Comte succeeded in following his own methodological dictates. Determined as he was to keep history abstract, he was kept away from the data that might have been relevant to his purpose. Convinced that Europe was the most highly developed society and that all societies were bound to have the same history (because human nature was everywhere the same), he felt justified in confining his attention to European history. Convinced, again, that society is a closely integrated organic whole with functionally related parts, he tried to simplify his task by attending to only one facet of European history—the intellectual. Comte's history, therefore, turns out to be a history of science, and the yield is his dubious law of the three stages—theological, metaphysical, and positive—through which the various branches of knowledge must pass.

Historiographers could find much to criticize in Comte's procedure. His knowledge of and patience with the bothersome details, even of intellectual history, were not equal to the ambitious task he set himself. Comte realized when he came to write the *Positive Polity* that he had not made good on his promise to validate historically what his analysis of human nature and his application of the comparative method had suggested. The following remarkable statement reveals the low regard for the petty empirical study of history that was so characteristic of nineteenth-century evolutionists:

If the present volume [Comte wrote in the *Positive Polity*] be compared with the historical part of my fundamental treatise, it will be found that while the general coordination becomes here more profound and more complete, the special explanations are less fully worked out. In the last respect, my Philosophy of History, in this its definitive shape, does not fulfil my former promises (*Phil. Pos.* iv. 3); for I undertook that there should be more details and proofs here than in the first sketch; to which, on the contrary, I am now obliged to refer my readers for that information. I understand better than I did then the true conditions of the philosophic regime, and I see that coordinated assertions, which I formerly regarded as a purely provisional presentation of my doctrine, must be the normal form of all really systematic exposition. The progress I have achieved has procured me a certain authority; and my conceptions are sufficiently matured. I am entitled therefore to proceed with the same freedom and rapidity as my principal ancestors, Aristotle, Descartes, and Leibniz, who confined themselves to a definite expression of their views, leaving the verification and development of them to the public.[38]

Spencer and Comte summarized the nineteenth-century philosophy of social evolution. Basically similar ideas appear at the same time in the great anthropological literature of the period. The pioneer work of such figures as Tylor, Morgan, Bastian, and McLennan centers around the propositions that the mind of man functions everywhere in the same way, that culture is a product of mind, that culture growth therefore follows parallel paths among different peoples, and that an arrangement of ethnographic descriptions can thus serve, roughly, to represent a history of culture. Dedicated as they were —and perhaps for extraneous reasons—to the study of primitive tribes, anthropologists were particularly interested in the recovery of origins and early stages in the historical process, but the systematizers did not lose sight of the broader anthropological objective of constructing a complete history of man and his works.

Much of this anthropological literature was based upon an ethnography vastly superior to that of either Comte or Spencer, and it was also marked by a far more sophisticated attention to methodological problems. It was, therefore, in this branch of inquiry that serious difficulties were first presented concerning the efficacy of evolutionism as a universal key to the historical problem. Edward Burnett Tylor is a notable case in point.

Although it may be correct to classify Tylor, finally, as an evolutionist, the questions and problems he raised while seeking to maintain that position, particularly in his earlier work, tend to overshadow his evolutionism. His announced purpose was to explain a present condition of culture (in Europe) by recourse to its very early history. Since there were no written records available for remote times, other sources of information had to be sought. Tylor, like Comte, considered the possibility of understanding institutions as "direct products of the human mind," but he rejected this procedure as generally untrustworthy. Then, in a noteworthy passage, he observed that cultural phenomena are the products of a "complication of events" and so must be understood through a "laborious piecing together of their previous history." One way of getting at that history lay in internal evidence of historical contacts between peoples. Evidence of such contacts might be discerned in an analysis of cultural similarities. This at once involved Tylor in the vexing problem of distinguishing among similarities arising from (1) the "like working of men's minds under like conditions," (2) blood relationships, and (3) contact. He pointed out that similarities had value as historical evidence only, of course, when they could be identified as results of common derivation or contact; and his early work was devoted to an unsuccessful attempt to make the distinction.[39]

This cautious historical sense becomes attenuated in Tylor's later work, notably his *Primitive Culture*. Here he was concerned with defending the savage as an historical document and with meeting current arguments that savagery represented a deteriorated cultural state rather than an original condition of mankind out of which civilization had gradually evolved.[40] His prodigious effort to accomplish this by identifying "survivals" of savagery in civilization prompted a host of folklorists to use their hitherto merely quaint materials in support of the evolutionist doctrine.[41]

Tylor's caution is not evident in the ethnological work that immediately followed him. A wholesale hunt for origins and stages in a developmental cultural series was undertaken with little thought given to Tylor's insistence upon probing the "complication of events" that must explain the present or even to Comte's requirement that the comparative method be accompanied by "philosophic" historical investigation. Despite occasional important doubts and caveats, the core of evolutionist doctrine remained a dominant theme in social science at the beginning of the twentieth century.[42]

Serious misconceptions of the idea of social evolution as a theory of history arise from associating it with the work or influence of Charles Darwin.[43] All of the central concepts of the theory were formulated and in full use long before 1859. The classical evolutionists in both sociology and anthropology either failed to refer to any notion of the evolution of biological species or they specifically denied dependence on the idea. Comte believed in the fixity of species. Spencer, as noted above, presented his "law of progress" two years before publication of the *Origin of Species* and was at that time in doubt about its applicability to life forms. Tylor claimed, with ample justification, that his work was unrelated to Darwin's. The historical sketch in the first portion of this chapter suggests that the major components of the idea of evolution have persisted from classical times in European thought.

Darwin and nineteenth-century social evolutionists shared, to some extent, a common intellectual heritage, but it would be easier to derive Darwinian theory from social theory than the reverse.

The question of historical priority, however, is perhaps irrelevant here. It *is* important to notice that Darwin's theory of change dealt with a theoretical problem quite distinct from the one conceived by social evolutionists. Darwin sought to explain the existence in the present of different *kinds* of organisms. He spelled out the mechanics of a process of change that would account for the differences. Social evolutionists, on the other hand, never accepted the problem of differences. Their aim was to trace the course of development of a single entity: Society. Differences for the social evolutionist were differences in degree of maturity achieved by individual representatives of the same kind of thing. There is a strong biological flavor to social evolutionism, but this stems from an analogy drawn between the history of society and the growth of an *individual* organism, not the history of species or organisms.

This is not to say that Darwin had no influence on social theory. For one thing, his depiction of change as slow and proceeding by infinitely fine gradations was quite in keeping with the social evolutionists' picture of a continuous and eventless process. His necessary dependence on indirect rather than direct historical evidence paralleled, in a way, the social evolutionists' self-imposed rejection of empirical-historical evidence. The immediate acceptance and fame of Darwin's work bolstered the confidence of social evolutionists as they noted these superficial resemblances. But social evolutionism remained what it had been before Darwin.

The rise of that school of social thought known as Social Darwinism is another matter. Here Darwin's impact is more evident (although even in this case we might be doing Malthus, who decisively impressed Darwin, an injustice). Concepts like "natural selection," "the struggle for existence," and "survival of the fittest" could easily be used to express, with new dignity and authority, the old idea that life is harsh and that the provisions made by nature for determining winners and losers should not, and cannot in the long run, be altered by social intervention. This general idea was exploited in tracing the origins of institutions—particularly the state—as well as in demonstrating the natural path of social improvement. Scholars like Gumplowicz, Ratzenhofer, and even Oppenheimer, presented elaborate conflict theories that largely bear a Darwinian stamp. The strictly laissez-faire social philosophies of Spencer or Sumner likewise sought support in the scientific surety of Darwin's great discovery.[44]

The fact that social Darwinists, in addition to their emphasis on the conflict aspect of social life, were also in many respects social evolutionists in the traditional, pre-Darwinian sense should not be allowed to obscure the independence and distinctiveness of the social-evolutionistic thesis. That social theorists who sought to apply some specific Darwinian concepts in an analysis of social processes "misinterpreted" Darwin is clear enough. But any suggestion that the broad evolutionist theme in humanist studies is a byproduct of Darwin's work simply does violence to the history of European social theory.

In assessing the grand theories of progress and evolution of the eighteenth and nineteenth centuries and their relevance to contemporary social theory, it is perhaps well to start on a positive note. Adverse criticism has been bitter enough, and it has often been superficial. We should bear in mind that the evolutionists were, after all, consciously addressing themselves to a fundamental question that usually escapes attention in this day of technically elaborate empirical social science. They were asking how it is that any people comes to be civilized. Their acceptance of Europe as the civilization to be explained narrowed their vision, but even the question of how Europe, in the course of a few centuries, had undergone such a striking social and cultural alteration is legitimate and of practical significance. There is a strong note of pride in the early literature, but the pride is not unjustified. Nor was it accompanied, in the theory under discussion here, by any contention that European civilization resulted from innate racial qualities peculiar to Europeans.[45] The problem was stated in historical terms: European civilization was conceived to be the result of the operation of a process in time.

Having thus stated an historical problem, however, evolutionists pursued it in unhistorical fashion. Instead of examining the history of Europe and comparing that with the histories of other peoples, with a view to explaining both similarities and differences in the light of what had happened, they chose to view Mankind and History as unities. They decided that discrete historical events were unmanageable as scientific data and sought, therefore, to discover process in the operation of immanent forces. They undertook to give form to this process by an arrangement of types instead of an arrangement of events. They sought generalizations about process through a comparison of types rather than a comparison of histories.

The basic concepts that led to these decisions constitute the core of evolutionism. The view that history is unitary and that historical *events* are unique dictated the basic procedure. The particular content of evolutionary doctrine—the idea that process is the kind of change that is analogous to biological growth—is in keeping with these judgments about history, but it is not required by them. Special procedures or concepts like the comparative method, the simple-complex criterion of growth, the doctrine of survivals, or the thesis of parallel development are only responses to problems raised by the basic decision to "do history" without historical evidence.

The fact that evolutionists violated cultural or social context when they tore traits or institutions from their settings in order to construct developmental sequences—the fact that "function" was ignored—is but incidental.

To point to this frailty as a reason for the demise of evolutionism is to miss the fundamental point, for the implication is that careful attention to function could legitimize the procedure.[46] Poor ethnography did not enhance the value of nineteenth-century anthropological works, but neither was it responsible for the inadequacy of evolutionism as historical explication.

The failure of evolutionism lies in the fact that it was just what its earlier exponents called it—"conjectural history." Historical research of any kind, and particularly the historical research in which sociologists or anthropologists are interested, must, of course, be accompanied by theory. But the theory must be of a sort that invites test by concrete evidence of what happened.[47] The theory of social evolution resists such testing by specifically denying the relevance of *event* to *process* and by directing attention instead to timeless elements in structure and function as sources of insight into what "must" have happened.

If sociologists are to avoid the very real pitfalls of classical evolutionism, it will be by accepting the universe of human social experience as a plurality of histories that can be compared for the purpose of reaching generalized descriptions of actually observed processes.

Notes

1. Auguste Comte, "Philosophical Considerations on the Sciences and Savants," in his *System of Positive Polity,* trans. by John H. Bridges, et al. (London, 1875–1877), IV:599.
2. Herbert Spencer, *An Autobiography* (London: Williams and Norgate, 1904), II:107.
3. T. Bendyshe, "The History of Anthropology," in *Memoirs Read before the Anthropological Society of London, 1863–1864* (London, 1865), p. 335.
4. Edward Burnett Tylor, *Researches into the Early History of Mankind and the Development of Civilization,* 3d ed. (New York, 1878), p. 1; *Primitive Culture,* 2d ed. (New York, 1873), I:5.
5. John Stuart Mill, *A System of Logic* (London: Longmans, Green, 1900), Bk. VI, ch. 10, No. 2, p. 595.
6. This is a persistent theme in the critical writings of Comte, Spencer, Mill, Tylor and other nineteenth-century social philosophers. Conventional historians replied on occasion; while the exchange was often lively it was barren of results. For some of the details see Kenneth E. Bock, *The Acceptance of Histories* (Berkeley and Los Angeles: University of California Press, 1956), chaps. 1–3.
7. Francis Darwin, ed., *The Life and Letters of Charles Darwin* (New York: D. Appleton, 1896), I:534.
8. See, especially, the *Physics,* II:1–4, 8, and the *Politics,* I:2.
9. Thucydides, *The Peloponnesian War,* I:1–6. See comments of E. E. Sikes, *The Anthropology of the Greeks* (London: D. Nutt, 1914), p. 10. Adam Ferguson took Thucydides as a methodological model for the recovery of origins and early development: *An Essay on the History of Civil Society,* 8th ed. (Philadelphia, 1819), 143–144, 146–147.

10. See the abundant evidence in A. O. Lovejoy and George Boas, *Primitivism and Related Ideas in Antiquity* (Baltimore: Johns Hopkins, 1935).

11. See especially, *The City of God,* trans. by John Healey (Edinburgh: John Grant, 1909), X:xiv.

12. The contrast is emphasized in most treatments of the idea of progress. See, for example J. B. Bury's classic *The Idea of Progress: An Inquiry into its Origin and Growth* (London: Macmillan, 1920).

13. René Descartes, *Discourse on Method* (Everyman's Library, New York, 1934), pp. 33–36.

14. See, for example, the argument of Bernard LeBovier de Fontenelle, "Sur l'histoire," in *Oeuvres,* nouvelle éd. (Amsterdam, 1764), 9:238–254.

15. Lucien Lévy-Bruhl, "The Cartesian Spirit and History," in Raymond Klibansky and H. J. Paton, eds., *Philosophy and History* (Oxford: Clarendon Press, 1936).

16. The history of the "Quarrel" has been fully treated. See, for example, J. B. Bury, *op. cit.;* Jules Delvaille, *Essai sur l'histoire de l'idée de progrès jusqu'à le fin de xviiie siècle* (Paris: F. Alcan, 1910); H. Rigault, *Histoire de la querelle des anciens et des modernes* (Paris, 1856). Significant excerpts from the original literature are contained in F. J. Teggart, *The Idea of Progress: A Collection of Readings,* rev. ed., with an Introduction by George H. Hildebrand (Berkeley and Los Angeles: University of California Press, 1949).

17. This is not the place to consider the various theories of polygenesis, physical environment, and diffusion first advanced by Europeans to explain cultural differences or similarities.

18. Joseph François Lafitau, *Moeurs des Sauvages amériquains, comparées aux moeurs des premier temps* (Paris, 1724); William Robertson, *The History of America* (London, 1777).

19. Turgot, "Tableau philosophique des progrès successifs de l'esprit humain"; "Plan d'un ouvrage sur la géographie politique"; "Plan de deux discours sur l'histoire universelle"; in *Oeuvres de Turgot et documents le concernant, avec biographie et notes,* Gustave Schelle, ed. (Paris: F. Alcan, 1913).

20. Cornelius de Pauw, *Recherches philosophiques sur les Américains, ou mémoires intéressants pour servir à l'histoire de l'espèce humain* (Berlin, 1770); Adam Ferguson, *An Essay on the History of Civil Society,* 8th ed. (Philadelphia, 1819 [1767]); Henry Home, *Sketches of the History of Man* (Edinburgh, 1774); Adam Smith, *An Inquiry into the Nature and Causes of the Wealth of Nations;* Condorcet, *Esquisse d'un tableau historique des progrès de l'esprit humain,* in his *Oeuvres complètes* (Paris, 1804). For a thorough treatment of the Scottish contribution to this notable literature, see Gladys Bryson, *Man and Society: The Scottish Inquiry of the Eighteenth Century* (Princeton: Princeton University Press, 1945).

21. For a typical critique of conventional historians, see Condorcet, *op. cit.,* VIII:314.

22. Ferguson, *op. cit.,* pp. 1, 147.

23. A classic statement of the point appears again in Ferguson, *op. cit.,* pp. 11–12. Adam Smith's derivation of the division of labor from a natural "propensity to truck, barter, and exchange" is a good case in point. See *Wealth of Nations,* I, ii. Bernard Mandeville offers a delightful parody of the psychogenetic method in his *Fable of the Bees.*

24. Auguste Comte, "Plan of the Scientific Operations Necessary for Reorganizing Society," in his *System of Positive Polity, op. cit.,* IV:555.
25. Herbert Spencer, *An Autobiography, op. cit.,* I:384–385.
26. E. B. Tylor, *Primitive Culture,* I:32.
27. For the distinction that Spencer drew between traditional historiography and sociology as "scientific" history, see his "Perverted History," in *Facts and Comments* (New York: D. Appleton, 1902); "What Knowledge Is of Most Worth?" in *Education: Intellectual, Moral, and Physical* (New York: D. Appleton, 1908); "The Social Organism," in *Essays: Scientific, Political, and Speculative* (New York: D. Appleton, 1899–1904), Vol. I.
28. *The Study of Sociology* (New York, 1874), p. 330.
29. "Progress, its Law and Cause," in *Essays,* I:10, 14–15.
30. *Ibid.,* pp. 19–35.
31. *Ibid.,* pp. 35–38, 60.
32. *The Principles of Sociology* (New York: D. Appleton, 1910), I:592–593.
33. *Ibid.,* II:242–243.
34. *Ibid.,* I:550–556.
35. A concise statement of his general position on these points appears in his "Plan of the Scientific Operations Necessary for Reorganizing Society," *op. cit.* For his assertion of the unilinear character of evolution, see *Cours de Philosophie Positive,* 4e éd. (Paris, 1877), IV:266, 318–319, 558 and *Positive Polity,* III:532.
36. *Cours,* IV:343–344; *Positive Polity,* III: 532; "Plan of the Scientific Operations . . . ," *op. cit.,* IV:581–584.
37. Comte's argument on the relationship between the comparative and historical methods appear in *Cours,* IV:316–323.
38. *Positive Polity,* III:xi.
39. Tylor, *Researches into the Early History of Mankind.* See especially: 1–5, 53, 87, 169, 204, 275, 373.
40. *Primitive Culture,* I:2, 25, 32.
41. See Margaret T. Hodgen, *The Doctrine of Survivals* (London: Allenson, 1936).
42. Examples from the literature: Charles Letourneau, *Property: Its Origin and Development* (London: W. Scott, 1892); Andrew Lang, *Modern Mythology* (London: Longmans, Green, 1897); James George Frazer, *The Golden Bough,* abridged ed. (New York: Macmillan, 1922); *Psyche's Task,* 2d ed. (London: Macmillan, 1913); R. R. Marett, *The Threshold of Religion,* 2d ed. (London: Methuen, 1914); Jane Ellen Harrison, *Ancient Art and Ritual* (New York: H. Holt, 1913); F. B. Gummere, *Beginnings of Poetry* (New York: Macmillan, 1901); Thorstein Veblen, *The Theory of the Leisure Class* (New York: Macmillan, 1899); Robert Briffault, *The Mothers: A Study of the Origins of Sentiments and Institutions,* 3 vols. (New York: Macmillan, 1927); Paul Caullet, *Éléments de Sociologie* (Paris: Marcel Rivière, 1913).
43. See Kenneth E. Bock, "Darwin and Social Theory," *Philosophy of Science,* 22 (April, 1955), pp. 123–134, especially the statement that "the conception of social change as manifesting itself in successive stages, tying origin and present together, and the dissociation of events and happenings from this process, clearly indicate the identification of change with growth." The notion of growth rather than the theory of the evolution of species is the *tertium comparationis.*

44. Ludwig Gumplowicz, *The Outlines of Sociology*, trans. by F. W. Moore (Philadelphia: American Academy of Political and Social Science, 1899); *Der Rassenkampf* (Innsbruck: Wagner'sche Universitaets-Buchhandlung, 1883); Gustav Ratzenhofer, *Soziologische Erkenntis* (Leipzig: F. A. Brockhaus, 1898); Franz Oppenheimer, *The State*, trans. by John M. Gitterman (Indianapolis: Bobbs-Merrill, 1914). For Spencer's influence on Sumner and other American social Darwinists, see Richard Hofstadter, *Social Darwinism in American Thought*, rev. ed. (Boston: Beacon Press, 1955).

45. Social evolution was incompatible with racial theory; it depended upon an acceptance of the unity of mankind. The comparative method could not be used if differences were regarded as anything but differences in degree of growth along a common trajectory. Some evolutionists occasionally toyed with the notion that certain tribes might have been retarded by inferior mental endowment, but this was inconsistent with their basic position, and they quickly returned to the idea of psychic unity. For a discussion of the point see K. Bock, "Cultural Differences and Race," *Commentary*, 23 (Feb. 1957), pp. 179–186.

46. Thus Bronislaw Malinowski's suggestion that evolutionary inquiry should be preceded by a functional analysis of culture. "Culture," *Encyclopedia of the Social Sciences*, IV:621–645. See also A. R. Radcliffe-Brown, "The Present Position of Anthropological Studies," in *The Advancement of Science: 1931* (London: British Association for the Advancement of Science, 1931), p. 22: "It seems to me evident that we cannot successfully embark on the study of how culture changes until we have made at least some progress in determining what culture really is and how it works."

47. In his critique of Rivers' unqualified diffusionism, Alexander Goldenweiser made the point that applies to evolutionism as well. "What could be done in theoretical physics, where the conceptual serviceability of a theory was the test of its validity, could not be done in a historical reconstruction, where the specific probability of a theory with reference to a particular historical setting was the only possible test." "Four Phases of Anthropological Thought: An Outline," *Papers and Proceedings, Sixteenth Annual Meeting, American Sociological Society*, XVI (1921), p. 63.

Joseph Maier   CYCLICAL THEORIES

CLEARLY FORMULATED THEORIES of progress and evolution emerged in the eighteenth and nineteenth centuries, but cyclical and conflict theories of history are very old. There were learned as well as simple men in many climes and times who believed they could discern a plot, a conflict, a recurrent rhythmic movement, not only in life, but in the whole realm of being. The examples are readily at hand: the beat of the pulse, the swing of the appetites, the succession of the seasons, the processes of organic growth and decline, and the even mightier cycles of the outer universe. Might not these rhythms have their counterpart in social phenomena? In the fluctuating rates of marriage and divorce, births and deaths, prices and crime, the recurrences of prosperity and recession, the rise and fall of empires and political movements?

Much effort has been expended in the attempt to discover the regularity of a pattern behind these phenomena. From Confucius and Lao-tse to Plato and Aristotle, from St. Augustine and St. Thomas to Machiavelli and Hobbes, from Montesquieu and Adam Smith to Kant and Comte, from Marx and Bagehot to several thinkers of our own time, men have sought to discover the law and meaning of history somewhere between the Scylla that the meaning of history lies outside history and the Charybdis that history has a multiplicity of equally valid or invalid meanings. Nor have all rhythmical theories been of one principal kind. There are dichotomies, such as order-disorder, war-peace, and the Chinese Ying and Yang. There are the more popular three-phase rhythms, or triads, such as appearance-growth-decline, ancient-medieval-modern, theological-metaphysical-positive, thesis-antithesis-synthesis. And there are four- five- and six-phase rhythms, such as childhood-youth-manhood-old age and monarchy-tyranny-oligarchy-democracy-mob rule. There is no doubt that this list could be expanded.

The most striking of these rhythms, the closed cycle of rise, maturity, and decline, as it is said to apply to human groups and entire cultures, is the principal subject matter of this paper. Its purpose is to examine some representative cyclical theories with a view to ascertaining the extent to which the alleged principle of social change is (1) historically accurate and capable of explaining phenomena, (2) primarily a form of inadequate organic analogy, and (3) sometimes a fruitful, albeit limited, hypothesis designed to crystallize and organize further thinking, always subject to verification, modification, or refutation.

Have historical processes been considered to have any direction, as far as the classical civilizations of Greece and Rome are concerned? The zeal with which the Greeks pursued the ideal of an unchanging and eternal object of knowledge might easily deceive us about their lively interest in the laws and institutions which filled their world. To be sure, the general tendency of their thought was unhistorical, if not antihistorical. If history is concerned with what men have done in the past, its objects belong to a world of change, a world where things are here today and gone tomorrow. Moreover, what is transitory cannot be demonstrably known. History, Aristotle said in a famous passage questioning the very intelligibility of its subject matter, tells us merely "what Alcibiades did or had done to him."[1] It is a mere collection of empirical facts. By comparison, Aristotle continued, poetry is far superior and more scientific, as it extracts from such facts a universal judgment. Man wants to know not only what happened, but why and by what fixed and universal principles it happened.

This does not mean that the Greeks cared little for history. Their pursuit of the eternal was as eager as it was precisely because they had an unusually vivid sense of the temporal. "They lived," Collingwood reminds us, "in a time when history was moving with extraordinary rapidity, and in a country where earthquake and erosion change the face of the land with a violence hardly to be seen elsewhere: They saw all nature as a spectacle of incessant change, and human life changing more violently than anything else."[2] It is this realization that nothing in life remains unchanged that might have made the Greeks sensitive to history.

History is a Greek word, meaning inquiry, and as a scholarly enterprise it is a Greek invention. It is the use of this word in the very title of his work that made Herodotus the father of historiography. In the passage in which several Persians are pictured as discussing the relative merits of monarchy, aristocracy, and democracy, most of the standard arguments appear: Monarchy tends to deteriorate into "haughty tyranny"; the license of the tyrant, "stirring strange and unwonted thoughts in the heart of the worthiest of men," leads to democracy. But democracy readily degenerates into "the wantonness of a rude unbridled mob." A government put into the hands of "the best men" is surely preferable, and "it is plain" that the rule of the one best man, "monarchy, is the best government."[3] By the time this manner of theorizing about government and history appears in Plato and Aristotle, it is part of every literate Greek's ABC.

But this cyclical outlook of a ceaseless coming-to-be and passing-away in the affairs of men, in which the processes of history were assimilated with the processes of nature, is not a theory of historical development, an inquiry into the past with the aim of discovering a process of continuing growth, or a theory of historical causation. It is true that Thucydides conceived his history as "an everlasting possession" of mankind, "a true picture of the events which happened, and the like events which may be expected to happen hereafter in the order of human things."[4] And Polybius, who undertook to write a "universal history," even more strongly believed that all polities were subject to an inexorable "law" of "growth, zenith, and decadence, and the time, circumstance, and place in which each of these may be expected to occur."[5] That all mixed forms of government tended to degenerate in "definite" ways, for monarchy to become tyrannous, for aristocracy to turn oligarchical, and so forth, is, as we have noted, an early Greek thought. However, that this method was, as Polybius believed, especially applicable to the Roman constitution is clearly an error. The cyclical scheme does not fit the development of the Roman constitution at all. So far as historical accuracy is concerned, Polybius grasped only a passing phase of the constitution he examined.[6]

Thus, in the Greek view, what may be gleaned from history are not any axioms of cause and effect. It is the "moral" lesson that an excess in one direction is likely to be followed by a change into its opposite, that "a high pitch of prosperity and undisputed power" is likely to prove "the beginning of a deterioration."[7] The Greeks thought that this was a matter of common observation. All that Herodotus would say of the power that ordains decay and change unto all things is that it was "full of jealousy, and fond of troubling our lot."[8] The Greeks could see no direct significance in the changes that time brings into human affairs, and "because there was no sense of the past, there was equally no sense of the future."[9] More than three centuries after Polybius, Marcus Aurelius would express the Graeco-Roman view of the "cyclic regeneration of the universe" in these words: "Our fathers had no fuller vision, neither will our children behold any new thing . . . the man of any understanding who has come to two-score years has in effect beheld the uniformity of all things past and all things to come."[10] Aristotle thought that catastrophes sooner or later wipe out all civilizations, and his emphasis on the importance of the stellar revolutions logically led to the notion of recurrent limited cycles rather than to any large-scale theory of the trend of general history. Greek philosophy was profoundly influenced by the notion of the Great Year, at the end of which all the planets would once again have the same position as today. And when this happened the belief was that all events would repeat themselves, since everything is dependent upon nature.[11]

In contradistinction to the Greeks, the modern conception of history has its roots in the Biblical story of Jahveh and of the world which He creates as the scene for the unfolding of a divine plan. God creates man in His own image to rule the earth, and He selects some of the seed of Abraham to be a priestly people to serve Him and the rest of mankind. On the one hand, early Christianity changed this conception of history in replacing the idea of a Messianic future by the assured faith that the Kingdom of God is already within us. On the other hand, however, later Christianity viewed the past primarily as a preparation for Christ's second coming, secondarily as a prelude for the temporal organization of the Church. In the continuous struggle between the Heavenly City and the Earthly City, with the Church as the Heavenly City on earth, St. Augustine pictured the history of mankind. "This dualism has been maintained not only by good Churchmen, but also by the modern followers of Voltaire and Condorcet. The latter only interchanged the roles of the two cities, picturing the Church as the power of darkness which by its superstitions has opposed the natural light of human reason, and picturing the earthly city of Science as the source of light."[12]

The development of cyclical theory may be said to have manifested itself in two principal models, the astronomical one of the Greeks and the biological one of the moderns, with the Judaeo-Christian idea of mankind, after the fall of Adam, moving toward ultimate redemption as a corrective to the latter. The philosophy of a Muslim thinker of the fourteenth century constitutes a midpoint. In the work of Ibn Khaldun, who "discovered and mastered the fundamentals of sociology some five centuries before Auguste Comte coined the word,"[13] we meet a very self-conscious effort to get at "the inner meaning of history,"[14] an effort directly concerned with the "subtle explanation of the causes and origins of existing things" and the "how and why of events."[15] It tries to demonstrate "how and why dynasties and civilization originate" and everything "concerning the reasons for change and variation in past periods and within religious groups, . . . towns and hamlets, strength and humiliation, large numbers and small numbers, . . . nomadic and sedentary life, actual events and future events, all things expected to occur in civilization."[16]

The cornerstone of Ibn Khaldun's "new science" of culture is his concept of *asabiyah,* that is, group feeling or social solidarity.[17] The strength of its solidarity ultimately determines the superiority of one group over another, as it also determines the leadership within a given group. With the natural "compassion and affection for one's blood relations" at its source, solidarity expands under the threat of external aggression and is affirmed in the ever renewed fight for supremacy and survival.

Against this background, Ibn Khaldun develops the notion of a governing life-cycle of civilization. He believes that states or "dynasties" grow and decline like living organisms. The life-span of a polity, he argues, is about the same as that of an individual, the biblical one hundred and twenty years, or three generations of forty years each. The first generation retains the desert qualities of toughness and savagery, with its group feeling fully intact. The second changes from desert to sedentary culture, from a life of strenuous privation to one of luxury and plenty, and while its solidarity "is broken to some extent," it still retains some of the old virtues. But in the third generation, the toughness and solidarity of the desert are so completely forgotten that it may appear as if they had never existed. The fourth generation starts the cycle of growth, maturity, and senility all over again. To make the biological analogy more striking still, Ibn Khaldun says that growth and decline of culture is much like the changes in the life-cycle of the silkworm, "like the silkworm that spins and then, in turn, finds its end amidst the threads itself has spun."[18]

It has been said that Ibn Khaldun anticipated Spengler, Sorokin, Toynbee, and Brooks Adams in formulating "a law of civilization and decay." He is even credited with having found the key to "the secret which so many modern theorists claim to have discovered anew: why it is that cultures rise and fall in much the same manner that living organisms live and die, and how we can predict, and if possible avert, the final outcome."[19] Alas, "the secret" is not disclosed. Even if we grant that Ibn Khaldun's "actual laboratory for the induction and testing of his theories of culture was the history of the Arabs generally and, more specifically, of the petty kingdoms and states that had mushroomed in the Muslim West,"[20] the claim that his was a "universal history" is not thereby sustained. Also, the constant reiteration of God's name is much more deeply grounded in the whole outlook of Ibn Khaldun than can be explained by reference to the circumstance that he had to write "esoterically" in order to avoid offending the sensibilities of Muslim orthodoxy. Muhsin Mardi is probably correct in saying that what Ibn Khaldun expected from history does not go beyond assisting him in applying the standards and goals he had learned from the political philosophy of Plato and Aristotle and that "he turned to history to learn how and to what extent he could apply the immutable standards which transcend history."[21]

The picture changes with Vico's *New Science,* which appeared in 1725. This work anticipates not only the fundamental ideas of Herder, Hegel, Dilthey, Michelet and Croce, but also the more specific discoveries of Roman history by Niebuhr and Mommsen, the interpretation of mythology by Bachofen, the reconstruction of ancient folk life through etymology by Grimm, the historical understanding of laws by Savigny, of the ancient city by Fustel de Coulanges, and of class struggles by Marx and Sorel.[22] It remains "one of the few works of original genius in the entire history of social theory."[23] The originality of Vico's *New Science* will be appreciated against the background of the Cartesian philosophy which was in vogue in the eighteenth century. Vico did not question the validity of mathematical knowledge, but he did impugn the Cartesian theory of knowledge with its implication that no other kind of knowledge was possible. He did so on the principle that *verum et factum convertuntur,* that is, we know intimately and certainly only that which we have caused or made—a condition wherein the true, or *verum,* is identical with the created or *factum.* Following from this, mathematics is certainly intelligible to man because its objects are constructs created by the mathematician. Extending the premise a step further, nature is ultimately intelligible only to God because He created it. But what about history, the "common nature of the nations," which is the principal concern of Vico's science?

Even the remote beginnings of history, says Vico, are eminently adapted to be an object of human knowledge because "in the night of thick darkness enveloping the earliest antiquity, so remote from ourselves, there shines the eternal and never failing light of a truth beyond all question: that the world of civil society has certainly been made by men, and that its principles are therefore to be found within the modifications of our own human mind."[24] Vico views the historical process as one whereby men build up systems of language, custom, law, and the like. History, to him, is the history of human societies and their institutions. Here, then, we reach "for the first time a completely modern idea of what the subject-matter of history is . . . The fabric of human society is created by man out of nothing, and every detail of this fabric is therefore a human *factum,* eminently knowable to the human mind as such."[25]

Precisely because the essence of man and nations is what it is by historic development, historical knowledge in general is possible. Vico's *New Science* "therefore comes to describe at the same time an ideal eternal history traversed in time by the history of every nation in its rise, development, maturity, decline and fall . . . Now, as geometry, when it constructs the world of quantity out of its elements or contemplates that world, is creating it for itself, just so does our Science (create for itself the world of nations), but with a reality greater by just so much as the institutions having to do with human affairs are more real than points, lines, surfaces, and figures are."[26]

According to Vico, the regular, typical course of human history in general, and of every culture in particular, proceeds "with the greatest equality and constancy" through three phases: the age of gods, the age of heroes, and the age of men. It leads from anarchy to order, from savage and heroic customs to rational and civilized procedures where industry prevails over agriculture, prose over poetry, a morality of peace over a morality of war. This development, however, is a development without fulfilment. It is followed by a new barbarism. The *corso* is followed by a *ricorso,* a recurrence which is, at the same time, a resurgence. The new barbarism is quite different from the heroic barbarism of the imagination; it is a "barbarism of the reflection." The barbarism of the Middle Ages is not simply a duplication of the pagan barbarism of early Greece and Rome; it is differentiated by everything that makes it distinctively an expression of the Christian mind.[27] Thus Vico puts the normal course in the following way: "Men first feel necessity, then look for utility, next attend to comfort, still later amuse themselves with pleasure, thence grow dissolute in luxury, and finally go mad and waste their substance."[28] But sometimes Providence supplies a remedy by ordaining that "there be found among these peoples a man like Augustus to rise and establish himself as a monarch." Or it decrees that "they become subject to better nations, which, having conquered them by arms, preserve them as subject provinces."[29] Or, if a nation is "rotting in that ultimate civil disease and cannot agree on a monarch from within and is not conquered and preserved by better nations from without," then Providence "for their extreme ill has its extreme remedy" at hand, the *ricorso* to the "primitive simplicity of the first world of peoples," the state of piety and faith.[30]

The cyclical movement observed by Vico is thus not a mere cycle of fixed phases, but a spiral. For this reason, Collingwood noted, the cyclical law does not permit us to forecast the future.[31] History, to Vico, repeats and does not repeat itself. It does not repeat itself in that it comes round to each new phase in a form different from what it had been before, and, as in Hegel's dialectical scheme, it repeats itself, but ever on another level and with ever-changing modifications. In the end, however, we must ask ourselves how valid Vico's three-phases doctrine really is. Is it not gleaned from an idealized concept of Roman history? Does the same principle apply "with the greatest equality and constancy" to what Vico called the history of remote and obscure periods? Suppose we grant that the Homeric period of Greek history and the European Middle Ages were both "heroic" in that they both had a morality based on the idea of personal prowess and fealty, an agricultural economy, a ballad literature, a warrior aristocracy, and so forth. Is it true that in order to find out more than the Odyssey and Iliad can tell us about the Homeric age we should do well by studying the Middle Ages and seeing to what extent we can apply what we have found there to the remote beginnings of Greek civilization? Is it true that by studying modern savages we can learn what ancient savages were like in the face of the fact that these modern savages are as removed in time and place from the ancients as we are ourselves?

What is generally referred to as "historical consciousness" is a late product of human civilization, in fact, not much older than the eighteenth century and Vico's *New Science*. When we now turn to a discussion of the modern cyclical theories of Hegel, Pareto, Brooks Adams, Spengler, Toynbee, and Sorokin, it must be said that while they are distinguished by a profound historical consciousness, their appreciations of the cycles of human history do not easily lend themselves to scientific proof either. They are fruitful historical hypotheses, and nothing more.

The common core of all the classical systems of European sociology is the idea that the existing social order is a historical category, a link in a chain of social forms, possessing its own dynamism and "inner contradictions." That is true for the thought of St. Simon and Comte, as well as of Lorenz von Stein and Karl Marx. Herder laid the groundwork for this idea, which was most systematically elaborated by Hegel. Contrasting historical change with changes in nature, Hegel maintains that historical change is "an advance to something better, more perfect," whereas mutation in nature "exhibits only a perpetually self-repeating cycle."[32] Historical change is therefore identical with development. The principle of development implies that there is a latent "potentiality striving to realize itself." While this is true of every living being, the highest form of development is reached only when self-consciousness exercises mastery over the whole process. The thinking subject "produces itself, expands itself actually to what it always was potentially."[33] How does it do that in history? The thinking subject lives in history, and the state furnishes the existential conditions of its historical life. The state exists as the universal interest amid individual actions and interests. At first the state appears as an immediate, "natural" unity, a golden youth. At this stage, social antagonisms have not yet intensified and individuals find satisfaction in the state without consciously opposing their individualities to the commonwealth. Unconscious, that is, potential freedom prevails, and actual freedom comes only with the unfolding of self-consciousness, with thought as the vehicle of the transformation. Sooner or later, however, the free rationality of thought must come into conflict with the rationalizations of the given order of life. This is the dialectic, the eternal law of history.[34]

For Hegel, whatever is is right; but this only means that what exists is a

necessary moment in the unceasing advance to something better. It is for man
to examine everything he has produced, every institution he has willed into
being, discover its essence, and carry it forward in accordance with the demands of reason. The highest potentialities of man are realized only in society.
When we examine contemporary civil society, however, we find that it is the
scene of unmitigated group egoism and that it has only imperfectly achieved
the "unity of the universal and subjective will." It contains an immanent contradiction: the *bellum omnium contra omnes,* the different segments of civil
society warring and competing with one another. Through this contradiction,
"by means of its own dialectic, the civic community is driven beyond its own
limits."[35]

Hegel stressed the recurrence of the same problems and of the same forms
of social life in different civilizations, but there are also dissimilarities. He
believed that every civilization was characterized by one specific dominating
concern, which left its imprint on all ongoing activities. In emphasizing the
differences between different forms of expression of the "Universal Spirit," he
stressed the essential sameness of all aspects of social life. Sameness in difference and difference in sameness is the essential point in the Hegelian dialectic.

While it is easy to appreciate how much of modern thought is owed to
Hegel's conception of reality as consisting of processes, of movements, with
everything being subject to change and development, it is important to remember, however, that all political, economic, social and historical categories
are, with Hegel, philosophical categories. In the end, history itself becomes a
mere moment in his total philosophical system, which culminates in the Absolute Spirit: Art, Religion and Philosophy. "World History," he says, "exhibits
the development of the consciousness of freedom on the part of Spirit, and of
the consequent realization of that freedom."[36] The rhythm and plot of history
which empirical enquirers are not able to detect, is clear to Hegel from the
outset. It derives from "the simple thought of reason, that reason rules the
world, and consequently that world history too is a rational process."[37] What
is meant by "a rational process" in this context is apparently that the outlines
of history, though perhaps not its details, are deducible from philosophical
premises. Reason is here the idealistic "free" reason of man, which is without
any intelligible connection with the real process of history. When it is brought
into relation with the empirical world, it appears as a timeless, static element.
"It is not the universal Idea that is implicated in opposition and combat, and
that is exposed to danger. It remains in the background, untouched and un-
injured."[38] This is what Hegel calls the "cunning of reason." As for man's
role in this process, he is nothing but the "means" in the process of the self-
realization of the Idea. In this way the historical process, where states, peoples
and individuals are but "the unconscious tools and organs of the universal
spirit"[39] and where "the Idea pays the penalty of determinate existence and of

corruptibility, not from itself, but from the passions of individuals,"[40] leads beyond itself into the realm of the Absolute.

In the sense that the Idea is ever present and above all limitations of time, the Hegelian philosophy of history allows no real passage from the present to the future. It fixates upon the present and treats it as a mere thing which neither needs nor is subject to process and development; it transforms a seemingly dynamic dialectic into a static metaphysic.[41] Hegel professes to tell us about the plot of history. But since history is an uncompleted process, how can its overall plot be empirically discovered? It is true, Hegel briefly observed, that "America is the land of the future where, in the ages that lie before us, the burden of the world's history will reveal itself."[42] He may be right, but it is not clear how these ages may be fitted into his scheme.[43] It would rather seem that the stoppage of the dialectic in the present is deeply woven into the structure of Hegelian logic. To Hegel, truth is "the bacchanalian revel where not a soul is sober," but it is paradoxically the kind of revel that can be characterized as a state of "transparent unbroken calm,"[44] for every phase of it is "endowed with the entire wealth of Spirit."[45] His philosophy of history is substantially a metaphysical adaptation of the Christian view. History is the unfolding of God, and God is primarily a logician unfolding Himself in Hegel's dialectical logic.[46] As the world-drama requires antagonists, the Absolute creates His own antithesis in the process of unfolding, and in that struggle the synthesis is produced. History moves on in an unending spiral, revealing its full plot and rhythm in an eternal present and yet not quite revealing it but waiting to reveal it in unique detail "in the ages that lie before us."

If Hegel had portrayed history as a dialetical process moving toward the realization of freedom, with different nations coming successively to the fore and each making its contribution to the ultimate end, Pareto, too, was convinced that history proceeds by cycles or undulations. In contrast to Hegel, however, he stresses sameness exclusively. By that token he falls behind Hegel in the appreciation of the historical process, and, for all his seeming scientism, his assumption of a cyclical movement takes no less than Hegel's dialectic the form of metaphysical assertion.

According to Pareto, three types of cycles may be distinguished—accidental, short, and long. Cyclical movement, he believes, may be observed throughout social life, but he begins its consideration with economic cycles. Accidental cycles are started by transitory facts, such as the revolution of 1848 or the war of 1870. Since their causes are transitory, so are their effects. Short cycles are the well-known business cycles, but Pareto is more concerned with long cycles. He observes that the period of 1852–73 was generally favorable, the one of 1873–97 unfavorable for business, while the period of 1898–1911 showed an ascending trend. But he cannot say much about former periods because data are lacking. Again, the whole of the modern period is contained in one still larger trend of economic ascendency, beginning with the discovery of America, which in itself was an accident of history.[47] In the last analysis, however, economic cycles seem to be determined by the movement of residues and the circulation of elites.

The theory of the circulation of elites is perhaps the core of Pareto's social thought. He starts with the simple factual observation that since men differ from one another in physical strength as well as scientific and artistic talent, they will differ in economic ability, general intelligence, and fitness to govern. He goes on to say that the economic, social and political differentiation of society corresponds to the natural differentiation in abilities. "Today," he observes,[48] "the ideas of Lapouge, Ammon and others, though partly erroneous and imperfect, have the great merit of having emphasized this important fact, the ignoring of which profoundly vitiates all democratic theories." Pareto is, of course, opposed to the vision of unilinear human perfectibility. But there arises a puzzling problem. If elites *ex definitione* are the very best there is, why then do they degenerate so conspicuously in the course of history? "Aristocracies," says Pareto,[49] "do not last. For one reason or another, after a certain time they disappear."

Since elites cannot persist, they must change. How? Here, Pareto transfers the ideal-typical economic situation to the sphere of "illogical actions," which is society. In a societal environment where competition is completely free, the gifted will rise and the nongifted fall. But the free circulation of the elites can never be reached, not even in a system of economic liberalism. Politics inevitably enters into economic relations, and in a sheer struggle for power a completely free circulation of elites is impossible by definition. At best, there is intelligent admission of the best elements of the lower classes into the ruling elite. Consequently, elites tend to become "closed"; they get corrupted and fall prey to their rising opponents. Generally, an elite relying on courage, force, violence, is followed by a bourgeois, plutocratic elite, depending on ruse, intrigue, and ideology, and vice versa. The social equilibrium is constantly being disturbed by the accumulation of "inferiors" in the upper class or "superiors" in the lower. Change finally comes when the elites do not have the residues adapted for governing while the lower classes do.

To prove his point, Pareto adduces examples from Italian, Greek, and Roman history, and there is no question about the facts he cites. But they serve to *illustrate* rather than *prove* his theory, and it is doubtful whether the history of other civilizations, such as those of ancient Egypt, India, or China will serve the latter purpose.[50] The circulation of elites remains an interesting idea, much akin to Nietzsche's doctrine of "eternal recurrence," but without Nietzsche's expectation that the "superman" will fulfill and break the cycle. "It suffers the general imperfection of instinctivist theories; they put something into human beings and then explain all conduct by what they have put in."[51] In this it is reminiscent of Ibn Khaldun's treatment of the subject.[52] Assuredly, Pareto is more pessimistic than Vico and Hegel. In his scorn for the idea of progress, in his view of the cyclical movement of social phenomena, the complete recurrence of the "essential" facts of history, he shows a strong affinity with the Greeks and an even stronger one with Spengler.

In the very first sentence of *The Decline of the West,* Spengler announces that he is attempting "for the first time" to predetermine history. History itself, he believes, makes such an attempt possible. Instead of one linear time, Spengler assumes as many "times" as there are historical civilizations—eight high civilizations, to be exact, since primitive societies may be neglected as "historyless." The fate of each is to fulfill the life-cycle of any organism, from birth to death. That, quite naturally, applies also to our own Western civilization, which has passed its peak and has nothing to look forward to but its inevitable decline and doom. It is directed neither by the will of God nor by the will of man. Its "sublimity" consists in this very development from rise and flowering to ultimate disintegration. To that extent Spengler's cyclical theory is thoroughly Greek.

But Spengler has also a peculiar "sense of the future,"[53] a dynamic and infinite Faustian conception of history, radically different from the static finiteness of classical Apollonian culture. He does not view the decline of the West with detachment. He invites his fellows to will and love their fate, even promote and fulfill it. No ancient ever fancied that the fate of decline should be willed and chosen, "for fate is either really fate, and then it is futile to decide upon it, or it is a self-chosen destiny, and then it is no unavoidable fate."[54] Hence Spengler's pathos grows from "the confusion of the will to a future, still open to possibilities, with the acceptance of a definite outcome."[55] Fundamentally, however, his outlook is biological. The word "humanity" is to him but an empty phrase. The great civilizations, Spengler maintains, are unique, unconnected, self-contained organisms. Not even science and technology show accumulations transcending the limits of one civilization. A civilization "blooms on the soil of an exactly definable landscape, to which plantlike it remains bound" and dies when it has "actualized the full sum of its possibilities in the shape of peoples, languages, dogmas, arts, states, sciences."[56] The biological phrases referring to the life-cycle of each civilization are meant to be understood quite literally. A civilization flowers and withers as surely and inevitably as any organism.[57]

No space can here be devoted to pointing out the specific errors of fact and the general distortion of history committed by Spengler. Most historians of repute have rejected his work and the organismic version of an all-inclusive cyclical theory. Also, Spengler's alleged affinity to the social Darwinists and to Gumplowicz is more apparent than real.[58] The *tertium comparationis* in each case is conflict theory, but the social Darwinists' progress-piety contrasts sharply with Spengler's pessimistic-heroic, almost Wagnerian, outlook; and Gumplowicz' assumption of the polygenetic origin of mankind is by no means as absolute as Spengler's conviction that each culture so stamps "its material, its mankind, in its own image" that people who belong to one cannot understand, and are hostile to, the achievements and modes of thought of the other.[59] Gumplowicz is concerned with the transformation of ethnic into class antagonism, which places him in the vicinity of Marx,[60] and with the circulation of elites within political states, which relates him to Pareto, to Gaetano Mosca,[61] and even to Ibn Khaldun.[62]

With more justice it may be said that Spengler's historical pessimism is a dramatic echo of the more resigned *fin de siècle* pessimism of Brooks Adams in *The Law of Civilization and Decay*. Surveying and interpreting social change from the Romans to modern times, Adams sees a cycle of phases through which human society must, apparently, pass in its oscillations between "barbarism" and "civilization," or, what amounts to the same thing, in its movement from a condition of physical dispersion to one of concentration. As societies differ in the manifestation of energy, in the earlier stages of concentration it is fear that appears to be the channel through which energy finds the readiest outlet, and, "accordingly, in primitive and scattered communities, the imagination is vivid, and the mental types produced are religious, military, artistic." As consolidation advances, fear yields to greed, and the economic organism tends to supersede the emotional and martial. Thenceforward, capital becomes autocratic, energy vents itself through those organisms best fitted to give expression to the power of capital. "In this last stage of consolidation, the economic, and, perhaps, the scientific intellect is propagated, while the imagination fades, and the emotional, the martial, and the artistic types of manhood decay."[63]

That martial virtues become submerged in monied interests, that the personal element is being replaced by the rational in the course of a civilization's development—these ideas may be said to anticipate Max Weber's view of social evolution in terms of a continuous growth of the rational habit of mind and his belief that rationalization was "our destiny."[64] They are also suggestive of thoughts which find more subtle and sophisticated treatment in Georg Simmel's *Philosophie des Geldes*. For Weber and Simmel, however, these are ideal-typical generalizations, covering many though by no means all phases of life, and not an all-encompassing "law of civilization and decay." When Adams writes: "No poetry can bloom in the arid modern soil, the drama has died, and the patrons of art are no longer even conscious of shame at profaning the most sacred of ideals,"[65] the images that come to mind are rather Spengler's spectacle of a shallow "civilization" of technique and trade replacing the profound "culture" of art, music, and literature, and Sorokin's vision of a "sensate culture" at its peak and inevitably nearing its end.

Like Spengler's, the work of Toynbee and Sorokin on the genesis of civilization is written under a compelling awareness of its decline; and in the sense that they suffer from the same "confusion of the will to a future, still open to possibilities, with the acceptance of a definite outcome," both Toynbee and Sorokin are, as it were, Spenglerians. Where Spengler saw eight civilizations, Toynbee finds twenty-one. They all have come and gone, repeating a recurrent cycle of birth and growth, breakdown and disintegration. The elites within each civilization meet challenge and response, resort to withdrawal and return, are subject to rally and rout, sub-rally and sub-rout, down to the bitter end, in precisely three-and-a-half beats. They have all perished, except Western civilization, about which, although it has already experienced one-and-a-half beats, Toynbee leaves us in doubt. He is less pessimistic than Spengler, though. As a professed Christian, he rejects Spengler's biological analogy. When civilizations break down, he says, it is not because of any cosmic law, but through their own actions: they exhaust themselves as their response to successive challenges becomes ossified.

Organicism, evolutionism, and a Christian outlook combine into a complex amalgam in Toynbee's interpretation of history.[66] Primitive societies, he says, "may be likened to people lying torpid upon a ledge on a mountainside, with a precipice below and precipice above." By contrast, his twenty-one civilizations, "specimens of a species" belonging to a single "genus" all, "may be likened to companions of these 'sleepers of Ephesus' who have just risen to their feet and have started to climb on up the face of the cliff."[67] They have direction, they know the road. What road and what direction? To Toynbee it is quite clear that "the consummation of history" consists in "accomplishing the transformation of Sub-Man through Man into Super-Man."[68] For this, he says, is "the goal towards which 'the whole creation groaneth and travaileth' (Romans VIII, 22)."[69]

Assuredly, to this "empirical student of history," history is not merely the history of civilizations; it actually "passes over into theology."[70] History is religious in nature and, more especially, God become man in Christ is its sense and essence. Civilizations are the "handmaids" of religion. Likening religion unto a chariot, it looks to Toynbee "as if the wheels on which it mounts towards Heaven may be the periodic downfalls of civilizations on Earth. It looks as if the movement of civilizations may be cyclic and recurrent, while the movement of religion may be on a single continuous upward line. The continuous upward movement of religion may be served and promoted by the cyclic movement of civilizations round the cycle of birth, death, birth."[71]

If we accept this conclusion, it opens up what Toynbee himself admits to as "a rather startling view of history." If civilizations are the handmaids of religion and if the Graeco-Roman civilization served as a handmaiden by bringing Christianity to birth before it finally went to pieces itself, then "the civilizations of the third generation may be vain repetitions of the Gentiles." It now appears to Toynbee that it is not the historical function of higher religions to minister, as chrysalises, to the cyclic process of the reproduction of civilizations, but the other way around: "It is the historical function of civilizations to serve, by their downfalls, as stepping-stones to a progressive process of the revelation of always deeper religious insight, and the gift of ever more grace to act on this insight."[72] The moment they have brought a higher religion to birth, "the societies of the species called civilizations have fulfilled their function." On this showing, indeed, "our own Western post-Christian secular civilization might at best be a superfluous repetition of the pre-Christian Graeco-Roman one, and at worst a pernicious backsliding from the path of spiritual progress."[73]

If Toynbee's "rather startling view of history" is decidedly more Christian though hardly more empirical than that of Spengler, his grand formula of "Challenge and Response" appears similarly not evolved from inside history but "is applied, as it were, from the outside; and its applicability, let alone its power to explain the facts, is often more than doubtful."[74] Perhaps, as Howard Becker has pointed out, this formula is very similiar to the socio-psychic mechanism of "crisis," as used by W. I. Thomas.[75] There is no question about its partial psychological value in enabling us to distinguish between individuals who can cope with a changing environment and those who cannot. Even in regard to cultures it is a convenient metaphor conveying the edifying moral truth that the successful life is a continuous succession of problems met and solved. None of this makes it an empirical law, however. Unless, as Sidney Hook says, "we can define what constitutes a successful response, unless we can say in advance what kind of unsuccessful response to what kind of problem spells disaster for a culture, unless we can formulate a hypothesis concerning the determinate conditions under which a creative response will or will not be made, we have hardly made a beginning towards a scientific study of the rise, growth, and decline of cultures. It may be that we do not know enough to speak confidently about laws that hold for cultures as a whole. But we do not know more when we resort to myths or to capricious intrusions of the creative spirit to account for what at the moment we cannot explain."[76]

Indeed, the most essential criticism that has been made of Toynbee refers to his claim that *A Study of History* was based on empirical methods. When you fish in a cauldron, says Pieter Geyl, you cannot select, and to select is exactly what Toynbee is doing all the time: "He selects the instances which will support his theses, or he presents them in the way that suits him, and he does so with an assurance which hardly leaves room for the suspicion, not only that one might quote innumerable others with which his theses would not bear company, but especially that those cases he does mention can be explained or described in a different way so as to disagree no less completely with his theses."[77]

It may be that Toynbee has given to sociologists "a magnificent example of the possibilities of culture case-study in historical sociology."[78] For all the inaccuracies that have been noted,[79] there has been much praise of Toynbee's many brilliant and illuminating interpretations of data he knows best, that is, those of Greek and Roman history. What is true for several and separate "histories," however, need not be so for all history. Possibly, as heuristic constructs or ideal-types, Toynbee's "laws" of the rise and decline of civilization are more or less fruitful for the understanding of a historical reality, depending on whether or not one shares his theological assumptions and proclivities.

We now turn to Sorokin, the other great exponent of comparative sociology and the culture case-study method. No other scholar has engaged in such extensive and intentive studies of cyclical theories, and with as much careful scrutiny and penetrating criticism.[80] His long list of social cycles is well-nigh complete. Institutions, ideas, population, distribution of national income, art, philosophy, science, psychology—all of these would be subject to the swing of the pendulum. Sorokin classifies civilizations into two main types: the "ideational" and the "sensate." The course of history is seen as one in which civilizations traverse a number of stages, from growth to maturity to decline and transformation, in a continuous though somewhat irregular fluctuation between sensate and ideational, with a transitional "idealistic" civilization between them. Obviously, none of these types has ever actually existed in pure form. They are rather, once again, "ideal types," with historical cultures approaching but never fully exemplifying the Ideational or Sensate. For example, Greek culture, in all the compartments of life, art, and thought, before the sixth century B.C. was predominantly Ideational (good); after the fourth century B.C. it was predominantly Sensate (bad).

All the main fluctuations of each compartment of the cultures studied by Sorokin "are all but manifestations of the change of the system of the whole culture, somewhat analogous to many anatomical, physiological and mental changes which occur when an organism passes from, say, childhood to maturity."[81] History moves, but does not move permanently in one direction. A sensate culture reaches its "limit," and by the operation of "immanent change" gives birth to a new culture, that is, the old values of ideationalism, which, in turn, will make room for a new sensate culture. Societies and cultures change because it is their "nature" to change, each being "a system that has its own immanent law and logic of change."[82]

In his apocalyptic conception of social change, the "Christian anarchist" Sorokin does not differ essentially from Spengler and Toynbee. He, too, sees the present status of Western culture and society as showing the "tragic spectrum of the beginning of the disintegration of their sensate supersystem" and predicts that their nearest future "will pass under the sign of the *dies irae, dies illa* to a new ideational or idealistic phase." Among the thirteen forecasts presumably based on the impressive number of statistics, graphs and calculations presented throughout his work, Sorokin makes the following: Contracts and covenants will lose the remnants of their binding power; rude force and cynical fraud will become the only arbiters of all values and of all inter-individual and intergroup relationships; freedom will become a mere myth for the majority and will be turned into unbridled licentiousness by the dominant minority; governments will become more and more hoary, fraudulent, and tyrannical, giving bombs instead of bread; Beethoven and Bach will become appendices to the eloquent rhapsodies of advertised laxatives, gums, and cereals; the material standard of living will go down.[83]

Whether Sorokin will be ultimately right or wrong is not the question here. The question is rather this: can the Hobbesian "state of nature" he projects really be predicted, and chiefly on the basis of calculating the sensate elements of a culture, that is, things an "ideationally" oriented observer does not like, such as biology, behaviorist psychology, psychoanalysis, empiricism and so forth? Is not the conclusion that Western civilization is in decline and due for "crisis-catharsis-charisma-resurrection" rather the one point fixed and determined beforehand in his categorial scheme?

It is Sorokin's final criticism of Toynbee that the latter failed to "translate" *A Study of History* into "the more accurate terms of real sociocultural systems and of the great rhythm of Sensate-Idealistic-Ideational supersystems of culture."[84] Sorokin may be right in this. His terms *are* more adequate for the purposes of sociological analysis. Yet, some of the same difficulties we have noted above in connection with Spengler and Toynbee continue to plague us. For one, Sorokin's categorial scheme, far from showing objective detachment, appears to be primarily a value scheme whose two basic poles are ideational (good) and sensate (bad). The impression is thus conveyed that the historical phenomena were studied not in order to understand their specific "law and logic of change" but rather in order to "grade" them.[85] Furthermore, is it enough to say that a culture changes from sensate to ideational or vice versa because it is its *nature* to do so? What, precisely, is the explanatory value of the principle of "immanent change" and "self-adjustment" according to which everything changes anyhow, irrespective of external influences and identifiable events?[86] Any principle of social change would seem to attain historical relevance only if it served to explain *specific* social changes.

Having examined some of the principal exponents of the cyclical view of history, we should now be in a position to assess some of the strengths and weaknesses of that view. Is it possible to lay bare the secret of the rhythm of history as such? The existence of all-inclusive cycles can neither be asserted nor denied *a priori*. That institutions and ideas come into being, flourish and wither is as the Greeks noted, a matter of nature and observation. However, no law seems to govern the speed of such transformations, and the facts of history cannot be shown to conform to any single fixed pattern. At first glance, then, the whole effort to demonstrate the operation of any determinate cycles of history would appear to have been a fantastic waste of time and effort. This it most decidedly was not. Whatever the specific shortcomings of the cyclical thinkers we have discussed, it cannot be denied that at least their indirect influence on modern historiography and historical sociology has been formidable. By stressing the importance of viewing historical facts as a coherent and functional whole, they contributed immensely to the development of these disciplines. Their efforts must be characterized as an attempt to comprehend history from the outside. But some of their ideas, those of Hegel in particular, showed a depth of insight which later historians were to turn to excellent use. The suggestion, for example, that, in studying the culture of a given people at a given time, we can find in the conception of an *ethos* or a folk-spirit the connecting link between phenomena previously thought to be wholly separate, has proved a fertile source of empirical hypothesis, and may thus be said to have shed real light on some dark places in history.[87]

What, then, is our conclusion concerning the cyclical theories of social change? These theories seem to be intermediate between the view of history as a record of man's degeneration and the doctrine of perpetual progress, for neither of these trends is capable of infinite extension. It attributes, as we have seen, to every culture or civilization the characteristics of infancy, maturity, and senescence, and it invokes the principle of limited possibilities to deny the emergence of real novelty in the world. But here we are confronted by two principal difficulties.

For one, the notion of a life cycle of civilizations assumes that external occurrences cannot change the course of a civilization. That is not even true for the path of a planet, to say nothing of the path of a civilization. To be sure, the order of the periods of a human life is immutable. But the analogy between the individual life cycle and the life cycle of a civilization is unclear and indefinite. "In Societies, of whatever kind, there seems to be no such necessary or essential Tendency to Dissolution. The human body is naturally mortal; the political body only so by Accident . . . There appears nothing in the internal Construction of any State, that tends inevitably to Dissolution, analogous to those Causes in the human Frame, which lead to certain Death."[88] The criteria by which we can judge whether a person is still alive, or has departed for the happy hunting ground, are precise and definite, but *when* did Judaism become fossilized and Greek civilization go the way of all flesh? Besides, historically, no two known civilizations have traversed the supposed cycle in the same way, for no two civilizations have started at the same point. Later generations have learned in some measure from the experiences of the preceding ones.

Furthermore, we have become distrustful of grand historical generalizations altogether. Among social scientists and historians it is now recognized that discoveries are made and knowledge acquired, not by constructing comprehensive laws, but by enunciating hypotheses which open the way to fresh inquiry. Instead of searching for an encompassing body of knowledge which would settle issues once and for all, we might better entertain "the more modest hope of advancing from one fragmentary hypothesis to another, isolating our facts through the medium of our interpretations, and testing our interpretations by the facts."[89] In any case, we are far from knowing enough to speak confidently about laws, cyclical or otherwise, that hold for cultures singly or culture generally. Yet there is insight in the cyclical view of history, in the notion that both progress and degeneration occur in the course of human development, that neither is of infinite extent, and that in so far as we can subject various periods of history to abstract questions with a limited range of possible answers, some of our answers are bound to recur. We agree with Morris R. Cohen that "recurrences relative to a given abstract factor are not a sufficient guide to the writing of history, since they cannot exhaust the concrete fullness of any event or period, but they are the stuff out of which generalization in the social sciences emerges. So qualified, the theory of cycles or undulations may guard us against the more violent extremes of optimism and pessimism. . . ."[90]

Notes

1. Aristotle, *On the Art of Poetry*. Transl. by Ingram Bywater (Oxford: The Clarendon Press, 1909), 27.
2. R. G. Collingwood, *The Idea of History* (Oxford: The Clarendon Press, 1946), 22.
3. Francis R. B. Godolphin, ed., *The Greek Historians* (New York: Random House, 1942), I, 199–200.
4. *Ibid.*, I, 576.
5. Polybius, *The Histories*. Transl. by Evelyn S. Shuckburgh (London: The Macmillan Co., 1889), I, 461.
6. George H. Sabine, *A History of Political Theory* (New York: Henry Holt & Co., 1958), 155.
7. Polybius, *op. cit.*, I, 507.
8. Francis R. B. Godolphin, *op. cit.*, I, 15.
9. Edward Hallet Carr, *What is History?* (New York: Alfred A. Knopf, 1962), 145.
10. Marcus Aurelius Antoninus, *To Himself*. Transl. by G. H. Rendall (London: The Macmillan Co., 1923), 140–141.
11. Morris R. Cohen, *The Meaning of Human History* (La Salle, Ill.: The Open Court Publishing Co., 1947), 11.
12. *Ibid.*, 12.
13. Gerson D. Cohen, "Ibn Khaldun: Rediscovered Arab Philosopher," *Midstream*, V (1959), No. 3, 77.
14. Ibn Khaldun, *The Muqaddimah*. Transl. by Franz Rosenthal (New York: Pantheon Books, 1958), I, 6.
15. *Ibid.*
16. *Ibid.*, 13.
17. Don Martindale, *The Nature and Types of Sociological Theory* (Boston: Houghton Mifflin Co., 1960), 132.

18. Ibn Khaldun, *op. cit.*, I, 297. Cf. Kamil Ayad, *Die Geschichts und Gesell-schaftslehre Ibn Khalduns* (Stuttgart: Cotta, 1930), 163.
19. Gerson D. Cohen, *op. cit.*, 81.
20. *Ibid.*
21. Muhsin Mahdi, *Ibn Khaldun's Philosophy of History* (London: George Allen & Unwin Ltd., 1957), 295.
22. Karl Löwith, *Meaning in History* (Chicago: University of Chicago Press, 1949), 115.
23. *The New Science of Giambatista Vico.* Transl. from the Third Edition by Thomas Goddard Bergin and Max Harold Fisch (New York: Doubleday Anchor Books, 1961), xiii.
24. *Ibid.*, 52.
25. R. G. Collingwood, *op. cit.*, 65.
26. *The New Science*, 62–63.
27. R. G. Collingwood, *op. cit.*, 68.
28. *The New Science*, 37.
29. *Ibid.*, 381.
30. *Ibid.*
31. R. G. Collingwood, *op. cit.*, 68. Cf. also Richard Peters, *Der Aufbau der Weltgeschichte bei Giambatista Vico* (Stuttgart: Cotta, 1929), *et passim.;* Max Horkheimer, *Anfänge der bürgerlichen Geschichtsphilosophie* (Stuttgart: W. Kohlhammer, 1930), 95–114.
32. Hegel, *The Philosophy of History.* Transl. by J. Sibree (New York: The Colonial Press, 1899), 54.
33. *Ibid.*, 55.
34. Herbert Marcuse, *Reason and Revolution* (New York: Oxford University Press, 1941), 238–239. Cf. also Ernst Troeltsch, *Der Historismus und seine Probleme* (Tübingen: J. C. B. Mohr, 1922), 241–277, 333–358, 619–623.
35. Hegel, *Philosophy of Right.* Transl. by S. W. Dyde (London: G. Bell & Sons, 1896), 164.
36. Hegel, *Philosophy of History*, 66.
37. *Ibid.*, 9.
38. Hegel, *Sämtliche Werke* (Stuttgart: F. Frommann, 1927–1940), XI, 63.
39. Hegel, *Philosophy of Right*, 343.
40. Hegel, *Philosophy of History*, 33.
41. Joseph Maier, *On Hegel's Critique of Kant* (New York: Columbia University Press, 1939), 95.
42. Hegel, *Philosophy of History*, 90.
43. W. H. Walsh, *Philosophy of History* (New York: Harper Torch Books, 1960), 152.
44. Hegel, *The Phenomenology of Mind.* Transl. by J. B. Baillie (London: S. Sonnenschein & Co. Ltd., 1910), I, 44.
45. *Ibid.*, II, 821.
46. Morris R. Cohen, *op. cit.*, 13.
47. Franz Borkenau, *Pareto* (London: Chapman & Hall 1936), 158.
48. Pareto, *Mind and Society* (New York: Harcourt, Brace & Co., 1935), No. 2206.
49. *Ibid.*, No. 2053.
50. Franz Borkenau, *op. cit.*, 151.
51. W. Rex Crawford, "Representative Italian Contributors to Sociology" in H. E.

Barnes, ed., *An Introduction to the History of Sociology* (Chicago: University of Chicago Press, 1948), 567.

52. H. E. Barnes and Howard Becker, *Social Thought from Lore to Science* (New York: D. C. Heath & Co., 1938), 1, 277.

53. Oswald Spengler, *The Decline of the West* (New York: Alfred A. Knopf, 1939), 137.

54. Karl Löwith, *op. cit.*, 12.

55. *Ibid.*

56. Spengler, *op. cit.*, 106.

57. Henri Frankfort, *The Birth of Civilization in the Near East* (New York: Doubleday Anchor Books, 1956), 6–7.

58. Ludwig Gumplowicz, *Ausgewählte Werke*. Ed. by G. Salomon (Innsbruck: Universitätsverlag Wagner, 1928), Vorwort *et passim*. Cf. Ludwig Gumplowicz, *Outlines of Sociology*. Transl. and Ed. by Irving Horowitz (New York: Paine-Whitman, 1963).

59. Spengler, *op. cit.*, 21.

60. The linkage of Marx and Gumplowicz was brought about by Gumplowicz' pupil Franz Oppenheimer. Cf. Franz Oppenheimer, *Der Staat* (Frankfurt / Main: Ruetten & Loening, 1912); English transl. by John M. Gitterman (Indianapolis: The Bobbs-Merrill Co., 1914).

61. Gaetano Mosca, *The Ruling Class*. Transl. by Hannah D. Kahn (New York: McGraw-Hill Book Co., 1939).

62. Ludwig Gumplowicz, *op. cit.*, IV, 90–188: "Ibn Chaldun, ein arabischer Soziolog des XIV. Jahrhunderts." Gumplowicz was the discoverer of Ibn Khaldun as a sociologist. About the influence of Khaldun and Vico's theory of *ricorso* on Gumplowicz, cf. Horowitz, *op. cit.*, Introduction, 27–28.

63. Brooks Adams, *The Law of Civilization and Decay* (New York: The Macmillan Co., 1910), viii-x.

64. Max Weber, "Science as a Vocation," in Logan Wilson and William L. Kolb, *Sociological Analysis* (New York: Harcourt, Brace & Co., 1949), 15. Cf. also Howard Becker's ideal-typical distinctions between "isolated sacred" and "accessible secular" societies in "Processes of Secularization," *Sociological Review*, XXIV (1932), 138–154, 226–286; and his "Current Sacred-Secular Theory and Its Development," in Howard Becker and Alvin Boskoff, eds., *Modern Sociological Theory* (New York: The Dryden Press, 1957), 133–184.

65. Brooks Adams, *op. cit.*, 383.

66. Henri Frankfort, *op. cit.*, 14, 17.

67. Arnold J. Toynbee, *A Study of History* (London: Oxford University Press, 1934–61), I, 19.

68. *Ibid.*, I, 159.

69. *Ibid.*, III, 381.

70. Arnold J. Toynbee, *Civilization on Trial* (New York: Oxford University Press, 1948), v.

71. *Ibid.*, 235.

72. *Ibid.*, 236.

73. *Ibid.*

74. Henri Frankfort, *op. cit.*, 21.

75. H. E. Barnes, "A. J. Toynbee: Orosius and Augustine in Modern Dress," in H. E. Barnes, ed. *op. cit.*, 724.

76. Sidney Hook, "Mr. Toynbee's City of God," *Partisan Review*, VI (1948), 692.

77. Pieter Geyl, *Debates with Historians* (Groningen: J. B. Wolters, 1955), 97–98.
78. H. E. Barnes, ed., *op. cit.*, 729.
79. For example, by Pieter Geyl, *op. cit.*, 112–119, and Henri Frankfort, *op. cit.*, 19–21.
80. Especially in his *Social and Cultural Dynamics* (New York: American Book Co., 1937–41) and *Contemporary Sociological Theories* (New York: Harper & Bros., 1928).
81. Sorokin, quoted in Barnes and Becker, *op. cit.*, 786.
82. *Ibid.*
83. P. A. Sorokin, *Social and Cultural Dynamics*. One-volume Edition. (Boston: Extending Horizons Books, 1957), 699–701.
84. Pieter Geyl, A. J. Toynbee, P. A. Sorokin, *The Pattern of the Past: Can We Determine It?* (Boston: The Beacon Press, 1949), 126.
85. Hans Speier, "The Sociological Ideas of P. A. Sorokin," in H. E. Barnes, ed., *op. cit.*, 892.
86. P. A. Sorokin, *Society, Culture, and Personality* (New York: Harper, 1947), 704–705. Cf., however, Alvin Boskoff in Howard Becker and Alvin Boskoff, *op. cit.*, 292–293.
87. W. H. Walsh, *op. cit.*, 153.
88. John Brown, *An Estimate of the Manners and Principles of the Times* (Boston, 1758), 107.
89. Edward Hallet Carr, *op. cit.*, 77.
90. Morris R. Cohen, *op. cit.*, 263–264; cf. Rudolf Bultmann, "Optimismus und Pessimismus in Antike und Christentum," *Universitas*, XVI (August 1961), 811–833.

Robert V. Daniels MARXIAN THEORIES OF HISTORICAL DYNAMICS

MARXISM IS ONE of the most remarkable systems of social thought produced in the nineteenth century, not least because it incorporates many of the outstanding historical and philosophical premises of its day. It is an attempt to analyze and explain the whole of history—or the whole of Western history—scientifically. It incorporates the new economic and technological interest of the century, with its emphasis on the conditions of ordinary life. It is optimistically evolutionary, a cyclical variant of the faith in progress, complete with an eighteenth century heaven-on-earth at the end of the line. Finally, it is an attempt to use the scientific analysis of history as a political weapon in the struggle for a revolutionary reconstruction of society. It is still being used as a political weapon, and powerful emotions are bound to it. However, this neither waives nor prevents objective inquiry into the actual substance and significance of Marx's work. Careful analysis of Marx's writings and the development of the Marxist movement reveals, in fact, that the actual meaning of his doctrine has been lost or misrepresented in the tumultuous course of its history.[1]

Marx's Work and the Evolution of Marxism

Marx's system of thought was not the cast-iron structure which both disciples and critics have frequently assumed it to be. Indeed, its many points of vagueness, incompleteness, and even self-contradiction have permitted diverse interpretations and emphases respecting the master's meaning. Not surprisingly, Marx's thought had its own historical development, with different successive directions of emphasis and considerable evolution in the meaning of his basic concepts.

Marx's first period, extending from his graduation from the University of Berlin in 1841 to the publication of *The Poverty of Philosophy* in 1847, was one of philosophical preparation. This was the period in which he worked his way from Hegelianism into the now familiar problem of "alienation," and thence (with help from Engels) into emphasis on economic conditions, the class struggle, the liberating role of the proletariat, and the ideal society of communism. The *Poverty of Philosophy,* published in 1847, represents the first fully developed model of Marx's philosophical system.

Marx's second period, from 1847 to 1852, was clearly political. Practically all his writing in this period was occasioned by his work in the revolutionary movement preceding and during the upheaval of 1848, and by his interest in the aftermath of the revolutions in France and Germany. His philosophy was still implicitly activist, with major attention to the problems of leadership, organization, and political action for both the revolutionary and conservative forces.

After 1852 Marx entered his third major period, when he settled down in the British Museum to study the economic development of capitalism, with the intention of demonstrating the inevitability of its collapse. By 1865 he had done practically all his work on *Das Kapital* (Volume I was published in 1867, while Volumes II and III remained incomplete and unpublished until after his death). It was during this third period, with his effort to establish the natural laws of capitalism and the proletarian revolution, that Marx's work came nearest to the deterministic image of his thought which posterity has inherited.

Marx's fourth period, slightly overlapping the third, commenced in 1864 with his renewed interest in active politics within the context of the International Workingmen's Association. This and other currents in the European labor movement, plus the revolutionary crisis in France, absorbed most of Marx's attention until 1872. During this period he emphasized the possibilities of gaining and/or holding proletarian state power through democratic procedures.

After 1872 Marx's creative work lapsed almost completely, a striking fact that most of his biographers have glossed over. In this later period Engels produced most of his own independent work—*Anti-Dühring, The Origin of the Family, The Dialectics of Nature,* and so forth. It has been assumed that Engels was working in close concert with Marx and that all this material represented Marx's own point of view and was approved by him, but in view of the evidence of Marx's illness, depression, and inactivity, there is good reason to doubt that Marx really exercised such influence over Engels. On the contrary, it has been convincingly argued by George Lichtheim and Maximilien Rubel that Engels was creating his own more generalized and deterministic version of the doctrine, considerably at variance with Marx's own more activist outlook.[2] In this, Engels and those who followed him obviously reflected the atmosphere of mechanistic scientism and the evolutionary faith in progress which prevailed in late nineteenth-century European thought. Finally, in his last years, long after Marx's death, Engels undertook to correct the overdeterministic impression of Marxism which had taken hold in Social-Democratic circles.

In the forty years following the death of Engels, Marxism was subject to the most diverse interpretations and profound metamorphoses, so much so that we can regard Marx's most committed Communist disciples as real Marxists only by defining as Marxism any profession of belief in any idea *called* "Marxist." The theoretical interest in latter-day Marxism lies in the various treatments of the problem of historical law and individual action, to which we will turn in a later section. Apart from this, the main theoretical contribution of Marx's successors was concerned with the relationship between countries at different stages of economic development. This problem encompassed the neo-Marxist theory of imperialism; Marxist attempts to clarify the problems of nationality, national minorities, and international class loyalty; and, above all, the application of the Marxian schema to Russia in its state of early capitalist development. The Bolshevik revolution was carried out under the theoretical rationale that Russia was the "weakest link" in the "chain of imperialism" and that a workers' uprising there would precipitate the long-awaited international revolution.

The accession of Marxists to power in a manner and setting scarcely envisioned by the prophets initiated a fundamental transformation in the meaning and function of Marxist theory as the Russians comprehended it. Marxism ceased to be the intellectual projection of individuals and became the official rationale of state policy under circumstances in which it was virtually a state religion. Such were the enforced manipulations of theory, after Stalin achieved his ascendancy in 1928, that subsequent pronouncements of Soviet Marxism cannot be taken seriously as genuine philosophical efforts.

History and the Structure of Society

The core of Marx's theory of history, a point of view to which he adhered with but slight shifts of emphasis from the mid-1840s to the end of his life, is the doctrine of "historical materialism." Marx and Engels had clearly established this approach when they wrote in *The German Ideology* in 1845–46: "The social structure and the state are continually evolving out of the life process of definite individuals, but of individuals not as they may appear in their own or other people's imagination, but as they really are, i.e., as they are effective, produce materially, and are active under definite material limits, presuppositions, and conditions independent of their will." Against the prevailing philosophical idealism of their epoch Marx and Engels exclaimed that "life is not determined by consciousness, but consciousness by life."[3]

Economic conditions and economically oriented actions, therefore, constituted the "base" of the social structure and profoundly influenced all other aspects of human existence and activity. Marx succinctly expressed this model of the social system in the Preface to his *Contribution to the Critique of Political Economy,* published in 1859: "In the social production which men carry on they enter into definite relations that are indispensable and independent of their will; these relations of production correspond to a definite stage of development of their material powers of production. The sum total of these relations of production constitutes the economic structure of society—the real foundation, on which rise legal and political superstructures and to which correspond definite forms of social consciousness. The mode of production in material life determines the general character of the social, political, and spiritual processes of life."[4]

The hierarchical model of the levels and interrelationships of social phenomena which Marx here presents is impressive and still useful. The question, however, of the preponderant direction of influence between the levels is much more debatable. Marx's own meaning has been disputed. Some writers see his historical scheme reduced to a purely technological determinism where all significant social changes are traceable ultimately to changes in the techniques of production.[5] One thing that is clear is that Marx did not mean that human behavior was exclusively determined by economic motives and interests; his point was to stress the overriding necessities and limits which economic conditions imposed on all human activities.

A second cardinal principle in Marx's sociology, along with his stress on the economic base, was his doctrine of classes and the class struggle. "The history of all hitherto existing society is the history of class struggles," he and Engels declared at the opening of the first section of *The Communist Manifesto.*[6] Classes were the fundamental social units, each generated by economic conditions and defined by a particular relationship to the resources and forces of production, i.e., by whether its members owned property, what kind of property, or how they worked for the owners of property. Every form of society would tend to crystallize into two sharply opposed classes—the haves and the have-nots. These classes and their antagonisms—slave-owners vs. slaves, nobility vs. serfs, capitalists vs. proletarians—Marx regarded as the principal dynamic forces in history. The history of any society was seen as being produced by the struggles between its classes, the increasing self-consciousness and determination of the subordinate class, and the ultimate revolutionary battle between the classes.

The class struggle created by the conditions of production and property ownership in turn governed the basic characteristics of a society's political and economic life. The state itself was explained as a product of the class struggle. "The state arose from the need to hold class antagonisms in check," Engels wrote in *The Origin of the Family, Private Property, and the State* (1884), "but as it arose, at the same time, in the midst of the conflict of these classes, it is, as a rule, the state of the most powerful, economically dominant class, which, through the medium of the state, becomes also the politically dominant class, and thus acquires new means of holding down and exploiting the oppressed class."[7] Thanks to the use of political power by the ruling class to maintain its dominance, the class struggle must take a political form, and victory for any rising class necessarily depends on political revolution which under most circumstances will be violent.

Ideas no less than political power were for Marx weapons in the class struggle, selected and publicized on the basis of class interest: "The ideas of the ruling class are, in every age, the ruling ideas . . . The dominant ideas are nothing more than the ideal expression of the dominant material relationships . . . , and thus of the relationships which make one class the ruling one. . . ."[8] This use of ideas to serve the class is not meant to be cynical; the ruling class actually persuades itself that the ideas corresponding to its interests are eternally and absolutely valid. Here is the essence of Marx's highly significant theory of "ideology," as a system of "illusions" justifying the dominance of any ruling group as eternally necessary and proper. It has been the fate of Marxism in the Communist states to become, in a more literal way than its founder ever imagined, the ideology of a new totalitarian and bureaucratic social system.

The Sequence of Societies

Marx's notions of levels of social life and their interaction represent his conception of the structure of society at any given moment—i.e., the structure of the particular "socio-economic formation" characterized by a given mode of production and the corresponding class and property relationships, government, and ideas. Over the span of historical time he distinguished a series of different socio-economic formations, each with its characteristic economic, social, political, and ideological make-up. The beginning of the process was presumed to be the primitive communal economy of tribal society which, with the rise of private property and class differentiation, yielded to a series of class societies. "In broad outline," Marx wrote in the Preface to the *Critique of Political Economy,* "we can designate the Asiatic, the ancient (slave-owning), the feudal, and the modern bourgeois methods of production as so many epochs in the progress of the economic formation of society."[9] After the last—bourgeois or capitalist—phase of history, analysis becomes prediction, as Marx looked forward to an inevitable revolution by the proletariat and the appearance of an altogether new socialism based on the economics of large-scale industrial production.

This scheme of the succession of social systems presents a number of difficulties. We will return later to the question whether it is supposed to be universally true, and to the problem of the validity of slicing up historical development into such sharply opposed phases. For the moment it should be noted that Marx vastly oversimplified the transition from "feudalism" to "capitalism" and that he failed to comprehend the political and social nature of five centuries of complex European history between the thirteenth and eighteenth centuries. A more general weakness of the scheme is that social systems of presumably great diversity—the Asiatic, the ancient, and the feudal—were all actually based on the same general conditions of production, i.e., ox-and-plow agriculture. Marx does not seem to consider the possibility that great differences in social organization could develop—for military reasons, for example—independently of economic conditions.

Historical development from one social stage to another was explained by Marx through the operation of the forces analyzed in his model of the social structure. The prime mover was change in the techniques or resources of production, which generated new social forces and interests pressing for a change in the institutional structure. We find this formulated again in that remarkable epitome of Marx's whole philosophy, the Preface to *The Critique of Political Economy:* "At a certain stage of their development the material forces of production in society come into conflict with the existing relations of production or . . . with the property relations within which they had been at work before. From forms of development of the forces of production these relations turn into their fetters. Then comes the period of social revolution. With the change of the economic foundation the entire immense superstructure is more or less rapidly transformed."[10]

Revolution is thus the characteristic form of the final, political transition from one socioeconomic formation to another, and such transition is the basic explanation for the phenomenon of social revolutions, such as the English and the French. Marx took the French revolution as his model, and here the bourgeois class factor is obvious, but the farther afield one proceeds from that model, back or forward in time, the less his class analysis of revolution actually holds up. In any case, Marx attributed no supra-historical power to revolutions, and no new class could rise to the top until conditions were ripe for it: "No social order ever disappears before all the productive forces for which there is room . . . have been developed, and new, higher relations of production never appear before the material conditions of their existence have matured in the womb of the old society."[11]

The Analysis of Capitalism

The major part of Marx's life work, which consumed most of his energy in the 1850s and 1860s, and left him too exhausted to make any significant contribution after that time, was the detailed application of his system of social analysis to the history and current trends of European capitalism. Starting with the premise that capitalist society was destined to be overthrown by the rising forces of the proletariat, Marx threw himself into the effort to establish historically and empirically "a process of natural history" with its "natural laws of capitalist production . . . , tendencies working with iron necessity towards inevitable results."[12] Herein lay the purpose of his voluminous economic studies on the labor theory of value, the theories of surplus value and capitalist exploitation, and the trends of capitalist accumulation and profit.

With the historical development of capitalism Marx's theory of social stages acquires empirical foundation. His views of the societies preceding and presumably following capitalism rest only on a few general comments and are quite conjectural or, in Ernst Troeltsch's estimate, "teleological."[13] Capitalism took shape, Marx found, in the interstices of the feudal system, but its critical development occurred in the process of "primary capitalist accumulation." This, according to Marx, was based on the dispossession of individual peasants and craftsmen by capitalistic landlords and merchant-employers who took over the resources and markets of the old "petty-bourgeois element." The latter, reduced to the status of a propertyless proletariat, were compelled to work for wages at the minimum subsistence level, and so provided the necessary labor force for capitalist industry.

For all its horrors of greed and exploitation, on which Marx so graphically expands, capitalism performed for him an indispensable progressive function —that of developing the powerful new productive forces of scientific technology and large-scale enterprise. Thanks to his self-imprisonment in the labor theory of value, Marx did not clearly appreciate the possibilities of multiplying the productivity of labor through capital reinvestment (with correspondingly enhanced bargaining power and welfare potential), but he saw in the large-scale factory organization of production a source of both efficiency and social cohesion that was the essential condition for progress toward the goal of socialism.[14]

In the most crucial—and most questionable—part of his analysis, Marx maintained that the inner laws of capitalist development would lead the system into a state of deepening crisis wherein the inability of a system of private ownership to realize the productive potential of a system of large-scale social production would become increasingly apparent. Two of the considerations making for such a crisis were unconvincing even in his own presentation and soon disproven by events—the "law" of the increasing immiseration of the proletariat, and the "law" of the declining rate of profit, both of which depended on the dubious support of the labor theory of value and the notion that wages tended to rise hardly, if ever, above the subsistence level. Marx conceded that absolute immiseration might not take place, and his predictions then rested on the expectation of "relative" immiseration where the bourgeoisie advanced in wealth faster than the proletariat, so that the gulf between them was broadened.[15] A third point stressed by Marx proved to be a much more serious threat to capitalism—the business cycle and its tendency to ever more serious recurrences of depression.

The great irony of Marx's critique of capitalism is that the economic theory in which he invested most of his effort is dubious in the extreme, while the sociological comments which he made briefly and in passing have lasting merit. Apart from his economic analysis, Marx observed a revolutionary social effect of capitalism in its steady concentration of the proletariat into larger and more self-conscious groups, while capitalist enterprise itself was amalgamating in the direction of trusts and monopolies. The workers would combine into unions and increasingly acquire political class consciousness: "This mass unites, it is constituted as a class for itself. The interests which it defends are the interests of its class. But the struggle between class and class is a political struggle."[16] "The development of modern industry," Marx and Engels declared in the *Manifesto,* "therefore cuts from under its feet the very foundation on which the bourgeoisie produces and appropriates products. What the bourgeoisie, therefore, produces, above all, is its own gravediggers."

The natural outcome of capitalism, Marx remained convinced, was the proletarian revolution and the creation of the classless society of socialism. He wrote in the closing pages of Volume I of *Capital,* "Centralization of the means of production and socialization of labor at last reach a point where they become incompatible with their capitalist integument. This integument is burst asunder. The death knell of capitalist private property sounds. The expropriators are expropriated."[17] The revolution might take a nonviolent form, and might even come by gradual stages. Marx hailed any meliorative measure such as Parliament's limitation of the working day in England as a victory for the socialist principle, but he looked for the day when the proletariat would take power through a democratic republic, destroy the remains

of capitalist property and begin to realize the presumably unlimited potential
of socialized industry.

After some educating by Engels, Marx consciously based his discussion
of capitalism and its fate on England as the "classic" case, and readily admitted differences of detail between England and the other countries of
Europe and North America.[18] In effect, he was using England as a Weberian
ideal type. He made no attempt to apply his analysis outside of Western
Europe and America as a universal law. When he was appealed to for his
opinion on Russia in the 1870s, he rejected the attempt to "metamorphose my
historical sketch into a historico-philosophic theory of the general path every
people is fated to tread . . ."[19] While the dynamics and fate of capitalism
were inexorable wherever the system took hold, its rise was not generally inevitable, and Russia might still preserve the peasant commune as the basis for
a direct transition to socialism. Otherwise, "if Russia continues to pursue
the path she has followed since 1861 [toward capitalism], she will lose
the finest chance ever offered by history to a people and undergo all the
fatal vicissitudes of the capitalist regime."[20]

By the 1890s it was clear to the Russian Marxists that Russia had become
irrevocably committed to a capitalistic development, and the problem of
fitting the special Russian case into Marx's analysis of capitalism became
the subject of voluminous controversy. The most original contribution to the
discussion was Trotsky's "law of combined development" and his "theory
of permanent revolution." Trotsky took Western Europe as the ideal type
and noted the uneven and telescoped nature of Russia's development, concluding that a proletarian revolution in Russia could be anticipated at an
early date.[21]

In broadest perspective Marx's view of history does not present, as so
often thought, an unilinear path of obligatory stages. A distinct alternative to
the sequence ancient-feudal-bourgeois is offered in his notion of "Asiatic society," where the political state and urban civilization developed upon the
economic base of communal village agriculture. Marx's German-American
disciple K. A. Wittfogel has elaborated the Asiatic concept into a theory of
"agromanagerial" society whose most recent manifestation is none other
than the Communist regime in Soviet Russia.[22] This is Wittfogel's view; Marxism proper is strictly a theory about capitalism and its fate, leaving the question of why capitalism emerges in a particular time and place indeterminate.

The Dialectic Process

The manner of looking at history which Marx employed throughout his
economic and social analysis was the philosophy of "dialectics," which
he had borrowed from Hegel. For Hegel the dialectic process of "thesis,"
"antithesis" and "synthesis" represented the logical development of the

Absolute Idea, of which human history was merely the material manifestation. Marx, like most of his student contemporaries at the German universities, was steeped in Hegelianism, but he rejected Hegel's philosophical idealism and instead took dialectics as a way of looking at the realities of human history. "In direct contrast to German philosophy, which descends from heaven to earth, here we ascend from earth to heaven," Marx and Engels wrote in *The German Ideology*.[23] Marx made the oft-repeated statement that he found Hegel standing on his head and turned him right side up.

The meaning of dialectics in Marx's hands was that all human existence is in flux, without eternal truths or institutions, that the meaning of the part depends on the whole, that change, development, and progress take place by way of contradiction and conflict, and that the resulting change leads to a higher unity. In particular, Marx viewed the class struggle and the transition from one social system to another as a dialectical process, in which the ruling class viewed as "thesis" evoked its own "negation" in the challenger class and thus led to a synthesis through revolutionary transformation resulting in a higher organization of elements from the old order.[24]

The dialectical approach to history at best was a stage on the road to social science, and in its suggestion of a historical demiurge shaping the universal course of events it was hardly conducive to the truly scientific frame of mind which Marx professed. It did convey a sense of the dynamic interaction of all the complex phenomena in the social system, if only in metaphysical terms.[25] There is a strong tendency in the dialectical point of view to abstract sharp stages or forces out of the continuity and gradations in the social process and then to explain the process on the basis of these stages and forces in dialectical conflict. Among other things, this makes violent conflict and abrupt, revolutionary change appear to be the normal thing, and encourages misleading oversimplification of the course of history and the structure of society. It was the dialectical approach which compelled Marx to concentrate so heavily on the internal workings of capitalism, to try to demonstrate the "inevitable" emergence of the proletarian negation out of capitalism which the dialectical view called for.

One of the most obvious difficulties in Marx's theory of history is the question why the dialectic process stops after the proletarian revolution. Presumably the proletariat embodies qualities, such as alienation from all property interest, which will enable it to put an end, for all time, to the dialectical antagonisms on which social change had heretofore depended. This involves the question of Marx's faith in the proletariat, to which we shortly return, and also leaves unanswered the question whether and how social progress will continue after the proletarian revolution. At one point Marx speaks of "social evolution" without "political revolution."[26] The Chinese Communists, facing a particularly difficult future of economic development after their accession to power, tried to resolve this problem in the 1950s by inventing the category of "non-antagonistic contradictions" to explain social progress after the demise of the old regime.[27]

Marx never got around to the systematic elaboration of the dialectical philosophy which he hoped to write, and it was left to Engels, after Marx's creative period was over, to generalize and defend the dialectic method. In Engels' treatment the dialectic process became more nearly automatic and implicitly universal, not only with regard to human history but to the world of nature and natural evolution as well. At the same time, the dialectical struggle of forces within a system was transformed into a plainly mechanistic cause-and-effect interaction, with overtones consistent with late nineteeenth-century scientific evolutionism and the faith in automatic progress.[28] The mechanistic emphasis thereafter prevailed among most Marxists, including the Bolsheviks, until after the Russian Revolution.

The interpretation of the dialectic process became a subject of acute philosophical and political controversy in Soviet Russia in the late 1920s, when the prevailing "mechanistic" viewpoint associated with Nikolai Bukharin and the Communist right wing came under attack by the new school of "dialecticians." Through two successive phases of controversy, each settled by the intervention of the party leadership, the official Soviet view of dialectics was revised to lay great stress on the dialectical "jumps" or discontinuities between the different successive phases in the history of society. This meant in practice that the Soviet regime considered itself released from the laws of value that prevailed under capitalist economics, and was free to direct the course of economic development by deliberate planning.[29]

The Proletariat and Its Mission

To the critical reader it is apparent that a preconceived conclusion lies behind Marx's whole dialectical conception of history and revolution. At the very outset of his career as a philosopher he had committed himself to the need for radical social change—initially, it seems, in reaction to religion and the conditions of social oppression which made the "illusory happiness" of religion necessary. "The immediate *task of philosophy*," Marx wrote in 1842, "once the *saintly form* of human self-alienation has been unmasked, is to unmask self-alienation in its *unholy forms*."[30] Thus the great moral necessity for mankind was its "emancipation" from illusion and alienation.

To accomplish this total liberation Marx looked for a genuine social force, a force with no stake in the existing order and its illusions, and this force he found in the new industrial working class, the proletariat.[31] Under the influence of the French utopian socialists he committed himself to the abolition of private property in production, and he devoted one of his major early works, *Economic and Philosophical Manuscripts* of 1844, to a critique of the dehumanizing effect of the "alienation" imposed on employers and

employees alike by the capitalist system of production. Even with his elaboration of a more thoroughly dialectical and deterministic analysis of capitalism, Marx remained at heart the impassioned moralist, railing against the
evil of capitalist exploitation, as in the following quotation from *Capital:*
". . . In its blind, unrestrainable passion, its werewolf hunger for surplus labor,
capital oversteps not only the moral, but even the merely physical maximum
bounds of the working day . . . Capital cares nothing for the length of life
of labor power. All that concerns it is simply and solely the maximum of
labor power that can be rendered fluent in a working day. It attains this
end by shortening the extent of the laborer's life as a greedy farmer snatches
increased produce from the soil by robbing it of its fertility."[32] In short, the
capitalist world was evil; the proletariat would have to destroy it; and history
and economics must be made to yield up the scientific "laws" which would
show how this would "inevitably" come to pass.

Through his dialectical analysis of capitalism, Marx was satisfied that
the proletariat as the "negation" of the bourgeoisie would grow in numbers,
organization, and self-consciousness, and prepare itself with the guidance
of philosophers like himself to seize political power when the growing contradictions of capitalism, expressed in increasing concentration and deepening crisis, should set the stage for revolution. The function he proclaimed for
the Communist League in 1848 was to educate and unite working class
parties everywhere, to prepare them for the task "to raise the proletariat to
the position of the ruling class, to establish democracy." When this stage is
reached, "the proletariat will use its political supremacy to wrest, by degrees,
all capital from the bourgeoisie," so that finally, "after class differences have
been eliminated", . . . "the public power will lose its political character".
There are then no longer property rights and class exploitation to enforce.[33]

On the actual manner of the proletarian seizure of power, not to mention
the nature of the subsequent "dictatorship of the proletariat," Marx was never
very explicit, though he did give increasing attention as time went on to the
possibilities for revolution by democratic means. "We do not deny," he declared in Amsterdam in 1872, "that there are countries, such as America,
England, and—if I understand your institutions correctly—Holland, where
the workers can attain their goals by peaceful means."[34] When the Paris
Commune rebelled in the spring of 1871 and set up a short-lived revolutionary regime, Marx hailed it as the actual model of a worker's government.
It had, as he saw it, eliminated all the repressive functions of the old state
and created a new administration with its officials directly responsible to the
democratic electorate and held to the level of "workmen's wages."[35] Engels,
near the end of his life, made the commitment to democratic methods quite
definite: "History has shown us to have been wrong. . . . The mode of
struggle of 1848 is today obsolete in every respect. . . ." Street fighting was
largely out, and universal suffrage had proved to be the workers' most effec-

tive weapon. "The irony of world history turns everything upside down. We, the 'revolutionists,' the 'overthrowers'—we are thriving far better on legal methods than on illegal methods and overthrow."[36]

With the consummation of the revolution, the mission of the proletariat as such would come to an end. Abolishing private property and the class differences which rested on it, the proletariat itself would cease to exist as a class; the proletarian negation of capitalist society would be dialectically super-seded by the classless society of communism. This did not mean mere col-lective ownerhip and forcible equalization, which Marx denounced as "general private property" and "envy and leveling [that] in fact constitute the essence of competition," where "the role of worker is not abolished, but is extended to all men." Soviet Russia with all its emphasis on "state property" seems to fall into Marx's category of "crude communism," which he called "only a phenomenal form of the infamy of private property." True "communism," he maintained, is "the positive abolition of private property, of human self-alienation, and thus the real appropriation of human nature through and for man."[37]

Marx was not so utopian as to expect all social problems to end im-mediately after the revolution. He noted in his "Critique of the Gotha Pro-gram" of 1875 that the "bourgeois right" of payment according to the individual's labor would still be necessary "in the first phase of communist society as it is when it has just emerged after prolonged birth pangs from capitalist society." Only in the "higher phase of communist society," when labor had become natural, its internal differentiations diminished, and its product more abundant, "only then can the narrow horizon of bourgeois right (law) be left behind and society inscribe on its banners: "From each ac-cording to his ability, to each according to his needs."[38] In the usage of Lenin and the Communist movement after 1917 this distinction between the two post-revolutionary phases was sharpened, with the application of the terms "socialism" and "communism" to designate the earlier and later phases, respectively.[39] "Socialism" in this special sense was extended by the Soviet authorities to denote a long "transitional period," and only under Khrushchev since 1959 has the program of effecting the "transition of communism" been officially initiated. In terms of objective sociology, of course, this phraseology, like most of the Marxian theory as applied to the actual Com-munist society, has become an arid scholastic exercise with little relevance to reality.

Marx's theory of the proletarian revolution raises a number of questions which strongly suggest that his certainty in the victory of the proletariat was a preconceived act of faith rather than a scientific conclusion. We have already noted the problem of the suspension of the dialectic process which is pre-sumably governed by the higher social nature of the proletariat as the only class capable of bearing the mission of ending the class struggle. Lying behind all this was Marx's original commitment of his moral hopes to the victory of the proletariat. By the logic of Marx's own conception of history, there was no reason to expect the proletariat to follow the bourgeoisie as the new dominant class. Feudalism had not been overthrown by the peasants whom the nobles exploited, but by a new minority group based on new conditions of production and new forms of property—the capitalists. To follow the parallelism, one should look for still another dominant minority, basing its power on the conditions of large-scale production, to supplant the capitalists step by step, with the proletariat or whoever succeeded them under the conditions of modern technology kept under firm control by the new ruling class. This is the direction in which some neo-Marxist thinkers have proceeded to analyze contemporary "post-capitalist" society in both Communist and non-Communist countries.

Actually, Marx relied on the idea that the proletariat as a non-propertied class would not be tempted to wield exploitative power. Marxism has rested on an emotional foundation of this kind from its very beginning in the early 1840s—faith in the mission and victory of the proletariat, or whatever is called the proletariat. Lacking this, no one can call himself a Marxist; with it, almost anyone can. It is this enduring "proletarian" emotionalism that has given continuity to the professedly Marxist movement of the Communists, even though the proletarian quality of the movement has finally become an elaborate fraud. The social systems ruled by the Communists are far from constituting Marx's ideal society, and are not likely to lead on to that society in the foreseeable future. They would seem to represent a complete departure from the Marxian image of a free and just social order, in terms of the institutional structure of society, the nature of the power-bearing groups, and the relationship between politics and economics. In the Communist system the fate of society is determined by the political power of the holders of bureaucratic office—the so-called "New Class."[40]

Determinism and Freedom: Marx and Engels

In a number of crucial respects the Soviet interpretation of Marxism, no less than the development of Soviet political practice, has raised major questions as to the meaning Marx originally intended for his scheme of history. The most difficult problem in the understanding of Marx is his conception of the economic laws of history and their determining effect on other aspects of life. Controversy has been chronic on this issue among non-Soviet writers on Marxism, while the Soviet regime under Stalin produced a complete revision in its view of the true doctrine, from the most extreme determinism to a highly activist emphasis on the role of political organization and leadership.

Marx's writings of the 1840s were, for all their economic emphasis, decidedly activist. Economic life was a form of action—the most important—

and the economic conditions which shaped men were at the same time the product of human action. The old materialism, Marx complained, "forgets that it is men that change circumstances, and that the educator himself needs educating."[41] In fact, activism was Marx's metaphysical justification for stressing the economic factor, on the ground that men were "the authors and actors of their own history,"[42] and had to be understood as concrete economic and social experience had shaped them. In the "manifesto" Marx and Engels constantly speak in terms of the conscious activism of the proletariat, armed with the weapon of philosophy which must struggle for its revolutionary emancipation.

The dialectical interaction of conscious action and social conditions which Marx tried to express assumed, in the later stages of his economic work, an increasingly deterministic tone, at least as regards the formation of the proletariat and the breakdown of capitalism. Marx became more and more deeply ensnared in the logical inconsistency of the activist revolutionary effort on the one hand and, on the other, the "science" of the laws of history which made the revolution appear inevitable and independent of the actions or ideas of any individual. Neither Marx nor any of his followers made clear what they meant by "laws" of history: they failed—and the Communists still fail—to distinguish between the conditional "if . . . then . . ." laws in which the propositions of natural science are usually couched, and the absolute "law" of a foreordained course of events. While Marx quite probably meant the former, he allowed his directives to sound more like binding predictions. Engels and the Social Democrats definitely understood the proletarian revolution as an historical inevitability, subject only to the uncertainties of timing and possible bloodshed. For Engels and for the ensuing Marxist orthodoxy the conscious action of the proletariat was itself the product of determining social conditions, as Engels suggested in his *Anti-Dühring:* "[The] conflict between productive forces and modes of production . . . exists, in fact, objectively, outside us, independently of the will and actions even of the men who have brought it on. Modern socialism is nothing but the reflex, in thought, of this conflict in fact; its ideal reflection in the minds . . . of . . . the working class."[43]

Despite his deterministic language, Marx himself acknowledged in many contexts the role of non-economic powers, particularly political action. His idea of "primitive capitalist accumulation," in which individual producers were dispossessed in order to get capitalist enterprises going, presumes the deliberate intervention of political force. "Force," he wrote in this connection, "is the midwife of every old society pregnant with a new one. It is itself an economic power."[44]

Of more contemporary import, Marx developed in his journalistic comment on the politics of France between 1848 and 1851, a concept of "Bonapartism" as the independent state machine standing over and above the strife of more or less evenly balanced social classes.[45] In their comment on the Paris Commune, Marx and Engels put great stress on the proper political steps by the proletariat in order to "safeguard itself against its own deputies and officials" and prevent even the revolutionary state from transforming itself "from the servant of society into the master of society."[46] Such remarks implied that there was a fork in the historical road *after* the proletarian revolution, and that political action alone would decide whether the revolutionary society took the true path or was diverted into a bureaucratic perversion. In 1916 Nikolai Bukharin offered another perspective of politically determined alternatives on the basis of the concentrated capitalist economy—either evolution toward "militaristic state capitalism," or the diversion of the course of history by the proletarian revolution and the destruction of the bourgeois state.[47]

From this point of view it is not hard to describe Soviet society as the proletarian revolution gone wrong, where the revolutionaries failed to prevent the state from becoming the master of society and the emergence of what Bukharin foresaw as "a new Leviathan, in the face of which the fantasy of Thomas Hobbes seems like child's play."[48] At any rate there is considerable anticipation in Marxian theory for the present situation where, as Sidney Hook states it, "in the very interests of the socialist society which Karl Marx anticipated, . . . it is not the mode of economic production but the mode of political decision which is of decisive importance."[49] Just as a variety of social and political systems could stand as the institutional superstructure over ancient agriculture, so is it possible to choose among a variety of political and economic forms, democratic or totalitarian, resting on the economic base of modern industry.

Marx never resolved the dialectical ambiguity in his philosophy between determinism and voluntarism, and his writings offered ample basis for his followers to stress either the one or the other. In the 1880s and 1890s, the trend was heavily deterministic, and Engels found it necessary to state certain reservations toward historical materialism, though in so doing he gave the doctrine a reading that was much more in line with Newtonian mechanism than with dialectical philosophy. He made it clear, for one thing, that economic laws did not require uniform economic determination of the actions of individuals. He wrote in 1890, "History is made in such a way that the final result always arises from conflicts between many individual wills, of which each in turn has been made what it is by a host of particular conditions of life. Thus there are innumerable intersecting forces, an infinite series of parallelograms of forces which give rise to one resultant—the historical event." Thus the individual might have entirely free will, but be powerless to affect the social process "which works, as a whole, unconsciously and without volition."[50] Engels was here groping toward something like the modern notion of statistical laws of causation, valid in the case of large numbers though not necessarily for the individual instance.

More significant for the Marxian system was Engels' concession regarding the role of the social superstructure. He denied that Marxism meant that economics was the only determining factor and noted that the political and intellectual forces of the superstructure "also exercise their influence upon the course of the historical struggles and in many cases preponderate in determining their *form*. There is an interaction of all these elements in which, amidst all the endless host of accidents . . . , the economic movement finally asserts itself as necessary."[51] Political force, as Marx had long before noted, could decisively accelerate or impede economic and social development: "Or why do we fight for the political dictatorship of the proletariat, if political power is economically impotent?"[52]

A further refinement by Engels was the notion of a "leap to freedom" attendant upon the proletarian revolution. "With the seizing of the means of production by society," he wrote in *Anti-Dühring*, ". . . the struggle for individual existence disappears. Then for the first time man, . . . emerges from mere animal conditions of existence into really human ones. The whole sphere of the conditions of life which environ man, and which have hitherto ruled man, now comes under the domination and control of man, who for the first time becomes the real, conscious lord of nature because he has now become master of his own social organization. . . . It is the ascent of man from the kingdom of necessity to the kingdom of freedom."[53] Presumably, in the chiliastically expected "society of the free and the equal," an enlightened societal response will be shaped in such a way that economics will no longer be the prime determinant of man's decisions. But the practical question is how the social decision is actually arrived at, that is, who makes the plans and what power enforces them. This question is left unanswered behind an implicit Rousseauean assumption of an automatic general will.

Determinism and Freedom—"The Epigoni"

By the time of Engels' death in 1895, the deterministic version of "classical Marxism" had taken firm hold as the official theory of the Social Democratic parties, especially in Germany. Karl Kautsky, the chief Social Democratic theoretician, expounded the rigorous laws of "inevitable" proletarian victory. He still spoke of the proletarian revolution as an abrupt and decisive overturn, but hoped to achieve it without violence. Kautsky was convinced that the best that proletarian leaders could do to facilitate the final outcome was to improve and use the instruments of political democracy.[54] Less dogmatically, the Italian economist Antonio Labriola took historical materialism simply as the best approximation to a developmental science of society, including a Marxist explanation of Marxism itself: ". . . The materialist conception of history arises . . . not as a personal and tentative opinion of two writers, but as the new conquest of thought by the inevitable suggestion of a new world which is in process of birth, that is to say the proletarian revolution. . . ."[55]

Kautsky's "orthodox" fusion of Marxian revolutionary prognosis and peaceful political practice soon evoked sharp criticism on both sides.[56] On the Right, Eduard Bernstein broke fundamentally with Marx's dialectical identification of the desirable and the inevitable. This "revisionism," under the influence of neo-Kantian ethics, posed socialism as an ethical goal not necessarily guaranteed by any laws of history and to be realized rather through persistent democratic gradualism.[57] Bernstein's "evolutionary socialism" has prevailed in both the practice and in the theory of all the West European Socialist parties, and they have thereby ceased to be dogmatically Marxist.[58]

Before 1917 the Marxist left wing was much less influential, but it foreshadowed the later activist reinterpretation of Marxism in Russia. Rosa Luxemburg and a number of Dutch Marxists (Anton Pannekoek, Herman Gorter), reflecting the anarcho-syndicalism which was then influential in many parts of Europe, laid increasing stress on direct "mass action" and the general strike to effect the proletarian revolution.[59]

The Russian interpretation of Marxism represented by Georgi Plekhanov was ultra-determinist. Plekhanov ignored most of Marx's qualifications about the role of noneconomic factors in history, and all of Marx's implications that world history need not be unilinear. To him Marxism was a water-tight dogma of the coming of capitalism and of the emergence of proletarian socialism after capitalism had completed its course.[60] Lenin followed Plekhanov in theory, although in his stress on the role of the disciplined revolutionary party there was a new current of implicit activism which echoed Marx's early attitude and also drew on the earlier voluntaristic philosophy of the nineteenth-century Russian revolutionary movement.[61] To justify the "vanguard" function of the party Lenin belittled the "spontaneity" of the working class and maintained, in direct though unwitting contradiction to Marx, that "political class consciousness can be brought to the workers *only from without,* that is, only from outside of the economic struggle, from outside the sphere of relations between workers and employers."[62] In 1917 he was to rest all his hopes on the "art" of insurrection.[63]

Despite the voluntaristic implications of the Bolsheviks' successful revolutionary action in Russia, Communist theory under Bukharin's leadership remained highly deterministic for another decade. Bukharin totally rejected the possibility of free will and accident in history. "When Marxists organize the Communist Party and lead it into battle," he argued, "this action is also an expression of historical necessity."[64] Bukharin's position was echoed by Soviet academic circles under the leadership of the "mechanist" school of philosophers and the archdeterminist historian Pokrovsky. The latter endeavored to explain every significant development in the Russian past as the product of economic conditions and the class struggle.[65]

Some European Communists were more prepared to recognize the voluntaristic implications of the Soviet experiment. The influential Hungarian literary critic Georg Lukacs, who had come directly from philosophical Hegelianism to Communist action, viewed the class struggle as a test of ideas and strength, with indeterminate outcome. The dominance of the "objective forces" of economics, he asserted, held true only for the nineteenth century, of which Marxism was thus a time-bound philosophical reflection. Proletarian victory would depend on "a struggle . . . for society's consciousness," in which historical materialism would be a "spiritual weapon," but force, or political power, would be decisive.[66]

Lukacs' approach was independently paralleled by Antonio Gramsci, the founding hero of Italian Communism. Gramsci condemned strict economic determinism as "primitive infantilism," a philosophy which might console the workers in defeat, but which would become a "clear and present danger" when the "subordinate group becomes the ruling group, responsible for the economic activity of the masses." He insisted on the decisive role of the social superstructure and the "struggle of political 'hegemonies'," though he differed from Lukacs in laying primary stress not on force but on intellectual effort, with the Catholic Church as his model.[67]

Similar deviations of voluntaristic frankness have appeared from time to time among British Marxists and in Communist East Europe.[68] The Polish "revisionism" of 1956–57 represented by Leszek Kolakowski was bitterly critical of determinism as an apology for political crime.[69] During the same period the East German sociologist Jürgen Kuczynski alleged that the idea of the masses making history was "a false, technicist, and economistic conception." He put primary stress on "the few whose spirit is not asleep," who made history "by bringing about the spiritual, i.e., conscious progressive change of social relations . . . on the basis of the production relations determined by the productive forces."[70] Finally, the Hungarian economist Eric Molnar went so far as to suggest that conscious political action could even suspend the laws of the development of capitalism in such a way that the predictions of immiseration and crisis were no longer valid.[71]

The obscurantist fury with which thinkers like Lukacs and Kuczynski were condemned by the Soviet authorities illustrates why the development of Marxist theory in the Communist orbit since the late 1920s cannot be approached in the usual terms of intellectual history. Theory under the circumstances of Stalinist and post-Stalinist totalitarianism is an instrument of politics, broadly manipulated and forcefully imposed as a system of propaganda and indoctrination. The fate of Marxism in the Communist states was to become, in a more literal way than its founder ever imagined, the ideology, or "false consciousness," of a new bureaucratic social system.

After Party intervention in the "philosophical controversy" of 1928–29 outlawed deterministic mechanism in favor of dialectical "jumps," and thus paved the way theoretically for Stalin's "revolution from above," Soviet thinking shifted rapidly toward a pragmatic conservatism, which included a legalistic and nationalistic rationale of the state and social authority. Along with all other efforts at a genuine economic interpretation of social phenomena, Pokrovsky's deterministic and anti-nationalistic interpretation of history was condemned in 1934–36. In 1934 Stalin explicitly denounced any attempt to explain the government's troubles and limitations in terms of "objective conditions."[72] Under the cloak of the deterministic Marxian liturgical language an essentially voluntaristic interpretation of history in terms of leaders, ideas, governments, nations, and missions, became the Soviet standard.[73] The Khrushchev regime has in no essential way modified this standpoint, though during de-Stalinization the role of the leader was played down for propaganda purposes and the role of the "party" and the "masses" as composed of equally free, willful and creative historical actors was played up.[74] Chinese Communism has left the deterministic Marxian approach even further behind, as evidenced by Peking's emphasis on the importance of the "proletarian spirit," even in the total absence of a proletariat in the established sense, and the efficacy of "correct thought" and "rectification" programs for purposes of wedding the entire populace to the boundless ambitions of the new state.[75]

The Significance of the Marxian Approach

As we consider Marxism historically it becomes clear that there can be no single Marxian orthodoxy. Marx himself was not "orthodox" by the standard of the late nineteenth-century interpretation of his theory. If he is viewed not as a prophet or as the anti-Christ, but only as a complex figure in the history of thought, it is possible to recognize his epochal though time-bound achievement as a social philosopher and a social critic, without subscribing to any of his particular theories, predictions, or political programs.

Probably Marx's most substantial contribution to social science is his model of the various levels of phenomena in the social system—economic base, class structure, political and ideological superstructure—and his conception of the interaction among these levels. From this standpoint, each aspect of life can be viewed in relation to every other, and none need be neglected. Herbert Butterfield writes, "The chief contribution of the Marxists has been that they, more than anybody else, have taught us to make our history a structural piece of analysis. . . ."[76] Marx's theory of ideology, in particular, opens the way to the whole area of the sociology of knowledge.[77]

The other major element in Marx's sociology, his conception of the sequence of class-dominated societies, is far less useful, except where it belabors the obvious, regarding the transition from feudalism to capitalism. His concept of class is ill-defined and arbitrary, and the dialectical approach to history cuts a complex development up into stages of artificial simplicity. Dogmatic Marxists have usually become the prisoners of Marx's particular class and period concepts, and have therefore been unable to interpret new departures, except within the confines of the Marxian frame of reference. Ironically, Marx himself was not so bound at all, and readily suspended the scheme in writing about matters as diverse as French politics and the Russian peasant commune. Marx has his enduring sociological significance not in the literal limits and laws of his system, but in the awareness of economic pressures and social antagonisms which he, more than any other thinker, impressed upon all Western social science since his day.

Notes

1. For a number of valuable suggestions incorporated into this paper I am indebted to Professor Werner J. Cahnman, Rutgers University, and to Professor Carl Landauer, University of California in Berkeley.
2. George Lichtheim, *Marxism: An Historical and Critical Study* (New York: Frederick A. Praeger, 1961), 234–258; Maximilien Rubel, "The Present State of Marxological Studies" (Cambridge, Mass.: Harvard University Russian Research Center, March 24, 1961).
3. Marx and Engels, "The German Ideology," in Lewis S. Feuer, ed., *Marx and Engels: Basic Writings on Politics and Philosophy* (New York: Doubleday Anchor Books, 1959), 246–247.
4. Marx, *A Contribution to the Critique of Political Economy* (New York: International Library Publishing Co., 1904), 11.
5. Cf., e. g., Carl Landauer, *European Socialism: A History of Ideas and Movements from the Industrial Revolution to Hitler's Seizure of Power*, 2 Vols. (Berkeley and Los Angeles: University of California Press, 1959), I, 144. A divergent interpretation is contained in Erich Fromm, *Marx's Concept of Man* (New York: Frederick Ungar, 1961), 1–86.
6. Marx and Engels, *Manifesto of the Communist Party* (New York: International Publishers, 1948), 9.
7. Engels, *The Origin of the Family, Private Property, and the State* (Moscow: Foreign Languages Publishing House, 1954), 280.
8. Marx and Engels, "The German Ideology," 280.
9. Marx, *A Contribution to the Critique of Political Economy*, 13.
10. *Ibid.*, 12.
11. *Ibid.*
12. Marx, *Capital: A Critique of Political Economy* (Chicago: Kerr, 1906; republished, New York: The Modern Library, n.d.), author's preface to the first (1867) edition, 13, 15.
13. Ernst Troeltsch, *Der Historismus und seine Probleme* (Tübingen: J. C. B. Mohr, 1922), 336. Troeltsch speaks about a superficially constructed relapse into a teleological conception of dialectics; all that Marx does, he continues, is to have the period of the class struggle preceded by a Morgan-type original communism and succeeded by a Fourier-type idealized communism.
14. Cf. *Capital*, I, 836.

15. Marx, "Wage Labor and Capital" (1847), in Marx and Engels, *Selected Works*, I, 96–98.
16. Marx, *The Poverty of Philosophy* (London: Twentieth Century Press, 1900), 158.
17. *Capital*, I, 837.
18. *Lichtheim*, 58.
19. Marx to the Editorial Board of the Fatherland Notes, Nov. 1877, *The Selected Correspondence of Marx and Engels*, 1846–1895 (New York: International Publishers, 1942), 354.
20. *Ibid.*, 353. Marx's theory of capitalist development might be described in Robert Merton's terms as a "theory of the middle range," applicable to one given society, not to society at all times and in all places.
21. Trotsky, "Prospects of a Labor Dictatorship" (1906) in *Our Revolution* (New York: Holt, 1918). Cf. Trotsky's later and more definite formulation of the "law of combined development" in Chap. I of his book, *The Russian Revolution*, now available (in an abridged version) in a Doubleday-Anchor edition (Garden City, N.Y.: Doubleday & Co., 1959).
22. See Wittfogel, *Oriental Despotism* (New Haven: Yale, 1957), and "The Marxist View of Russian Society and Revolution," *World Politics*, July 1960, 487–508.
23. Feuer, 247.
24. See particularly Marx, *The Poverty of Philosophy*, 86–89, 100–102, 159; and *Capital*, I, 837.
25. See Alfred G. Meyer, *Marxism: The Unity of Theory and Practice* (Cambridge, Mass.: Harvard University Press, 1953), 31–39.
26. Marx, *The Poverty of Philosophy*, 159–160.
27. See Mao Tse-tung, "On the Correct Handling of Contradictions among the People," *People's China*, July 1, 1957, supplement, 4.
28. The classic delineation of this process is contained in Ernst Troeltsch, *op. cit.*, 314ff.
29. Gustav A. Wetter, *Dialectical Materialism: A Historical and Systematic Survey of Philosophy in the Soviet Union* (New York: Frederick A. Praeger, 1958), 130–136, and R. V. Daniels, *The Conscience of the Revolution: Communist Opposition in Soviet Russia* (Cambridge, Mass.: Harvard University Press, 1960), 360–362.
30. Marx, "Toward the Critique of Hegel's Philosophy of Right," in Feuer, 263.
31. *Ibid.*, 265–266.
32. Marx, *Capital*, I, 291.
33. Marx and Engels, *Manifesto of the Communist Party*, 30–31.
34. Quoted in Landauer, I, 133.
35. Marx, *The Civil War in France* (1871; New York: International Publishers, 1940), 57.
36. Engels, Introduction to the 1895 edition of Marx's "Class Struggles in France, 1848 to 1850," in Marx and Engels, *Selected Works*, I, 123, 136.
37. Marx, "Economic and Philosophical Manuscripts" (1844), in Erich Fromm, *Marx's Concept of Man*, 125, 127.
38. Marx, "Critique of the Gotha Program," *Selected Works*, II, 566 (Edition prepared by the Marx-Engels-Lenin Institute, Moscow 1933, under the editorship of V. Adoratsky).
39. See Lenin, "The State and Revolution," *Selected Works*, I–II, 294–300.
40. As expounded, *inter alia*, in Trotsky, *The Revolution Betrayed* (New York:

Doubleday & Co., 1937); James Burnham, *The Managerial Revolution* (New York: John Day, 1941); Milovan Djilas, *The New Class* (New York: Frederick A. Praeger, 1957); Max Shachtman, *The Bureaucratic Revolution* (New York: Ronald Press, 1962).

41. Marx, "Theses on Feuerbach," in Feuer, 244.
42. Marx, *The Poverty of Philosophy,* 94.
43. Engels, *Anti-Dühring* (Moscow: Foreign Languages Publishing House, 1954), 371.
44. Marx, *Capital,* I, 824.
45. Marx, "The Eighteenth Brumaire of Louis Bonaparte," *Selected Works,* I, 333–334. Cf. at this point Marx's contemporary and co-Hegelian Lorenz von Stein and his three-volume *Geschichte der Sozialen Bewegung in Frankreich von 1789 bis auf unsere Tage* (Leipzig, 1850); new ed. with Introduction by Gottfried Salomon (Munich: Drei Masken Verlag, 1921); abridged Engl. transl. by Kaethe Mengelberg, *The History of the Social Movement in France,* 1789–1850 (Totowa, N.J.: The Bedminster Press, 1964).
46. Engels, 1891 Introduction to Marx's *Civil War in France,* 20–21.
47. Bukharin, "On the Theory of the Imperialist State," in R. V. Daniels, *A Documentary History of Communism* (New York: Random House, 1960), I, 85–86.
48. *Ibid.,* 85.
49. Sidney Hook, Introduction to the 1962 edition of *From Hegel to Marx* (Ann Arbor: University of Michigan Press, 1962), 8–9.
50. Engels to Joseph Bloch, September 21–22, 1890, *Correspondence,* 476.
51. *Ibid.,* 475.
52. Engels to Conrad Schmidt, October 27, 1880, *op. cit.,* 484.
53. Engels, *Anti-Dühring,* 392–393.
54. See, e.g., Kautsky, *The Class Struggle* (1891; Chicago: Kerr, 1910).
55. Labriola, "Historical Materialism," in *Essays on the Materialist Conception of History* (1896; Chicago: Kerr, 1908), 158.
56. Alfred G. Meyer, *Marxism: The Unity of Theory and Practice,* Chap. 6.
57. See Bernstein, *Evolutionary Socialism, A Criticism and an Affirmation* (New York: Huebsch, 1909).
58. Of course, independent Marxist theorists in the West have continued in a more or less orthodox fashion, e.g., John Strachey, *Contemporary Capitalism* (London: Victor Gollancz, 1957); Paul M. Sweezy, *The Theory of Captialist Development* (New York: Oxford University Press, 1942, and Monthly Review Press, 1956); Max Shachtman, *op. cit.*
59. See, e.g., Luxemburg, *Reform or Revolution* (1899; New York: Three Arrows Press, 1937).
60. See Plekhanov, *The Development of the Monist View of History* (1895; Moscow: Foreign Languages Publishing House, 1956), and *The Role of the Individual in History* (1898; London: Lawrence and Wishart, 1940).
61. See R. V. Daniels, "Lenin and the Russian Revolutionary Tradition," in Hugh McLean, Martin E. Malia, and George Fischer, eds., *Russian Thought and Politics* (Harvard Slavic Studies, IV; The Hague: Mouton, 1957).
62. Lenin, "What is to Be Done?" (1902), *Selected Works,* Vol. I, Part 1, 287.
63. See Lenin, "Marxism and Insurrection" (Sept. 26–27 [old style], 1917), *ibid.,* vol. II, part 1, 167, 173.
64. Bukharin, *Historical Materialism: A System of Sociology* (New York: International Publishers, 1926), 51.

65. See Pokrovsky, *Brief History of Russia* (1920; New York: International Publishers, 1933).

66. Lukacs, "Der Funktionswechsel des historischen Materialismus," in *Geschichte und Klassenbewusstsein* (Berlin: Malik, 1923), 229–232.

67. Gramsci, "Preliminaries to a Study of Philosophy," in Carl Marzani, ed., *The Open Marxism of Antonio Gramsci* (New York: Cameron Associates, 1957), 30–31, 43–44. See also Gwyn A. Williams, "The Concept of 'Egemonia' in the Thought of Antonio Gramsci," *Journal of the History of Ideas,* October, 1960.

68. See, for example, Maurice Dobb, "Historical Materialism and the Role of the Economic Factor," *History,* Feb. 1951.

69. See Kolakowski, "Responsibility and History," *East Europe,* Feb. 1958.

70. Kuczynski, "Der Mensch, der Geschichte macht," *Zeitschrift für Geschichtswissenschaft,* No. 1, 6.

71. Molnar, "Some Economic Problems of Contemporary Capitalism" (Budapest, 1959), discussed in *The New York Times,* Jan. 10, 1960.

72. Stalin, "Report to the Seventeenth Party Congress," in *Problems of Leninism* (Moscow: Foreign Languages Publishing House, 1940), 529.

73. See Klaus Mehnert, *Stalin vs. Marx* (London: Allen and Unwin, 1952). For an elaboration on the replacement of determinism by voluntarism compare Robert V. Daniels, "Fate and Will in the Marxian Philosophy of History," *Journal of the History of Ideas,* Vol. XXI, No. 4 (Oct.–Dec. 1960), 538–552.

74. See, e.g., O. V. Kuusinen, et al., eds., *Fundamentals of Marxism-Leninism* (Moscow: Foreign Languages Publishing House, 1961).

75. See Robert Lifton, "Thought Reform of Chinese Intellectuals," *Journal of Asian Studies,* Nov. 1956.

76. Herbert Butterfield, *History and Human Relations* (London: Collins, 1951), 79.

77. See Karl Mannheim, *Ideology and Utopia* (New York: Harcourt, Brace & World, 1936).

Robert N. Bellah   DURKHEIM AND HISTORY

HISTORY WAS ALWAYS of central importance in Durkheim's sociological work. Without understanding this, a full appreciation of his contribution to sociology is impossible. From his earliest to his latest work, Durkheim urges the closest rapprochement between sociology and history.[1] In one of his earliest published papers[2] he stresses the importance of history for sociology and of sociology for history.[3] In the Prefaces of Volumes I (1898) and II (1899) of *L'Année Sociologique,* he lays down the policy of including a large proportion of historical works among the books reviewed, a policy from which *L'Année* never deviated, and addresses his colleagues: "It has appeared to us that it would

Abridged and reprinted with the permission of the author and the American Sociological Association from the *American Sociological Review,* Vol. 24, No. 4 (August 1959). The paper was originally read at the Durkheim-Simmel Centenary Session of the annual meeting of the American Sociological Society, August, 1958.

be useful to call these researches to the attention of sociologists, to give them a glimpse of how rich the material is and of all the fruits which may be expected from it."[4] In 1905 he calls to his students' attention the importance of history for the understanding of the sociology of education,[5] and in 1912 he speaks of the crucial importance of history for the sociology of religion.[6] And in his last paper, "Introduction à la morale" of 1917, Durkheim once again notes the fundamental significance of history for the understanding of man.

Sociology and History: Methodological Considerations

At several points Durkheim went so far as to question whether or not sociology and history could in fact be considered two separate disciplines. In the Preface to Volume I of *L'Année* he quotes the great historian, Fustel de Coulanges—to the effect that "the true sociology is history."[7] Durkheim approves of this on the condition that history be treated sociologically and, in a subsequent article, he traces the tendency of the writing of history during the last half of the nineteenth century to become in fact more and more sociological.[8] His most extreme statement on the subject was made in the course of a discussion held by the French Society of Philosophy in 1908 where, in reply to the statement of a distinguished historian, he said: "In his exposition, M. Seignobos seemed to oppose history and sociology, as if they were two disciplines using different methods. In reality, there is nothing in my knowledge of sociology which merits the name, which doesn't have a historical character. . . . There are not two methods or two opposed conceptions. That which will be true of history will be true of sociology."[9] When reviewing some articles by Salvemini, Croce, and Sorel, however, he draws the distinction between the two fields that he maintained more or less constantly: history is concerned with the particular; sociology with types and laws, that is, with comparative structure and analytical theory, with the study of things not for themselves, but as examples of the general. But he adds that these are not two disciplines but two points of view which, far from excluding each other, support and are necessary for each other, although they should not be confused.[10]

But Durkheim did not merely preach. Almost all of his own researches draw heavily from historical and ethnological sources and are in fact organized in a historical framework. This is true, for example, of his sociology of the family,[11] his treatment of the division of labor,[12] his theory of punishment,[13] his discussion of property and contract,[14] his sociology of education,[15] his sociology of religion, his study of socialism.[16] Even *Suicide*,[17] which depends more on contemporary data than almost any other of his studies, derives its conceptual scheme in part at least from hypotheses about very long-term changes in the structure of solidarity in society.

If Durkheim was not an ahistorical theorist neither was he just another philosopher of history whose work stimulated little concrete historical research. Durkheim's profound influence on two generations of anthropologists and sociologists is well known, but what is perhaps less well known is his equally profound influence on cultural history—Hubert's work on the Celts, Granet on China, Harrison and Cornford on ancient Greece, Maunier on North Africa, and many others.[18] Of course, Durkheim advocated comparative historical studies relevant to problems of analytic theory, not a narrow historicism.

What is the theoretical groundwork of Durkheim's lasting concern with history in his sociological thought? His Latin thesis contains an early formulation of his position: "There are two types of conditions which move social life. One is found in present circumstances such as the nature of the soil, the number of social units, etc.; the other is found in the historical past (*in praeterita historia*). And in fact just as a child would be different if it had other parents, societies differ according to the form of the antecedent society. If it follows a lower society it cannot be the same as if it had issued from a very civilized nation. But Montesquieu, having not known this succession and this kinship of societies, entirely neglected causes of this type. He didn't take account of this force from behind (*vis a tergo*) which pushes peoples and only paid attention to the environing circumstances (*circumfusa*)."[19] He then points out that Comte was equally mistaken in the opposite direction in thinking that placing a society in an historical series was in itself sufficient for sociological explanation.

The position maintained in the Latin thesis, however, was inherently unstable. In saying that both the historical past and the social milieu are causal factors in sociological explanation, Durkheim seems to be adopting an eclectic "both/and" position which leaves the fundamental antinomy unresolved. But in as early a work as the *Rules of Sociological Method* he adopted a stable position which he maintained with consistency thereafter. In the *Rules* he decisively rejects both causal finalism, which seeks to account for the emergence of sociological phenomena in terms of the use or advantage which will result from them,[20] and historical determinism which explains sociological phenomena as the product of an inevitably operative sequence of stages.[21] In opposition to both of these types of explanation, Durkheim holds to the position that only efficient causes are admissible in scientific explanation. Thus he maintains that only currently operative variables can account for the emergence of social phenomena and that neither a hypothetical sequence of past historical stages nor a hypothetical future utility can do so. Causes, then, are to be found only in the currently operative social milieu, or, as we might say, in the social system, a position which some have taken as Durkheim's renunciation of history.[22]

Durkheim, however, had by no means renounced history. This is shown by his insistence, on the one hand, that currently operative variables cannot be understood without a knowledge of their history and his deepening understanding of those variables themselves, on the other. The Preface of Volume II of *L'Année* is instructive in this regard. Immediately after having commended historical researches to the attention of sociologists, he says:

> Perhaps, it is true, the busy sociologist will find this procedure uselessly complicated. In order to understand the social phenomena of today . . . , isn't it enough to observe them as they are given in our actual experience and isn't it a work of vain erudition to undertake research into their most distant origins? But this quick method is full of illusions. One doesn't know social reality if one only sees it from outside and if one ignores the substructure. In order to know how it is, it is necessary to know how it has come to be, that is, to have followed in history the manner in which it has been progressively formed. In order to be able to say with any chance of success what the society of tomorrow will be . . . , it is indispensable to have studied the social forms of the most distant past. In order to understand the present it is necessary to go outside of it.[23]

Durkheim repeatedly warned that to study the present from the point of view of the present is to be enslaved by all the momentary needs and passions of the day.[24] It is necessary to go into the past to uncover the deeper lying forces which, though often unconscious, are so largely determinative of the social process. Durkheim compares this stricture with the necessity of studying the past of an individual in order to understand the unconscious forces at work in him, thus urging a sociological analogue to the psychoanalytic method.[25]

But history is not only essential to the understanding of the present. History is central to sociology by the very nature of the sociological method, namely, that it is *comparative*. This is precisely the point that Durkheim makes in Chapter VI of the *Rules*. There he argues that the comparative method is above all the appropriate method for sociology and, more specifically, within the general logic of comparative analysis, the method of concomitant variation[26]—a position which the subsequent history of sociology has largely borne out. But Durkheim was always acutely aware of the problems of analysis and definition in sociological work. He therefore criticizes those sociologists and anthropologists who understand the comparative method to consist in the indiscriminate collection of facts and who believe that the sheer weight of documentation can prove anything. Durkheim, rather, insists that comparison can only be meaningful when the facts compared have been carefully classified in terms of a systematic and theoretically relevant typology. This means, for him, especially the typological classification of whole societies or what he calls "social species."[27] Durkheim's work in this area, while far from definitive, did lay down some of the essential guidelines. His basic principle of classification, that of morphological complexity, as he plainly saw, has both analytical and genetic implications. The arrangement of social types or species shows a rough sequence, in that the more complex types emerge from the simpler. But there is no suggestion of "inevitable stages": the genetic concept was not tainted with unilinear evolutionism.[28]

How, then, is the comparative method to be applied in sociology? It can, according to Durkheim, be used in a single society "when absolutely necessary" if certain conditions obtain, namely, when there are data for a considerable period of time and when the data themselves reveal extensive systematic variation, as in the case of suicide.[29] Results obtained from several societies of the same species are desirable in confirming the generalizations reached on the basis of a single case. But by far the best use of the comparative method, from Durkheim's point of view, is its application to an extended series of social types, involving a wide range of historical and ethnographical material.

To explain a social institution belonging to a given species, one will compare its different forms, not only among peoples of that species but in all preceding species as well. . . . This method, which may be called "genetic," would give at once the analysis and the synthesis of the phenomenon. For, on the one hand, it would show us the separate elements composing it, by the very fact that it would allow us to see the process of accretion or action. At the same time, thanks to this wide field of comparison, we should be in a much better position to determine the conditions on which depend their formation. *Consequently, one cannot explain a social fact of any complexity except by following its complete development through all social species.* Comparative sociology is not a particular branch of sociology; it is sociology itself, in so far as it ceases to be purely descriptive and aspires to account for facts.[30]

Here, as so often, Durkheim overstates his case. There are clearly some problems for which the historical and comparative method is less relevant than others. Still, it is important to remember that most of his empirical work was carried out in terms of just such a method of extended comparison, and that the great theoretical advances which have inspired so much valuable work in anthropology, history, and sociology directly emerged from the use of that method.

Thus, although Durkheim stresses that only currently operative variables can be accepted as causes of social phenomena, he insists with equal vehemence that such variables can only be understood by a comparative analysis involving a recourse to history. So in Durkheim's mature view there are not two alternative modes of explanation of social phenomena, one in terms of sociological function, the other in terms of the historic past. There is only one method of explanation, at once both sociological and historical.

We may now turn to an analysis of the chief types of social cause with which Durkheim worked, an analysis which will take us even more deeply into Durkheim's conception of the role of the historical in sociology. For here Durkheim went quite far in the direction of developing a theory of social change—which, presumably, static functionalists are not allowed to do.

In the early period, roughly from the *Division of Labor* through *Suicide,* Durkheim gives primary emphasis to morphological variables in the explanation of social causes. Schnore has recently published an excellent analysis of Durkheim's views on morphology and structural differentiation; only the briefest summary is necessary here.[31] Durkheim isolates two especially important morphological variables: the number of social units or the "size of a society"; and the degree of interaction taking place between the units of the system, which he calls "dynamic" or "moral" density. In general, as size and dynamic density increase, competition between unspecialized units engaged in the same activities also increases. Structural differentiation is then seen as an adaptive response to this increased competition: by specializing in different activities the units no longer come in conflict. Although his conception is schematic and oversimplified, Durkheim is unquestionably correct in seeing structural differentiation in response to adaptive exigencies as a major aspect of social change.[32] This concern with structure, far from obscuring the problem of change, actually illuminates it.

Durkheim saw that the focus of structural differentiation is economic organization; but he also saw that structural differentiation had a profound effect on the total society and that it always involved important elements which were in no immediate sense economic. Examination of some of these noneconomic aspects of structural differentiation provides better understanding of Durkheim's conception.

Family, Individual, and Differentiation

In Durkheim's conception the starting point of the process of structural differentiation is the undifferentiated segment that he tends to identify with a "diffuse clan." This is the beginning of the development of the family as an institution.[33] The diffuse clan has economic, political, religious, and other functions, as well as functions which, on the basis of our form of family (which Durkheim called "conjugal" and we sometimes call "nuclear"), are today often referred to as *familial*. Durkheim therefore believes that it is somewhat confusing to name the diffuse clan a "family" since by that term we mean something so different. He does recognize the existence of the nuclear family within such a unit but finds it weak in structural differentiation and institutional legitimacy compared with the family in our society. As the process of division of labor proceeds Durkheim sees the successive differentiation of religious, political, and economic functions away from the kinship unit itself. But together with these external changes there are also internal changes. As familial relations become disentangled from relations to property, political authority, and the like, they become more personalized. The external environment reaches into the family in the form of the state, which affords protection from abuse even within the family. Under these circumstances the conjugal family in modern society is enabled to carry out its indispensable function, namely the moral training of children or, as we would say, "socialization," and the provision of moral and emotional security for all family members.[34] So brief a summary gives no idea of the richness of the comparative material which Durkheim presents in support of his argument. But the essential position is that in the process of structural differentiation the family does not merely lose functions but becomes a more specialized unit playing a vital role in more complex societies, although not the same role as in simpler societies. Not only does this analysis increase our understanding of the family, it adds an important principle to the theory of structural differentiation—namely, that when in the course of differentiation, a unit appears to lose important functions, it is not necessarily a weakened version of its former self; it may be a new, more specialized unit, fulfilling important functions at a new level of complexity in the larger system.

A similar conclusion may be drawn from the consideration of Durkheim's views on the changing position of the individual in society as the result of structural differentiation. This is a subject to which Durkheim devoted considerable attention, references to it being found in a great many of his books and articles. Taken as a whole, his work on this subject constitutes an important contribution to the "sociology of personality," or, as it may be put, a historical and comparative social psychology.[35] Durkheim's great problem in this area is to explain the emergence of individualism on a sociological basis, avoiding both the abstract philosophical and purely psychological analyses of his predecessors.

The core of the problem is touched in *The Division of Labor*. Individuality is at its minimum in the undifferentiated segment characterized by mechanical solidarity; here a single *conscience collective* guides all individuals alike. In a differentiated society where the division of labor and organic solidarity have become important, the sphere of the *conscience collective* has shrunk and individual differences are not only tolerated but encouraged. How does this occur? In the first instance, Durkheim cites a number of morphological factors. One aspect of the increase of dynamic density (the degree of interaction between units in a social system) is increased physical mobility. As individuals move away from their place of origin the hold of the older generation, defenders of tradition (itself the stronghold of the *conscience collective*), is weakened and consequently individual differences can occur more easily—especially in the process of urbanization.[36] Another aspect of urbanization allowing greater individual variation is the anonymity afforded by large population aggregates, which renders the individual less subject to rigid traditional controls.[37] In addition to these rather negative causes Durkheim adduces certain important positive factors. One of these is the emergence of the state, which he sees as an essential prerequisite for the emancipation of the individual from the control of the undifferentiated segment. The state, seeking to extend its own influence at the expense of the primary and secondary groups which immediately envelop the individual, operates to secure the rights of individuals against such groups. If the state destroys the secondary groups, however, it becomes even more oppressive than they were. Durkheim sees a dynamic balance between the state and secondary groups as maximizing individuality.[38] As society becomes more voluminous it tends to become more universalistic—and here is another positive factor. Law, for instance, when it must apply to a vast empire must be more generalized than are the local customs of a petty hamlet. Religion, too, if spread over a wide area, must have a universal appeal and not be restricted by narrowly local and particularistic concerns. But a more generalized and abstract law and religion will bind the individual less closely than the minutely specific customs of the undifferentiated segment.[39] Implicit throughout the *Division of Labor* is the notion that the performance of complex differentiated functions in a society with an advanced division of labor both requires and creates individual variation, initiative, and innovation, whereas undifferentiated segmental societies do not.[40]

These more or less morphological hypotheses may serve as an introduction to Durkheim's sociology of the individual. His understanding of this problem was greatly deepened as he became aware of a second main type of causal variable, noted below. The foregoing discussion, however, is sufficient to indicate that Durkheim not only introduced a series of stimulating hypotheses about the role of the individual, but also added further important corollaries to the theory of structural differentiation. One of the most important of these is what Talcott Parsons calls "institutionalized individualism."[41] This is the notion that the emergence of individuality involves the shift from one kind of social control to another, not the weakening of social control itself. Durkheim, then, stressing the necessity of conformity in some sense for social order, turns our attention from the false issue of conformity *versus* nonconformity to a consideration of various types of conformity, including, of course, the pathological possibility of overconformity.

For our purposes, however, the point of special interest in Durkheim's views on the family and the role of the individual, for example, is that the basic analytic concepts of morphology[42] and social differentiation, which supply the basis of so much of Durkheim's work, apply, as he uses them, both to current functioning and to long-term historical change. Here are concrete examples of that method of extended comparison which Durkheim advocated. If the concepts which have emerged from these comparisons—the types of solidarity, the types of suicide, and so on—have proven useful in the analysis of the functioning of social systems, these same concepts when organized around the master idea of structural differentiation have made very important contributions to our understanding of social change.

Religion, Collective Representations, and Social Change

The second major type of social cause which Durkheim isolated, and which occupied him increasingly in his later years, is the *representation collective*. As is well known, Durkheim's interest turned increasingly to religion, especially primitive religion, and it was in relation to this interest that the idea of collective representation takes on prominence.[43] It seems likely that Durkheim's concern with problems of structural differentiation turned his interest to religion. At any rate his work on religion is closely related to that earlier concern, as indicated in the preface of Volume II of *L'Année*.[44] Durkheim is interested in discovering in religion, especially primitive religion, that undifferentiated whole from which the elements of social life gradually differentiated. (Durkheim twice speaks of this phenomenon in connection with the importance of the discovery of the unicellular organism in biology.) It is in this context, then, that we can understand why Durkheim came to devote so much attention to religion in the Australian clan, attention that led to the production of his greatest work, *The Elementary Forms of the Religious Life*. As early as the 1880s, Durkheim had seen what he called the "diffuse clan" as the simplest form of kinship structure. By 1898 he had come to view the clan as more fundamentally a religious group than a consanguineal one. With the example of the Australian clan and its religious life, he undertook to analyze the social analogue of the unicellular organism, the basic structural type from which all other social structures have differentiated.[45]

For fifteen years Durkheim used Australian totemism as a "laboratory" in which to study with minute precision the relations between religion, social structure, and personality. During that time he mastered the concrete empirical data to such an extent that *Elementary Forms* anticipated discoveries made by Australian fieldworkers only several years later, and profoundly influenced subsequent work in this field.[46] And it was during these long and painstaking experiments on Australian totemism that Durkheim made some of his most fundamental sociological discoveries—the symbolic nature of the sacred, the theory of ritual, the role of religion in the internalization of values, and so on. It is impossible here to give even a superficial summary of the *Elementary Forms*. We can only cite a single point of method and discuss the major contribution to the theory of social change—our theme—which emerged from Durkheim's study of primitive religion.

Durkheim clearly regarded the *Elementary Forms* as a vindication of his genetic method. He said on one occasion that he understood the Australian primitives better than he did modern France.[47] He found the fundamental facts simpler and the relations between them easier to grasp than in a more complex society.[48] Unfortunately, he was unable to carry out his method extensively, that is, by a series of studies of religion in societies of successively more complex types. He did give some suggestions along these lines, however, some of which are noted below.

Turning to the main contribution to the theory of social change emerging from his work on religion we must consider the idea of *collective representations*. This idea appears in 1898—when Durkheim was deeply concerned with the sociology of religion. One of the earliest uses of the concept is in

"La Prohibition de L'Inceste," an article which appeared in that year, and is the first paper drawing heavily on Australian sources. Both in this paper and in another publication in 1898, "Individual and Collective Representations," the fundamental point is made that while collective representations (which Durkheim later called "ideals" and which we might call "values"— although the original conception was broader than these terms suggest) arise from and reflect the "social substratum" (the morphological variables of the earlier period) they are, once in existence, "partially autonomous realities" which independently influence subsequent social development. Thus Durkheim, in the concept of collective representations, made the fundamental discovery of culture as an element analytically independent of social system,[49] although the full significance of this insight remained somewhat obscured by his use of the word "social" to apply to both elements.

With the creation of the concept of collective representations Durkheim made a twofold contribution to the theory of social change. First and better known, he greatly increased our understanding of how collective representations arise by showing their relation to morphological features. (In this, incidentally, he anticipated Mannheim by more than twenty years.) The greatest impact of the *Elementary Forms* on the study of primitive religion and on early societies in the ancient Mediterranean, the Far East, and elsewhere, was of this sort. But Durkheim, never a devotee of one-way determinism,[50] also saw clearly that collective representations have a reciprocal influence on social structure and are independent variables in the process of social change. This is stated explicitly as early as 1898[51] and receives something like a theoretical formulation in 1911.[52] But the richest and most exciting elaboration of this view appears in that little known but extremely important book, published twenty years after Durkheim's death, *L'Évolution Pédagogique en France,* composed of lectures written in 1904 and 1905.

In this work Durkheim takes the history of French education as an index to the history of the French spirit and of the social and cultural framework out of which it arose: here is an intricate and sensitive analysis of the interplay of morphological and representational factors in the development of French culture from the early middle ages to the nineteenth century. In accordance with his penchant for origins, he begins by showing that French education first appeared in the church. He demonstrates how certain fundamental features of the Christian world-view colored the conception of the school as a place for the education of the total personality, a conception which still survives. Here a representational element is used as a fundamental point of reference without any attempt to explain it morphologically.[53] There follows an interesting discussion of how the morphological factors involved in the political unification of Charlemagne and the religious unification of the high middle ages are related to the structure of the school system and to the predominance first of grammar and then of logic in the curriculum, although in this analysis he takes full account as well of cultural factors.[54] Subsequently, the changes in social structure involved in the breakdown of the medieval system and the several cultural tendencies of the Renaissance are considered as alternative answers to the problems raised by the breakdown.[55] The analysis of the factors involved in the French cultural synthesis of the seventeenth century is especially brilliant; and since the spirit of modern French culture derives from that period, this discussion is helpful in understanding the France of today as well as Durkheim's thought.[56] A final example—there are many others—of Durkheim's historical sociology in this work is his analysis of the relation between Protestantism and the rise of "realistic education," especially the teaching of science. In linking the orientation of Protestantism to science Durkheim independently reached a conclusion better known from the studies of Weber and Merton.[57]

Two general conclusions may be drawn from Durkheim's treatment of such problems, which have reference to the theory of social change. One is his insistence that collective representations, once institutionalized, are capable of exerting an influence over an exceptionally long period of time and in the face of many social and cultural changes. He held, for example, that even modern secular ideas of duty, morality, and the like were derived from fundamentally Christian ideas, since Christianity was the chrysalis of Western culture itself, and that these ideas are quite different from the ethical views of the classical pagan world. Again, he maintained that the Cartesian spirit held a certain cultural dominance in France in spite of the tremendous political and economic revolutions which occurred after its formulation. The second general conclusion is that as long as the social system is running smoothly the accepted system of collective representations will not be questioned. Only when the old system is breaking down, when there is a great deal of turmoil and social ferment, new systems of ideals become formulated, and then contribute to the establishment of a newly stabilized social system.[58] Durkheim's conclusions about the role of collective representations in social process together with his conception of structural differentiation, I believe, provide the outlines of a fruitful theory of social change and suggest the direction of future work in the development of such a theory.

Notes

1. What Durkheim meant by "history" will, it is hoped, become clear during the course of this paper. At this point it may merely be noted that he was not committed to any special conception of history such as the "historical individual" of German historicism or the trait atomism of the "historical" anthropologists.
2. "Introduction à la Sociologie de la Famille," *Annales de la Faculté des Lettres de Bordeaux*, 10 (1888), pp. 257–281.
3. *Ibid.*, pp. 262–265, and pp. 276–278.

4. Preface, *L'Année Sociologique,* 2 (1899), p. v.

5. *Education and Sociology* (New York: The Free Press, 1956), pp. 152–153.

6. *The Elementary Forms of the Religious Life,* (New York: The Free Press, 1947), p. 3.

7. Preface, *L'Année Sociologique,* 1 (1898), p. iii.

8. "Sociologie et sciences sociales," *Revue Philosophique,* 55 (1903), pp. 465–497 (with P. Fauconnet).

9. Discussion of "L'Inconnu et l'Inconscient en Histoire," séance du 28 Mai, 1908, *Bulletin de la Société Française de Philosophie,* 8 (1908), p. 229.

10. *L'Année Sociologique,* 6 (1903), pp. 123–125. The relevant passage is as follows: "It is necessary, then, to choose. History can only be a science on condition that it raise itself above the particular; it is true that then it ceases to be itself and becomes a branch of sociology. It merges with dynamic sociology. It can remain an original discipline if it limits itself to the study of each national individuality, taken in itself and considered in the diverse moments of its becoming. But then it is only a narrative of which the object is above all particular. Its function is to place societies in the state of remembering their past; this is the eminent form of the collective memory. After having distinguished these two conceptions of history, it is necessary to add further that more and more they are destined to become inseparable. There is no opposition between them, but only differences of degree. Scientific history or sociology cannot avoid direct observation of concrete facts and on the other hand national history, history as art, can only gain by being penetrated by the general principles at which sociology has arrived. For in order to make one people know its past well, it is still necessary to make a selection among the multitude of facts in order to retain those that are particularly vital; for that some criteria which presuppose comparisons are necessary. Similarly, to be able with greater sureness to discover the way in which concrete events of a particular history are linked together, it is good to know the general relations of which these most particular relations are examples and applications. There are not, then, in reality two distinct disciplines, but two different points of view, which, far from excluding each other mutually presuppose each other. But this is no reason to confuse them and attribute to the one what is the characteristic of the other" (pp. 124–125).

11. "Such are the general conclusions of the course: The progress of the family has been to be concentrated and personalized. The family becomes more and more contracted at the same time that relations take on a more and more exclusively personal character, along with the effacement of domestic communism. As the family loses ground marriage on the contrary is strengthened." "La Famille Conjugale," *Revue Philosophinque,* 90, p. 14. The material is drawn from classical, ancient German, medieval, and modern sources. See also Georges Davy, *Sociologues D'Hier et D'Aujourd' hui* (Paris: Alcan, 1931), Part II, "La Famille et la Parenté d'après Durkheim," pp. 104–158.

12. *The Division of Labor in Society* (New York: The Free Press, 1949). The concepts of mechanical and organic solidarity are developed from an essentially historic framework, and a wide range of historical material is presented as evidence.

13. "Deux lois de l'évolution penale," *L'Année Sociologique,* 4 (1901), pp. 65–95. The laws are "The intensity of punishment is greater the less advanced the

society and/or the more absolute the central power" (p. 65) and "Punishments which involve deprivation of liberty and of liberty alone, for periods of time variable according to the gravity of the crime, tend more and more to become the normal type of repression" (p. 78). Evidence is drawn from the ancient Near East, India, Greece, Rome, medieval and modern Europe.

14. *Professional Ethics and Civic Morals* (New York: The Free Press, 1958), Chapters XI–XVIII.

15. Especially his *L'Évolution Pédagogique en France* (Paris: Alcan, 1938), two volumes. This is a major work of Durkheim, unfortunately too little known. It is in fact nothing less than a history of the French spirit in its sociological setting. As his major essay in what might formally be called "history," the book is especially rich in implications for the relation between history and sociology.

16. *Le Socialisme* (Paris: Alcan, 1928). This is the beginning of an unfinished *history* of socialism.

17. (New York: The Free Press, 1951).

18. Most of the writers cited have worked on problems in connection with the emergence of early societies from a "primitive" background. The hypotheses put forward in "De Quelques Formes Primitives de Classification: Contribution à l'Étude des Représentations Collectives," *L'Année Sociologique,* 6 (1903), pp. 1–72 (with Marcel Mauss), and *Elementary Forms, op. cit.,* have been especially fruitful.

19. *Quid Secundatus Politicae Scientiae Instituendae Contulerit* (Bordeaux: Guonouilhou, 1892), p. 69. A French translation of "The Contribution of Montesquieu to the Establishment of Social Science" is to be found in E. Durkheim, *Montesquieu et Rousseau: Précurseurs de la Sociologie,* editor and translator Armand Cuvillier (Paris: Riviere, 1953). This translation is superior to that of F. Alengry, *Revue d'Histoire Politique et Constitutionelle,* 1 (1937), pp. 405–463. A similar formulation is to be found in *Professional Ethics and Civic Morals, op. cit.,* pp. 1–2.

20. Durkheim's reserved and cautious use of the concept of function eliminates at least nine-tenths of the objections made to functionalism. See *The Rules, op. cit.,* pp. 89–97.

21. *Ibid.,* pp. 115–121. This is the fundamental ground of his opposition to any unilinear theory of social evolution.

22. This interpretation of the passages under consideration has several times been put forward by M. Georges Davy, e.g., in "L'Explication Sociologique et le Recours à L'Histoire d'après Comte, Mill et Durkheim," *Revue de Metaphysique et de Morale,* 54 (1949), esp. pp. 346–353; in the Introduction to *Professional Ethics, op. cit.,* esp. pp. xxix-xxx (first published in French in 1950); and in the Introduction to *Montesquieu et Rousseau, op. cit.* Nevertheless one of the clearest presentations of Durkheim's real position was put forward by M. Davy himself at a much earlier date; see *Emile Durkheim,* Choix de Textes avec Etude du système sociologique par Georges Davy (Paris: Louise-Michaud, 1911), esp. pp. 31–51.

23. P. v. The application of this stricture to a great deal of contemporary sociological work is obvious. Don Martindale has recently given an example in showing how American urban sociology would have benefited from historical research in understanding some of its own chief problems. See

his Introduction to Max Weber's *The City* (New York: The Free Press, 1958).

24. Here again the contemporary application, in a day when "policy" considerations determine more than a little sociological research, is obvious.

25. E.g.: "But we know today that in order to know ourselves well, it is not enough to direct our attention to the superficial portion of our consciousness; for the sentiments, the ideas which come to the surface are not, by far, those which have the most influence on our conduct. What must be reached are the habits, the tendencies which have been established gradually in the course of our past life or which heredity has bequeathed to us; these are the real forces which govern us. Now, they are concealed in the unconscious. We can, then, succeed in discovering them only by reconstructing our personal history and the history of our family. In the same way, in order to be able properly to fulfill our function in a scholastic system, whatever it may be, it must be known, not from the outside, but from within, that is to say, through history. For only history can penetrate under the surface of our present educational system; only history can analyze it; only history can show us of what elements it is formed, on what conditions each of them depends, how they are interrelated; only history, in a word, can bring us to the long chain of causes and effects of which it is the result." *Education and Sociology, op. cit.*, pp. 152–153. See also *L'Évolution Pédagogique en France, op. cit.*, Vol. I, pp. 15–19.

26. The *Rules*, pp. 129–136.

27. Durkheim's insistence on taking the total society as his theoretical frame of reference was one of his major contributions, as Talcott Parsons has recently pointed out with respect to mechanical and organic solidarity in "Durkheim's Contribution to the Theory of Integration of Social Systems," in Kurt H. Wolff (ed.), *Durkheim, 1858–1917* (Columbus: Ohio State University Press, 1960), 118–153. On this point the Latin thesis contains some valuable observations: "Montesquieu follows one rule of method which present social science must retain. . . . [He] has well seen that all the elements form a whole of a sort that when they are taken separately and apart from others they cannot be understood; that is why he doesn't separate law from morality, from religion, from commerce, etc., nor above all from the form of the society which extends its influence to everything social. Different though they are all the facts express the life of one and the same society; they correspond to diverse elements or organs of the same social organism. If one refrains from seeking how they realise their harmony and their reciprocal influence one cannot determine the function of each. Indeed one lets their nature escape completely, because they seem to be realities endowed with their own existence while they are only elements of a whole." *Montesquieu et Rousseau, op. cit.*, pp. 102–104. We are still far from having learned this lesson.

28. A satisfactory typology of societies remains to be achieved, though it is one of the first tasks of sociology as Durkheim clearly saw. All comparative work which does not use at least an implicit typology is severely limited. This stricture applies to at least some of the cross-cultural survey studies which use, say, "400 societies," but where we have no idea how comparable these societies in fact are in terms of structural types. It is safe to say that an adequate typology will be based on the most *generally* applicable concepts of sociological theory *and* will be genetically valid. It is in the work

of Max Weber rather than Durkheim that the most fruitful beginnings of
a satisfactory typology are to be found.

29. The *Rules*, p. 136.

30. *Ibid.*, pp. 138–139. Italics in the original.

31. Leo F. Schnore, "Social Morphology and Human Ecology," *American
Journal of Sociology*, 63 (May, 1958), pp. 620–634. I wish to underscore
Schnore's conclusion as to the importance of Durkheim's theory of structural differentiation and the necessity of developing structural taxonomies,
adding that these are crucial not for ecology alone but for general sociology.

32. Durkheim, *Division of Labor, op. cit.*, Book II, Chapter 2; *The Rules*, pp.
92–93, 112–115. Parsons and Smelser have recently pushed the theory of
structural differentiation considerably forward. See Talcott Parsons and
Neil J. Smelser, *Economy and Society*, (New York: The Free Press, 1956),
Chapter 5; and esp. Neil J. Smelser, "Revolution in Industry and Family:
An Application of Social Theory to the British Cotton Industry, 1770–
1840," unpublished Ph.D. dissertation, Harvard University, 1958. In the
latter work Smelser treats certain social movements as reactions to strains
generated in the process of social differentiation, a point which Durkheim
anticipated in his *Le Socialisme, op. cit.*

33. Durkheim's lectures on the family (discussed by M. Mauss in "In Memoriam,
L'Oeuvre inédite de Durkheim et de ses collaborateurs," *L'Année Sociologique*, new series, 1, pp. 7–29) unfortunately were never published. His
sociology of the family therefore must be reconstructed from the items
mentioned in notes 3 and 11 above, from his "La Prohibition de L'Inceste
et ses Origines," *L'Année Sociologique*, 1, 1898, pp. 1–70, and from scattered remarks in other works. See esp. the article by Davy cited in footnote
11 above.

34. Cf. Davy, *Sociologues D'Hier et D'Aujourd'hui, op. cit.*, pp. 153–154. Parsons
and Bales in seeing the modern type of family as the result of a process
of specialization and its main functions as those of "pattern maintenance"
and "tension management" are very close to the Durkheimian view. See
Talcott Parsons and Robert F. Bales, *Family, Socialization and Interaction
Process* (New York: The Free Press, 1955), Chapter 1.

35. To cite only some of the chief references on this subject: *Division of Labor,
op. cit.*, esp. pp. 283–303, 345–350, 386–388; *Suicide, op. cit.*, esp. pp.
152–276; "Deux lois de l'evolution penale," *op cit.*; *L'Education Morale*
(Paris: Alcan, 1925); *Professional Ethics and Civic Morals, op. cit.*, pp. 55–
75. Durkheim's works on the sociology of the family and of religion are
also relevant. Marcel Mauss carried forward Durkheim's work in this area
by undertaking an historical and comparative analysis of the concept of
the "self" as found in the following societies: the Pueblos, the Indians of
Northwest America, Australia, India, China, and Rome; and as the concept is treated by Stoics, Christians, and modern European philosophy. See
"Une categorie de l'esprit humain: La Notion de personne, celle de 'Moi',"
in M. Mauss, *Sociologie et Anthropologie* (Paris: Presses Universitares de
France, 1950), pp. 331–362.

36. *Division of Labor*, pp. 291–297.

37. *Ibid.*, pp. 297–301.

38. *Professional Ethics*, pp. 55–64.

39. *Division of Labor*, pp. 287–291. Here Durkheim seems to be getting at a
very important aspect of normative systems, namely their level of generality,

whether or not his overly simple morphological explanation of the problem is acceptable. See Howard Becker, "Current Sacred-Secular Theory and Its Development" in H. Becker and A. Boskoff, editors, *Modern Sociological Theory in Continuity and Change* (New York: Dryden, 1957), Chapter 6. Becker's distinctions between proverbial and prescriptive, on the one hand, and principial, on the other, seem to be concerned with what Durkheim is here discussing.

40. Recent work by Morris Janowitz on long-term changes in military organization tends to bear out some of Durkheim's ideas. As military units change from the old undifferentiated infantry to the complex organization geared to the use of modern weapons, control of individuals becomes less formal and rigid and involves more participation and initiative. His finding that repressive corporal punishment tends to diminish in modern armies supports Durkheim's contention in "Deux Lois." See Morris Janowitz, "Changing Patterns of Organizational Authority: The Military Establishment," *Administrative Science Quarterly*, Vol. 3, No. 4 (March 1959).

41. Parsons, "Durkheim's Contribution," *op. cit.*

42. See Durkheim's introductory note on "Morphologie Sociale," *L'Année Sociologique*, 2 (1899), pp. 520–521, where he points out that morphology cannot be a static science and that history and comparative ethnography are essential to it.

43. According to Davy: ". . . he undertook the study of religious phenomena only after having written the *Division* and *Rules* and it is this new study which revealed to him the importance of ideal factors." *Emile Durkheim*, *op. cit.*, p. 44. Actually, Durkheim's interest in religion is already clearly in evidence in *Division;* and even in one of his first articles, "Les Études de Science Sociale," *Revue Philosophique*, 22 (1886), pp. 61–80, there is a long and interesting discussion of Spencer's theory of religion. Nevertheless, Davy is almost certainly right that religion became a central concern of Durkheim only after the late 1890s.

44. *L'Année*, Vol. II, pp. iv-v. Following the preface of *L'Année*, Durkheim shows the relation between kinship and religion in "La Prohibition de L'Inceste," *op. cit.* (1898), between punishment and religion in "Deux Lois," *op. cit.* (1901), between categories of thought and religion in "De Quelques Formes," *op. cit.* (1903), between property, contract, and taxation and religion in *Professional Ethics*, pp. 145–195, and in the *Elementary Forms* (1912), he provided a summary of the whole problem, including the religious source of morality.

45. Of course, Durkheim did not view the Australian clan as a fossilized survival of the exact structure from which all other structures differentiated. Rather, in line with some of his ideas discussed above, he considered the Australian clan to be an example of a social *type*. Taking his results at a sufficient level of generality, then, we find them validly applicable to the "single-celled" type of society—all more complex societies must have descended from some society of this type. Further, although Durkheim held that the Australian social structure was in certain key morphological respects simple, he was well aware of the considerable complexity of this system, especially as to kinship. Lévi-Strauss, in this regard, refers to ". . . Durkheim's important article 'La Prohibition de L'Inceste' where anthropologists may find a remarkably clear interpretation of the genesis of the Australian

eight-class systems through the cross-cutting of a matrilineal dichotomy based on filiation, and a partrilineal fourfold division based on residence." (C. Lévi-Strauss, "French Sociology," in G. Gurvitch and W. E. Moore, editors, *Twentieth Century Sociology*, New York: Philosophical Library, 1945, p. 517.) In general, moreover, Durkheim understood that "simple" structures are in their own way complex: "When Spencer states that the universe goes 'from homogeneity to heterogeneity,' this formula is inexact. That which exists at the origin is also heterogeneous, but it is a diffuse state of heterogeneity. The initial state is a multiplicity of germs, modalities and different activities, not only mixed but, so to say, lost one in another, in such a way that it is extremely difficult to separate them: they are indistinct from one another. Thus in the cell of unicellular beings all the vital functions are gathered together: all are found there only they are not separated; the functions of nutrition and the functions of relation [integration?] seem blended and it is difficult to distinguish them. . . . In social life this primitive state of undifferentiation is even more striking still." *Pragmatisme et Sociologie, op. cit.,* p. 191. This passage dates from 1914 and indicates that Durkheim was aware of relatively recent developments in biology, the complex functions of unicellular organisms becoming well known only in the early years of the century.

46. See Lévi-Strauss, *op. cit.,* pp. 521–522, 536. Such distinguished Australian fieldworkers as Radcliffe-Brown, A. P. Elkin, and W. L. Warner have acknowledged Durkheim's remarkable contributions to the Australian field.

47. "L'Inconnu et l'inconscient en histoire," *op. cit.* M. Seignobos found this assertion quite incredible.

48. *Elementary Forms*, pp. 6–7. Although Durkheim's method was "genetic," he was not a victim of the genetic fallacy. He never lost sight of his rule that social causes could only be understood in terms of current functioning. He knew that structures inherited from simpler societies might have quite different functions in more complex ones. As an example of his clarity on this fundamental point see his "La Prohibition de L'Inceste," *op. cit.,* pp. 66–70.

49. This point is so crucial that we quote the relevant passage from "Individual and Collective Representations": "Also, while it is through the collective substratum that collective life is connected to the rest of the world, it is not absorbed in it. It is at the same time dependent on and distinct from it, as is the function of the organ. As it is born of the collective substratum the forms which it manifests at the time of its origin, and which are consequently fundamental, naturally bear the marks of their origin. For this reason the basic matter of the social consciousness is in close relation with the number of social elements and the way in which they are grouped and distributed, etc.—that is to say, with the nature of the substratum. But once a basic number of representations has been thus created, they become, for the reasons which we have explained, partially autonomous realities with their own way of life. They have the power to attract and repel each other and to form amongst themselves various syntheses, which are determined by their natural affinities and not by the condition of their matrix. As a consequence, the new representations born of these syntheses have the same nature; they are immediately caused by other collective representations and not by this or that characteristic of the social structure.

The evolution of religion provides us with the most striking examples of this phenomenon. It is perhaps impossible to understand how the Greek or Roman Pantheon came into existence unless we go into the constitution of the city, the way in which the primitive clans slowly emerged, the organization of the patriarchal family, etc. Nevertheless the luxuriant growth of myths and legends, theogonic and cosmological systems, etc., which grow out of religious thought, is not directly related to the particular features of social morphology. Thus it is that the social nature of religion has been so often misunderstood." (*Sociology and Philosophy,* New York: The Free Press, 1953, pp. 30–31.) This passage deserves the closest study; in itself it is enough to acquit Durkheim of the charge of "sociologism."

Apart from the two papers cited above, one other occurrence of the term "collective representation" may date as early as 1898, namely, *Professional Ethics,* pp. 48–50, which was drafted, according to Mauss, between November, 1898 and June, 1900. I have not found the term used before 1898, although there are various foreshadowings, e.g., in the discussion of religion in *Suicide, op. cit.,* pp. 157–160. Durkheim's discussion of Montesquieu's idea that different social types have different integrating ideals (e.g., "virtue" in the ancient city, "honor" in the monarchy, and "fear" in despotism), which occurs in the Latin thesis, may be a forerunner. The treatment of socialism in *Le Socialisme,* written in 1895–96, seems to move in the same direction, but the term "collective representation" is not used. Durkheim's fullest treatment of what is in fact his theory of culture is in the core passage of the *Elementary Forms,* Book II, Chapter VII, pp. 205–239. Lévi-Strauss believes that even in this passage Durkheim is not quite fully aware of the analytical independence of symbolism: "Society cannot exist without symbolism, but instead of showing how the appearance of symbolic thought makes social life altogether possible and necessary, Durkheim tries the reverse, i.e., to make symbolism grow out of society." (*Op. cit.,* p. 518.) I would question Lévi-Strauss's view, but to explain my reasons would require a more extended analysis of the passage in question than is possible here. It is shown below that Durkheim did use morphological (social) and representational (cultural) elements as independently variable in a number of instances.

50. The old chicken and egg problem concerning material and ideal factors was never an issue for Durkheim at a time when it was agitating many lesser minds. On the reciprocal nature of causation see the references cited in *Pragmatisme et Sociologie,* p. 196, note 1.

51. "La Prohibition de L'Inceste," *op. cit.,* p. 69.

52. "Value Judgments and Judgments of Reality," *Sociology and Philosophy, op. cit.,* pp. 80–97.

53. *L'Évolution,* Vol. I, Chapters II and III.

54. *Ibid.,* Chapters IV–XIII.

55. *Ibid.,* Vol. I, Chapter XIV; Vol. II, Chapters I–IV.

56. *Ibid.,* Vol. II, Chapters V–VIII.

57. *Ibid.,* Vol. II, Chapter IX.

58. This conclusion was anticipated in *Suicide,* pp. 157–160, and esp. in *Le Socialisme,* pp. 248–352, where Durkheim finds socialism, religious revival, sociology, and the historical method, diverse though they are, all reactions to the great social changes brought on by the industrial revolution and all in one way or another attempts to understand and cope with the new

situation. The relation between this view and Weber's idea of charismatic leadership should not be overlooked—Durkheim stresses the features of social disturbance. Weber the charismatic response, but they are two sides of the same process.

Werner J. Cahnman   MAX WEBER AND THE
METHODOLOGICAL CONTROVERSY
IN THE SOCIAL SCIENCES

IN RECENT DECADES MAX WEBER has become known as a major proponent of social action theory, but his writings have been translated into English in bits and pieces in such a way that the total aspect of his work has been obscured.[1] As a consequence, a static and atomized Weber has emerged, divorced from the historical background against which he must be understood. However, in the present context, there is more at stake than the proper interpretation of a single theorist. Max Weber's basic concepts of "understanding on the level of meaning" and of the "ideal type," and especially of rational social action as the paradigm of an "ideal type," are the result of a century-long discussion about the nature of history as a branch of knowledge. An awareness of this discussion is indispensable for the evaluation of the relations between history and sociology. As a matter of fact, Max Weber's (and, to some degree, Ferdinand Toennies') brand of sociology, that is, sociology as a generalized conception of socio-cultural reality, emerges as one of the answers, perhaps as *the* answer, to problems which agitated many of the best minds for a considerable period of the time.

Obviously, the story of how this came about, if told in full, would transcend the limits of a survey article. The main locale is Germany, but there are related developments in England which would bear scrutiny. Further, there is a most variegated philosophical background to the story, extending from Hobbes and Kant via many intermittent links to Dilthey and Rickert which, for lack of space as well as competence, can be merely referred to here and there in the account that follows. However, since practically all philosophies and philosophically relevant theoretical systems which have a bearing on the methodology of historical research and the nature of historical

Harry H. Bash of the University of Pennsylvania has rendered valuable service in helping to collect and evaluate the literary sources which have been used in preparing this paper; I am sure it could not have been written without his assistance. The author is indebted to Professor Robert K. Merton, Professor Richard Jung, and the late Professor Paul Honigsheim for valuable advice.

knowledge have been surveyed in masterly fashion by Ernst Troeltsch, it would seem permissible to ask the reader to consult this work for a more comprehensive kind of information.[2] The following discussion is restricted to outlining the principal approaches which serve to put into relief the methodological controversy in the social sciences.

Romanticism, Idealism, and the Theory of History

The revolutionary impact which the romantic movement of the early nineteenth century has had on modern thought can hardly be overrated. By romanticism, we mean the revulsion against uniformity, generality, calculated simplicity, and the reduction of living phenomena to common denominators; the aesthetic antipathy to standardization; the abhorrence of platitudinous mediocrity. More positively: the attentiveness to the detailed, the concrete, the factual; the quest for local color; the endeavor to reconstruct in imagination the distinctive lives of peoples remote in space, time, or cultural condition; the cult of individuality, personality, and nationality; indulgence in the occult, the emotional, the original, the extraordinary.[3] The repercussions of this volcanic outburst of individualized energy are still with us: in modern music and art, in progressive education, in existentialist philosophy, in psychoanalysis, in a host of nationalistic and charismatic movements. Both the loosening of standards and the quest for a new "community" are romantic in character. The sentence, ascribed to the poet Novalis, "where you are *not,* there is happiness," has often been quoted as the essence of the romantic spirit.

In the context of the social sciences, the romantic revolution has had a profound impact on the development of the academic disciplines of history, geography, and anthropology. Of these, history arrests our attention, not so much *per se,* but because the "historical method" at that point began to claim the dignity of a universal approach to the study of human affairs. Symptomatic of this approach is the "historical school of law," whose basic philosophy is expressed in Carl von Savigny's words: "There is no absolutely singular and separate human existence; rather, what may be considered singular, or individual, from one point of view, is part of a larger whole, if seen from another point of view. Accordingly, every individual human being, at the same time, must be thought of as member of a family and a people ["folk"], as the continuation and evolution of the epochs of the past."[4]

Accordingly, the historical school of law opposed the idea that institutions are the result of conscious reflection and deliberate planning. Law in particular, if it was not to be disruptive of societal bonds, should aim not at systematization and codification, but should be conceived of as the result of slow "organic" growth out of custom and usage; that is, as an expression of the "mores" and, indeed, the entire "culture" of a people. This is the meaning of the often-quoted term *"Volksgeist."*[5] There is much here that anticipates Sumner's dictum that "the mores are always right," but historically the connection is rather with the counter-image which English common law seemed to provide to the *Code Napoléon*. Especially pertinent is Edmund Burke's reference to the "policy of our constitution to claim and assert our liberties as an entailed inheritance derived to us from our forefathers and to be transmitted to our posterity . . ."; this "policy" appeared to him as "the happy effect of following nature, which is wisdom without reflection and above it."[6] Burke's influence on Savigny, Eichhorn, and other leading spokesmen of the "historical school of law" is attested to by Carl Menger, one of the protagonists of the *"Methodenstreit,"* but it is interesting to note that Burke's German translators, A. W. Rehberg and Friedrich Gentz, rendered the term "partnership"—in the celebrated Burkean phrase in which a nation is defined as "a partnership of past, present, and future generations—as *"Gemeinschaft."*[7] This is the unromantic origin of a romantic concept. What was true continuity in England became a yearning for it in Germany.

What has been said about the study of law and institutions also applies to the study of linguistics, another favorite object of the "historical," or holistic, approach. Language is an expression of "culture," as we would say. In the "historical" approach, then, the individual manifestation is seen as part of a whole rather than as the application of a general law. In this context, one can understand why the eminent historian Georg von Below, contemporary and counterpart of Max Weber, could say that he derived his brand of sociology directly from romantic thought.[8] In defining sociology as the study of relations between individuals, on the one hand, and the groups and collectivities to which the individual belongs, on the other, he expressed the opinion that sociology is an "approach" to societal data rather than an independent branch of knowledge—an approach which emphasizes that the actions of individuals do not originate in the individuals themselves but are derived from the nonvolitional and transmitted reality of their groups. (One must note the unabashedly collectivistic nature of this definition as against Max Weber's definition of "social action" as merely "oriented" to the actions of others.) Von Below credits the romantic inspiration with the discovery of the twin concepts of "collectivity" and "personality," the *tertium comparationis* being that both are distinguished by uniqueness and unity. In other words, they have the quality of "historical" phenomena.

Sociology as an independent academic discipline only intermittently adopted a comparable approach, most notably in the Durkheimian concept of *représentations collectives*. One cannot understand Durkheim's position in sociology if one overlooks his indebtedness to De Bonald, to Maistre, to Boeckh, to Fustel de Coulanges.[9] Cultural anthropology, a related discipline to which Durkheimian sociology had a particularly strong affinity, is much more clearly romantic and collectivistic in inspiration, and the historiography of the nineteenth century rests squarely upon the foundations of romantic thought. However, a difficulty arises at this point in that romantic philosophy expresses the world-view of the artist more adequately than it does the world-view of the scientist.

To be sure, the new historiography contained positivistic, or scientistic, elements inasmuch as it stressed reliance on factual data and a rigorous critique of sources, that is, inductive procedure—the slow ascent from the particular to the universal—as against the lofty, deductive reasoning of the philosophers. But Wilhelm von Humboldt, in his influential essay "*Ueber die Aufgabe des Geschichtschreibers*," following Schelling, added that to ascertain what actually happened was to present merely the raw material of history, not history itself.[10] To give "*Gestalt*" to disconnected data, that is, to infuse them with life, the historiographer would have to become creative. In this regard, he was to be compared to the poet: he must internalize reality in order to reorganize it independently in the light of a constructive "idea." Humboldt, a linguist of distinction, observed that it might seem "objectionable" to confound the spheres of the scholar and the artist in such fashion, but he saw "the difference which neutralized the danger" in the circumstance that historical imagination, in contrast to the imagination of the poet, was to be guided by trained experience; it was to become "the art of combination." To combine properly, that is, with a view to arriving at the correspondence of a living "*Gestalt*," was to "understand." Precisely how this was to be done, however, remained unsaid.

Humboldt's views were shared by the dean of nineteenth-century historiographers, Leopold von Ranke, as evidenced by the famous concluding sentences of Ranke's essay "The Great Powers."[11] They were considered a guiding star by the systematizer and defender of the historical method, J. G. von Droysen. Droysen's concise *Grundriss der Historik,* first published in 1867, translated into English in 1893, is a *magna charta* of the historical method.[12] Foreshadowing Dilthey, the essence of the historical method is defined by Droysen as "*forschend zu verstehen*," that is, to establish facts on the basis of strict rules of evidence and to infer from these exterior manifestations the moving force which is in the mind of man. This is said to be possible because the researcher who attempts to understand is a total personality like his object (§10). But the mechanism of understanding differs from the act of understanding, which is more than explanatory; it is creative (§11). Generally, according to Droysen, historical research does not explain the later as necessary sequence to the earlier, the actual phenomena as repetitive instances of general laws. Such sequences do exist; but if this were all that was to be said about it, human life, deprived of liberty and responsibility, would lack moral character (§37).

In the third quarter of the nineteenth century, this kind of humanistic realism was bound to clash with the claim of Comtean sociology to be a "new history," conceived in the spirit of positive science. In his *History of Civilization in England,* H. T. Buckle, referring to Comte as a trail blazer for what needed to be done "to raise the standard of history," complained that while in all other fields of inquiry the need for generalization was universally admitted, so that the laws could be discovered by which the facts are governed, "the unfortunate peculiarity of the history of man [was] that, although its separate parts have been examined with considerable ability, hardly anyone has attempted to combine them into a whole and ascertain the way in which they are connected with each other."[13] Buckle was trying to show that environmental factors accounted for man's behavior. His work was presociological inasmuch as it centered attention on determinants of social action rather than on social action itself, but at the time it appeared it stood for the "sociological," or "materialistic," interpretation of history and was widely read.

Droysen, in an impassioned review of Buckle's work—published with other pertinent essays in the Appendix to *Grundriss*—attacked Buckle not on substance, but on method and, through method, on approach.[14] He doubts that the procedures employed in the physical and biological sciences are the only methods which can claim to be scientific in character; in fact, he denies that they are applicable to the human realm. No science, he asserts, is a mere collection of isolated facts; history, in particular, shows that the human ego does not exist by itself, but is a part of larger wholes, that the past of the collectivities which encompass man and his works continues to live in the present, and that the moral categories, which are in evidence everywhere, must be recognized as autonomous values. Droysen's reply has "the touch of the poet," even as he tries to come to grips with the requirements of the scientific method. But where Buckle is self-assured, Droysen is groping. His answers are not free of contradictions; for instance, how "freedom of the will," combined with "divine providence," maintains itself in the face of environmental "circumstances," is not explained. Even more serious was the admission that the theoretical foundations of the procedures by which the affairs of man may be studied are by no means firmly established. Such a theory, which would formulate "not the laws of history, but the rules of historical research," was expected from renewed efforts in the future.[15]

Efforts in this direction were made in the generation following Droysen, especially by Dilthey, Windelband, Rickert, and Simmel.[16] It is not the purpose of this paper to enter into a detailed analysis of these philosophies as they bear on the problems of historical knowledge, and of their agreements and disagreements.[17] What is important in the present context is that, as a result of their epistemological clarification of basic concepts, such as "nature" and "culture," "law" and "event," "science" and "history," a new sociology was ushered into existence, which turned its back on any attempt to ascertain the "laws" of "historical" development—now recognized as self-contradictory

—and instead developed a methodological approach to historical research based on the establishment of sociology as a formal system of "social relations" (Toennies, Simmel) or of "social action" (Max Weber). In Max Weber's definition, which is widely accepted, action is considered "social" only if and insofar as it is meaningfully oriented to the action of others; otherwise, we are confronted with a mere reaction to *stimuli,* which may be socially relevant, but does not constitute social action.[18] The moral, that is, the value-oriented element in history, so fervently defended by Droysen as the essence of history, is herewith preserved.

This moral, or "historical," quality of "social action" is further fortified methodologically in Max Weber's definition of sociology as "a science which attempts to understand social action on the level of meaning" (*"deutend verstehen"*). The word *deutend* is here decisive, as the affinity between Droysen's definition of the historical method as *"forschend verstehen"* and Weber's definition of the sociological method as *"deutend verstehen"* can hardly be overlooked. The German word *"forschen"* points to the painstaking procedures of factual research, thus precluding reliance on mere "intuition" as the basis of "understanding."[19] The word *"deuten"* links "meaningful interpretation" to its scientific goal, namely "causal explanation." But Max Weber goes a step further. As he puts it in the notes to his definition, "meaningful interpretation" looks for evidence (*"Evidenz"*), that is, any mode of proof, or confirmation, which may carry conviction. According to Max Weber, such evidence can be "either of a rational (logical, mathematical) or of an empathic, emotional, artistic-receptive character."[20] Following Dilthey and Simmel more than Windelband and Rickert at this point, Max Weber leans over backwards to accommodate the Humboldtian and Rankean tradition in historiography.[21] He recovers his positivistic posture immediately by establishing "rational social action" as the "ideal type" of *all* social action; but, as will be shown later, his "rationalism" is merely formalistic, not substantive, in character. We must now turn to delineating the genesis of the concept of the "ideal type" in the famous *Methodenstreit,* the methodological controversy in the social sciences.

Socio-Economic Institutionalism versus Theoretical Economics

The *Methodenstreit* is concerned with the relations between the "historical " and "theoretical" approaches in the social sciences. It arose within the field of what was then called "Political Economy," but as a result of the arguments and counterarguments in which the combatants engaged, institutional economics and a historically oriented sociology made their appearance.[22] That the controversy should have arisen in the field of economics is not surprising. The modern science of economics had come to the fore in the "age of reason," *pari passu* with the growth of the entrepreneurial classes and that "civic society" which seemed to base its existence neither on custom and tradition nor on political authority, but on the interplay of individual interests. These interests could be isolated from other social forces and it was possible to show that they were not only "reasonable" in themselves but that their summation yielded intelligible "laws" which explained the formation and fluctuation of prices in a market and, more especially, the monetary rewards for the disposal of fixed and fluid capital, landed property, and manual labor, respectively. The underlying nominalistic assumption was that the social world was an aggregate of individual wills, which, if acting "economically," that is, in accordance with the principle of the relative scarcity of the productive factors, could be presumed to be acting rationally; and that, if such were the case, enlightened self-interest would serve the ends of society, as far as the economic sphere was concerned, better than any other principle or motive.

All this sounded like a revelation at the time, but, as can be seen in retrospect, this position, which is here produced in great brevity and without reference to the objectification which the theory underwent from Smith to Ricardo, raised a great many questions. Was "rational economic action," as "supposed" by classical theory, the expression of a universally valid "law" of human behavior? Was it to be conceived as a theoretical model? Or was it to be understood as a theoretical model which, at the same time, reflected the "nature" of economic processes, that is, the reality of economic life? Or was it an "ought-to-be," a guideline for economic policy? All these elements were present, lending themselves to enthusiastic advocacy, but also provoking critical doubts and determined opposition.

In the camp of the advocates, the Smithian and Ricardian theoretical models were soon transformed into doctrinaire recipes, imposed upon a reluctant reality. They were used as a club by which to beat down corporate entities, such as guilds or unions, and to ward off state intervention that threatened to interfere with the "pursuit of happiness." This was not classical, but "vulgar" economics, to use the contemptuous Marxian expression, but the dividing line between the two was blurred. However, confusion was more confounded in the other camp. To be sure, there was solid ground on which to base a stand in opposition. Whatever its scientific merits, a purely chrematistic economics clashed everywhere, except perhaps in the English midlands and in some port cities, with older patterns of thought and action, which may best be characterized by pointing to the derivation of the term "economics" from the Greek *oikos,* that is, a self-contained, family-based household.[23] Within such a household, purely economic considerations were subordinated to moral goals which are "shared" and "transmitted" in a particular culture. Accordingly, the historians of culture, especially the adherents of the "historical school" in Germany, drew attention to "the scantiness of authority which the institution of private property in its present form can derive from history; and to urge on broad scientific and philosophical grounds a reconsideration of the rights of society as against the rights of the individual." These were the words of Alfred Marshall;[24] in the two or three generations preceding him, the kind of society which served as a model for collectivistic philosophies had been rediscovered in Greek, Roman, Germanic, and Celtic antiquity as well as in the experience of the British India Service by such scholars as August Boeckh, A. H. L. Heeren, G. L. von Maurer, N. D. Fustel de Coulanges, and Henry S. Maine.[25] We shall return to the collectivistic theme presently. At this juncture, it should merely be noted that Henry Maine's terms, "status" and "contract," have become an inheritance of sociology; but Ferdinand Toennies—who learned a great deal from Maine, and after him, Max Weber—went a step further.

Ferdinand Toennies was not directly involved in the *Methodenstreit,* but his major work might have made the entire controversy seem unnecessary, if it had been understood properly at the time of its first appearance (1887).[26] Toennies was aware of the arguments of natural law as well as the counterarguments of the historical school against the generalizations of natural law: he realized that the rationalistic approach, while identical with scientific procedure, was far from exhausting the varieties of social action.[27] He devised the concepts of "essential will" and "arbitrary will" and their institutional counterparts of *"Gemeinschaft"* and *"Gesellschaft,"* as formal, or "normative" concepts in sociology. Thus, "family," "clan," "village," "friendship" may serve as approximate examples of *"Gemeinschaft,"* but they are *"Gemeinschaft"* only to the extent to which they coincide with the ideal conceptual image of *"Gemeinschaft."* "City," "state," "industry," "public opinion" may serve as examples of *"Gesellschaft"* in the same way. In other words, viewed in the light of "normative" concepts, actual societies, especially of the *"Gesellschaft"* type, are always mixed. Yet, the formal aspect of the terms used and their historical connotation are inseparable. According to Toennies, human societies have developed, or are going to develop, from *"Gemeinschaft,"* that is, from primitive agrarian communism, or communal village organization, through "individualism," which he considers only as an "ideal limiting point," to *"Gesellschaft,"* that is, an associational society. Ultimately, *"Gesellschaft"* may turn out to be a planned, bureaucratic, or "socialistic," society, but on its way to that goal the voluntaristic element, as exemplified in commercial activities, prevails.

This amounts to saying that "arbitrary," reflection-based, rational processes, apart from their value as a conceptual model, also indicate an increasingly potent historical trend. Max Weber says the same thing when he views "in a certain sense and within certain limits . . . the entirety of economic history as the history of the nowadays victorious economic . . . rationalism."[28] In this sense, the theoretical construct summarizes a historical process; "formal" sociology is transformed into "cultural," or historical sociology. It is remarkable that "value judgments," so strenuously disavowed by both Toennies and Weber as formalists, recur in this context with a vengeance. Toennies characterizes the trend toward *"Gesellschaft"* as a process of "aging"[29] while Weber considers the heyday of capitalism in the nineteenth century as "the dawn of the iron age."[30]

Perhaps we have been anticipating too much, but the complexity of the mature conclusions of Toennies and Weber in a way exonerates their predecessors in the discussion on methodology. We are going to summarize the principal points of this discussion by referring chiefly to the two protagonists of the *Methodenstreit:* Gustav Schmoller, the leader of the "younger historical school," and Carl Menger, the initiator of the Austrian branch of "marginal utility theory."[31] But while Menger can stand by himself, we will have to refer to Roscher, Knies, and Hildebrand, the representatives of the "older historical school," along with Schmoller, chiefly because Max Weber's subsequent polemical remarks were directed against Menger, on the one hand, and against Roscher and Knies, on the other, while they spared Schmoller, probably because of the latter's dominant position in the *"Deutsche Gelehrtenrepublik."* As far as polemics against untenable positions of the "historical school" are concerned, Max Weber sides largely with Menger, but he turns against him when he develops his own concept of the "ideal type," which is a vindication of the implicit methodological assumptions of historical research.

It is most important to realize that the historical school of economics, "older" or "younger," does not present a unified ideological front. The reason lies in the nature of the field of economics itself, which is generalizing in procedure and nominalistic in assumption and thus contrasts not only with the emphasis on the "unique," but also with the collectivistic tendencies and artistic aspirations which are of the essence in history writing. German students of theoretical economics received intensive training in historical fields at the same time; in addition, they lived in a country which even in the second half of the nineteenth century was not yet fully drawn into the capitalistic nexus, and they thus retained their attachment to an older economics of the all-inclusive "household." The very terms *"Volkswirtschaft"* and *"Volkswirtschaftslehre"* ("national economy" and "national economics"), which were used by German authors, point in that direction; Karl Buecher's theory of stages—"household economy," "city economy," and "national economy"—viewed the later stage as an enlargment of the former. Roscher had defined the purpose of his work as "the description of what peoples and nations have wanted and felt regarding economic matters, the goals which they pursued and reached, the causes which have made them pursue and reach these goals."[32] Carl Menger later correctly pointed out that this kind of naive realism barred the road to the formation of scientific laws in economics since single economic units, not collectivities, were the carriers of economic action.[33] Schmoller, in reviewing Roscher's work, emphasized that, contrary to what is required for quantitative procedures, "qualitative observation" faced the difficulty that "collectivities," not merely individuals, had to be analyzed; but, more sophisticated than Roscher, he added that "out of a thousand inexhaustible details" one had to grasp what is "important, typical, general, and to combine it imaginatively" (*"in Bildern"*).[34]

However, the differences between the "important," the "typical," the "general" are not further pursued. In another context, Schmoller distinguished between "exact causal knowledge," proceeding from the parts to the whole, which explains immediate causal sequences, and a "teleological principle of reflection," proceeding from the whole to the parts, which does not impart certain knowledge, but is indispensable for the elucidation of "ultimate causes and purposes." The concept of "organism," he added, was such a teleological, or idealistic, construct.[35] Here, a linkage between Kantian idealism and neo-Kantian formalism becomes visible; but the approach is groping and eclectic, not synthetic, in character.

Indeed, eclecticism marks the methodological approaches of the "historical school of economics" throughout. In his paper "Roscher and Knies and the Logical Problems of the Historical School of Political Economy,"[36] Max Weber points out that Roscher (incorrectly) believed, as did his disciples Bruno Hildebrand and Karl Knies, in collective action as a reality in and of itself, rather than as a resultant of individual actions while he (correctly) conceived of historical generalizations as aiming at the significant rather than the generic; but Weber also showed that it was not Roscher's intention to replace the generalizations of the classical economists, which are generic in character, with a historical typology and even less with historical descriptions of "unique" situations of an economic nature. What Roscher and his disciples, including Schmoller, disliked was the use by theoretical economists of the "deductive," or "philosophical," method, meaning the reasoning from general premises to either actual occurrences or policy propositions which would bend economic actuality to prescriptive rules.[37] That this was not so much the procedure of Smith and Ricardo as the one of their doctrinaire successors, is here beside the point. What is decisive is that Roscher as well as Schmoller, far from intending to replace "theory" with "history," believed rather that the application of the "historical method" would help economists to arrive at a better, that is a more general, theoretical formula in the future. Roscher thought that "Adam Smith and his immediate successors established the rule, but that the newer writers [i.e., historians and socialists] undermined it by means of a multitude of exceptions" and that the need was now "for such an enlargement of the rules that the exceptions could be included in it."[38] In other words, theory, instead of being an abstraction from reality, was to become identical with reality itself. Ironically, Roscher termed this procedure, which is as unhistorical as it is anti-theoretical, the "historical" or "physiological" method.

In view of this stated position, Carl Menger is correct when he points out that the historical school of economics bears only superficial similarity to the historical school of law.[39] It is true that the fundamental organicism of the representatives of the historical school of law was shared by the representatives of the historical school of economics, but there the similarity ends—or almost ends. Whereas consistently held organicist views—from Savigny to Sumner—lend themselves to conservative politics, corresponding views on the part of "historical" economists were compatible with a liberal stance in politics and especially with the fervent advocacy of welfare state measures in the field of social legislation. To be sure, the latter inclination might be interpreted as an emphasis on "security" versus "adjustment" and a spiral return, as it were, to the "larger community,"[40] but there is overwhelming evidence in the writings of "historical" economists that their historicism is largely empiricism and their methodological approach naturalistic in character.[41] Roscher goes so far as to speak of "natural laws" of history.[42] This would tend to make of history a "positive science" along Comtean lines —a position which, in Max Weber's view, amounts to a contradiction in terms.

Later, Roscher's parallelism of history and physiology was superseded by the parallelism of history and psychology, first under the influence of Wundt, then under the influence of Dilthey. The latter especially emphasized that whereas nature was "outside" of us and therefore "foreign" to us, "society was our world" because historical experience was psychic experience writ large.[43] Even though Schmoller reviewed Dilthey favorably, Schmoller's view of psychology hardly assimilated the elements of a sociology of "understanding" which were contained in it.[44] For him, "scientific psychology" meant a science dealing with the varieties of verifiable experience. It meant "empiricism," as opposed to "rationalism," the diligent assembling of "facts" which "speak for themselves" as opposed to premature theorizing from "one-sided" premises.[45] The "one-sidedness" resided in the assumption on the part of classical as well as "marginal utility" theorists that only one "psychological" factor, namely "acquisitiveness," or "self-interest," was operative in economic action. In his argument against Menger, Schmoller predicted a bright future for theoretical economics, but only "through the utilization of the entire historical-descriptive and statistical material, which is now being brought into shape, not through further distillation of the already a-hundred-times distilled rules of the old dogmatism."[46] Menger agreed with Schmoller on the psychological foundation of economic phenomena, but insisted that the "one-sided" reliance on "self-interest" was proper scientific procedure.[47] He further accused Schmoller of "detail-mongering" ("*Kleinmalerei*") and predicted that no "exact theory" could be derived from it.[48] This is undoubtedly true, but it is equally true that the emphasis on the un-

biased attention to original sources, which the historical school fostered, led
to the investigations of the *Verein fuer Sozialpolitik,* in some of which Max
Weber participated, to Le Play's independent investigation of workingmen's
budgets, to Tooke and Newmarch's phenomenal *History of Prices,* and to the
entire social survey movement which, starting with Booth's *Life and Labour
of the People of London,* contributed much toward the appreciation of social
reality.

If Schmoller were classified as a sociologist rather than as an economist,
many of the pieces in his writings which are otherwise puzzling would fall
in line.[49] The connecting link is provided by institutional economics. Institu-
tionalism owes much to romanticism and the historical school, especially to
the trend toward "culture history" which was born of both. It contains elements of universalism as well as empiricism. "Essentially," says Schmoller,
"political economy (*Volkswirtschaft*) includes government and society, custom
and law; it cannot rest on the shaky foundations of dreamt-up robinson-
ades."[50] Schmoller missed the meaning of economic theory (or any other
theory in the social sciences), which either "isolates" one factor in order to
arrive at an "exact theory," as Carl Menger had put it, or establishes an
"ideal type" of social action, as Max Weber would say; but he focused the
attention of social scientists on the need of applying to the full reality of social
life the results gathered by the "isolating" and "abstracting" procedures of
the theorists. Max Weber, in naming the collective work which he was to edit
toward the end of his career *Grundriss der Sozialoekonomik* and including
his expanded essay "Economics and Society" in it, has thereby put the cap-
stone on Schmoller's work. The study of what is "economically conditioned"
and "economically relevant"—in contradistinction to what is purely "economic"—[51] became the subject matter of sociology.

Max Weber's relation to Carl Menger and what he stands for is not so
easily characterized. Weber mentions Menger at various points, if only ob-
liquely and without doing full justice to Menger's contribution.[52] Where he
meets him head on, he refers to him, somewhat darkly, as "the creator of the
[marginal-utility] theory."[53] Weber argued as a latter-day disciple of the historical school, trying to rectify the school's regrettable inconsistencies, but
his sharpest disapproval was directed against mistaking theoretical concepts
for segments of reality itself. Indeed, Menger's position served as a paradigm
for that kind of misconception. To be sure, Menger's criticism of the belief
that out of the sheer amassing of "facts" would arise at some future day of
glory the magnificent edifice of an all-inclusive theory had been much to the
point. The "empirical-realistic" trend in theoretical endeavors, according to
Menger, could only lead (a) to "empirical laws," that is, the knowledge of
factual regularities in the sequence and co-existence of phenomena and (b)
to "*Realtypen,*" that is, basic forms, or typical images of reality, with a greater
or lesser scope for deviations.[54] But such empiricism, he added, could not

lead to the formulation of "exact laws," according to which "what has been observed in one case must invariably recur, if exactly identical factual conditions are maintained."[55] Menger further insisted that the difference between the theoretical sciences of nature and of society rested with the phenomena they investigated, not with the methods they used.[56]

Weber agreed with the recognition, which is inherent in Menger's statements, that it is equally impossible to replace the historical knowledge of reality with the formulation of "exact laws" and to arrive at "exact laws" by a mere comparison of historical observations, but he objected to Menger's claim that reality, while not deducible from a single set of "exact laws" (as, for example, the laws of economic theory), might be deducible from an aggregate of such "laws," that is, from theoretical statements encompassing all the segmental factors which are operative in human affairs.[57] Indeed, the knowledge of the totality of a historical situation, including the causal relations involved, if at all attainable, cannot possibly be the result of a summation of theoretical principles because even if one were to heap concept upon concept *ad infinitum,* no semblance of life could be derived from such a mountain of lifelessness. Menger, as much as Schmoller, was under the spell of "scientific psychology" whereas Weber thought that human motives, far from "explaining" the emergence and the operation of social institutions, could be made comprehensible only on the basis of institutional analysis. For that purpose, the tool of the "ideal type" was forged.

Max Weber's Sociology: A Positivistic
Interpretation of Idealism

As a student of law and economics, and especially because of his early interest in economic history and in the history of law, Max Weber could not help being sensitive to the implications of the methodological controversy among leading economists which agitated the scholarly community in Germany at the start of his academic career. The issue at stake was the reconciliation of the idealistically based, but at the same time meticulously accurate, historiography of the nineteenth century with the accepted scientific code, which required conformity with the laws of causality. In line with these intentions, the papers on Roscher and Knies attempted to demonstrate that the intermixture of historical and naturalistic elements was unsatisfactory from the standpoint of historical logic, not only—as Menger had shown earlier—from the standpoint of theoretical clarity. The paper "Objectivity in the Theory of the Social Sciences and of Social Policy" carried the argument against Menger; it was in this context that the concept of the "ideal type" was first developed.[58]

According to Weber, Menger was caught in a double "prejudice": that naturalistic "laws" are possible of establishment in the cultural sciences and that such "exact laws" are conditioned "psychologically," that is, in the case of theoretical economics, on the "egoistic," or "acquisitive" drive.[59] In contradistinction, Weber maintained that the propositions of abstract economic theory are a special case of a kind of concept construction which is peculiar to the cultural sciences. This does not necessarily exclude the formulation of theoretical propositions in the field of economics as "exact laws"; but it must be recognized that another interpretation is called for insofar as these propositions are relevant in a socio-cultural context.[60] In this case, economic theory does not express a "law," but presents a "model"; it offers "an ideal image of events in the commodity market under conditions of a society organized on the principles of an exchange economy, free competition and rigorously rational conduct."[61] We are dealing here with an accentuation, or enhancement (*Steigerung*), of actually existing elements of reality—in this case of "rational action"—to the point of their fullest potentiality, amounting to the image of an "utopia." This definition of economic theory at the same time defines the "ideal type." The "ideal type," then, is not a description of concrete reality, or even of the essential features of such a reality (*eigentliche Wirklichkeit*); it is not a "hypothesis"; it is not a "schema" under which a real situation, or action, is subsumed as one instance; it is not a generic concept or a statistical average. Rather, it is "an ideal limiting concept with which the real situation or action, is compared," so that it may be properly appraised in line with the categories of "objective possibility" and "adequate causation."[62] In *Economics and Society,* where the earlier methodological disquisitions are presented in a condensed way, it is said that ideal typical constructions delineate "what course human action of a certain kind *would* take, if it were strictly purposive—rationally oriented, undisturbed by error or emotions, and *if,* furthermore, it were unambiguously oriented toward one single, especially an economic, purpose."[63]

Again, as an example of such constructions he offered the concepts of the "pure" theory of economics. All of this amounts to saying that "rational social action," exemplified in the ideally conceived economic situation, is the prototype of the "ideal type." This does not involve a "rationalistic bias," however. "Rational social action" merely serves as a base type while concrete social action, whether founded on erroneous calculation or decidedly nonrational, that is, traditional or affectual, enters as a variant.[64] The term "variant" in this context does not denote a deviation from "regular" aspects of reality; it stands for *all* of reality, as against the "ideal type" which, as a concept, is deprived of "real existence."

If one holds that the principles of pure economic theory are universally valid laws, it follows that they are operative at all times and under all circumstances, if other variables are held constant, and that they cannot, for this reason, be considered as mere aids for the causal analysis of concrete reality. As already stated, this is not Max Weber's position. In substantial agreement with Toennies, but also with such American sociologists as Park and Becker, Weber regards the market model as typical of a *Gesellschaft* type of society and therefore inapplicable to traditional societies. It is also considered inapplicable to a "charismatic" situation, which Weber characterizes as "specifically foreign to economic considerations" (*"spezifisch wirtschaftsfremd"*).[65] The further qualification must be added that, of all historical societies, only modern occidental society approximates the typical "associational society" to a significant degree.

Consequently, "pure" economic theory of eighteenth and nineteenth century derivation, in Weber's opinion, expresses primarily the "idea" of a historically given society which is uniquely oriented on the principles of rational action, namely, modern capitalism.[66] It would not be incorrect to say that "formal" and "historical" aspects converge in Weber's ideal-typical construction, but it should be understood that the formal aspect remains subordinated to the historical one. The academic discipline of sociology may be said to rest on the assumption that the establishment of concepts and types of a "formal" nature, including "ideal types," is an end in itself. In a wider sense, however, the validity of the concept rests with its applicability to concrete situations, in line with the principles of "objective possibility" and "adequate causation." Consequently, concepts of this kind need not be verified in each and every instance, as would be the case if they were abstract natural laws. They are just as valuable if they are not verified, or verified only to a degree, because they are primarily heuristic in nature; they are formed *ad hoc,* and have no independent and timeless validity. They serve the purpose of making concrete cultural, or historical, situations accessible to human "understanding."[67]

Not every concept used in the investigation of concrete reality is in the nature of an "ideal type"; but the boundary lines between "ideal types" and "individual concepts," or "relatively historical concepts"—to use Rickert's term—are fluid.[68] By "individual concepts," we mean such clearly dated and localized concepts as "the American Civil War" or "the battle of Gettysburg," which are the stock-in-trade of historians; by "relatively historical concepts," or "historical totality concepts," we mean concepts referring to relatively undated and nonlocalized collective phenomena, or configurations, like "the Protestant ethic," "Chinese literati," or "Indian castes." Even such a comparatively broad and seemingly undated and nonlocalized concept as "ethical prophecy" ["missionary prophecy"] belongs in this context because it refers primarily to ancient Hebrew prophecy.

Alexander von Schelting has pointed out that concepts of this sort have a "double face": if seen from the outside, that is, compared with other historical configurations, they express the uniqueness of a single collective phenomenon; while seen from the inside, that is, with reference to the multitude of events within such a configuration, they assume a rather general, possibly even a generic character. He further maintains that only the completely generalized concept of "rational social action," and perhaps (by way of contrast) "traditional" and "charismatic" social action, deserves the designation as the true and only "ideal type."[69] (We called it, somewhat more cautiously, the "prototype" of the "ideal type.") At this point, however, Schelting's position is open to doubt. For, while it is correct to say that terms like "economic man" or "price formation under the condition of free competition" represent neither absolutely nor relatively historical individuals, even these very general terms are not considered by Max Weber to be equally relevant to all times and places, but chiefly to a historical configuration called "modern capitalism."[70] One must therefore conclude that the "ideal type," even in its most generalized expression, shares to some degree the characteristics of "historical totality concepts."[71]

Schelting may be quite right in asserting that ideal-type concepts and historical-totality concepts should be kept rigorously apart, but this constitutes an extension, not an interpretation, of Weber. Four other such extensions, two constructive and two critical, may be mentioned here. One, by Arthur Spiethoff, puts the emphasis on "historical reality concepts," or "real types."[72] According to Spiethoff, the multiplicity of socio-economic phenomena and their transformations may be encompassed by a series of "typical examples," or "economic styles" ("*Musterbeispiele*" and "*Wirtschaftstile*"), which reflect not an exemplary utopia, as would "ideal types," but actual configurations: they are "corresponding images" ("*Abbilder*") of concrete reality. For every socio-economic style a theory may be formulated, for instance a theory of capitalistic development, while a truly general theory would have to combine such partial and realistic, or "historical," theories in highly abstract statements. A corresponding image emphasizes the regular as well as the essential features of concrete reality, but differs from our "ideal type" insofar as it must include "disturbing elements"; comparable to an artist's painting, the "ideal type" must not. Spiethoff's economic *Gestalt* theory is a sophisticated elaboration of Schmoller's empirical emphasis. However, while accommodating "exact theory" in Menger's sense more readily than Max Weber would have been inclined to do, it is hardly the synthesis of "scientific" and "historical" approaches which Max Weber had in mind. Spiethoff's aim is to arrive at limited, that is, "historical" theories rather than at theoretically valid heuristic propositions.

Contrary to Spiethoff and more in line with Schelting, Howard Becker attempts to reduce the involvement of the "ideal type" with time and locale by emphasizing its character as a tentatively "constructed type."[73] What is accentuated here is not so much the historical singularity of ideal-typical models as the pragmatic utility of bringing the greatest possible number of isolated phenomena under a concept of considerable generality. The "prediction of the recurrence of social phenomena," irrespective of time and place, is the goal.[74] This position is likely to lead away from Weber's as well as Spiethoff's intentions, which are directed at the understanding of processes of historical significance but also of historical limitation. Becker admits that the social scientist can work only with *relatively* undated and nonlocalized types, but the example which he offers of a "constructed type," namely the one of a "marginal trading people," ranges far and wide across time and space. It is so general that it explains less of the concrete reality of Jews, Armenians, Parsees, Chinese, Greeks and Scots than of the nature of marginality itself. One huge step further, Sjoberg's "constructed type" has shed all tentativeness: the "pre-industrial city" is an inflexibly constructed procrustean bed upon which every urban reality from Katmandu to Florence is stretched.[75] The type has become an end in itself and the "reification" of concepts, a danger which Max Weber strove to avoid, is an accomplished fact.

Critically speaking, Carlo Antoni would seem to score a most telling point.[76] Analyzing Max Weber's sociology of the city, he maintains that the ideal type of the "citizen," namely, the urban middle classes in medieval northern Europe, is "useful for the analysis of this population in its historical individuality and as such is no longer ideal but real"; and he concludes that sociology is thereby "resolved into history." Indeed, the occidental "city"— and likewise modern "bureaucracy"—is seen by Max Weber as an incident in the development of "modern capitalism" which, in turn, is characterized by a prevalence of purposive rationality in social action unparalleled at any other time and place in the memory of man. But the possible coincidence of the ideal and the real at one particular instance in history does not invalidate the usefulness of ideal-typical construction in relation to a series of other instances where the ideal and the real are to some degree, or even widely, apart. If this is conceded, the convergence of historical and sociological research in ideal-typical construction is vindicated.[77]

Compared with Antoni, Firey's related argument is of considerable complexity. It resumes the culturally oriented opposition of the historical against the theoretical school of economics without, however, directly referring to Max Weber.[78] Firey's chief targets are the "methodologically rationalistic theories" of human ecology, especially the "pure" theory of the location of industries, as formulated by Max Weber's brother, Alfred Weber.[79] This theory is constructed along the line of Ricardian economics, assuming free movement of goods and services and rational, i.e., cost/price-oriented, social action. Firey admits that it is legitimate scientific procedure to specify certain premises as given and to conclude from these to unknown variables even though the premises do not present themselves to direct observation. The theoretical ecologist, he says, may "limit himself to the study of those locational processes which would operate *if* space were only an impediment and social systems . . . only economizing agents." But when Firey denies that this is a "pure" theory, applicable to all times and places and instead asserts that it is a historically conditioned "capitalistic" or "contractualistic" theory, he not only disregards the heuristic value of models—but argues also against himself. If "pure" ecological theory adequately describes spatial adaptation in a contractualistic value system, it is neither "anemic" nor historically "wrong," as Firey, following Sombart at this point, asserts. Rather, we are confronted with the coincidence of a pure theory of rational action and a historical situation of high rationality. Even more than in the case of Antoni, such coincidence does not preclude the use of a "pure" or ideal-typical model for the analysis of situations which are culturally divergent.

We must forego here further elaboration. What, we may rather ask, is the meaning of Weber's gigantic effort in terms of the history of ideas? Talcott Parsons has outlined the development of the concept of "social action" from Alfred Marshall to Max Weber as a key concept in sociology, but in replacing typological conceptualization as a means with systematic sociology as an end he has departed from Max Weber's notion of the role of sociology among the social sciences. Parsons correctly calls to mind Weber's fear that "organic sociology" might induce "illegitimate reification,"[80] but this hardly justifies the statement that Weber's "general polemical animus" was directed against the "idealistic position," that is, against the principles underlying the position taken by the historical school.[81] Max Weber counted himself among the "children" of the historical school; he came to fulfill and not to destroy. He was a restorer of "idealism"; his objection against the representatives of the historical school was that they regarded "empirical," that is, historical and statistical investigation as *a* means—even as *the* means—to the end of theory construction. For Weber, the roles were reversed: he believed concepts to be not ends in themselves, but means to the end of recognizing significant relations of an individual-concrete character.[82] Consequently, Weber's "animus" was directed against the assumption that scientifically valid concepts necessarily would have to be of a "monistic," that is, a "naturalistic" character.[83]

The reason why this has not been immediately evident to interpreters is that in attempting to formulate the non-naturalistic logic of human relations in history, Max Weber had to clear away a number of misconceptions. He brushed aside any attempt to mix "idealistic" and "naturalistic" concepts as merely demonstrating their mutual incompatibility.[84] While he recognized the essentially "holistic" approach inherent in historiography, to designate it for this reason—in the Rankean and Humboldtian fashion—as "art" rather than as "science" appeared to him as a renunciation of historiography's claim to the logical validity of its findings.[85] Finally, he rejected the elevation of the *Volksgeist* to the dignity of an ultimate cause because he saw in it an unwarranted "reification" of holistic concepts.[86] Social action remained the action of individuals; collectivities, like "family," "nation," "government," "joint stock company" and so forth were defined as "probabilities" ("*Chancen*") that under certain circumstances a certain kind of action may take place with regard to them, and no more.[87]

However, turning the argument the other way round, Max Weber conceded that in the mind of individual actors collectivities are real as a motivating force; he could have added that they are "real in their consequences." In this view then, in Kantian fashion, collectivities are considered as "ideas" which, while not "real" in any existential sense, nevertheless are "necessary" for our understanding of reality. In this regard, Max Weber follows Schmoller, not Menger; he goes beyond Schmoller in that he does away with uncritical empiricism, returning to the "idealistic" position, as it were, on a new level of scientific validation. The new level is reached in ideal-typical construction and involves the interpretation of holistic images in nominalistic terms. The question as to whether and to what extent Max Weber has succeeded in establishing this veritable *coincidentia oppositorum* as the cornerstone of the social sciences will provide work for social scientists for a good time to come.

Notes

1. The writings of Max Weber, insofar as they are available in English, are listed in the "Bibliographical Note on The Writings of Max Weber" which is appended to Reinhard Bendix, *Max Weber—An Intellectual Portrait* (Garden City, N.Y.: Doubleday & Co., 1960). A complete bibliography of Max Weber's writings in German is contained in the appendix to Marianne Weber, *Max Weber—Ein Lebensbild* (Tuebingen: J. C. B. Mohr, 1926). The lucid introduction of Talcott Parsons in *Max Weber, The Theory of Social and Economic Organization,* translated by A. M. Henderson and Talcott Parsons (New York: Oxford University Press, 1947) should be consulted, although its main concern differs from the one pursued here. Recently, Parsons has moved much nearer to the interpretation arrived at in the present paper in his introduction to Max Weber, *The Sociology of Religion,* translated by Ephraim Fischoff (Boston: Beacon Press, 1963). The preface of the translator of this edition and the appendix on "The Background and Fate of Weber's *Wirtschaft und Gesellschaft*" are likewise worthy of consideration.
2. Ernst Troeltsch, *Der Historismus und seine Probleme* (Tuebingen: J. C. B. Mohr, 1922).
3. The best account in English of the revolutionary impact of romanticism on occidental thought which is known to me is contained in Arthur O. Lovejoy, *The Great Chain of Being—A Study of the History of an Idea* (New York: Harper, 1960; first ed. 1936), chaps. X and XI, esp. p. 293. The German literature on the topic is legion.
4. Carl von Savigny in *Zeitschrift fuer Geschichtliche Rechtswissenschaft* (Berlin, 1815), I, 3ff.
5. Carl von Savigny, *Ueber den Beruf unserer Zeit zur Gesetzgebung* (Heidelberg, 1814).
6. Edmund Burke, *Reflections on the Revolution in France.* Coll. Works (London, 1792), III, 58ff.
7. Cf. Otto Brunner, *Neue Wege der Sozialgeschichte* (Goettingen: Vandenhock and Ruprecht, 1956), 227, and Gunnar Rexius, "Studien zur

Staatslehre der historischen Schule," *Histor. Zeitschr.* (1911), Vol. 107.
Gentz translated Burke's "partnership" as *"Gemeinschaft"*; Adam Mueller
took over the term from Gentz; and Toennies from Mueller.

8. Georg von Below's views on romanticism, sociology, and history are found
in *Die Deutsche Geschichtschreibung von den Befreiungskriegen bis zu
unseren Tagen* (Leipzig: Quelle & Meyer, 1916); "Soziologie als Lehrfach,"
*Schmoller's Jahrbuch fuer Gesetzgebung, Verwaltung und Volkswirtschaft
im Deutschen Reich* (1919), Vol. 43, 1271ff.; "Der Streit um das Wesen
der Soziologie," *Jahrbuecher fuer Nationaloekonomie und Statistik* (1926),
Vol. 124, 219ff.; "Die Entstehung der Soziologie," *Deutsche Beitraege zur
Wirtschafts-und Gesellschaftslehre* (Jena: Gustav Fischer, 1928), Vol. 7.

9. The connection of Durkheim with romantic thought is best indicated in
Robert A. Nisbet, "Conservatism and Sociology," *American Journal of
Sociology,* Vol. 58, No. 2 (Sept. 1952), 167–175. It should be noted, however, that romanticism and conservatism, while historically overlapping, are
not conceptually identical. There is the ferment of decomposition in romanticism, but also the desire for reconstruction; and decomposition is the
work, reconstruction the aim of revolutionaries. Durkheim's "conservatism"
is therefore more in doubt than his indebtedness to romanticism. On the
other hand, it should be noted that, while Durkheim's terms of "mechanical"
and "organic" solidarity bear comparison with Toennies' terms *"Gemeinschaft"* and *"Gesellschaft,"* the value emphasis is on the former by Toennies
and on the latter (*"Gesellschaft"* = *"organic solidarity"*) by Durkheim. One
of the reasons why Durkheim's affinity to romantic—and idealistic—
thought has been played down may be that German and French scholars
used to be habitually antagonistic to each other. However, Charles Gide
and Charles Rist, *A History of Economic Doctrines,* 2nd ed. (London:
George C. Hurop & Co., 1948), 392 or *Histoire des Doctrines Économiques,*
5th ed. (Paris: Recueil Sirey, 1926), 462, draw attention to the similarities
as well as the dissimilarities between Durkheimian sociology and the
historical school of economics.

10. Wilhelm von Humboldt, *Ueber die Aufgabe des Geschichtschreibers,* Ges.
Werke (Berlin, 1841), Vol. I; cf. Ernst Troeltsch, *op. cit.,* 243–277;
Edward Spranger, "Wilhelm v. Humboldt's Rede ueber die Aufgabe des
Geschichtschreibers und die Schelling 'sche Philosophie," *Histor. Zeitschr.*
(1908), Vol. 100, 541ff; Paul Honigsheim, "Schelling als Sozialphilosoph
und seine Auswirkungen in Deutschland" *Koelner Zeitschrift fuer Soziologie* (1953–54), Vol. 6, 1–11; Joachim Wach, *Das Verstehen—Grund-
zuege einer Geschichte der hermeneutischen Theorie im 19. Jahrhundert,*
3 vols. (Tuebingen: J. C. B. Mohr, 1926–1933), Vol. I 227ff.

11. Leopold von Ranke, *Die Grossen Maechte* (Inselbuecherei No. 200, Leipzig,
1916). Ranke stressed the ascent from careful factual research involving
attention to particulars to "imaginative reconstruction" (*"Anschauung"*) of
an entire course of events; each is considered indispensable to the other. Cf.
Sigmund Neumann, "Die Stufen des preussischen Konservatismus," *Historische Studien* (Berlin, 1930), Vol. 190, 7ff.

12. J. G. von Droysen, *Grundriss der Historik* (3rd ed. Leipzig, 1883; first ed.,
1858); transl. by E. B. Andrews as *Outline of the Principles of History*
(Boston: Ginn & Co., 1893).

13. Henry T. Buckle, *History of Civilization in England* (2 vols., New York,
1871; first ed. 1857–61), Vol. I, 3.

14. J. G. von Droysen, "Erhebung der Geschichte zum Rang einer Wissenschaft," *Grundriss der Historik, op. cit.,* 47ff. Cf. "Natur und Geschichte," *op. cit.,* 69ff.

15. J. G. von Droysen, "Kunst und Methode," *op. cit.,* 81ff.

16. An excellent brief analysis in English of the controversy about "nature" and "history," from Buckle and Droysen to Windelband and Rickert, is contained in Fred Morrow Fling, "Historical Synthesis," *Am. Hist. Review* (Oct. 1903), Vol. 9, No. 1, 1ff.

17. Ernst Troeltsch, *op. cit.,* 509–530, 550–565, 572–596 *et passim.*

18. Max Weber, *Wirtschaft und Gesellschaft [W.u.G.]* (Tuebingen: J. C. B. Mohr, 1922), 1, 2; A. M. Henderson and Talcott Parsons (transl.), Max Weber; *The Theory of Social and Economic Organization,* 88, 90.

19. Joachim Wach, *op. cit.,* III, says that its "systematic character" differentiates *forschend verstehen* from ordinary procedures of understanding.

20. Max Weber, *op. cit.,* 2; Henderson and Parsons, *op. cit.,* 90.

21. In the introductory note to *W.u.G.,* Weber *expressis verbis* refers to Georg Simmel, *Probleme der Geschichtsphilosophie* (Munich and Leipzig: Duncker & Humblot, 1923), but not to Dilthey; however, cf. Renate Wanstrat, "Das Sozialwissenschaftliche Verstehen bei Dilthey und Max Weber," *Schmoller's Jahrbuch* (1950), Vol. 70, 19ff. That Max Weber knew Droysen's "Historik" must be assumed; but Droysen's influence on Dilthey, Rickert, and Simmel is confirmed by Joachim Wach, *op. cit.,* I, 261, III, 137. The influence extends both to the nature-culture dichotomy and to the concept of "understanding" which is derived from it.

22. The literature concerning the *"Methodenstreit"* is fully quoted in Gerhard Ritzel, *Schmoller versus Menger—Eine Analyse des Methodenstreits im Hinblick auf den Historismus in der Nationaloekonomie* (Doctoral Diss., University of Basel; printed Frankfurt, 1950); a lucid, brief account is found in Charles Gide and Charles Rist, *op. cit.,* 383ff.; a somewhat essayistic treatment in Joseph A. Schumpeter, *Economic Doctrine and Method* (New York: Oxford University Press, 1954), 152ff., and in Edgar Salin, *Geschichte der Volkswirtschaftslehre* (4th ed., Bern: A. Francke, 1951), 126ff.; cf. Felix Kaufmann, *Methodology of the Social Sciences* (New York: Oxford University Press, 1944), esp. chaps. X and XVI and Wilhelm Dilthey's concise statement in *Gesammelte Schriften* (Leipzig, Berlin, Stuttgart: B. G. Teubner, 1921–60), Vol. I, 49.

23. Otto Brunner, *op. cit.,* 42ff.; cf. Max Weber, *W.u.G.,* 54, 189, 518 *et passim* and Ferdinand Toennies, *Community and Society* (quoted below), 54.

24. Alfred Marshall, *Principles of Economics* (1st ed., London and New York: Macmilian, 1890), 67ff.

25. August Boeckh, *Die Staatshaushaltung der Athener* (Berlin, 1817; Engl. transl. *The Public Economy of Athens,* London, 1828); A. H. L. Heeren, *Ideen ueber die Politik, den Verkehr und den Handel der vornehmsten Voelker der alten Welt* (Vienna, 1817; Engl. transl. *Historical Researches into the Politics, Intercourse and Trade of the Principal Nations of Antiquity,* London, 1833–34); G. L. v. Maurer, *Geschichte der Markenverfassung in Deutschland* (Erlangen, 1853); *Geschichte der Hofverfassung in Deutschland* (Erlangen, 1862–63); *Geschichte der Dorfverfassung in Deutschland* (Erlangen, 1865–66); *Geschichte der Staedteverfassung in Deutschland* (Erlangen, 1869–71); N. D. Fustel de Coulanges, *La Cité Antique* (Paris, 1864; Engl. transl. 1874; now available in a Doubleday Anchor edition);

Henry S. Maine, *Ancient Law* (London, 1861); *Village Communities in East and West* (London, 1871).

26. Ferdinand Toennies, *Community and Society* (transl. and ed. by Chas. P. Loomis, East Lansing: Michigan University Press, 1957); the introduction and notes contained in that edition are particularly valuable. Cf. Talcott Parsons, *The Structure of Social Action* (New York and London: McGraw-Hill, 1937), 686ff.

27. Toennies renders account of the origin of his theoretical convictions in "Mein Verhaeltnis zur Soziologie," in Richard Thurnwald, *Soziologie von Heute* (Leipzig: C. & L. Hirschfeld, 1932); cf. Rudolf Heberle, "Das Soziologische System von Ferdinand Toennies," *Schmollers Jahrb.* (1951), Vol. 75, 385ff.; of additional interest is Ferdinand Toennies, "Ethik und Sozialismus," *Archiv fuer Sozialwissenschaft und Sozialpolitik* (1907), Vol. 25, 513ff. and (1909), Vol. 27, 895ff., because of the combination of idealism and socialism that is contained in it, coupled with a pronounced criticism of the historical school.

28. Max Weber, *Wirtschaftsgeschichte* (Munich and Leipzig: Duncker & Humblot, 1923), 15. The sentence is found in the opening chapter, dealing with "basic terms," which remained untranslated.

29. In "Mein Verhaeltnis zur Soziologie" Toennies rejects the imputation of value judgments in this regard, emphasizing that in actual societies *"Gemeinschaft"* and *"Gesellschaft"* types of social organization are always mixed. But in the same paper, historical currents are indicated also and the trend of thought is not entirely clear.

30. Max Weber, *General Economic History* (transl. Frank H. Knight, New York: The Free Press, 1950), 369.

31. Menger's case was ably presented to American readers in Eugen v. Boehm-Bawerk's paper "The Historical versus the Deductive Method," *Ann. of the Am. Ac. of Pol. and Social Science* (July 1890–June 1891), Vol. I, 244ff.

32. Wilhelm Roscher, *Grundriss zu Vorlesungen ueber die Staatswirtschaft nach geschichtlicher Methode* (Goettingen, 1843), Vorwort, IV.

33. Carl Menger, *Untersuchungen ueber die Methode der Sozialwissenschaften und der Politischen Oekonomie insbesondere* (Leipzig: Duncker & Humblot, 1883), 83ff. The English edition: Carl Menger, *Problems of Economics and Sociology*. Ed. with intro. by Louis Schneider (Urbana, Ill.: University of Illinois Press, 1963) has been published after this paper was completed.

34. Gustav Schmoller, *Zur Literaturgeschichte der Staats und Sozialwissenschaften* (Leipzig: Duncker & Humblot, 1888), 165; reviewing Roscher.

35. Gustav Schmoller, *op. cit.*, 139, 140; reviewing Lorenz v. Stein.

36. Max Weber, *Gesammelte Aufsaetze zur Wissenschaftslehre* [*G.A.W.*] (Tuebingen: J. C. B. Mohr, 1922), 1ff.

37. Gustav Schmoller, *op. cit.*, 147ff. *et passim.* Schmoller's position is not altogether clear. He accuses the classical economists of "rationalism" (144), "abstraction" (149, 249), "dogmatism" (279), but he also accuses them of a merely "mechanistic" procedure (144) and he contrasts this procedure to the "teleological-dialectic" procedures of Hegel and his followers; the latter, as the former, are said to lead to nothing but "abstract categories" (144). He dislikes both Hegel and Ricardo and praises Roscher for using the "totality of cultural phenomena" as background for a "realistic," that is, a "historically" based science of economics (144). Roscher's argument against the "philosophers" is found in *Das Leben, Werk und Zeitalter des Tukydides* (Goettingen, 1842), 19, 24. It may not be uninteresting to note

at this point that Charles H. Cooley shared the distrust of Schmoller and his school against the "economic theorist" who appeared to him "like a man who should observe only the second hand of a watch; he counts the seconds with care, but is hardly in a position to tell what time it is." However, Cooley also thought that the methods of the historical school are "too empirical to hold out much prospect of an adequate theory of process." *Sociological Theory and Social Research* (New York: Henry Holt, 1930), 251ff.

38. Wilhelm Roscher. "Der gegenwaertige Zustand der Wissenschaftlichen Nationaloekonomie und die notwendige Reform derselben," *Deutsche Vierteljahrschrift* (Stuttgart und Tuebingen, 1849), 174ff.
39. Carl Menger, *op. cit.*, 200ff.
40. Rupert B. Vance, "Security and Adjustment; The Return to the Larger Community," *Social Forces* (May 1944), Vol. 22, No. 4, 363–370.
41. Wilhelm Roscher, *op. cit.;* Carl Menger, *op. cit.*, 100ff., 209ff.; Max Weber, *G.A.W.*, 1ff., esp. 17.
42. Wilhelm Roscher, *Grundriss zu Vorlesungen ueber Staatswirtschaft nach geschichtlicher Methode* (1843), IV, 2, 5 *et passim.*
43. Wilhelm Dilthey, *Ges. Schriften, op. cit.*, V, 253. For an English account of Dilthey's thought, cf. H. A. Hodges, *Wilhelm Dilthey: An Introduction* (New York: Oxford University Press, 1944).
44. Schmoller also reviewed favorably Simmel's *Philosophie des Geldes,* expressing satisfaction that this "psychological approach to socio-economic phenomena" had originated in Schmoller's seminar.
45. Gustav Schmoller, *op. cit.*, 147; *Grundriss der Allgemeinen Volkswirtschaftslehre* (Munich and Leipzig: Duncker & Humblot, 1920), 117 *et passim.*
46. Gustav Schmoller, *op. cit.*, 279.
47. Carl Menger, *op. cit.*, 71ff.
48. Carl Menger, *Die Irrthuemer des Historismus in der deutschen Nationaloekonomie* (Vienna, 1884), 37.
49. Heinrich Herkner, "Gustav Schmoller als Sociologe," *Jahrbuecher fuer Nationaloekonomie und Statistik* (1922), Vol. 118, 1ff., esp. referring to one of Schmoller's last works, *Die Soziale Frage—Klassenbildung, Arbeiterfrage, Klassenkampf* (Munich und Leipzig: Duncker & Humblot, 1918).
50. Gustav Schmoller, *op. cit.*, 283, 287, VIII *et passim.* In terms of institutional economics, the point can indeed be made that collectivities, such as Maine's "village communities," are the units of social action and that such action takes place along traditional lines, not according to economic rationality; insofar as individuals act in this context, they do so as executors of communal decisions.
51. Max Weber, *G.A.W.*, 162, 163; Edward A. Shils and Henry A. Finch, *Max Weber on the Methodology of the Social Sciences* (New York: The Free Press, 1949), 64, 65.
52. Max Weber, *G.A.W.*, 3, 12, 42, 372 ("Die Grenznutzlehre und das psychophysische Grundgesetz"); Weber says that "Menger presented excellent ideas which, however, were not carried to their methodological conclusion."
53. Max Weber, *G.A.W.*, 187 (Shils, 87).
54. Carl Menger, *op. cit.*, 36, 37.
55. Carl Menger, *op. cit.*, 40.
56. Carl Menger, *op. cit.*, 39.
57. Max Weber, *G.A.W.*, 188 (Shils, 88).
58. Max Weber, *G.A.W.*, 146ff. (Shils, 49ff.).

59. Max Weber, *G.A.W.*, 187ff. (Shils, 87ff.); 131, 360ff.
60. This is a slightly different way of putting it than the one of Joseph A. Schumpeter, *History of Economic Analysis* (New York: Oxford University Press, 1954), 819.
61. Max Weber, *G.A.W.*, 190 (Shils, 89).
62. Max Weber, *G.A.W.*, 190, 191, 192, 194 (Shils, 90, 93).
63. Max Weber, *W.u.G.*, 4 (Henderson and Parsons, 96). This formulation is based on *G.A.W.*, 371; cf. 130, 496.
64. Max Weber, *W.u.G.*, 2, 3 (Henderson and Parsons, 92). Max Weber uses the word "*Stoerung*," which may mean "variant" as well as "disturbance." What is "disturbed" is conceptual purity. Parsons uses the term "disturbance" which, however, may give rise to misinterpretation. Cf. *G.A.W.*, 496.
65. Max Weber, *W.u.G.*, 142 (Henderson and Parsons, 362).
66. Max Weber, *W.u.G.*, 211, 360; not translated. *G.A.W.*, 176, 192 (Shils, 75, 91).
67. Max Weber, *G.A.W.*, 170, 172, 191, 202, 203, 204, 212, 214 (Shils, 69, 72, 90, 101, 102, 103), 287, 370 *et passim; W.u.G.*, 9 (Henderson and Parsons, 109).
68. Alexander v. Schelting, *Max Weber's Wissenschaftslehre* (Tuebingen: J. C. B. Mohr, 1934), 333ff.; cf. 73.
69. Max Weber, *W.u.G.*, 10 (Henderson and Parsons, 110); A. v. Schelting, *op. cit.*, 356ff.
70. "The historical significance of the capitalistic period and hence the significance of marginal utility theory (as well as of any other economic theory) for the understanding of that period rests with the fact that . . . under present conditions of life *the approximation of concrete reality to the theoretically established principles is steadily increasing* (italics mine), involving the fate of ever larger strata of the world's population, and it appears that this trend will continue." Max Weber, *G.A.W.* ("Grenznutzlehre"), 371.
71. Werner Bienfait, "Max Weber's Lehre vom geschichtlichen Erkennen," *Histor. Studien,* 194 (Berlin, 1930), differentiates between "epochal phenotypes," which are identical with "individual concepts," "epochal genotypes," such as "medieval Christianity" or "occidental capitalism," and "ideal phenotypes," like "marginal utility theory" or "ethical prophecy." I would classify the latter among "epochal genotypes," as would Schelting, but I am inclined to agree with Bienfait that Max Weber emphasizes the "ideal phenotype" in his methodological treatises, but tends toward "epochal genotypes" in his actual research. This may be a source of the "confusion" in interpretation about which Bendix, *op. cit.*, 281, complains.
72. Arthur Spiethoff, "Die Allgemeine Volkswirtschaftslehre als geschichtliche Theorie," *Schmoller's Jahrbuch* (1932), Vol. 56, 891ff.; and "Anschauliche und reine Theorie und ihr Verhaeltnis zueinander," *Synopsis, Festgabe fuer Alfred Weber,* Edgar Salin, ed. (Heidelberg: Lambert Schneider, 1948). Cf. Schelting, *op. cit.*, 73. For an English version, see Arthur Spiethoff, "The Historical Character of Economic Theories," *Journal of Economic History* (Winter 1952), Vol. XII, No. 2, 891ff., and Frederick C. Lane and Jelle C. Riemersma, *Enterprise and Secular Change—Readings in Economic History* (Homewood, Ill.: Richard D. Irwin, 1953), chaps. 25 and 26 ("Introduction to Arthur Spiethoff" and "Pure Theory and Economic Gestalt Theory. Ideal Types and Real Types"). A. S., one time assistant to Schmoller and the latter's successor as editor of Schmoller's *Jahrbuch,* has made a reputation for himself with "historical" theories in the field of

business cycle research and real estate economics. Cf. Schumpeter, *History of Economic Analysis, op. cit.,* 816.

73. Howard Becker, *Through Values to Social Interpretation* (Durham, N.C.: Duke University Press, 1950), 106–114.

74. Paul Honigsheim, "In Memoriam Howard Becker," *Koelner Zeitschrift fuer Soziologie and Sozialpsychologie,* 12, Jahrg. 1960, Heft 3, 3–8.

75. Gideon Sjoberg, *The Preindustrial City—Past and Present* (New York: The Free Press, 1960), 21, 63, 108 *et passim.*

76. Carlo Antoni, *From History to Sociology,* transl. Hayden V. White (Detroit: Wayne State University Press, 1959), 182, 183.

77. Cf. my review of Carlo Antoni's book in *Sociological Review* (Feb. 1960), Vol. 25, No. 1, 120. My contention is borne out by Max Weber's letter to Georg von Below of June 21, 1914, wherein he expresses the opinion that "what is specifically characteristic of the medieval city . . . can really be developed only through the statement of what is lacking in the other (ancient, Chinese, Islamic) cities." He considers this procedure to be "the very modest comparative work" which sociology can do for history. The letter is published in Georg v. Below, *Der Deutsche Staat des Mittelalters* (Leipzig: Ouella & Meyer, 1925), XXIV, and is in part reproduced in English in Reinhard Bendix, "Max Weber's Interpretation of Conduct and History." *Am. Journal of Sociology* (May 1946), Vol. 51, No. 6, 518ff.

78. Walter Firey, *Land Use in Central Boston* (Cambridge: Harvard University Press, 1947), 229ff.

79. Alfred Weber, *Theory of the Location of Industries,* transl. by Carl Joachim Friedrich (Chicago: University of Chicago Press, 1929); cf. Walter Firey, *op. cit.,* 22ff.

80. Talcott Parsons, *Essays in Sociological Theory, Pure and Applied* (New York: The Free Press, 1949), 81–82. However, the "functional" approach, for which Parsons pleads, is itself organicist in character and hence subject to a similar objection.

81. Talcott Parsons, *The Structure of Social Action,* 601ff., esp. 602.

82. Max Weber, *G.A.W.,* 205 (Shils, 106); cf. 168, 171, 185, 203 (Shils, 69, 72, 86, 101).

83. When Weber argues against representatives of the historical school, he speaks with great respect, merely trying to rectify the logical inconsistencies in the work of the revered masters. This is done with regard to Roscher, Knies, Schmoller, Eduard Meyer, and also Ranke (*G.A.W.,* 214). I am in agreement, at this point, with Albert Salomon, "Max Weber's Political Ideas," *Social Research,* Vol. II, 368. But when Weber speaks about the "naturalistic prejudice," and the "naive faith" of its addicts, his attitude is openly antagonistic, ranging from mild condescendence to sarcastic contempt. An example for the latter is the paper on "Energetische Kulturtheorien" (*G.A.W.,* 376ff.), which is directed against the "allegedly exact sociological method" of O. Ostwald and E. Solvay and what Weber considers its "Comtist and Queteletist" inspiration. The difference between Droysen's argument against Buckle and Weber's argument against the *epigoni* of the monistic "faith" is that Droysen is apologetic while Weber is aggressive.

84. Max Weber, *G.A.W.,* 41.

85. *Ibid.,* 209 (Shils, 107).

86. *Ibid.,* 9, 10, 210 (Shils, 99, 102, 107).

87. Max Weber, *W.u.G.,* 6, 7, 9 (Henderson and Parsons, 102, 103, 107).

Serge Hughes   THE EVALUATION OF SOCIOLOGY IN
                     CROCE'S THEORY OF HISTORY

THE SYMPATHY BENEDETTO CROCE SHOWED for Max Weber's insistence on
an explicit methodological analysis of the basic concepts of sociology was quite
in keeping with the spirit of his own philosophy. Sociology, like the theory of
history, necessarily involved an examination of principles; and Croce was
sure that an investigation of social phenomena which went about its work
without sufficiently taking into account the point of view and accomplishments of other disciplines had no business considering itself a valid field
of knowledge. At best, a work-a-day pragmatism unconcerned with relating
its work to the findings of other investigations could come to some *grosso
modo* approximations, not rigorous truths; and this narrow outlook, in turn,
could not but deal perfunctorily with any outside objections. In this narrow
version of sociology, objections could only be put aside as indefinitely post-
ponable, or not very relevant, or, with more open condescension, as subject
matter for disciplines for which the sociologist had no respect.

Croce was speaking from experience. Particularly at the turn of the century, it was not hard to come across unoriginal Italian sociologists who
went to great pains not to conceal their contempt for "non-scientific"
disciplines; and there was undeniable merit in Croce's retort that this crude
form of sociology was little more than an extreme case of myopia.

It might have been expected though that, with the decline of "scientific"
sociology in the Comtean and post-Darwinian manner, Croce's hostility would
correspondingly diminish. It did not. His sympathy was exclusively for what
Weber sought to do, not for what he did, and he rejected Weber's sociology
quite as firmly as he had preceding forms.

There are many reasons for this attitude. The problem of the extent to
which a new science has to theoretically justify its presuppositions and procedures is surely complicated; and apparently neither Croce, nor Weber, nor
their contemporaries, have said the final word on the subject. There is still
enough common sense and polemical passion left to account for a number of
volumes on the problem. There is a point, however, in trying to understand

Croce's thought on the matter, to see why his reservations on sociology were so firm or so obdurate as to make him reject even a sociology methodologically as sophisticated as that of Max Weber; an intransigent attitude, it might be mentioned, that made even some of his most unsuspicious followers wonder whether the historian-philosopher had not finally succumbed to the *esprit de système*.

It would not do, in this connection, to rely entirely on Croce's dictum that there need be no conflict between history and sociology, that all that is required is that the historian judiciously use the sociologist's suggestions. It is not easy to specify just what "judiciously" means in this ambiguous dictum and, at any rate, it is not something that can be understood by cautiously avoiding all philosophy.

To avoid the treacherous ground of philosophy, however, is precisely what most sociologists are tempted to do when they take a stand behind the sensible but not entirely adequate maxim that, if the choice was between epistemological clarification and "concrete" sociology, sociology would have to be the first choice. And so the sociologist, with an almost innate mistrust of speculative thought, will all too easily go one step further and "sociologically" explain away Croce's attitude toward sociology and the attendant difficulties of that discipline in Italy.[1] Sociology, in this view, has had no success in Italy because of a power group of philosophical Idealists who have effectively barred the way for a liberating Positivism and, with the aid of a passive religious tradition, firmly suppressed any possible academic recognition of sociology as a science. There may be some crumbs of truth in this conspiracy-explanation, but it is disconcerting to learn that the existence of an opposition must be considered as a danger to new truths, and that academic recognition is a *condition sine qua non* for the proper development of any new discipline.[2]

Turning from this type of "explanation" to a more proper one is not to make the task easier; and if there are other means, they should be used. For the present, however, there does not seem any better approach than to meet Croce on his own grounds—on philosophic grounds. There does not seem to be any more reliable way to understand Croce's notion of what the relationship between history and sociology should be. It may help, in this connection, to remember that sociology, after all, had epistemological preoccupations from the very beginnings, and gives every sign of continuing to have them. If early sociological theory was weak on its epistemological side, this insufficiency should be corrected, not ignored. The spirit of Gramsci's criticism, though quite uneven, can serve as a model. It met Croce, or it sought to meet Croce, on his own grounds, which included a discussion of Croce's reform of the Hegelian dialectic—and Gramsci was working from the dubious vantage point of economic determinism.[3]

There are few scholars in the Anglo-American tradition, however, who have much familiarity with German Idealism, and with Hegel in particular. The American sociologist, consequently, like his colleague, the historian, will probably be forced to rely initially on the "expertise" of a professional epistemological analysis. For while American historians have appreciated the general spirit of Croce's historiography, particularly at the height of the anti-objective history movement, they have prudently left the examination of his theoretical postulates to philosophers.[4]

Since Croce's philosophy of Spirit is no more familiar to sociologists than it is to historians, a brief sketch of the system may be useful. That system is commonly and justly considered an elaboration of Hegel's thought, and the question of the extent to which it is or is not a critical elaboration is very much a matter for discussion. The traditional problem of Being and Knowing was certainly among the least important aspects of Hegel's thought for Croce. Almost fideistically idealist by temperament, Croce had no trouble in considering Being as Knowing, philosophy as idealism alone, and Reality as nothing other than Spirit. With this basis as a point of departure, Croce conceived the task of philosophy as the study of the structure of Spirit.

Philosophy, to this point, was primarily epistemological, and Croce accordingly elaborated his notion of the Theoretical and Practical Spirit, the former concerned with knowing, the latter with doing. There were no causes in the Spirit, but degrees, developments; and the degrees of the Theoretical were the intuitive and the conceptual, and that of the Practical, the volitional and the ethical.

As epistemological analysis, the system has found very few defenders among contemporaries. Absolute idealism is no longer as popular today as it was in the late nineteenth century and not only philosophers rejecting absolute idealism, immanence, and the notion of Spirit have made telling criticisms; from within the Hegelian camp, and from Gentile, who first introduced Hegel to Croce, criticism became increasingly sharp.

A good deal of that criticism centered on the notion of the Theoretical Spirit, on the impossibility of conceiving a pure intuition and its concomitant dialectic opposite, the pure concept; on the arbitrariness of considering intuition as absolute uniqueness, the concept as pure universal; and on the excessively schematic division of all knowledge as either intuition or concept.

These speculative objections to Croce's Theoretical Spirit are not quite as irrelevant to the sociologist and historian as they may seem to be. These very objections can, in fact, provide a rather useful springboard for a sustained critique of Croce's attitude towards sociology.

If all knowledge is either intuition or concept, the problem is to decide on the validity of such concepts as class, laws, causes, and recurrent patterns. Croce had no doubt as to the answer. These concepts, not being concepts of the universal, could not be valid concepts; they were pseudo-concepts, useful for volitional activity, practical activity, but devoid of any real cognitive value. To invalidate pseudo-concepts, then, the concepts which are the very stuff of sociology and history, is to invalidate a good part of sociological investigation.

There was, to Croce's credit, a very sound aspect of his notion of pseudo-concepts. It was directed against the "scientism" of the late nineteenth century, the pretense that history and sociology had to become imitators of the natural sciences, usually physiology or some vague idea of biology, in order to be true science;[5] and it was also an attempt to protect his doctrine of the unique nonrecurring nature of history. For in deciding whether history should be considered as a science or art, as a knowledge of the universal or the individual, Croce had taken his stand on history as intuition, that is, as knowledge of the individual, the unique—and had thereby put up a rather high wall between history and sociology. That wall is no longer considered necessary or advisable today, when a general edifying modesty prevails among the natural sciences particularly; and there is a common reluctance on the part of any discipline to act as a model for others. Historians today can be grateful to Croce for that defense, but that gratitude does not go so far as the acceptance of the dubious theory of the pseudo-concepts, nor, for that matter, of Croce's complicated theory of the uniqueness of history, which is something more than a *caveat* against excessive theoretical generalizing.

The situation has so changed today, in fact, that the historian in general is quite willing to defend, together with the sociologist, notions of "laws" and "causes" as concepts essential to both disciplines.

For Croce, the concept of cause is properly restricted to the natural sciences and serves exclusively classificatory purposes, since those sciences can tell us nothing about reality, which can only be Spirit. There can be no other proper use of the concept, except, of course, in an admittedly imprecise way.

As for laws, they too can be no more than a practical approximation, useful for action, not insight. Historical laws are consequently quite indefensible, for they demonstrate either truisms or arbitrary notions and ignore the essential uniqueness, the constant creativity of history.

As long as Croce's criticism of the concept of cause remains a criticism of Taine's use of the notion—and it was the French historian who represented in Croce's eyes the *reductio ad absurdum* of Positivist historiography—the point is well taken: to argue that the more inclusive the category of explanation the more scientific the cause is to use "cause" in a way that would be anathema to most historians. But to argue that the notion of cause should be put aside because it is an endless postponing of explanations which never come to the ultimate one, is not at all convincing—and a particularly incongruous Aristotelian argument for an absolute idealist. The historian and sociologist do well, then, to retain a cautious notion of cause, a limited not overabstract cause, one conditioning factor in an interconditioning complex: a radical empirical denial of any kind of monocausality.

A similar defense can be made for a guarded and sophisticated concept of law as a common recurrent pattern of behavior within the definite limitations of a given historical situation. Needless to say, sociologists can applaud with good conscience the strictures of Croce for those sociologists who, at the turn of the century, were obsessed with the quest for absolute laws.[6]

The most unexpected and the most persuasive demonstration of the merits of the defense of a judicious notion of cause and law, however, comes from Croce himself, whose theoretical strictness did not, happily, always find a counterpart in concrete historical work. Not satisfied with the doctrine of history as intuition, Croce elaborated the idea of history as that in which intuition, problem and concept—principally a political-ethical problem— were interrelated. In the *History of the Kingdom of Naples,* perhaps Croce's finest historical work, the much-maligned concepts of laws and causes, out of sheer necessity, occupied a central place.[7] In this work, Croce conceived the problem as the determination of the nature of the political-ethical strength of the Kingdom of Naples in the course of its development, the extent to which it was an effective political-ethical force, the reasons for its failure to assume the initiative in the process of national unification, and the implications of that failure for his times. The problem required an analysis of the interaction of economic forces, social classes, ideologies and political forces— in a word, a sociological and historical approach in which the use of concepts of law, cause, class, and type were indispensable.

In a more detailed way, the *History* sought to give a full account of the origin, development, successes and failures of a moral-political aristocracy, an elite which was such because of the supremacy of its political-ethical ideal.[8]

The analysis of Croce is deservedly famous, though perhaps its rigorously anti-Marxist tone has not always been properly appreciated. The idea of the *ceto medio,* one of the three classes of that society together with the *basso popolo* and the aristocracy, is not that of an economic class. The *ceto medio,* in fact, was not considered as a compact, homogeneous unit but was composed of types—the *buon signori,* the anarchical barons, and the law-abiding ones. There were class conflicts within the state, and the monarchy made use of them to maintain power, but the monarchy was, in turn, affected by the political action and theory of the *ceto medio* so as to depend on that group, and not the aristocracy, for its vitality.

Among the definite causes for the collapse of the Kingdom, Croce lists an insufficiently strong alliance between the *ceto medio* and the monarchy, and the *ceto medio's* abrupt abandonment of a judicious and moderate liberalism for a radical and rationalistic French Jacobinism which inevitably brought about a hardening of the monarchy's stand. The sudden reversal of the political philosophy of the *ceto medio* was, no doubt, for Croce the most decisive factor in the explanation of the failure of the Neapolitan monarchy to play a directive role in the Italian *Risorgimento*.

The *History,* then, which does not sharply separate historical and sociological procedures, is a superb illustration of the use of concepts which Croce minimized in theory. There is no question that it could even serve as illustration of a historical law, to wit, that a political science and a political class though influenced by economic factors could rise above them; that political science could be more than ideology; and that the political action of an elite might be more than an extension of class interest. This defense of the autonomy of thought against a Marxist devaluation that would reduce political theory to a more or less complicated reflection of an economic "praxis" is a constant element in Croce's theory of history.

Croce had come to and squared his accounts with Marx at a very early stage in his development, as shown in his essays on Marxism in *Il materialismo storico e l'economia Marxistica.* Dazzled at first by the sweep of Marx's vision, fascinated by Marx's use of the Hegelian dialectic, impatient to understand economics, he had for a while, for a very short while, shown enthusiasm for what he termed Marxist sociology. And then, and not too gradually, he virtually rejected Marxism *in toto:* the economic interpretation of history, the analysis of economics, the "scientific" nature of Marx's political program, and the Marxian notion of capitalism. Through Marx, Croce deepened his study of Hegel; and it was Hegel properly understood, Croce eventually concluded, who showed the crassness of Marx's interpretation of the dialectic.

Above all, Croce fought in Marx the reduction of science to ideology, that is, to ideologies as moments or instruments of class conflicts. On this point Croce became increasingly intransigent, willing to see in Marx only an advocate of an abstract normative sociology or a political Utopia. The other aspects of Marx, and particularly Marx's concern for political-sociological problems of a modern industrial society, his concern for the problem of alienation, his interest in the problem of rationalization, were a closed book for Croce. The Marxist experience became one element in the epistemology of the Practical Spirit; and after Croce had elaborated his philosophy of politics, the theory of the *classe dirigente* ("ruling class") that was remarkably similar to Gaetano Mosca's thought on the subject, he minimized out of all proportion the relevance of class ideology and oversimplified the nature of political parties.[9]

It is this lack of interest, and his concern to defend autonomous knowledge that help explain his hostility to Pareto's sociology. Croce was not only scandalized at what he considered the philosophical naiveté of Pareto, who did not subscribe to absolute idealism, or at Pareto's obstinate refusal to make of the notion of utility in economics a qualitative rather than a quantitative concept. He was very much convinced that the sociology of Pareto was founded on a simplistic, mechanistic psychology which was overconcerned with irrational motivation and the forms of rationalization.[10]

Similarly, any sympathy he felt for Durkheim's studies were checked by the French sociologist's attempt to connect the validity of a discipline with its social usefulness or his claim to have discovered the specific nature of the social fact.[11] There is no doubt that Croce considered these sociologists as tainted with Marxist weaknesses, for all their professed anti-Marxism.

There is evidence, though, that even Croce himself, for all his exorcizing of Marxism, did not fully free himself from the influence of the author of *Das Kapital*.

In the Practical Spirit, the notion of the "useful" or the "volitional" as a pure, autonomous form is one of the more vulnerable parts of the system; and it is a weakness that is not much attenuated by studying its dialectic opposite, the "ethical" will, which is moral because it aims at the universal, not the individual. The superiority of the ethical will—its universalist character—is so generic as to be useless for the political sociologist and historian.

This "volitional" will, for Croce, becomes the basis of politics or the State, embodying the irredeemable instruments of pure power. This concept of politics and State was the only one, according to Croce, that could do justice to the requirements of the autonomy of politics, and the demands of justice. There should be no confusion of the ethical and useful will; they were separate and distinct. An abstract moralism might raise objections to placing such an absolute barrier between the two wills, but that objection, Croce felt, was adequately disposed of by Marx, whose one great contribution was his demonstration of "the right of history to drag and crush individuals."[12] In complete sympathy with Marx's mistrust of the supposedly "ethical" State, Croce at this point, with dubious coherence, after having rejected virtually all Marxian thought, accepted Marxian *Realpolitik;* and he considered all discussions of whether social forms embody a kind of ethics superior to the ethics of the individual or whether individual ethics should inform the social group as pointless.

In this connection, Croce was not altogether incoherent in guardedly accepting Sorel's syndicalism as a temporary substitute for his short-lived enthusiasm for the Marxist proletariat. Had history proved the syndicates to be the true *classe dirigente,* Croce would have been very right indeed.

In its main outlines Croce's system, his reflections on history and sociology, his political philosophy which could with equal composure advocate Sorel's syndicalism[13] or a moderate *Risorgimento* Liberalism, remained unchanged until, and some time after, the decisive advent of Fascism. The experience of Fascism had more impact on Croce than any experience in the realm of autonomous ideas.

After an initial passive approval of Fascism, Croce became thoroughly disillusioned and set about revising parts of his thought, making it a more solid base for an unrelenting anti-Fascism. The doctrine of politics as pure power was no longer presented as crudely as it had been as recently as World War I; the "abuses" of nationalism became a recurrent theme; the moment of consent, and not force, was emphasized; and in season and out of season Croce became the advocate of the Parliamentarian Liberalism that had come to an end in 1925, and had come under increasing fire from the Fascists, the Communists, and the *Popolari*.

Yet, this gradual change at no point involved recantation. Croce never disavowed the philosophy of the Spirit, much less any part of the doctrines of pseudo-concepts and the "useful" will. He did not once see any difficulties in the problems raised in distinguishing the "true" useful from the "false" useful,[14] and he believed he could retain the doctrine of politics as pure power and still be in a position to criticize excesses. In this spirit, he had no misgivings in criticizing the work of the German contemporary historian he most esteemed, Meinecke, as weakened by an indefensible notion of a conflict between political and personal morality.[15]

Croce's famous historical work of this period, the *Storia d'Italia 1871–1915,* published in 1928, may be considered as primarily a polemic against Dorso, Gobetti, Salvemini, and Sturzo, all of whom found much more to criticize in the Italy of that period than Croce, and also as a vindication of the excellence of Croce's thought; for he did believe that most of the cultural anarchy of recent times was traceable to a philosophic decadence, the dismissal and ignorance of the German Idealist tradition, and to a political obscurantism which was the consequence of not knowing how properly to understand socialist doctrine. In brief, he considered Fascism as a symptom of a general decadence in which those who had been too concerned with the irrational, with rationalizations, and with messianic politics, had their share of blame; and Sorel was one name among such.

But Croce did not intend to stop with such defensive measures. To understand the decline, to defend those values of the nineteenth century which his contemporaries repudiated, was the task to which he next dedicated himself in *Storia d'Europa nel secolo decimonono (History of Europe in the Nineteenth Century).* This was the least concrete of all of Croce's histories, the most abstract as a history of cultural ideals, the least interested in any sustained sociological investigation. It was, in effect, the prologomenon to the next development in Croce's historiography, history as the history of Liberty.

It was a foreseeable development. Because Croce felt that it was his duty to provide for and act as custodian of values temporarily eclipsed, which would one day surely be taken up again by a *classe dirigente,* he fashioned a theory which he had long denounced as bad philosophy and poor history: a philosophy of history.[16]

The philosophy of history was not altogether out of character with the tenor of Croce's thought. Croce did not spare sarcasm at any evolutionary sociology and especially at the whole corpus of Herbert Spencer's work and his biologically tinged idea of evolution; but he himself had a very clear idea of progress and evolution in philosophy which had to be observed for the sake of coherence. Thus, philosophy—to be philosophy—had to be immanent and idealistic, or at least striving in that direction; and any metaphysics that was dualistic and transcendent was *ipso facto* inferior philosophy. Again, there was in Croce a distinct evolutionary point of view with respect to the relationship between religion and philosophy; the first was an inferior, mythical form of knowledge, the latter was the rational and clear transformation of that antecedent and inadequate form. But the theory of Liberty was a grandiose application and extension of any such aspects in Croce's thought. It was a dithyrambic philosophy of history, in which Spirit was no longer conceived as the realm of the uniquely unpredictable or ethical-political problem of contemporary significance, but as an inexhaustible source of values for an elite—values constantly created anew, values whose final victory was assured. Liberty was religion in the sense of a creed and an ethics in conformity with it, and like most religions it was positive: it denied decadence.

Liberty so conceived was not one with any contingent historical form. It exhausted itself in no historical form. Neither a moment nor an institution, it was the direction of Spirit and Spirit itself; that is, constant creativeness. What appeared to be decadence was no more than a temporary ebbing, a momentary loss of vitality which prepared the way for a resurgence of strength; decadence in brief was a spur, a prodding to a greater progress.

For all its buoyant optimism, and perhaps in part because of it, Croce's history-liberty equation has found few champions today. Critics were not wanting to point out that the theory succeeds, like other philosophies of history, in discovering in history what had been put there previously. A liberty-essence—something more than the sum of all its historical manifestations—like the Marxist doctrine of the proletariat or Comte's three-stage evolution is assumption, is hope, not demonstrable doctrine. In a concrete historical setting, that kind of liberty is not luminously self-evident, as Croce's polemic with Einaudi demonstrated all too convincingly: for Einaudi argued quite coherently that Croce's Liberalism necessarily implied economic liberalism, and Croce's contention that he was free to accept or reject economic liberalism was a very apt example of how multiform and ambiguous his cult of liberty could turn out to be in actual application.

Vulnerable to criticism, like all philosophies of history, the theory of liberty does not even successfully account for the problem of decadence. More than a step backward, decadence from this point of view is only illusion, since Spirit is always positive. To explain the possibility and physiognomy of illusion Croce had to resort to a rather involved theory of error; moreover, the application of this positive historicism concerned itself predominantly with histories of literature and general culture, never with a detailed political-sociological history. Croce never felt that he could apply this positivist interpretation to the history of Fascist Italy.

Novel in scope and dimension, the theory of liberty was still constructed of traditional materials. The individual, as in previous theories, remained no more than a moment of the Spirit, one with the historical situation, no "freer" than in some absolutist deterministic sociologies which Croce continued to condemn to the last as blasphemy against the constant creativity of the Spirit.

Under Fascism, and after World War II, Croce dedicated himself completely to the elaboration and, to the extent possible, the implementation of the religion of Liberty. He did not keep in too close contact with new developments in philosophy and historiography. Had he spent more time on them, his discouragement no doubt would have grown heavier. Yet, in his last years there was discernible in his attitude a growing indifference to the speculative problems of absolute idealism and a preference for concrete historical research.

It is quite possible that if he had meditated on the sociology of Max Weber in these years he would have found much to his liking. Weber, like Croce, had respect for the historically unique. He, too, appreciated the need for epistemological clarity and thoroughness. Like Croce, Weber had no reluctance in working in a number of fields; and both felt very much the need of coming to grips with the thought of Marx. Weber's sociological concepts—concepts useful for the orientation of historical investigations and for the understanding of the behavior of individuals with respect to the meaning they give to their actions—were hardly crude positivistic sociological notions; and Weber himself had taken notice of Croce's work up to a point. There are even points of resemblance between Croce's volitional action and Weber's *zweckrationales Handeln,* and some analogies between Croce's Liberty and Weber's identification of reason and liberty.

But even if he had been younger, there is the strong probability that Croce's systematic temper would have precluded any radical about-face in any fundamental convictions. Preoccupied with other matters, and loyal to Hegel, it was enough for him to realize that Weber's sociology rested principally on Rickert, Windelband, and Dilthey to lose interest.[17] Those philosophers were for Croce tired epigones, and nothing enduring could come from building on their foundations.

Though he never made an explicit criticism of Weber's sociology, he most certainly would have considered indefensible the idea of a value-free descriptive sociology ultimately dependent on values not susceptible of philosophical verification; and the epistemological implications of Weber's notion of archetypes would hardly have won his approval.

Still, there are grounds for believing that if there is any dialogue possible between Croce and a good part of modern sociology, it would have to be done through the mediation of Weber; and though the work of distinguishing the spirit of Croce's thought from the letter is difficult and delicate, such a detailed analysis and confrontation might bring to light as yet unsuspected relations and possibilities.

There is no such possibility of *rapprochement* between Croce and the followers of an ahistorical psychological sociology. It is precisely this very sort of psychological-sociological approach, in fact, that justifies Croce's warnings to the social disciplines not to seek to do without epistemological analysis and not to neglect the concrete historical dimension of a meaningful social theory.

There is scant chance that Croce's theory of history and his ideas on sociology will ever be more frequently studied than they are now. This is understandable, especially in the American context, but still deplorable,[18] for whatever conclusions one may come to with respect to Croce's fundamental Idealism, he does merit close study. In a time when discoveries and insights in one field are left too often unrelated to the knowledge of other disciplines, he stressed, like Weber, the constant need of systematic thought; and in an age of intense specialization he was a refreshing example, again like Weber, of a thinker willing to pursue a problem even when that problem trespassed into a specialist's domain. And at his very best, and most persuasive, he demonstrated the shortcoming of any history or sociology which presumed to abstract too much from the concrete and nonrecurring individual aspect of all history. That demonstration alone should be a permanent acquisition for historian and sociologist alike.

Notes

1. Cf. Victor A. Rapport, S. C. Cappannari, and L. W. Moss, "Sociology in Italy," *American Sociological Review*, Vol. 22, No. 4 (August 1957). Also, for edifying contrast, E. Pennati, "L'ultima polemica fra idealismo e sociologia," *Il Politico* (December 1951); cf. further Franco Ferrarotti, "Sociology in Italy: Problems and Perspectives," in Howard Becker and Alvin Boskoff, eds., *Modern Sociological Theory in Continuity and Change* (New York: Dryden, 1957), pp. 695–710.
2. Giambattista Vico, the author of the *Principii d'una Scienza Nova* (1725), which can properly be considered one of the great Italian treatises on sociology, evidently was not familiar with these prerequisites.
3. Cf. A. Gramsci, *Il materialismo storico e la filosofia di Benedetto Croce* (Torino: Einaudi, 1948).
4. Cf. as an example of a critical evaluation of the metaphysical basis of Croce's historiography, M. Mandelbaum, *The Problem of Historical Knowledge* (New York: Liveright, 1938).
5. Cf., for example, Croce's demolition of Ferrero's *Grandezza e decadenza di Roma* (Milano, 1902), in *Storia della storiografia italiana*, Vol. II (Bari: Laterza, 1947), pp. 149–152. Notice by contrast his cautious criticism of the more skillful sociological histories of Salvemini and Volpe. (*Ibid.*)

6. Cf. F. Ferrarotti, "Introduzione alla sociologia come scienza," in *Quaderni di Sociologia*, 1951.

7. Croce, *Storia del Regno di Napoli*, 3rd ed. (Bari: Laterza, 1925).

8. Cf. Croce's Preface to Mosca's *Elementi di scienza politica* (Bari: Laterza, 1953).

9. Cf. Gaetano Mosca, *The Ruling Class*. Transl. by Hannah D. Kahn (New York: McGraw-Hill, 1939) and James H. Meisel, *The Myth of the Ruling Class: Gaetano Mosca and the "Elite"* (Ann Arbor: University of Michigan Press, 1958).

10. For Croce's argument with Pareto on the philosophic basis of value, cf. "Sul principio economico—due lettere al Prof. V. Pareto," in *Materialismo storico ed economia marxistica* (Bari: Laterza, 1946), pp. 225–247. Croce had no use at all for Pareto's attempt to give a sociological amplification of his economics. Cf. his review of Pareto's *Trattato di sociologia generale* in *Conversazioni Critiche*, Vol. IV (Bari: Laterza, 1932), pp. 167–170.

11. Cf. Croce's notice of Durkheim's studies on suicide in *Conversazioni Critiche*, Vol. I (Bari: Laterza, 1942), p. 273.

12. "Contributo allo critica di me stesso," in *Etica e Politica* (Bari: Laterza, 1945), 383.

13. Cf. S. Hughes, *The Role of French Culture in the Development of Croce's Thought* (Library of Congress Microfilm 55–1132), 96–119, 146ff.

14. Cf., e.g., De Ruggiero-Croce polemic on Croce's judgment on the Inquisition, in *Nuova Europa*, No. 6.

15. Cf. Croce's review of Meinecke's *Die Idee der Staatsraison in der neueren Geschichte*, in *Conversazioni Critiche*, Vol. IV (Bari: Laterza, 1932), pp. 95–101.

16. For a rather full elaboration of this stage of Croce's historiography, cf. *La storia come pensiero ed azione* (Bari: Laterza, 1943), particularly "La storia come storia della liberta," pp. 46–50.

17. The treatment of Weber in C. Antoni's *Dallo storicismo alla sociologia* (Sansoni, 1950), with Preface by Croce provoked a new polemical exchange between sociologists and Idealist philosophers. Cf. N. Abbagnano, "Riposta a Carlo Antoni," *Quaderni di Sociologia*, No. 3, 1952, and E. Pennati, *op. cit.* Also cf. W. J. Cahnman's review of Antoni's work in *American Sociological Review*, Vol. 25, No. 1, February 1960, and Mazlosh's long review of same in *History and Theory*, Vol. I, No. 11, 1961. An English translation of Antoni's book, with Croce's Foreword, was published by Hayden V. White under the title *From History to Sociology* (Detroit: Wayne State University Press, 1959).

18. However, for those who want to try, here is a list of those works of Croce which are available in English:

Philosophy of the Practical: Economics and Ethics (London: Macmillan, 1913).

Logic as a Science of Pure Concept (London: Macmillan, 1917).

Aesthetic (London: Macmillan, 1922).

History, Its Theory and Practice (New York: Russell & Russell, 1960). These are the four volumes of which the *Filosofia dello Spirito* is composed.

Historical Materialism and the Economics of Karl Marx (New York: Macmillan, 1914).

What Is Living and What Is Dead in the Philosophy of Hegel (London: Macmillan, 1915).

Conduct of Life (New York: Harcourt, Brace, 1924); cf. *Frammenti di Etica* (Bari: Laterza, 1922).

An Autobiography (Oxford: Clarendon Press, 1927); cf. "Contributo alla Critica di me stesso" in *Etica e Politica* (Bari: Laterza, 1930).

History of Italy 1871–1913 (Oxford: Clarendon Press, 1929).

History of Europe in the Nineteenth Century (New York: Harcourt, Brace, 1933).

History as the Story of Liberty (London: Allen & Unwin, 1941; New York: Russell & Russell, 1955).

It might further be advisable to consult the passages referring to Croce in R. G. Collingwood, *The Idea of History* (Oxford: Clarendon Press, 1946; paperback ed., New York: Oxford University Press, 1959). Among writers in the English language, Collingwood is most knowledgeable of, and most sympathetic to, the approach of Croce.

Alvin Boskoff   RECENT THEORIES OF SOCIAL CHANGE

BY THE VERY NATURE of their respective disciplines, both sociologists and historians have been concerned with one or more aspects of social change. Indeed, much of the theorizing and interpretations about nations and societies have inevitably involved the domain of social change, either as borrower or contributor. But, as the preceding chapters demonstrate, the history of thinking about social change is dominated by dogma, parochialism, wholesale psychologizing, and rationalization of political or social objectives. The result has been a general revulsion against the study of social change *per se;* students of history and sociology instead tend to pursue their diligent search for patterns, coherent descriptions, correlations, and configurations, adverting to questions of dynamics and dramatic process on an *ad hoc* basis. The latter approach has satisfied few practitioners and likewise leaves the observer of both disciplines with a sense of conventionally ordered chaos and vicarious frustration.

But one positive consequence of the earlier period of theorizing is the identification of a range of relevant variables associated with processes of social change. With varying degrees of clarity and reliable information, earlier approaches to social change were concerned with political organization, warfare, migrations, technology, class systems, ideologies, the nature of specific elites, and religion. The fundamental problem, then, was to provide a framework within which these important aspects of social change could be accommodated, not merely for intellectual symmetry, but for practical application by students of specific societies and societal types.

In view of this background, "recent theories" of social change can be approximately dated from 1920 to the present. Furthermore, it may be useful to classify these theories into three analytically separable varieties, though it should be clear at the outset that these approaches do not follow a consistently chronological order.

Phase One: External Theories of Social Change

Understandably, among the first comprehensive theories of social change in this period, the dominant motif was the crucial role assigned to *diffusion*.[1] The sources and "causes" of both specific and general categories of change were largely conceived to be external to given societies or cultures. In retrospect, two reasons for this viewpoint seem to be quite relevant. First, this period was heir to the now discredited notion that cultural and social developments throughout long stretches of human experience were more often the result of borrowing and transculturation than of independent invention and creativity. While a considerable controversy raged on this issue among anthropologists, historians, and philosophers, the diffusion hypothesis in its variant forms was the more persuasively presented—and was likewise more congenial to implicit or explicit attitudes toward historical development held by leading writers of the late Victorian and Edwardian eras. Second, and perhaps as important, is the relative scarcity of attempts to focus analysis on societies and nations as indigenous systems of change and development. The major exception to this trend, of course, was the Marxian theory of economic determinism and its consequences for stratification and institutional change.

One of the best representatives of this approach is Frederick J. Teggart who is still somewhat unique as a historian concerned with developing a theory of social change. Teggart's major postulate was that significant change can be conceptualized as a *process* in which established institutions and patterns of thought are challenged by novel experiences and values. As a process, the key phase is not the eventual substitution of new patterns for old ones, but rather the *period of transition,* in which the practical opportunity for change occurs.[2] Consequently, Teggart's theory sought to provide a generalized analysis of the factors in transitional periods of nations or civilizations.

According to Teggart, change can be traced to any set of events that constitute an *effective intrusion* in some established social order. To initiate a process of change, intrusions must "disrupt" the ongoing ensemble of groups, values, and activities. Within his system apparently, only *migrations* of ethnically or culturally distinctive peoples provide sufficient challenge to produce the unique phenomena of transition: pressure and conflict at specific loci (geographical and functional) of "invaded" societies.[3]

The consequences of effective intrusion by migration, according to Teggart, appear on several levels, though there is an implied attempt to posit a serial order of development. Migration inevitably creates a juxtaposition of divergent value systems. A direct result is a period of conflict (presumably of several kinds, including violence) between groups holding opposing objectives and values. But conflict serves to weaken the authority of established forms. In time, old customs come to be viewed as inadequate and a spirit of criticism arises. These processes are accompanied by a release from former controls, which is expressed by assertions of heightened individuality and self-expression.[4] And, by implication, this "freedom" permits the development of new social and cultural arrangements, which are somewhat independent of the initial intrusions.

Teggart's analysis of social change seems to have been generally designed for societies in early stages of civilization, and particularly for those that have been strategically located on classical migration routes (e.g., Southeastern Europe and Southwest Asia). Robert E. Park, one of the most influential sociologists in recent American history, largely accepted Teggart's framework, with echoes of such theorists as Gumplowicz and Ratzenhofer, but with an empirical focus on modern societies and the significance of intrusions for urban development.

For Park, human affairs and the complex organizations that provide guidelines to social behavior are conceptualized in comparative *locational* terms. That is, interactions between persons and groups occur (1) in a *geographic* context, thereby involving different degrees of *distance;* and (2) in a culturally defined "social space" in which different status positions may be regarded as different opportunities to interact with others and to occupy space. With such a framework, social change can be translated into patterns of "movement" in space and status structures.[5] The relation between spatial and status spheres is, however, not consistently analyzed by Park.

If migration remains the key process of social change for Park, as for Teggart, the former tries to explain both the *causes* and *consequences* of migration. In short, Park treats migrations as *internal* to "transmitting" societies and *external* to "receiving" societies. By contrast with Teggart, Park views migrations as not necessarily "original causes" of transition. Indeed, he notes that migrations are more or less spontaneous responses to profound disturbances in economic and social arrangements.[6] But the general origins of such disturbances are left unexplored, since Park was clearly more concerned with the social and cultural *products* of population movements.

Specifically, Park focused on social changes connected with the growth and differentiation of modern urban areas. Since urban growth was, until recently, a consequence of migration, Park sought to uncover a generalized pattern of changes derived from urbanward migration in the modern era. Social change was then reduced to a theoretically cohesive cycle of distinctive social processes, behavior patterns, and their social products.[7]

The first phase following migration itself is *contact* of diverse groups, marked by irritation and "social unrest." Such contact necessarily entails changes in relations for both resident and migrant categories. In general, the migrant is liberated from previous social influences and value systems and therefore behaves more individualistically, or even in an unpredictable manner.

A second phase of change occurs when migrants are defined by residents as competing for available space and facilities—in short, as a threat to established forms of social relations. This marks the beginning of what Park calls "collective behavior," the processes by which established forms lose their potency and new kinds of social organization are experimentally created (cf. Teggart's concept of "transition").

Social change proceeds to a third phase in which migrants and residents respectively try to introduce or suppress variations by force or threat of force —*conflict*. However, a fourth general phase is characterized by attempts to reduce conflict. This objective is realized through more or less temporary and expedient *innovations in social relations, values, and opportunities*. The phenomena of segregation (voluntary or involuntary), compromise, conciliation, toleration, and mediation are examples of *accommodative* mechanisms in social change.

Finally, according to Park, selected types of accommodation may become sufficiently successful in practice to achieve sanctioned acceptance of (1) the new social and cultural patterns and (2) the migrants who initiated the overall social change process.

This generalized schema of social change, though focused on urbanization, was also adapted to processes of social change in historical societies and nations. Following a tradition of analysis formed by such men as Comte, Spencer, Toennies, and Durkheim, Park viewed change as a long-term process in which a *sacred societal type* becomes transformed into a *secular type*. The former is relatively immune to change until its members migrate to more complex societies, or migrants from the latter invade previously isolated communities. In either case, heightened mobility serves to weaken the moral monopoly of established forms—in Park's phrase "mobility secularizes relations which were formerly sacred."[8] The processes discussed above may then be conceived as rough stages of secularization, the consequence of which is a society accustomed to mobility, to greater social complexity, and to the normality (and desirability) of change. But this transformation is not without problematic by-products. One such consequence is the phenomenon of the *marginal man,* who is psychologically exposed by virtue of having discarded "sacred" practices and not having achieved commitment to a socially acceptable alternate set of values. The marginal man may therefore complicate social change by one of two types of deviation: rebellious behavior (directly violating accepted norms); or innovative behavior (seeking to create new norms for social approval).[9]

A second by-product of change to which Park and his students devoted much attention is that of intergroup antipathies in the form of prejudice and discrimination. Park briefly developed a theory of the inevitable but transitional nature of ethnic conflicts—as a consequence of migration and accompanying dislocations, rather than of human failings or differential racial abilities. Briefly, Park explained the rise of prejudice against minority migrant groups as a reflection of *resistance to change* on the part of adherents to established patterns. In line with his phase theory of social change, discrimination (and to some extent prejudice as well) on the basis of ethnic difference tends to be replaced by accommodative and assimilatory phases. But Park, following Gumplowicz, suggested that ethnic divisions are ultimately superseded by *class* and socio-economic differences and conflicts.[10]

Howard Becker, a student of Park, followed the general tradition of Teggart and Park for thirty years. However, Becker developed his own approach by focusing on varieties of societal types, while largely ignoring Park's schema of social change processes. Essentially, vulnerability to external influences remains a key conception; but migration of peoples is only one mechanism of accessibility. Becker contends that modern mass communications are similarly significant in initiating transition and change.[11]

The novel, yet largely supplemental, features of Becker's approach to social change may be summarized in perhaps two major segments. First, and more basic, is his recognition that *attitude toward change* (readiness or reluctance) constitutes a major variable in any serious analysis of long-term processes of change. Indeed, a rather complex typology of societal types (based on the sacred-secular dichotomy)[12] was progressively worked out with primary attention to this variable.

It should be clearly recognized that Becker disclaimed any quest for "the causes" of social change. In particular, he did not even attempt a *generalized explanation* of variations in attitudes toward change. However, we find occasional references to specific situations of change, in which Becker suggests the importance of a charismatic leader, a strong emphasis on rationality, the presence of crises, the opportunities afforded by division of labor, efficient systems of communication, and, of course, intrusions provided by population movements.[13]

Primarily, however, Becker chose to analyze processes of social change by focusing on a series of *socially relevant personality types,* which reflect both (1) different phases of the change process and (2) different degrees of receptivity to new values and organizations. Again, the origins of these types and the processes or conditions under which any type achieves increase in numbers or greater salience are matters that Becker did not seek to investigate.

Essentially, Becker identified seven personality types in change processes that accompany a shift from sacred to secular societal types.[14] With one exception, these personality types are presented in logical order, and, according to Becker, in an approximate sequence of normal development.

1. *Amoral or unmoral type.* This category is not necessarily a first product of externally caused social change. It consists of persons who, for various reasons, had not been properly socialized for established groups. (Examples: children from some broken homes; some children from slum areas; genuine cases of psychopathic personality).

2. *The desocialized or demoralized type.* This category includes persons who have unlearned old values as a consequence of freedom from traditional controls and extreme crisis situations (unemployment, incarceration, war, etc.) The behavior of these persons is marked by unpredictability, violence, and apparent aimlessness. (Examples: some relatively recent urban migrants from isolated rural areas; some prisoners of war; some occupation forces).

3. *Semi-socialized or segmented type.* Here we have evidence of *partial* adjustment to conditions of change by compartmentalizing adherence to traditional values from experimentation with new or nonsanctioned means in limited areas of activity. This semi-schizophrenic social type is supremely encouraged where the social division of labor is complex (urban areas, for example) and where rigorous means of identifying and controlling deviation are absent. According to Becker, the segmented type vaguely feels the discomfort of these inconsistencies and therefore seeks "salvation" in irresponsible sexual adventures, heightened use of vicarious satisfactions (in spectator sports, mass media, and various types of gambling), and in emotionally satisfying cults and fads formed by charismatic leaders.

4. *The marginal or transitionally socialized type.* This type has partly renounced the old ways and yet only partly accepts available alternatives in values and appropriate attitudes. The notion of change as desirable is strong, but fixation on an adequate substitute for tradition persists as a basic problem for such persons, particularly if marginal persons are (as is often the case) members of socially "inferior" categories. But marginality may result in a search for perspective, for objectivity—or the quest for social recognition. In the former case, we may find as a positive response creativity in literary and intellectual spheres, and as a negative response the development of personal dissociation from environmental problems (i.e., mental deviation). In the latter case, on the other hand, the marginal type may develop charismatic traits and a novel collection of adherents from the segmented category; such a symbiotic relationship in social change would repay closer analysis.

5. *The regulated or "convert" type.* New or different practices are embraced with enthusiasm by persons of this type, who usually react with distaste to the values (and their adherents) they have renounced. This uncritical

acceptance of change is a new form of sacred pattern. The religious convert, the newly naturalized citizen, the *nouveau riche* are a few examples.

6. *The decadent or "sophisticated" type*. The basic attitude among persons of this type is a "compulsive search for variety" without apparent satiation. Change for change's sake alone, change as an antidote for boredom, experimentation well beyond the normally accepted bounds of propriety and decency—these are distinctive traits of a type that has converted change into monotony, and monotony into a dominant motive for further change. In general, this type derives from (but does not exhaust) the economic and social elite of a society, "whose status shields them from the more immediately disastrous consequences of their erratic conduct" (e.g., some millionairesses, some Proustian survivals in central European nobility, and some film stars).

7. *The liberated or emancipatedly stable type*. At this point we reach an "ideal" personality type, whose description and evaluation have taxed the analytic talents of such writers as Thomas and Znaniecki, Fromm, and Riesman. The liberated type represents a balanced orientation to tradition and change, and a concern for continuity between the established and the emerging variety of alternatives. He maintains a core of stability on what he conceives to be essential matters (family, occupation, etc.), with a periphery of variation, change, and adaptability in nonessentials (clothing, leisure, gadgets and appliances). In the face of vast opportunities for variation and congenial whims, as well as the safety of rigidity, he desires instead a measure of creativity and responsibility. As Becker suggests, in the modern era the liberated type is likely to be attracted to the "discipline of science" or a career in political or commercial statesmanship (the secular "man of action").

Social change, then, is a process of assimilating new patterns by developing a *range* of social personality types. Change therefore involves simultaneous ingredients of traditional practices, approved and nonapproved deviant forms, and even some disciplined creativity. At some points, the production of desocialized and decadent types may usher in a period of *normlessness,* or confusion in response to the challenge of change. But Becker regards this as a temporary phenomenon; normlessness is unbearable to its victims, who seek further change (in the form of new values and social groupings) as an antidote to undesirable consequences of former changes ("the normative reaction to normlessness").[15]

Phase Two: Broad "Internal" Theories of Social Change

Becker's approach to social change increasingly redirects attention to "internal" processes of change, though largely on a classificatory or descriptive plane. In the '30s two theorists, a historian and a sociologist, presented systematic theories that tried to provide *explanations* of broad developments in complex historical societies. Let us first turn to the historian, Arnold Toynbee.

Though Toynbee has been criticized severely on various grounds,[16] both factual and methodological—in addition to his disturbing mixture of religious, philosophical, and objective aims—there remains a body of responsible theorizing that merits continuing attention. The key proposition for Toynbee is that *significant change* (both "growth" and "decline" types) is not external," i.e., due to environment, racial differences, or migration, but derives from *attitudes* toward change *within* a given society.[17] The *source* of different attitudes toward change, is, however, not clarified by Toynbee; these attitudes are *givens* whose consequences are crucial for students of society.

Social change conceived first as a process of achieving progressive complexity is for Toynbee a result of a creative minority, who invent successful solutions to problems of their socio-geographic environment ("challenge and response"). But a creative minority can only contribute to development by (1) interposing a period of temporary isolation—voluntary or involuntary—from routine matters for thought and undisturbed experimentation ("withdrawal"); and (2) applying the fruits of innovation—values, techniques, policies—to specific problems of adaptation ("return").[18] By implication, since Toynbee does not discuss this point, the existence of a creative minority and the opportunity for its "withdrawal" reflect *antecedent processes of specialization,* which make possible the segregation of one or more social categories (e.g., a leisure class, a literate minority, a pariah group) from the tasks associated with mere survival.[19] The development of specialization *itself* is a social change that requires some explanation.

If a nation's creative minority remains "creative" (though an understanding of this motive is likewise not pursued by Toynbee), it is stimulated to seek other problems and challenges for further inventive solutions. In this way, the minority becomes increasingly differentiated from the larger society, in experience, confidence, and prestige. Likewise, the more difficult the problems that are encountered, the more likely appropriate solutions will be specialized in structure and, presumably, in the types of groups required to carry them out. Briefly, then, "developmental" social change is, descriptively, a process of acquiring (1) greater differentiation and specialization of activities, values, techniques, and social organizations within a society and (2) a consequent increase in societal mastery of its environment and a concomitantly greater ability to control change from "external" sources.[20] Causally, developmental social change results from the workable and socially accepted creations of an elite that (1) is capable of identifying challenges accurately, (2) maintains an opportunity to find productive isolation, and (3) understands and acts upon the necessity of pursuing the "new" problems that become visible from the vantage point of antecedent solutions.

A second variety of social change, which is "regressive" by contrast with the previously discussed type, derives from the failure of creative minorities either to accept available challenges or to devise appropriate solutions. Toynbee asserts that a successful minority—at some time—inevitably finds its success a handicap for subsequent challenges. Two factors seem to underlie this "nemesis of creativity." First, except for unusual cases of creative leadership, the creative minority tends to emphasize those skills and viewpoints that *previously* proved highly successful. Second, and this is rather implicit in Toynbee's work, successive problems tend to be somewhat differentiated from one another and thereby require appropriately specialized approaches and techniques.[21] Consequently, further processes of change await the replacement of self-satisfied minorities by more venturesome types.

A complacent minority rarely abdicates its position; it instead substitutes *force* for creativity and thereby initiates a characteristic set of social changes. Increasingly relying on coercion, the formerly creative minority becomes a dominant minority, which develops a universal state as its major means of retaining power and influence. The resultant repressions and frustrations tend to produce variably organized "internal proletariats," drawn from the lower or specially disadvantaged categories. The responses from segments of the society so produced are of two sorts:[22] (1) the eruption of counter violence in the form of riots, rebellions, bitter strikes; and (2) the development of new religious organizations that claim universality, ultimate solutions. Social changes, then, in Toynbee's view, consist of competitive and accommodative relationships between stratified segments of society.

If, for Toynbee, the nexus of social change is the character of a crucial elite, or elites, the essential locus of change for Pitirim A. Sorokin is the peculiar structure of total societal systems. Essentially, Sorokin analyzes human phenomena—the stuff of history—into agents (people), vehicles (material items), and meanings (the values assigned to experience). Of these, the most important is meanings, which Sorokin defines as shared attitudes about the nature of reality (cultural premises).[23] Change is therefore *sociocultural;* that is, a compound of changes in social relations and systems of values.

Sociocultural change reflects the character of the broadest sociocultural systems—not groups or institutions, or even single nations, but *supersystems,* which are defined as logical and meaningful complexes of values underlying and organizing the operation of interdependent groups. The supersystem is roughly equivalent to Toynbee's concept of civilization. But the major feature of genuine supersystems is their relative degree of internal integration and self-determination. Consequently, change is of two types: the *development* of one variety of supersystem; and the *substitution* of one supersystem by alternative forms.[24] This likewise recalls Toynbee's distinction between *change as growth or progression* and *change as decline.*

For the first type of change, Sorokin posits a generalized sequence of ideation (creation of new meanings), objectification (transforming meanings into some material representation), and socialization (the inculcation of these meanings in a given population).[25] However, change by substitution or replacement is by far more crucial in Sorokin's theoretical system. Three major principles are brought to bear, plus several assumptions or assertions of a distinctly metaphysical character.

A central principle is the inevitable process of *immanent,* or internal, change in supersystems. For Sorokin, each type of supersystem (Ideational, Idealistic, and Sensate) develops more or less cumulative variations that are characteristic of that type alone. Sorokin insists that meanings and values normally change first. To this he adds the observation that noticeable changes first appear in "small subsystems" (specialized groups or elites, by implication), then in institutional systems, and finally in the supersystem as a whole.[26]

However, two further considerations complicate this simplistic type of explanation. On the one hand, external factors may interfere with immanent developments, but principally as facilitators or delayers of ongoing change processes—in the case of already integrated supersystems. But with or without external influences, sociocultural change reflects the principle of limits. This is a viewpoint that is broadly acceptable, but, unfortunately, it is difficult to apply with assurance in specific instances. According to Sorokin, reality (which refers to the interactive factors experienced or experienceable by human groups) possesses sensory and ideational aspects, stable and dynamic aspects, freedoms and restraints. Any supersystem selects a focus on one part of these pairs and develops by further refinement of these aspects. But this specialized focus "possesses the germs of its own decline," for the societies involved thereby lose touch with other important aspects of reality.[27] The principle of limits, then, suggests that (1) societies generally develop along roughly *unilineal* cultural lines and (2) after a certain point in such development, dominant values and related social organizations are no longer able to adapt to the demands of a broader reality. In Toynbee's words, the supersystem at this juncture cannot produce successful responses to challenges of the environment (reality); indeed, by implication, this coincides with the development of an uncreative minority, which clings to previously practical, but one-sided and now outdated cultural premises.

In short, Sorokin's theory of change rests on a dialectic process in which, on the one hand, change is a consequence of self-determined, creative experimentation on limited themes and, on the other, change is an adaptation to the limitations of environing systems. From a practical standpoint, the student of specific social changes must be able to locate such changes in the proper phase of the career of typical supersystems. However, he is not thereby required to seek (1) the proximate causes of emphasis on certain values rather than others, and (2) the ways in which sociocultural change *revises* reality.

Phase Three: The Search for Significant Mechanisms of Internal Change

In the past twenty years, theorists of social change have tended to accept the internal approach and also have generally agreed on the necessity of discovering the mechanisms by which parts or aspects of human social systems promote and assimilate change. As a result, the former emphasis on leadership and elites, on migrations, and on inevitable cycles of development have been largely discarded. The major contributors to this revised approach include such men as Znaniecki, MacIver, and Mannheim. But their efforts may be said to provide significant clues that require interpretation and some attempt at codification. Let us first turn to Znaniecki.

Florian Znaniecki, a philosopher who became a sociologist well before 1920, has advanced two or three clear-cut and interrelated propositions that are both simple and practicable.

1. A basic notion is that social change requires the study of networks of social actions, rather than of "values abstracted from those actions."[28] In this way, change is an intelligible human process to which specific persons contribute by changes in behavior.

2. A crucial characteristic of social change, therefore, is some process of *creativity,* in which persons redefine practical situations as a guide to and accompaniment of social actions. Creativity in a broad sense is widespread, but its "causes" and conditions are not well understood.[29] But however creative ideas originate, their *consequences* for social change are traceable by means of a systematic framework.

3. For Znaniecki, the context of change is any social system composed of actions regularly performed by persons for a *social circle* of persons who are affected by those actions. Social change therefore occurs in one of two forms.

(a) *Creative change* represents the development of new actions or new social effects by innovators (e.g., the city manager, the foundation executive, the efficiency expert, the marriage counselor).

(b) *Incidental or unplanned change* involves not new actions but changes in the evaluation or effects of such actions on other members of the group. For example, the military in our society and the merchants in late medieval Europe achieved greater recognition and prestige without significant change in *their* behavior or values.

In either case, social change is, for Znaniecki, a product of a continual evaluation of specific social roles by the rest of the social system or its representatives. However, Znaniecki is particularly concerned with specifying the relevant variables in this process. Empirically, social change involves alterations in any of the following components of social roles:[30]

(a) The social circle—its size, needs, and facilities.

(b) The social function of the role—the relation between performance of a role and its evaluated satisfaction of some explicit need of the social circle.

(c) Social status—the cluster of rewards (material and psychological) conferred by the social circle for performance of a given social role.

Since each of these is variable, change may arise in two ways. Persons may come to emphasize different components of their roles at different periods of time—e.g., the status aspect as over the social function aspect. On the other hand, for reasons that Znaniecki does not explore, the social circle may develop revised interpretations of its needs and interests, altered judgments of a role's contributions, and/or changed allocations of rewards to incumbents of certain roles. All of these contingencies, therefore, rest on fundamental processes of redefinition and re-evaluation of social experience.

Robert M. MacIver places the process of re-evolution in a *strategic* position for the analysis of social change. The *materials* or *preparatory conditions* of change include such familiar variables as population movements, natural catastrophes, innovations in ideas and values, and mechanical or technical inventions. But the *precipitant* or catalyst of change is the process by which these candidates for change are perceived and selectively evaluated by a widening range of individuals and groups. This is the crucial phenomenon of *dynamic assessment.*[31]

A comprehensive theory of dynamic assessment has not been constructed by MacIver, though some of its elements seem to be at hand in his book *The Web of Government*. First, significant variations in basic values ("myth") and in manipulation of the environment ("technique") are reciprocally related. Thus, technological changes tend to respond to prevailing values; and dominant values reflect to some extent a narrowing of perspectives related to experience with customarily employed technologies.[32]

However, myth (or value-impregnated beliefs regarding behavior) operates as a major component of dynamic assessment through the development of a *myth of authority*[33] congenial to projected changes in other values and techniques. MacIver explains the creation of new authority myths as a response to changes in "the situation," i.e., the challenges or pressures provided by the socio-physical environment. Yet the situation must be interpreted as necessitating alterations in prevailing myth. Once a new myth of authority is accepted, dynamic assessment tends to convert a linkage of values and techniques into "deviant" behavior.

In addition, the political mechanism—government, which is considered to be a key component of technique—intrudes at this point in the social change process to control—by facilitation or obstruction—(1) the *rate* at which deviant social behavior is transmitted and (2) the manner in which technological and cultural derivatives reverberate through other aspects of a total society or nation.[34]

Yet government is likewise a product of myth and the situation. It is therefore responsive to changes in other institutional areas, just as the latter ultimately reflect major trends in the nature of political power. MacIver seems to suggest, further, that the relative importance of dynamic assessment and government in social change may vary. Thus, social changes due to behavioral applications of collective dynamic assessments may be incorporated into the structure of society without major contributions from, or effects on, the formal political order.[35] But there is a point, as yet quite indefinite, beyond which social changes cannot be assimilated without a congenial *revision* in the political order (e.g., in the myth of authority, centralization of controls, personnel). In summary, then, social change is a practical consequence of the variable cooperation between (1) new dynamic assessments from any portion of society and (2) the political institution.

Both Znaniecki and MacIver sought to provide analyses of long-term changes, with a consequent focus on the positive mechanisms of change. Two anthropologists, Godfrey and Monica Wilson, have instead applied their field work on acculturation in southeast Africa to a theoretical scheme that centers on transitional phases of change (rather than on causal mechanisms) and on the normal tensions and conflicts that accompany significant change. In doing so, they give theoretical prominence to a greatly disregarded aspect of society —*scale*.

The scale of a society refers to its size, but more directly to (1) its degree of internal specialization, (2) intimacy and impersonality in social relationships, and (3) the opportunity for geographic and social mobility of its members. Thus large-scale societies possess intricate division of labor, considerable proportions of formalized, impersonal social contacts, and high mobility.[36] While social changes serve to produce broad changes in scale over long historical periods, the Wilsons are more concerned with the more immediate relations between change and scale.

In line with a familiar tradition, the Wilsons identify the general causes of change as innovations in ideas and values, new techniques or new applications of existing technologies, and unassimilable conflicts between subgroups in society.[37] Whatever the source, the acceptance of innovation often produces *unevenness of scale*, i.e., greater complexity in some parts of the social structure, without corresponding increases in complexity in other parts. For example, industrial changes during the eighteenth century were not accompanied by adjustive political and religious developments. According to the Wilsons, the resulting "disequilibrium" tends to present people with the necessity of supporting practically contradictory concepts, values, and behavior patterns. When this condition is sufficiently widespread, it constitutes "radical oppositions," which cannot be controlled either by segregation of groups and institutional activities, or by centralized power and coercion.[38]

Clearly, the theory of problematic transition is mainly applicable to simple societies that experience intensive stimuli for change. But the Wilsons also theorize that rapid change does not produce similar effects in large-scale or highly complex societies. For, the greater the scale, the greater the diversity of autonomous spheres of social experience.[39] Consequently, innovations do not necessarily create radical oppositions and conflicts. What aspects of social structure, then, explain the special nature of social change in complex societies?

One of the most ambitious attempts toward furnishing an answer to this problem, and also an internal theory of social change, may be found in the work of the Hungarian-born German-British sociologist Karl Mannheim. While Mannheim did not develop a systematic presentation of this approach, he has provided four sets of interrelated theoretical clues that deserve greater attention than they have received.

Mannheim's most basic concept refers to society as a dynamic system of interdependent "parts," verbalized by many analysts as "principles of organization" (e.g., division of labor, centralization of authority) and by Mannheim as *principia media*.[40] These principles, or complexes of social and cultural variables in specific societies, possess two important attributes. On the one hand, they reflect opportunities (and limitations) for proximate institutional and societal developments. But secondly, the *principia media* form *historically specific hierarchies,* so that future developments tend to proceed along lines "directed" by superordinate principles for given periods of time.[41] Thus, a technologically oriented society will be more likely to develop variations in material techniques than in political ideologies.

For Mannheim, therefore, social change is often undramatic and gradual —a working out of persistent sets of *principia media*.[42] However, changes in the hierarchy of principles may likewise occur slowly and with little warning to most participants, but eventually reach a point of turmoil and the need for new decisions.

Regardless of source, social change is said to be mediated by the organizational capacities of concrete societies. The next problem, therefore, concerns the patterns of functioning by which *principia media* serve as links in the over-all change process. Mannheim employs three types of approach to an understanding of the "transmission belts" that convert potentiality into altered systems of behavior.

(a) One significant dimension is the level of thinking that is, or becomes, dominant in a given era and among the key persons or groups.[43] *Chance discovery* refers to the simplest mode of response to new situations: trial and error undirected by clear conceptions of problems or of possible alternative solutions. A second level, *invention,* involves conscious development of *specific* "satisfactory" solutions (technical or evaluational) based on some prior acceptance of a goal and analysis of limited problematic situations. *Planning,* the most complex level, is marked by recognition of the *interdependence* of situations and the search for solutions that can be applied to strategic points in the system of situations. Obviously, each of these levels involves a different degree of receptivity to change and also a different contribution to the speed and effects of given change processes.

A related means of analyzing the "internal" transmission of change is through careful study of social techniques.[44] By social techniques Mannheim means the organized "practices and agencies" that consciously or unconsciously influence the behavior of persons and the nature of the social relationships in which they regularly participate. By implication, social techniques are responsive to specific social and cultural changes, and also serve to implement and institutionalize these changes. Two aspects of social techniques are theoretically important for Mannheim. One is the *range of application,* from narrow circles of traditional, personal relationships to a mass, impersonal type of control. The second aspect concerns the *control mechanisms* associated with social techniques: direct vs. indirect and subtle forms of influencing behavior (e.g., gossip vs. advertising).[45]

But levels of thinking and social techniques function most significantly in strategic elites. Therefore, Mannheim gives special emphasis to the dynamics of the composition and role of various elites and "intellectuals" in complex societies. According to Mannheim, earlier social changes affect elites and their ability to interpret or translate these changes to larger contexts in two respects: (1) the significant reduction or increase in the number of elite groups, with corresponding changes in the influence wielded by any elite; (2) changes in selection of elite members—e.g., in *criteria* of selection (family, ability, seniority, etc.), in breadth of experience (local vs. cosmopolitan background)—as these changes are reflected in the elites' attitude toward adjustments to past social changes.[46]

In short, Mannheim's theory of social change assigns crucial importance to the processes by which antecedent change produces derivative changes, through alterations in the nature and functioning of leadership (elites). But the changing character of elites in periods of transition does not receive a causal explanation. Instead, Mannheim suggests that transition is marked by multiple possibilities of development, that the emergence of one line rather than others is a matter for which hypothesis remains unaided by appropriate facts.

Summary and Conclusions

The nature of specific social changes and the essential character of social change processes can be fruitfully regarded as facets of the same intriguing problem: how can we understand the development of *shifts* in ideas, practices, organizations, and problems for any nation or society (past or present) in which we have some interest? While such a problem does not exhaust the professional objectives and related skills of either sociologists or historians, it does constitute a significant and enduring meeting ground for these two fields. What, then, is the major import of the previously discussed theories and orientations for modern historians and sociologists?

Perhaps the most general contribution is an implicit or explicit rejection of unexamined determinisms, both of the vague type (e.g., evolution) and specific monistic forms (e.g., economic or technological determinism).[47] This is surely related to an increasing reluctance to search for ultimate causes or principles and a corresponding concern for more immediate contexts of description and analysis. Thus, migration, diffusion, invention, race, climate, and the like are no longer seriously employed as *crucial* explanations for social change.[48]

Indeed, we can note in recent theories a salutary concern for *transitional periods or phases* of social change as a means of revealing the multiple potentialities for variation and the processes by which *one* of the practical alternatives emerges.[49] At this point the study of pressures, conflicts, strains, etc., becomes a crucial empirical problem, calling on the most varied skills in data gathering and evaluation known to sociologists and historians.

But this revised emphasis also involves a necessary theoretical focus on the social actions and dominant motives of specific categories of persons during transitional periods. In particular, these theories strongly suggest the necessity of determining the connections between strategic persons and groups, on the one hand, and available control mechanisms (e.g., government, communications systems) on the other—as these operate to obstruct or facilitate processes of social change. In this way, too, these theories stress the *contingent* nature of social changes and the importance of seeking the conditions and consequents of *derivative byproducts* in the varied compartments of social organization.

Finally, the more recent theories of social change represent a strong tendency among various students of society to renounce the traditional but unsuccessful shortcuts to a proper understanding of developments in human affairs. A philosophy of history in any of its familiar metaphysical or ideological forms, with its characteristic disdain for carefully evaluated fact, is conspicuously out of grace. Likewise, the "abstracted empiricism" of chroniclers (in history) and some pollsters and surveyers (in sociology), with their narrow devotion to brute fact, receives little support from this body of theory.[50] Indeed, by ignoring the cloudy atmosphere of philosophies of history and yet aspiring beyond the trackless morass of the empiricists, the study of social change gives promise at last of developing a distinctively *human scale* and perhaps of explanations that are both understandable and demonstrable.

Notes

1. Robert H. Lowie, *The History of Ethnological Theory* (New York: Rinehart, 1937), chaps. 10, 11.
2. Frederick J. Teggart, *Theory and Processes of History* (Berkeley: University of California Press, 1941), pp. 278–279.
3. *Ibid.*, pp. 151, 195–196, 272.
4. *Ibid.*, pp. 279–290.
5. Robert E. Park, *Human Communities* (New York: The Free Press, 1952), pp. 166, 173.
6. Robert E. Park and Ernest W. Burgess, *Introduction to the Science of Sociology* (Chicago: University of Chicago Press, 1921), p. 54; Robert E. Park, *Race and Culture* (New York: The Free Press, 1950), p. 10.
7. Park and Burgess, *loc. cit.;* Park, *Race and Culture,* p. 350.
8. Park, *Race and Culture,* pp. 12–13, 351.
9. *Ibid.*, pp. 354–355.
10. *Ibid.*, pp. 116, 233.
11. Howard Becker, "Processes of Secularisation," *The Sociological Review* (British), 24 (April–July and October, 1932), pp. 138–154, 266–286.
12. Howard Becker, *Through Values to Social Interpretation* (Durham: Duke University Press, 1950), chap. 5.
13. *Ibid.*, pp. 69–71. Cf. Roscoe C. Hinkle, "Howard Becker's Approach to the Study of Social Change," *Sociological Quarterly,* 2 (July 1961), pp. 155–180.
14. *Ibid.*, pp. 78–91; Howard Becker, *Man in Reciprocity* (New York: Praeger, 1956), chap. 14.
15. Becker, *Man in Reciprocity,* pp. 182–183; Howard Becker, "Normative Reactions to Normlessness," *American Sociological Review,* 25 (December 1960), pp. 803–810.
16. See Harry E. Barnes, *An Introduction to the History of Sociology* (Chicago: University of Chicago Press, 1948), chap. 37; Ashley Montagu, ed., *Toynbee and History* (Boston: Porter Sargent, 1956); Pieter Geyl, *The Pattern of the Past* (Boston: Beacon Press, 1949).
17. Arnold J. Toynbee, *A Study of History,* abridged by D. C. Somervell (New York: Oxford University Press, 1947), p. 49.
18. *Ibid.*, pp. 67–68, 217–241.
19. See, e.g., Leslie A. White, *The Evolution of Culture* (New York: McGraw-Hill, 1959), chap. 12.
20. Toynbee, *op. cit.,* pp. 187–189, 241–246.
21. *Ibid.*, pp. 307–309, 367–368.
22. *Ibid.*, pp. 371–375.
23. Pitirim A. Sorokin, *Society, Culture and Personality* (New York: Harper, 1947), pp. 41–63, 580; Pitirim A. Sorokin, *Social and Cultural Dynamics* (New York: American Book Company, 1937–1941, 4 vols.).
24. Sorokin, *Society, Culture and Personality,* pp. 635–644.
25. *Ibid.*, pp. 537–578.
26. *Ibid.*, pp. 659–660, 696–699.
27. *Ibid.*, pp. 704–705.
28. Florian Znaniecki, *Cultural Sciences* (Urbana: University of Illinois Press, 1951), p. 183.
29. *Ibid.*, pp. 198–204, 372.

30. Florian Znaniecki, *The Social Role of the Man of Knowledge* (New York: Columbia University Press, 1940), chap. 1; Florian Znaniecki, "The Social Roles of Innovators." Address given before the Midwest Sociological Society, April 1953, Omaha, Nebraska.

31. Robert M. MacIver, *Social Causation* (Boston: Ginn, 1942), p. 163.

32. Robert M. MacIver, *The Web of Government* (New York: Macmillan, 1947), pp. 4–16, 39–42.

33. *Ibid.*, pp. 143–145, 298, 447–452.

34. *Ibid.*, p. 294.

35. *Ibid.*

36. Godfrey and Monica Wilson, *The Analysis of Social Change* (Cambridge: Cambridge University Press, 1945), pp. 24–26.

37. *Ibid.*, pp. 83–100, 132–133.

38. *Ibid.*, pp. 125–127, 132. Cf. William F. Ogburn, *Social Change* (New York: Viking Press, 1950 ed.), pp. 200–213. Ogburn's theory of cultural lag is the classic American discussion of the problem of differential change. See the discussion of Ogburn's theory by Don Martindale, "Social Disorganization: The Conflict of Normative and Empirical Approaches," in Howard Becker and Alvin Boskoff, eds., *Modern Sociological Theory* (New York: Holt, Rinehart & Winston, 1957), pp. 349–354.

39. Wilson and Wilson, *op. cit.,* pp. 108, 134; Alvin Boskoff, "Social Indecision: A Dysfunctional Focus of Transitional Society," *Social Forces,* 37 (May 1959), pp. 305–311.

40. Karl Mannheim, *Man and Society in an Age of Reconstruction* (New York: Harcourt, Brace, 1940), pp. 173–187.

41. Cf. Sorokin, *Society, Culture, and Personality;* Melville J. Herskovits, *Man and his Works* (New York: Knopf, 1947), chap. 32.

42. Mannheim, *op. cit.,* p. 12.

43. *Ibid.*, pp. 150–152.

44. *Ibid.*, p. 247.

45. *Ibid.*, pp. 252–259, 274–327.

46. *Ibid.*, pp. 86–96. See also William Kornhauser, *The Politics of Mass Society* (New York: The Free Press, 1959).

47. A comprehensive review is in Pitirim A. Sorokin, *Contemporary Sociological Theories* (New York: Harper, 1928).

48. However, for a modification of this statement, compare W. J. Cahnman, "The Rise of Civilization as a Paradigm of Social Change," in this volume.

49. Ludwig von Bertalanffy, *Problems of Life* (New York: Wiley, 1952), pp. 143–183.

50. Hans Meyerhoff, ed., *The Philosophy of History in our Time* (Garden City: Doubleday Anchor, 1959); Paul Barth, *Die Philosophie der Geschichte als Soziologie* (Leipzig, 1921); C. Wright Mills, *The Sociological Imagination* (New York: Oxford University Press, 1959), chap. 3; E. K. Francis, "Prolegomena to a Theory of Social Change," *Kyklos,* 14 (1961), 213–230.

INTRODUCTION

IN PRESENTING A SELECTION of historical writings by sociologists and by some historians who write in a sociological vein, we were guided by a number of principles. First, our intention was to present research papers. We are aware that a great many excellent treatises exist concerning the principles underlying the writing of history, the nature of historical processes, and the relations between history and the social sciences. But since the problem of whether a knife cuts a cake can only be solved by actually cutting the cake with it, we decided that what was to be demonstrated was the effectiveness with which sociologically oriented authors use the conceptual tools of the social sciences in order to come to grips with the reality of historical situations. We wanted to show that a multiplicity of such situations had been mastered and that the result was good historiography.

Second, we wanted to show not only that the understanding of history would be served by sociological conceptualization, but also that sociology was likely to gain from historical study. If it is true that social scientists are interested in discovering the general in the particular, then the generalizations can neither disregard the individual case nor can they be based on cases whose occurrence is restricted in time and place. Historical data are therefore indispensable, if valid theory is to emerge. However, it should be obvious from the selections presented that the quest for theory is to be pursued with moderation. As Kenneth Bock puts it, rather than analyzing history in the abstract singular, "histories" must be accepted in their concrete plurality.[1] Correspondingly, one should not expect historical data to yield a single grand theory of societal development. What appears in the here and there of spatial-temporal reality is a variety of social actions; and theories answering to the challenge contained in them, therefore, ought to emerge in the plural.

Third, we wanted to take particular notice of a hitherto neglected area in American social science, and also to make clear that the American effort is worldwide in connotation. Consequently, American contributions are em-

1. Kenneth E. Bock, *The Acceptance of Histories: Toward a Perspective for Social Science* (Berkeley and Los Angeles: University of California Press, 1956).

phasized, but not to the exclusion of others—two British, one French, one Latin-American, one Chinese, and one Israeli scholar are represented among the authors. However, one of the British scholars is American-trained and three of the others (Castro, Ch'u, and Ben-David) have worked and published in the United States. Conversely, some of the American scholars received part of their training in other countries. At any rate, whether the authors are American or not, the topics are worldwide in scope. There are pieces on the Far East, the Middle East and Africa, on Mediterranean antiquity, on medieval and modern Europe, and on the Americas. It is doubtful whether a similar publication in any other country would have done as much justice to the New World as we have to the Old.

In many ways, World War II marks a watershed in American life and thought. As a result, changes occurred in sociological writing which became more clearly discernible in the postwar years. It would seem not amiss, therefore, to note that the contributions included in the anthology that follows are from the last two decades, the only exception being the opening piece by Marc Bloch. But Marc Bloch, who but for his death before a Nazi firing squad would be a contemporary of all of us today, is as much a forerunner of things to come as he is the bearer of a message of earlier days. It seemed fitting to pay homage to what he stands for. He leads the other authors of our selections not only in the recognition that history as a discipline should use more precise methods of interpretation than it thus far has employed,[2] but also in the recognition that it is the task of sociology to assist in the understanding of historical processes, not to replace historical investigation with sociological theory. The pieces which follow should be read with this consideration in mind.

The order in which the contributions appear does not follow conventional lines of classification in either history or sociology. We do not proceed from the oldest records to the newest, although we consider sequence after other considerations have taken precedence. We have attempted to combine some pieces from Asia, Europe, and the Americas with others from the same continents, but not at the expense of conceptual coherence. Neither have we attempted, as was our earlier intention, to classify according to sociological categories, such as stratification, institutions, race relations, the family, social movements, and so forth, because this might have led to crossfiling of those contributions which belong in more than one conceptual category. Rather, as researchers, we have followed the lead of the data themselves, as one contribu-

2. Marc Bloch, "Pour une histoire comparée des sociétés européennes," *Revue de synthèse historique*, XLVI, 1928, 15–20. English translation in Frederic C. Lane and Jelle C. Riemersma (eds.), *Enterprise and Secular Change* (Homewood, Ill.: Richard D. Irwin, Inc., 1953), pp. 494–521. Cf. Marc Bloch, *Apologie pour l'histoire ou métier d'historien*, (Paris: Colin, 1949). English translation by Peter Putnam, *The Historian's Craft* (New York: A. A. Knopf, 1953).

tion seemed to suggest the next in a continuing argument which combines the individual pieces into a whole that transcends the sum of the parts. As a result, the chapter subheadings, suggestive of possible conceptualization, are not preconceived and the resulting theory remains historical in character.

1. Feudalism and Power in Various Societies

The first section opens with a selection from Marc Bloch's *Feudal Society*. Page after page from this sparkling work could have been included, but the choice fell to Bloch's discussion of "Feudalism as a Type of Society." There are many aspects to this chapter. Feudalism is described here as a "historical totality concept" (Rickert) or a "real type" (Spiethoff), that is, as a unique configuration of traits. Moreover, European feudalism of the tenth to thirteenth centuries, as it evolved in large parts of France, Germany, the Low Countries, and England, is taken as prototypical of a kind of society which in rudimentary or attenuated form also appeared in less feudalized outlying regions of Europe. European feudalism is further seen dialectically as replacing antecedent kinship societies and continuing in significant survivals and revivals in later centuries.[1]

But feudalism is also treated as an ideal-typical concept, at least in a tentative way. One might say that what Max Weber would have termed ideal-typical procedure, Bloch, following Durkheim, designates as the comparative method.[2] He compares European feudalism not only to kinship-based societies, to relatively less feudal parts of medieval Europe, and to societies dominated by representative institutions, but also to non-European feudalisms, such as the feudalism of Japan. In the chapter which is here reprinted, Bloch's conclusion is that feudalism was by no means a unique cluster of events and processes occurring once and never again in history. However, in the chapter which follows in *Feudal Society*, the emphasis is on the complementary statement that, while Japanese feudalism remains closely akin to that of the West, there is no denying the fact that the vassal's submission in Japan was much less contractual in nature than in the West and that the divine power of the Emperor was left altogether outside the structure of lord-vassal arrangements. In Bloch's hands, then, the comparative method is far from being content with forced analogies which are sometimes even invented by the postulating of some kind of necessary parallelism between a number of social developments. On the contrary, the comparative method culminates in the observation of differences.

The other pieces in the section, all of them dealing with feudalism and other forms of power, must be seen in comparison with the chapter from Bloch.

Sigmund Diamond, writing about French Canada, refers directly to Bloch. Diamond's over-all problem, which he has been working out in studies of Virginia, Quebec, and Massachusetts, is the creation and growth of new societies on historically virgin soil. This, in itself, is a comparative venture, but French Canada is different from the two Anglo-Saxon settlements in that the emphasis there is not so much on a new enterprise or a new society, but on the transplantation of the elements of a feudal society to a new environment. Diamond shows how French feudalism, having served its purpose in Europe, became dysfunctional under frontier conditions and of necessity generated new forms of social organization. The feudalism of Quebec, molded after the one of France, in meeting with the forces of a very different environment, brings forth an American society. Here, the historical dialectic is observed almost under laboratory conditions.

Norman Jacobs implicitly takes up Bloch's suggestion concerning Japan, but his incentive stems from Max Weber's thesis about the origin of modern capitalism. However, without referring to Bloch, Jacobs adopts Bloch's derivation of capitalism from the element of contractual obligation which is present already in feudalism. Further, his thesis is consistent with the conclusions of one of the foremost experts on Japan's economic development, Thomas C. Smith,[3] who explains some of the major features of the industrialization of Japan from previous change in agrarian conditions. Jacobs employs the historical, as well as the comparative, method tracing, on the one hand, the essentials of the social structure of modern Japan to feudal antecedents and contrasting Japan with the "oriental," that is, patrimonial-bureaucratic society of China, on the other;[4] the similarities of Japan and the West stand out in this procedure. Compared with Diamond, Jacobs' approach assumes a somewhat inflexible quality. But his use of ideal-typical categories is precise and clear.

The other pieces in this section continue the analysis of power structure in Asiatic societies. Bryce Ryan's paper on Ceylon describes a value system as dissimilar from the one of Japan as it is from the one of the West and thus offers a negative proof of Jacobs' thesis. Robert M. Marsh's paper on formal organization in Chinese society is remarkable for the use which it makes of Max Weber's ideal-typical concepts of bureaucratic and patrimonial societies in order to show the limitations within which these concepts are applicable in concrete situations. Marsh's method is the one of quantitative social science, as contrasted to the humanistic approach of Tung-tsu Ch'u. The latter should be taken as representative of the attempt, stimulated by Robert Redfield, to bring together humanists and social scientists in a common study of large-scale civilizations. The humanists, Redfield says, see civilization "through the works of its most reflective and creative minds, the social scientists attend to what is done and thought by the many plain people."[5] If this is so, Professor Ch'u combines the qualities of the humanist and the social scientist in an admirable way. The same may be said about the veteran British historian H. A. R. Gibb, one of the foremost living experts on the Middle East. Gibb's and Bowen's analysis of government and social structure in Islamic society is a classic example of the perfect blend of the historical and sociological methods which a knowledgeable social historian can achieve.

Notes

1. Cf. Marc Bloch, *Feudal Society,* translated by L. A. Manyon (Chicago: University of Chicago Press, 1960), Chapter XXXIII: "The Persistence of European Feudalism."
2. F. C. Lane and J. C. Riemersma, *op. cit.;* concerning Bloch's profound admiration of Durkheim, cf. *Annales d'histoire économique et sociale,* III, p. 590.
3. Thomas C. Smith, *The Agrarian Origins of Modern Japan* (Stanford: Stanford University Press, 1959).
4. For a statement based on both Karl Marx and Max Weber, cf. Karl A. Wittfogel, *Oriental Despotism—A Comparative Study of Total Power* (New Haven: Yale University Press, 1957).
5. Cf. Robert Redfield and Milton Singer, Foreword to G. E. von Grunebaum, *Islam—Essays in the Nature and Growth of a Cultural Tradition* (New York: Barnes and Noble, 1961).

Marc Bloch   **FEUDALISM AS A TYPE OF SOCIETY**

1. Has There Been More Than One Feudalism?

IN THE EYES OF MONTESQUIEU, the establishment of "feudal laws" was a phenomenon *sui generis,* "an event which happened once in the world and which will perhaps never happen again." Voltaire, less experienced, no doubt, in the precise formulation of legal definitions, but a man of wider outlook, demurred. "Feudalism," he wrote, "is not an event; it is a very old form which, with differences in its working, subsists in three-quarters of our hemisphere."[1] Modern scholarship has in general rallied to the side of Voltaire. Egyptian feudalism, Achaean feudalism, Chinese feudalism, Japanese feudalism—all these forms and more are now familiar concepts. The historian of the West must sometimes regard them with a certain amount of misgiving. For he cannot be unaware of the different definitions which have been given of this famous term, even on its native soil. The basis of feudal society, Benjamin Guérard has said, is land. No, it is the personal group, rejoins Jacques Flach. Do the various exotic versions of feudalism, which seem to abound in universal history today, conform to Guérard's definition or to Flach's? The only remedy for these uncertainties is to go back to the origins of the problem. Since it is obvious that all these societies, separated by time and space, have received the name "feudal" only on account of their similarities, real or sup-

Reprinted from *Feudal Society* by Marc Bloch, translated by L. A. Manyon, by permission of The University of Chicago Press, Chicago, 1959, and Routledge & Kegan Paul Ltd., London, England.

posed, to Western feudalism, it is the characteristics of this basic type, to which all the others must be referred, that it is of primary importance to define. But first it is necessary to dispose of some obvious instances of the misuse of a term which has made too much noise in the world not to have undergone many perversions.

In the system which they christened "feudalism," its first godfathers, as we know, were primarily conscious of those aspects of it which conflicted with the idea of a centralized state. Thence it was a short step to describing as feudal every fragmentation of political authority; so that a value judgment was normally combined with the simple statement of a fact. Because sovereignty was generally associated in the minds of these writers with fairly large states, every exception to the rule seemed to fall into the category of the abnormal. This alone would suffice to condemn a usage which, moreover, could scarcely fail to give rise to intolerable confusion. Occasionally, indeed, there are indications of a more precise notion. In 1783 a minor municipal official, the market watchman of Valenciennes, denounced as responsible for the increase in the price of foodstuffs "a feudality of great country landlords."[2] How many polemists since then have held up to public obloquy the "feudalism" of bankers or industrialists! Charged with more or less vague historical associations, the word with certain writers seems to suggest no more than the brutal exercise of authority, though frequently it also conveys the slightly less elementary notion of an encroachment of economic powers on public life. It is in fact very true that the identification of wealth—then consisting mainly of land—with authority was one of the outstanding features of medieval feudalism. But this was less on account of the strictly feudal character of that society than because it was, at the same time, based on the manor.

Feudalism, manorial system—the identification here goes back much farther. It had first occurred in the use of the word "vassal." The aristocratic stamp which this term had received from what was, after all, a secondary development, was not strong enough to prevent it from being occasionally applied, even in the Middle Ages, to serfs (originally closely akin to vassals properly so called because of the personal nature of their dependence) and even to ordinary tenants. What was then only a kind of linguistic aberration, especially frequent in somewhat incompletely feudalized regions like Gascony or Leon, became a more and more widespread usage, as familiarity with genuine vassalage faded. "Everyone knows," wrote Perreciot in 1786, "that in France the subjects of lords are commonly called their vassals."[3] Similarly it became customary, in spite of etymology, to describe as "feudal rights" the burdens to which peasant holdings were subject. Thus when the men of the Revolution announced their intention to destroy feudalism, it was above all the manorial system that they meant to attack. But here again the historian must interpose. Though an essential element in feudal society, the manor was in itself an older institution, and was destined to last much longer. In the interests of sound terminology it is important that the two ideas should be kept clearly separate.

Let us therefore try to bring together in broad outline what we have learned about European feudalism, in the strict sense of the word, from its history.

2. The Fundamental Characteristics of European Feudalism

The simplest way will be to begin by saying what feudal society was not. Although the obligations arising from blood relationship played a very active part in it, it did not rely on kinship alone. More precisely, feudal ties proper were developed when those of kinship proved inadequate. Again, despite the persistence of the idea of a public authority superimposed on the multitude of petty powers, feudalism coincided with a profound weakening of the State, particularly in its protective capacity. But much as feudal society differed from societies based on kinship as well as from those dominated by the power of the State, it was their successor and bore their imprint. For while the characteristic relationships of personal subjection retained something of the quasi-family character of the original companionage, a considerable part of the political authority exercised by innumerable petty chiefs had the appearance of a usurpation of "regalian" rights.

European feudalism should therefore be seen as the outcome of the violent dissolution of older societies. It would in fact be unintelligible without the great upheaval of the Germanic invasions which, by forcibly uniting two societies originally at very different stages of development, disrupted both of them and brought to the surface a great many modes of thought and social practices of an extremely primitive character. It finally developed in the atmosphere of the last barbarian raids. It involved a far-reaching restriction of social intercourse, a circulation of money too sluggish to admit of a salaried officialdom, and a mentality attached to things tangible and local. When these conditions began to change, feudalism began to wane.

It was an unequal society, rather than a hierarchical one—with chiefs rather than nobles; and with serfs, not slaves. If slavery had not played so small a part, there would have been no need for the characteristically feudal forms of dependence, as applied to the lower orders of society. In an age of disorder, the place of the adventurer was too important, the memory of men too short, the regularity of social classifications too uncertain, to admit of the strict formation of regular castes.

Nevertheless, the feudal system meant the rigorous economic subjection of a host of humble folk to a few powerful men. Having received from earlier ages the Roman *villa* (which in some respects anticipated the manor) and the German village chiefdom, it extended and consolidated these methods whereby men exploited men, and combining inextricably the right to the revenues from the land with the right to exercise authority, it fashioned from all this the true manor of medieval times. And this it did partly for the benefit of an oligarchy of priests and monks whose task it was to propitiate Heaven, but chiefly for the benefit of an oligarchy of warriors.

As even the most perfunctory comparative study will show, one of the most distinctive characteristics of feudal societies was the virtual identity of the class of chiefs with the class of professional warriors serving in the only way that then seemed effective, that is as heavily armed horsemen. As we have seen, of the societies where an armed peasantry survived, some knew neither vassalage nor the manor, while others knew them only in very imperfect forms—as in Scandinavia for example, or the kingdoms of northwestern Spain. The case of the Byzantine Empire is perhaps even more significant because its institutions bore the stamp of a much more conscious, directing thought. There, after the anti-aristocratic reaction of the eighth century, a government which had preserved the great administrative traditions of the Roman period, and which was furthermore concerned to provide itself with a strong army, created tenements charged with military obligations to the State —true fiefs in one sense, but differing from those of the West in that they were peasant fiefs, each consisting of a small farm. Thenceforth it was a paramount concern of the imperial government to protect these "soldiers' properties," as well as small holdings in general, against the encroachments of the rich and powerful. Nevertheless, there came a time toward the end of the eleventh century when the Empire, overwhelmed by economic conditions which made independence more and more difficult for a peasantry constantly in debt and further weakened by internal discords, ceased to extend any useful protection to the free farmers. In this way it not only lost precious fiscal resources, but found itself at the mercy of the magnates, who alone were capable thereafter of raising the necessary troops from among their own dependents.

In feudal society the characteristic human bond was the subordinate's link with a nearby chief. From one level to another the ties thus formed—like so many chains branching out indefinitely—joined the smallest to the greatest. Land itself was valued above all because it enabled a lord to provide himself with "men" by supplying the remuneration for them. We want lands, said, in effect, the Norman lords who refused the gifts of jewels, arms, and horses offered by their duke. And they added among themselves: "It will thus be possible for us to maintain many knights, and the duke will no longer be able to do so."[4]

It remained to devise a form of real property right suitable for the remuneration of services and coinciding in duration with the personal tie itself. From the solution which it found for this problem, Western feudalism derived one of its most original features. While the "men of service" who surrounded the Slav princes continued to receive their estates as outright gifts, the fief of the Frankish vassal, after some fluctuations of policy, was in theory conceded to him only for the term of his life. For among the highest classes, distinguished by the honorable profession of arms, relationships of dependence had assumed, at the outset, the form of contracts freely entered into between two living men confronting one another. From this necessary personal contact the relationship derived the best part of its moral value. Nevertheless, at an early date various factors tarnished the purity of the obligation: hereditary succession, natural in a society where the family remained so strong; the practice of enfeoffment which was imposed by economic conditions and ended by burdening the land with services rather than the man with fealty; finally, and above all, the plurality of vassal engagements. The loyalty of the commended man remained, in many cases, a potent factor. But as a paramount social bond designed to unite the various groups at all levels, to prevent fragmentation and to arrest disorder, it showed itself decidedly ineffective.

Indeed in the immense range of these ties there had been from the first something artificial. Their general diffusion in feudal times was the legacy of a moribund State—that of the Carolingians—which had conceived the idea of combating social disintegration by means of one of the institutions born of that very condition. The system of superposed protective relationships was certainly not incapable of contributing to the cohesion of the State: witness, the Anglo-Norman monarchy. But for this it was necessary that there should be a central authority favored, as in England, not only by the fact of conquest itself but even more by the circumstance that it coincided with new material and moral conditions. In the ninth century the forces making for disintegration were too strong.

In the area of Western civilization the map of feudalism reveals some large blank spaces—the Scandinavian peninsula, Frisia, Ireland. Perhaps it is more important still to note that feudal Europe was not all feudalized in the same degree or according to the same rhythm and, above all, that it was nowhere feudalized completely. In no country did the whole of the rural population fall into the bonds of personal and hereditary dependence. Almost everywhere—though the number varied greatly from region to region—there survived large or small allodial properties. The concept of the State never absolutely disappeared, and where it retained the most vitality men continued to call themselves "free," in the old sense of the word, because they were dependent only on the head of the people or his representatives. Groups of peasant warriors remained in Normandy, in the Danelaw, and in Spain. The mutual oath, strongly contrasting with the oaths of subordination, survived in the peace associations and triumphed in the communes. No doubt it is the fate of every system of human institutions never to be more than imperfectly realized. Capitalism was unquestionably the dominant influence on the European economy at the beginning of the twentieth century; yet more than one undertaking continued to exist outside it.

Returning to our feudal map, we find between the Loire and the Rhine, and in Burgundy on both banks of the Saône, a heavily shaded area which, in the eleventh century, is suddenly enlarged by the Norman conquests of England and southern Italy. All around this central nucleus there is an almost regular shading off till, in Saxony and especially in Leon and Castile, the stippling becomes very sparse indeed. Finally the entire shaded area is surrounded by blank spaces. In the most heavily shaded zone it is not difficult to recognize the regions where the regularizing influence of the Carolingians had been most far-reaching and where also the mingling of Romanized elements and Germanic elements—more pronounced here than elsewhere—had most completely disrupted the structure of the two societies and made possible the growth of very old seeds of territorial lordship and personal dependence.

3. A Cross-Section of Comparative History

A subject peasantry; widespread use of the service tenement (i.e., the fief) instead of a salary, which was out of the question; the supremacy of a class of specialized warriors; ties of obedience and protection which bind man to man and, within the warrior class, assume the distinctive form called vassalage; fragmentation of authority—leading inevitably to disorder, and, in the midst of all this, the survival of other forms of association, family and State, of which the latter, during the second feudal age, was to acquire renewed strength—such then seem to be the fundamental features of European feudalism. Like all the phenomena revealed by that science of eternal change which is history, the social structure thus characterized certainly bore the peculiar stamp of an age and an environment. Yet just as the matrilineal or agnatic clan or even certain types of economic enterprise are found in much the same forms in very different societies, it is by no means impossible that societies different from our own should have passed through a phase closely resembling that which has just been defined. If so, it is legitimate to call them feudal during that phase. But the work of comparison, thus involved, is clearly beyond the powers of one man, and I shall therefore confine myself to an example which will at least give an idea of what such research, conducted by surer hands, might yield. The task is facilitated by the existence of excellent studies which already bear the hallmark of the soundest comparative method.

In the dark ages of Japanese history we dimly perceive a society based on kinship groups, real or fictitious. Then, toward the end of the seventh century of our era, under Chinese influence a system of government is founded which strives (exactly as the Carolingians did) to maintain a kind of moral control over its subjects. Finally, about the eleventh century, the period begins which it has become customary to call feudal and whose advent seems (in accordance with a pattern with which we are now familiar) to have coincided with a certain slackening of commercial activity. Here, therefore, as in Europe, "feudalism" seems to have been preceded by two very different forms of social organization; and, as with us, it was profoundly influenced by both. The monarchy, though it had less connection than in Europe with the feudal structure proper—since the chains of vassalage terminated before reaching the Emperor—subsisted, in law, as the theoretical source of all power; and there also the fragmentation of political authority, which was fostered by very old habits, was held to be a consequence of encroachments on the State.

Above the peasantry a class of professional warriors had arisen. It was in these circles that ties of personal dependence developed, on the model furnished by the relations of the armed retainer with his chief; they were thus, it appears, marked by a much more pronounced class character than European "commendation." They were hierarchically organized, just as in Europe; but Japanese vassalage was much more an act of submission than was European vassalage and much less a contract. It was also more strict, since it did not allow plurality of lords. As these warriors had to be supported they were granted tenements closely resembling the fiefs of the West. Some times even, on the pattern of our *fiefs de reprises,* the grant was purely fictitious and involved in fact lands which had originally belonged to the patrimony of the pretended recipient. These fighting men were naturally less and less willing to cultivate the soil, though as in Europe there were to the end exceptional cases of peasant "vavasours." The vassals therefore lived mainly on the rents from their own tenants. There were too many of them, however—far more, apparently, than in Europe—to admit of the establishment for their benefit of real manors, with extensive powers over the people. Few manors were created, except by the baronage and the temples, and being widely scattered and having no demesne, they recalled the embryonic manors of Anglo-Saxon England rather than those of the really manorialized regions of the West. Furthermore, on this soil where irrigated rice fields represented the prevailing form of agriculture, the technical conditions were so different from those of Europe that the subjection of the peasantry assumed correspondingly different forms.

Although far too brief, of course, and too absolute in its appraisal of the contrasts between the two societies, it seems to me that this outline nevertheless enables us to reach a fairly firm conclusion. Feudalism was not "an event which happened once in the world." Like Europe—though with inevitable and deep-seated differences—Japan went through this phase. Have other societies also passed through it? And if so, what were the causes, and were they perhaps common to all such societies? It is for future works to provide the answers.

Notes

1. Montesquieu, *Esprit de Lois*, XXX, I; *Voltaire, Fragments sur quelques révolutions dans l'Inde*, II (ed. Garnier, XXIX), p. 91.
2. G. Lefebvre, *Les paysans du Nord*, 1924, p. 309.
3. For example, E. Lodge, "Serfdom in the Pyrenees," in *Vierteljahrschr. für Soz. und W. G.*, 1905, p. 31; Sanchez-Albornoz, *Estampas de la vida en Leon*, 2nd ed., p. 86, n. 37; Perreciot, *De l'état-civil des personnes*, II, 1786, p. 193, n. 9.
4. Dudo of Saint-Quentin, ed. Lair (*Mém. Soc. Antiquaires Normandie*, XXIII), III 43–4 (933).

Sigmund Diamond   OLD PATTERNS AND NEW SOCIETIES:

VIRGINIA AND FRENCH CANADA

IN THE SEVENTEENTH CENTURY

I

THE HISTORY of sixteenth- and seventeenth-century colonization provides an almost unique opportunity for the study of certain problems in social organization. The very requirement, as in the case of the British and French in North America, to establish settlements "where none before hath stood," or, as in the case of the Spanish in Central and South America, to devise a mode of accommodation with pre-existing societies, imposed the necessity of considering problems of social organization with a clarity and directness rarely before achieved. Nor was this entirely a matter of necessity. The creation of new societies raised thought about appropriate forms of organization to a new level of consciousness, not only because the situation created the need, but also because it created the opportunity. Man had now the possibility, so at least it seemed, of making a fresh beginning. Was it really necessary that he be forever burdened with the residue of the iniquity and folly of past history? Was it not possible to devise a new form of social organization in which at least some of the less desirable characteristics of the old would be eliminated? From consciousness of both necessity and opportunity came the impetus to create forms of social organization appropriate to achieve the ends held by the

Condensed and reprinted from "An Experiment in 'Feudalism': French Canada in the Seventeenth Century," with the permission of the author and publisher from the *William and Mary Quarterly*, Williamsburg, Virginia, January 1961.

leaders of colonization ventures—whether corporations, private individuals invested with almost regal authority, or the crown.

How were the members of the new societies to be recruited? How were they to be motivated to accept the obligations attached to their positions in these new societies? How was order to be maintained between persons of different status? What should be the proper balance among ethic, reward, and sanction in getting persons to behave in the proper fashion? Would the family detach persons from their loyalty to the colonizing organization, or would it increase their satisfaction with their lot in the New World? What special features of social organization would have to be created to accommodate the new societies to sponsorship by joint-stock companies, and how might these be different in colonies undertaken by individuals or by government?

Simply to state these questions is to suggest that implicit in the history of early modern colonization is the problem of planned social action, and that this history may be re-examined with the view in mind of analyzing the discrepancy between the plan for the new society and the actual outcome of the effort to apply the plan. If, as appears to be the case, the effort to plan certain aspects of a social system may have unanticipated effects elsewhere in the system—effects that may negate the very purposes of the planners—an examination of the sources of these unanticipated effects may reveal to us more than we now know of the ways in which the different parts of a society are related, and how that society worked.

II

The conclusions that emerged from the first of our studies may be briefly stated.[1] Virginia in the early seventeenth century is an example of a social system established in accordance with the model of a commercial organization, in which the behavior of the members was expected to be determined entirely by their positions within the organization. At the outset, the planners of the venture sought to strip from people all attributes save the one that really counted in the relationship the Company wished to impose on them— their status in the organization. Behavior was expected to conform to a set of prescriptions, the major characteristic of which was that the rights and obligations of persons depended on their position within the organization. In order, however, to induce persons to accept positions within the organization, concessions—land, marriage, political rights—had to be offered, and no longer could social relations be determined exclusively by the positions persons held within a single system—the organization of the Company. Each concession created a new status, each new status involved the person in a new system of relations, and behavior was determined not by a single position within a single relationship, but by the totality of positions each person held in a network of sometimes complementary, sometimes incompatible relationships. The Company had been faced with the dual task of recruiting a labor force and motivating it to work for the ends it was created to achieve and, at the same time, of maintaining the order and discipline that were essential for its organizational integrity. The solution it adopted for the first problem made it impossible to solve the second, for ultimately the point was reached at which the settlers came to feel that the new relationships in which they were involved were of greater importance than the Company relationship. At that point, they were no longer willing to accept the legitimacy of their organizational superiors, and the burden of achieving order and discipline had now to be borne by a new form of social organization.

Our concern here will be to compare the early history of Virginia with that of French Canada in the seventeenth century; more specifically, it will be to see if the mechanism that was responsible for the transition of Virginia from organization to society—an alteration in the behavior of persons as the unanticipated result of a change in their status—was responsible as well for the failure of French Canada to maintain the forms its planners so ardently desired.

In New France, as in Virginia, the first persistent instrument used to achieve the purposes of colonization was the chartered commercial company. Society was brought to both Jamestown and Quebec in the ships of a commercial company, in both cases for the same reasons and with much the same consequences. The form of organization devised by the company proved incapable not only of balancing the somewhat contradictory objectives of the merchants—and others—who invested and the government which patronized, but even of solving the strictly business problem of recruiting the supplies of capital and labor necessary for the survival of the company. To take but one example, the great Company of One Hundred Associates, the most prominent of several that failed in New France before 1663, undertook by the terms of its charter to transport four thousand settlers between 1627 and 1642. It was, however, unable to devise a form of social organization that could reconcile its own interests in deploying its labor force into the most profitable economic pursuits with the interests of the government in fixing immigrants to the land and in establishing a polity, and with the interests of the population in receiving as many as possible of the rewards for undertaking the hazardous task of bringing society to a wilderness. Colonization under commercial auspices was considered a failure, and with the demise of the company in 1663, it devolved upon the government in France, as it had upon the government in England in the case of the Virginia Company in 1624, to create a more adequate form of social organization. The cost of recruiting a population, of supplying it, of motivating it to work, of defending it against its enemies became a charge upon government and not upon private business.[2]

What followed was a remarkable experiment in creating a society according to plan, an attempt to utilize existing institutions—religion, family, land tenure, law—and to adapt them, under government auspices, to the objectives of the planners and the needs of an immigrant population under frontier conditions. The administrative demands entailed in such an effort were staggering. Hundreds of manuscript volumes of home and colonial decrees and an even larger mass of correspondence, court decisions, and other official documents stand today as mute testimony to the scope of the attempt. What, above all, characterizes the plan is that it bore so clearly the stamp of that passion for rationality—the desire to achieve order, symmetry, and harmony—which is the hallmark of bureaucratic endeavor. It would be anachronistic and yet truthful to describe the objective of the French authorities in Canada after 1663, not as the creation of a society to be governed by political means, but as the creation of an administrative system in which persons would have fixed positions in a table of organization, would behave in the way deemed appropriate for those positions, and would be manipulated, deployed, and disciplined by measures more compatible with the requirements of a formal organization than of a society.

Relying upon the loyalty of their direct subordinates and the self-discipline of the population, the metropolitan authorities aimed at the creation of a society in Canada in which the vast majority of persons would be firmly fixed to the land, would live peaceably in their villages, and would respond obediently to the commands of their superiors. The reins of legitimate power were held firmly in the hands of the administrative authorities and their designated surrogates, and any tendency toward the development of competing authority, even when it conformed to practices already established in France, was rigorously suppressed.[3]

Every aspect of life in Canada was subject to rational calculation and was alterable by purposeful action. Political institutions, the family, Indian affairs, the range of permissible trades and occupations, the amount of prestige and honor to be associated with each particular status in the society were all carefully regulated. The behavior of each major segment of the population was prescribed in the minutest detail, even to the point of regulating the order of precedence in religious and secular ceremonies, the appropriate forms of address, and the types of weapons that each might bear. The total corpus of these regulations betrays the assumption, central to the conception of the administrator, that each person is essentially the occupant of a position in an organization and that his behavior can be made to conform to the needs of the system for order and stability.

In short, what was planned was a society in which all persons would be under a jurisdiction and patronage that were at once French, royal, and orthodox. Stability would be guaranteed by each person's having a precise place and acting in accordance with the behavior defined as appropriate to that place. The elements of this society were, of course, diverse—government regulation of economic activity, a special system of land tenure, an elaborate code of law, an established church, royal patronge of the institution of the family—and every effort was made to weld them together into an organization in which discipline would be achieved because each man would remain loyal to the institutions to which he was attached.

The fur trade, which had been at once a blessing and a curse to the colony, was the subject of endless consideration by government officials. Although the form of regulation varied, the trade was controlled at virtually all times so as to restrict the number and influence of persons engaged in it. The privileged few were thus to be attached to the government with the ties of gratitude that flow from profit, while the mass of the population would not be diverted from the performance of necessary agricultural tasks.[4] The *coureurs de bois* were to be quarantined so that their lawlessness could not contaminate what was hoped would be an obedient agricultural society. Men who desert the land to enter the forests, said Talon, are men "without Christianity, without sacraments, without religion, without priests, without laws, without magistrates, sole masters of their own actions and of the application of their wills . . ."[5]

Population growth, recognized by government officials as indispensable to increasing agricultural production and, at least indirectly, to reducing the overhead costs of administering the colony, was promoted through immigration, encouragement of marriage, family subsidies, and attempts to mobilize the Indians into the labor force. The policy of "Francisation," which included conversion, domiciliation, intermarriage with the Indans, and their education in the ways of the white man, was undertaken in the hope that, made tractable by their re-education, the Indians would swell the labor force. It quickly became evident that the policy had failed, and that population growth would have to come about through immigration and natural increase.[6]

In 1668 Colbert suggested to Talon that those "who may seem to have absolutely renounced marriage should be made to have additional burdens and be excluded from all honors; it would be well even to add some marks of infamy." The Intendant was quick to take the hint; bachelors were barred from the right to hunt, fish, trade with the Indians, and even to enter the woods. By the act of the Sovereign Council of Canada, "any inhabitant having in legitimate marriage ten living children, not priests, *religieux* or *religieuses* shall be paid three hundred livres a year, and those who have twelve shall be paid four hundred livres a year." Fathers whose sons were not married by the age of twenty or whose daughters were still vestals at the age of sixteen were to be fined and summoned to the court every six months.[7]

But to encourage marriage the government would have to take the initiative in providing women, unless it were willing—which it was not—to tolerate "a thousand disorders in the settlements . . . where the women are very glad to have several husbands and where the men cannot get even one wife." Marriage, it was anticipated, would not only increase the birth rate but would lead to a more settled and orderly life.[8] As in Virginia, therefore, the government assumed the responsibility of shipping from France *demoiselles* for the military officers and what pious Mother Marie de l'Incarnation called *"une marchandise mêlée"*—mixed goods—for the ordinary settlers, something more than a thousand altogether.[9]

Still, French Canada's population growth, dependent overwhelmingly upon natural increase and very little upon immigration, lagged far behind that of the British North American colonies and even behind Canadian requirements. As late as 1710 Governor Philippe de Rigaud, Marquis de Vaudreuil, complained that there was not enough labor for the seigniors to cultivate even half their estates; six years later he was recommending that condemned salt smugglers in France be shipped as indentured servants at the expense of the farmers-general. In 1733 Governor Charles de la Boische, Marquis de Beauharnois, and Intendant Gilles Hacquart echoed the complaint: "The scarcity of men and the high wages of both agricultural and urban labor considerably diminish the revenues of landlords and merchants." Despite every effort of a government that exhorted and a people that produced, the population of French Canada amounted to only about 5 per cent of the population south of the St. Lawrence River by the middle of the eighteenth century.[10]

But neither government regulation nor family attachments were, in the view of the French authorities, sufficient to maintain social discipline; religion, too, was counted on to disseminate an ethic calculated to remind each man to keep to his allotted place. From the beginning of New France, the Roman Catholic Church was given major responsibility for enforcing the ban on Protestants in Canada, and the zealousness with which it responded to the task of rooting out unorthodoxy in both its Jansenist and Protestant forms revealed that secular as well as religious discipline was its proper concern. The importance of orthodoxy from the religious viewpoint was self-evident. "On the side of the state," wrote Bishop François Xavier de Laval, "it appears to be no less important. Everyone knows that Protestants in general are not so attached to His Majesty as Catholics . . . To multiply the number of Protestants in Canada would be to give occasion for the outbreak of revolutions."[11]

Doctrinal conflict was minimized, therefore, by screening prospective immigrants, but the Church played a no less significant role in disciplining colonists once they had arrived. The keynote was sounded in a letter from Louis XIV to Bishop Laval: "As I have been informed of your continued care to hold the people in their duty towards God and towards me by the good education you give or cause to be given to the young, I write this letter to express my satisfaction with conduct so salutary, and to exhort you to persevere in it." The nature of this education may be inferred from the list of virtues commended to boys, drawn from the rulebook of the Petit Séminaire in Quebec: "humility, obedience, purity, meekness, modesty,

simplicity, chastity, charity, and an ardent love of Jesus and his Holy
Mother." All schools but one were under control of the church, and that
single exception—the School of Mathematics and Hydrography—passed
under its influence early in the eighteenth century.[12]

In its role as custodian of morals and, though its pretensions in this
area were disputed, of law,[13] the church went even further. It regulated the
style of clothing; it censored books, it established with meticulous accuracy
the order of priority of both religious and secular officials on ceremonial
occasions; it attacked usury and supported its attack by refusing confession
to usurers; it shipped back to France immoral men, including those who were
so unmindful of their situation in life as to fall in love with more highly
placed girls; and it attempted to cultivate an ethic of obligation and obedience, of simplicity and austerity.[14]

Most important of all, however, it threw the weight of ecclesiastical discipline behind the effort to fix the population into assigned positions; the
sanction of excommunication itself was invoked against those who left the
land without permission and traded illegally for furs with the Indians. Although there were disputes between secular and religious officials when
either tried to exercise authority that pinched the other, they were as one in
recognizing the importance of the church in disciplining the inferiors of both,
in urging upon them acceptance of a code of beliefs that would confine their
behavior within the limits desired by higher authority. Finally, in its capacity
as landowner, the church assumed the role of model seignior, and attempted
by the force of its own example to influence the behavior of other landlords. By 1750 the church held over two million arpents of land, more
than one-third of all the grants that had been made.[15]

But the most characteristic institution of the old regime in Canada—
the one that gave tone to the entire society—was the seignioral system. There
was much in it that was reminiscent of medieval feudalism, but only reminiscent. Feudalism in France was an organic growth; in Canada it was a
transplanted institution, and the French administration saw to it that in the
transplanting it was pruned of less desirable characteristics. The French
monarchy had established itself in the teeth of feudal opposition and was in
no mood now to offer the seigniors sufficient independence and power so as to
require repetition of the experience. When Governor Tracy and Intendant
Talon drew up their "Project de Règlement" in 1667, they warned that since
"obedience and fidelity [two words obscured] are more likely to suffer at-
tenuation in distant provinces of the state than in the neighbors of the
Sovereign Authority, which resides mainly in the person of the prince and has
more force and virtue there than in any other person, it is the part of prudence
to prevent in the establishment of the growing state of Canada all those vexa-
tious revolutions which might render it monarchical, aristocratic, or democratic, or even—by a balanced power and authority between subjects—

divide it into parts and give rise to such a dismemberment as France suffered by the creation of such sovereignties within the kingdom as Soissons, Orleans, Champagne, and others."[16] In their concern lies the clue to the essential difference between French and Canadian feudalism. The landed seignior in Canada was entitled to many of the rights possessed by his counterpart in France—potential membership in the nobility; ceremonial rights like fealty and homage; judicial rights like holding private courts; and more lucrative rights such as the collection of rents and mutation fines, the imposition of labor services, and the monopoly of all milling—and the enforcement of these rights was presumably guaranteed by the extension to Canada of the law code known as the Custom of Paris and the beneficent protection of the royal authority. Nevertheless, the position of the Canadian seignior was far different from that of the French.

The right to have a private court was his, but the use of the term *haute, moyenne, et basse justice* in Canada must not delude us into thinking that it held the same meaning as in France. The existence of the competing royal court eventually limited private jurisdiction to relatively simple cases about seigniorial dues and obligations, and even in these the habitant had free right of appeal to the royal court. Nor were the profits of justice as lucrative in Canada as in France; where population was sparse, the opportunity to squeeze income from it in the courts was limited by the small number of cases and by the fear that too much repression would cause the seignior's labor force to move to the lands of a less exacting landlord.

Even the conditions under which he held land and could legitimately demand payments from his sub-infeudees were different from those in France. Squirm though he might, never could the seignior wholly evade the scrutiny of the intendants, who were determined to prevent the payments owed by the *censitaires,* the peasants, from becoming too burdensome. Even more, his power to dispose of his own domain was limited in such a way as to reduce his maneuverability and to make him essentially an agent of the Crown in the achievement of its purposes. After several preliminary gestures, the King, through the Arrêts of Marly in 1711, decreed that all seigniorial grants not settled and developed through sub-infeudation would revert to the Crown, and that the payments to seigniors from sub-infeudated lands must be uniform and limited.

As with the seigniors, so with the *censitaires*. They, too, had rights and obligations differing somewhat from their brothers' in France. They had to clear the land lest it revert to the seignior; they owed him rent and mutation fines; they worked for him and gave him part of their catch of fish; they paid him deference; they were not allowed to engage in the fur trade. Yet, their duties were less onerous than in France, and they were protected from excessive exploitation by a solicitous officialdom. Besides, the prospect of improvement was such, so it was anticipated, as to induce them willingly to accept their position. The seigniorial system in Canada was transformed by the authorities into an agency of land settlement, an instrument for peopling the country, and a mechanism for insuring social stability.[17]

III

How did the system actually work? If long-term stability and social discipline were the objectives desired by the authorities, they were not the objectives attained.

The *sine qua non* of successful colonization was the mobilization of an adequate labor force. In Canada, as in British North America, experiments in the use of forced labor and of the local Indians failed, and it soon became necessary to recruit labor by voluntary means.[18] To do so, however, such substantial concessions had to be made that the real position occupied by the labor force in the new society was utterly different not only from its position in Old World society but even from what the planners of the system had intended.

The companies before 1663 recognized the necessity of offering incentives, but sought to minimize them in an effort to keep costs low. Louis Hébert, the Paris apothecary who became the first settler at Quebec, had been offered full support for himself and his family for a period of two years plus two hundred crowns per year for three years as inducements to emigrate. After he arrived, however, the company imposed harsher terms: he was given only one hundred crowns per year; his entire family and his servant were required to work for the company for three years, after which time he was required to sell all his produce to the company at prices current in France; he could work on clearing his land and building his house only when the chief factor did not need his services; he was not to engage in the fur trade; and he was to offer his professional services free of charge to the company.[19]

Samuel de Champlain had been quick to see that the terms were not sufficiently attractive to encourage immigrants. "The Companies having refused to give them the means of cultivating the land," he wrote, "had thus taken away all reason for them to become settlers. At the same time, these Companies gave out that there were numerous families in the country; the truth is that, being entirely useless, they served only to count, and burdened the settlement more than they helped it. . . . That was not the way to create a great desire on the part of anyone to go and people a country, when a man cannot have any free enjoyment of its returns . . . "[20]

Those who came at their own expense had the promise of land and even, if they performed "notable service" in the interests of the authorities, of titles and patents of nobility. If, as now appears to be the case, most of the *engagés* did not have the promise of land at the time they agreed to their contracts of engagement, many did receive land after completion of their term of service; and, in any case, the wages they could expect in Canada allowed them a substantial increase in living standards.

The net effect of the administration's policy was to introduce slackness rather than rigidity into the society, even to the point of seriously compromising its own ability to obtain revenue. The state *corvée* had to be curtailed, eventually suppressed, for fear that word of its existence would restrict emigration from France and would antagonize the labor force, which, in another capacity, was counted on to provide militia service. The billeting of soldiers, always a source of complaint, was progressively limited until in 1683 it was entirely abolished and became a regular fixed charge upon the state. Direct payments in the form of seigniorial rents and ecclesiastical tithes were reduced considerably below the level prevailing in France.[21] Indeed, *liberté* and *tranquilité*—eventually the major objectives of colonial policy—were seen as attainable only by offering concessions to induce a labor force to migrate and increase its productivity. "Such are the means of attracting colonists and keeping them," wrote M. Petit in his treatise on colonization. "But the most important of all is gentleness and moderation in the government, in extending its hand so that the colonists find, at least in the legitimate use of authority, compensations for the harshness of their labor and the sacrifice of their health in establishments recognized as so useful to the state."[22]

Despite all inducements, the population of Canada never reached the desired quantity and quality. From beginning to end, the reports to the authorities bemoaned the scarcity of labor and its lack of discipline. The problem of maintaining an adequate labor force was made even more difficult by the flight into the wilderness of those who were expected to remain fixed to the land. Throughout the eighteenth century, when the population of able-bodied adult males was always pathetically small, an average of three hundred men were absent each year, won over to the freedom of forest life, deserters to the English, or seekers after their fortune in Louisiana.[23] Above all, however, the problem of disciplining labor and raising its productivity was exacerbated by the refusal of the populaton to behave in an expected manner.

The continued loyalty of the seignior to the system depended on his ability to profit from his privileges, and his privileges were such as to require a large and expanding population. But in Canada, unlike France, land was plentiful and people scarce; and the competition was among seigniors for tenants and not among tenants for land. Even the land system itself conspired against the desire of the authorities to fix people to the land and against the ability of the seigniors to make their living from it. The estates, laid out in parallelograms with the short side fronting on the St. Lawrence River, became split up into ever-narrowing ribbons of farms as, with the passage of time, they were divided among heirs; and agricultural productivity suffered accordingly. Instead of wealth and the grandeur of privileged status, poverty was the lot of most seigniors. "It is necessary to help them," wrote

Denonville to Seignelay, "by giving them the means of . . . livelihood for, in truth, without that there is great fear that the children of our nobility . . . will become bandits because of having nothing by which to live."[24]

What was a bad situation to begin with was worsened by the propensity of many seigniors to adopt a style of life better in accord with their expectations than with realities. "The Gentlemen that have a Charge of Children, especially Daughters," wrote Baron La Hontan, "are oblig'd to be good Husbands, in order to bear the Expence of the magnificent Cloaths with which they are set off; for Pride, Vanity, and Luxury, reign as much in *New France* as in *Old France*."[25] "One finds here no rich persons whatever," Father Pierre F. X. de Charlevoix wrote. "In New England and the other British colonies there reigns an opulence by which the people seem not to know how to profit; while in New France poverty is hidden under an air of ease which appears entirely natural. The English colonist keeps as much and spends as little as possible; the French colonist enjoys what he has got, and often makes a display of what he has not got."[26]

To persist in behaving in New France in ways that were appropriate to Old France was to fly in the face of reality. When the Sieur de Frédéric, captain in the Carignan-Salières regiment and nephew of its colonel, punished a habitant for complaining to the Intendant about injury done to his crops when Frédéric rode over his land, he doubtless felt that the propriety of his behavior could not be impeached. He was, however, returned to France by Intendant Talon.[27] In France, conscience required that sympathy be extended to peasants whose fields were trampled by seigniors. In Canada, the reverse was true: "divers persons so [abuse] the goodness of the seigneurs of this island [Montreal], who allow them such freedom, that they hunt and fish everywhere on the superior's private domain . . . where they kill the pigeons on pretence of their being other game, and break down all the fences, even threatening the overseer, a most worthy man placed there by the seigneur."[28] So widespread was the abuse that the seigniors had to beg the protection of the authorities.[29]

The protection to the ego offered by keeping up appearances at all costs rather quickly reached its limits. Louis Hamelin, the seignior of Grondines, was himself reduced to working his own mill when his miller was called to military service.[30] Even such notable families as Saint-Ours, Verchères, Repentigny, and Aubert de la Chesnaye were impoverished and forced to besiege the King with petitions for military commands, judicial posts, licenses to trade in furs, pensions—anything that might provide income. Others gave up entirely and returned to France.[31] When the owners of the seigniory of Monts-Pelées donated it to the Dames Religieuses de la Miséricorde de Jesus, they wrote wistfully and pathetically: "the present donation is made because the donors find themselves at a very advanced age which does not permit them to work to gain their livelihood and because the little property they have is not sufficient to produce enough income to support them in sickness or in health for the rest of their days; they are, moreover, abandoned by all their relatives and friends."[32] In the circumstances, the seigniors began to behave not as their role prescribed, but as conditions seemed to require.

They violated their obligations to their tenants, attempting to exact from them rights to which they were not entitled. They "grant to their habitants leave to cut timber on the ungranted lands, on condition that they pay 10 per cent of the value of the boards obtained therefrom," Intendant Michel Bégon wrote Victor Marie d'Estrées, president of the Conseil de Marine, in 1716. "When they concede woodlands they reserve for themselves all the oak and pine timber thereon without compensation to the habitants, and they are able to exact any price they please for this wood. . ."[33] They attempted to squeeze more labor through the *corvée* than they were entitled to, made attractive verbal promises to the habitants and then stiffened the terms in writing, induced tenants to clear land for pasture which they later sold, and extorted illegal payments.[34]

Instead of using land for agriculture and settlement, they used it for speculation. Without themselves making any improvements or insisting that their tenants do so, the seigniors, so the local authorities reported to Paris, encouraged the habitants to buy and sell land so that they might collect the mutation fine that went with every change in ownership.[35] "There will always be some people," Intendant Jean Bochart de Champigny informed Minister Louis de Phélypeaux, Comte de Pontchartrain, in 1691, "who will seek land concessions in distant places . . . for the sole purpose of going there to trade . . . without thought of settling."[36]

Instead of doing their duty in the preservation of law and order, the seigniors connived with lawbreakers. Fearful in Canada as in the Antilles that the establishment of too many taverns would distract workmen and increase delinquency, the authorities sought to use the seigniors as direct agents of social control. "The trade of tavern-keeper has attracted all the rogues and lazy people who never think of cultivating the land," Denonville write Seignelay in 1685: "far from that, they deter and ruin the other inhabitants. I believe, Monseigneur, that in the villages, the Seigneur should hire and dismiss the tavern-keeper according to his good and bad conduct, and the Seigneur would be responsible for him. I know of seigneuries where there are only twenty houses and more than half are taverns . . ."[37] But instead of upholding the law against tavern-keepers, they helped them to break it; as, indeed, they helped others also to break the law. "I must not conceal from you," Intendant Jacques Duchesneau wrote Colbert, "that the disobedience of the *coureurs de bois* has reached such a point that everybody boldly contravenes the King's interdictions . . . I have enacted ordinances against the *coureurs de bois;* . . . against the gentlemen . . . who harbor them; and even against those who have any knowledge of them, and will not inform the local judges. All has been in vain; inasmuch as some of the most considerable families are interested in them . . ."[38]

In classic feudalism, institutions and rules existed which empowered the seigniors to compel obedience. Marc Bloch has observed:

Now, in the hands of the seigniors the almost unrestricted exercise of the rights of justice placed an infinitely powerful weapon of economic exploitation. It reinforced their power of command, which in the language of the time . . . was called their "ban." "You can compel us to observe these rules" (those relating to the oven), the inhabitants of a village in Rousillon tell the Templars, masters of the place, in 1246, "even as a seignior can and ought to compel his subjects." . . . Among the multiple applications of this discipline, one of the most significant and, in practice, the most important, was the formation of seigniorial monopolies . . . With very sure instinct, the jurists, when they began in the thirteenth century to create a theory of society, found themselves in agreement in linking the *banalités* with the organization of justice. The right to judge had been the strongest prop of the right to command.[39]

These were the rules and institutions that permitted the seigniors to maintain distance between themselves and the *censitaires* and that compelled the latter to accept the discipline imposed on them. In Canada, these institutions did not exist—or, at least, they existed in a most attenuated form—and it proved impossible to subject *censitaires* to a discipline that implied a far wider distance between themselves and their superiors than in fact was the case. Not only were the seigniors' traditional monopolies emptied of meaning and their authority curbed by the administration, but the *censitaires* now competed directly with them in areas that had once been their private preserve. It was the *censitaires,* not the seigniors, who were appointed to the position of *capitaine des milices,* a post that involved the exercise of civil as well as military authority; and the complaints of the seigniors, faced with declining prestige, were to no avail. "You should," wrote Minister Jérôme de Pontchartrain to Governor François de Galiffet of Three Rivers, "make the seigniors of the parishes in your jurisdiction understand that the *capitaines des milices* must not communicate to them the orders that they receive from the governors and intendants before executing them; that is not due to them and they have no right to demand it of the *capitaines,* who might do so as a matter of courtesy, however, when it is of no interest to the service."[40]

The *censitaires* hunted and fished almost at will, they were occasionally called in to offer advice on government policy, and they were urged to report all "torts, exces, violances" committed by the seigniors.[41] Small wonder, then, they responded to their new situation by surrounding themselves with some of the trappings of the status that had so long been denied them. Though the government appealed to their own self-interest in urging them to concentrate on the production of cattle, pigs, and sheep, and though it imposed ban after ban on the raising of horses, they continued to breed horses and to ride through the countryside, as if in unconscious remembrance of the age-old connection between *cheval* and *chevallerie*.[42]

That the Canadian *censitaire* had ceased to be a French peasant received stunning confirmation in the eighteenth century, but by then time had run out on the French government. Taking pity on those displaced Acadians who had managed to return to France, the government devised a variety of plans to attach them "à la glèbe de France," all of which involved tenurial terms far superior to those of the generality of peasants and at least one of which was drawn up on the basis of the most advanced physiocratic theory. Each attempt to place the Acadians on the land proved a fiasco, for the way in which they had assimilated their own history made them unfit to assume the status of peasant. "I think, really, that the Acadians are mad," wrote the Commissaire Général in 1772. "Do they imagine that we wish to make seigniors of them? The intention of the government is to put them on the level of the cultivators in the provinces where they might be established, giving them the means to subsist by their labor. They seem offended by the fact that we wish to treat them like our peasants."[43]

Instead of obedience to the seignior, there were *mutinerie et l'indépend-ence*. The state, too, on occasion felt the wrath of its citizens,[44] and even the church, though protected by the loyalty of the people to Catholicism, became the target of popular hostility. When Bishop Laval introduced the French tithe into Canada in 1663, the resistance was so widespread that he was quickly forced to offer concession after concession—reduction from one-thirteenth to one-twentieth and finally to one-twenty-sixth; exemption of fish, eggs, timber, and livestock; and a five-year exemption on newly cultivated land. For more than fifty years the conflict raged between church and habitants, and not even the refusal to grant absolution to those who withheld the tithe or who paid in spoiled wheat could quell the "great murmuring at the door of the church." "Many individuals," wrote Duchesneau in 1677, "through plain disobedience . . . and scorn of the church not only refuse to pay the tithes, but are even carried away to the point of violence." As late as 1727 the inhabitants of the parish of St. Antoine-de-Tilly had to be *ordered* by the Intendant to pay their tithes to the curé.[45]

Worst of all, their disobedience took the form of wholesale desertion of agricultural tasks. Despite the severe sanctions imposed by church and state. increasing numbers of people, "excited by the bad example of the *coureurs de bois* and by the profits that they had made," left the field for the forest in search of furs. In the year 1680 approximately one-third of the adult male population had escaped the discipline of society by entering the, fur trade. At no time does the proportion of the adult male labor force engaged in trapping and hunting seem to have been less than one-quarter or one-fifth.[46] Not only did they deplete an already inadequate labor force, but they infect those who remained with the example of their rebelliousness. "We are

Cesars, being nobody to contradict us," said Pierre Radisson, greatest of all the *coureurs de bois*.[47] If his was a self-image too elevated for the many to aspire to, they felt themselves at least to be captains of their own fate. "The genius of the people of New England," Minister Maurepas wrote to Beauharnois in 1728, "is to work hard at cultivating the land and to establish new settlements one after the other . . . The inhabitants of New France think differently. They would like always to move forward without getting tangled up in interior settlements, because they gain more and are more independent when they are more remote."[48] "One part of our youth is continually rambling and roving about," wrote Father Charlevoix, "and . . . it infects them with a habit of libertinism, of which they never entirely get rid; at least, it gives them a distaste for labour, it exhausts their strength, they become incapable of the least constraint, and when they are no longer able to undergo the fatigues of travelling . . . they remain without the least resource, and are no longer good for anything. Hence it comes to pass, that arts have been a long time neglected, and great quantity of good land remains still uncultivated, and the country is but very indifferently peopled."[49]

Litigious, independent, insubordinate, the habitants joined the seigniors in making a mockery of the behavior defined for them. No longer were they willing to act as instruments of those who planned the system; they acted now out of concern for their own survival or improvement. At times, as we have seen, they deliberately violated the norms of their society; at times, they violated them unwittingly because, under conditions of rapid change, it became problematic as to how the norms were to be applied. But the society was turned upside down when its sworn defenders themselves subverted it. "Profit, my dear Vergor, by your place," wrote Intendant François Bigot to Louis Du Pont du Chambon, Sieur de Vergor, commandant of Fort Beauséjour; "trim, lop off; all power is in your hands; do it quickly so that you may be able to come and join me in France and buy an estate near mine." Instead of enforcing the laws against illegal fur traders, the intendants permitted them to carry on and they cut themselves in on the profits. They traded in flat violation of the orders they received from Paris. "Trading is prohibited to persons in office," wrote the President of the Navy Board. "They are placed there only to protect it, not to carry on even the most legitimate, and for the strongest reasons should abstain from dealing in concessions and monopolies that they ought to prevent with all their power . . . What is certain is, that . . . it can only be regarded as criminal on the part of all those who have taken part in it or those who have favored it or even fostered it, and above all for persons employed in the service . . ."[50]

The circle was complete when what had once been regarded as deviance came later to be recognized as the norm. "I believe," wrote Denonville to Seignelay, "that Monseigneur should not determine to cease to give letters of nobility but that it would be well to give them only to those who will . . .

enter into whatever commerce makes a noble in this country." In 1685 the Canadian noblesse—which had been created as the apex of the seignioral system—was allowed without derogation of rank "to engage in commerce by land as well as by sea, to buy and sell goods wholesale as well as retail." Never did the French nobility obtain such blanket permission to trade, and such permission as they did obtain came later than in Canada.[51]

So disrupted had the society become, then, and so profitless to its sponsors, that only the merchants of the seaport towns of France objected when Canada was lost to the British. On February 10, 1763, the very day the Treaty of Paris was signed, Voltaire wrote Étienne François, Duc de Choiseul: "Permit me to compliment you. I am like the public; I like peace better than Canada and I think that France can be happy without Quebec."[52]

IV

The French government was faced with the twofold problem of maintaining order and stability in Canada and of motivating its subjects to perform the tasks given them. It sought to assign each man a status, the behavior of which was defined and regulated; when men behave according to prescription, each can act toward the other with the certainty that his own behavior will be understood and with the expectation that the other's responses will be the appropriate ones. At the same time, however, the government was faced with the necessity of recruiting a labor force, and the means it used involved offering such a variety of concessions and incentives that the position of the labor force in the society that was actually created was utterly different from its position in the society that had been contemplated. The government of France, like the General Court of the Virginia Company of London, was fully conscious of its problems, but—again like the Virginia Company—the solution it adopted for the problem of motivation made it impossible to solve the problem of order. Rigor and severe discipline, the distinguishing characteristics of the first social order in Canada as in Virginia, broke down in the face of the need to recruit a *voluntary* labor force. By her own actions, France created in Canada a social basis for disobedience, a society in which deviance became the only means of survival and of taking advantage of such opportunities as existed.

In a sense, a drama was taking place on the North American continent that had been played out before in Europe. At various times in late medieval and early modern Europe, especially in periods of considerable stress, the seigniors had to offer concessions to their tenants, even to the point of enfranchisement, to prevent, by their emigration to "free" lands, the loss of their labor force. In 1439 the Hospitaliers de la Commanderie de Bure enfranchised their serfs of Thoisy: "all the 'houses and barns which are at the said Thoisy have been burned and destroyed . . . and no one wants to live

. . . in the town . . . in this way everyone withdraws and goes to live in free places.' " In 1628, when the Sire de Montureux-les-Gray, in Comte, freed his serfs, he did not conceal his hope that the "enfranchised village will be 'better inhabited and populated,' and, 'consequently,' that the seigniorial rights 'would produce greater revenue.' "

"Misery was sometimes the creator of liberty," says Marc Bloch.[53] So it undoubtedly was in Europe; in North America, the need to recruit a voluntary labor force was the mother of liberty.

Notes

1. Sigmund Diamond, "From Organization to Society: Virginia in the Seventeenth Century," *American Journal of Sociology,* LXIII (1957–58), 457–475.
2. For the early history of colonization under commercial auspices, see H. P. Biggar, *The Early Trading Companies of New France* (Toronto, 1901), *passim;* George M. Wrong, *The Rise and Fall of New France* (New York, 1928), I, 242–248, 253–255, 361–384; Dorothy A. Heneker, *The Seigniorial Regime in Canada* (n. p. 1927), 49–63; J. M. S. Careless, *Canada: A Story of Challenge* (Cambridge, Eng., 1953), chap. 3; Henri Blet, *Histoire de la colonisation française* (Paris and Grenoble, 1946), 20–26; William B. Munro, *The Seigniorial System in Canada* (New York, London, and Bombay, 1907), 17–22. For a discussion of the relationship between the form of social organization and the objectives of colonization, see Georges Hardy, *Histoire sociale de la colonisation française* (Paris, 1953), 16; S. D. Clark, *The Social Development of Canada* (Toronto, 1942), 1–14; W. T. Easterbrook and Hugh G. J. Aitken, *Canadian Economic History* (Toronto, 1956), 47–48. On devices calculated to increase labor productivity by providing incentives, see Paul-Émile Renaud, *Les Origines économiques du Canada* (Mamers, 1928), 306–309; Compagnie des Iles d'Amérique, "Mémoire sur le Canada," 1666, Archives du Ministère de la France d'Outre-Mer, Ser. F²A, Carton 15, Archives Nationales, Paris. Archives du Ministère de la France d'Outre-Mer is hereafter cited FOM.
3. Renaud, *Origines économiques,* 93; Blet, *Colonisation,* 126–127; Mason Wade, *The French Canadians,* 1760–1945 (New York, 1955), 18–19; Gerard Filteau, *La Naissance d'une nation* (Montreal, n. d.), I, 79–81. ". . . it is to be feared that as a result of engaging in trade the inhabitants will live a good part of the year in idleness, whereas if they had no such freedom to engage in trade it would be necessary for them to apply themselves in cultivating their lands." Colbert to Talon, Apr. 1, 1666, FOM, Ser. C¹¹A, fol. 200. As late as the eve of the final struggle with the British for the mastery of Canada, the King of France was still exhorting his officials to make the progress of agriculture their first concern; see, for example, the extracts from the royal correspondence in *Report Concerning Canadian Archives for the year 1905* (Ottawa, 1906), I, 73, 165, 202.
4. For an excellent summary view of the Canadian fur trade, see Easterbrook and Aitken, *Economic History,* 39–45, 76–78, 87–89, 112–124. See also R. M. Saunders, "Coureur de Bois: A Definition," *Can. Hist. Rev.,* XXI (1940), 123–131; Emile Salone, *La Colonisation de la Nouvelle France,* 2d ed. (Paris, n. d.), 250–261; Clark, *Social Development,* 25–43; Wrong,

New France, II, 541–542; Charles A. Julian, *Les Français en Amérique,* Centre de Documentation Universitaire (Paris, n. d.), II, 26–28.

5. Quoted in Pierre-Georges Roy, ed., *Ordonnances, Commissions, etc., etc., des gouverneurs et intendants de la Nouvelle-France, 1639–1706* (Beauceville, 1924), I, 107–109; Donald Creighton, *A History of Canada* (Boston, 1958), 79; M. Patoulet to Colbert, Jan. 25, 1672, FOM, Ser. C¹¹A, III, fol. 274.

6. Renaud, *Origines économiques,* 226–229; Salone, *Colonisation,* 115–116; R. Mousnier, *Les Européens hors de l'Europe de 1492 jusqu'à la fin du xviie siècle* (Paris, n. d.), I, 129–130.

7. Colbert quoted in Francis Parkman, *The Old Regime in Canada* (Boston, 1922), 287–288. The Council's act is in Arrêt of Apr. 13, 1669, FOM, Ser. C¹¹A, III, fol. 26–29. That Colbert's decree was not entirely a dead letter may be seen from the verdict in the case of François le Noir, of La Chine, summoned before the court on the charge that, though unmarried, he had traded with the Indians. Le Noir confessed, but was released on his promise to marry within three weeks of the arrival of the next ship bringing women from France or payment of a financial forfeit to the church and hospital at Montreal. He lived up to his promise and married Marie Charbonnier of Paris. Parkman, *Old Regime,* 287–288.

8. Frontenac to Colbert, Nov. 2, 1672, FOM, Ser. C¹¹A, fol. 257; Talon to Colbert, Oct. 20, 1667, *ibid.,* II, fol. 316; Wrong, *New France,* I, 394–396.

9. Quoted in Parkman, *Old Regime,* 284. See also Isabel Foulché-Delbosc, "Women of New France," *Can. Hist. Rev.,* XXI (1940), 132–149; Clark, *Social Development,* 52; Munro, *Seigniorial System,* 70–71. For an account of the shipment of these women as it was in historical reality and in the minds of men, see Gustave Lanctot, *Filles de joie ou filles de roi . . .* (Montreal, 1952). Immigration to French Canada 1608–1760 amounted to just over 10,000, while total population reached the 65,000 mark in 1763; *Censuses of Canada, 1665–1871* (Ottawa, 1876), IV, 2–67; see also Georges Langlois, *Histoire de la population canadienne-française* (Montreal, 1934), 59–60; Ivanhoe Caron, *La Colonisation du Canada sous la domination française* (Quebec, 1916), 56–57; Paul Veyret, *La Population du Canada* (Paris, 1953), 10–12. Recent studies indicate that women in Canada did not enter the marriage market much before their sisters in France, but they performed well, once in it. At no time between 1660 and 1770 did the birth rate by decade fall below 47.3 per 1,000, and twice it exceeded 60 per 1,000; Jacques Henripin, *La Population canadienne au début du xviiie siècle,* Institut National d'Etudes Démographiques, Cahier No. 22 (Paris, 1954), 39, 96–101. See also Sr. Pastoulet to Minister Pontchartrain, Nov. 11, 1699, FOM, Ser. C¹¹A, III, fol. 64–65.

10. H. A. Innis, *Select Documents in Canadian Economic History, 1497–1783* (Toronto, 1929), 302, 360; "Pour Peupler et défricher le païs," FOM, Ser. C¹¹A, II, fol. 45ff.; William B. Munro, *Documents Relating to the Seigniorial Tenure in Canada, 1598–1854* (Champlain Society, *Publications,* III [Toronto, 1908]), 151–152; Maurepas to Beauharnois and Claude Dupuy, May 27, 1728, FOM, Ser. D²D, I; Wade, *French Canadians,* 20; Frégault, *Civilisation,* 39. The farmers-general were private contractors to whom the king leased the right to collect taxes in return for a fixed payment to the state.

11. Mémoire of the Bishop of Quebec, 1670, *Collection de manuscrits,* I, 204–

205. See also *Report Concerning Canadian Archives for 1905,* I, 192; Wade, *French Canadians,* 13; Filteau, *Naissance d'une nation,* 169–170; Walter Alexander Riddell, *The Rise of Ecclesiastical Control in Quebec* (Columbia University, *Studies in History, Economics, and Public Law,* LXXIV [New York, 1916]), 44–45, 73–75.

12. Quoted in Parkman, *Old Regime,* 426–427; Riddell, *Ecclesiastical Authority,* 83–84.

13. For a discussion of church-state controversies over such matters as the liquor trade with the Indians, the right of precedence in civil and religious ceremonies, and the like, see, for example, Wrong, *New France,* I, 347–351; Jean Delanglex, *Frontenac and the Jesuits* (Chicago, 1939), *passim;* Parkman, *Old Regime,* 166–168; and the royal instructions to administrators in Canada, *Supplement to Report on Canadian Archives for 1899,* 92, 245, 248.

14. H. Têtu and C. O. Gagnon, *Mandements, lettres pastorales, et circulaires des évêques de Québec* (Quebec, 1887), I, 106–108, 114–115, 167–174, 275–281, 318, 330–331, 334–335, 363–365, 382–384; Roy, ed., *Ordonnances,* II, 328–30; Salone, *Colonisation,* 134–135; Wrong, *New France,* II, 531–532, 538–540.

15. Munro, *Seigniorial System,* 180–181; Salone, *Colonisation,* 314–316; Heneker, *Seignorial Regime,* 197–200. One "arpent de Paris" is equivalent to approximately five-sixths of an English acre.

16. "Projec de règlement fait par M[ess]rs. de Tracy et Talon pour la justice et la distribution des terres du Canada," Jan. 24, 1667, Nouvelles Acquisitions Français, 9271, fol. 60V⁰–61R⁰, Bibliothèque Nationale, Paris. This collection is hereafter cited as NAF.

17. Munro, *Seigniorial System, passim;* Heneker, *Seigniorial Regime,* 142–150; Munro, *Documents,* lxxvii–cxii.

18. H. P. Biggar, comp., *A Collection of Documents Relating to Jacques Cartier and the Sieur de Roberval* (Public Archives of Canada, *Publications,* XXCIII, No. 14 [Ottawa, 1930]); R. M. Saunders, "The First Introduction of European Plants and Animals into Canada," *Can. Hist. Rev.,* XVI (1935), 394–395; Leon Vignols, "La Mise en valeur du Canada à l'époque française," *Revue d'histoire économique et sociale,* XVL (1928), 732.

19. Biggar, *Early Trading Companies,* 105. On early company colonization, see also Wrong, *New France,* I, 242–248; Munro, *Seigniorial System,* 22–27; Salone, *Colonisation,* 55–61.

20. H. P. Biggar, ed., *The Works of Samuel de Champlain* (Champlain Soc., Pubs. [Toronto, 1933]), V, 326–327.

21. Vignols, "Mise en valeur," 780–782.

22. M. Petit, *Mémoires sur l'administration des colonies françaises en Amérique et projets de legislation pour les d. colonies,* Manuscrits Français, 12081, fol. 314–315, Bibliothèque Nationale, Paris. The reason for the government's ban on the arbitrary arrest of habitants was its recognition that the practice was "wholly contrary to the wealth and augmentation of the colonies . . ." Ordinance of May 7, 1679, FOM Ser. C¹¹A, V, fol. 99.

23. Filteau, *Naissance d'une nation,* II, 192–193. For the complaints of the seigniors that the absence of able-bodied men was intensifying the labor shortage, see Duchesneau to Colbert, Nov. 13, 1681, FOM, Ser. C¹¹A, V, fol. 298.

24. Quoted in Clark, *Social Development,* 72.
25. Quoted in *ibid.,* 71.
26. Quoted in Parkman, *Old Regime,* 459–460.
27. Talon to Colbert, Oct. 1667, FOM, Ser. C¹¹A, II, fol. 318–319. "On the judgment that the King will pass on the conduct of this officer depends the security and tranquillity of the colonists of Canada," Talon added.
28. Dollier de Casson, *A History of Montreal, 1640–1672,* trans. Ralph Flenley (London, Toronto, and New York, 1928), 29.
29. Roy, ed., *Ordonnances, I,* 183–184, 224–226; Arrêt of July 6, 1676, FOM, Ser. C¹¹A, IV, fol. 148–149. For the effect of the poverty of the Canadian sengnors in weakening their position against the church, as compared with the French seigniors, see E. R. Adair, "The French-Canadian Seigneury," *Can. Hist. Rev.,* XXXV (1954), 201–204.
30. Heneker, *Seigniorial Regime,* 192.
31. "Demands des officiers, 1696," FOM, Ser. D²C, XLIX, foll. 33–38; List of petitions, FOM, Ser. D²D, I, foll. 18–19; List of petitions, 1694 et seq., FOM, Ser. C¹¹A, CXX, foll. 1–200; Salone, *Colonisation,* 233–234, 236–237, 310–313.
32. Pierre-Georges Roy, ed., *Inventaire des concessions en fief et seigneurie . . . ,* Archives de la Province de Québec (Quebec, 1927–29), III, 158.
33. Quoted in Munro, *Seigniorial System,* 135.
34. Vignols, "Mise en valeur," 745–747; Munro, *Documents,* 153–156, lxxvii–lxxix, Salone, *Colonisation,* 360–361; Heneker, *Seigniorial Regime,* 125–430.
35. Munro, *Documents,* 169–174, liv–lix, lxxix–lxxxii; Heneker, *Seigniorial Regime,* 186–188.
36. Quoted in Clark, *Social Development,* 66.
37: Quoted in *ibid.,* 60. See also Leon Vignols, "Les Antilles françaises sous l'ancien régime: les cabarets et leurs grands protecteurs," *Revue d'histoire économique et sociale,* XV, (1927), 359–365; Roy, ed. *Ordonnances, I,* 86–88, 200–201.
38. Nov. 2, 1679, FOM, Ser. C¹¹A, V, fol. 38.
39. Marc Bloch, *Les Caractères originaux de l'histoire rurale française* (Paris, 1955), I, 82–84.
40. Quoted in Frégault, *Civilisation,* 176–177. See also *Report Concerning Canadian Archives for 1904,* Appendix K, 59; Filteau, *Naissance d'une nation,* I, 89–90; Benjamin Sulte, "The Captains of Militia," *Can. Hist. Rev.,* I (1920), 241–245.
41. Roy, ed., *Ordonnances, I,* 83–84; Wrong, *New France,* II, 646–651; *Supplement to Report on Canadian Archives for 1899,* 71; Ordinance banning arbitrary arrest of habitants, May 7, 1679, FOM Ser. F³, V, fol. 234–235.
42. "Extrait du mémoire au Beauharnois et Hocquart," Apr. 22, 1732, FOM, Ser. F³, XII, fol. 16; Vignols, "Mise en valeur," 758.
43. Quoted in Ernest Martin, *Les Exiles acadiens en France au xviiiᵉ siècle et leur établissement en Poitou* (Paris, 1936), 85–86. For indirect evidence of the improvement in the position of the French peasant in Canada, arguing from population theory, see John T. Krause, "Some Implications of Recent Work in Historical Demography," *Comparative Studies in Society and History,* I, (1958–59), 164–188.
44. Frégault, *Civilisation,* 69, 165.

45. A. L. Burt, "The Frontier in the History of New France," Canadian Historical Association, *Annual Report* . . . *1940* (Toronto, 1940), 96–97; "Inventaire des documents concernant l'église du Canada sous le régime français," *Rapport de l'archiviste* . . . *de Québec pour 1940–41* (Quebec, 1941), 402; Roy, ed., *Ordonnances*, I, 213, 70–74, 177–178; Têtu and Gagnon, *Mandements*, I, 47, 160–161, 275–281, 491–492. See also Filteau, *Naissance d'une nation*, I, 163; "Inventaire des documents concernant l'église," *Rapport de l'archiviste de Québec, 1939–40* (Quebec, 1940), 205, 218, 245; *ibid.*, *Rapport de l'archiviste de Québec, 1941–42* (Quebec, 1942), 182, 251, 261, 273; *Supplement to Report Concerning Canadian Archives for 1899,* 362; *Report Concerning Canadian Archives for 1904,* Appendix K, 140–141; Ordinances of Tracy and Talon, Aug, 23, Sept. 24, 1667, FOM, Ser. F³, III, foll. 349–352; Arrêt de Conseil Supérieur de Québec, Nov. 18, 1705, *ibid.*, VIII, foll. 390–391; Requests of habitants to reduce tithes, *ibid.*, CXLII, foll. 56, 69–71; Ordinances forbidding insults to the clergy, Oct. 23, 1730, *ibid.*, XI, fol. 343; "Requête des habitants du Canada," FOM Ser. C¹¹E, II. fol. 18; Duchesneau to Seignelay, Nov. 13, 1680, FOM, Ser. C¹¹A, V, foll. 177–179.

46. Instructions of the King to Governor Louis Hector de Callières, May 25, 1699, in *Collection de manuscrits*, II, 323; Langlois, *Population canadienne-française*, 81–84, 246; Filteau, *Naissance d'une nation*, II, 128–131; Frégault, *Civilisation*, 91–95. "I desire you to use all the authority of your office to put an end to hunting and to punish in accordance with the full rigor of my ordinances all those who are captured while hunting. . ." Louis XIV to Duchesneau, June 2, 1680, FOM Ser. C¹¹A, V, fol. 209.

47. Quoted in Creighton, *Canada*, 82.

48. Quoted in Frégault, *Civilisation*, 118.

49. Quoted in Clark, *Social Development*, 47. See also, "Mémoire attribué à Raudot," FOM, Ser C¹¹A, CXXII, foll. 82–83. A similar development took place in Louisiana. Marcel Giraud, *Histoire de la Louisiane française*, I, (Paris, 1953), 136–138, 207, 213–214, 265–266.

50. Quoted in Wrong, *New France*, II, 827; *Report Concerning Canadian Archives for 1905,* I, Pt. vi, 289–290. See also Delanglez, *Frontenac*, 200–207; Francois Xavier Garneau, *History of Canada*, trans. Andrew Bell, 3d ed. (Montreal, 1866), I, 546–547; Clark, *Social Development*, 64.

51. Quoted in Clark, *Social Development*, 72; Royal Decree, Versailles, May 1, 1685, NAF, 9328, fol. 75; Marc Szeftel, "La Règle de vie exemplaire des nobles et l'évolution sociale de la France de l'ancien régime," *Revue de l'Institut de Sociologie*, XVL (1936), 607–608. See also A. Couillard-Desprès, *La Noblesse de France et du Canada* (Montreal, 1916).

52. M. Devèze, *Histoire de la colonisation française en Amerique et aux Indes au xviiiᵉ siècle*, Centre de Documentation Universitaire (Paris, n. d.), 78–79.

53. The quotations are from Bloch, *Caractères originaux*, I, 113–114. For similar conditions in Germany, see James Westfall Thompson, "East German Colonization in the Middle Ages," *American Historical Association, Annual Report* . . . *1915* (Washington, 1917), 140; Geoffrey Barraclough, *The Origins of Modern Germany* (Oxford, 1949), 276–277. See also F. L. Carsten, *The Origins of Prussia* (Oxford, 1954), 38, 40, 68, 80, 83; G. F. Knapp, *Die Bauernbefreiung und der Ursprung der Landarbeiter in den älteren Theilen Preussens* (Leipzig, 1887).

Norman Jacobs   MODERN CAPITALISM AND JAPANESE
DEVELOPMENT

JAPAN AFTER 1868 fulfils the criteria of a modern, industrial capitalist society. That is to say, Japanese capitalism is a distinctive social and economic organization differing from what preceded it. Among its characteristics are the control of production and marketing under the ownership and operation of capitalists or their agents, in a process of continuous production directed toward the attainment of rational profit. This point is of importance for all institutional areas, but we explore the question most thoroughly in connection with the aspect of exchange and property. Modern industrial capitalism is not characteristic of the modern occident alone.

In so far as values can be isolated and correlated with behavioral norms, no system of values which positively favored modern capitalism *as such* can be said to have existed in Japan prior to the mid-nineteenth century. On the contrary, all the contemporary subjective systems of behavior, even if they were not concerned with problems other than capitalism, were directed to extolling behavior patterns which were the very opposite of capitalist behavior.

The question of whether or not Japan, under these circumstances, developed capitalism *spontaneously* has been discussed ever since the promulgation of Max Weber's theory. Before this issue is taken up, we must observe that the comparison must not be in terms of the structure of capitalism which existed in western Europe at the time when Japan belatedly developed capitalism in the nineteenth century. Rather, it is western Europe at the inception of capitalist organization which may legitimately be compared with the Japanese capitalism of that period. It is the *type of social and economic organization, not the stage of technological development,* that determines the answers to the question with which the present study deals.

The school which believes that capitalism was of spontaneous generation in Japan points first to the introduction of iron and the beginnings of a modern iron industry at Hirado, replacing both the earlier technology and the antecedent systems of industrial organization. Moreover, by 1850 (that is, before the introduction of the western influence) the traditional domestic system was being replaced in certain instances with production based on futures, in units employing up to a hundred people, and utilizing a modern banking system for credit and investment.

Condensed and reprinted with the permission of the author and the publisher from *The Origin of Modern Capitalism and Eastern Asia* by Norman Jacobs, Hong Kong University Press, Hong Kong, and Oxford University Press, New York, 1958.

Those who maintain on the other hand that modern capitalism as we know it is a foreign importation into Japan, can demonstrate that the pre-1850 development just referred to affected, at most, only a small proportion of the population; that it was predominantly a domestic system, replaced by western machinery and techniques only after 1850; and that it was this later organization which determined the capitalist nature of modern Japan. Even today a large part of Japanese industry is based on the techniques of the older system.

Reverting to this question later, we wish only to state at this point that to argue the problem of the origins and development of modern capitalism in terms of the criteria and the manner of posing the question proposed by Weber, is to emphasize only one aspect, out of several—and not the most telling aspect, in our view.

A preferred point of departure is the fact that Chinese society did not develop modern capitalism but only succeeded in introducing certain technological, not sociological, capitalistic innovations into the social structure. Whether there be "spontaneous generation" or not, not all societies *accept* capitalism, even when that capitalism "knocks at the door," as Weber and others allege.

The criteria and method for differentiating capitalist and non-capitalist societies must therefore be other than the traditional ones. The solution here suggested is, in respect of method, to distinguish pre-capitalist or noncapitalist societies into at least two discontinuous types of social systems; and seek criteria to determine whether or not pre-capitalist societies *can* or *cannot* develop capitalism. The question of whether or not Japan did or did not develop capitalism spontaneously is thus converted into the question of whether Japan and China could or could not develop it in the first instance, and why.

Our conception of modern capitalism, in the spirit of Weber, continues to be that of a system which is not universal in time or place, and hence not due to human nature in a cultural stage of development. It continues to be, moreover, that of a system of social and economic organization and not a system of technology alone. On the other hand, it is now not primarily that of a system differing in degree from all pre-capitalist social and economic organization, but of one which (like true pre-capitalist organization) differs primarily in *kind* from all those systems which do not (and in our view cannot) develop capitalism.

On both logical and methodological grounds, this difference has been demonstrated to be due to a difference in *positive* values. On logical grounds alone, it cannot be considered sufficient to demonstrate a connection (in our terms a functional relationship) between values and empirical behavior in one instance, and to conclude from that that the absence of those values implies the absence of the connected behavior; for, in simple logical terms, the behavior may arise from other causes or origins. On methodological grounds, we maintain that social systems which do not develop capitalism are distinctly and positively different *in kind even in their pre-capitalist stage* from social systems which do develop capitalism.

The positive values referred to are a series of interdependent propositions. In a society which develops modern capitalism these are present *prior* to the inception of that capitalism; in a system that does not develop capitalism, they are totally *absent* and are *replaced* by *equivalent* non-capitalist and anti-capitalist propositions of a positive kind.

As these values define *possibility,* and refer equally to the pre- and post-capitalist phases of the societies which do develop capitalism, they are not original and coincident with the inception of modern capitalism. Moreover, they cannot be linked to a system of religious values alone. Historically, the religious values of Japan in the mid-nineteenth century, if they can be related to non-religious behavior at all, were concerned with the problem of the establishment of a modern centralized state. Capitalism was useful in this, and capitalism found the State-Centralization move useful to it; but there is no positive logical link between Japanese religion and the rising capitalist forces as such.

Historically, Japan did not break with traditionalism in the development of modern capitalism. Rather capitalism fitted into the traditional social structure, breaking that pattern only in so far as was necessary to carry out the functions of capitalism. The present study's system of positive values does not stipulate that the absence of traditionalism is a criterion for the presence of modern capitalism in a particular society. Rather it is a certain difference in *kind* between two or more societies, even if those societies are traditional, that determines the possibility of whether or not they will or will not develop capitalism.

Also, contrary to the usual analysis, feudalism is not the arch enemy of capitalism, but happens (speaking perhaps chiefly historically, not so much out of logical necessity) actually to be the earlier phase of those societies which do develop capitalism. From the standpoint of the origins of the possibility of capitalism, the underlying generalized value systems of both feudalism and capitalism are identical, as contrasted with those of the societies which do not develop capitalism.

Max Weber and others state that the formal difference between feudal gilds and capitalist commercial organs is of the essence in determining the rise of modern capitalism. That is, weak Chinese gilds are interpreted as facilitating the possibility of capitalist organization, since their very weakness made it easier for the anti-gild economic forces to destroy them. In contrast, the strong feudal gilds and their entrenched power impeded the rising capitalist and his market control. The two systems of analysis and interpretation are based on identical empirical data.

In shifting the focus of the analysis it is not attempted here to "refute" Weber; it is not desired to discuss what are or are not the positive criteria for the spontaneous generation of modern capitalism. The present writer believes there was spontaneous generation of capitalism in Japan, but does not pursue the question, considering that on that basis it is not possible to adequately account for both the Japanese case (and with it the case of western Europe) and the Chinese case. There is obviously a diversity of cultural backgrounds between Japan and western Europe, with respect to religion; and an absence of positive and indigenous capitalist values in Japan at the period of inception. These are cornerstones of Weber's theory. It is not possible, on this basis, simultaneously to account for the absence of capitalism in China.

In order to establish our value system for determining similarity and difference, we have therefore to pose a novel criterion and method, not only for the overall analysis but also in the various elements. Recourse is to the hypothesis of a certain school of sociological thought which has attempted to establish at least two basic society-types which are discontinuous and have no temporal relationship with each other, in contrast to the "stage" theory of nineteenth-century sociology.

It is an irony that the origins of this school of thought may be found in the Chinese sections of Weber's work. There, he interprets religious values in the broader sense of the "sacred," covering the values underlying all aspects of Chinese society, not just religious values in the narrow technical definition. But, as often in Weber's works, this is in the form of random or implicit observations, not in a systematic presentation of Chinese society as a whole. It is to the credit of Professor K. A. Wittfogel, a student of Weber, that the general theory of these principles has been tentatively systematized into what Wittfogel has termed the "oriental mode of production" or "oriental society." In this interpretation, China would be an example of an oriental society, and modern western Europe and Japan would be included in another discontinuous society-type.

In the present study, Japan has been selected as the example of one type, of which western Europe is a member, and China as the example of a so-called "oriental" type. The conclusions for Japan can be transferred directly as conclusions for the origins and development of western European capitalism, and the conclusions on China may be applied to another similar type of society (e.g., India). Thus we have established formulations generalized enough to be universally applied (Japan and western Europe versus China in particular) yet specific enough to be meaningful in terms of one concrete society (Japan or any society in western Europe versus China or India, etc.)

The positive values which are the prerequisites for the absence or (potential) presence of capitalism in the two social systems may be summarized as follows:

CHINA   JAPAN

1. Exchange and Property

is characterized by an ethically accepted assumption that production and exchange are to be substantively manipulated in the name of public service, through either ownership or interference by a ruling authority.

is characterized by control of production and exchange dispersed among a number of independent, semi-autonomous economic groupings, such that cooperation and coordination are necessary to maximize economic development.

2. Authority

is characterized by the assumption that the right to public office is determined by moral and intellectual considerations, and that office is monopolized by a self-asserted elite, oriented to the fulfillment of the needs of the people.

is characterized by an ability successfully to administer and coordinate independent, politically oriented groupings.

3. Occupation

is characterized by a differentiation (determined by an elite) of certain roles in the division of labor as honorable and other roles as dishonorable.

is characterized by the assumption that all roles in the division of labor are honorable, though not all roles are privileged.

4. Stratification

is characterized by honorable roles alone being entitled to corporate protection of economic-political rights and privileges.

is characterized by all occupational groupings being able to assert, and possibly win, corporate protection of rights and privileges.

5. Kinship

is characterized by the forced division of landed property among all male heirs.

is characterized by the descent of landed property through one male heir (feudal) or the separation of property and status (industrial).

6. Religion

is characterized by concern with man's external adjustment to the social order, determined by, and administered entirely by an elite.

is characterized by concern with man's inner, personal adjustment to an other-world order, administered by a number of competing religious associations.

7. Integration and Stability

is characterized by monopoly of the sanction to determine an integrated and stable social order, in the hands of an elite.

is characterized by the sanction for an integrated and stable social order in the hands of the agency which manifests ability to solve the existing problem of order (that is, political coordination and control).

It is not implied that the absence of the values and the correlated behavior in one system means their presence in the other system.

Though we have departed in many instances from Max Weber's position, especially on the most crucial point—the interrelation of ascetic Protestantism and the origins of modern capitalism—the overall structure of the present study is definitely derived from Weber's sociology of religion and his other works. The point is to find the best utilization of the master's teachings.

Thus, the historical-comparative method which makes use of Far Eastern materials, enables us to arrive at conclusions which are more generalized, universal and valid than those to be drawn by remaining bound to the experience of western Europe, or to so-called primitive societies elsewhere, in which crucial points of social organization are not available for comparison, and are therefore overlooked, or surrendered to "human-nature" or "advanced-society" interpretations.

The Far Eastern data may be of great value not only from the standpoint of adjusting conclusions, but also that of adjusting theory and method. For example, difference between societies is not, analytically, just a matter of cultural difference. An autonomous, logically "pure," sociological approach is legitimate and empirically worthwhile. The social evolutionists' dogma of a unilinear society, unfolding in stages, has no universal validity on either logical or empirical grounds; it is based on quantitative, i.e., nonsocial criteria, either cultural or technological. Novel sociological concepts and methods may be more useful in a comparative analysis, so that significant differences and similarities may be brought out in relief, in the light of new questions. Some of these concepts and tools are suggested in the present study; particularly the concepts of "honor" and "dishonor," and the method of the corporate analysis of class.

Finally, not only are the Far Eastern data of definite utility to the general field of sociology, but sociology (not simply social history), in its turn, is of definite utility to the Far Eastern discipline. The present study has attempted to resolve a problem which is very familiar to the Far Eastern specialist—the question why modern capitalism developed in Japan and not in China. The implications of the problem and the solution are of great significance to the contemporary observer of the Far Eastern scene faced with such questions as what relationship Chinese communism may bear to the traditional social structure of China.

Bryce Ryan   SOCIAL VALUES AND SOCIAL CHANGE IN CEYLON

CEYLON IS IN MANY RESPECTS the most developed country of South Asia. Its international credits arise from an efficient plantation sector; it is a nation of literates, with a reasonably informed electorate, excellent transportation and communication facilities, and a low death rate. Yet outside the tea economy, largely in British hands, Ceylon has not moved rapidly toward either industrialization or efficient agriculture. With a majority of the population in peasant villages, Ceylon imports most of her food requirements. Natural increase is close to three per cent, among the world's highest, while growth in the economy is faltering and retarded.[1] To escape absolute decline in living levels and a rising death rate, Ceylon has no alternative; the economy must be rationalized—and very rapidly. Optimism is not justified by events. It is the thesis of this paper that one significant retarding force lies in an institutionalized value cluster relating to status, achievement and work. Reference will be confined to the Sinhalese, the predominant ethnic group in Ceylon.

The historic status-achievement-work value matrix in Ceylon is nourished by the institutions of government, education, marriage, social class and caste. Its basic character may be described in the following five propositions:

1. Wage employment and entrepreneurial activity, except cultivation, in any private concern is grossly inferior in status to equivalent work within the governmental institution.

2. Work or productivity as such is without normative significance; hence, idleness and unproductive work or activity lack negative moral flavor.

3. Manual employment other than agriculture, even when not vocational, is generally degraded.

4. Thrift, and savings, are typically directed toward consumption rather than investment.

5. Wealth in land is more honorable and secure than is any alternative form of capital investment.

It may not be argued that the Sinhalese are less achievement motivated than most other peoples. Rather, their values have yielded a type of achievement motivation which is dysfunctional in the contemporary setting.

Studies of occupational prestige consistently demonstrate the high valuation of government service and the low valuation of self-employment and employment in private industry.[2] When village school children rated different

This paper, slightly abridged for this edition, was read at the 54th Annual Meeting of the American Sociological Association in Chicago, 1959.

occupations on a scale of 0–100, the government doctor was rated 81, the private medical practitioner, 61. Of 38 occupations, the government doctor ranked second, the doctor in private practice ranked eighth. A chief clerk in a government department ranked fourth and an average clerk tenth. An average clerk in an insurance company ranks seventeenth. Menial occupations show similar differences.

In a study of vocational preferences and ambitions, T. L. Green queried a large sample of youth in four provinces.[3] In the urbanized Western Province only 75 per cent of the boys expressed a preference for government employment. Elsewhere the desire was stronger. Many had no very specific vocational objectives beyond this. In the writer's study of a peasant village, also in the most urbanized region, over 90 per cent of the fathers chose similarly for their sons.[4] Murray A. Straus, studying Ceylon University entrants, found that 2 per cent of the men wished to enter business.[5] None expressed an interest in Ceylon's major industry, planting. Nearly two-thirds cited some government employment and others planned on professional careers in government related activities, e.g., law. For most university students in any field, an academic career has been in vain if it does not culminate in a government job. Entrepreneurial pursuits other than landed proprietorship are usually viewed with feelings which range from distaste to disgust.

In villages, buying cheap and selling dear is akin to cheating ones kinsmen and neighbors. In the city it is crass and undignified, especially for an educated person. An honors graduate of Ceylon University, asked by his father if he wished to take over his lucrative business, observed: "How would I ever hold my head up again when I walked down the street and heard people whisper, 'there goes John Singho, Bachelor of Arts, Mudalali' " (businessman). The excellent University of Ceylon has never recognized business administration or management as a field of study. Nor, so far as I am aware, had the suggestion of a chair of business administration ever been seriously made until 1957 when the Ceylon Chamber of Commerce went on record favoring it.[6]

Whenever work must be done, Sinhalese can work very hard but in no kind of endeavor is there a feeling that productive activity is itself ennobling, dignifying or spiritually enriching. There is no feeling for "the calling." There is little feeling for enjoyment in work itself and hence it is not surprising that high proportions of youth simply do not care what they do just so long as it is white collar and in government service. Even few university students have strong vocational interests in a Western sense. Where such interests exist they are likely to be frustrated by a hiring policy in which type of training means less than achievement in liberal education generally, outside of certain highly technical areas.

Attitudes toward productive investment are equally dysfunctional in a situation requiring rapid economic growth, especially in the absence of a satisfactory relationship formula between private capital and public finance.[7]

This attitude has to do with investment of effort as well as money. Commonly a farmer will not use available techniques to enhance production if they involve more labor. Frequently this has been related to an iniquitous tenant system, but not always.[8] Likewise dysfunctional is the attitude toward savings, which tend to be viewed in terms of future consumption, retention for dowry, or family crisis. When peasants were asked how they would treat a windfall of 500 rupees, only about one-third cited anything like capital improvement, or investment.[9]

While the status-achievement-work ethos here described would seem to be weaker than previously, it is yet a force supported by existing institutions. In an island which has been under European domination and influence for four centuries these values may seem surprising. For a fuller understanding, let us consider the impact of colonial rule upon the indigenous value system.

The traditional status system can be viewed as a hierarchical series of ascribed situses within which achievement was possible.[10] The situses themselves held differing prestige positions. Caste membership was purely ascribed and it conditioned the achievement of family and feudal honors. Thus the status-laden names of Sinhalese families reflect achieved honors befitting caste but these honors once achieved often come to give hereditary prestige. The character of high caste names is indicative of the indigenous achievement system.[11] Bandaranayaka might mean "great treasurer of the kingdom"; and among Ge or "clan" names, "keeper of the king's storehouse," "scribe," and "chief scribes," are lines of high status today. According to Reimers, honorific names were taxed and they made significant contribution to the island's revenue.

Robert Knox, an English captive of the Kandyan king from 1660 until his escape in 1679, gives us a detailed account of the virtually untouched interior.[12] He says that achieved honors were graded by the caste of the aspirant, and that the drive to achieve must have been intense, at least among the relatively high born. Knox reported that the king frequently elevated to high office those whom he intended to soon "cut off." "Howbeit altho they know and see this before their eyes daily, yet their hearts are so haughty and ambitious, that their desires and endeavours are to ascend until the highest degrees of honour: tho that be but one remove from Death and utter Destruction. And the Women's ambition is so great also, that they will put their Husbands on to seek for Preferment urging how dishonorable it is for them to sit at home like Women, that so they may have respect, and be reputed for great Ladies."[13]

Despite hazards, higher office also brought landed estates under vassalage to the King. In the mid-nineteenth century, Tennent noted that even then the economic ambition of a Kandyan chief was not to mass property but to acquire land; "and land is prized not for produce, as represented by its value in money, but in proportion to the number of retainers and dependents it will feed."[14]

If the record demonstrates immense concern with achievement and its symbolic accoutrements, it gives no hint that economic enterprise or work was ever a route to prestige, nor that the accumulation of wealth was much sought after. Knox, and many after him, remarked upon the infinite capacity of the Sinhalese to absorb leisure while opportunity knocked and knocked.[15] The early trade of Ceylon seems to have been concentrated in the hands of Arab traders. And even Knox, the captive, had no difficulty in setting himself up as a hatmaker and peddler among his captors and profiting rather handsomely by enterprise which few or none cared to emulate.

While there was indeed honorable work outside the king's appointment, this did not include profit making, hired employment of any kind, or any hand-dirtying occupations other than agriculture. Working for hire seems to have been institutionalized in caste alongside the most degraded occupations. Most nongoverning occupations other than agriculture were linked with low caste status. There was no merchant caste within the hierarchy.

The Portuguese entered the Ceylon Low Country in the early years of the sixteenth century bent upon salvation of the heathen, and the spice trade. It was the handful of Muslim traders who recognized their threat far more than the Sinhalese.[16] Low Country chiefs were mollified by assurances that the ancient customs and their own prerogatives would be protected. The Portuguese, and to a considerable extent the Dutch after them, largely accepted the social order as they found it. The Europeans fitted hand-in-glove into the established feudal and caste hierarchy. Even those natives who might have wished to trade were hindered by the Dutch monopolies.[17] The new rulers were gratified to find that native leaders demanded little pecuniary reward so long as magnificent titles and medals were granted them and their ancestral powers remained undisturbed. Neither the Dutch nor the Portuguese, however, succeeded in taming the interior provinces and even the conquering British found the Kandyans intransigent.

Entering Ceylon at the start of the nineteenth century, the British were plagued by "British conscience" and a false certainty that all men desired to better their condition.[18] Feudalism for the first time did not provide a long range pattern for exploitation. On expropriated land, opened up by a retained forced labor system (*rajakaraya*), the British established a capitalistic plantation industry. It was expected that a competitive labor force would develop in a thriving market economy. But the British reckoned without regard for the Sinhalese ethos. These natives performed miserably, according to the standards required by nineteenth-century economic theory, and Ceylon must have made a notable contribution to the stereotype of the indolent native lying open-mouthed under the laden fruit tree. This is precisely how the "natives" behaved when confronted with a competitive economy based on profit making, capital accretion and hired labor. To work for money involved motivations foreign to them, as well as a punctuality and regimentation which conflicted with their own loosely structured standards. Labor for the coffee and later the tea plantations was imported from India to create one of the substantial minorities of contemporary Ceylon, the Indian Tamil.

Tennent in 1846 observed that pecuniary motivation failed to inspire even fishermen, although they were in fact enmeshed in the market economy. He demonstrated that the reduction and eventual abolition of the fish tax resulted not in greater income but, "contrary to principles of political economy," in reduced catches.[19]

To be sure, the British did not consistently encourage local enterprise. The early taxes on production and on immovable property and the virtual expropriation of vast land tracts for British corporate development were not calculated to shift many Sinhalese into productive endeavor.[20] But, in fact, whenever the British moved in opposition to the established status hierarchy they met trouble. And with their own interests intimately bound to plantation development and very little involved with the economy of the village, the part of wisdom was to forget the model of the economic man and utilize the values and motivations which really worked in this unusual climate. The British required little of the natives beyond continued tranquillity, since their concern was chiefly with plantation production for export worked by a tame transported labor force.[21]

Under British rule the status system was modified and a money economy spread. But the Sinhalese obsession with honorable office, clerical employments, and prestige symbolism were useful while their continued lack of enterprise affected British plans mainly in that it reduced the threat of indigenous competition. While European planters and businessmen offered a model for the Sinhalese, it was not a model which many could find applicable to themselves. On the other hand, a British gentry turned civil servant was within their ken.

The autobiography of Solomon Dias Bandaranaike, father of the late Prime Minister, is much to the point here.[22] He was Maha Mudaliyar (Chief Chief) for thirty-two years, serving jointly as ADC to eight consecutive British governors. Solomon Dias Bandaranaike's *Remembered Yesterdays* recounts a life seemingly spent largely in celebrating royal visitors, soothing troubled countrymen, attending coronations, and racing horses. What Governor North wrote of the Maha Mudaliyar in 1798 was no less true in 1907:

Every order I give him is executed, and whatever takes place on the Island is communicated by him to me. The only pecuniary rewards which he and the inferior Moodliars look to from the government are small *accomodessaos*. Their great object is to gain marks of distinction such as sabres, gold chains, medals, etc. . . .[23]

In the late British period, as in earlier times, the lesser folk might aspire to scribeships and inspectorships. Nowhere has clerkdom been more hallowed than under the colonial government, nor more omnipresent. Even the lowly errand boy received a flaming sash and great badge of office—and a pension too. Sir Emerson Tennent in 1847 fulminated at the army of useless clerks in government service.[24] On a visit to one provincial capital he found that all clerks in the establishment were engaged in writing eight thousand copies of pay lists in quadruplicate in order to close the accounts of a recently deceased road officer. No one so far as I know has yet reported a government clerk who quit due to the unproductive monotony of his employment.

As British rule reached the villages, it continued to support the concepts of clean, honorific service in the king's employ. Local ascribed status relationships and reciprocities have slowly diminished but are far from extinct. Though the money economy spread, mental and enterprising occupations rose little from a status in which their degradation was institutionalized. The occupational status system was, and is, supported by the institutions of family honor and dowry. While it cannot be said that colonial rule enhanced these ethos-supporting institutions, it can be argued that the colonial system of education worked directly and deliberately to preserve the value of honorific service. Schools were designed as the training ground for government clerks.

One consequence of English education was to support an urban upper and lower class division in which separation was by a cultural as well as a prestige gulf. Class position in Ceylon is not a matter of degree on a simple prestige continuum. Trousers and sarong belong to two different standards of living, two worlds of discourse, and hence two worlds separated by a hiatus in status. The cost and limited accessibility of English education contributed to the rigidity of this structure and also to the preservation of a still different class, the peasant, honored in theory but less so in practice.[25] The very process of secondary and higher education, even for the fortunate coolie or peasant, meant systematic indoctrination in the values and skills, especially linguistic, of the clerical elite. Teachers' attitudes reflect the old prestige system as does the content of curriculum itself.[26] Education at its lowest level has been geared to the production of inferior clerks; at its highest level to the production of genteel civil servants.

Marriage and family systems were never deliberately reformed to vitalize the status-achievement order. However, traditional family values have had an amazing persistence in Ceylon.[27] The loosely structured Sinhalese kinship and marital family concepts were easily adapted to colonial, and even urban, conditions. Traditional conceptions of familial honor and the custom of dowry became intimate parts of the new occupational-achievement order. Practically all Sinhalese husbands expect dowry. From the groom's standpoint, dowry is his reward for achieved status. From the bride's standpoint—or rather from her kinsmen's standpoint—it is the price for maintaining or improving familial prestige. In practice this means that a family of no consequence except wealth will seek a well-placed government servant for their son-in-law. The prestige of an occupation is better measured by dowry than by income. Consequently, an educated youth who pursues a career in business finds his chances of getting a desirable and well-dowered wife considerably reduced. Family honor and dowry drive youth toward the government sinecure. A really highly placed government servant can reasonably command a dowry of a hundred thousand rupees or more.

In this exposition of an ethic which is antithetical to that of Protestant Christianity, it may seem surprising that no significance has been attached to religion. It should be clear, however, that there can be nothing in Sinhalese religious values which prevents strong secular ambitions.[28] The particular status-achievement-work ethos of the Sinhalese has no support in religion comparable to the Protestant supports of capitalism. The Sinhalese ethos instead is rooted in a historic social structure redefined under colonial administration. It is supported deliberately in the enacted institutions of education and government and less deliberately in the institutions of family and caste.

With the present rise of nationalism in Ceylon there may well be an increase in forces counteracting the traditional ethos. Thus a reversion to indigenous languages in the schools and in government, replacing English, and the Ceylonization program in industry, may work toward the breakdown of the old class structure and offer increased stimulation to Ceylonese in the fields of industry and commerce. The very suggestion, which has been made, of a university chair in Business Administration is noteworthy. Increasing attention is being given to vocational education. These movements are new and their potential effects therefore obscure. Barring revolutionary upheavals, the old ethos will probably persist for some time to retard rationality in investment and status rewards for productivity and enterprise.

Notes

1. See Burton Stein, "Problems of Economic Development in Ceylon," *Ceylon Historical Journal*, Vol. III, January and April 1954, 286–330. Theodore Morgan, "The Economic Development of Ceylon," *The Annals*, Vol. 305, May 1956, 92–100. Although Morgan concludes on an optimistic note, his observations provide scant foundation for it. Also see the report of a mission organized by the International Bank for Reconstruction and Development, *The Economic Development of Ceylon* (Baltimore: Johns Hopkins Press, 1953).

2. Various studies carried out independently by T. L. Green, Murray Straus, and B. Ryan cited in this connection. The data cited in this paragraph are taken from an unpublished study by the writer.

3. "Education and Social Needs in Ceylon," *University of Ceylon Review*, Vol. X, October 1952, 297–316. Cf. T. L. Green and Chitra Wickramasooriya, "The Vocational Attitudes of Ceylonese Graduate Teachers," *University of Ceylon Review*, Vol. XI, January 1953, 10–16.

4. B. Ryan, L. D. Jaysena and D. C. R. Wickremesinghe, *Sinhalese Village* (Coral Gables: University of Miami Press, 1958), p. 176.

5. "Family Characteristics and Occupational Choice of University Entrants as Clues to the Social Structure of Ceylon," *University of Ceylon Review*, Vol. IX, April 1951, 125–134.

6. Ceylon National Chamber of Commerce, "Programme For Progress," *The Ceylon Economist*, Vol. 3, May 1957, 281–298.

7. In a fully socialized economy the drive toward government employment *per se* and the reluctance of private wealth toward industrial and business enterprise might not be serious. Capital is not fully regimented in Ceylon and in those areas where government has entered industry the results have not been heartening. The collaboration of government and private capital has not been entirely satisfactory either. A leading Colombo Newspaper, the *Ceylon Observer*, as recently as May 3, 1959 reports the failure of such a joint scheme for the production of car batteries, a project which experts are said to have found economically sound.

8. Few studies of agricultural problems fail to report the effects of the tenure system. Recently a drastic Paddy Lands Bill has been passed which among other effects is designed to ameliorate this condition. See, J. B. Kelegama, "The Economic Significance of the Paddy Lands Bill," *The Ceylon Economist*, Vol. 4, January 1958, 80–124.

9. *Sinhalese Village*, pp. 173–174.

10. Bryce Ryan, *Caste in Modern Ceylon* (New Brunswick: Rutgers University Press, 1953), esp. Chapter 13.

11. E. Reimers, "Some Sinhalese Names and Surnames," *Journal of The Ceylon Branch of the Royal Asiatic Society*, Vol. XXXI, 1930, 437–454. Taxation of names possibly refers to the Dutch Period.

12. Robert Knox, *An Historical Relation of Ceylon* (James Ryan edition, Glasgow, 1911). Cf. esp. p. 83. (The first edition of this work appeared in London, 1681.)

13. *Ibid.*, p. 86.

14. Sir J. Emerson Tennent, *Ceylon* (London: Longmans, Green, Longman and Roberts, second edition, 1859), Vol. II, p. 410.

15. *Op. cit.*, p. 51.

16. Tennent, *op. cit.*, p. 9.

17. *Ibid.*, p. 58, 487.

18. The dilemma of "British conscience" is evident in a variety of writers. Cf. *Caste in Modern Ceylon*, pp. 79–81. Dr. Ralph Pieris has presented a superb analysis of the clash between British ideology and the Sinhalese ethos during the early years of colonization. See Ralph Pieris, "Society and Ideology in Ceylon during a 'Time of Troubles,' " *University of Ceylon Review*. This paper is in three parts beginning Vol. IX, July 51, pp. 171–185, and continued in two consecutive issues.

19. *Op. cit.*, p. 131 and pp. 148–149.

20. See Pieris, *op. cit.*, especially Vol. X, January 1952, pp. 179–102. Cf. A. B. Perera, "Plantation Economy and Colonial Policy in Ceylon," *The Ceylon Historical Journal*, Vol. 1, July 1951, 46–58.

21. Tennent, *op. cit.*, p. 410.

22. *Remembered Yesterdays*, Being The Reminiscences of Maha Mudaliyar Sir Solomon Dias Bandaranaike, K.C.M.G. (London: John Murray, 1929).

23. Cited by Ralph Pieris in "Administration of Justice and of Revenue on the

Island of Ceylon Under the Dutch Government ('The Cleghorn Minute')
Introductory Note," *Journal of the Ceylon Branch of the Royal Asiatic
Society,* New Series, Vol. III, Pt. II, June 1954, pp. 125–152.

24. *Op. cit.,* pp. 172–173.

25. No account is taken here of the landed aristocrat. He survives particularly in
Kandyan areas. There is however a persistent tendency for these families
to validate their position through governmental employments and politics.
See for example *The Autobiography of Tikiri Banda Panabokke* edited by
P. B. Panabokke and J. A. Halangode (Kandy, undated, and *The Autobiography of Sir Tikiri Banda Panabokke* (Kandy, 1939–1949) [writ-
ten?]. Sir Tikiri was the son of the elder Panabokke, a great Kandyan
patriot. Descendant of a noble family, the elder Panabokke worked diligently to reestablish family wealth and to serve his people in government
office. Sir Tikiri makes no secret of his driving ambition—for honorific
title and ultimate knighthood. Family investment appears to have been,
and to have remained, strictly in the form of land and plantation development.

26. Cf. T. L. Green, "The Vocational Attitudes of Ceylonese Graduate Teachers,"
University of Ceylon Review, Vol. XI, January 1955, 10–16.

27. Cf. S. J. Tambiah and Bryce Ryan, "Secularization of Family Values in
Ceylon," *American Sociological Review,* 22, 1957, 292–299.

28. Milton Singer has made a similar argument in reference to Hinduism and has
documented it in great detail. Many of the same points apply to Buddhism.
Milton Singer, "Cultural Values in India's Economic Development,"
Annals, 305 (May 1956), 81–91.

Robert M. Marsh

FORMAL ORGANIZATION AND PROMOTION IN CHINESE SOCIETY

Introduction

RECENT SOCIOLOGICAL RESEARCH on formal organization has concentrated on
modern, Western, highly industrialized societies. As a result, an important part
of Max Weber's theory of bureaucracy—that dealing with "pre-bureaucratic"
forms of administration[1]—has been seriously neglected. It is true that research
on contemporary bureaucracies has already contributed important refinements
and extensions of Weberian analysis. However, parallel developments in the
study of pre-bureaucratic forms of administration are needed. This should include the analysis of formal organization (a) in the *historical* empires and

Reprinted from *The American Sociological Review,* Vol. 26, No. 4, August 1961, with the
permission of the author and the American Sociological Association.

states, e.g., ancient Egypt and Rome, Imperial China, Sassanid Iran, the Byzantine Empire, etc.; and (b) in *contemporary* less-industrialized and non-
Western societies. The present study is of the first type, and concerns the problem of the determinants of advancement in the nineteenth century Chinese
Imperial bureaucracy.[2]

Determinants of Advancement

A formal organization, whether modern (rational-legal) or traditional, is
hierarchically organized. Members of the administrative staff move "up" and
"down" this hierarchy over time. Our dependent variable is the *differential
advancement* observable among the members of any administrative staff. The
higher the rank reached by officials, the greater their degree of advancement.
Our independent variables are those factors that determine advancement, that
explain differentials in rank reached among officials.

For Weber, what were these factors? In the *modern bureaucratic* type of
administration, "There is a system of 'promotion' according to seniority or to
achievement, or both."[3] We shall refer to seniority and achievement as
bureaucratic determinants of advancement. In the pure type of *traditional*
administration, on the other hand, "There is no regular system of appointment
and promotion on the basis of free contract."[4] "There is such a thing as 'promotion' only according to the arbitrary grace of the chief."[5] In the sub-type of
traditional administration of which Weber saw China as an example—patri-
monial-praebendal administration[6]—promotion could depend upon "a certain
social status . . . and . . . the corresponding sense of honor of a distinctive
social group."[7] The consequence would be a "guild-like closure of officialdom
typically found in patrimonial and . . . praebendal officialdoms of the past."[8]

Thus far, one might conclude that, for Weber, promotion in modern
bureaucratic administration was primarily dependent upon seniority or
achievement, but primarily dependent upon factors *other than* seniority and
achievement in traditional administrations. Yet this conclusion would do violence to Weber's analysis. A closer reading of Weber reveals three important
points. First, he *qualified* his characterization of traditional administration:
promotion occurs only according to the arbitrary grace of the chief "*except
under certain circumstances when the administrative staff is organized on a
basis of praebends.*"[9] Second, he made the empirical observation that in patri-
monialpraebendal administration "it is common for slaves and freedmen to
rise even to the highest positions."[10] To the extent that this is so, patrimonial
administration does not exhibit a "guild-like closure." Third, slaves and
freedmen might frequently rise to the highest positions because in patrimonial
administrations "it is possible to maintain a system of promotion on a basis of
seniority or of particular objectively determined achievements,"[11] just as in
modern bureaucracies.

Weber suggested, then, that seniority and achievement could operate strongly enough even in traditional patrimonial bureaucracies to ensure men of varying social origins relatively *equal* access to high office, once they had entered officialdom in the first place. In our terminology, advancement in both modern and patrimonial administration might be *bureaucratically* determined. All determinants of advancement other than seniority and achievement will be referred to as *extra-bureaucratic* determinants. In the analysis to follow, the following variables will be treated as extra-bureaucratic determinants of advancement: (1) The *purchase* of substantive posts by officials. The sale of office was sanctioned by the formal structure of the Chinese bureaucracy; yet purchase is treated as an extra-bureaucratic determinant of advancement because it represents the intrusion of officials' *pecuniary* status, and not necessarily their seniority or achievement. (2) *Family background,* on the assumption that the social origins of officials and their achievements in office vary more or less independently of one another.[12] (3) *Age of officials,* on the assumption, again, that this varies more or less independently of their achievement in office. (4) *Method of recruitment* to the bureaucracy, whenever this entails special favors, preferential treatment, instead of the universal application of achievement norms.

It should be clear that these variables are not *extra*-bureaucratic determinants because they stem only from outside the organization; they may also stem from *within* the organization in question. Such variables are extra-bureaucratic in the sense that they are *extraneous* to the two *bureaucratic* determinants of promotion—seniority and achievement. This distinction accords well with that current in the field of formal organization, in which patterned deviations from the formal structure or rules are seen as stemming from either the external adaptation of the organization, or from the internal, informal structure of the organization, or both.[13] It should also be made clear that the distinction between bureaucratic and extra-bureaucratic determinants is an analytical one, drawn by the scientific observer. It need not correspond to officials' subjective definitions of "legitimate" and "illegitimate" influences on advancement. The influence of purchase or family background is, for reasons stated above, an extra-bureaucratic influence, whether or not the officials in question viewed it as a legitimate influence.

Weber did not specify the relative impact of these bureaucratic and extra-bureaucratic variables upon advancement in the Chinese bureaucracy. He left this question open, of course, because he simply lacked the necessary empirical data. If we examine the formal norms concerning personnel and promotions during the Ch'ing dynasty (1644–1912), it appears that advancement was bureaucratically rather than extra-bureaucratically determined, in the main. The formal norms required that merit ratings be drawn up triennially for all officials. In any given year, the only officials eligible for the normal one-half rank promotion were those with *both* seniority and a first-class recommendation from their superiors and from the Board of Civil Office and the Censorate. Promotions occurred within a nine-rank hierarchy, with the highest posts in rank one and the lowest in rank nine. Each rank was divided into two grades, designated 1a, 1b, 2a, 2b, etc. Officials who had already attained the seniority of, say, a 5a-rank post were eligible for promotion to a post one-half rank higher, i.e., to a 4b-rank post, *providing* that they also had received a high rating on the formal criteria of merit: personal conduct (*shou*), ability (*ts'ai*), service record (*cheng*), and were not overage or infirm.

To what extent did the *actual* patterns of promotion in the Ch'ing bureaucracy reflect the primacy of these formal rules of seniority and merit? Alternatively, to what extent did promotion and advancement reflect the primacy of extra-bureaucratic determinants, such as family background and purchase of office? Previous research on this problem has dealt, for the most part, only with individuals or specific cliques or factions of officials. Other studies have provided valuable insights, but have dealt with earlier periods of Chinese history, with high officials rather than a cross-section of officials of all ranks, or with status mobility in the examination system rather than officialdom *per se*.[14] The present paper is a preliminary report of my attempt to analyze systematically the advancement of all ranks of officialdom.

Method and Data

A sample was drawn of 1,047 officials from the Chinese government directories known as *T'ung Kuan Lu*. Of the total sample, 39 officials were listed in the 1778 Shantung Province *T'ung Kuan Lu*, the remaining 1,008 officials appeared in directories for the period 1831–1879. Historical conditions varied during this period, but for statistical reasons and for reasons of space will not be considered here. The sample will be treated as a whole rather than broken down into small time periods.

Table 1 shows that the sample closely approximates the actual hierarchic distribution of provincial officialdom in the nineteenth century.

Table 1—Universe and Sample Distribution of Officials by Rank

Rank	Provincial Officials: All China*	PROVINCIAL OFFICIALS: T'UNG-KUAN LU SAMPLES**						All T'ung-Kuan Lu Samples
		1778	1831	1837	1859	1871	1879	
1–4	7%	—	10%	14%	11%	18%	22%	13%
5–6	17%	—	25%	21%	14%	33%	19%	20%
7–Unclassed	76%	100%	65%	65%	75%	49%	59%	67%
Total	100%	100%	100%	100%	100%	100%	100%	100%
No.	20,471	38	110	318	302	164	98	1,020

* Based on estimate by Chang Chung-li, *The Gentry in 10th Century China*, unpublished Ph.D. dissertation, University of Washington, 1953. This estimate includes all civil and military officials in the 18 provinces, but not Bannermen.

** No information on rank was available for 27 officials.

Findings and Discussion

Influence of Bureaucratic Variables on Advancement. (1) *Seniority.* There is a correlation between seniority and advancement ($\sqrt{T_b} = .233$).[15] Table 2 shows that the longer officials served, the more likely they were to be

Table 2—The Relation between Seniority and Advancement

Rank Reached	Amount of Seniority 0–12 YEARS		13–24 YEARS		OVER 24 YEARS	
	Number	Per Cent	Number	Per Cent	Number	Per Cent
1–4	9	3	54	19	43	26
5–6	35	14	66	23	49	29
7–Unclassed	214	83	163	58	75	45
Total	258	100	283	100	167	100

promoted to a higher rank post. (Rank one through four posts are *high* posts, rank five and six posts are *middle-rank* posts, and rank seven through nine and "unclassed" (*wei ju liu*) posts are *low* posts.)

(2) *Achievement.* Our only independent measure of achievement is highly unsatisfactory.[16] It is the *age* of a man when he became a *chin shih* ("advanced scholar"), i.e., when he attained the highest level in the competitive examination system. (Becoming a *chin shih* was one of the most prestigeful ways of securing initial appointment to the bureaucracy.) Our assumption, which may be quite erroneous, is that the earlier in life a man succeeded in attaining the *chin shih,* the greater would be his subsequent achievement as an official. Table 3 shows that among the 146 officials who became *chin shih*

Table 3—The Relation between Age at Chin-shih and Advancement

Rank Reached	Age When Chin-shih Was Received UNDER 25		26–35		OVER 35	
	Number	Per Cent	Number	Per Cent	Number	Per Cent
1–4	6	43	25	31	5	10
5–6	2	14	10	12	7	14
7–Unclassed	6	43	46	57	39	76
Total	14	100	81	100	51	100

—16 per cent of the total sample—there was a correlation between "achievement" and advancement ($\sqrt{T_b} = .210$). The earlier in life one became a *chin shih,* the more likely one was to reach high-rank posts, and vice versa.

Influence of Extra-Bureaucratic Variables on Advancement. (1) *Purchase of substantive posts.* Weber noted how widespread this phenomenon was in traditional administrations: in antiquity, priesthoods were sold at auction; appropriation of office by pledging was significant in the Papal States, and in the Parlaments of France as late as the eighteenth century; the purchase of officers' commissions continued in the British army well into the nineteenth century.[17]

In early Ch'ing China only relatively empty titles and honors, and some low posts, could be purchased. By the mid-nineteenth century provincial ranks and even substantive posts (*shih kuan*) from the fourth rank down could be purchased.[18] A commoner, for example, in 1843 could purchase the fourth rank post of Circuit Intendant for 30,000 taels silver.[19]

Table 4—The Relation between the Rank of Posts Purchased and Advancement

| | Rank of Posts Purchased | | | | | |
| | RANK 4–6 | | RANK 7–UNCLASSED | | NO PURCHASE | |
Rank Reached	Number	Per Cent	Number	Per Cent	Number	Per Cent
1–4	31	26	9	4	91	16
5–6	80	67	32	13	77	13
7–Unclassed	8	7	208	83	417	71
Total	119	100	249	100	585	100

Table 4 shows that officials who purchased middle-rank posts were more likely than those who purchased only low posts to reach high posts. Indeed, the latter group was less likely to reach high posts than were officials who had never purchased a post. ($\sqrt{T_b} = .299$)

In Table 4, almost all the officials who had purchased middle-rank posts were either in those ranks or in *high* rank posts. In contrast to the officials who had purchased the highest posts purchasable (middle-rank posts), the great majority of both non-purchase officials (71 per cent) and of low purchase officials (83 per cent) were in *low* ranks posts.

There is another way of viewing this. Although officials who purchased middle-rank posts were more likely to be in middle- or high-rank posts than were either low-purchase or non-purchase officials, since only 12 per cent of the sample purchased middle-rank posts, these middle-rank purchase officials comprised only 24 per cent of all high rank officials in the sample. The bulk of officials in the highest four ranks—69 per cent—were non-purchase officials.

What was the influence of purchase *per se,* irrespective of the *rank* of the post purchased? Of the sample, 28 per cent were recorded as having resorted to purchase once during their official careers and another 10 per cent more than once; the other 62 per cent had no record of purchase of substantive posts. If we compare those who ever purchased posts with those who never purchased, we find that purchase was most instrumental in enabling officials to move from low-rank posts up into middle rank posts ($\sqrt{T_b} = .213$). But since posts above the fourth rank were not purchasable, we find that purchase officials were not more likely than non-purchase officials to reach these high rank posts (unless the purchase officials purchased fourth through sixth-rank posts.)

(2) *Family Background.* We shall measure the influence upon advancement of four different aspects of family background: general position, official

rank, strength of official tradition, and distaff influence. To understand the influence of the general social position of one's family, we must briefly characterize the system of stratification in China in the nineteenth century.[20] At the top were the members of the Manchu, Mongol, and Chinese Banners, descendants of the Banner military organization created by the Manchus at the beginning of the Ch'ing period. Men born into Banner families formed an hereditary, caste-like elite. Below Bannermen and their families were the traditional Chinese elite, consisting of government officials, degree-holders and local elite, and their families. The remaining 98 per cent of the population held the legal status of commoners. While there were differences in wealth and influence *among* commoners, they are here treated as a single stratum, partly because the necessary economic data are lacking, but also because the *legal* criterion of ranking (Bannermen; officials and degree-holders; commoners) was a crucial one in Ch'ing stratification.

If we examine how this criterion of stratification in the wider society influenced advancement within the bureaucracy, we note that Bannermen outdistanced Chinese from official and degree-holding families ($\sqrt{T_b} = .231$), but the latter did *not* rise higher than Chinese from commoner families. Table 5 shows that virtually as large a proportion of commoners' sons as of the sons of officials and degree-holders reached high rank posts.

Table 5—The Relation between Family Background and Advancement

	FAMILY BACKGROUND								
					All Other Chinese				
	Manchu Bannermen		Chinese Bannermen		Official Families		Degree Families		Commoner Families	
Rank Reached	N	%	N	%	N	%	N	%	N	%
1–4	23	36	10	27	59	12	21	10	13	10
5–6	22	34	7	19	107	21	38	18	18	14
7–Unclassed	19	30	20	54	340	67	154	72	99	76
Total	64	100	37	100	506	100	213	100	130	100

Table 6—The Relation between Highest Rank Reached by Forebears and Advancement

| | Highest Rank of Father, Grandfather, and Great-Grandfather | | | | | |
| | RANK 1–3 | | RANK 4–UNCLASSED | | COMMONERS | |
Rank Reached	Number	Per Cent	Number	Per Cent	Number	Per Cent
1–4	32	30	58	12	13	10
5–6	24	23	105	21	18	14
7–Unclassed	49	47	327	67	99	76
Total	105	100	490	100	130	100

($\sqrt{T_b}$ for entire table $= .139$; $\sqrt{T_b}$ for columns 1 vs. 2 $= .21$.)

A second aspect of family background was the rank in the bureaucracy which one's father, grandfather, and great-grandfather had reached. Was it more important for an official to have *one high-ranking* official forebear than to have more than one official forebear, but all in lower rank posts? Table 6 reveals that high-ranking forebears gave an official an advantage both over officials with low-rank official forebears and also over those with commoner forebears. Having official forebears in the fourth through ninth ranks, however, did *not* enable an official to rise higher than officials from commoner families.

A third aspect of family background that might influence advancement was the *strength* of the official tradition in one's family, among the father, grandfather, and great-grandfather. Two officials in Table 5 might both be classified as from an "official family," but one may have had only one official ancestor while the other may have had forebears all of whom were officials. This factor of the strength of official tradition was introduced by Kracke in 1947.[21] Table 7 shows that it does not determine advancement in the *T'ung Kuan Lu* sample.

Table 7—The Relation between Strength of Official Tradition in Family and Advancement

	Strength of Official Tradition in Family*							
	PREVALENT		STRONG		MINOR		NONE	
Rank Reached	N	%	N	%	N	%	N	%
1–4	48	15	32	17	12	14	34	10
5–6	82	26	32	17	16	19	57	17
7–Unclassed	190	59	126	66	58	67	239	73
Total	320	100	190	100	86	100	330	100

* Prevalent: fa, gfa, and ggfa all officials; or fa and gfa officials; or fa and ggfa officials.
Strong: gfa and ggfa officials; or fa only an official.
Minor: only gfa or ggfa an official.
None: neither fa, gfa nor ggfa officials.

Table 7 shows that almost as high a percentage (10 per cent) of officials from commoner families as of officials with a "prevalent" official tradition in their families (15 per cent) reached high rank posts. It is true that only 59 per cent of the officials with "prevalent" official tradition in their families, as compared with 73 per cent of the officials from commoner families, were in low-rank posts. But the overall relationship between "strength of official tradition in the family" and an official's advancement was very low ($\sqrt{T_b} = .095$).

The fourth aspect of family background that we tested was the influence of having official forebears on the distaff side, e.g., mother's brother, mother's uncle, etc. We found that distaff influence on one's advancement was also insignificant ($\sqrt{T_b} = .091$). Officials from commoner families reached high posts almost as frequently (10 per cent) as did officials with distaff official influence (14 per cent). And among officials with any given "strength" of official tradition in their families—prevalent, strong, or minor—those *with* official forebears on the distaff side were not significantly more likely than those *without* distaff official influence to reach high posts.

(3) *Recruitment Path.* Officials who entered the bureaucracy through special privileges had significantly greater chances of reaching high posts than officials who were recruited through any other method, including the competitive examination system ($\sqrt{T_b} = .219$). These privileges included *Yin-sheng* (sometimes bestowed upon the descendents of officials in the three highest ranks) and *Kuan hsüeh-sheng* (students in the school for Bannermen).

Table 8—The Relation between Recruitment Path and Later Advancement

	SPECIAL FAVOR[1]		Type of Recruitment Path HIGHER COMPETITIVE EXAMINATIONS[2]		LOWER EXAMINATIONS AND PURCHASE[3]		UP FROM THE RANKS AND "OTHER"[4]	
Rank Reached	N	%	N	%	N	%	N	%
1–4	16	67	65	13	33	10	16	15
5–6	4	16.5	79	16	80	25	27	25
7–Unclassed	4	16.5	361	71	212	65	64	60
Total	24	100	505	100	325	100	107	100

[1] Yin-sheng and Kuan hsüeh-sheng.
[2] Chin-shih, chü-jen and kung-sheng.
[3] Chien-sheng, sheng-yuan and purchase.
[4] Up from the ranks of clerks. "Other" includes those recommended for appointment as "filial, incorrupt, and upright," and those recommended for their military merit, etc.

Table 8 shows that 67 per cent of the *Yin-sheng* or *Kuan hsüeh-sheng* officials reached high rank posts, in contrast to only between 10 per cent and 19 per cent of officials recruited from any other path. This finding that *Yin-sheng* and *Kuan hsüeh-sheng* had a marked career advantage over officials recruited by all other means is, however, not as momentous as it may seem. For extremely few officials benefited by this means of recruitment: only 2 per cent of my total sample. As Wittfogel has noted, "The Ming and Ch'ing emperors reduced the Yin prerogative to a shadow of its former self."[22]

(4) *Age of officials.* There were charges during the nineteenth century that, at least in Peking, high rank posts were monopolized by doddering old men. This was not the case for our sample of provincial officials: of the 132 officials in high posts, only 13 per cent were 60 years old or over; 76 per cent were between 40 and 59 years old, and 11 per cent of these high-ranking officials were under 40 years old. Whatever the veneration of age in Ch'ing culture in general, there was only a low relationship ($\sqrt{T_b} = .133$) between age and advancement. As might be expected, even this small relationship between age and advancement is seen to be spurious when seniority is held constant.

One possible source of error in our findings was that while we were analyzing career advancement, many officials in our sample were only in an *early* stage of their careers. Did the role of the several determinants of advancement *differ* as between early and late career stages? We found this *not* to be the case when we repeated the above analysis for a sub-sample of older officials (those over 50 years old). Thus, our conclusions are free from this source of error.

We may now summarize our findings by showing the zero-order correlations ($\sqrt{T_b}$) between the several independent variables (both bureaucratic and extra-bureaucratic) and the dependent variable, advancement, or rank reached.

Bureaucratic Variables	
Seniority	.233
Age at *Chin-shih*	.210
Extra-Bureaucratic Variables	
Rank of post purchased	.299
Family background[a]	.231
Recruitment path[b]	.219
Purchased vs. never purchased posts	.213
Family background[c]	.139
Age of officials	.133
Family background[d]	.095
Family background[e]	.091

[a] Banner families vs. all other families.
[b] *Yin-sheng* and *Kuan hsüeh-sheng* vs. all other recruitment paths.
[c] Highest rank among father, grandfather and great-grandfather.
[d] Strength of official tradition among immediate forebears on both sides of the family.
[e] Distaff official influence.

The following attributes were found most often among the officials who rose highest in the Chinese bureaucracy (i.e., to rank 1–4 posts); 1. the purchase of middle-rank posts, the highest purchasable; 2. seniority; 3. Banner family background; 4. recruitment through the special privilege of *Yin-sheng* or *Kuan hsüeh-sheng;* 5. attainment of the coveted *chin-shih* early in life, if at all. Let us look more closely at only the *three extra-bureaucratic* attributes related to advancement (attributes 1, 3 and 4). We noted earlier that these three attributes gave men a systematic advantage in their careers, but that none of these attributes was very widely distributed among the total sample. Purchase of substantive posts gave men an edge in advancement, but only 12 per cent of the sample purchased the relevant posts. Banner family background was also advantageous, but again, only 10 per cent of the sample were from Banner families, only two per cent of the sample could benefit from the third attribute, recruitment as *Yin-sheng* or *Kuan hsüeh-sheng.* To what extent were these three extra-bureaucratic advantages *clustered* in the same individuals? A simple index of Extra-Bureaucratic Status Advantages was constructed by scoring each rank one through four official one point for each of the three status advantages he had. Thus, an official from a Banner family who was recruited as a *Yin-sheng* or a *Kuan hsüeh-sheng,* and who had purchased fourth through sixth rank posts received a score of three points; an official with only two of these advantages two points, etc.

Thus, half of the officials in the highest four ranks were neither from

Index Score		N	%
3	Highest status advantages	3	2
2		13	10
1		50	37
0	No status advantages	69	51
	Total	135	100

Banner families, nor recruited as *Yin-sheng* or *Kuan hsüeh-sheng,* nor officials who had purchased middle-rank posts during their careers. Another one-third (37 per cent) of these high officials had *one* of these three status advantages; only 12 per cent had more than one status advantage. The lack of these particular status advantages, then, did *not* necessarily prevent an official from reaching the highest posts.

Purchase is the only (extra-bureaucratic) factor which is more strongly related to advancement than is the bureaucratic factor of seniority. If we hold purchase constant, we can observe whether the original relationship between seniority and advancement ($\sqrt{T_b} = .233$) holds up or is reduced. The relation between seniority and advancement *within* various purchase sub-groups is as follows:

$$\sqrt{T_b} =$$

1. Among officials who purchased 4–6 rank posts   .217
2. Among officials who purchased only 7–9 rank posts   .248
3. Among officials with no record of purchase   .272

Controlling for purchase has enabled us to *specify* further the relationship between seniority and advancement: the relation is not a spurious one; it is slightly weaker among officials who purchased middle-rank posts, but it is *stronger* among officials who purchased only low posts or did not purchase at all. Thus, advancement *did* depend upon seniority as well as on purchase, though officials who purchased well were somewhat less dependent upon seniority for their advancement than were those who never purchased posts.

The final question to be dealt with here is: what is the *relative* influence of (a) the two bureaucratic variables and (b) the several extra-bureaucratic variables, upon advancement? For various statistical reasons, only five of the eight extra-bureaucratic variables could be adapted to a multiple correlation analysis. The measure of multiple correlation used is $\sqrt{T_b}$, the same as used above for our zero-order correlations.

Variables
1. Advancement (dependent variable)
2. Seniority
3. Age at *chin-shih* degree
4. Rank of post purchased
5. Family background: Banner families vs. all others
6. Family background: highest rank reached by immediate forebears
7. Age of the official
8. Family background: strength of officials tradition in family

Results: $\sqrt{T_b}$ 1.23   = .447
$\sqrt{T_b}$ 1.45678 = .574

The above multiple correlations indicate that the combined predictive power of the two bureaucratic variables (2 and 3) on advancement is less than the combined predictive power of the five extra-bureaucratic variables (4 through 8). Advancement was somewhat more strongly related to extra-bureaucratic than to bureaucratic variables.

Conclusion

Weber did not specify his propositions concerning promotion in patrimonial administrations. Instead, he held that *either* bureaucratic factors (seniority and achievement) or extra-bureaucratic factors (a certain social status, the arbitrary grace of the chief, etc.), or both, could operate. He did not specify the *conditions under which* one or the other of these factors would have primacy as a determinant of advancement in patrimonial administration. In the case of nineteenth century China, advancement was determined somewhat more by extra-bureaucratic than by bureaucratic factors.

We should, however, resist any facile conclusion that, in contrast to traditional bureaucracies, bureaucratic influences have primacy over extra-bureaucratic influences in modern bureaucracies, i.e., in industrial societies. Britain's "higher civil service"—the Administrative Class—has long been heavily recruited from the upper strata of the population.[23] Promotion in an American industrial plant was shown to be based not upon any definite formal procedure, but upon such informal criteria as ethnic-group affiliation, religion, participation in specific out-of-plant activities, political affiliation, etc.[24] Favoritism may be resorted to in United States federal civil service appointments because of the inadequacy of formal merit ratings. And the adding of extra points to the civil service grades of veterans was a widespread form of extra-bureaucratic influence following World War I in the United States. Of the veterans appointed, from one-sixth to one-eighth earned less than the passing civil service grade of 70.[25] Thus, more comparative research is needed, in which earlier studies of different types of bureaucracies are re-examined, and new studies conducted, in the light of our distinction between bureaucratic and extra-bureaucratic variables.

The comparative analysis of recruitment and advancement in different types of formal organization will also have important implications for the study of social stratification and mobility, and vice versa.

Notes

1. Traditional and charismatic forms of administration were seen as pre-bureaucratic. The sub-types of traditional administration were gerontocracy, patriarchalism, patrimonialism, sultanism, and feudalism. See Max Weber, *The Theory of Social and Economic Organization* (New York: Oxford University Press, 1947), pp. 324–386; *From Max Weber: Essays in Soci-*

ology (New York: Oxford University Press, 1946), pp. 196–264; "Die drei reinen Typen der legitimen Herrshaft," in *Staatssoziologie* (Berlin: Duncker and Humblot, 1956), pp. 99–110.

2. For earlier phases of the writer's research in this area, see Robert M. Marsh, "Bureaucratic Constraints on Nepotism in the Ch'ing Period," *Journal of Asian Studies*, 19 (February, 1960), pp. 117–133, and *The Mandarins: Circulation of Elites in China* (New York: The Free Press, 1961).

3. Weber, 1947, *op. cit.*, p. 334.

4. *Ibid.*, p. 343.

5. *Ibid.*, p. 345.

6. In patrimonial administration officials have the status of personal dependents of the emperor or chief, in contrast to feudalism, where there is a relationship of fealty between the ruler and his relatively autonomous, self-equipped vassals. Weber defined "praebendal" as the support of the administrative staff largely by the private appropriation of fees and taxes derived from office, rather than by a formally fixed salary.

7. Weber, 1947, *op. cit.*, p. 351.

8. Weber, 1946, *op. cit.*, p. 200.

9. Weber, 1947, *op. cit.*, p. 345.

10. *Ibid.*, p. 343.

11. *Ibid.*, p. 251.

12. There is some evidence that this assumption is valid for Chinese officialdom. Outstanding officials (as judged by expert raters) were not more likely to come from privileged families than were the general run of officials.

13. See F. J. Roethlisberger and W. J. Dickson, *Management and the Worker* (Cambridge: Harvard University Press, 1939); Philip Selznick, *TVA and the Grass Roots* (Berkeley: University of California Press, 1949); R. K. Merton, *et al.*, *Reader in Bureaucracy* (New York: The Free Press, 1952), several papers.

14. K. A. Wittfogel, *New Light on Chinese Society* (New York: International Secretariat, Institute of Pacific Relations, 1938); K. A. Wittfogel and C. S. Feng, *History of Chinese Society, Liao, 907–1125* (Philadelphia: American Philosophical Society, 1949); K. A. Wittfogel, *Oriental Despotism* (New Haven: Yale University Press, 1957); E. A. Kracke, Jr., "Family vs. Merit in the Civil Service Examinations under the Empire," *Harvard Journal of Asiatic Studies*, 10 (September, 1947), pp. 103-123; W. Eberhard, *Conquerors and Rulers* (Leiden: E. J. Brill, 1952); O. B. van der Sprenkel, "High Officials of the Ming," *Bulletin of the School of Oriental and African Studies*, 14 (Part I, 1952), pp. 87–114; Ping-to Ho, "Social Mobility in China, 1368–1911," *Comparative Studies in Society and History*, 1 (June, 1959), pp. 330–359.

15. Tau_{-b} measures the degree of relationship between variables, and is useful when comparing two or more tables with varying numbers of rows and columns. It was introduced by Goodman and Kruskal, in "Measures of Association for Cross Classifications," *Journal of the American Statistical Association*, 49 (December, 1954), pp. 732–764. Like other measures, T_b varies between $+ 1.0$ and $- 1.0$, but since T_b shows a lower degree of association than other measures, e.g., Pearson's C, the square root of T_b is more comparable to other standard measures and is used here.

16. Even in modern bureaucracies the achievement or performance of personnel is one of the most difficult variables to measure, both practically and

theoretically. Weber could speak of "objectivity determined achievement" in his ideal-type analysis, but few administrators or students of organization are sanguine on this matter. L. D. White concludes that none of the forms of merit-ratings yet devised, except production records for manual-mechanical operations, has eliminated subjective judgments. *Introduction to the Study of Public Administration* (New York: Macmillan, 1949).

17. Weber, 1947, *op. cit.*, p. 350.
18. Hsu Tao-ling, *Outline Essay on the History of Chinese Law* (Taipei, 1953), pp. 131–132 (in Chinese).
19. Hsieh Pao-chao, *The Government of China, 1644–1911* (Baltimore: The Johns Hopkins Press, 1925), pp. 107–111.
20. For a more complete analysis of social stratification in China between 1600 and 1900, see Robert M. Marsh, *The Mandarins, op. cit.*, chapters 3 and 4.
21. Kracke, *op. cit.*
22. Wittfogel, *op. cit.*, 1957, p. 350.
23. R. K. Kelsall, *Higher Civil Servants in Britain* (London: Routledge and Kegan Paul Ltd., 1955).
24. O. Collins, "Ethnic Behavior in Industry: Sponsorship and Rejection in a New England Factory," *American Journal of Sociology*, 51 (January, 1946), pp. 293–298; Melville Dalton, "Informal Factors in Career Achievement," *American Journal of Sociology*, 56 (March, 1951), pp. 407–415.
25. W. E. Mosher and J. D. Kingsley, *Public Personnel Administration*, rev. ed. (New York: Harper, 1941), pp. 240–242.

Tung-tsu Ch'u   CHINESE CLASS STRUCTURE AND ITS
                         IDEOLOGY

THIS PAPER uses Chou dynasty sources, together with a few Han works, to analyze certain theories of social stratification which had an enduring influence on Chinese political life. After the collapse of Chou feudalism, China's class structure was modified by historical changes in the degree and the channels of social mobility and in the factors which formed classes and determined the individual's status. Yet certain general patterns of social stratification persisted, together with traditional tenets of ideology.

1. Division of Labor and Social Stratification

The Confucian school denied that there could be a society of uniformity and equality. Instead it believed that human beings were different in intelligence, ability, and morality. Some were wise and some simple; some were

Condensed and reprinted from *Chinese Thought and Institutions*, edited by John K. Fairbank, copyright 1957, by permission of The University of Chicago Press.

virtuous and some vicious. There was a natural hierarchy. Consequently, people in a society could not all be given the same roles and treated as equals.

"Work is what people dislike; gain and profit are what they like," says Hsün-tzu. "If there is no distinction of occupation, then people will have difficulty in getting work done."[1] Social organization therefore required a division of labor and the assignment of different kinds of work to people, in a rational way.

Basically there were two types of work, the mental and the physical. Farmers, artisans, merchants, and others pursued the second type. It was their function to produce goods or render services. On the other hand, there was a group which was not expected to engage in production. This group included scholars and officials, whose function it was to study and to acquire virtue. Obviously the physical labor, which needed little training, could be performed by average men, whereas only the more talented were qualified to perform mental work. This kind of labor was considered to contribute the most to society and was therefore highly respected. The role of this class was characterized as that of the "great man," "the superior," or *chün-tzu,* in contrast to the role of the "small man," or *hsiao-jen.* The former group not only was superior but was also expected to be served and supported by the latter. This led to a relationship of subordination and superordination. Statements such as the following were common in Chou times:

Superior men diligently attend to the rules of propriety [*li*], and men in an inferior position do their best.[2]

It is a rule of the former kings that superior men should labor with their minds and smaller men labor with their strength.[3]

The great men devote themselves to governing, and the small men devote themselves to labor.[4]

In an age of good government, men in high stations give preference to men of ability and give opportunity to those who are below them, and lesser people labor vigorously at their husbandry to serve their superiors.[5]

The commoners, the artisans, and merchants, each attend to their profession to support their superiors.[6]

Furthermore, the division of labor was politically oriented. Mental labor was linked with governing. This was clearly pointed out by Mencius in the following statement, which has been frequently quoted:

Great men have their proper business, and little men have their proper business. . . . Some labor with their minds, and some labor with their strength. Those who labor with their minds govern others; those who labor with their strength are governed by others. Those who are governed by others support them; those who govern others are supported by them. This is a principle universally recognized.[7]

Thus, to him, "if there were not men of a superior grade, there would be none to rule the countrymen. If there were not countrymen, there would be none to support the men of superior grade."[8]

Since the role of *chün-tzu* was more important to society, and since the *chün-tzu* assumed more responsibility than a member of the other group, naturally more rewards were distributed to him. He enjoyed more prestige. He was also given more and better material comforts.

Most ancient Chinese philosophers and statesmen merely argued that the labor of the two groups deserved different rewards. Probably Hsün-tzu was the only one who attempted to give a systematic explanation as to why consumption should be differentiated in society—an explanation which went beyond the usual argument that one's reward should correspond to one's contribution. He related it to the scarcity of things and the impossibility of satisfying all human beings without discrimination. "People desire and hate the same things. Their desires are many but things are few. Since they are few, there will inevitably be strife."[9] He also says:

Man by birth has desire. When desire is not satisfied, then he cannot be without a seeking for satisfaction. When this seeking for satisfaction is without measure or limits, then there cannot but be contention. When there is contention, there will be disorder; when there is disorder, then there will be poverty.[10]

Therefore the problem was how to meet human wants and keep society in order. Hsün-tzu thought that the problem could not be solved by treating all human beings alike and distributing things equally among them. In the circumstances, things would not be sufficient to satisfy all.

When social statuses are equal, there will not be enough for everybody. When men's power is equal, there will be no [way to achieve] unification. When people are equal, no one will be able to command the services of others. . . . Two nobles cannot serve each other, and two humble persons cannot command each other. This is a law of nature. When people's power and position are equal and their likes and dislikes are the same, things will not be sufficient to satisfy everyone, and hence there cannot but be strife. Strife will lead to disorder and disorder will lead to poverty.[11]

Thus the only way to solve the problem and to maintain the social order was to make social positions distinct and definite and to distribute things according to status. Hsün-tzu emphasized over and over the importance of "making social distinctions plain and keeping the people together."[12] The essential thing, then, was to have some way to insure that each one in the society would find his correct position, assume his duty, and satisfy his wants.[13] This was the function of *li*, the purpose of which was to make social distinctions clear and to regulate men's desires according to their statuses.[14]

2. Achievement as the Criterion

According to the above theories advocated by Confucianists, the criterion for social status should be achievement, not ascription. This has been described by Parsons as the "particularistic-achievement pattern."[15] Theoretically speaking, only the wise and virtuous were qualified for mental work and entitled to the task of governing. Virtue was the fundamental basis for appointing officials. Mencius thought that a ruler should "esteem virtue and honor virtuous scholars, giving the worthiest among them places of dignity, and the able, offices of trust."[16] To Hsün-tzu, "one's rank must correspond to his virtue, and his salary must correspond to his rank."[17] And the greater one's wisdom and virtue, the higher his rank and salary. It was remarked by Mencius that "when the state is in good order, men of little virtue are submissive to those of great. and those of little worth to those of great."[18] And Hsün-tzu put it this way:

One's grade should be determined by his virtue and his appointment to office should be according to his ability, making everyone assume his function and get into his proper position. The men of greater wisdom should be feudal lords, and the men of lesser wisdom should be made ministers.[19]

It was said that in a kingly state "a man without virtue would never be honored; a man without ability would never be made an official; and a man without merit would never be rewarded."[20] On the other hand, "if a man's virtue does not correspond to his rank, or if his ability does not correspond to his office, or if his reward does not correspond to his merit," Hsün-tzu observes, "there is no misfortune greater than this."[21] A fair social order and good government could be attained only when it was certain that the virtuous were wealthy and honored and that the unworthy were poor and humble. In such an orderly society, poverty and humbleness would be indexes of unworthiness and inability, and things of which to be ashamed. That is why Confucius said, "When a country is well governed, poverty and a mean condition are things to be ashamed of."[22] A person would then be ashamed of his wealth and nobility only when the state was ill governed and corrupt.[23]

However, there is always a discrepancy between this ideal pattern advocated by the Confucianists and the actual system of stratification. Shun, who is frequently referred to by the Confucianists as an example of perfect coordination between virtue and reward, was a man of such great virtue that "it could not but be that he should obtain the throne, that he should obtain those riches, that he should obtain his fame, that he should attain to his long life."[24] However, a man of great virtue did not always enjoy such rewards. Confucius, whose virtue was that of a sage, did not hold a post corresponding to his virtue and ability. Thus there was no mechanism to guarantee that a man of great virtue would occupy a high post, no matter how orderly the society might be. This certainly puzzled the ancients, and reasons were sought to explain the discrepancy. Wang Fu, a Han scholar, says:

It is not necessary that the so-called virtuous men or *chün-tzu* must always enjoy high position and high salary, must be wealthy, noble, and glorious. These are [attributes] which a *chün-tzu* should have, nevertheless they are not what a *chün-tzu* must have. It is not necessary that the small man always be poor, humble, and exposed to cold, hunger, humiliation, and distress. These are what a small man should be, nevertheless they are not what a small man must be.[25]

A similar attitude was held by another Han scholar, Wang Ch'ung, who attributed the unexpected discrepancy to opportunity.

Integrity is always found among the virtuous; opportunity is not always there when one seeks to enter upon an official career. To be virtuous or not virtuous is a matter of ability; to meet or not meet [an opportunity] is a matter of chance. There is no guarantee that a person of great talent and pure behavior will be honored; there is no guarantee that a person of slight ability and impure behavior will be humbled; the talented and pure may not meet [with opportunity] and may be down in low positions; the incompetent and the impure may meet [with opportunity] and be up above others. . . . Entrance to official career depends upon meeting opportunity, and nonentrance depends upon not meeting it. One who is in an honorable post is not necessarily virtuous; it is because he has met [with opportunity]. One who is in an inferior post is not necessarily unintelligent; it is because he had not met [with opportunity].[26]

3. The Structural Background

The above are theories arguing that stratification is a requirement for the existence of society. Now let us discuss the structural background of this ideology.

First of all, it should be pointed out that the above-mentioned theories were formulated in the feudal period, in which the ranks and manors of the feudal lords and other nobles were hereditary. A commoner was born to be a commoner and never could become a nobleman. Thus it was remarked in the *Kuan-tzu* that the son of a *shih* was always a *shih,* that of a farmer always a farmer, that of an artisan always an artisan, and that of a merchant always a merchant.[27] These theories which emphasized the different roles of *chün-tzu* and small men and the importance of maintaining such differences obviously reflected the class structure of the society. They might be either an explanation of the situation expressed in the social structure or a rationalization of the privileges of the ruling class.

Here we are confronted with the most difficult problem involved in ideological analysis, for we have no way of identifying a rationalization. How can we prove one to be such unless an explicit confession is made by the person who advances the theory? However, any thought has an existential basis.[28] If we can locate the social bases of ideas and relate them to the ideas, we may be led to focus our attention on certain problems which would otherwise have been entirely overlooked. We may locate a man's social position and see whether he identifies himself with the characteristic thinking of the social group of which he is a member, i.e., whether he identifies himself with the interest of his own group. We may also explore the various social factors such as occupational role, style of life, relations of production, power structure, etc., to determine whether they are related to a man's verbal expression.

Now, we know that all statements found in the *Tso-chuan, Kuo-yü,* and other classics like those quoted above were voiced by members of the ruling class (e.g., Liu-tzu, Chih Wu-tzu, Yen-kung, and Kuo) or else by persons closely associated with that group (e.g., Mencius and Hsün-tzu). Their social position can be easily located. Our problems are: Do their statements represent the interest of a privileged group? Do they aim to justify its privileges, to consolidate its status and power, or to rationalize its control over and exploitation of the ruled class?

Creel has argued that Confucius was not an advocate of feudalism. However, he points out that "Confucius never directly denounced feudalism."[29] On the other hand, Confucious clearly stated, "I follow Chou."[30] His emphasis on the primacy of "ratifying names"[31] certainly was based on the concept that "there is government, when the prince is prince, and the minister is minister."[32] His statement which complained about the transfer of power from the Son of Heaven to the feudal lords, from the latter to the ministers, and from them to the subsidiary ministers, clearly indicates that he was not in favor of the disorder of his time and that he advocated the restoration of the traditional feudal order.[33] Mencius' advocacy of the "well-field" system[34] and of hereditary salaries for the descendants of officials[35] was also an indication of his attitude toward feudalism.

It should be pointed out that any theory which encourages the ruling class to give up its privileges is incompatible with feudalism. The productive system in a feudal society, by definition, calls for the exploitation of serfdom. Otherwise, it would be impossible for the feudal lords to be supported, and it would be impossible for the scholars of the lowest class (*hsia-shih*) to have "an emolument equal to what they would have made by tilling the field."[36] In short, the style of life which characterized the ruling class could not be maintained without feudalism. This point can best be illustrated in Mencius' own case; he was once a minister in the state of Ch'i and, while not holding an office, as pointed out above, was closely associated with the ruling class. This kind of association made it possible for Mencius "to go from one prince to another and live upon them, followed by several tens of carriages and attended by several hundred men."[37] Without some explanation or rationalization, this style of life, which was clearly marked off from that of the masses, certainly could not be justified. Questions might even be raised among those who were closely associated with the privileged class, not to mention the unprivileged and the exploited groups. Thus one of Mencius' disciples was puzzled by his extravagant way of life and questioned whether it was proper for a scholar performing no service to accept such support. To this Mencius replied:

"If there be not a proper ground for taking it, a single bamboo-cup of rice may not be received from a man. If there be such proper ground, then Shun's receiving the kingdom from Yao is not to be considered excessive. Do you think it was excessive?"

[P'eng] Keng said, "No. But for a scholar performing no service to receive his support notwithstanding is improper." Mencius answered, "If you do not have an intercommunication of the productions of labor, and an interchange of men's services, so that one from his over-plus may supply the deficiency of another, then husbandmen will have a superfluity of cloth. If you have such an interchange, carpenters and carriage-wrights may all get their food from you. Here now is a man, who at home is filial and abroad respectful to his elders; who watches over the principles of the ancient kings, awaiting the rise of future learners—and yet you will refuse to support him. How is it that you give honor to the carpenter and carriage-wright, and slight him who practices benevolence and righteousness?" P'eng Keng said, "The aim of the carpenter and carriage-wright is by their trades to seek for a living. Is it also the aim of the superior man in his practice of principles thereby to seek for a living?" "What have you to do," returned Mencius, "with his purpose? He is of service to you. He deserves to be supported and should be supported."[38]

In another case, Mencius was asked by another disciple why it was that the superior man ate without laboring in the fields. Mencius answered:

When a superior man resides in a country, if its sovereign employs his counsel, he comes to tranquility, wealth, honor, and glory. If the young in it follow his instructions, they become filial, obedient to their elders, true-hearted and faithful— what greater example can there be than this of not eating the bread of idleness?[39]

The above two quotations may be examined as expressing theories formulated by Mencius to explain the important role performed by the *chün-tzu* in his society. The situation in which these statements were made may give us some hints as to their motivation, although these may be far from conclusive. We may assume that, when one's privilege is questioned and challenged, it is necessary to find reasons with which to defend it or justify it. The element of rationalization seems more explicit in this case than in other cases where the situation in which statements were made remains obscure to us. Mencius may or may not have been conscious of his rationalization, but his statements, whether we call them rationalizations or theories, apparently were put forward by him to defend and to justify the privileges of the upper class. They represented the class interest of the privileged group.

Our discussion shows that the theories expressed in connection with the division of labor and social stratification corresponded to the structure of the feudal society; they fit each other harmoniously. However, there was one point of discrepancy between the social structure and one of these theories, namely, that the achievement pattern advocated by the Confucianists, which emphasized the importance of virtue and merit, was in conflict with the ascription pattern, which was characteristic of feudalism. If one's status and reward were determined at birth, then they had nothing to do with personal qualification and achievement. These theories could not be justified unless all nobles were men of virtue and intelligence. This could not always be the case. Confucius' and Mencius' remarks on the government conducted by the ruling class implied that it fell far short of the ideal pattern. Confucius and his followers emphasized that the government should be in the hands of the most virtuous, such as Yao and Shun. This was their Utopia; yet they could do little about it.

On the other hand, Confucius was successful in causing some changes in class structure and social mobility by extending to commoners the kind of education which hitherto had been accessible only to nobles. He educated a group of commoners and made them members of the *shih* group, qualified to enter on official careers.[40] Most of his disciples were men of humble origin.[41] When knowledge was no longer monopolized by the nobles, then the commoners were given a new opportunity for social mobility. As a matter of fact, a number of his disciples, such as Jan Ch'iu, Tzu-lu, Tzu-yu, Tzu-hsia, Yuan-Ssu, Tzu-chien, Tzu-kao, Tsai Wo, and Tzu-kung, either became stewards (*chia-ch'en* or *tsai*) of the nobles or occupied official posts of higher rank.[42] Under the principle that, when one has "completed his learning [he] should apply himself to be an officer,"[43] the cultivation of virtue and the special training for the *chün-tzu* had a practical value in promoting one's status and changing one's role. However, one could enter only the lower stratum of the political hierarchy. Power was still in the possession of the big families.

A more radical change took place in the late Chou period of the warring states. The feudal order was greatly weakened, if not completely destroyed, through the violent process of political struggle. As the legitimate order of the feudal system was no longer respected by the powerful feudal lords and their ministers, the top stratum of the political hierarchy was upset. At the same time, there was also a change at the bottom of the stratified order. A number of commoners with extraordinary talent and unusual ability were able to impress the rulers of the various states and push their way into the upper stratum. Many prominent intellectuals, including Tzu-hsia, Shun-yü K'un, P'eng Meng, Hsün tzu, Tsou Yen, and other scholars, who were honored as guests or teachers of the rulers, enjoyed superior prestige as well as material comfort, although they were not appointed officials.[44] Some others were able to become high officials. Fan Sui, Ts'ai Tse, Su Ch'in, Chang I, Lü Pu-wei, Sun Pin, Po Ch'i, Wang Chien, and others whose background was that of commoners became chancellors and generals of the state. As pointed out by Chao I, this was the first time in Chinese history that men of humble origin could ever occupy such top posts.[45]

This unprecedented change certainly gave a new basis for the justification of the theories of achievement and social mobility. It was for this reason that the situation was somewhat redefined by Hsün-tzu. In the earliest days, as seen in the usage of Confucius and others, the meaning of *chün-tzu* referred to either virtue or status or both.[46] The new definition given by Hsün-tzu, however, almost completely disregarded status; his emphasis was on the side of virtue, that is, personal qualification. Thus we read in his works:

Although a man is the descendant of a king, duke, or *shih ta-fu,* if he does not observe the *li* and righteousness, he must be classified as a commoner; although he is a descendant of a commoner, if he accumulates learning, rectifies himself and his conduct, and is able to observe the *li* and righteousness, then he must be classified as a minister, chancellor, or *shih ta-fu.*[47]

Another change occurred in Han times. First of all, with the exception of a limited number of kings and marquises, official posts were not hereditary. Thus they were no longer monopolized by the big families. Although there was no regular system of civil service examination, the offices were bestowed, in principle, according to merit. Men of special qualifications could be either recommended as students in the Imperial Academy or directly recommended as candidates for official appointment. In the first case, those students of the Erudits who had excellent academic records were qualified for official appointment.[48] In the second case, people could be recommended by the local governments and the offices of the central government under various categories such as "virtuous, wise, square, and upright," "filial and pure," or "extraordinary fine talents."[49] Besides, scholars of extraordinary reputation were sometimes summoned to court by special decree.[50] By these means a formal channel for social mobility was set up. These opportunities had been unknown in the past.

A mechanism to facilitate and regulate "free competition" by means of a regular examination system was not set up until the Sui and T'ang periods. Theoretically, this opportunity was, with a few exceptions, open to all. This system was considered the most rational measure ever worked out to select men of ability. It was assumed that the talented and the learned would be able to pass the examinations; on the other hand, if one failed, it meant that he was not qualified. This popular belief at least served one purpose. It minimized the discrepancy between the actual degree of social mobility and the ideal pattern.

4. Class Structure: Officials and Commoners

Now let us examine the class structure after Chou times. Did the theories discussed above continue to play an important role in the actual stratification of Chinese society after the collapse of feudalism? To what extent was the social order conditioned by these social theories? Did the class structure correspond closely to the ideal pattern? Can the theory of two classes, i.e., the ruling class and the ruled, serve to describe the class structure? Were there only two classes in the society, or were there more?

The doctrine which distinguished between mental and physical labor was widely accepted and played a dominant part in China's social stratification for many centuries as a criterion in determining the prestige of one's occupation. Mental labor was highly respected, whereas physical labor was looked down upon. Physical labor was, so to speak, a status disqualification.

At the same time, the sharp demarcation between the ruling class and the ruled continued to operate. The officials, the backbone of the ruling class, were the superiors; commoners were inferiors. Officials themselves were conscious of their superior status, which was also admitted by the commoners. There was little social communication between the two groups, and intermarriage was rare.

The difference between the two groups can also be observed by objective criteria. The officials, together with their family members, had a style of life quite different from that of commoners, so that they could be clearly marked off from the latter. The style of life was not conditioned economically, as is the situation in modern capitalist society. Instead, it was regulated legally under sumptuary laws.[51] Thus a monopoly over the superior way of life by a privileged group was legitimized. The official class was guaranteed the exclusive enjoyment of it, unthreatened by any propertied class. The sumptuary laws served to minimize or limit the exercise of economic power to such an extent that wealth alone did not guarantee the right to consume. For example, it was emphasized in the *Kuan-tzu* that "one may have a virtuous and honorable body, but he dare not use [a nobleman's] garment if he does not possess a noble rank; one's family may be wealthy, but he dare not use his money if he does not receive an official salary."[52] It was also mentioned in an edict of Emperor Ch'eng of Han that "the sage kings distinguish the *li* so as to put the superior and the inferior in order, and they differentiate the carriages and horses so as to mark out the virtuous. Though one has wealth, if he has not a superior [status], his use of it is not allowed to go beyond the regulations."[53]

Officials were also given other legal privileges. They were exempted from *corvée* service. They could not be arrested and investigated without the approval of the emperor.[54] Neither were they subject to corporal punishment. The punishment could be canceled by giving up official rank or by paying a fine. These procedures were given in detail in the codes of various dynasties.[55] The inequality between the officials and the commoners was most striking in the fact that the punishment of a commoner who injured an official was heavier than in ordinary cases in which both parties were commoners.[56]

From the above discussion we may conclude that the officials and the commoners were two different status groups, whether in terms of prestige, or style of life, or legal privileges.

However, it would be a mistake to think that China was a two-class society. Were there only two classes? The answer must be in the negative. All the theories seeking to justify the privileges of the ruling class were focused on the respective statuses and roles of the rulers and the ruled. They were not concerned with the different statuses within the ruled class. From the standpoint of the power structure, all the "four people" (*ssu mln*) might be considered as one homogeneous group—all of them were the ruled. However, sociologically speaking, in terms of social stratification they could not be considered one class. First, not all persons in the same occupational group enjoyed the same status. Witness the difference between wealthy merchants and small shopowners or peddlers. Similar variations also characterized the farmers: to include landowners, owner-cultivators, tenants, and hired laborers in a single class would certainly be misleading. Furthermore, numerous occupational groups were all classified as commoners. Obviously, neither their roles in the society nor their statuses were the same. Different occupations were accorded different degrees of prestige. The traditional order of scholars, farmers, artisans, and merchants itself already suggested that there was a stratified difference in prestige. The status of the nonofficial scholars was the highest among the commoners, because they were the only group engaged in mental labor. They were considered the best elements among the commoners—the elite. The occupation of farmer, artisan, merchant, butcher, and the like was considered physical work, and their statuses were therefore inferior. This kind of classification, in which the officials were distinguished from the commoners and, among the latter group, the scholars were again marked off from the others, is quite similar to Pareto's classification of governing and nongoverning elites, on the one hand, and the nonelite, on the other.[57]

Among those who performed physical labor, farmers were held to be the most productive, and therefore their status came next to that of the scholars. Artisans and merchants, whose efforts were considered less productive, had an unfavorable position and were looked down upon by the society, especially by the intellectuals. An example may be cited from the *Family Instructions* of Lu Yu, in which he advised his descendants that they should devote themselves to study and make a living by teaching, that it was all right for them to become farmers, but that they should never be engaged in the "small men's business of the marketplace," which he considered would be a great disgrace to his family. He also expressed concern about the fate of his descendants who might be "degraded to the marketplace or reduced to government runners."[58] During certain periods, merchants were particularly discriminated against. They were allowed neither to wear silk nor to use horses in Han times.[59] Similar restrictions against horseback-riding were also invoked against merchants and artisans in the T'ang dynasty.[60] And at times, these two occupational groups, as well as butchers and sorcerers, were forbidden to take the civil service examinations or enter upon an official career.[61] However, the stratified order described above was an ideal pattern. The actual situation was much more complicated. The inferior status of merchants in Chinese history has usually been exaggerated. In spite of the fact that their class position did not correspond to their status,[62] the influence of their wealth cannot be overlooked. It must have had some effect on their status and style of life.

Statesmen frequently complained that the merchants, by the possession of great wealth, had violated the sumptuary laws and enjoyed what they were not entitled to. Merchants in Han times were accused of wearing embroideries and silks.[63] It was also mentioned in a T'ang edict that many merchants and artisans rode on horses which bore rich decorations.[64] With these deviations in mind, it is not difficult for us to imagine what status a wealthy merchant actually had in the society. For, if the style of life peculiar to the privileged class was no longer monopolized by it, then the status order was already threatened. Their trespass against the regulations meant that the merchants were successful in sharing the honor of the superior status group, to which they were not entitled legally. The fact of close communication between merchants and officials can also be documented.[65] Association with the most honored group must have greatly enhanced the prestige of merchants in society. In these circumstances we can hardly imagine that merchants had an inferior status among the commoners. That a wealthy merchant usually had a status superior to that of a farmer, who was supposed to be in a higher position but was actually exploited by him, was well illustrated in a Han memorial of Ch'ao Ts'o.[66]

All these facts lead us to think that probably the merchants were discriminated against not simply because they were despised by the ruling class but because their economic power constituted a constant threat to those whose privileges were legally protected. All the efforts at discrimination and the repeated warnings may be looked upon as a reaction on the part of the elite to the danger of the merchants' intrusion into the status group. The latter made jealous and vigorous efforts to guard their status and privileges.[67]

It may also be pointed out that the status of merchants did not remain the same all the time. They must have enjoyed a higher status in periods such as the Ming and Ch'ing, when there was no unfavorable sumptuary law against them, when they were not excluded from the privilege of taking the civil service examinations, and when there was a growth of industry and commerce which greatly strengthened their financial power. All these factors must have contributed to the improvement of their status and the enhancement of their social mobility.

Thus it is obvious that the commoners, though as a group they had a social and legal status inferior to that of the officials, may be subdivided. There were differences in occupational prestige. Moreover, wealth, though not a determining criterion of Chinese stratification, nevertheless influenced in some degree the status of different occupational groups as well as that of persons in the same occupational group. Unfortunately, we have only fragmentary knowledge about the prestige of various occupations. There are evidences that certain occupations were superior in prestige, whereas certain other occupations were inferior.[68] But we are unable to compare the prestige of the various occupations and thus to reconstruct a scale of occupational prestige in stratified order. Such a study would require the subjective judgment and evaluation of the various occupations in the society, either in terms of accorded status or in terms of subjective self-ranking, and these are impossible to obtain in a historical study.

5. Class Structure: "Mean" People

Finally, there was the lowest stratum in the social pyramid. This group was comprised of slaves, prostitutes, entertainers, government runners, and such regionally defined groups as the *yueh-hu,* or singers and music players, in Shensi and Shansi, the "beggars" in Kiangsu and Anhwei, the "lazy people"[69] in Chekiang, the boatmen[70] in Kwangtung, the "permanent servants"[71] in Hui-chou, Ning-kuo, and Ch'ih-chou of Anhwei Province, and others. Their occupations, which were merely to serve or entertain others, were considered nonproductive and as making the least contribution to society. They were therefore placed lowest on the prestige scale and labeled "mean" people. Certain families ruled that any one of their members who chose to become an actor, prostitute, or government runner was to be expelled from the clan, since engaging in any of these mean occupations was considered a serious disgrace to the whole group.[72] The social distance between the "mean" people and the common people was great. Intermarriage between the two strata was socially and legally forbidden. Social mobility was very slight. In fact, the "mean" people formed a caste more than a class.

Moreover, the "mean" people were the negatively privileged class. They were excluded from taking the civil service examinations,[73] a prohibition which made it impossible for them to enter upon an official career. Their children were similarly deprived.[74] Thus the best avenue for social mobility was closed to them. Under sumptuary law they were allowed to have only the most humble style of life. If the style of life peculiar to the officials gave them special social honor, then we may say that the style of life peculiar to the "mean" group, such as a certain specified color or decoration, was designed particularly to give the bearers social dishonor, so that they would not be mixed up with the "good" people. For instance, a black gown[75] or green scarf[76] was a symbol of humiliation and an indication of inferior status. Nor were the "mean" people given the same treatment as commoners before the law. Every dynastic code held that a slave who had injured or killed a commoner was to be punished more severely than in ordinary cases between equals, whereas a commoner who had injured or killed a slave was to be punished less severely.[77] The same principle also operated in cases of illicit intercourse.[78]

6. The Bureaucratic Power Basis

From the above discussion it is obvious that the superior-inferior relationship in traditional Chinese society was based on occupational categories. The officials had the highest status. The scholars, farmers, artisans, merchants, and other occupational groups, known as the common people or "good" people, came next. They may be divided into substrata. Then, in the lowest stratum, there were the "mean" people.

There was a close correlation between the distribution of power and the distribution of statuses.[79] In other words, bureaucracy was the source of prestige and privilege. Those persons permitted to enter the bureaucracy had the highest social status and enjoyed the most privileges. The scholars had the highest status among the commoners because their training constituted the basic qualification for civil administration. Thus they were the potential candidates for membership in the bureaucracy. That was why the possessor of a degree under the examination system had a status superior to that of a scholar without a degree; he was a step closer to the power structure than the ordinary scholar. It has been keenly observed by Max Weber that "social rank in China has been determined more by qualification for office than by wealth."[80] Unlike the commoners who, with a few exceptions, at least in theory could take the examination and enter officialdom, the "mean" people were excluded from such privileges. In terms of political power they were permanently barred from entering the power structure. Thus they had the most inferior status in society. It is not exaggerating to say that the hierarchy of prestige corresponded closely with the hierarchy of power. We cannot understand and interpret social stratification in traditional China if the stratification system is not considered in terms of power. In this sense, then, the "ruling class and the ruled class" dichotomy is a key concept in Chinese social and political thought, and its sociological significance should not be overlooked.

Notes

1. *Hsün-tzu* (*Ssu-pu Ts'ung-k'an* ed. [hereinafter cited as "SPTK ed."]), chap. 6, p. 2b; H. H. Dubs, *The Works of Hsün-tzu* (hereinafter cited as "Dubs") (London: Arthur Probsthain, 1928), p. 152.
2. A statement of Liu-tzu. See *Ch'un-ch'iu Tso Chuan Chu-su* (*Ssu-pu pei-yao* ed. [hereinafter cited as "SPPY ed."]), chap. 27, p. 6a; James Legge, *The Chinese Classics* (hereinafter cited as "Legge") (5 vols.; London, 1861–72), V, Part I, 381–82.
3. A statement of Chih Wu-tzu. See *Tso Chuan Chu-su*, chap. 30, p. 16a; Legge, V, Part II, 440.
4. A statement of Yen-kung. See *Kuo-yü* (SPTK ed.), chap. 4, p. 1a.
5. *Tso Chuan Chu-su*, chap. 32, p. 2b; Legge, V, Part II, 458.
6. A statement of Kuo. See *Kuo-yü*, chap. 1, p. 16a.

7. *Meng-tzu Chu-su* (SPPY ed.), chap. 5B, pp. 1b–2a; Legge, II, 125–26.
8. *Meng-tzu Chu-su,* chap. 5A, p. 5a; Legge, II, 120.
9. *Hsün-tzu,* chap. 6, pp. 1b–2a; Dubs, p. 152.
10. *Hsün-tzu,* chap. 13, p. 1a; Dubs, p. 213.
11. *Hsün-tzu,* chap. 5, p. 3b. Cf. Dubs, pp. 123–24.
12. *Hsün-tzu,* chap. 6, p. 2a. Cf. Dubs, p. 152.
13. *Hsün-tzu,* chap. 2, p. 22a–b; Dubs, p. 65.
14. Thus *li* was defined by Hsün-tzu as follows: "*Li* is to nourish. A great man enjoys nourishment and also likes discrimination. And what is meant by discrimination? The answer is that a graded sequence be set up for the noble and the humble, that there is a difference between the elders and the young, and that whether the individuals are poor or rich, unimportant or important, all will be appropriate" (*Hsün-tzu,* chap. 13, pp. 1b–2a; cf. Dubs, p. 214). For a more detailed discussion on the meaning and function of *li* see Ch'ü T'ung-tsu, *Chung-kuo Fa-lü Yü Chung-kuo She-hui* (Shanghai: Commercial Press, 1947), pp. 217ff.
15. Talcott Parsons, *The Social System* (New York: The Free Press, 1951), pp. 195–98.
16. *Meng-tzu Chu-su,* chap. 3B, p. 1b; Legge, II, 73.
17. *Hsün-tzu,* chap. 6, p. 4b. Cf. Dubs, p. 121.
18. *Meng-tzu Chu-su,* chap. 7A, p. 6a; Legge, II, 172.
19. *Hsün-tzu,* chap. 8, p. 7a–b.
20. *Hsün-tzu,* chap. 5, p. 9a–b. Cf. Dubs, p. 131.
21. *Hsün-tzu,* chap. 12, pp. 7b–8a. Cf. Dubs, p. 194.
22. *Lun-yü Chu-su* (SPPY ed.), chap. 8, p. 3a; Legge, I, 76.
23. *Lun-yü Chu-su,* chap. 8, p. 3a.
24. *Li-chi Chu-su* (SPPY ed.), chap. 52, p. 7b; Legge, I, 263.
25. Wang Fu, *Ch'ien-fu Lun* (SPTK ed.), chap. 1, p. 10a.
26. Wang Ch'ung, *Lun-heng* (SPTK ed.), chap. 1, p. 1a.
27. *Kuo-yü,* chap. 6, pp. 3b–5a.
28. For the significance of this concept in approaches to the sociology of knowledge, see R. K. Merton, *Social Theory and Social Structure* (New York: The Free Press, 1949), p. 223.
29. H. G. Creel, *Confucius, the Man and the Myth* (New York: John Day, 1949), p. 148.
30. *Lun-yü Chu-su,* chap. 3, p. 5a; Legge, I, 24.
31. *Lun-yü Chu-su,* chap. 13, p. 1a–b; Legge, I, 127–28.
32. *Lun-yü Chu-su,* chap. 12, p. 4a; Legge, I, 120.
33. *Lun-yü Chu-su,* chap. 16, pp. 2b–3b; Legge, I, 174–75. Cf. Hsiao Kung-ch'üan, *Chung-kuo Cheng-chih Ssu-hsiang Shih* (2 vols., Shanghai: Commercial Press, 1945), I, 43–44.
34. *Meng-tzu Chu-su,* chap. 5A, p. 5a–b; Legge, II, 120–21.
35. *Meng-tzu Chu-su,* chap. 2A, p. 8a; 5A, p. 4b; Legge, II, 38, 118.
36. *Meng-tzu Chu-su,* chap. 10A, p. 3a; Legge, II, 250–52.
37. *Meng-tzu Chu-su,* chap. 6A, p. 4b; Legge, II, 145. In another instance, the king of Ch'i was willing "to give Mencius a house, somewhere in the middle of the kingdom and to support his disciples with an allowance of 10,000 *chung*" (*Meng-tzu Chu-su,* chap. 4B, p. 4a; Legge, II, 226).
38. *Meng-tzu Chu-su,* chap. 6A, pp. 4b–5a; Legge, II, 145–46.
39. *Meng-tzu Chu-su,* chap. 13B, p. 3a–b; Legge, 343–44.
40. Confucius himself made the remark that "in teaching there should be no dis-

tinction of classes" (*Lun-yü Chu-su,* chap. 15, p. 6a; Legge, I, 169). Cf. Feng Yu-lan, *A History of Chinese Philosophy,* trans. Derk Bodde (Peiping: Henri Vetch, 1937), pp. 47–52.

41. Ch'ien Mu, *Hsien-Ch'in Chu-tzu Hsi-nien K'ao-pien* (Shanghai: Commercial Press, 1935), p. 77.

42. *Lun-yü Chu-su,* chap. 6, pp. 2a, 3b; chap. 11, pp. 3b, 5b; chap. 13, p. 4a; Legge, I, 50, 53, 106–7, 110; *Shih-chi* (Po-na ed.), chap. 67; *Han-shu* (Po-na ed.), chap. 88, p. 2a.

43. *Lun-yü Chu-su,* chap. 19, p. 2b; Legge, I, 208.

44. Here we may cite the case of Marquis Wen of Wei, who honored Tzu-hsia as his teacher, and the case of the group of scholars who were received by the rulers of Ch'i at Chi-hsia. They were not officially appointed, but they received the salary of *shang ta-fu* and were treated nicely (see *Shih-chi,* chap. 46, pp. 13b–14a; chap. 74, p. 5a; Huan K'uan, *Yen-t'ieh Lun* [SPTK ed.], chap. 2, 13b; cf. Ch'ien Mu, *op. cit.,* pp. 215–21.

45. Chao I, *Nien-erh Shih Cha-chi* (SPPY ed.), chap. 2, p. 9a–b.

46. Cf. Hsiao Kung-ch'üan, *op. cit.,* I, 49–50.

47. *Hsün-tzu,* chap. 5, p. 1b.

48. *Han-shu,* chap. 88, pp. 4b–6a.

49. Hsü T'ien-lin, *Hsi-Han Hui-yao,* chaps. 44, 45; *idem., Tung-Han Hui-yao,* chap. 26.

50. *Hsi-Han Hui-yao,* chap. 44; *Tung-Han Hui-yao,* chap. 26.

51. For details see Ch'ü T'ung-tsu, *op. cit.,* chap. 3.

52. *Kuan-tzu* (SPTK ed.), chap. 1, p. 14a.

54. *Han-shu,* chap. 10, p. 13b.

54. *Ibid.,* chap. 1B, p. 10b; chap. 8, p. 24a; chap. 12, p. 3a; *Hou-Han-shu* (Po-na ed.), chap. 1A, p. 30b; *Hsü Han-chih* (Po-na ed.), chap. 26, p. 12; *Sung-shih* (Po-na ed.), chap. 199, p. 22a; *Ming-lü Chi-chieh Fu-li* (1908 ed.), chap. 1, pp. 6a, 11a–b; *Ta-Ch'ing Lü-li Hui-chi P'ien-lan* (1872 ed.), ch. 4, p. 25a.

55. *Wei-shu* (Po-na ed.), chap. 111, p. 12b; *Sui-shu* (Po-na ed.), chap. 25, pp. 9a, 18a; *T'ang-lü Su-i* (Lan-lin Sunshih ed.), chap. 2, pp. 10b–13a; *Sung Hsing-t'ung* (Liu-shih Chia-yeh-t'ang ed.), chap. 2, p. 11a; *Ming-lü Chi-chieh,* chap. 1, pp. 19a–23a; *Ta-Ch'ing Lü-li,* chap. 4, pp. 7a–b, 10a, 48a–b, 60a.

56. *T'ang-lü Su-i,* chap. 21, pp. 11a, 14a–b; *Sung Hsing-t'ung,* chap. 21, pp. 10a, 12b; *Ming-lü Chi-chieh,* chap. 20, p. 11a–b; *Ta-Ch'ing Lü-li,* chap. 27, pp. 31a–32a.

57. Vilfredo Pareto, *The Mind and Society,* trans. Andrew Bongiorno and Arthur Livingston (4 vols., New York: Harcourt, Brace Co., 1935), III, 1419ff.

58. Lu Yu, *Fang-weng Chia-hsün* (*Chi-pu-tsu-chai Ts'ung-shu* ed.), pp. 2a, 9b.

59. *Han-shu,* chap. 1B, p. 11b; 24B, p. 3a.

60. *Hsin T'ang-shu* (Po-na ed.), chap. 24, p. 12b.

61. Merchants were not permitted to enter on an official career, according to Han regulations (*Han-shu,* chap. 11, p. 3b; chap. 24B, p. 3b; chap. 72, p. 16b; *Hou-Han-shu,* chap. 81, p. 36a); neither were sorcerers (*Hou-Han-shu,* chap. 83, p. 15a). Artisans and merchants were not permitted to be officials in Sui and T'ang times (*Sui-shu,* chap. 2, p. 10b; *Chiu T'ang-shu* [Po-na ed.], chap. 43, pp. 3b, 7a; chap. 177, p. 18b; *Hsin T'ang-shu,* chap. 45, p. 1a; chap. 181, p. 5a). Under Sung, artisans and merchants were not qualified for the *chin-shih* examination (*Sung-shih,* chap. 155, p. 3a). In the

Liao dynasty, physicians, diviners, butchers, and merchants were also excluded from the privilege of taking examinations (*Liao-shih* [Po-na ed.], chap. 20, p. 4b; chap. 27, p. 4b).

62. Here we adopt the terminology of Max Weber. "Class" refers to the possession of property, and "status" refers to prestige (see H. H. Gerth and C. W. Mills, *From Max Weber: Essays in Sociology* [New York: Oxford University Press, 1946], pp. 181ff.; A. M. Henderson and Talcott Parsons, translators, Max Weber: *The Theory of Social and Economic Organization* [New York: Oxford University Press, 1947], pp. 424–29).

63. *Han-shu*, chap. 48, p. 14a.

64. Wang P'u, *T'ang Hui-yao* (*Wu-ying-tien Chü-chen-pan* ed.), chap. 31, p. 15a–b.

65. *Han-shu*, chap. 24A, p. 11b; chap. 57A, p. 1b; chap. 59, p. 4b; chap. 91, p. 8a–b. It was remarked in an early Ch'ing source that two wealthy families of Wan-p'ing, Ch'a and Sheng, were fond of associating with the *shih ta-fu* and that they were accused by the censors for this reason (Chao-lien, *Hsiao-t'ing Hsü-lu* [1880 ed.], chap. 1, pp. 63b–64a).

66. Ch'ao Ts'o's memorial reads: "At the present time the laws and regulations (of the government) disesteem the merchant, but the merchant is already rich and honored. (Laws and regulations) dignify the farmer, but the farmer is already poor and disesteemed. Thus what usage honors is what rulers disesteem; what offices (*li*) debase is what law dignifies" (*Han-shu*, chap. 24A, pp. 11b–12a; N. L. Swann, *Food and Money in Ancient China* [Princeton, N.J.: Princeton University Press, 1950], p. 166).

67. Max Weber has noted the effect of economic power on status as follows: "Yet if such economic acquisition and power gave the agent any honor at all, his wealth would result in his attaining more honor than those who successfully claim honor by virtue of style of life. Therefore all groups having interests in the status order react with special sharpness precisely against the pretensions of purely economic acquisition. In most cases they react the more vigorously the more they feel themselves threatened" (Gerth and Mills, *op. cit.*, p. 192).

68. Cf. nn. 58 and 59.

69. The "lazy people" (*to-min*) in Chekiang and the "beggars" (*kai-hu*) in Kiangsu and Anhwei were the same kind of people. Actually they were not beggars. Their main occupation was to render services to others at weddings or funerals. Most of the women supported themselves by dressing the hair of women of ordinary families or by being the *Pan-niang*, the maid who accompanied a bride (Shen Te-fu, *Yeh Hou Pien* [1827 ed.], chap. 24, pp. 29b–30a; *idem.*, *Pi-chou-hsuan Sheng-yü* [*Hsueh-hai Lei-pien* ed.], chap. C, p. 10a).

70. The boatmen (*tan-hu*) are said to have been aborigines of the south, the *Nan-man*. Fishing, gathering of oysters, and collecting pearls were their major occupations. They were not treated as equals by the common people and were not allowed to live on the land by the native Chinese. The boats were their homes (T'ao Tsung-i, *Cho-keng Lu* [*Ching-ti Pi-shu* ed.], chap. 10, p. 5a; Ku Yen-wu, *T'ien-hsia Chun-kuo Li-ping Shu* [SPTK ed.], ts'e 29, pp. 107–8; Ch'ü Hsuan-ying, *Chung-kuo She-hui Shih-liao Ts'ung-ch'ao* [3 vols.; Shanghai: Commercial Press, 1937], II, 389–91).

71. Legally the "permanent servants," *shih-p'u* or *pan-tang*, were neither considered slaves nor classified as "mean" people. However, they were treated by the

local populace as "mean" people and were compelled to render services to a family. When they enrolled for examination or purchased an official title, they were always accused by the commoners, who complained that they were "mean" people and not entitled to such privileges. An edict was issued in 1727 to assure their free status. Later, in 1810, however, a distinction was made in the law between two categories: those who were still kept by a master and rendered service in the latter's family were treated as slaves and were allowed to enter the examinations or to purchase an official title only three generations after manumission. On the other hand, those who were not kept by a master and did not render service at the time were treated as free people and were entitled to the above-mentioned privileges three generations later (for details see *Ch'ing Shih-lu* [1937 ed.], Shih-tsung, chap. 56, pp. 23b–28b; Jen-tsung, chap. 223, p. 25a–b; *Ta-Ch'ing Hui-tien Shih-li* [1886 ed.], chap. 158; *Hu-pu Tse-li* [1831 ed.], chap. 3, p. 27a–b; *Hsueh-cheng Ch'üan-shu* [1812 ed.], chap. 43, pp. 29a–30a; *Ta-Ch'ing Lü-li*, chap. 8, p. 18a–b; chap. 27, pp. 59a–62b).

72. E.g., see *Yun-yang Chang-shih Liu-hsiu Tsung-p'u* (1887), chap. 3, p. 2b.

73. *Liao-shih*, chap. 20, p. 3b; *Yuan-shih* (Po-na ed.), chap. 81, p. 9a; *Yuan Tien-chang* (*Ta-Yuan Sheng-cheng Kuo-ch'ao Tien-chang*, 1908), chap. 31, p. 15b; *Ming-shih* (Po-na ed.), chap. 3, p. 9a; *Hsueh-cheng Ch'üan-shu*, chap. 43, pp. 1a, ff.

74. According to Ch'ing law, the children of prostitutes, entertainers, and government runners were not allowed to participate in the civil service examinations. Any member of such a family who entered for an examination or purchased an official title was dismissed and given one hundred strokes (*Ta-Ch'ing Lü-li*, chap. 8, p. 16b; *Hsueh-cheng Ch'üan-shu*, chap. 43, pp. 1a, 4a, 5a–b). Although the *yueh-hu* in Shensi and Shansi, the *kai-hu* in Kiangsu and Anhwei, the *to-min* in Chekiang, and the *tan-hu* in Kwangtung were removed from the category of "mean" people in 1723, 1729, and 1730, respectively, they were not allowed to participate in the examinations immediately. Their descendants could have this privilege only after a lapse of four generations from the time of their change of occupation (*Tu-Ch'ing Hui-tien Shih-li*, chap. 158; *Hsueh-cheng Ch'üan-shu*, chap. 43, pp. 4a–5a).

75. In Ming and Ch'ing times black gowns were worn by the government runners, the so-called *tsao-li* (*Ming Hui-tien* [1587 ed.], chap. 61, p. 39b; *Ming-shih*, chap. 67, p. 23a).

76. It was required in the Yuan dynasty that a male member of the family of a prostitute wear a blue scarf (*Yuan Tien-chang*, chap. 29, p. 8b; *T'ung-chih T'iao-ko* [Peiping: National Peiping Library, 1930], chap. 9, pp. 4a–5a). In the Ming dynasty a green scarf was worn by the actors belonging to the *Chiao-fang-ssu* (*Ming Hui-tien*, chap. 61, 39b; *Ming-shih*, chap. 67, p. 23a).

77. *T'ang-lü Su-i*, chap. 17, p. 7a; chap. 22, pp. 2a–5b; *Sung Hsing-t'ung*, chap. 17, p. 6b; chap. 22, pp. 2b–5a; *Yuan-shih*, chap. 104, p. 7a; chap. 105, p. 13a–b; *Ming-lü Chi-chieh*, chap. 19, p. 5b; chap. 20, pp. 22a–b, 25a–26a; *Ta-Ch'ing Lü-li*, chap. 26, p. 17b; chap. 27, p. 58a–b; chap. 28, pp. 2a–4a.

78. *T'ang-lü Su-i*, chap. 26, pp. 11b–12a, 13b; *Sung Hsing-t'ung*, chap. 26, pp. 14b, 16a; *Yuan-shih*, chap. 104, p. 10a–b; *Ming-lü Chi-chieh*, chap. 25, pp. 8b, 11b; *Ta-Ch'ing Lü-li*, chap. 33, pp. 31a, 40a.

79. For a discussion of the correlation between power and status in a society, see Kingsley Davis, *Human Society* (New York: Macmillan, 1949), p. 95.

80. Gerth and Mills, *op. cit.*, p. 416.

H. A. R. Gibb

and

Harold Bowen

GOVERNMENT AND SOCIAL
STRUCTURE IN THE ARAB
PROVINCES OF THE
OTTOMAN EMPIRE

THE WESTERN OBSERVER, accustomed to an organized social hierarchy, and inclined to pursue the ideal of stability through a system of mutual rights and duties between the different classes and social groups, braced by legal safeguards and checks, and sanctioned by some participation in the control of the legislating and administrative bodies, can find nothing comparable to such a system in the Ottoman Empire. He is therefore apt to conclude that the Ottoman regime was essentially a system of exploitation, injurious to the social and economic welfare of the subjects, that it not only lacked any guarantees for life and property against the violence, cupidity, or caprice of the soldiery, but in effect made agriculture, industry, and commerce their helpless victims. Legal redress, it was assumed, could not be looked for from courts whose officers were a byword for venality and corruption, and whose decrees, moreover, were illusory, since they depended for enforcement upon the goodwill of the very administration and soldiery against whom they were directed. Such is the impression conveyed by all, or almost all, the travelers and writers of the eighteenth century.[1] More especially do they marvel that any people could endure the rule of such a caste as the Mamlûks, in which the ordinary evils of the Ottoman administration were intensified by the servile origin and violent character of the governors and by the instability of their power.[2]

A perusal of the contemporary oriental documents and of the careful descriptions and analyses which were compiled by the French officials during their period of administration of Egypt[3] makes it clear that the Turco-Mamlûk administration was in itself by no means the capricious and irresponsible tyranny which has so frequently been held up to obloquy. It is true that, theoretically, no system of government could be worse or could more quickly lead to economic disruption and anarchy than that of foreign slave-born military despots, linked by no ties of nature to the country and people they exploited, and with no ambitions but power and wealth. Yet, in

Reprinted with permission from *Islamic Society and the West: A Study of the Impact of Western Civilization on Moslem Culture in the Near East* by H. A. R. Gibb and Harold Bowen, Vol. I, *Islamic Society in the Eighteenth Century,* published by Oxford University Press, 1950, under the auspices of the Royal Institute of International Affairs.

fact, by the middle of the eighteenth century, Egypt had lived for more than five hundred years under the Mamlûk system, and was still far from relapsing into anarchy.[4] The level of her economic prosperity had undoubtedly declined during this half-millennium (in large measure owing to causes external to Egypt itself),[5] large areas of land had gone out of cultivation, and it is probable that the population had been appreciably reduced.[6] Had it not been for the Ottoman conquest, a breakdown might perhaps have taken place much earlier; but we have reason to believe that, by reducing the crushing burden of taxation and by maintaining a fairly regular system of administration, the establishment of Ottoman supremacy guaranteed (at least down to the beginning of the eighteenth century) to the population of the Arabic provinces a period of relative tranquillity after the disasters of the later Mamlûk, Timûrid, and Türkmen regimes.

Yet the paradox remains of a government, generally apathetic, unprogressive, and careless of the welfare of its subjects, and often arbitrary and violent in its dealings with them, and a society upon whose institutions and activities such a government had little or no effect. The explanation is to be found in the very lack of a complex, all-embracing political organization. As we have already suggested, we may visualize Moslem society as composed of two coexisting groups, the relations between which were for the most part formal and superficial. One group formed the governing class of soldiers and officials, the other the governed class of merchants, artisans, and cultivators.[7] Each was organized internally on independent lines, and neither group interfered with the organization of the other in normal circumstances. From time immemorial the governing class had lived on a percentage of the produce of the land, supplemented by various duties on goods, and the social structure of the other class had accommodated itself to this situation. In spite of political and dynastic revolutions, stability was ensured by the fact that under all changes of sovereignty the existing bureaucracy remained in being, and maintained the traditional practices with a minimum of alteration.[8] The new masters stepped into the places vacated by their predecessors; the titles to assignments of land were redistributed, but the relations between landlord and peasant, official and artisan, remained on the whole unchanged. The extreme conservatism of the bureaucracy is nowhere more clearly seen than in Egypt, where the respective functions of the Moslem accountants, the Jewish gold dealers and bookkeepers, and the Coptic tax assessors and collectors in the eighteenth century were practically what they had been in the tenth. From the outside it looked as though the *Pasha* or *Bey* could do as he pleased; in practice he was restrained from excessive abuse of his power partly by his own reverence for tradition and acceptance of traditional usage as binding,[9] partly by the steady pressure of the bureaucracy, who had learned by experience that a certain standard of agricultural and industrial productivity was in their own best interests. Changes of dynasty, even, were not without their compensations. During a long period of uninterrupted dynastic rule, abuses naturally crept in and multiplied, sometimes to an extent which threatened social stability. The advent of a new dynasty swept these away and revitalized the old system; usually the energy and foresight of its founder resulted in a number of minor reforms in addition. Such had been the case in the Ottoman conquest, and the real defect of Ottoman rule was that it had lasted too long.

A further consequence of this state of affairs was that the Ottoman conquest did not result in the Ottomanization of the Arabic lands. A Turkish military aristocracy was no new phenomenon in either Egypt or Arab Asia, but even the bureaucracy never became thoroughly Turkicized. On the contrary, we find that the Turkish (or rather Bosniak) garrisons, intermarrying generation after generation with the Arab inhabitants, became absorbed into the local population, apparently even to the extent of forgetting their Turkish tongue. The old administrative cadres retained both their traditional functions and their Arabic idiom. The careful reader of Cabartî's chronicle cannot fail to be struck by the persistence of the technical administrative terms of the medieval Mamlûk Sultanate, and it is very questionable whether a knowledge of Turkish extended far outside the ranks of the senior officials. The increasing predominance of the Mamlûk troops[10] still further, if anything, counteracted any tendency towards Ottomanization, since they deliberately cultivated the tradition of pre-Ottoman times.[11] In Syria, however, Ottoman influence was much stronger, but here too, except in Aleppo and the northern districts,[12] it scarcely penetrated below the ranks of the governing class. Even the aristocratic families among the 'ulemâ of Damascus, though in frequent relations with the Turkish 'ulemâ and intermarrying with Turkish families, resented the introduction of Turkish usages,[13] and only those who had studied in Constantinople were familiar with the Turkish language.[14]

The interposition of the bureaucracy thus shielded the mass of the population—cultivators, artisans, merchants—from the effective intervention of the military power in their organization and activities. Over a long period of centuries they had created an independent organism, so solidly based and yet so resilient that its stability was never in danger. On this social and economic basis the structure of Islamic society was built up; the foreign slaves, foreign rulers and administrators, and foreign merchants formed only the superstructure, which could be supported without risk of collapse, so long as the foundations remained intact.

To describe the structure of this society in any detail would as yet be premature. It is evident upon closer examination that we have to deal, not with a closely knitted organism, even within the restricted limits of a single province, but rather with a vast number of small social groups, which may almost be described as self-governing. A recent investigator has defined such a society as "consisting mainly of territorial and genealogical communities, rooted in thousands of more or less isolated centers, mostly villages, which are autonomous units, almost self-sufficient in their religious, social, political, and economic life."[15] It will be part of our task to analyze more fully elsewhere the triple relationships involved in this system—those between the individual and the group, between the groups themselves, and between the different groups and the administration, but certain common features may be indicated here.

In the first place the groups carried none of the social and religious exclusiveness of the Indian castes, and are not to be regarded as in any way analogous to the latter. There is indeed a tendency towards the marking-off of the military forces as a superior caste, but even this is offset very considerably by their normal social relationships; and amongst the social groups themselves any similar tendencies seem to be foreign to the mentality of Western Asia. This is again reflected in the religious equalitarianism adopted by Islâm, which has in turn strengthened the resistance to caste ideas, if it has not wholly prevented the classification of social grades. The absence of rigid caste barriers gave sufficient flexibility to the system to allow exceptional talent or personality to make its way up; and there are enough examples in our very restricted material of persons who, born into one group, attained to some position in another, to justify us in asserting that there was at all times a certain movement within and between the individual groups.

Nevertheless, for the enormous majority of persons, their station in life, their occupation, and their economic position were regulated by the accident of birth. A son normally followed his father, a daughter was generally married within the village or craft group. Consequently where these groups were of long standing (and there were few which were not), the tie of common occupation was almost always strengthened by that of blood, and the craft or village community—if not too large—was constituted by members of a single family more or less widely branched. Such a constitution enabled the effect of the rigid Islamic law of inheritance, namely to decompose property into minute fractions, to be mitigated by constant recombination, and rendered the community more compact and homogeneous. On the other hand, the already powerful control of tradition over the conduct of the individual member of the group was intensified by the family ties which linked him to the other members, and by the disciplinary sanctions which the family was in a position to exercise. In these circumstances initiative was not so much stifled as nonexistent, since every consideration combined to persuade each member that in the maintenance of the established order lay his own best interests, and nothing ever came to his observation or knowledge which might induce a belief that a better order could exist.

The relations in which the separate groups stood to one another were less uniform. Groups with different economic functions—such as cultivator and artisan, artisan and merchant—were obviously linked by the natural or traditional economy of their provinces, which was almost always of a simple and direct kind. The normal interchange of services was conducted in the cities usually on a money basis, in the country districts very often for produce in kind. Except for these, and for the common participation of local groups in local religious ceremonies or the more specialized association of two or three groups in a religious fraternity, there seems to have been extraordinarily little direct contact between the various groups. Each inhabited its own quarter in the city, or its own village or section of a village in the country, and, in certain districts at least, the existence of factional feuds set up a positive barrier to social intercourse.

Administratively, each group had a chief member, an elected or appointed şeyḫ or leader, through whom all its relations with the governing authorities were conducted. The holder of an assignment of land acted through the village şeyḫ or şeyḫs, who were held responsible for the maintenance of order and the collection of the taxes. Each industrial and merchant corporation had likewise its şeyḫ, with the same administrative and taxing functions, who dealt with the relevant officer of government either directly or through a superior şeyḫ possessing jurisdiction over a number of corporations. In every case, again, these relations were fixed by tradition, and for the most part strictly adhered to. The very looseness of this organization was one of the chief safeguards of the social structure. Any violence on the part of a military officer, a government official, or a band of Arab marauders could normally affect only individual groups; when it expended itself, the groups rapidly recovered. In extreme cases, if the original group were entirely dissolved, a fresh group was formed, and—provided the violence was not renewed—set to work to rebuild the shattered economic tissue. When this happened too frequently (as was the case in the later medieval period) it caused a shrinkage in the numerical strength and economic capacity of the social structure as a whole, but did not destroy it. In general, therefore, the conduct of government touched only the surface of its life; here and there temporary dislocations might be caused, and a grasping and short-sighted policy might and did produce local contractions by allowing land to fall out of cultivation or forcing the stoppage or transfer of a branch of industry. But so long as the groups themselves, with their traditional organs of administration, remained intact, and so long as the intervention and extortions of the military governors were limited to the profits and spared the capital and the means of livelihood themselves, the social organism showed a marvelous power of recuperation.

The predominating role of traditional usage in all these relations, internal and external, has been sufficiently emphasized above. Its precise character necessarily varied from group to group and from place to place, even within the same district. There can be little doubt that in many groups this tradition went back far behind the Islamic era; in Upper Egypt, especially, its roots lay in the ancient Pharaonic civilization. Among the industrial groups, on the other hand, the traditional usages as a whole derived from the Middle Ages, though specific practices might be of earlier origin. But it was not merely the fact of its antiquity that made traditional usage all but absolute; indeed it was generally quite sufficient for a usage to be once established, even at a most recent date, for it to enjoy the same prescriptive character. Its potency lay in its association with the religious ideas of governors and governed alike; not primarily in the sense that the religious authorities of Islam gave a religious or quasi-religious sanction to each and every usage,[16] but rather that reverence for tradition was the doctrine most characteristic of and most strongly stressed in Islamic teaching. The close association of the religious and social structures will be examined later, but enough has been said to show that, for all its apparent fragility, even a Turkish or Mamlûk governor might hesitate to lay a sacrilegious hand on tradition.

It is not surprising that so intimate an association, governed by unwritten sanctions, should have escaped the notice of European travelers, whose contacts with Moslem society were most superficial.[17] But it is of importance for us to appreciate it thoroughly, as it is typical of the institutions of Islamic society and government generally. *"Point de lois fixes. . . ."* No written laws, whether with penal or other sanctions; in their place a network of traditional relations, maintained only by the common will, yet which had survived eight centuries of dynastic vicissitudes and conquering armies, and still regulated the conduct of both society and government. Similarly, in other fields, where at first sight there appears to be nothing but unregulated confusion, and even, to the Western eye, a total disregard of law and justice, we shall find custom and tradition setting recognized limits to conflicting jurisdictions and dictating what may not be done and what may be done, even though technically against the written law. In the last resort, it is a difference in the conception of law, and in the function of administrative law in particular, that is at the bottom of the misunderstanding.[18]

Such a system, on the other hand, possessed serious and inescapable drawbacks, quite apart from the personal suffering and economic loss resulting from its repeated violation by members of the governing and military classes. It perpetuated the gulf which separated the people from the government,[19] producing at best an apathetic acquiescence in it on their part, as a necessary evil, but not infrequently offering a foothold to elements of social opposition. Their direct relations with it were limited to the field of taxation, often extorted with violence[20] and supplemented by oppressive *avanias*. On the side of the government we have already seen its results in a similar apathy towards the interests of the subjects and an absence of all incentive to improvement or reform. But since the situation could not long remain stationary, the balance was continually shifting against the people by constant small encroachments. One institution, it is true, remained to form a positive link between them, and in a measure endeavored to redress the balance—the religious institution.

The second criticism to be brought against the system is its hostility to change and consequent stifling of initiative. If we may judge by the analogous situation in intellectual life, originality was not wholly nonexistent but it was suppressed in the supposed interests of the group, or if it could not be suppressed was ignored, and its achievements suffered to disappear.[21] We shall never know, in any probability, whether some Arab Jacquard devised an improved loom or some Turkish Watt discovered the power of steam, but we can confidently assert that, if any such invention had occurred, it would have been entirely without result. The whole social organism, in fact, was one characteristic of, and only possible in, a stationary or retrograde civilization, and herein lay its essential weakness. It is not an exaggeration to say that after so many centuries of immobility the processes of agriculture, industry, exchange, and learning had become little more than automatic, and had resulted in a species of atrophy that rendered those engaged in them all but incapable of changing their methods or outlook in the slightest degree.

It was this incapacity, rather than unwillingness, to learn[22] that above all characterized Asiatic Moslem society in the seventeenth and eighteenth centuries. Its sterilized brain could not effectually conceive any idea that lay outside the narrow range of its experience and tradition, nor could it meet any situation which deviated from the path traced by routine. So long as the Ottoman provinces lived in a closed intellectual, economic, and social order, the system continued to serve its purpose, though with steadily diminishing returns. But during the course of the eighteenth century various factors combined to disturb the existing equilibrium, more especially in the economic and military spheres, and created new problems which the old organization was totally unable to deal with. The result was to render the social order the helpless victim of violent solutions by which its protective covering of tradition was torn away and its institutions were exposed to destruction.[23]

Notes

1. But it must be remembered that their statements relate almost entirely to the last half of the eighteenth century, when the old structure was being rapidly undermined.
2. Of the numerous amiable descriptions of the Egyptian Beys, that of George Baldwin may serve as a sample: "The Mamaluks, a set of swineherds, vagabonds, any thing; kidnapped in the mountains of Mingrelia, Circassia, Georgia, and brought young into Egypt; sold, circumcised, and trained to the career of glory; their road to honour, apostacy; their title to power, assassination and a contempt of death; no stability, no order, no character among them, but a constant thirst and jealousy of command." *Political Recollections Relative to Egypt* (London, 1801), Preface, 50–1.—Cf. Volney, i. 157–8; and Lockroy, *Ahmed le Boucher,* pp. 4–6, whose account is false in all material particulars.

3. Although they too shared the general opinion of the Turco-Mamlûk administration.

4. The Mamlûk system of "fiefs" or "assignations" was introduced into Egypt by Saladin (regn. 1171–93) and with subsequent modifications (in 1315 and again, after the Ottoman conquest, in 1517 and 1526) remained substantially the same until the period of Mehmed 'Alî.—Cf. C. H. Becker, "Steuerpacht und Lehnswesen" in Islamstudien, i. 234 sqq. and the monographs of Poliak.

5. The most serious blow being the opening up of the Cape route to India in 1497, with the consequent diminution of the Indian transit trade in the Red Sea.

6. It is scarcely possible to gain more than a very rough idea of the population of Egypt in the Middle Ages, but in the fourteenth century it is not likely to have exceeded four millions. In 1800 it was estimated, after careful calculation, at a little over 2,400,000 (Chabrol, 8), but reasons will be given later for regarding this figure as an underestimate.

7. The place held by the "men of religion" is discussed below (ch. viii).

8. Hence the indifference shown by the population of Egypt to political changes and the quarrels of the Beys, remarked on by all travellers; e.g., Sonnini: "The tradesman neither quitted nor shut up his shop; and the mechanic worked coolly at his door, without giving himself the smallest concern respecting the combatants" (English trans., p. 428). But the factional feuds of the Janissaries at Damascus and elsewhere were a different matter.

9. It may be thought that this could hardly apply to the Mamlûks, but on the contrary they were, as many passages in Cabartî show, equally strongly attached to tradition.

10. It is remarkable that as late as the eighteenth century they were still called, even in Syria, by the medieval name Guzz.—Haidar, i. 93; Cab., passim; Lane, Mod. Egypt, chap. iv, first sentence.

11. The most striking illustration of this is the inscription of 'Alî Bey in the Mausoleum of the Inmâm el-Sâfi'î in Cairo, where he is called by the ancient wazirial and Caliphial titles "azîz miṣr . . . al-mutawakkil 'ala'llâh . . . al-ḥâkim bi'amri'llâh" (G. Wiet in Bull. de Inst. d'Eg., xv 182–3).

12. The famous Turkish historian Na'îmâ (d. 1716) was a native of Aleppo, and Murâdî mentions several Turkish poets at Aleppo and its environs. Since the Middle Ages there has always been a considerable Turkish element in the population of Northern Syria.

13. e.g., Murâdî, ii. 98.

14. Cf. Murâdî, ii. 187 foot.

15. A. D. A. de Kat Angelino, Colonial Policy (tr. G. J. Renier, The Hague, 1931), i. 67–8. The passage quoted contains as follows (slightly abridged): "Great religions like Islam have superimposed a common veneer of general religious culture, without, however, causing them to lose the peculiar shade of mystical-magical feeling of their own particular life. Tradition, status, and the interests of the group determine the place and function of the individual, and as a rule heredity transfers them. Aptitude and inclination are not consulted, so that talent is rarely given the chance of unfolding itself."

16. It might be questioned whether they ever expressly sanctioned a great many of the traditional usages in village and town, but there can be no doubt that the local men of religion, whether of the 'ulemâ, or of the Ṣûfîs, or of both, did in fact throw their weight upon the side of tradition, and officially con-

doned the traditional usages even when (like those at the cutting of the Halîc at Cairo) they were pre-Islamic and animistic in origin.

17. Cf., e.g., Volney's generalization: "Il n'y a point de lois fixes; et ce cas, qui est commun à toute l'Asie, est la cause radicale de tous les désordres de ses gouvernements" (i. 455). The statement is, in point of fact, not inaccurate, but it sees only the negative and not the positive side of the relationship.

18. See *Gibbs and Bowen*, ch. x, i.

19. It did not, however, create this gulf, which was a legacy to Islamic civilization from its imperial predecessors in Western Asia, deepened by the establishment of Turkish military hegemony from the eleventh century.

20. So traditional had this practice become that observers agree in asserting that the Egyptian peasant refused to pay his taxes until they were exacted by violence, and was regarded with contempt by his fellows if he did so.

21. A typical example is offered by the physician Ibn el-Nafîs (d. A.D. 1288), who discovered the principle of pulmonary circulation; but it was entirely ignored by the physicians of the following generations, and his name and work were both forgotten.—(See *Supplement* to *Encyc. of Islam*, s.v.)

22. But it encouraged an unwillingness to learn, out of an exaggerated estimate of its own perfection. A striking example is given by the historian Cabartî, who asserts (as an explanation of the mechanical advances made in Europe) that in 1159/1746 a number of Franks came to study mathematics under his father and on their return to Europe taught what they had learned, and 'translated it from theory into practice, inventing by means of it marvellous devices such as windmills, machines for drawing heavy weights, for raising water from wells, &c.' (i. 397, foot/iii. 191).

23. Compare Cabartî's grievance against 'Alî Bey that "he rent established customs and violated usages, destroyed ancient houses, and abolished the old sound ways" (i. 258/ii. 235), although, in comparison with subsequent events, he looks back to his time with regret (i. 383 foot/iii. 162–3).

2. Empire, Nationality, and Religion

The organization of this section is chronologic as well as thematic, even though chronology is subordinate to the requirements of conceptualization. The individual pieces range in time and place from societies of classical antiquity to the Middle East, Africa, medieval and modern Europe, and North America. But the prime notion to be derived from a comparative perusal of these pieces is their interlinkage in theme rather than their sequence in time. Alvin Boskoff's paper "Social Indecision in Two Classical Societies" is scientific in method but humanistic in scope in that it utilizes the analysis of transitional society in Greek and Roman antiquity for the purpose of making us understand better the problems which our own transitional society is facing. The lesson is Goethe's:[1]

Denn der Mensch, der zur schwankenden Zeit auch
    schwankend gesinnt ist,
Der vermehret das Uebel und breitet es weiter
    und weiter.

(If in times of decision a man's mind's undecided,
He'll surely compound the evil and spread it farther
    and farther.)

Social indecision is a corollary of historical change, but it is also a social problem in itself.

In contrast to Alvin Boskoff, Robert C. Nisbet is not primarily concerned with application or comparison, but his aim, nevertheless, is theoretical as well as historical. He analyzes the change from a kinship society, where the *patria potestas* is the highest and religiously sanctioned authority, to a military *imperium*, where the state recognizes only individuals who are subject to its centralized power, not intermediary forces, such as the autonomous family. As he describes the process for Rome, the cradle of the legal institutions of the western world, there is no doubt that he delineates the formative period of our own society. The process is historical in nature inasmuch as it is constitutive only for the western world, but it has been repeated wherever a western social system has come into contact or collision with a kinship society.[2]

It is instructive to note that in Werner J. Cahnman's paper "Religion and Nationality" the very same process is described from another aspect. What is viewed as subject to change in Nisbet's paper, appears in Cahnman's paper as continuity. Nationality as a territorial principle—the heritage of Rome—is contrasted to nationality as a familial or religious principle, analogous to the Turkish *millet*, which itself represents only a second growth from much older roots. Influences stemming from Durkheim's interpretation of religious institutions are here fused with ideal-typical methodology. Eastern institutions are considered as paradigmatic and as such are compared with related phenomena in the West, even as the underlying principle is described as becoming attenuated and at times stifled or submerged outside—and recently, also inside—the original area.

What is merely indicated in Cahnman's paper is worked out more fully in Thomas F. O'Dea's paper on the Mormons. Church, sect, and incipient nationality are combined in the remarkable phenomenon of Mormonism. Another similarity between the Cahnman and the O'Dea papers lies in their closeness to the influence of Robert E. Park. O'Dea's cautionary attitude with regard to abstract schemata in sociology would have been shared by Park.

The remainder of the papers in this section are concerned either with nationality or with religion. Regarding nationality, Florian Znaniecki's paper "The Origin of National Culture Societies" is a classic statement. It is taken from his book *Modern Nationalities,* which is little known although it belongs to the very best among Znaniecki's writings and is one of the most lucid statements we have on the topic of nationality. Immanuel Wallerstein's paper on African nationalism complements Znaniecki's statement in an important direction which was not quite discernible at the time Znaniecki's book was written—although that was only a decade ago.

With the phenomenon of nationality thus clarified, the three remaining papers return to the phenomenon of religion, each in a different way. Leonard W. Moss's and Stephen C. Cappannari's paper on "The Black Madonna" has an anthropological bent which we welcome since we do not see anthropology as essentially different from sociology, except perhaps insofar as the anthropologist's predilection for the concept of culture makes him more inclined to think in total situations than is customary among sociologists. Further, this paper connects the world of antiquity with the world of the Middle Ages and may therefore stand as an example for the continuity of symbolic expression which underlies even a seemingly radical shift in meanings. Joshua Trachtenberg's chapter on usury shows religious interpretation and economic activities closely intertwined. Initially, religion defined the situation, but then the socio-economic consequences gained a momentum of their own until Hitler's genocide made it clear that the identification of the Jew and the Devil had never been eradicated from the Western mind. Norman Birnbaum's paper "The Zwinglian Reformation in Zurich," likewise, connects religion and economic life, but the lesson is chiefly methodological in nature. Max Weber's thesis concerning the linkage between the Protestant ethic and the spirit of capitalism is here tested in a specific historical context. The procedure is exemplary in its cautious weighing of all factors inherent in the situation, and the outcome is a definite contribution to historical understanding. Theory is a guide here, but not a master.

Notes

1. "Hermann and Dorothea," Tenth Song.
2. Cf. Henry S. Maine's classical statement in *Ancient Law, its Connections with the early History of Society and its Relations to Modern Ideas* (3rd Am. ed., New York: Henry Holt & Co., 1879; 1st English ed., London, 1861).

Alvin Boskoff   SOCIAL INDECISION IN TWO

CLASSICAL SOCIETIES

IN THE QUEST for a deeper comprehension of social change as a process, the social sciences have developed a nonevolutionary series of guiding concepts which distinguish societal types according to their respective susceptibilities and responses to innovation. *Folk Society* refers to a simply organized, relatively isolated society which is removed from sources of major innovation both

Reprinted with permission from *The Midwest Sociologist*, Spring 1953.

by choice and opportunity. Toward the other extreme is the *State Civilization,* which has achieved a high degree of complexity and formal organization in its constituent institutions because of its accessibility to and hearty acceptance of cultural and social innovations. However, while all societies experience some degree of development, it has been noted that certain degrees of transitional development are accompanied by unique features which constitute another type: *Transitional Society.* This type might be defined as that stage of society which manifests substantial modification from *either* of the preceding types, but involves in addition a continued inability to assimilate numerous changes without enormous tensions and conflicts.[1]

Transitional society is marked by social crises which remain unresolved under the following conditions: (1) constituent individuals and groups become particularly devoted to relatively minor problems; (2) they remain largely unaware of major problems; and (3) if the necessary awareness is achieved, they resort to irrational, "nativistic" solutions which intensify the crisis. The sum of these reactions, which are highly visible only in transitional society, I call "social indecision," since they involve postponement of the more realistic decisions which provide stability after crisis.[2]

Social indecision is mirrored in political affairs (domestic and foreign), in the development of conflicting ideological systems, in trends of crime and dishonesty, in mental disease, and certain types of suicide. To illustrate the phenomena of social indecision and to test the validity of the first two criteria, I have selected as historical case studies (1) Greece in the crucial fifth and fourth centuries B.C. and (2) the Roman Empire from the third to the eighth centuries A.D. It should be noted that these societies represent *alternative* transitional developments: Greece evolving from its basic folk-like society; and Rome disintegrating from a state civilization into the folk society of succeeding feudalisms.

I. Transitional Greece

From the tenth to the sixth centuries B.C., Greece experienced a cultural transformation which can be described as "progressive secularization." Gradually, the folk-like units developed into more complex city-states as the economic bases were altered and as the tribal groups were seen to be more clearly inappropriate. A pastoral economy was slowly replaced by the liberating techniques of agriculture and the priceless products of settlement, security, and surplus. By the eighth century, a flowering of Greek commerce led the way to significant social developments which clearly distinguished the Greeks from their Mycenean forebears. The use of money in a market economy stimulated large capital demands and intensive competition for land. Meanwhile, minute subdivision of small peasant lands was followed by inefficient agriculture, heavy rural debts, and soon a surplus peasantry. These economic difficulties resulted in two centuries of sponsored colonization in the Black Sea region, Egypt, and the western Mediterranean.[3]

The "nomads" were becoming a practiced people, creating a complexity, however, that could not be easily tamed. Solon's reforms (594 B.C.) mitigated the position of debtors in Attica, but his encouragement of exports divided the aristocracy into warring factions. The landowning nobility, raised on the barter system, resented the new-found wealth of the commercial aristocracy and particularly the flagrant riches of the Alcmaeonidae.[4] This conflict of landowner and merchant, which was to have significance in the fifteenth through the nineteenth centuries as well, reflected a major crisis in Greek development, whose solution by tyranny tended to hasten the process by which the society became more complex.

On the whole, the tyrants of the late seventh and sixth centuries B.C. should be viewed, not as aberrations, but as a form of adjustment to deep-seated changes; and despite the modern connotation of "tyrant," an unbiased reading of Greek history must reveal the important role of these nonlegitimized leaders. Tyranny stimulated Greek development negatively by breaking the tribal hegemony; positively, by encouraging trade, coinage, manufacture, art, philosophy, by originating foreign policy for the *polis,* by founding colonies, and by extending the fruits of citizenship to wider categories of people.[5] The strength and determination which underlay Greek victory in the Persian Wars were perhaps created by the tyrants and their cultural innovations. But this was to be the last great example of social decision in Greek experience.

Victorious Greece, like later victors, was unable to move beyond her victories. The fifth century—glorious in drama, poetry, architecture, and philosophy—was fatal to further development; emerging from tribal depths, Greece gathered might with a spurious unity which quickly revealed itself in a long process of critical indecision. Whatever the causes—class struggle, ancient ethnic antipathies, untutored democracy—as a society, Greece entered a transitional period of profound problems, tensions, aimlessness, and political stagnation.

The Problem of Political Accommodation. Perhaps the most immediate problem was a satisfactory political accommodation of class and occupational groups in the expanding *polis.* The development of mass armies and extensive commercial enterprise demanded a diminishing role of the established aristocrats,[6] but the creation of a realistic democracy was thwarted both by the Eupatrids and their opponents.

In Athens, for example, the aristocrats invited Spartan intervention and when this failed, *ostracism* was designed to check popular leaders. But the continued use of ostracism as a party weapon literally stripped Athens of able leaders from both camps. The political instability following Pericles' death (429 B.C.) thus gave entrée to the questionable leadership of Cleon. Nicias, Alcibiades, and Cleophon.[7]

The Athenian democracy produced a continued political morass characterized by incompetence, irresponsibility, and retaliation. Having shackled the Areopagus and installed the Council of Five Hundred, the Athenians succumbed to the demagogues, whose total lack of positive ideas was equaled by ineptness in civil and military affairs. During the fateful conflict with Sparta, for example, the rich landowners favored a defensive war aimed at eventual peace. But the merchants and their supporters brought superior pressure for "definite triumphant aggression" led by politicians like Cleon, whose military improvisations left strategy the "sport of programmes, promises, and personal ambitions." After the demagogic bungling of the Sicilian campaign, the Athenian aristocrats staged a *coup d'état* (the reign of the oligarchic Four Hundred) followed by a temporary regime of terror, startling incompetence and, ultimately, treason. The enraged populace deposed the oligarchy, but only to fall prey to Cleophon, who prolonged an unhappy war in the face of earnest peace proposals by Sparta.[8]

The inconclusive conflict between democracy and oligarchy during the disastrous wars lifted Athens to the pinnacle of futility. Popular suspicions of reversion to despotism seemed to be confirmed by every pointless maneuver. After 410 B.C. these fears provoked a series of secret associations in which each member solemnly swore resistance to oligarchy and death to its supporters. Thus began a wild search for potential traitors, marked by malicious gossip, character assassination, and a torrent of legal suits against irresponsibly accused offenders—mainly men of prominence and property. As a result, so many were banished that retaliatory plots from abroad constantly menaced an already fragile political structure.

The Crucial Problem of Foreign Policy. Though the Greeks never applied their vaunted genius to internal problems of the *polis,* this failure was overshadowed by an epic inability to appraise with any clarity the crucial problems of foreign policy. The mainland Greeks maintained a questionable isolationism during the Ionian revolts from Persian domination, thereby neglecting to reduce the menace of Persian expansion to the west. However, the problems of foreign policy were soon focused on the mainland. Essentially, the Greek situation after 465 B.C. demanded a close defensive alliance, led by city-states capable of contributing continuous, realistic direction, and of inspiring confidence in constituent states.

Neither Athens nor Sparta satisfied both prerequisites; and their fruitless rivalry served merely to postpone the problem of effective union. Sparta longed for military leadership of Greece, but her basic parochialism and fear of local rebellions doomed her to the role of pretender. Athens, on the other hand, was in the forefront of change and therefore contemplated wider horizons. Yet within Athens and other allied cities, class conflicts continually plagued the architects of foreign policy, aggravating the rivalry of Athens and Sparta and finally provoking the civil wars.

Recognizing the political incompetence of Sparta, Athens under Themistocles and Pericles embarked on a crusade of Hellenic confederation. However, in misinterpreting the psychology of fifth century Greece, in converting its allies into subjects, Athens created a political vacuum which even force could not adequately fill. Indeed, imperious Athens permitted no secession from the empire, as the rebellious Samians were to discover. Instead of the original military contributions, the allies were compelled to make money payments of "gratitude" which, after 444 B.C., were used by Pericles to adorn the Acropolis. Timely relaxations of tribute eased difficult moments, but the allies were increasingly restive. They came to resent Athenian interference in judicial matters, though this calculated solicitude was originally considered a convenience. In addition, Pericles severely restricted Athenian citizenship, thereby discouraging ties of loyalty between Athens and subject cities.

Consequently, the Peloponnesian Wars were indecisive conflicts between rival incompetents, each of which desired to implement its unique misinterpretation of Grecian problems, to be custodian of a political disorder it was unable to understand, except in military terms. But pursuit of these narrow objectives for two generations reduced Greece to a calamitous impotence; and when the Long Walls between Athens and Piraeus were razed as a symbol of Athenian defeat, Sparta limped along as the guarantor of the "politics of atomization."[9]

By 355 B.C. Greece found itself once more in a sixth century world of problems, but with a more compelling deadline presented by the menace of Macedonia. Yet Greece had clearly failed to establish a balance of power among its leading states; instead it developed a fatal indecision which was nurtured by opposing political programs. When Persia was relatively weak under Artaxerxes, the Athenian populace, strangely seconded by Isocrates, clamored for a crusade against Persia. Soon after, Isocrates called upon Athens to renounce her imperial pretensions, to eschew alliances for a "splendid isolation" that would insure peace. To this set of feeble alternatives was added the manifest need, proclaimed by Demosthenes, to halt the power of Philip. But since the Athenian assembly remained the pawn of successive demagogues, Athens gave less attention to policy than to her theatrical festivals. Bungling in Thrace opened an inevitable corridor to lower Greece, and belated aid to the strategic city of Olynthus placed Philip only a few hours' march from Athens. Demosthenes' counsels finally triumphed in 338 B.C., but a hasty alliance with Thebes was no match for the Macedonian phalanx and cavalry at Chaeronea.[10] Thus was Greece stripped of a fumbling autonomy and prepared for her eventual immersion in the Roman Empire.

The Problem of Ideological Conflicts. These political *culs de sac* in transitional Greece were accompanied by ideological conflicts which derived from and contributed to the arrested development of Greek society. The mainland's essential philosophical homogeneity, based on the Homeric religious structure, began to disintegrate as early as the seventh century B.C. under the impact of economic and military changes. Since ideas are wrought from the interplay of experience and acquired needs, these changes introduced tensions and opportunities which demanded more specialized representation. A growing conflict emerged between defensive ideals (ideologies) and those which were directed toward substantial change in Greek society (utopias). As Greece moved into the fifth century, the flowering of ideational diversity came to be focused on a handful of roughly parallel issues: change vs. the *status quo ante;* religion and magic vs. "natural" philosophy; oligarchy vs. democracy; practical realism vs. escapism.

Vague philosophies of change were imported from Ionia during the age of the tyrants, but these were effectively countered by aristocratic notions of *arete,* bolstered in part by Pythagorean and Eleatic conceptions of order and "illusory change." With the development of a bourgeois aristocracy, the utopia of a society based on acquired intellectual qualities and individualism provided a *rationale* for commercialism. Yet this early phase of the Sophistic movement coagulated into a bald justification of a new *status quo* when the *nouveaux riches* had attained political power. By the end of the fifth century, Sophist teachings were in fact popularly linked with defenders of the oligarchy.[11] At the same time, a carelessly formulated imperialist democracy, led by Pericles and ruined by successive demagoguery, heralded the growing power of sailors, traders, and the urban proletariat, whose horizons extended far beyond those of the complacent aristocracy. For our purposes, Socrates is important as a critical utopian who derided the ignorance, the aimlessness, the incompetence of fumbling utopians. A final criticism, launched by Isocrates in the fourth century, was retrospectively utopian; embodying the outlook of the propertied class, he preached a return to the diluted oligarchy of the Areopagus and the rigid conservatism of his model polity—Sparta.

As the fourth century advanced, Greek intellectuals continued to wrestle with suitable utopias, but the *demos* was confused by conflicting ideas it could not adequately appraise. It came to distrust philosophy and philosophers and relapsed into the exaggerated religious bigotry that culminated in the heresy trials of Anaxagoras, Diagoras, Socrates, Protagoras, and possibly Euripides. Stunned by military defeats and the menace of future wars, Greece clung to religious orthodoxy, but also carried on wide experiments in orgiastic religion, magic, and mysteries—"the pleasures and comforts of the primitive."[12]

The latter half of the fourth century produced yet two more utopias which were perhaps too late and too impractical. Plato's ideal State discouraged excessive individualism and envisaged the leadership of intelligent statesmen grounded in philosophy and dedicated to policies which would procure harmony between classes. Its success depended on a prior development of improved morality and a Greek union regulated by a common public law. Similarly based on Socratic criticism of the democracy, the Cynics constructed

their utopia on a reasoned individualism. They espoused a wholesale renunciation of Greek society, with its grades and distinctions, for a world state and
citizenship, but—like Plato—neglected to indicate practical paths to utopia.[13]

II. The Roman Empire in Transition

Unlike the Greeks, the Romans developed sufficient unity to defeat their
enemies and, by the genius of Augustus, forestalled the social paralysis inherent in numerous civil wars. Supremely conscious of empire, Augustus proceeded to recast Roman institutions in the interest of intelligent integration.[14]
The encouragement of urbanization in the provinces produced greater cultural
homogeneity and sufficient military recruits for a newly constituted army directly under the emperor. In the economic sphere changes were less evident,
though an increasing emphasis was placed on free labor in Rome. And, recognizing the vagaries of army commanders, senatorial vacillation, and the irresponsibility of tongue and purse, Augustus wrestled with the problem of continuity by careful designation and training of an imperial successor.[15] By A.D.
14, therefore, Roman society had reached a degree of conscious formal organization which social indecision had denied to the Greeks. But the linea-
ments of state civlization did not long survive their architect.

During the next two centuries the empire toyed intermittently with catas-
trophe, though the surface of imperial control appeared reasonably calm. One
of the earliest indications of potential regression was an acquiescent Senate,
which seemed fearful of sharing responsibility in the administration of the
empire under the Julii and Claudii. While this was in part a result of encroachment by the emperor, senatorial abdication of power received wide approbation from the provinces. However, this development erased an important agent
of social decision, thereby providing freedom of judgment for the emperor or
the army, unchallenged by those with superior education and experience.
Consequently, both the respected and the degenerate emperors of this period
espoused questionable policies whose repercussions were no less significant because they were sometimes delayed. As the second century ended, such policies had materially altered the work of Augustus and poised the Roman Empire in the direction of critical transition.

Though it is difficult to fix a precise date, the empire was clearly becoming a transitional society in the first third of the third century A.D. The very
nature of the empire stimulated a series of simultaneous, interlocking problems which comprised a sternly itemized invoice of change for those willing to
note the costs. But while the emperors as a group seemed aware of such problems and the attendant social evils, their lack of a systematic policy merely
aggravated social crises until they became unendurable.

Perhaps the most flagrant problem was the bloody question of imperial
succession. From the Severi to Diocletian, imperial leadership creaked under

the capricious suffrage of the legions and an occasional attempt to transmit the *imperium* through family or adoption. Diocletian's plan of voluntary abdication in favor of carefully selected "Augusti" and "Caesars" was soon repudiated by love of power and careless selection. Instead, the army reassumed an elective power which was vaguely modified by the practice of co-optation during the fourth and fifth centuries.

The Problem of the Military. In a society largely based on military might, the constitution and quality of the army became a continuous source of concern.

While the Flavians had recruited their legions from the best educated, more "civilized" classes of the urbanized provinces, the army of the second century was gradually transformed into a conscript army of peasants and landowners who were truly "provincial." During the reign of the Antonines, such an army was well-disciplined and moderately successful, but it became a vicious force in the crises of succession. On the death of Commodus, the imperial power teetered in the hands of conflicting provincial armies anxious to elevate their commanders. Solely dependent on his soldiers, therefore, Septimius Severus impaired their fighting ability by catering to their irresponsible demands with bribes and important political posts. The next half-century, from Caracalla to Aurelian, witnessed the fruits of military anarchy: the legions as impotent units; infiltration of poorly armed barbarians in Italy, Gaul, etc., and the rise of upstart emperors in almost every province. By the end of the fourth century, military efficiency was so poor that barbarian mercenaries (the *foederati*) were hired. The latter, however, served under their own chiefs and constituted a constant menace to their employers.[16]

As a result of its military basis, the empire was regularly confronted with the alternatives of expansion or stability, of offense or a fluid defense against frontier tribes. Trajan's costly wars convinced Hadrian and his successors that military policy should be reversed. Instead, permanent fortifications were scattered along the frontiers, but with a consequent dispersion of the legions that prevented quick mobilization of a striking force at any critical point. This was apparently the signal for the numerous frontier raids which plagued Marcus Aurelius and succeeding emperors. And the exigencies of defense prompted the enforced barbarization of the legions. By the middle of the third century, defense of the provinces became uncoordinated and branded with failure; the provincials therefore transferred their allegiance to more efficient local authorities during the chaotic years of Valerian and Gallienus. The Roman army, then, had largely disintegrated; in the next century it had neither the might nor the morale to halt the undisciplined, badly armed, and surprisingly scanty barbarian "hordes."[17]

The Problem of Economic Organization. If essential political links were poorly forged, the empire in its transitional stage so grossly misinterpreted economic problems that no genuine functional interdependence between the units of empire was ever achieved. The basic difficulty, a stagnant agricultural system, was recognized by Nerva and Trajan, but their efforts seemed only to invigorate the *latifundia*—with their archaic technology, enslavement of the peasantry, and a growing self-sufficiency that was inimical to extensive trade. The wholesale confiscation of vast estates by Septimius Severus sustained these evils and led to chaotic migrations by impoverished farmers. Guided by the peculiar economic bias of numerous generations, Diocletian and Constantine responded to crisis by attaching the peasantry to the land. Such a policy was not only inept, but was also unenforceable, for many peasants continued to escape to the towns. To fill vacant lands, therefore, later emperors recruited tenants from the Germans, whose ignorance of agriculture was matched only by the emperors' imprudent economics.[18]

Imperial leaders, it must be remembered, formed a squirearchy; their attitudes were conditioned by investments in real estate and the ancient antipathy to industry and commerce. The emperors, therefore, tended to intervene in agricultural matters, but retained a *laisser faire* policy with respect to trade.

Since no attempt was made to induce a balance of trade between Rome (and Italy) and the provinces, the Italian peninsula followed the path of decay which had first been clearly traced in the time of Trajan. Subsidies to agriculture and the village system actually restricted urban industry and commerce, since the free peasants of the rural districts were an excellent source of business. Diocletian's Edict of Prices, a major exception to *laisser faire* in non-agricultural matters, vainly aimed to discourage industry in the eastern empire by constricting wages and profits through an elaborate, unrealistic, and unenforceable system of maximum prices. By the fourth century, therefore, industry had become ruralized: limited in scope to the villa; and immune to technical advancement.

With the absence of any decisive economic policy, the problem of imperial revenue gained critical significance in the third century. Administrative autonomy for urban units of the empire therefore succumbed to the extension of an imperial bureaucracy whose major function was taxation. Beginning with Septimius Severus, urban officials (*curiales*) were made personally responsible for meeting urban tax quotas. Since industry and commerce were declining and exemptions were granted by the emperor to large landholders and tenants on imperial estates, the urban middle class was unwillingly caught between excessive demands and quickly vanishing incomes. The hapless *curiales* consequently sought asylum in the army, in religious orders, and even in semi-serfdom, but the Theodosian Code and its amendments sealed most avenues of escape. A desperate social caste, stripped of fortune, mobility, and status, became bound to fortress-like cities in a regime of terror and hopelessness.[19]

The consequent ruin of the middle classes sharply outlined the focal problem of the empire: the future of its cities. But from the Severi onward, the significance of urbanization for a strong empire was largely ignored. As the emperors and their armies were increasingly drawn from the ruralized provinces, an unyielding reliance on force and landed privilege replaced the reasoned decisions of Augustus and several of his successors of the first century A.D. Wars and prodigality destroyed the economic bases of urban centers. More important, during the early fourth century the provincial aristocracy (*clarissimi*) were permitted—with the connivance of high officials—to establish extensive *private* jurisdictions of unassailable power and prestige. This "villa system" served to shift the locus of power and allegiance to local potentates who thereby attracted increasing numbers of individuals and village communities eager to secure adequate protection and relief from municipal taxation. Valentinian and Honorius failed to halt this crystallization of the empire merely by levying fines and threatening confiscation. By the fifth century, the empire had lost the inter-urban linkage which was its core; it had become a loose collection of rural localisms whose intermittent alliance in Germanic kingdoms was later initiated by force and then abrogated by autarchic baronies.[20]

The Problem of Ideological Conflict. Contrary to expectation, the period of transition was not well marked by ideological conflicts. Indeed, with the exception of the religious realm, this era was so barren of ideas that it might be styled the "Tinplate Era" of Roman thought and literature, in contrast to the Gold and Silver periods.[21] But the absence of rival philosophies is not derived from an identity of interests; nor can it be fairly attributed to the direction of change which Roman transitional society represents, *i.e.,* from state civilization to folk society. The peculiar character of the empire, which precluded the production of ideas in at least three ways, offers a more tenable explanation. (1) Perhaps the most striking element was the provision of nonintellectual outlets for disadvantaged groups in the empire: the army for rural peasantry; the church for the urban proletariat. In the latter case, the proliferation of heresies in the fourth and fifth centuries was quite incidental to the broader problems of social adjustment.[22] (2) The de-emphasis on urban development and the onerous, inescapable responsibilities of the bourgeoisie combined to deprive the city of unique functions: the spirit of inquiry, dissent, and intellectualism. (3) The highly privileged *clarissimi,* the feudal magnates of the villa, displayed the disinterest in ideas which seems so closely associated with secure social monopoly; unchallenged by utopian protests, they had little need for ideological rationalization of their sanctioned position.

Summary

Postponement of relevant social decisions, therefore, stimulated a transitional society (third to eighth centuries) that was neither Roman Empire nor yet feudal simplicity. If the Greeks had briefly fashioned a tenuous veneer of state civilization over a basic folk society, the Roman emperors in their conservatism had progressively worn away the texture of organized social complexity. If Greek society crumbled under the changes it had devised, the Roman Empire discarded its heritage of change in a desperate attempt to preserve a complexity whose continuance demanded acceptance and integration of change. Both situations of social indecision are crises of transitional society which inevitably deepen to social disintegration when "postponement" becomes the principal humor of the agents of social decision. And that, if we care to recognize it, may be the supreme lesson of the ancient world.

Notes

1. Alvin Boskoff, "Structure, Function, and Folk Society," *American Sociological Review,* XIV (December, 1949), 749–759.
2. Alvin Boskoff, "The Postponement of Social Decision in Transitional Society," *Social Forces* (March 1953).
3. M. Rostovtzeff, *A History of the Ancient World* (Oxford: The Clarendon Press, 1930), 199–201.
4. Alfred Zimmern, *The Greek Commonwealth,* rev. ed. (Oxford: The Clarendon Press, 1931), 130–140; Werner Jaeger, *Paideia: The Ideals of Greek Culture* (New York: Oxford University Press, 1945), Vol. I, 224–225.
5. Zimmern, *op. cit.,* 142, 152–154, 178; J. B. Bury *et al., Cambridge Ancient History (CAH),* (New York: Macmillan, 1925), Vol. III, 549–552; vol. IV, 62–65.
6. Cf. Max Weber, *General Economic History* (New York: The Free Press, 1950), 324, 328–329.
7. CAH, vol. IV, 139–140, 151–153.
8. CAH, vol. V, 107–190, 348–349; Thucydides, *The Peloponnesian Wars* (New York: Modern Library, 1934), Books IV and VII.
9. Werner Jaeger, *Demosthenes* (Berkeley: University of California Press, 1938), 11.
10. *Ibid.,* 52–53, 73, 106–107, 123, 138–140, 162, 165: Jaeger, *Paideia,* Vol. III, 126, 130, 282.
11. Sir Ernest Barker, *Greek Political Theory* (London: Methuen, 1947) 69, 71–75.
12. E. R. Dodds, *The Greeks and the Irrational* (Berkeley: University of California Press, 1951), 189–195; Martin P. Nilsson, *A History of Greek Religion* (Oxford: The Clarendon Press, 1925), 275.
13. Barker, *op. cit.,* 105–108; Plato, *The Laws; The Republic* (Oxford: The Clarendon Press, 1875), Vols. III, V.
14. CAH, vol. X, 176–180, 206–207.
15. *Ibid.,* chapters VIII, XVIII.
16. M. Rostovtzeff, *Social and Economic History of the Roman Empire* (Oxford: The Clarendon Press, 1926), 103, 122–123, 351–355; Arthur E. Boak, *A History of Rome to 565 A.D.* (New York: Macmillan, 1922), 337–338.
17. Boak, *op. cit.,* 247, 258–259, 276; Tenney Frank, *Rome and Italy of the Empire* (Baltimore: Johns Hopkins Press, 1940), 303.
18. Frank, *op. cit.,* 85, 297; James W. Thompson and Edgar N. Johnson, *An Introduction to Medieval Europe* (New York: Norton, 1937), 13–14.
19. Samuel Dill, *Roman Society in the Last Century of the Western Empire,* 2nd ed., (London: Macmillan, 1933), 229, 245, 253–259; Rostovtzeff, *Social and Economic History,* 333, 358.

20. Thompson and Johnson, *op. cit.*, 14, 186–187, 229, 232.
21. See J. W. Duff, *A Literary History of Rome from the Origins to the Close of the Golden Age* (New York: Scribner's, 1909); J. W. Duff, *A Literary History of Rome in the Silver Age,* 2nd ed. (New York: Scribner's, 1930).
22. *Cf.* an account of the clash between paganism and Christianity in the fourth century by Andrew Alföldi, *A Conflict of Ideas in the Late Roman Empire* (New York: Oxford University Press, 1952).

Robert A. Nisbet   **KINSHIP AND POLITICAL POWER**

IN FIRST CENTURY ROME

I

I PROPOSE in this paper to deal with a problem that has long been of interest to historians and sociologists of legal institutions: kinship authority (*patria potestas*) and its decline in ancient Rome. Quite apart from the intrinsic interest of the subject, we can learn much from it, I believe, of what is more generally involved in the shift of authority from one institution to another, in the rise of legal individualism, and in the dislocation of important social groups from functional significance in a social order.

Exactly a century ago, Sir Henry Maine gave brief but striking attention to the problem, and his own statement is worth repeating. Whereas, Maine pointed out, we find the house father possessing in early Rome the *jus vitae necisque,* the power of life and death, over his children and others under his power, along with comparable authority in other spheres—economic, religious, and educational—the Imperial Age reveals the decline of the *patria potestas* to a level scarcely greater than that to be found in the modern family.

The unqualified right of domestic chastisement has become a right of bringing domestic offenses under the cognizance of the civil magistrates; the privilege of marriage has declined into a conditional veto; the liberty of selling has been virtually abolished, and adoption itself, destined to lose almost all its ancient importance . . . can no longer be effected without the assent of the children . . . in short we are brought very close to the ideas which have at length prevailed in the modern world.[1]

It would be difficult to state the problem more concisely, and, as we shall see, Maine has some penetrating observations to make on the factors involved in the decline. The principal objections to Maine's presentation—apart from a lack of data that more recent scholarship has supplied—are, first, the view he takes of the general nature of change and, second, the strict and uncompromising legalism of his treatment.

Like most of his contemporaries, Maine wrote under the spell of the evolutionary perspective. He regarded change in an institution as endogenous, proceeding as does growth in an organism, in a slow, gradual, and continuous manner. Past phases of any social institution are deemed to be immature or imperfect, mere steps in a development whose true and proper nature lies ahead. Thus, Maine tells us, the *patria potestas* could not have been a durable institution; it was inherently unstable and imperfect. The essential problem of change is not that of accounting for actual transformation in the *patria potestas* but rather "to guess at the causes which permitted the *patria potestas* to last as long as it did by rendering it more tolerable than it appears."[2]

This leads to the second difficulty of Maine's approach—that of dealing with his subject in an exclusively legal manner. Writing as a lawyer—albeit a broadly educated one—Maine chose to regard the *patria potestas* as a power much like sovereignty in the modern state—abstract, impersonal, and remote —rather than as an institution embedded in religion, morality, and economics. It was because Maine fixed his attention almost strictly on the power aspects that the problem of the *patria potestas* could appear as one of accounting for the length of time it was able to maintain itself, rather than that of uncovering the historical forces which were in fact necessary for the dislocation of one of the most durable institutions in all Roman history.

Most subsequent students of the Roman family have dealt with the subject in substantially the same terms. Sociologists, in particular, have done so in the same way that they have handled social change in general—as the consequence of internal forces and tensions, only moderately and perhaps catalytically affected by external factors.[3]

Major social change is not, however, the consequence of internal tensions, nor of immanent variations and mutations proceeding in ways best known to biologists. It is, on the contrary, the result of intrusion, external impact, or conflict.

It will be the primary purpose of this paper to show that the *patria potestas,* far from being unstable and driven to its decline by innate difficulties, was in fact a powerful and tenacious institution, one that did not change in any important respect until it was subjected to the force of another—and eventually greater—authority, the military *imperium*. It was the unequal conflict between these two forces, as we shall see, that transformed the kinship system in Rome and, with it, the basis of the larger society.

II

We have no difficulty in describing the nature and significance of the *patria potestas* in the Republic—that is, the period down to approximately the end of the first century B.C. An imposing body of scholarship gives us a clear and detailed view of our subject. What has too often been overlooked or underemphasized, however, is the key role of the *patria potestas* in the larger structure of power in the total society of the Republic. As we shall see, the fateful change in kinship authority came only where there began to take place a massive rearrangement of this larger structure of power.

To properly see the picture of early Roman society, [Strachan-Davidson writes]

we must imagine a number of households, each united under its own *paterfamilias*. Inside the household the father is the sole judge, beholden to no one for his actions and performances. . . . No Roman writer ever attributed the *patria potestas* either to the magistrate, whether king or consul, or to the sovereign people itself, and there is no trace of the power exercised by the state authorities developing out of those exercised by the head of the family.[4]

Strachan-Davidson's last point is an important one to our problem. So many anthropologists and historical jurists in the modern world have treated political sovereignty as if it were the simple outgrowth of family authority that the essential separateness of the two has been minimized or overlooked. In the final section of this paper, I will expand upon the significance of this separateness to the problem of change. Here it suffices to emphasize that the *patria potestas* was an original and autonomous power within Roman society, drawing its vast authority over individual behavior from immemorial tradition, not from any higher agency within the Roman state.

Strictly speaking, the *patria potestas* was much more than power. It stood for the unity of the family, its continuity in time, and as the irreducible atom of society as a whole. The word for father, *pater,* did not connote generation, but authority and protection. The basis of the Roman family, Fowler has emphasized, was the right of ownership, inseparable "from the idea of land settlement and therefore essentially *das Hauswesen,* the house itself, with persons living in it, free or servile, with their land and all their property, all governed and administered by the *paterfamilias,* the master of the household."[5]

The centrality of the family in law was reinforced by its agnatic character. The framework of the Roman family was not common birth; blood brothers were not *ipso facto* members of the same family. Two people were related agnatically if they were in the *patria potestas* of the same man, or if there was some common ancestor in whose power they would both have been were he still alive. Thus, given Roman male succession, a father and his brother were agnates; so were a father and his son. But a Roman male and his married daughter or sister were not agnatically related. For there was only cognatic relationship, and to this the Romans, in the Republic, attached little importance of any kind, and no legal importance whatsoever.

The reason for strict insistence upon the agnatic tie in all matters of law, property, and religion is not far to seek. The organization of Roman society would have been disrupted if men had claimed relationship to their mother's blood relatives. For then a person would have fallen under more than one *patria potestas,* with all the related confusion that would prevail in a society that did not possess a centralized political power over persons. "As long as the family was an *imperium in imperio,* a community within a common-wealth, governed by its own institutions of which the parent was the source, the limitation of relationship to the agnates was a necessary security against a conflict of laws in the domestic forum."[6] It was only after the public power penetrated and became eventually sovereign in private matters that the principle of agnation could be safely abandoned. And, as history records, by the second century of the Empire, the agnatic relationship meant little more than it does in modern society. It had ceased to be the center of gravity of Roman society.[7]

Individualism did not exist in the Republic—legally, economically, mor-ally, or socially. Tradition united with overt authority in making each Roman feel, first, a member of a group, with duties, and, only second, an individual with rights. Until very late in the Republic the family bore responsibility for most individual offenses, and it was the prime agency of ret-ribution for injuries suffered by one of its members. Not until 149 B.C. did true criminal law make its appearance, in the statute known as the *Lex Calpurnia de Repetundis,* resulting in the establishment of the first *Quaestio Perpetua*—that is, a permanent commission for consideration of public crimes. Prior to this date such offenses were dealt with by the Senate as a whole, much as they did with any other public responsibility.[8] In the execution of criminals, even when the offense was against the whole state (treason, for example), it was the family itself that served as the vehicle.

Over and over we find the actual execution of punishment, capital or otherwise, committed to the relatives of the culprits instead of being carried out by servants of the state. The noticeable point is that this occurred not only with those who were under the *potestas* of father or husband . . . but with women who were *sui juris,* but who were nevertheless put to death or banished by *propinqui* or *cognati.*[9]

Repeatedly we are struck by the autonomy of the family in the law and custom of the Republic. Magistrates and censors could exhort, but little more.

The officers of the commonwealth, the consuls and other magistrates, did not dare cross the threshold of a father's house; they assumed no power to interfere within his doors. The head of the family was its sole representative; he alone had *locus standi* in the tribunals of the state. If a wrong was done by or to any member of his family, he and not they must answer for it or demand compensa-tion.[10]

The legal majesty of the *patria potestas* could not have endured as long as it did, and been as difficult to dislodge in the end, had it not been for roots in the religious, economic, and social life of Rome. This is the point that has been too often overlooked by historians and jurists. And when the *patria potestas* did come to an end as a major part of Roman society, it did so, as we shall see, within a larger context of change that included religious and economic, as well as political dislocations.

Thus, religion, throughout most of the Republic was hardly more than a spiritualization of family life, reaching back to earliest ancestors and forward to the unborn. Public pontiffs had few and limited rights of supervision. The *Lares* and *Penates,* being gods of the household were private; ceremonies were secret. Nothing violated the priestly authority of the father over his hearth, and religion was deemed as inextinguishably a function of kinship as was life itself. Birth, marriage, and death were the ceremonial high points, and in each ritual the authority and unity of the family were, in effect, reaffirmed. No child was born into the family; he had to be accepted. What else were death rites but the means whereby one left the earthly members of the family to join the departed—who were deemed not the less living for their eternal stay elsewhere? To allow others—strangers—into the religion of the hearth was to risk alienation of the departed; and for a family to fail to make food offerings at each meal to the gods of the household, or, most direly, to permit the sacred flame to go out, was to risk extinction of the departed souls. Similarly, marriage, far from creating a new family, was the ceremony (purely private) whereby the young woman, the intended wife of a son under power, was, in effect, cleansed of the worship under which she had previously lived, and made the subject of a new religion, that of her husband.[11]

Finally, and equally crucially, property and wealth were regarded as possessions of the family, never of individuals. At no time in the Republic could a son under power, however important he might be in military or public affairs, or whatever his age, legally own property. Nor could he even retain income personally earned, unless with the consent of the father. Beyond this, there was the strict limitation of rights of inheritance. Property could not easily be alienated from the agnatic family. Law and custom joined in stress upon the corporate, kinship character of property.[12]

Let us summarize briefly the character of the society within which the *patria potestas* flourished. (1) It was the very opposite of an individualistic society, for the family was the irreducible unit in law, economics, religion, as well as other functional areas. (2) It was a society strong in descriptive law —tradition, convention, custom—rather than prescriptive law. (3) Pluralism, rather than monism, was the essence of the social system, although we should not underestimate the ease and effectiveness with which the early Romans could mobilize into military unity. (4) It was a society based upon legal decentralization rather than centralization, a condition emanating naturally from its pluralism. For the *patria potestas* could hardly have flourished in a society where the power of the state directly impinged upon each individual.

III

So much for the background of the problem. We must turn now to the events and changes which specifically and decisively changed the character of the *patria potestas* in Rome and, with it, the foundations of order in Rome. Our subject is intimately involved in the social transformation which characterized the end of the Republic and the rise of the Empire at the very end of the 1st century B.C.

We can do no better than quote some words of the Roman historian, Dio Cassius, as the means of introducing this section. "So it was," he wrote of the fateful accession of Augustus in 27 B.C., "that all the power of the people and the Senate passed over to Augustus, and from that day pure monarchy was established."[13] Monarchy is perhaps not the word we would apply to a personal absolutism founded, not upon tradition or right of succession, but rather upon military power united with popular appeal to the masses that is best known as Caesarism. Julius Caesar had offered the vision, and, for a moment, the actuality of absolutism founded upon mass appeal; Augustus Caesar now supplied both the blueprint and the implementation of a form of totalitarian power that was to survive in one form or another for half a millennium.

The façade of the Republic was maintained in the form of the Senate, but after 27 B.C., as Rostovtzeff, among others, has emphasized, the crucial elements were "the now permanent army and its commander-in-chief, the Emperor Augustus, *Imperator Caesar divi filius Augustus. . . .* The army was the master of the State, and, in the restored Roman republic, the Emperor ruled wholly through the army and for so long as the army was willing to keep him and obey."[14] There was, to be sure, much to recommend the new form of government. A century of bitter, destructive civil wars among the rival military commanders—based, as Rostovtzeff has pointed out, upon no social programs or objectives; merely the struggle for absolute supremacy in the state—had so thoroughly weakened the traditional foundations of the commonweal that effective rule by the Senate was impossible. It is, of course, tribute to the majesty of the idea of the Senate that Augustus strove to make his government at all times seem to rest upon the Senate. But every Roman historian who touched upon the matter makes clear that, in fact, Augustus was the unrivalled and absolute ruler of Rome. All else was convenient fiction.

Time does not permit an examination of all the changes which were the consequence of the penetration of Augustan political power into the recesses of the social structure in Rome. Our specific concern here is the *patria potestas* and the role of the family in the new order. It is enlightening, however, to note by way of preface that changes in the *patria potestas* were themselves parts of a larger program that involved also the reconstitution of social classes in Rome, new foundations of property and wealth, the character of religion, and even the social origin of members of the Senate. As Pelham has written, legislation on the family "formed an integral part of the general policy of social and administrative reconstruction in Rome and Italy which Augustus kept steadily before him from the beginning to the end of his long reign, and it is only in connection with that policy that it can be properly studied and understood."[15]

I will merely summarize the consequences of this broad program. There was, first, the centralization of political power. No longer would Rome be, in political terms, a decentralized and cellular society as it had been for centuries in the Republic. In the same way that the Senate had been supplanted by the Emperor as the effective source of public power, so would all other social bodies that lay intermediate to the individual and the government: social classes, gilds, and the family itself. Gradually there took form the doctrine that was, within a century, to become the basis of the texts of Roman jurists (the texts which, after their codification in the age of Justinian, were to comprise the powerful and historically significant code of Roman law). The essence of this doctrine was the axiom that law—in contrast to mere custom or tradition—flows from the sovereign alone, who must be, by definition, above the law.

Second, and functionally related to the doctrine of centralized sovereignty, was the rise of legal individualism. A century of social atomization caused by civil war and political turmoil greatly facilitated this, but the theoretical essence of legal individualism lay in the idea, closely related to the idea of sovereignty, that individuals alone are the true units of the state, not social units; and such individuals, and all the relations among them, exist under the contemplation of the legal sovereign. Everything between the state and the individual inevitably had, now, an insecure existence, for it was the state alone that could give sanction to a corporate unity. From this fateful perspective of legal individualism arose, within a century, the important doctrines of legal fiction and legal concession. By legal fiction was meant the proposition that no social group, however old and embedded in tradition, has true or real character. It is a concept in the contemplation of the sovereign—nothing more, so far as law is concerned. Reality lies in individuals, not groups. More important was the related but distinguishable idea of concession. Those groups and only those groups may legally exist whose foundations have been created, so to speak, by specific concession of the sovereign.

This is, stated simply and baldly, the Roman doctrine of corporations, and it means, in the words of the great Maitland, that "all that stands between the individual and the state has but a derivative and precarious existence." I do not suggest that this momentous doctrine, which was to aid the transformation of Europe a thousand years later with the revival of Roman Law, took its full shape in the Age of Augustus. We must wait a century for this. But there can be no doubt that the specific measures of centralization and individualization that took place in Roman polity under Augustus, at the end of the first century B.C., were the true source of later legal formulations.[16]

What happened to the *patria potestas* in 18 B.C. is of a piece with the other measures which were being taken to bring power firmly into the central government over association and classes throughout society. If public order was to be restored and Rome's greatness secured in the world, there must be no *imperium in imperio,* no social allegiance, not even the agnatic family, which could detract from necessary political centralization.

The professed object of the famous *Leges Juliae* in 18 B.C.—and in particular the two laws *de adulteriis* and *de maritandis ordinibus*—was moral: to clean up the moral delinquencies and to restore marriage to its once proud estate. We need not question motive. The austerity of Augustus' personal life—unchallenged by contemporaries—is perhaps sufficient proof of this. But neither can we overlook the fact that in the establishment of these laws on morality and marriage, we are dealing with the first *official* limitations in Roman history of the historic authority of the *patria potestas* over these matters. It must further be kept in mind that the new laws, far from being isolated manifestations of moral reform, constitute an integral part of that larger reconstruction of Rome which, whether dealing with water supply, fire control, education, religion, or corn dole, was to lead to complete centralization. As Pelham has written:

When we turn to the measures of reform adopted by Augustus it becomes clear that his efforts were by no means limited to the removal of the obstacles which impeded the growth of material prosperity or the repression of the vices which disgraced society. Great statesman as he was, he realized from the first the necessity, if either the political system which he had established was to stand or his other reforms were to have any lasting effect, of creating in a people demoralized by faction and civil war a healthy and vigorous public feeling.[17]

For centuries, however imperfectly at times, the sole authority over adultery and other moral matters had been the power of the corporate family. Exile for personal delinquencies was not uncommon, but it was a power wielded under the authority of the *patria potestas,* not by a public magistrate nor even by the Senate unless damage to the commonweal had been done. Similarly, responsibility for marriage, for its motivation as well as for its operation, was, as we have also seen, a sacred function of the family. No public officer intruded into the decisions and ceremonies involved.

Now, at a stroke, these matters are brought within public jurisdiction. In the case of adultery, the nature of the offense was defined, the procedure fixed which was to be followed when a case arose, and the penalty laid down.

For the primitive and probably decaying jurisdiction of the *pater familias* [writes Pelham] and the equally primitive right of private vengeance where the guilty parties were caught in the act, the *Lex Julia* aimed at substituting the more regular procedure of the law.[18] So it did, but it also, as Pelham himself points out, suggests, as do Augustus' other social and moral reforms, his anxiety not merely to restore social order by assigning to each class an appropriate career, a definite status, and definite privileges, but to connect each class with himself and his rule by special ties.

So far as we know, the first object of the new law was Augustus' own daughter, a young woman who, apparently, deserved exile for the reasons given. But the genius of the punishment lay in the fact that, having just established a public law which for the first time in history arrogated such punishment to the public agency, any possible sting in its first application was taken away by the familiar spectacle of a father exiling his own daughter. Further genius was shown when, for a time, he showed considerable mercy in dealing with others guilty of adultery, turning them over to their own families. But the all important precedent had been set, and under the head of *de pudicitia* in the law, various other regulations governing public decency —behavior at public games and shows, women's attendance at athletic contests, extravagances in dress, and undue expenditures on banquets—were passed under the authority of the *Leges Iuliae*.[19]

The same kind of transfer of authority is to be seen in the sections on marriages. Here too the ostensible aim is the encouragement of marriage and the production of children, an aim on which Augustus could indeed claim the sanction of ancient custom and opinion. The aim had more than once, in earlier times, been made the subject of exhortation by various censors. But there is more in the Augustan decree. For the first time in history marriage becomes a matter of state concern and supervision. Marriage is made obligatory upon all men between the ages of twenty and sixty and upon all women between twenty and fifty. Childlessness in men over twenty-five and in women over twenty was made punishable. Widows and divorced women were also ordered to remarry within a specified time. "To enforce these regulations a system of penalties and rewards was devised. The unmarried were declared incapable of inheriting property or accepting legacies; the childless were mulcted of half the amount of such bequests."[20]

Perhaps even more significant was the limitation placed upon the right of marriage among certain classes, specifically with persons who were not freeborn. Marriage between the freeborn and those who were not—the freedmen were a large and growing class—was forbidden to patricians. Marriages to freedmen were forbidden not only to senators but to their children, grandchildren, and great-grandchildren. Here too it might be said that the aim was moral—the reduction of the license that had grown up, often leading to the exploitation of the lower class member as well as to dilution of ancient families. But, from our point of view the result is the same: for the first time the state intervened in a matter that had been traditionally private, reserved to the *patria potestas*.

The penalty forbidding the unmarried from inheriting property was, of course, an invasion of what we have seen to be the autonomy of the family in matters connected with its own property and income, and it is closely related to a separate act of Augustus during this period. This was the *peculium castrense,* which permitted the sons under power to retain all booty, income, and property they had acquired during military service. It will be remembered that at the basis of the *patria potestas* was its economic solidarity, the corporate possession of property by the family alone, not its individual members. In this decree, plainly, lie the beginnings of economic individualism and, with it, of contractualism, a concept that was also to become primary in later Roman law codes. Later emperors, beginning with Hadrian, were to extend this right of individual ownership to all public employees and civil servants, eventually to all citizens. Not unrelated to Augustan decrees on property and family were those touching on membership in the Senate. Senatorial status was no longer inherited through family lines; it was to be conferred by the Emperor.[21]

There was, finally, the religious aspect of the *patria potestas.* As we have seen, family authority was deeply rooted in the religion of the *Lares* and *Penates.* Privacy of the corporate religion of the family was one of the very pillars of the *patria potestas.* This, too, was radically modified. In 12 B.C. Augustus became Pontifex Maximus, thus uniting the political and religious life of the commonweal. But far more important from our point of view is the political penetration of the family hearth. Images of Augustus began to make their appearance within family domiciles, thus giving root to the novel and exotic efflorescence of emperor worship, a form of religion in the East that had aroused the revulsion of Romans a century or two before.

Along with the image of the *Lares* and *Penates* was placed that of Augustus. So this "genius" shared with the *Lares* the libations poured in their honor and the offerings placed for their acceptance. The worship which thus established Augustus as a household god in the homes of the people and gave him a place in one of their oldest worships was admirably fitted to serve his interests and those of the empire on a larger scale.[22]

Thus, in three decisive ways, the *patria potestas* was challenged by the military *imperium*—in control of marriage and descent of family property; in the fragmentation of economic ownership; and, finally, in the invasion of the religious sphere. All of these momentous changes took place in the decade, 18 to 8 B.C., and they are at the heart of that simultaneous rise of individualism and political centralization in the Empire.

Relations between the state and the individual became ever more direct. The various situations in which the juridical person found himself affected him alone, and there was no more need to break or form any bond with a jealous and exclusive family group. Being no longer the foundation of the Republic, the *paterfamilias* ceased to interpose between the individual and the state. . . .[23]

IV

Let us turn, finally, to the question of what social forces, over a considerable period of time, had combined to form the effective bases of the Augustan decrees? Obviously these decrees did not take effect in a society totally unprepared for them. Change in an institution or concept may be the consequence of impact and intrusion from external forces, but conditions for the assimiliation of this intrusion must be present—as studies of diffusion have made clear.

Here it is tempting to take refuge in such abstractions as secularism, commercialism, and religious skepticism in Rome during the century or two leading up to Augustus. These, it is said rightly enough, formed the context that alone permitted acceptance of the radical Augustan inroads on the family and other forms of association. No one familiar with the history of Rome in this period would doubt that such generalized forces were indeed involved.

Without pretending to exclude these forces, I would like, however, to put the matter in somewhat different terms—terms that are at once more precise and more sociological. I shall illustrate this in a context that had been potentially present in Roman society from earliest days. This is the conflict between the *patria potestas*—the ancient authority of the family, and the *imperium militiae*—the authority over soldiers that came into being at the outbreak of any war.

The *imperium militiae* was not, strictly speaking, military power alone. "The Romans," writes Strachan-Davidson, "knew no such thing as a severance between supreme military and supreme civil authority. They merely distinguished between the space inside the walls (*domi*) and the rest of the world which was comprehended in the locative case by the word *militiae* 'on service.' This full imperium, then, governs all the world, less the city of Rome."[24] So much is true, but the fact remains, and it is crucial, that it was in a military context that "the rest of the world" became of significance to the Romans, and, more important, it was in its intrinsic military role that the *imperium militiae* first conflicted with the *patria potestas*.

I stressed earlier the fact that the public power did not and could not deal with the multitude of private and social matters that came under the *patria potestas*. The opposite, however, is also true, and here I present a brilliant clarifying insight from Maine:

In every relation of life in which the corrective community might have occasion to avail itself of his wisdom and strength, for all purposes of counsel and war, the *filius familias,* the son under power *was as free as his father*. It was maxim of Roman jurdisprudence that the *patria potestas* did not extend to the *jus publicum*. Father and son voted together in the city, and fought side by side in the field; indeed, the son, as general, might command the father, or, as magistrate, decide on his contracts and punish his delinquencies.[25]

Here, I suggest, is a potential conflict of roles, a tension, that lies at the heart of our subject. So long as the public role of the *filius familias,* the son under power, was minimal, just so long was the claim of the *patria potestas* upon his allegiance an unqualified and undistracted one. There could be little conflict of authority and role. On the other hand, all that tended to maximize the son's public role—either in quality or extent—tended equally to weaken the prestige and moral authority of the *patria potestas* if only because of the greater relative sphere of matters in the son's life over which the *patria potestas* had no influence.

We are justified in assuming from the evidence that it was in times of war that the maximization of a son's public role—and, correspondingly, his sporadic releases from the *patria potestas*—was heightened. Historically, as we know, war puts a premium upon the services of the young, not the old. Ordinary civil affairs in Rome, like ordinary business affairs, could be, and were, handled by those who were *sui juris,* those who held the *patria potestas* and were not under it. The most honored title indeed of the members of the Senate was the *Patres Conscripti.* But in war, different requirements prevail, and when warfare is extended and intensified, as it became in the later Republic, these requirements can become decisive.

The conflict between kinship society and the military is, as Jenks has brilliantly emphasized, one of the key conflicts of history.[26] Kinship society is inherently cellular—composed of compact and largely autonomous groups, families, clans, and *gentes*—whereas the military, as we find it in its earliest form is, by comparison, individualistic. Between the power of the commander and the individual soldier there is no intermediate authority, for such authority would weaken both the unity and the necessary directness of command. The very directness of the military *imperium* therefore induces a kind of potential individualism in social relations if only because of its corroding effects upon intermediate groups. In the second place, military society operates primarily in terms of command—not custom, tradition, and the *mores.* In the interstices of command, accordingly, there is a degree of moral freedom unknown in kinship society, which is governed not by prescriptive law, but by the less specific and infinitely more inclusive ties of custom which, by its nature, fills in every possible crevice. In short, there is a kind of secularizing and individualizing quality in military life.

In the third place, military society, unlike kinship, is, or by its nature aspires to be, rational in its distribution of function and authority; that is, whether explicitly or implicitly, both authority and function tend to fall into hands that are most competent, irrespective of considerations of age or social prestige. It does this, that is, if it is to be successful. Kinship society, on the other hand, tends, as we have seen, to accept seniority and age as the crucial qualities of leadership, with such matters as descent and inherited prestige close in importance. We may summarize the difference between the two societies by saying that in the first—kinship—it is ascribed status that counts, whereas in the second—the military—it is achieved status that is alone significant, if victory is the prime consideration.

We know that the Romans were well aware of the differences between the two types of society and the potential consequences of military service to kinship and ordinary civil authority. An ingenious variety of checks existed to prevent possible thrusts to ascendancy of victory-intoxicated returning soldiers. For centuries there was the custom by which no militia could form within the walls and no returning militia could enter the city gates until it had disbanded outside. When the individuals reentered the city, they were thus symbolically, as well as actually, freed from the *imperium* and once again under normal civil authority, and especially the *patria potestas*.[27] Such checks, however, whether customary or constitutional, could not forever withstand the growing number of wars, the increasing size of the forces themselves, and, perhaps most important, the constantly growing pressure for a regular standing army with continuous command.

One by one, from the end of the second century on, the old checks upon the military ceased to function. There began that fateful affinity between military service and popular following, between military triumph and political success, that, in Rome, as in many another society, was to have a transforming effect upon government and society. The key personage, undoubtedly, was the brilliant but ruthless Marius at the beginning of the first century B.C. "Marius was not content to supplement his army by drawing upon the 'bravest men of Latium' and recalling to the colors *evocati* or discharged veterans known to him by reputation. He employed another method of enlistment. The proletariat . . . now legally qualified for enrollment, were signed on for a definite period of service, in all probability for twenty years."[28] The soldier might be a citizen when he joined up, he might be uncomplainingly under civil and paternal power, but the mere length of service that he among tens of thousands of young Roman males was now to look forward to—making him in effect a mercenary, knowing little and caring less about traditional matters—would make him restive, to say the least, when he returned on furlough or following separation.

The army strongly detached from civil institutions, had chiefs who were absolute chiefs. Soldiers entered the service because they liked it; they hoped for loot and allotments of land. Who could give them this privilege? The General. So there grew up between the general and his men a closer association based not on the old discipline, nor even on the religion of the standard, but on mutual interest and greed.[29]

It is therefore, I suggest, in the rising incidence of war in Roman history, especially from the second century B.C. on, that we find the setting for the tensions that were eventually to reduce the *patria potestas* to innocuousness. For it was in the circumstances of increasing warfare that more and more sons under paternal power found themselves for lengthening periods of time under the *imperium militiae,* a form of authority that differed vastly from the *patria potestas* and provided, for all its own stringency, the essential conditions of that special type of individualism that was to sap the foundations of kinship society.

As Maine has reminded us,

the military tribune and the private soldier who were in the field three-quarters of a year during the earlier contests and, at a later period the proconsul in charge of a province and the legionaries who occupied it, cannot have had practical reason to regard themselves as the slaves of a despotic master; and all these avenues of escape tended constantly to multiply themselves . . . We may infer, I think, that a strong sentiment in favor of the relaxation of the *patria potestas* had become fixed by the time that the pacification of the world commenced on the establishment of the Empire.[30]

Notes

1. Sir Henry Maine, *Ancient Law*. First published in London, 1861. Everyman edition, pp. 81–82.
2. Maine, *Ancient Law,* p. 82.
3. This is, of course, one of the consequences of the continuous influence exerted upon European thought by the Greek concept of organism; from Aristotle down to contemporary functionalists in the social sciences, there is scarcely an exception to the view that change is inherent in the institution or culture.
4. James L. Strachan-Davidson, *Problems of the Roman Criminal Law* (Oxford University Press, 1912), Vol. 2, pp. 28–29, 38.
5. W. W. Fowler, *The Religious Experience of the Roman People* (London: Macmillan, 1911), p. 70.
6. Maine, *Ancient Law,* p. 88.
7. See Henry J. Roby, *Roman Private Law in the Times of Cicero and the Antonines* (Cambridge: University Press, 1902). See Bk. 2, Ch. 7 *et. seq.*
8. See Pandias M. Schisas, *Offences Against the State in Roman Law* (London: University Press, 1926), pp. 125–129. See also Maine, *Ancient Law,* p. 227.
9. Strachan-Davidson, *Problems of the Roman Criminal Law.* Vol. 1, p. 32. Poste writes (p. 402): "Injuries which in modern law are punished exclusively as crimes could throughout the history of Roman law be vindicated by the private party as private wrongs."
10. William A. Hunter, *Introduction to Roman Law* (9th Ed., London, 1934), p. 14.
11. By all odds the finest and most beautiful account of the religious basis of the Roman family may be found in Fustel de Coulanges' *The Ancient City*. See especially Bk. 2, Ch. 2.
12. See especially J. Declareuil, *Rome The Law-Giver,* translated by E. A. Parker (London: K. Paul, Trench, Trubner & Co., 1927), p. 156ff.; French ed. J. Declareuil, *Rome et l'organisation du droit* (Paris: La Renaissance du livre, 1924).
13. Dio Cassius, Liii, 17. Dio together with Tacitus and Suetonius form the basic source of all that we know of this fateful period.
14. M. I. Rostovtzeff, *The Social and Economic History of the Roman Empire* (Oxford: Clarendon Press, 1926), pp. 39–40, 41.

15. Henry F. Pelham, *Essays on Roman History* (Oxford: Clarendon Press, 1911), p. 94. The entire essay on the domestic policy of Augustus (pp. 89–151) is a brilliant sociological analysis of one of the greatest ages of change in Roman history.
16. See especially, Declareuil, pp. 152–54 and 354–55. Also P. Willems, *Le droit public romain* (Paris, 1888), p. 611f. F. W. Maitland dealt with the centralizing and the individualizing characteristics of Roman imperial law as profound forces of change in the rise of modern Europe. See *Collected Papers* (Cambridge University Press, 1911), Vol. 3, p. 309.
17. Pelham, "Domestic Policy of Augustus," pp. 95–96.
18. Pelham, p. 115.
19. See E. H. Haight, "Reconstruction in the Augustan Age," *Classical Journal,* Vol. XVII, pp. 335–376.
20. Pelham, p. 120.
21. On this momentous economic invasion of the *Patria Potestas* see James Hadley, *Introduction to Roman Law* (New Haven: Yale University Press, 1931), p. 213; also Declareuil, pp. 159–60.
22. Pelham, p. 109.
23. Declareuil, p. 314.
24. Strachan-Davidson, p. 100.
25. Maine, *Ancient Law,* p. 81. It is this kind of insight that makes Maine one of the great sociological minds of his age.
26. Edward Jenks, *Law and Politics in the Middle Ages* (New York: Henry Holt, 1908), p. 308f. My comparison of the two types of society here is greatly indebted to Jenks' work.
27. See Mommsen's treatment of this in his *History of Rome,* W. P. Dickson translation (New York: 1895), Vol. 1, p. 335.
28. H. M. D. Parker, *The Roman Legions* (Oxford: University Press, 1928), p. 24.
29. Lem Homo, *Roman Political Institutions* (New York: 1930), p. 164.
30. Maine, *Ancient Law*. p. 82.

Werner J. Cahnman   **RELIGION AND NATIONALITY**

I

SOCIETY IN THE WEST is based on a territorial principle which is the heritage of the Roman Empire. A child born on American soil, according to the prevailing *jus soli,* the law of the soil, is an American citizen. This, however, is not true of the East. A child born in Germany, say, of unnaturalized Polish parentage, according to the prevailing *jus sanguinis,* the law of blood (or

This paper was written at the suggestion of Professor Robert E. Park and read in its original form at the Fourteenth Annual Festival of Music and Fine Arts, Fisk University, Nashville, Tenn., April 1943. It is reprinted with permission from the *American Journal of Sociology,* Vol. XLIX, No. 6, May 1944. The notes have been overhauled and the last part reformulated for this edition.

kinship), remains a citizen of Poland if no naturalization is granted. Society
in the East is based on the concept of the "folk." We may call the territorial
principle the principle of the marketplace and designate the concept of the
folk as a personal concept derived from the concept of the family. In this sense,
we may speak about personal, as against territorial nationality.

It is in the light of these concepts that we are to understand some of Sir
John Hope Simpson's remarks in his survey on the refugee problem. Here is
what he says:

> It cannot be expected that social assimilation will be complete in the first
> generation but experience shows that in the second and third generation little
> difference persists in Western Europe and in overseas countries. This is not
> necessarily the case in Eastern Europe where the minority system, approximating
> the Turkish millet, is an obstacle to intermarriage and attendance at common
> schools, and isolates the group.[1]

In other words, social assimilation seems to be easier in a society of sellers
and buyers on the marketplace than in a society approximating what Sir
John calls the "Turkish millet." Apparently, the Turkish millet is regarded
as an ideal type when it comes to a consideration of nationalities and minorities in the East. We will, therefore, concern ourselves in this paper with a
definition and explanation of the millet system. We will follow up its roots in
the history of the region and briefly consider its development and decline, as
well as its persistence, in our time.

II

The millet system of the Ottoman Empire may be conceived of as a part
of the religious law of Islam. The world of Islam, roughly speaking, falls
into two sections—dar-ul-Islam, the world of peace and devotion, and dar-
ul-harb, the world of warfare. The world of Moslems is considered under an
obligation to engage in holy warfare until the dar-ul-harb progressively
diminishes as more and more of it is brought into the dar-ul-Islam.

In the dar-ul-Islam, however, non-Moslems, under sufferance, may continue to exist if they are not idolators but communities of the peoples of the
Book, that is to say, Christians and Jews.[2] They may be allowed to profess
their faith and to organize their family affairs according to their own customs;
but the theory has it that they stay on their lands only on lease, paying a
heavy tribute for themselves and for their lands to the Moslem state. They are
reduced to the status of Dhimmis, that is, persons protected by specific
covenants.[3]

The techniques of the sociology of knowledge serve to explicate this
ideology. It is the ideology of a conquering warrior tribe from the desert
which has swarmed in on the settled land and the trading townships and
oases. The Bedouins of Arabia, occupying Syria, Iraq, Egypt, and other

countries peripheral to Arabia proper, found themselves confronted with the central problem of administration in a region where desert and steppe, on the one hand, and stretches of fertile soil, on the other, are intermingled. They would have found themselves unable to cope with the problems of urban civilization had they not availed themselves of ways and means to put to good use the traditional skills and the taxpaying capacities of subjected, yet more sophisticated, populations.

Accordingly, religious life, in the Islamic as well as the pre-Islamic period, conforms to the social pattern of the region. The Bible abounds with stories depicting the interplay between the settled land and the desert. The life of the prophet Elijah marks one phase in that ever-recurring conflict. Elijah's God is the God of his fathers; we see him struggle against the Baalim of the hills, or, in other words, we see the Lord of history up against the spirits of the soil. The two deities interlocked and then separated. It may be said that the community of the Exiles in Babylon returned to the Lord of history after the spirits of the soil had deserted them. Thus, they retained their own status in a strange environment. Later, the "Prince of Exile," presumably of Davidic ancestry, was recognized under Sassanid rule in Babylonia and Persia.[4] It was likewise under Sassanid rule that the first agreement which can properly be said to institute a "millet" was concluded. It was the treaty of Milan between the Shah-in-Shah Jezdegerd and the *Catholicos* of the Assyrians. The Catholicos, or patriarch, became a political dignitary and, in addition to his ecclesiastical functions, was made responsible for the allegiance of his people to the ruler and the state. The Assyrians, or Nestorians, were granted freedom of worship and autonomous jurisdiction of civil cases among their members. In return, they would, as a community, pay taxes to the shah's treasury.[5]

The Sassanid rulers of Persia, themselves Zoroastrians, had found it advantageous to tolerate Christians and Jews who had fled to them in increasing numbers from the heresy-hunting regime which prevailed in the Byzantine Empire. They could count on the loyalty of their new subjects because they left their community life intact, and these new subjects, in turn, could swear allegiance to a ruler who was alien to them because they had no immediate territorial ambitions of their own. The Arab caliphs and later the Turkish sultans adopted this system, although not without gradually depressing the status of their dissenting subjects. Both Arabs and Turks were warriors with a following of primitive tribesmen, and, as a result, they were even more dependent on such a system, as well as more likely to abuse it, than the Persians had ever been.

The millet may be defined as the peculiar political organization which gave to non-Moslem subjects of the Ottoman Empire the right to organize into communities possessing delegated political power under their own ecclesiastical chiefs. The head of the millet was directly responsible to the state for the administration of all its subjects. Although the millet lacked territorial cohesion and military power and had, therefore, to be protected by the ruling warrior caste, it formed in many respects an autonomous unit within the state. Yet, the members of the millet were limited in their general citizenship by virtue of the very fact that the laws of personal statute were based upon religious sanctions.[6]

This seems to us a strange notion. In Western Christianity, the idea of the Kingdom of God is interpreted as referring to a purely spiritual realm with no political connection, but oriental Christianity and traditional Judaism, as well as Islam, do not dissociate religion from social life, from community ties, from civic status, and from law.[7] In our compartmentalized culture, religion has a special shelf, for exclusive use, so it seems, on Sunday mornings, to be forgotten completely after the midday meal. This, however, has never been so in the East. In early antiquity, two and a half millennia before Christ, Sumerian kings were priest-kings, heads of city-states that were at the same time religious entities. The king of Lagash was but the representative of the God of Lagash, king only in relation to the people, but priest in relation to the king of kings, the supreme ruler of the state who dominated the whole life of the people. Truly, Lagash was a "Kingdom of God," and so were Babylon, Moab, Ammon, and Israel. Moreover, public life was intimately connected with ancestral rites. The God of the fathers was venerated along with the God of the locality, as Robertson Smith and, in a larger sense, Émile Durkheim have shown.[8] Society, conceived not merely as an ecological or political phenomenon but envisaged primarily in terms of the enlarged family, retained its religious significance and was perpetuated through worship. Some extended kinship groups preserved their social and religious identities even after centralized states had subjugated wide territories and combined many tribal units within their imperial domain. It matters little whether these established units were based on actual common descent or not; the mere fact that they were founded upon an ancestral myth or, in other words, that their members believed in a common ancestor was enough to unite them with bonds of brotherhood.

Maybe we are touching here on a general truth. But the least that can be said is that the time aspect of society rather than the space aspect seems to have been stressed in the East. The Hebrew and Arabic terms for "world" indicate infinite time rather than infinite space, and the same seems to be true of other oriental languages. It may be said that in the East, religion, understood in terms of a time sequence rather than as a spatial uplifting from this valley of tears to the high heavens, is constitutive of nationality. Abraham was called by the voice of his God to leave the country into which he had been born and thus to become the father of a nation. The process was repeated when Moses led the slaves of Goshen up to Sinai, and it has been repeated ever since. Arab national consciousness has been called into being by the faith of Mohammed and has been revived by religious zeal on later occasions.

Surely, Islam did not invent the pattern in which religion and nationality are inseparably intertwined, but it has drawn upon the pattern of the region and intensified it. Social stratification along economic lines cannot rise to prevalence so long as the conditions of tribal law prevail. Yet, in spite of the ethnic basis of Eastern society, we find the apparent contradiction that race or color prejudice is foreign to Islam. The explanation is to be found partly in the ancient custom of adoption or naturalization; mainly, however, in the encouragement of conversion to a religion claimed to have universal applicability. Tribal patterns do not disappear, but they are overlaid by the conception of Islam as one great brotherhood. The rival tribes of ancient Mecca and Medina, the Quraish, the Aws and the Khazrajs, had to adjust to the demand that adherence to the faith, rather than birth, was henceforth to be the factor deciding whether an individual was to be included within the community or not.[9] Later, brown Javanese and black Africans were accepted under the banner of the prophet together with Arabs, Mongols, and Turks. Aided by the institution of polygyny, the Turks especially have drawn upon the female population of all subjected races, and on imported Negro women in addition, to fill their harems and bear their children. They have taken boys from Christian homes, to rear them in Islam and to have them incorporated into the ill-famed corps of the Janissaries, which was once the fiercest unit of their army. Many of the founders of modern Turkey had foreign mothers, as Enver, Talaat, and Kemal had Greek, Jewish, and Albanian mothers, respectively. If there ever has been a melting pot of races and peoples, it is certainly Turkey.

The dividing line in the East runs not so much between classes and races as between conquerors and conquered, or believers and disbelievers. Disbelievers are tolerated but segregated and forced into little subsocieties of their own. Racial and economic differentiations emerge only in a secondary way. Accordingly, the millet may just as well be defined as a church organized into a nationality as a nationality organized into a church.[10]

Examples are abundant. For instance, the Bulgarians preserved their nationality under their Bulgarian exarch; the Greeks looked up to their patriarch, when he put on the robes of the Byzantine ruler, as if he had been their king. The same is true with regard to the Armenians. The *Catholicos* of the Armenians, says an Armenian author, "is recognized as their national as well as religious chief. In this dual capacity, at the time of the Congress of 1878, he had sent to Berlin a representative, whose intervention had procured the insertion of Article 61 in the treaty."[11] On the other hand, the Maronites were simply the followers of Maron, and it was only subsequently that they developed into what is now the bulk of the Lebanese people. A monk called Jacobus Baradaeus initiated the Jacobite church, which was later constituted as the Jacobite millet and perpetuated solely by endogamy, since proselytizing was forbidden to disbelievers. The followers of Nestorius, who had been declared a heretic at the Council of Chalcedon, formed the Nestorian church of the East. They expanded, at one time, far into Central Asia; but in Persia and Turkey they were recognized as the Nestorian or Assyrian millet. Their remnants split into several denominations and today are known as the Assyrian people. For instance, the Elijah line of the Assyrians submitted to the Holy See in 1845, and the Turks were quick to recognize them as a separate millet under the name of Chaldeans. Numerous similar phenomena can be found within Islam, where, for instance, the sect of the Druzes, following a religious propagandist by the name of Darazi, developed into the Druze people and, temporarily, under the French mandate of Syria, even acquired some measure of territorial recognition.[12] In other words, all these religious or quasi-religious groups came to live in close proximity to one another, married only among themselves, and thus became in the course of time secondary ecological and kinship units. They became peoples.[13]

As a matter of fact, a Moslem Assyrian or Armenian could not exist. He became, by means of his change of faith, a Turk or an Arab; spoke, dressed, and behaved Turkish or Arabic. Even if an Armenian left his Armenian Gregorian church only to join one of the Protestant denominations that were proselytizing among the Armenians, he loosened, by so doing, the ties that bound him to the Armenian people. On the other hand, the Christian missions in Moslem lands were confronted with grave difficulties because for a Moslem to change his faith meant to lose his nationality.

Another example is provided by the Turkish-Greek population exchange after the first World War. It proved to be well-nigh impossible to discover who was Turkish and who was Greek except by the test of religion. Every Greek Orthodox family of Asia Minor, no matter what their racial or ethnic origin, had to leave for Greece; every Mohammedan family in Greece, most of them probably of the same stock as their "Greek" compatriots, were to be resettled in Anatolia. Even the sect of the *Doenmehs,* originally Jewish followers of the false messiah, Sabbatai Zevi, people who had embraced Islam but remained a strictly endogamous group, had to leave Salonica and to take up their residence in Izmir. In brief, religion, which at first can be observed as replacing tribalism, at a later stage fosters a new growth of ethnicity. The institutional expression of this development used to be called a "millet" in the administrative practice of the Ottoman Turks.

What can be seen in the purity almost of an "ideal type" in the countries formerly under Ottoman rule becomes somewhat blurred in the outlying areas of the "East" and it is by no means unknown even in the "West." The majority of the Moslem subjects of France in Algeria never acquired French citizenship because this would have deprived them of their religio-political status as Moslems. If a Tartar, Jew, Pole, or Latvian in the Czarist Empire took to the Greek Orthodox cross, he not only ceased to be a Mohammedan, Israelite, Roman Catholic, or Lutheran, respectively, but he also lost membership among his people and became a Russian. In Yugoslavia, the Roman Catholic Croats and Slovenes, on the one hand, and the Greek-Orthodox Serbs, on the other, have grown together politically, but the cultural divide persists. Roman Catholic Germans in the formerly Prussian province of Poznan tended to become Polonized while the Mazurs in East Prussia, speaking a Polish dialect but being Lutherans, had a German national consciousness. In the old German Empire, the "Permanent Diet," which convened in Regensburg from 1663–1806, was divided into a *Corpus Catholicorum* and a *Corpus Evangelicorum,* and religious division has remained one of the obstacles standing in the way of German political unification. Farther west, the strongest cases that come to mind are those of the Irish and the French Canadians. It has been said that if the English had stayed with Rome, the Irish would have turned Protestant.[14] In French Canada, the Archbishop of Quebec in some ways functions as a political, in addition to being a religious, representative of the French-Canadian people. In the United States, the Mormons in Utah might have developed from "sect" to "peoplehood," if it had not been for the late formation of the group in the railroad age.[15]

These are only some examples out of many. In a number of cases religion is a protective cloak for nationality; in others ethnicity is born of sectarian separation. In all these instances the institution of the "millet" serves as a useful reference.

To sum up our deliberations again in the words of Sir John Hope Simpson:

When the Assyrians petitioned the Council of the League [of Nations] that they might be allowed to live as a millet as they had done in the past, the Permanent Mandates Commission, taking a Western European view, concluded that the adoption of such a resolution would imperil the unity of the Iraqui State.[16]

In these words, which refer to the numerically insignificant but highly representative people of the Assyrians, we find the clash between East and West expressed in classical terms.

III

We can now draw some conclusions as to major trends in our time. The society of the East, based as it has been on the time-consecrated concepts of the folk and the family, has broken down, and the territorial society of modern nationalism—founded upon the principles established in the late Roman Empire, which were recovered by the French Revolution and centered around the marketplace and the military imperium—has had the upper hand throughout the nineteenth and twentieth centuries. The treaties that ended the first

World War have carried the French nation-state far into the East. Commercialism has opened up vast colonial areas and brought peoples and races who hitherto had lived side by side in a merely symbiotic relationship, into close contact with one another. Post-colonial nationalism has taken up the same trend with increased intensity. Territorial nationalism has put dynamite to folk societies and their diversified ancestral rites everywhere; it has conquered the minds and hearts of Eastern youth from Morocco to Indonesia. Turkey, once the seat of the caliphate, has become a lay republic combining the best and the worst of both Germany and France. The Turkish regime has killed Armenians, expelled Greeks, impoverished Jews, and attempts to "Turkify" what is left. Similarly, Nasser's Egypt has forced its Jewish, Italian, and Greek minorities out of the country, and even the ancient Coptic community is now discriminated against. In Algeria, whatever chances existed for the peaceful coexistence of Moslems, Christians, and Jews are shattered.

To be sure, there are exceptions to the rule. In Cyprus, Greeks and Turks have reached a tentative and exceedingly shaky *modus vivendi*—but not a common nationhood. In Lebanon, the various Christian and Moslem subgroups are jealously preserving their autonomy. The state of Israel retains the "millet" concept of separate ecclesiastical jurisdiction for religious communities, as far as matters of personal status are concerned; as a consequence, a territorially conceived Israeli nationality is as yet but faintly indicated. In India, Pakistan, Ceylon, and Burma, religious as well as linguistic divisions abound and are being constantly reinforced. However, the three smaller states of Cyprus, Lebanon, and Israel owe their existence largely to a precarious balance of external forces while the Indian subcontinent is in internal turmoil, with its definite political shape not yet decided. It is possible that in India, as well as in Europe, the nation-state of French revolutionary vintage is being superseded by a more inclusive territorial loyalty.

In the collision between "state" and both "tribe" and "millet,"[17] the city-state, later the nation-state, of the West has emerged victorious. It is now the tree that overshadows East and West. At the same time, the record of political nationalism looks like a failure. The principle of the identity of nationality and territory has brought human misery to the East, where ethnic groups interlock in such an inextricable way that dogmatic minds are driven to despair. As a result, tradition has been replaced as a guiding principle not so much by reason as by coercion. Populations that have lived side by side for centuries, even in the face of frequent conflict, have been uprooted from their homes, driven from one country to the other, starved and butchered by the millions, only to please the jealous God of Uniformity, who tolerates no other gods beside him. To be sure, the world we live in seems to be rapidly moving along the line of expanding political and economic units, such as the "Common Market," the "Inter-American System," the "Atlantic Community," and so forth. But this move from a familial to an ever-larger territorial base in society must not make us overlook the fact that the more intimate forces which have been operating throughout history are not dead; they are only pushed beneath the surface. They will reassert themselves because they are bound up with human nature. Where there is change, there must also be continuity, if normlessness is to be avoided. We must therefore note the need for cultural autonomy in the face of territorial unification.

Notes

1. John Hope Simpson, *The Refugee Problem: Report of a Survey* (London & New York: Oxford University Press, 1939), 540–41. Cf. C. D. Macartney, *National States and National Minorities* (London, 1934), 284.
2. These communities had no rights in a Moslem state, but were exempted from attack and "protected" on payment of a *jizya*, or poll-tax, as provided by the Koran, (9:29). Cf. Reuben Levy, *The Social Structure of Islam* (Cambridge: University Press, 2nd ed., 1957), 66–67.
3. R. J. H. Gottheil, "Dhimmis and Moslems in Egypt," in *Old Testament and Semitic Studies in Memory of William Rainey Harper*, ed. Robert F. Harper (Chicago: University of Chicago Press, 1908), II, 351–414; Reuben Levy, *Introduction to The Sociology of Islam*, 2 vols. (London: William & Norgate, 1931–33), esp. Vol. I, Chap. 1: "The Grades of Society"; Hamilton A. R. Gibb and Harold Bowen, *Islamic Society and the West*, 2 vols. (London-New York-Toronto: 1950), Vol. II, Chap. XIV; G. E. v. Grunebaum, *Medieval Islam—A Study in Cultural Orientation* (Chicago: University of Chicago Press, 1945), 180ff.; cf. also André Chouraqui, *La Condition Juridique de l'Israélite Marocain* (Paris: Presse du Livre Français, 1950), 47–55.
4. Salo W. Baron, *The Jewish Community*, 3 vols. (Philadelphia: Jewish Publication Society of America, 1942), I, 118ff., 157ff.
5. W. A. Wigram, *The Assyrians and Their Neighbors* (London: G. Bell & Sons, 1929), 51. Cf. Malech, *History of the Syrian Nation and the Evangelical-Apostolic Church of the East* (Minneapolis: 1910) and John Joseph, *Nestorians and their Muslim Neighbors—a Study of Western Influences on their Relations* (Princeton: Princeton University Press, 1961).
6. For other definitions of "millet" see James Thayer Addison, *The Christian Approach to the Moslem: A Historical Study* (New York: Columbia University Press, 1942), 62, 113; Macartney, *op. cit.*, pp. 58, 64, 284; Elliot Grinnel Mears (ed.), *Modern Turkey* (New York: Macmillan, 1924), pp. 98, 121, 419; *The Statesman's Yearbook* (London: 1940), 1350. A. Hourani's statement that only three "millets," the Greek, the Armenian and the Jewish, were organized prior to the nineteenth century is irrelevant in the present context: Cf. A. Hourani, "Race and Related Ideas in the Near East" in Andrew W. Lind, *Race Relations in World Perspective* (Honolulu: Univ. of Hawaii Press, 1955), 116–144; cf., also, John Joseph, *op. cit.*, 20, 27, who quotes from "Religion and Nationality," but fails to acknowledge the source. There is no definition of "millet" in the *Encyclopaedia of Islam*.
7. Reuben Levy *op. cit.*, p. 192.
8. William Roberston Smith, *Lectures on the Religion of the Semites* (New York: Macmillan, 1927), esp. Lect. II: "The Nature of the Religious Community

and the Relation of the Gods to Their Worshippers," 28ff.; cf. Émile Durkheim, *The Elementary Forms of the Religious Life: A Study in Religious Sociology,* transl. by Joseph Ward Swain (London: Allen & Unwin, 1954); now available in paperback edition (New York: Collier Books, 1961).

9. Reuben Levy, *op. cit.,* p. 271.
10. Wigram, *op. cit.,* pp. 51, 77, 93, 157, 161, 162, *et passim.* Wigram considers only the sequence: nationality-church although some of his examples would seem to indicate the sequence: church-nationality as well.
11. Boghos Nubar Pasha, "Armenians," in Mears (ed.), *op. cit.,* p. 70.
12. Philipp K. Hitti, *The Origins of the Druze People and Religion* ("Columbia University Oriental Studies," Vol. XXVIII [New York, 1928]).
13. Leo Dominian, *The Frontiers of Language and Nationality in Europe* (New York: Holt, 1917), 271ff.
14. As for the Irish case in the United States, cf. Ruby Jo Reeves Kennedy, "Single or Triple Melting-Pot? Intermarriage Trends in New Haven, 1870–1940," *American Journal of Sociology,* XLIX, No. 4 (January 1944), 331–39, and Lee Benson, *The Concept of Jacksonian Democracy: New York as a Test Case* (Princeton, 1961), pp. 165–207.
15. The complexity of the development of the Mormons from "near-sect" to "near-nation" is set forth in Thomas F. O'Dea, "Mormonism and the Avoidance of Sectarian Stagnation: A Study of Church, Sect and Incipient Nationality," *American Journal of Sociology,* LX, No. 3 (Nov. 1954), 285–293. Cf. E. K. Francis, "The Russian Mennonites: From Religious Sect to Ethnic Group," *American Journal of Sociology,* LIV, No. 2 (Sept. 1948), 101–107.
16. Simpson, *op. cit.,* p. 541, referring to the League of Nations, *Minutes of The Mandates Committee,* 22nd Session, 43, 375. Macartney, *op. cit.,* p. 284, relates that the representative of the British Colonial Office contributed to this wish of the Assyrians the splendidly ingenious remark that "the real difficulty lay in the fact that the Assyrians seemed to desire to live now as they had lived in the past." The unhistorical insistence of the Mandate Commission, certainly, did not provide for them any decent life at all. The massacres in Iraq were soon to follow.
17. René Maunier, *The Sociology of Colonies: Introduction to the Study of Race Contact,* ed. E. O. Lorimer, in International Library of Sociology and Social Reconstruction, ed. Karl Mannheim, 2 vols. (London: Routledge & Kegan Paul, 1949), II, 556ff., *et passim.* Cf. John Joseph, *op. cit.,* p. 148.

Thomas F. O'Dea   MORMONISM AND THE AVOIDANCE
OF SECTARIAN STAGNATION: A
STUDY OF CHURCH, SECT, AND
INCIPIENT NATIONALITY

ONE OF THE MANY CHURCHES founded in the region south of the Great Lakes
in the first half of the nineteenth century, the Church of Jesus Christ of Latter-
Day Saints, or the Mormon church, alone avoided the stagnant backwaters
of sectarianism. Founded in New York State in 1830 by a small group of
men, it has today more than a million members in the United States and in
its mission countries in Europe and the South Seas. It is the only religious
body to have a clear majority of the population in a single state (Utah),
and it has been the central and strategic group in the settlement of the inter-
mountain West. Of its numerous dissident bodies, five survive, the largest of
which has 100,000 members; the smallest, 24. The former, the Reorganized
Church of Jesus Christ of Latter-Day Saints, is an important denomination in
parts of the Middle West.[1] From its founding the Mormon church had set
out to establish the Kingdom of God on earth and had created—once in
Ohio, twice in Missouri, and once in Illinois—settlements in which this ideal
was to be realized, only to see them consumed by external conflict and internal
dissent. Finally, in 1847, the Mormons, harassed and persecuted, dispossessed
of all but faith, leadership, and superb organization, crossed the plains and
settled in the Utah desert. There, relying on these spiritual and sociological
assets, they established a regional culture area bearing the pronounced imprint of their peculiar values and outlook.

This article attempts to answer two questions: (1) What enabled the
Mormon church to avoid sectarianism? (2) If the Mormon church did not become a sect, is it then an ecclesiastical body or "church" in the sense in which
that term has been understood in the sociology of religion since Ernst
Troeltsch?[2] In answering these two questions, two others—of more general
interest—suggest themselves; the first of interest to sociological theory, the
second to the growing concern with interdisciplinary research: (3) Is the
accepted dichotomy, church or sect, conceptually adequate to handle the
empirical data in the sociology of religion? (4) Can sociological analysis alone

Reprinted from the *American Journal of Sociology*, 1954, pp. 285–293, by permission of The
University of Chicago Press.

adequately explain the emergence of one type of social structure as against another?

Presented here are the findings of a larger study of Mormon values and Mormon social institutions,[3] a study which involved an analysis of Mormon theology and religious teaching, the development of Mormon social institutions—ecclesiastical, political, economic, and educational—and a community study based upon participant observation in a rural village, the characteristic product of Mormon efforts at settlement in the West.[4]

Church and Sect

Ernst Troeltsch and Max Weber define a sect as a body of believers based upon contracted or freely elected membership in contrast to the institutional ecclesiastical body or church in which membership is ascribed. "Born into" and "freely chosen" signify the vital distinction. Park and Burgess, Simmel and von Wiese, and, following them, Becker elaborate this definition.[5] For them a church or *ecclesia* is characterized by the following: (1) membership on the basis of birth; (2) administration of the means of grace and its sociological and theological concomitants—hierarchy and dogma; (3) inclusiveness of social structure, often coinciding with ethnic or geographical boundaries; (4) orientation to the conversion of all; and (5) a tendency to compromise with and adjust to the world. The sect, on the contrary, is characterized by (1) separatism and defiance of or withdrawal from the demands of the secular sphere, preferring isolation to compromise; (2) exclusiveness, expressed in attitude and social structure; (3) emphasis upon conversion prior to membership; and (4) voluntary election or joining.

The sect is often persecuted and is always ascetic. It usually rejects hierarchy and endeavors to implement the "priesthood believers" in an egalitarian if narrow social organization. As H. Richard Niebuhr has observed, sectarianism, strictly defined, cannot outlast the founding generation[6] and, as Liston Pope has shown, often does not last it out.[7] The birth of children to the freely electing sectaries and the worldly success which so often crowns sectarian frugality and industry result in that adjustment to the world which Weber has called "the routinization of charisma." To cover this phenomenon, von Wiese and Becker introduce a third type, as does Niebuhr—the denomination. "Denominations are simply sects in an advanced stage of development and of adjustment to each other and the secular world."[8]

There have been attempts—often highly suggestive—to characterize the sectarian personality.[9] Von Wiese and Becker introduce a fourth type—the cult in which religion is private and personal; and Wach introduces another—the independent group. This latter is a semi-ecclesiastical body which starts out resembling a sect and through slow transformation and organizational differentiation becomes much more like a church. Wach's chief example is the Mormon church. This classification is perceptive, but arguments will be given below to show that it is inadequate.

Wach also points out the impossibility of applying any of the above criteria with rigor. Accepting the importance of sociological criteria and of theological and philosophical doctrines in differentiating sects from other religious bodies, he concludes that the characteristic attitude is most pertinent —an attitude which claims to be "renewing the original spirit of the absolute or relative beginnings" of a religious movement.[10] In what follows the criteria of von Wiese and Becker and of Wach are applied to Mormonism.

The Avoidance of Sectarianism

The Mormon church claimed to be a divine restoration of the Apostolic Church after centuries of apostasy. The mark of the new dispensation was contemporary revelation. Through the prophet, Joseph Smith, the Lord was believed to have called the elect. The result was the church which was founded in western New York, at the time a near-frontier and the scene of a great religious enthusiasm.[11] To its converts it offered security—a resolution of the outer conflict and inner turmoil of denominational confusion and one which claimed the sanction of divine revelation. Convinced of a covenant to build the Kingdom of God on earth, the Latter-Day Saints attempted to establish their settlements on the basis of the Law of Consecration, or United Order of Enoch, a plan announced by the prophet-founder which reconciled Christian socialism with private initiative and management.[12] This law was withdrawn in 1838 after some seven years of experiment marked by contentions and jealousies, and tithing was substituted for it.

The Mormon church placed great emphasis upon the restoration of Hebrew ideals and upon the revival of Old Testament practices and institutions. The Saints were, they believed, a modern Israel: called by God, party to the covenant, and about to be gathered unto Zion. Polygamy was but one, although the most notorious, example of such revivals. In restoration and peculiarity, two important aspects of the Mormon Gospel, the attitudes of renewal and exclusiveness characteristic of sects were palpably present.

While commitment to building the Kingdom was sectarian in so far as it required withdrawal from the world and refusal to accommodate to the routine demands of secular life, it certainly had other possible implications. The idea of a Christian commonwealth was capable of quite nonsectarian interpretation. Moreover, the withdrawal from "Babylon" did not involve a repudiation of worldly pursuits, for in the City of God, the New Jerusalem, business, family life, government, and even armed defense would be acceptable and accepted. Nature was not seen as corrupted, and the vitiating effect of original sin upon preternatural virtue was denied—a most unsectarian doctrine. Work and recreation were both accepted and sanctified. Against the sectarian notions of renewal and exclusiveness must be placed the nonsectarian possibilities of building a Christian society and the doctrine of human goodness—of total "undepravity."

Yet other groups had set out to build the Kingdom, and whatever nonsectarian possibilities lie hidden in the idea of a Christian commonwealth were never made apparent. How many sects built isolated little communities where prosperity followed upon the sectarian ascetic of work and thrift? Such settlements often reached a membership of a thousand and then stopped growing. Others experienced "swarming," that is, excess numbers, usually in excess of a thousand, migrated and established a new settlement emulating the mother-community but independent of its authority. This was the common sectarian fate. How were the Mormons to avoid it and realize the nonsectarian possibilities of their vision?

The Kirtland attempt to build the Kingdom failed because of internal dissent, external opposition, and economic distress—the last the most important. The Saints then migrated to Missouri and there at two points—Jackson County and Far West—endeavored to construct the New Jerusalem. Their strange doctrines claiming contemporary converse with God, their frugality and industry and consequent prosperity, their talk of making the region a "promised land," and their northern manners accentuated by rumors of abolition sentiments aroused the animosity of their neighbors. Consequently, they were driven from the land, and, crossing the Mississippi, the only eastward move in their long wanderings, they entered Illinois, where they built another city. Nauvoo, on the east bank of the river, saw the arrival of converts in great numbers, the first fruits of the European harvest. But there, too, hostility followed the Saints, and rumors that the leaders were practicing polygamy—rumors that turned out to be true—and a more defiant attitude from the Mormon leadership increased Gentile antagonism. In 1844 Joseph Smith was murdered at Carthage jail, and in the next three years the Saints were driven from Nauvoo. In 1847, after a period of disorganization and hardship, they migrated to Utah under the leadership of Brigham Young.

In the West the church gained the respite needed for its internal recovery and at the same time the relative isolation required for establishing a civilization whose institutions would be informed by Mormon conceptions and Mormon values. In the 1880's and 1890's, however, the Mormon-Gentile conflict broke out anew with considerable acuteness, the issues now being polygamy and the admission of Utah to the Union. After harsh federal legislation and prosecution of Mormon leaders, the church abandoned polygamy and accommodated itself to the demands of the larger American community into which it was reintegrated. Yet relative isolation had done its work—Utah and the surrounding region remained a Mormon culture area, although the implicit claim to it as an exclusive homeland was given up. Moreover, Mormon peculiarity and self-consciousness remained.

In this early period of Mormon history many marks of sectarianism were present: not only the attitude of renewal and exclusiveness but voluntary election as the basis of membership, withdrawal from the secular community, asceticism which placed a high value on hard work, persecution which increased in-group cohesion, and the conception of the priesthood of believers. The last doctrine, however, was not interpreted in terms of an egalitarian congregationalism. Rather it found expression in an hierarchical priesthood organization, authoritarian in structure and function. As the church grew, as its early charismatic leadership became more institutionalized in the leading offices, and as it had to stand against external threats, the early congregationalism gave way more and more to authoritarian rule.

What factors militated against the development of a typical sect in this situation? Two were already mentioned: (1) *the nonsectarian possibilities of building the Kingdom which could require so much subtle accommodation* and (2) *the doctrine of natural goodness, by way of which nineteenth-century American optimism entered Mormon religious consciousness to blend there with the chiliastic expectations of a restorationist movement.* Yet the former alone could not effect the avoidance of sectarianism, as the record of so many other groups makes so clear; nor could the latter, although, when combined with other factors effective in the concrete situation, both could affect the issue in a powerful and pervasive manner. These two factors combined with the following eight to effect the issue:

3. *Universal missionary understanding of the notion of "gathering the elect."*—The Mormon notion of peculiarity was exclusive, but it was not necessarily sectarian in the strictest sense. It was rather committed to missionary work—to calling the elect from the world. This was of great consequence when taken together with several other factors, despite its being a rather sectarian idea of missionary work.

4. *The temporal appropriateness of the doctrine in the late 1830's*— A generation before, the "gathering of the elect" might have been understood in terms of calling the elect from the neighboring counties. But in the second decade of the nineteenth century, American Protestantism had discovered a bigger world. The Mormons came upon the scene in time to inherit the newer and broader definition. The universal understanding of calling the elect combined with the new world-wide definition of the mission field worked against a sectarian issue.

5. *The success of missionary work.*—The ability of the Mormon Gospel to bring meaning and hope to many, in America and in Europe, especially England and Scandinavia, resulted in thousands of converts. With increased numbers, the notion of the holy city which the Saints were called to build now took on dimensions hardly compatible with sectarianism. Nauvoo had a population of 20,000 when Chicago had 5,000.

6. *The withdrawal of the Law of Consecration.*—Had the Law of Con-

secration worked, the Mormons might have built another successful communitarian settlement of which our history has seen so many. The failure of the Law, on the other hand, deprived them of a blueprint, rigid conformity to which could have been interpreted as the only permissible economic ethic, thereby lending a sectarian narrowness to their activities and inhibiting growth. Moreover, the Law was withdrawn by Joseph Smith in a revelation which still held up its ideals as the will of God. As a result the flexibility of charismatic leadership was transmitted to the institutionalized church in economic matters, and its spirit vivified economic experiment for the next century, while a killing economic literalism was successfully eschewed. This is all the more striking, since in scriptural interpretation Mormons have generally been literalists.

7. *The failures and consequent necessity of starting again.*—The need to start over again four times in sixteen years also contributed to flexibility, preventing a set routine from developing which could then have been imposed on new problems, thereby limiting growth and contributing to a sectarian atmosphere and structure. Combined with the withdrawal of the Law of Consecration, this made a dogmatism of minutiae impossible.

8. *The expulsion from the Middle West.*—The Middle West, the continent's most attractive ecological area, was destined to draw large numbers of non-Mormon settlers. In such a situation it would have been quite impossible for the Mormon church to have maintained any hegemony, spiritual, political, or economic. Instead it would in all likelihood have become one of a number of denominations accommodating to each other and to the secular world and thus would have been reintegrated into the general American community with which it shared so many common roots as another small and unimportant Protestant group.

9. *The choice and the existence of a large, unattractive expanse of land in the West.*—The Mormon leadership deliberately chose an unattractive region to gain the necessary respite that isolation would give and resisted the seductions of more pleasant prospects. The existence of this arid region was something over which they had no control. It was unquestionably a prerequisite for the future form of their community. The result was the opening-up of a huge area waiting to be converted from desert, supporting a scant nomadic population, to a Mormon culture area based upon irrigation farming. This also gave the necessary time in isolation for Mormon social institutions to emerge and to "set."

10. *The authoritarian structure of the church and the central government which it made possible.*—The existence of a charismatic leader in the early stages of Mormon church history whose right to rule was believed to be based upon divine election and the consequent authoritarian and hierarchical structure of church government permitted scattered settlement in the West under central direction. Such authoritarian characteristics were strengthened by the

external conditions of conflict and hardship. Centrifugal tendencies in the West were restrained when not completely inhibited. The priesthood structure and the routinization of prophetic rule might in other circumstances have been completely compatible with sectarianism, yet in the western settlement they combined with open and relatively empty and isolated land, and missionary success and consequent emigration, to make large-scale settlement possible under central government. This combination ruled out the last chance of sectarianism.

These last eight factors, then, combined to militate against a sectarian issue to the Mormon experiment and to bring into existence the Mormon church of the present day. Instead of becoming a sect, the church became the core of a large culture area. In these eight factors and their combination we have the answer to our first question.

Neither Church Nor Sect

The Mormon church is excluded by definition from the category of church or *ecclesia,* unless it has become one in the course of its development. Similarly with regard to the category of denomination: since we have defined denominations as "routinized sects," Mormonism, having avoided sectarianism, at the same time avoided denominationalism. However, to be of genuine interest, these two statements must be true in more than a formal sense—they must be more than mere analytical inferences from definitions. The question is then: Has the Mormon church become an ecclesiastical body in the course of its evolution?

Despite the avoidance of typical sectarian structure and isolation, the Mormon church has displayed and retained many sectarian characteristics. Most important are: (1) a sense of peculiarity, of election, and of covenant, which is reinforced by explicit theological doctrine; (2) a tendency to withdrawal from the Gentile world (this is now most frequently expressed in admonition and symbolic practices, yet it found large-scale expression in the Church Welfare Plan with which the Mormon church sought to meet the great depression as a separate body capable of considerable autarchy); (3) a commitment to "warning the world" and "gathering the elect," the implications of which have been more routine and less dramatic since the accommodation which followed the defeat of the church on the polygamy issue; and (4) chiliastic expectations, still important not only among rural groups but in the writings of some leaders of the church.

While the Mormons have never identified group membership with peculiarity of dress as sectarists have frequently done, the strict interpretation of Joseph Smith's no-liquor, no-tobacco counsel at the present day serves an analogous function and has become the focus of the expression of exclusivist sentiments. Moreover, although persecution has stopped, the memory of it preserves in-group solidarity and strengthens loyalty.

Yet despite the notae of the sect, the basic fact in Mormon history since 1890 has been the accommodation of the church to the demands of the larger Gentile community. The abandonment of polygamy—that camel at which so many strained but which became so identified with loyalty that all were willing to suffer in its defense—was the surrender of what had become the typical Mormon institution. Economic experimentation—the communism of the United Order, for example—became less characteristic of Mormon activities, and, in general, the secular demands of Babylon displaced the earlier enthusiasm for the New Jerusalem. Even the successes of earlier fervor strengthened the trend to accommodation. Having become the dominant group over a large culture area, the Mormon church experienced the conservatism of the successful, which was not likely to upset a working equilibrium. The involvement of church leadership in established political, economic, and educational institutions, the education of children, the comparatively long-established hierarchy and dogma—all display ecclesiastical features of Mormon organization. The demand for conversion and the aversion to the ecclesiastical practice of infant baptism were soon institutionally compromised in the baptism of the eight-year-old children of Mormon families.

This combination of sectarian characteristics with structure, policy, and circumstances similar to many *ecclesiae* suggests that the Mormon church is a mixture of the pure categories outlined in our typology. Joachim Wach, recognizing this problem—specifically about the Mormons and generally in such typologies—has characterized the Mormon church as an independent group with semi-ecclesiastical organization.[13] It is, for Wach, neither church nor sect; it is an independent group through whose organization its members have access to the necessary means of salvation.

In terms of theology and group structure there is considerable justification for Wach's classification. Yet, in larger terms, there is more to be said. The Mormon restoration was not only a Christian renewal; it was a Hebrew revival. Mormondom conceived itself as a modern Israel. This alone is not uncommon in Christian experience, and we are likely to take it for granted. Yet in the Mormon case, contemporary conditions of life were to give the revival of Hebrew ideals a more genuine content than would have been possible in smaller groups in less demanding circumstances. The acceptance of a model is always important in the patterning of subsequent behavior, and in the Mormon case the model of the chosen people could not but affect Mormon belief and behavior: polygamy is but the most notorious example.

Guided by this model, the Saints withdrew from the modern Babylon to build the modern Zion. Owing to circumstances over which they had little control, they found themselves wandering in the wilderness. They had sought but part of the Israelitish parallel; circumstances had provided the rest. For sixteen years they were driven about, attempting four times to build their city. Their size, the extent and duration of their suffering, and the way in which defeat several times crowned the most palpable successes combined to transform the bread and water of sectarian affliction into the real presence of national potentiality. Common effort in success and in failure, common suffering from elemental and human adversaries, even common struggle with arms against common enemies, all these lent to the symbolic emulation of ancient Israel an existential reality which devoted sectaries in more (or less) fortunate circumstances could hardly surmise. Mormonism lived its Exodus and Chronicles, not once but many times. It had its Moses and its Joshua. Circumstances had given it a stage upon which its re-enactment of biblical history was neither farce nor symbolic pageant.

Throughout this intense group experience—an experience which produced a genuine folk tradition in a decade and a half—Mormon family life and Mormon economic and political activity continued. During this time the Mormons courted and married, begat children and reared them, and established ties of consanguinity and affinity—made more numerous and complex by polygamy—which reinforced and impenetrated those of membership in the church. Economic activity, both cooperative and private, and political necessities, established further bonds. Moreover, in the years of wandering the Saints spent their lives in largely Mormon surroundings. This was even more true in the years that followed 1847, when geographical reinforced social isolation.

Fellowship in the Gospel became—and remains today—supported by and imbedded in a matrix of kinship. The circumstance of enforced nomadism and of successive resettlement, brought about by no design of the Saints and yet in close emulation of their Hebraic model, was experienced in a manner that would guarantee its transmission as informal family history as well as the more formally taught Church history. In each attempt at settlement a group increasingly conscious of itself as a chosen vessel established its holy city—its spiritual and temporal homeland—only to be driven out under circumstances that strengthened in-group loyalty and increased self-consciousness. In Utah a homeland was finally found where "the desert would blossom as the rose," and all previous Mormon history was reinterpreted as precursory of this final fruition in "the place which God for us prepared." The death of Joseph on the eastern side of the Mississippi was the final act of the first stage, as was that of Moses on the borders of the land of Canaan. It was the first stage in the development of incipient nationhood. The members of the Church of Jesus Christ of Latter-Day Saints had become—to use the significant term often used most casually by the Mormons themselves—the "Mormon people." Moreover, the Mormon people had found a homeland. The ties of religious faith were reinforced by those of blood and marriage, of common group memories often involving suffering and heroism, of common economic and cultural aspirations—and now by a region whose very physiognomy would become symbolic of another and perhaps greater group achievement, the successful settlement in the desert.

The Mormons were not completely unaware of what they had become. It is true that their American patriotism, which was an article of faith with them, inhibited any movement for national independence, and they tended to see their own religious homeland as part of a secular manifest destiny. Yet the latter was certainly subordinate to a religious conception of Zion in the mountaintops. In 1850 the Mormons established the state of Deseret—much larger than present-day Utah—and applied for admission to the Union. The covenant people would become an American state rather than an independent nation. In Nauvoo they had been virtually a state within a state through grant of a special charter from the Illinois legislature, and all previous attempts to build the city were characterized by considerable autonomy. The Civil War had not yet settled certain limitations of autonomy, nor had postwar developments in politics, economics, and technology made autonomy seem so far-fetched as one might imagine in today's conditions. Moreover, it must be recalled that, in moments of passion in the Mormon-Gentile conflict, separatism and secession were openly considered and that armed, if inconclusive, conflict with federal forces did take place.

The Mormons had gone from near-sect to near-nation. The Zionism of the nineteenth-century Mormons stopped short of the national fulfilment of the Jewish Zionism of the twentieth century. Yet the Saints had in large part realized the implications of the model which had guided them in such auspicious circumstances. If their own patriotism combined with their defeat in the Mormon-Gentile conflict to inhibit the full fruition of national sovereignty, Mormondom, nevertheless, became a subculture with its own peculiar conceptions and values, its own self-consciousness, and its own culture area. The Mormons, in a word, had become a people, with their own subculture within the larger American culture, and their own homeland as part of the American homeland.

Conclusion

We have now answered the first two questions. A peculiar concatenation of ten factors—ideal, matters of conceptions and values; historical, matters of unique concomitance or convergence in time; and structural, matters of social structure—combine to explain how the Mormon church escaped sectarianism. In escaping the fate of an isolated sect which had been the nemesis of so many other restorationist religious groupings, it did not become either a denomination or a church in the sense of the accepted definitions, although it displayed characteristics of both. Rather, the emulation of the Old Testament Hebrews in the unsettled conditions of the nineteenth-century Middle and Far West resulted in the emergence of a Mormon people—a phenomenon not unlike the emergence of nations and empires from religious groups in the past or in our own day. The development of nationhood, such as we have seen in contemporary Jewish Zionism, or in the fulfilment of the aspirations of Indian Islam, was inhibited by American patriotic convictions on the part of the Latter-Day Saints themselves and by the integrating power of the larger American community, yet the flare-up of separatist sentiment in the heat of conflict suggests the possibilities of development had circumstances been different.

What of the third and fourth questions asked above?

The dichotomy of church and sect and their derivatives—independent group and denomination—do not exhaust the possibilities which are offered by empirical research in the sociology of religion. The development of a people with a peculiar culture and with developed self-consciousness as well as a native region identified with themselves and their group "myth" is another possibility as was realized in the history of Mormonism.[14]

The final question is whether sociological analysis alone can adequately explain the emergence of one type of social structure as against another. Ten factors have been given as preventing the Mormon church from becoming a sect despite a theological and sociological tendency in the sectarian direction. Eight of these have been presented as particularly effective. It should be noted that, of these, all but the third and tenth factors are matters of historical contingency. That is, in the cases of factors 4 through 7 unique convergence of specific events must be considered in any adequate explanation. These matters could hardly have been predicted from, or be explained in terms of, a purely sociological frame of reference. It would seem that sociology in the uncontrolled field situation—and most significant problems are still in that category —must not attempt to solve its problems in terms of abstract schemata which do not take account of historical contingency and which abstract from time. From another point of view it may be said that intellectual analysis of the content of conceptions and values often gives a much richer understanding and a much safer lead concerning their implications for social action than do categorizations in terms of highly abstract schemata. Yet this difficulty seems less formidable than the historical. The inability of sociological analysis alone to predict or explain the emergence of one type of social structure as against another must be granted at least in the present example.

This concession has great significance for sociology, whether in the planning of research or in the training of specialists. It proves again the importance of interdisciplinary cooperation. This may be either what Linton used to call several disciplines under one skull or collaboration between social scientists and scholars across departmental lines. In larger research it must certainly mean the latter.

Notes

1. Elmer T. Clark, *The Small Sects in America* (New York: Abingdon-Cokes-bury Press, 1937). Clark gives the following dissidents besides the Re-organized Church: Bickertonites, Hedrickites, Strangites, and Cutlerites. None of these groups had over 1,500 members; the Cutlerites had about two dozen and practiced community of property.
2. See Joachim Wach, *The Sociology of Religion* (Chicago: University of Chicago Press, 1944), pp. 195ff.
3. This research was done as part of the Values Study Project of the Laboratory of Social Relations of Harvard University and was supported financially and otherwise by the project. It has been republished in Thomas F. O'Dea, *The Mormons* (Chicago, Ill.: University of Chicago Press, 1957).
4. See Evon Z. Vogt and Thomas F. O'Dea, "A Comparative Study of the Role of Values in Social Action in Two Southwestern Communities," *American Sociological Review*, XVIII, No. 6 (December, 1953), 645–54; and Lowry Nelson, *The Mormon Village* (Salt Lake City: University of Utah Press, 1953).
5. Robert E. Park and Ernest W. Burgess, *Introduction to the Science of Sociology* (Chicago: University of Chicago Press, 1921), pp. 50, 202–3, 611–12, 657, 870–74; Howard Becker, *Systematic Sociology: On the Basis of the "Beziehungslehre und Gebildelehre" of Leopold von Wiese: Adapted and Amplified* (New York: John Wiley & Sons, 1932), pp. 624–28.
6. H. Richard Niebuhr, *The Social Sources of Denominationalism* (New York: Henry Holt & Co., 1929), pp. 17ff.
7. Liston Pope, *Millhands and Preachers: A Study of Gastonia* (New Haven: Yale University Press, 1942).
8. Becker, *op. cit.*
9. See John L. Gillin, "A Contribution to the Sociology of Sects," *American Journal of Sociology*, XVI (1910), 236ff.; Robert P. Casey, "Transient Cults," *Psychiatry*, IV (1941), 525ff.; and Ellsworth Faris, "The Sect," Chap. V. of *The Nature of Human Nature* (New York: McGraw-Hill Book Co., 1937).
10. Wach, *op cit.*, pp. 194–96. For an excellent discussion of the church-sect problem see *ibid.*, pp. 195–205, and especially his later "Church, De-nomination, and Sect," Chap. IX in *Types of Religious Experience* (Chicago: University of Chicago Press, 1951), pp. 187–208.
11. Whitney B. Cross, *The Burned-over District: The History of Enthusiastic Religion in Western New York, 1800–1850* (Ithaca: Cornell University Press, 1950).
12. See Doctrine and Covenants 42:30–36; also 51:1–16; 70:3, 9; 104; 82; and 92. This is a standard scriptural work of the Mormon church and contains the revelations of Joseph Smith. See also Leonard Arrington, "Early Mormon Communitarianism," *Western Humanities Review*, VII, No. 4 (Autumn, 1953), 341–69; and also Arthur E. Bestor, Jr., *Backwoods Utopias: The Sectarian and Owenite Phases of Communitarian Socialism in America: 1663–1829* (Philadelphia: University of Pennsylvania Press, 1950).
13. *The Sociology of Religion*, pp. 194–97.
14. After I had worked through my data to the conclusion that Mormonism developed into something like an incipient nationality, I found the fol-

lowing paragraph in Park and Burgess, *op. cit.*, pp. 872–73: "Once the sect has achieved territorial isolation and territorial solidarity, so that it is the dominant power within the region that it occupies, it is able to control the civil organization, establish schools and a press, and so put the impress of a peculiar culture upon all the civil and political institutions that it controls. In this case it tends to assume the form of a state, and become a nationality. Something approaching this was achieved by the Mormons in Utah." Although Park did nothing more with the idea, its statement here leaves little to be desired in clarity—a strong argument in favor of more familiarity with the masters of American sociology!

Florian Znaniecki   **THE ORIGIN OF NATIONAL CULTURE SOCIETIES**

Who Initiates the Formation of a National Culture Society?

WHEN WE SURVEY THE HISTORY of nationalism during the last two hundred years, we notice that some nationalities began to manifest strong active solidarity much earlier than others. Thus, in Europe at the beginning of the nineteenth century common national culture was already a powerful bond uniting Frenchmen, Englishmen, Irishmen, Danes, Swedes, Poles, Czechs, Russians, Greeks, Hungarians; although some political and economic conflicts occurred within each nationality, they were less influential and lasting than conflicts between nationalities. Italian and German cultural solidarity, though already strong, did not overcome political divisions and conflicts until after the middle of the century. The cultural solidarity of Finns, Estonians, Letts, Lithuanians, Ukranians, Slovaks was fully manifested only in the twentieth century.

Outside of Europe no such solidarity existed a century and a half ago. The American colonies broke away from England while they still shared English culture. An original American culture soon began to develop, but ninety years ago it was not yet sufficiently strong as a social bond to prevent a civil war; however, during the last seventy-five years, its unifying influence has been steadily growing. In Spanish America, notwithstanding a common historical background of Spanish culture, separate sovereign states were formed; interstate wars and civil wars have been going on for more than a century, and only recently did new original national cultures begin to grow in some of them. In Asia, Chinese culture, which for centuries united a small group of intellec-

Reprinted with permission from Florian Znaniecki, *Modern Nationalities: A Sociological Study* (Urbana: University of Illinois Press, 1952), pp. 23–35.

tuals, is not yet sufficiently influential to unite the masses of Chinese people. Japanese unity proved strong, indeed, during the last fifty years, but we must remember that the people who share Japanese national culture have also some age-old common religious beliefs, and nearly all belong to a well-integrated political society. In India, the religious solidarity and separatism of Moslems and Hindus are more powerful than the ideal of a common Indian cultural nationality promulgated by nationalistic leaders. Of Islamic peoples, only the Turks already form a separate, united nationality; a distinctly Arabian national unity has only recently begun to develop.[1]

This brief survey indicates that, in order to compare national culture societies and reach sociological generalizations about them, we cannot simply study them as they exist right now or as they once did exist at any particular static cross-section of universal history. We must investigate them in the course of their gradual development from the time of their origin. A comparative analysis of this development shows that, however much the cultures differ, the processes of their social formation, growth, and integration manifest a striking similarity.[2]

In every instance hitherto investigated, the formation of a national culture society starts with a relatively small social nucleus whose influence slowly spreads until it eventually reaches millions of people. This nucleus is not constituted by any authoritative organized group, be it the government of a state, or the clerical hierarchy of a church, or an association of members of an economically dominant class. It originates with independent *individual leaders* in various realms of cultural activity, who gradually create a national culture in which a plurality of traditional regional cultures becomes partly synthesized. We call them leaders because and insofar as they attract circles of voluntary followers. They frequently gain also the support of socially powerful sponsors or patrons—princes, magnates, church dignitaries, men of wealth, statesmen, military commanders, heads of political parties.

As the national culture grows, these leaders, their followers, and sponsors who participate in its growth form an increasingly coherent intellectual community activated by the ideal of a culturally united and socially solidary national society, which should include all the people whose folk cultures are presumed to be essentially alike and who are supposed to share the same historical background. The realization of this ideal is expected to overcome the cultural isolation of local and regional communities, political divisions, religious differences, class conflicts.

Throughout this process new social groups become organized and existing groups modified, either to promote further development and perpetuation of the national culture or to integrate, expand, and defend the evolving society.

Let us survey, first, the various social roles of those intellectual leaders who contribute to the creative growth of a national culture.

The Social Roles of Men of Letters

We use the term "men of letters" to denote writers of aesthetic works. It is they who developed new literary languages from traditional regional dialects and produced distinctive nationalistic literatures. They did this by recording and synthesizing in writing the unwritten products of popular poetry, myth, legend, and story; by translating into the vernacular or imitating the aesthetic products of older literatures; and especially by their own original creations. These writers initiated national cultures in Western and Central Europe at the time when the only fully developed literary culture in these areas (apart from Hebrew culture, shared by scattered Jewish communities) was that of the Roman Catholic Church, which throughout its extent used Latin as a common language.

Of course, men of letters were not the only ones who contributed to the formation of new literary languages. Some early legal documents were written in the vernacular. Priests translated prayers and wrote sermons in a popular language which could be understood by inhabitants of a large region. Eventually, when the Reformation began, important contributions to the standardization, unification, and spread of national languages were made by Protestant leaders who translated the Bible into the vernacular in order to make it accessible to lay believers. Thus, John Huss and his successors translated it into Czech, Wycliffe into English, Luther into German. Catholics followed their example later, at a time when the national languages were already at least partly developed.

Now, why was the development of national cultures mainly due to writers of aesthetic literature? To answer this question adequately, we would have to explain the universal appeal, in traditional as well as in literary cultures, of epics, legends, fiction, lyric poetry, drama; and this is, of course, far beyond our present task. The significant point about the social roles of secular men of letters as initiators and builders of national culture is that, unlike religious writers and legislators, they had considerable freedom of innovation. Their agglomerated original contributions enriched the language in which they wrote, besides giving new aesthetic form and new content to the total literature which they were creating. At the same time, however, some linguistic standards and norms had to be accepted by all writers who used the same language; otherwise, this language would have no cultural unity or continuity. Consequently, after the Renaissance, dictionaries and grammars of modern national languages began to be composed on the model of dictionaries and grammars of ancient Greek and Latin.

The creative growth of national languages and literatures, however, was rather slow, especially when writers used different regional dialects as main foundations for a new literary language. This is well exemplified in France. French literature began in the eleventh century with the *Chansons de Geste,* epic stories about the achievements of military heroes, and later with lyric poetry. In the thirteenth century, two different literary languages were evolving in France: one based on southern dialects, popularly included under the name "langue d'oc"; the other on northern dialects, under the name "langue d'oeil."

Which of the competing regional dialects eventually triumphed and became accepted as the common national literary language depended, first, upon the number, as well as upon the wealth of form and of content, of the literary works created by the authors who used it; second, upon the support of influential sponsors who helped spread it over several regions. Thus, the literature of southern France ceased to grow after the Albigensian war, whereas the literature of northern France continued to grow, slowly at first, more and more rapidly during the sixteenth and seventeenth centuries, when its spread was sponsored by the kings of France.

The language originally based on the Tuscan dialect became universally recognized and accepted as the supreme common Italian language at the beginning of the fourteenth century, due to the many creative contributions written in that language, culminating in the works of Dante and Petrarch. The Norman conquest impeded the development of Old English, based on Anglo-Saxon dialects, and only in the fifteenth century did Modern English begin to grow creatively through new contributions. From about 1150 on, the German literary language, based on so-called High German (*hochdeutsch*), was sponsored by several rulers and autonomous cities, although only about 1500 did it gain general recognition as the national language, as shown by the fact that Luther used it for his translation of the Bible.[3] No such difficulty, however, in overcoming dialectical differences was found in Poland. Up to the end of the fifteenth century, Latin was the language used by nearly all Polish writers. When in the sixteenth century Polish national literature began to develop, most of the writers were nobles, and by that time the spoken language of the nobility was already quite uniform; only the regional dialects used by peasants continued to differ widely.

The evolution of new national languages and literatures was much slower in Eastern Europe. Greek became the religious literary language of the Greek Orthodox Church; but, unlike Latin, it remained at the same time a spoken language, used by several million people. There was no linguistic distinction between religious and secular language, and contributions to Greek literature continued to be made as long as the Byzantine Empire lasted. But after the Ottoman conquest, Greek secular literature practically disappeared; only in the nineteenth century did a new literature, written in modern Greek, begin to develop.

In order to promote the conversion of Slavs in the Danube region, Cyril and Methodius in the ninth century translated the Bible into a new written language which they introduced. It was based upon the Slavic dialects of this region, with an alphabet borrowed from Greek, but somewhat modified to fit the local dialects. This language, later called "Old Slavonic," was also used to spread Christianity among the Eastern Slavs north of the Balkans and remained for nearly a thousand years an almost changeless sacred literary language of all the Slavic peoples who did not adopt the Latin language as used by the Roman Catholic Church. In the course of time, secular works appeared, combining in various degrees this Old Slavonic with regional dialects; and eventually several national languages with distinctive literatures evolved but with one exception this evolution was interrupted or slowed down by extraneous influences. Thus, the Ottoman invasion of the Balkans stopped the incipient development of the Serbian and the Bulgarian literatures, which did not start again until the nineteenth century. The growth of the Ukrainian national literature was until recent times impeded by the influence of Polish culture in the west and repressed in the east by the Tsarist regime.[4] On the other hand, Russian literature, although it began to develop only in the eighteenth century, has been growing rapidly and continuously.[5]

The problem of developing a secular literary language to be used by all the people belonging to the same nationality has not yet been solved by Jewish or by Hindu leaders. During the development of Jewish national culture (as distinct from Hebrew religious culture), Yiddish literature has grown rapidly. But Zionist leaders refuse to accept Yiddish as the common literary language; they promote instead the revival of Hebrew not only as the sacred, but also as the secular, language. In India, the most widely spread literary language is Hindustani, but less than a third of the people of India understand it; moreover, it has two different divisions, one used by Moslems, the other by Hindus. Similarly, a dual trend is found in Ireland: Should Gaelic be fully revived or English used in Irish literature?[6] Of course, it may be said that a common language is not indispensable for social unity, as the example of Switzerland shows. But the Swiss form a political society, including three nationalities, not a national culture society.[7]

The example of older and more developed national culture societies has made leaders striving for the cultural independence and social unification of their own nationality fully aware of the importance of creating an original national literature. For instance, the growth of Norwegian literature has been recognized as the most important step in liberating the Norwegian people from the century-old cultural and social domination of the Danish national society.[8] After gaining political independence from Spain and Portugal, the striving of Latin American political societies for cultural independence was manifested sooner or later in efforts to develop original literatures of their own.[9] In British Canada, the creative growth of an original Canadian literature is considered the most important step toward the development of a separate Canadian nationality, united by a distinctive, independent culture of its own.

The Social Roles of Historians and Ethnographers

While a common written language and literature is a necessary condition of overcoming the separatism of local and regional collectivities with different folk cultures, it is obviously not sufficient to integrate socially such collectivities. The very idea that they should be united is founded upon the doctrine that, however much their folk cultures may differ, they are essentially similar as compared with those of other collectivities and that this similarity is essentially due to a common historical background. This doctrine is a joint product of ethnographers who study folk cultures and of historians who trace back the origin of these cultures and of the peoples who maintain them. Ethnography and history are both very old and from the beginning they have been interconnected.

Members of a tribe or a folk community are aware that their cultural products, customs, and mores differ from those of other tribes or communities with which they have been in contact and are in some measure acquainted. And, whenever there is considerable social mobility, especially mass migrations, tribes come into contact with other tribes, hitherto unknown, whose cultures differ more from theirs than the cultures of their neighbors do. They become increasingly conscious of the fundamental similarities underlying what in the light of these new contacts appear to be only minor differences. Such primitive ethnographic knowledge, however superficial and prejudiced, has been the original source from which comparative studies of culture have evolved.

As to primitive history, we know that all tribes and folk communities are conscious of a common past. Older members can name their predecessors for several generations back, and any important event affecting the life of the collectivity becomes part of the traditional knowledge transmitted from generation to generation. Of course, the more distant the past, the less reliable the oral history, until eventually it becomes mere legend. And in most collectivities with traditional cultures, we find myths and legends which explain the origin of the most permanent, important, and valuable components of their culture as creations of certain ancestors who, if not divine beings, were at least superhuman heroes. Such explanations have a dual significance; they strengthen the belief of members of the collectivity in the supreme validity of their culture and in their own superiority as heirs of such great ancestors.

When written history began, the historians were mostly priests, and they originally assumed a common descent of the people who shared the same religion, as they did in the Old Testament. Frequently, however, religious history was closely connected with the political history of the kingdom ruled by a sacred king. The separation of the two was partly achieved by Chinese historians, fully by Greek and Roman historians, who specialized almost entirely in political history. But the old connection between history and ethnography remained as exemplified by Herodotus' description of Persian, Egyptian, and other Eastern peoples. And nearly all Greek historians, even those who limited their histories to particular city-states or wars, considered Hellenes as culturally and hereditarily superior to Barbarians. During the Middle Ages, priests again assumed the function of historians, but political history remained distinct from the history of the Church, though strongly influenced by religious ideology. This is well exemplified by the two works of Grégoire de Tours, written in the sixth century: ten books on the *History of the Franks* and six books on the *Miracles* performed by Frankish saints.

When secular history began to be written by secular authors, it was primarily political, especially when historians functioned under the patronage of rulers, and much of it remains political to this day, though for different reasons, such as the facility of obtaining political and legal documents and of reconstructing from them political organizations. Gradually, however, cultural similarities and differences not coextensive with political divisions began to be taken into consideration by historians. Ethnographc knowledge of these similarities and differences was at first rather superficial, derived mostly from the observations of travelers (including merchants) and from contacts of natives with foreign travelers, immigrants, and invaders; only from the second half of the eighteenth century on did ethnographic studies of folk cultures begin to provide factual foundation for including some of these cultures in the same nationality and excluding others. For instance, Herder, who was both an ethnographer and a philosopher of history, used his studies of German folk culture as a basis for his conception of the historical unity and continuity of the German people. But even as early as the end of the fifteenth century, many intellectuals had already formed definite cultural stereotypes of "Italians," "Spaniards," "Frenchmen," "Englishmen," "Germans," etc., although the stereotypes naturally differed, according to the nationality to which the intellectuals themselves belonged. And this was the time when historians started to write histories of nationalities.

Italian historians, for example, who at first wrote exclusively histories of particular city-states, gradually began to write historical works dealing with Italy as a whole.[10] This was not merely because the Italian peninsula formed a definite territorial unit, but chiefly because of the common culture of Italian people, mainly derived from the dominant Latin culture of the Roman Empire. Later, some French historians included in the history of France, besides the state ruled by the kings of France, other areas which were not parts of this state but were inhabited by people who, whatever their regional differences, were presumably like the Frenchmen within the kingdom, because they had the common historical background of Romanized Gaul. This trend culminated in the early nineteenth century, and is well exemplified by the work of Théophile Lavallée on the history of the French since the time of the Gauls.[11]

German historians dealing with the history of the medieval empire conceived it from the very first as an empire "der deutschen Nation," under the obvious assumption that it was composed of people of common German descent and culture. Later, they began to write histories of the "German people" as a whole, culturally united long before the empire was formed. Thus, Sporschil wrote a work on the history of the Germans from the oldest times up to his day, beginning with the struggle against Rome in the second century B.C. After the Nazis came to power, Pastenaci published a book in German entitled *The Four-Thousand-Year-Old Kingdom of the Germans*.[12]

Polish historians to this very day have been primarily concerned with the history of all the peoples who have shared the common Polish culture, presumably rooted in a prehistoric past, notwithstanding their political division in the thirteenth century and the nonexistence of an independent Polish state from 1795 to 1918. Modern Russian history started in the eighteenth century as a history of the multiple nationalities in the Tsarist Empire,[13] but eventually Russia was conceived as culturally Russian, including all the peoples (mostly Slavs) who presumably already shared or were expected to share the culture of the dominant Great Russian nationality.[14]

Both historians and ethnographers usually tend to emphasize the distinctive character of their own nationality, and many of them are inclined to exalt it as superior to others, at least in some respects, just as religious thinkers, political thinkers, even tribal thinkers exalt their own societies.[15] This has been called by some sociologists "national megalomania." We shall mention here a few examples.

The superiority of Chinese people was for centuries taken for granted by Chinese historians; nor was this belief undermined by the Manchu conquest, since the conquerors accepted Chinese culture. In modern Europe, Italian scholars were probably the first to exalt their history, culture, and nationality, and many continue to do so still. This has provided comfort and confidence for all the people who were conscious of being Italians, especially at times of crisis, during periods of inner conflict and of foreign domination. This exaltation had three foundations. First, Italians were the heirs of Roman greatness. Dante initiated this conception, but it was fully developed only recently by Mussolini and his followers. Second, the creative growth of Italian national culture began relatively early in Italy and was for a long time a model which other nationalities imitated. Third, Rome was, and is, the world center of Catholicism, and Rome is Italian.

Quite a few French historians have exalted the total history of the French nationality. For instance, Lavallée in his preface to the *Histoire des Français* states: "I have considered France as exerting at all epochs the moral leadership of Europe, as having providentially the mission of progress, as always placed at the head of other nations so as to trace for them the road for the future; thus, the history of our country has been for me the history of humanity in the West." At about the same time, Hegel as philosopher of history was developing his theory that German civilization (a synthesis of two anti-thetic civilizations, oriental and Greco-Roman) was the supreme "objective" manifestation of the "Absolute Spirit." A century later, A. Willy and W. von Scholz published a work *Die grossen Deutschen,* five volumes of idealized biographies, proving the age-old supremacy of the Germans in every realm of culture.[16]

In Russia, about the middle of the nineteenth century, while so-called "Westerners" deplored the lag of Russian culture and urged it to follow the West, "Slavophiles" exalted the greatness of the Russian people as supreme representatives of the old Slavonic culture which was morally and spiritually superior to every other.[17] Later, as original Russian culture, especially litera-ture, music, and art, grew, the "West" lost its influence. After the October Revolution, Bolshevik historians at first disparaged the Russian national cul-ture developed during the Tsarist regime on the ground that it was "bour-geois"; but they soon revived its positive valuation, and naturally extrolled the new cultural developments under the Communist regime. By now Russian cul-ture is supposed to be far in advance of any other, according to the Soviets.

The emergence of nationalism in India was from the very first influenced by the intellectual leaders, who compared the history of Hindu civilization with the history of modern Western civilizations and exalted the former as representing the highest spiritual values in contrast to the latter, which are essentially materialistic.

Notes

1. For a general survey of the early stages of growing national solidarity in Asia, see Hans Kohn, *Geschichte der Nationalen Bewegung im Orient* (Berlin, 1928). Similar growth has started in several regions of Africa. According to J. Obrebski, "The great revolution of our times consists . . . in the formation of new national cultures and national culture groups." "The Sociology of Rising Nations," *International Social Science Bulletin,* No. 2, 1951, III, 238.
2. A number of my students supplemented my work by their own historical surveys of the evolution of particular nationalities, using the conceptual framework formulated in this chapter.
   The following nationalities were surveyed: American, during the colo-nial era, by Theodore Fish; Armenian, by Gregory N. Cross; Brazilian, by Joyce Hooper; Burmese, by Sheldon Davidson; Colombian, by Wilma Ernst; Indian, since independence, by Robert W. Fox; Irish, by V. Sutcher; Jewish, by Joyce Kaplan; Korean, by Edmund L. Szablowski; Lithuanian, by A. J. Krukas; Mexican, by Shirley Horwitz and Lois Sprout; Nigerian; by Joyce Wiener; Peruvian, by Earl Rubeking; Rumanian, by Philip Acker-man; Uruguayan, by Wilma Ernst; Welsh, by Jane Mueller.
3. A. F. C. Vilmar, *Geschichte der Deutschen National-Literatur* (Marburg-Leipzig, 1894).

4. Some Ukrainian historians trace its beginning to the twelfth century, e.g., Mitropolit Ilarion, *History of Ukrainian Literary Language,* in Ukrainian (Winnipeg, 1950). However, at that time, in consequence of many migrations, the specific regional dialects were not yet separated and stabilized. What later became a distinct and common Ukrainian literature was growing slowly, though the influence of Old Slavonic remained strong until the nineteenth century. For its full development in modern times, see, e. g., D. Doroshenko, *History of the Ukraine* (Edmonton, 1940); Michael Hrushevsky, *A History of Ukraine* (New Haven: Yale University Press, 1941).

5. See Alexander Brückner, *A Literary History of Russia,* trans, by H. Havelock (New York: Scribner, 1908). An excellent outline of the beginnings and subsequent growth of literature in Russia.

6. Douglas Hyde, *A Literary History of Ireland* (London, 1901); Ernst A. Boyod, *Ireland's Literary Renaissance* (New York: Day, 1916); Aodh de Blácam, *Gaelic Literature Surveyed* (Dublin, 1929); Emma Jane Williams, "The Celtic Renaissance" (manuscript). Systematic attempts to revive Gaelic continue to this day, not only in Ireland but among Irish immigrants abroad. For instance, in 1949, there were five Gaelic societies in New York (Austin Hershberger, manuscript).

7. Four, if we include Romansh, which is more a folk dialect than a literary language.

8. Cf. Anges M. Wergeland, *Leaders in Norway* (Menasha, Wis.: Banta, 1916); Einar I. Hangen, *The Origin and Early History of the New Norse Movement in Norway* (Menasha, Wis.: Modern Language Association, 1933); A. Sommerfelt, *The Written and Spoken Word in Norway* (Oxford, 1942).

9. Cf., e.g., R. Craig, *The Modernistic Trend in Spanish-American Poetry* (Berkeley: University of California Press, 1934); Isaac J. Barrera, *Literatura Hispano-americana* (Quito, 1934); Alfred L. Coester, *The Literary History of Spanish America* (New York: Macmillan, 1941); Julio A. Leguizamón, *Historia de la Literatura Hispano-Americana,* 2 vols. (Buenos Aires, 1945); Isaac Goldberg, *Brazilian Literature* (New York: Knopf, 1922); José Bezerra de Freitas, *História da Literatura Brasileira* (Pôrto Alegre, 1939); Erico Verissimo, *Brazilian Literature, an Outline* (New York: Macmillan, 1945).

It is curious that, while the literary works written in Portuguese by authors living in Brazil are treated as a separate "Brazilian literature," all the literary works written in Spanish by authors living in Central and South America are included under the general term "Spanish-American literature," instead of being particularized as "Mexican literature," "Peruvian literature," "Argentinean literature," etc. Can this be the manifestation of an incipient tendency to develop cultural solidarity among all the peoples in the Americas who share the Spanish literary language, over and above the cultural nationalism growing in the particular countries?

10. Francesco Guicciardini, *La Historia di Italia* (Florence, 1561), was the first historical work of this type, limited to the preceding years and not very optimistic.

11. Théophile Lavallée, *Histoire des Français depuis le temps des Gaulois jusqu'en 1830,* 1st ed. (Paris, 1838).

12. Johann Sporschil, *Geschichte der Deutschen von den ältesten Zeiten*, 5 vols. (Regensburg, 1859–60); Kurt Pastenaci, *Das viertausendjährige Reich der Deutschen* (Berlin, 1940).

13. Some minor outlines, e.g., Tatishchev. The first comprehensive history of the Russian state, exalting autocracy, was written by N. Karamzin, 12 vols. (1818–26).

14. As early as 1831, the poet Pushkin wrote that all the "Slavonic streams" were destined to merge in the "Russian Sea." By the end of the nineteenth century all Russian textbooks emphasized the predominantly "Russian" character of most of the inhabitants of the empire.

15. The significance of history in the development of modern nationalism was noticed some time ago. See, e.g., R. W. Seton-Watson, *The Historian as a Political Force in Central Europe* (London, 1922).

16. A. Willy and W. von Scholz, *Die grossen Deutschen* (Berlin, 1935–37). For a survey of such trends in German historiography, see Antoine Guilland, *Modern Germany and her Historians* (New York: McBride, 1915).

17. Khomyakóv, Kiréevsky, and Aksakov. Perhaps the most enthusiastic proclaimer of the greatness of the Russian "national spirit" was Dostoyevsky. Cf. Hans Kohn, *Prophets and Peoples* (New York: Macmillan, 1946), Chap. V.

Immanuel Wallerstein   THE SEARCH FOR NATIONAL IDENTITY IN WEST AFRICA: THE NEW HISTORY

THE STUDY of contemporary West African societies illustrates two aspects of the relationship of sociology to history. On the one hand, a valid understanding of the social structures and ideologies of the new nation-states is not possible without placing them in the historical context out of which, and with reference to which, they have evolved. On the other hand, West African history, or rather historiography, is adequately understood only by placing it in the context of the contemporary social structure and assessing the ways in which it affects this structure. It is with this latter issue, one in the sociology of knowledge, that we shall be most concerned here. The rise of nationalism and the creation of new nation-states in West Africa has led to a new concern for national history. Though some European scholars have made important contributions to this research, we shall deal more particularly with the work of the new generation of West African scholars, writing in both English and

Revised version of a paper presented at the Annual Meeting of the American Sociological Association, New York, August 1960, and originally published in *Présence Africaine*, Engl. ed., No. 6/7, 1960, 17–29.

French. This generation is both writing and rewriting its history, as indeed does every generation. But a post-revolutionary generation makes more radical revisions than others.

The English historian, Buckle, observed a century ago:

There must always be a connection between the way in which men contemplate the past, and the way in which they contemplate the present; both views being in fact, different forms of the same habit of thought, and therefore presenting in each age, a certain sympathy and correspondence with each other.[1]

The thesis of this paper is that when nations are "new," for example, when a colony achieves its independence, the loyalty of the citizens to the state is low both in intensity and in numbers of persons primarily oriented to national norms. One reason for this is the fact that the legitimation of the new system lacks the habituation of custom, which accrues to old states. Such habituation seems to be necessary even for modern states based on rational-legal legitimation. It is, so to speak, the nonrational basis of rational values. To the extent that a national identity of long duration can be "created," "found," "rediscovered," the sense of loyalty on the part of the citizens will be deepened. It is therefore not accidental that this period sees the revival of interest in national history, and places a particular emphasis on the search for national origins. We shall here illustrate this process at work in contemporary West Africa today. Similar processes have been noticed in other areas of the modern world.[2] One way to prove this hypothesis might be to undertake a comparative analysis correlating the revival of interest in national history and the emphasis on national origins with some index which would adequately measure the degree and nature of legitimacy accorded regimes. The necessary data for such a comparative analysis are not yet available. And the validity of a simple correlation of two such indices might be open to doubt. Another way is to try to trace the process of "the search for national identity" in as much detail as possible in one historical setting, thus indicating the specific relations of nation building and history writing. This is the path chosen in this paper.

To analyze developments in West Africa, we shall first look at the colonial situation and the cultural dilemmas it bred. This is the historical context out of which, and with reference to which, contemporary historical scholarship has evolved. We shall then proceed to discuss the new history in terms of the ways in which it affects the structures of the new nation-states.

European contact with West Africa dates from the fifteenth century but colonial administration was not established in most areas before the nineteenth century. Colonial administration created a new social structure within which social change occurred.[3] One of the most important changes wrought by the colonial power was the creation of a new elite, different from, and often antagonistic to, the traditional elite. This elite was trained in the European educational system created in the colonies by missionaries and administrators. A small percentage of those educated were sent on to further study in European universities.

One of the principal ways in which colonial rule was maintained was by creating a justifying ideology of cultural supremacy. The educational system was used to inculcate this ideology into the new elite. Thus the political, economic, and social inequalities of the colonial situation were reinforced by a doctrine of cultural inequality. The way history was taught was central to this process. During the colonial era, the history that was written tended to be the history of the colonial era. The history that was taught in European universities, and also in West African elementary schools, was the story of the coming of the European to West Africa, the clash of imperialist rivalries, the establishment of native administrations. The reason for this was very simple. It was assumed there was no other history. As late as 1951, a noted British scholar wrote:

Until the very recent penetration by Europe the greater part of the [African] continent was without the wheel, the plough and the transport animal; almost without stone houses or clothes except for skins; without writing *and so without history.*[4]

Throughout the twentieth century, however, archaeologists and art collectors were constantly making findings that commanded respect; thus, some attention had to be given occasionally to pre-colonial history. But more often than not, credit was attributed to non-Negro peoples. The Early Sudanic empires were said to be governed by Jews or Berbers.[5] Many Negro kingdoms were said to be the work of Hamites.[6] Attempts were made to prove Benin bronzes the work of the Portuguese, and Ife heads the work of the Egyptians.[7] In the case of the famous ruins of Zimbabwe found in Central Africa, there is a long history of efforts to attribute this high civilization to Arab or European civilization.[8] As K. O. Dike, the Nigerian historian, notes:

Many statements on Africa rest, not on the evidence of history or of ascertained fact, but on preconceived notions which in other contexts the scholars responsible would dismiss with the appropriate academic detachment.[9]

The work of anthropologists might have been a helpful corrective to such a bias. But the anti-historical and primitivistic bias that informed much ethnological research, particularly in West Africa, prevented this. As a contemporary West African sociologist has remarked:

One often has the impression that these first and great ethnographic works [of Westermann, Frobenius, Delafosse, Griaule] were nothing but a sort of vast phenomenology, vast compilations without a precise orientation as to the sociological objectives which interest us here. As for the fundamental criticism, one can only deplore the "committed" fashion in which these works have been undertaken.[10]

The historical assumptions made by these scholars tended to justify colonial rule not in terms of its military superiority but in terms of its inherent civilizing mission. Indeed, the noted French scholar Robert Montagne observes on this subject:

The politicians followed the scholars, made use of their labours and tried to find in them arguments to support action. History was made to justify the desire for conquest, and became an epic to the glory of the "white man"; although it is true that other white men sometimes made themselves the opponents of expansion, interpreted in a contrary sense the results of scholarship and predicted the emancipation of the people.[11]

Such scholarship permitted colonial policies—and in particular the educational system—to be directed to the production of "inferior white men."[12] It trained a generation of African intellectuals who half believed the myth of no African culture and no African history. And until recently, any attempt to dispel these myths ran up against very strong resistance.[13]

The emergence of a nationalist movement in the various West African colonies changed the intellectual climate within which this scholarship was pursued. The nationalist movement sought to create within the colony a sub-culture with values at variance with those of the colonial government. Eventually the nationalist movement came to power and its values became those of the new nation-state. In such a situation, African intellectuals began to reject the perspectives and restraints imposed in the colonial situation and to create a "new history," based on the assumption that the African past has glorious achievements to its credit which allow it to be considered on a par with the European past. While this assumption is not entirely new, and has had its exponents for some time,[14] it only became widely accepted in West Africa during the period following World War II, the time of the rise of the nationalist movement. The revival of history thus begins in the colonial era, gets impetus with the emergence of the nationalist movement, and is pursued even more actively after independence with the encouragement of the government of the now independent nation.

The new history aids the search for national identity in four ways. First, it aids the nationalist revolution in the period before independence by giving its values the legitimacy of tradition. Secondly, it helps to maintain the integrity of the new state after independence by reinforcing the affective ties of its citizens. Thirdly, it bolsters the intellectual cadres of the new nation in both periods by welding their own search for psychological integrity with the search for national identity. Fourthly, it enables the governments of the independent nations to pursue modernization by offering the glorification of the past as reassurance about the present. The following will amplify the four ways described above.

1. Just as the European historiography of the colonial era often served to justify the colonial regime, so did the developing nationalist movements see

the political value inherent in the revalorization of heroes and empires. Samory, whom the French saw as a rapacious and cruel warrior finally subdued, was presented by West African nationalists as the noble and heroic chieftain finally repressed by the invader. A revolutionary movement needs to create legitimate sources of deviant norms. The reinforcement of symbols already latent in the mass of the people is obviously the easiest and most effective way to do this.[15]

The revalorization of heroes is important not merely to legitimate deviance but also to assert the illegitimacy of the colonial norms. To denigrate colonialism, to tear down the whole framework of justifications of alien rule performed two essential tasks. It weakened, to some extent at least, the self-assurance of the colonizers, particularly in the metropolitan country. More importantly, it strengthened the nationalist resolve of West Africans themselves, especially the intellectuals who were most ambivalent, because of the conflicting values of their multiple reference groups. Thus we have seen the creation in the past fifteen years of many journals where the new history is published[16] and the publication of many serious monographs by West African scholars on West African pre-colonial and colonial history.[17] This has been supplemented by the growing amount of work by non-African historians, anthropologists and archaeologists[18] which is no longer as encumbered by the old prejudices of which Dike complained as recently as 1953.

2. Reinforcing national identity becomes even more important *after* independence. Independence revives the centrifugal tendencies which had been suppressed during the struggle for independence. The claim of the new governments to legitimacy is a rational-legal one, and this claim is as yet insecure. To reinforce the loyalty of the citizens, the governments feel the need to have recourse to tradition. So they seek to tie themselves closely to the past. In West Africa, Ghana and Mali have deliberately assumed the names of old empires of the Sudan.[19] The position of the charismatic leaders, key elements in maintaining the integrity of their countries, is reinforced by linking them to historical heroes. President Sékou Touré of Guinea claims to be the great-grandson of the warrior-hero Samory Touré. And it is said that President Modibo Keita, of the present-day Republic of Mali, is descended from Soundiata Keita, thirteenth-century founder of the ancient Mali empire.

Contemporary West African historians are in fact self-conscious about their role in building a nation. Dike observes that:

Every nation builds its future on its past; so the African must not only instinctively have faith in his own inheritance but must also satisfy himself by scientific inquiry that it exists.[20]

And Cheikh Anta Diop is even more explicit:

Only a true knowledge of the past can create in one's consciousness the sentiment of a historical continuity that is indispensable to the consolidation of a multinational state.[21]

3. Furthermore, the new history permits reassurance to all those, particularly intellectuals, who were socialized to the Western values of the colonial powers and then revolted against this political system, partly on the basis of Western values, partly on the basis of appeal to traditional values. Bringing African history into the mainstream of world history helps to alleviate the anomie of the intellectuals, a need defined by the historian Joseph Ki Zerbo:

The debt of those of us who have been sent for training by contact with the Western world is very heavy towards our compatriots. They expect of us that we bear witness for our people, that we aid them to find themselves in a world in full evolution and eventually to choose a path. But to find oneself and to orient oneself, it is good to stop a moment—to reflect on the path already taken. Hence the importance of memory. Intellectual life, memory, as Pascal says, is necessary for all the operations of the mind; but it is also indispensable for the cohesion of the personality. Take a man, wrench from him brutally all the facts registered and conserved by his memory. Inflict upon him, for example, a total amnesia. This man is no more than a man wandering in a world where he no longer understands anything, stripped as he is of any axis of reflection. Despoiled thus of his history, he is a stranger to himself; one will say that he is alienated and he is, in effect, in all the senses of this term.[22]

The internal conflicts of those educated in colonial school systems and involved in nationalist movements are perhaps transitional phenomena. A future generation, socialized in developing and independent nations, may feel a sense of confidence in their present and past that will permit a more fully analytic historiography. For the moment, it is often precisely the intellectuals, suffering from what has been called the "complex of the colonized," who tend most strongly to reassert traditional values, especially the glories of past history. In the search for their nation, the intellectuals also find themselves, thus lessening their alienation from the nation. The split between the intellectuals and the party cadres in new nations is thus mitigated. Counteracting the *anomie* of the intellectuals is another form of national integration.

4. Fourthly, the new history aids in the process of modernization by offering the history of the past as reassurance about the present. One of the biggest problems for new nations in the pursuit of modernization is that it involves the acquisition of certain skills and values associated with Western nations. The psychological image of the norms being assimilated is not, however, merely one of useful ideas borrowed from another culture subjugated by, equal to, or politically irrelevant to the receiving nation. This image, on the contrary, incorporates the ideas and values of the former colonial power; and so the moral implications of modernization include inevitably an element of abasement, an attempt to remove an inferiority to the West by adopting some of its secrets.

Modernization, under such conditions, is a big pill to swallow, especially since there remain many traditional forces in the new nations whose interests are not served by the process. In such a situation, men need reassurances about their own worth. They need to feel strong enough to accept the change. They need to believe that the changes advocated are comparatively minor in relation to the total set of national values. The revival of the past, of a remote past, plays a very large role in meeting this need.

History, of course, is a vast subject. One may write about many different things. Yet, in fact, West African historiography has taken a very particular path, that of what Biobaku calls the "fascinating"[23] search for origins. Ortega y Gasset, speaking of Spain and of Europe, noted:

> It is when a people is young, and in course of development that it is chiefly influenced by the past. . . . And it is not a short past that is envisaged, but one so long and with so vague a horizon, that no one has ever seen or remembers its commencement. It is, in brief, immemorial.[24]

In West Africa, some of these efforts started very early. Bishop Crowther in the nineteenth century was the first in a long line of writers, up to Biobaku, who have suggested that the Yorubas of Western Nigeria derived from Egypt.[25] The Reverend W. T. Balmer, in 1926, seems to be the first to suggest that the Akan peoples of the southern Gold Coast originated from the ancient empire of Ghana.[26] This claim was picked up later by Gold Coast intellectuals such as J. C. DeGraft-Johnson[27] and J. B. Danquah.[28] Danquah, as a politician, made this claim a central theme of Gold Coast nationalism. Cheikh Anta Diop expressed dissatisfaction with the historians who trace West African history only back to the fourth century A.D. and insisted on following it back to its Egyptian origins.[29] Dick Akwa was perhaps the most extravagant. In his work, Moses and Buddha became Egyptian Negroes; Christianity derived from a Sudanic people; and Nietzsche, Bergson, Marx, and the Existentialists were reflections of Bantu philosophy.[30] All this work testifies to what Balandier has called the "devouring claim to paternity."[31] The degree of scientific rigor employed in this research is variable. Danquah frankly states:

> At present, Akan claim to origin in Ghana is only a hypothesis, not yet a theory. But that does not prevent those who have eyes to see its truth. The Copernicuses, Galileos and Newtons of the hypothesis have probably been born, or are yet to be born. But while waiting to hear finally from them, we are entitled, with the modicum of knowledge in hand, to build on faith and express our sincere belief that it is the fairest and most reasonable solution of the origin of the Akan people.[32]

The search for origins enables Africans to claim respect from the West by identifying their fate with achievements already recognized by the West; they "look to the past to vindicate present claims to status and respect. . . ."[33] Cheikh Anta Diop has, for example, erected a vast world anthropology in his L'Unité culturelle du monde noir which proves that, by some of the very standards of the West, African civilization is superior. Diop sees the world as essentially divided into two basic cultural groupings: the Aryans (who include the Semites, and it seems the Asians and American Indians as well)

and the Southerners (*Méridionaux*) who are the Negro-Africans, which includes the ancient Egyptians. The Aryans, responding to a harsher climate,
have developed patriarchy which leads to the suppression of the woman and
a warlike morality. From this is derived the concept of sin and guilt, a
materialist religion, the tragic drama, the city-state, xenophobia, individualism, and pessimism. In contrast, the Southerners are basically matriarchal,
which liberates the woman; hence no sin, but a Dionysian approach to life
and religious idealism. With this goes a dedication to justice, the tale or fable
as the literary genre, the territorial state, xenophilia, social collectivism and
optimism. Again, the rigor of the evidence is less important than the social
function of the doctrines which are advanced in a scholarly fashion and
seriously entertained.

Thus, Diop's search for origins, step by step, turns the tables on the West.
If once the Africans had no history, it is now the Europeans who have
none, or at least none that is not ultimately derived from African sources.
"Everything teaches us that the Egyptians were Negroes, like the Ethiopians
and the other Africans; that Egypt has civilized the world."[34] Even technology,
presumably the great Western achievement, is traced to its Egyptian (Negro)
origins.[35] As once Egyptian origins were suggested to disprove Negro achievements, so now they are suggested precisely to prove them.

The search for origins, as a focus of historical research, is probably a
temporary feature of West African scholarship. Once West African independent nations have existed for some time, and thus their institutions are
sanctified by some tradition, they may be less interested in the constructs of
a remote past. Vercingetorix is still hailed in French schoolbooks, but the
glories of the French Revolution or even the Resistance may be more important as integrating myths. So too, in the perspective of time, the West
African struggle for independence, receding into the past, may be more
meaningful than more obscure and historically more dubious precedents. But,
in the present, the situation is different. As Rupert Emerson notes:

Surprisingly enough, the advocates of a return to origins not infrequently discover
at the end of their researches what they set out to find—a bridge by which they and
their coreligionists may easily and consistently move into the modern world
without abandoning the faith of their fathers.[36]

The crucial question, however, is whose tool is contemporary West African
historiography? In nineteenth-century Europe, "both conservative and liberal
used historical slogans to shape and sustain their ambitions."[37] It must be expected that the same thing will happen in the newly independent West African
states. It is too early to analyze the exact lines of division, although the
question of African unity may loom large. Already we find that Biobaku writes
of the origin of the *Yoruba* but Diop of the origin of the *African*. Diop indeed
makes his option clear:

When we shall have created . . . a sovereign continental and multinational state, we shall have to, whatever one may say, endow it with an ideological cultural superstructure which shall be one of its essential ramparts of security. That means that such a state will have to be, as a whole, aware of its past, which presumes the elaboration of a general history of the Continent, embracing the particular histories of particular nationalities.[38]

West African historians, by their influence on the elites of today and the masses of tomorrow, can be expected to have much influence on the boundaries and forms of the new West African nations.

Notes

1. From the *History of Civilization in England,* cited in Fritz Stern, *The Varieties of History: From Voltaire to the Present* (New York: Meridian Books, 1956), p. 15. Stern's book presents an overview of how European scholars rewrote not merely their history but their historiography.
2. Cf. B. Lewis, "History-Writing and National Revival in Turkey," *Middle East Affairs,* IV, 1953, 48–277; Cyril Black, ed., *Rewriting Russian History* (New York: Praeger, 1956); J. M. Van Der Kroef, "On the Writing of Indonesian History," *Pacific Affairs,* XXXI, 1958, 352–71.
3. For a fuller analysis of the impact of colonial administration, see the author's *Africa: The Politics of Independence* (New York: Vintage, 1961), Chaps. 2–4.
4. M. Perham, "The British Problem in Africa," *Foreign Affairs,* XXIX, July, 1951, 638. Italics not in original.
5. Cf. M. Delafosse, *Haut Sénégal-Niger,* 3 Vols. (Paris, 1912), Vol. I, p. 215, and Vol. II, pp. 22–25; *Negroes of Africa,* pp. 37–39, 46–47; E. W. Bovill, *Caravans of the Old Sahara* (London, 1933), pp. 27, 45, 47.
6. Cf. D. Westermann, *The African Today and Tomorrow* (London: International African Institute, 1949), 3rd ed., p. 12. G. Seligman notes that the Hamites were the "great civilizing force of black Africa from a relatively early period" and later that the Hamites are "Europeans." *Races of Africa* (London: Oxford University Press, 1957), 3rd ed., pp. 10 and 85.
7. Cf. K. O. Dike, "African History and Self-Government," II, *West Africa,* No. 1881, March 14, 1953, p. 225.
8. See the remarkable arguments of J. T. Bent in 1895: "We may consider that the builders of these mysterious structures were well versed in geometry and studied carefully the heavens . . . and this quite excludes the possibility of any negroid race having more to do with their construction than as slaves . . . for it is a well-accepted fact that the negroid brain never could be capable of taking the initiative in work of such intricate nature." Cited in Dike, *loc. cit.* Cf. also B. Davidson, *The Lost Cities of Africa* (Boston: Atlantic-Little, Brown, 1959), Chap. IX.
9. Dike, *op. cit.,* I, *West Africa,* No. 1879, February 28, 1953, p. 178.
10. N. Ablémagnon, "Les responsabilités du sociologue africain," *Présence africaine,* XVII–XVIII, août-novembre 1959, p. 209.
11. Robert Montagu, "The 'Modern State' in Africa and Asia," *The Cambridge Journal,* V, 10, July, 1952, p. 584.
12. Dike, *op. cit.,* III, *West Africa,* no. 1882, March 21, 1953, p. 251.

13. As Dike further notes: "The point is not that Africans have no history but that there is profound ignorance concerning it, and an almost pathological unwillingness to believe the evidence of it when presented. The study of African history and culture is confronted with formidable prejudices which militate against the spirit of scientific inquiry and retard research." *Op. cit.,* II, p. 225.

14. For example, American Negro scholarly interest in African history has been on the rise since the turn of the century. See Ulysses Lee, "The *ASNLH*," *The Journal of Negro History,* and, American Scholarly Interest in Africa, in J. A. Davis, ed., *Africa Seen By American Negroes* (Paris: Ed. Présence Africaine, 1958), pp. 401–418.

15. Cf. P. Decraene, *Le Panafricanisme* (Paris: "Que sais-je?" no. 847, Presses Universitaires de France, 1959), p. 35.

16. Among others, Transactions of the Historical Society of Ghana, Transactions of the Nigerian Historical Society, Sierra Leone Studies, Présence Africaine, Odù. There are also the many different publications of the Institut Français d'Afrique Noire (IFAN), and its former territorial affiliates.

17. Among others, S. C. Biobaku, *The Egba and Their Neighbors* (London: Oxford University Press, 1957); K. O. Dike, *Trade and Politics in the Niger Delta* (London: University Press, 1956); Cheikh Anta Diop, *L'Afrique noire pré-coloniale* (Paris: Ed. Présence Africaine, 1960); Jos. Ki Zerbo, "L'économie de traite en Afrique noire," *Présence africaine,* XI, décembre 1956-janvier 1957, pp. 7–31; Ly Abdoulaye, *La Compagnie du Senegal* (Paris: Ed. Présence Africaine, 1958); Ly Abdoulaye, *L'Evolution du commerce française d'Afrique noire dans le dernier quart du XVIIe Siècle* (Paris: Ed. Présence Africaine, 1959). Sylla Assane, "Une republique africaine au XIXe siècle (1795–1857)," *Présence africaine,* n.s., I–II, avril-juin 1955, pp. 47–65.

18. This is numerous and varied, although the work of R. Mauny should perhaps be singled out. Much of it is resumed in Davidson, *op. cit.* See the bibliography, *passim.*

19. Shortly after the creation of the Federation of Mali, *Notes africaines,* one of the publications of IFAN at Dakar (then the capital of Mali) devoted two successive issues to the history of the ancient empires. Cf. No. 82, avril 1959, and No. 83, juillet 1959. That same year, a children's book appeared by Andrée Clair, entitled *Le fabuleux empire du Mali* (Paris: Ed. Présence Africaine, 1959).

20. Dike, "African History and Self-Government," I, *op. cit.,* p. 177.

21. *L'Unité culturelle du monde noir* (Paris: Ed. Présence Africaine, 1959), p. 9.

22. J. Ki Zerbo, "Histoire et conscience nègre," *Présence africaine,* XVI, octobre-novembre 1957, p. 53.

23. S. O. Biobaku, *The Origin of the Yoruba* (Lagos: Federal Information Service, 1955), p. 5.

24. J. Ortega y Gasset, "The Sunset of Revolution," in *The Modern Theme* (New York: W. W. Norton, 1933), p. 103.

25. Biobaku, *op. cit.,* pp. 8ff.

26. *A History of the Akan Peoples of the Gold Coast* (London: Atlantis Press, 1926), pp. 3–28.

27. *African Glory* (London: Watts & Company, 1954), pp. 84–86.

28. Cf. "Akan Claims to Origins from Ghana," *West African Review,* XXVI, Nos. 338, 339 (Nov., Dec., 1955), pp. 968–970, 1107–1111.

29. Cf Diop, *Nations nègres, op. cit.,* p. 15 and *passim.*

30. *L'Itinéraire de la pensée nègre,* as cited in G. Balandier, *Afrique ambigue* (Paris: Plon, 1957), p. 280.

31. *Op. cit.,* p. 279. Similar claims by the Russians have been noticed extensively in the public press.

32. J. B. Danquah, "The Akan Claim to Ghana" (manuscript). Biobaku is more cautious: "The historian must never propose to lend himself to the politics of the moment, but he hardly needs to apologize if the African past turns out to be more glorious than one has in general wrongly thought." S. O. Biobaku, "Les responsabilités de l'historien," *Présence africaine,* XXVII–XXVIII, août-novembre 1959, pp. 98–99.

33. Dike, *op. cit.,* III, p. 251.

34. *Ibid.,* p. 19. Cf. also p. 249: "It is impossible to insist on everything the world—and in particular, the Hellenic world—owes the Egyptian world. The Greeks did nothing but take up and sometimes, to a degree, develop Egyptian inventions, all the while despoiling them, as a result of their [Greek] materialist tendencies, of the idealistic religious shell which surrounded them." De Graft-Johnson agrees that the Egyptians were Negroes (*op. cit.,* p. 7). So does W. E. B. Du Bois. Cf. *The World and Africa* (New York: The Viking Press, 1946), p. 106 and Ch. V, *passim.*

35. Diop, *op. cit.,* p. 253.

36. R. Emerson, *From Empire to Nation* (Cambridge: Harvard University Press, 1960), p. 160.

37. Stern, *op. cit.,* p. 18.

38. Cheikh Anta Diop, "Apports et perspectives culturelles de l'Afrique," *Présence africaine,* n.s., VII–IX–X, juin-novembre, 1956, pp. 342–43.

Leonard W. Moss

and

Stephen C. Cappannari

THE BLACK MADONNA: AN EXAMPLE OF CULTURE-BORROWING

THE EXISTENCE OF BLACK MADONNAS in various parts of the world has been noted by many authors. It should be explained that some of the so-called black madonnas are not actually black, but are dark brown in color. We have classified these representations of the Virgin Mary in three distinct categories.

First, there are the dark brown or black madonnas with physiognomy and skin pigmentation matching that of the indigenous native population. In this class we include such madonnas as Nuestra Señora de Guadalupe Hidalgo in Mexico and the various negroid madonnas found in Africa. Though the Catholic Church has never given official approbation to these representations,

Reprinted with permission from *The Scientific Monthly,* Vol. LXXVI, No. 6, June 1953, pp. 319–324.

they are tolerated, probably as one way of bringing religion closer to these populations.

Second, there are various art forms which have turned black as a result of certain physical factors. The change may have been brought about by (a) deterioration of the pigment (some of these madonnas have been repainted in the flesh tones only to turn black again); (b) smoke damage stemming from the use of votive candles in areas adjacent to the statues; (c) smoke damage resulting from a fire in the church; (d) oxidation of the silver used in the construction of the image; (e) other physical factors such as the accumulation of dirt over the ages.

Third, there are the miracle-working black madonnas. It is this class of madonnas that is investigated here. The hypothesis that there has been here an attempt to anthropomorphize the Virgin is not tenable, since the natives of these regions are caucasoid. The various physical explanations cited in our second group do not seem applicable to this category. One must also discard the physical explanation, which may differ with the various madonnas under question. In such cases we find: (a) There is no evidence for physical de- terioration of the pigment, no smoke damage, no oxidation, and so on. (b) Where there is evidence of such physical damage, the madonna has been repainted black.[1]

Of the madonnas in this third category, we have felt it necessary to eliminate two from further consideration in the development of an hypothesis. Bavarian legends hold that the "Black Mother of God" at Altötting was pre- served from smoke damage despite the ravaging of the church by flames in A.D. 907. The face, hands, and feet of this statue allegedly turned black "with age" at a later date. This explanation is deficient in that it fails to explain why the rest of the statue, in flesh tones, did not undergo similar deterioration. Moreover, according to Dr. George Lechler, who is familiar with this icon, the art form is that of the seventeenth century. He believes it to be a copy of an earlier form.[2]

The madonna at Czestochowa is darker of skin than most Central Euro- pean representations of the Virgin. However, the figure is distinctly thirteenth to fourteenth century Byzantine in form, and this skin coloring is a character- istic feature of varied Byzantine portraiture. According to Ernst Scheyer, who studied this madonna at the behest of the Polish government, the present image was restored in the nineteenth century.[3]

How the image got to Czestochowa is debatable. Local legend describes a miraculous appearance of the statue sometime in the fifteenth or sixteenth century. For those who would rather explore the alternative possibility of diffusion, it may be noted parenthetically that the Queen of Poland about 1515 was Bona Sforza, of Italian origin.

We wish to emphasize that all the black madonnas mentioned above are "miracle-working madonnas," and, with the exception of the Polish madonna, all these images are found in areas once occupied by the Roman legions. The bulk of this paper is centered on the madonnas of southern Italy, but let us note some of the history and legend attached to other black madonnas listed above.

The statue of Our Lady of Montserrat was supposedly carved by St. Luke, in Jerusalem (La Jerosolimitana), and legend holds that it was brought to Barcelona by St. Peter. The statue was removed from Barcelona during the Moorish invasion of Catalonia in A.D. 718. Hidden in a cave near Montserrat, it was rediscovered in 880. Earliest archival notations indicate that the image was black at least as long ago as A.D. 718.

Our Lady of the Hermits at Einsiedeln, Switzerland, exhibits a history that may be traced back as far as A.D. 835. St. Meinrad built a chapel to the Virgin that year. Local tradition, however, alleges that the statue was brought there by crusaders returning from the Middle East. This statue does not appear to be Byzantine in origin, nor does it give evidence of being a ninth-century German art form.

The Black Virgin at Chartres dates back to the fourth century. Early Christian travelers to that area found an altar supposedly erected by the Druids upon which was seated a woman holding within her arms the figure of a child. This pagan image was black in color. The cathedral at Chartres, founded in the fourth century, was dedicated to the Virgin and Child. Although the present statue of the Virgin at Chartres is depicted as black, it is of more recent origin.

The Sanctuary of the Madonna of Tindari occupies the site of a fifteenth century church that had been built on the ruins of a temple to Cybele. This ancient temple was mentioned in the writings of Strabo and Pliny. Greek influence in Tindari dates back to the founding of the city by the elder Dionysius in 395 B.C., and the city was colonized by Peloponnesian exiles driven from their homeland by the Spartans. This black madonna at Tindari is perhaps the most famous of the Sicilian images of the Virgin.

Castrogiovanni (now Enna), a corruption of the Arabic Kasr-Yanni, was the ancient Castrum Ennae. The mountain, upon which the town is situated, was the principal seat of worship for Demeter-Ceres. Founded about 664 B.C. by the Syracusans, the town was considered a choice prize by the many invaders of Sicily during the course of history. A temple to Ceres and Proserpina, built at the summit of the mountain, was the object of pagan pilgrimages before the introduction of Christianity in the eleventh century. The present church, Madonna della Visitazione, built by Queen Elenora in 1307, incorporates in its south wall a pillar from the old temple of Ceres. The present statue of the madonna adorning the church is of mid-nineteenth-century origin. This image of the Virgin is not black.

Ancient Enna was sacred to both Ceres and her daughter Proserpina. It was in this locale that the abduction of Proserpina by Pluto took place.

According to Greek mythology, Proserpina (Persephone) was called Saviour, having gone through death and resurrection. It is at Castrogiovanni that one finds the most interesting adaptations of pagan symbolism by the Catholic Church. Until the mid-nineteenth century, the images of Ceres and Proserpina were used in the church as the Virgin and Infant Jesus, despite the fact that Proserpina was female![4]

One writer, William Paton, has this to say about the ritual connected with the Castrogiovanni madonna:[5]

On the day of the fete of the "Madonna of all the Graces" her worshippers place before her statue large sheaves of grain and bunches of wild flowers, and form processions in her honor, composed of men in long white tunics, who carry flowers in their hands, make offerings of grain and other products of the soil before the altar in the churches . . . it seems most reasonable to believe that many of the old pagan rites have been preserved in their essential forms in Christian ceremonies of today . . . it is safe to say that Christian priests have added little to that ritual [of Demeter], have taken little from it, and today religious ceremonies practiced by the farming communities of Sicily are essentially the same as they were twenty-five centuries ago, with the exception that Christian saints have usurped the honors and dignities of pagan deities.

The history of the Region of Puglia shows frequent and prolonged culture contacts with the various culture groups that have occupied the Mediterranean basin. On this basis we look for indications of diffusion. Legend holds that around 975 B.C. Diomedi, King of Etolia (a section of ancient Greece), landed at Rodi and journeyed to the Temple of Minerva at Lucera. There he remained, established a kingdom, married the daughter of the King of Daunia, and built a temple to Ceres (goddess of grain). Diomedi also built temples to Calcante (god of prophecy) and Podalirio (god of medicine) at Castel Drione, site of San Severo.[6]

The region was occupied by the indigenous Italic tribes, the Pencezi and the Messapi. To the north were the Molise, in what is now the Region of Abruzzi. According to the local legend this area was first visited by the Phoenicians as early as the tenth century B.C. Phoenician temples to Ma or Ammar were utilized by the Greeks, who rededicated these same temples to the Cretan Rhea or Cybele. Cybele, the mother goddess, gave birth to Demeter, the Greek goddess of fertility, grain, and earth. It is pertinent to our thesis that there were actually two Demeters. One was the sorrowful Eleusinian mother. The second and more powerful was Demeter Melaina, the Black Demeter associated with the earth and fertility.

The Greeks built temples to Demeter in and around the area of Foggia Province. Lucera existed as a city-state independent of Rome until 400 B.C.; then she allied herself with Rome and later (319 B.C.) became a colony of the Roman Empire. It was during this period that a cult of the Egyptian Isis was introduced into this area by seagoing natives of Puglia. We should mention that Isis-Horus have been represented as black by the Egyptians.

Many scholars have observed resemblances between the Osiris myth of death and resurrection and the story of Jesus. Carl G. Jung suggested that the wife of Osiris, Isis, and her son Horus may be considered as an Egyptian anticipation of the Virgin-child complex.[7] Direct contact between Hebrews and Egyptians is described in the story of Joseph, who may be regarded as a vizier under a Hyksos king, during the second Intermediate Period of Egypt.

Herodotus suggested the connection between the Egyptian Isis and the Greek Demeter. While never explicitly acknowledged by the Romans, it seems evident that Ceres is a Roman adaptation of the Greek Demeter. At this point it should be stressed that the Roman Ceres was likewise depicted as black.

St. Peter, on his way to Rome in A.D. 42 installed Basso as the Bishop of Lucera. St. Basso reputedly built a cathedral to the Virgin Mary on the precise spot occupied by the Roman temple to Ceres. The cathedral was dedicated to the Madonna della Spiga (literally, sheaf of wheat, and later, ear of corn). It is not clear whether the church dedicated to the Virgin can be traced to St. Basso or St. Padro (A.D. 208–250). After the fall of Rome this area was occupied by the Eruli, Ostrogoths, Greeks, Longobards, Moslems, Greeks (again), Normans, and the forces of the Holy Roman Empire, in that order. Frederick II (grandson of Frederick Barbarossa) invited the Moslems into the area in 1225 and built a mosque for them on the site of the Cathedral of the Madonna della Spiga. The Anjou dynasty, which came to power after the death of Frederick II, compelled the Moslems to leave Lucera and rebuilt the mosque into the present-day Cathedral of San Francesco. The statue of the Virgin and Child was reinstalled in the Cathedral in 1300.

Santa Maria, the Patron Saint of Lucera, is credited with the liberation of the city from the Moslems by Charles II (Carlo Secondo d'Anjou). A second major miracle attributed to the statue is the end of an epidemic of cholera on July 13, 1837. The statue miraculously moved its eyes on that date and for two consecutive days thereafter, bringing to an end the plague which had ravaged the city. If *dulia* and *hyperdulia* (veneration and adoration) are accorded saints, then the only word for the degree of adoration of this image is that of *latria* (worship). The Madonna is worshipped for its power rather than the grace normally accorded the Virgin. It is showered with wheat, corn, and other sacrificial offerings on feast days, particularly on those feast days which coincide with the seasons of planting and harvesting. It is accorded powers relating to fertility (human, animal, and vegetal).

Elsewhere in southern Italy one finds other examples of these madonnas. The present-day church of Santa Maria di Siponto occupies the site of Sipontum, an ancient Roman colony. Because of flood threats, the city of Siponto was abandoned in A.D. 1256, and the inhabitants moved to Manfredonia two miles to the east. Records indicate that the present church was constructed prior to 1117. Before its reconstruction by Julius III in 1508, there are indications that the Saracens used the building as a mosque. The lower level of this church contains the tomb of Emilius Tullius (A.D. 593) and the miracle-working madonna. Local legends attest to the fertility powers of the icon. The origin of this statue is said to be Byzantine.[8]

At the summit of Monte Vergine, near Avellino, was the temple to Ceres in which the high priest Atys held sway as the Sibylline oracle. The mountain draws its name from one Virgilius, a poet, necromancer and compounder of herb drugs (l'Orto di Virgilio). Christianity was late in coming to this stronghold of pagan beliefs. In A.D. 1119 William of Vercelli dedicated the mountain to the Virgin Mary and founded a Benedictine abbey on the site of the temple to Ceres. Henry Swinburne, an English author and traveler, acknowledged the tribulations involved in establishing Christianity in this area.[9]

The missionaries sent among them to preach the faith of Christ found no means of conversion so easy and efficacious as those of admitting some of the names and ceremonies of the old church into the ritual of the new one. By thus adopting many tenets and forms of Paganism, they reconciled their proselytes to the idea of exchanging Jupiter for Jehovah, and their *lares* and *penates* for saints and guardian angels. To this expedient of priestcraft must be ascribed many strange devotions and local superstitions, still prevalent in Roman Catholic countries, which ought not to be confounded by the adversaries of that church with its real doctrines. All the truly learned and sensible persons of that communion reject, abhor, and lament such depravation; and, were it possible to reason rude minds out of hereditary prejudices, would long since have abolished them.

La Madonna di Constantinopoli (la Schiavona) is enshrined in the church, which contains four standing columns of *porta santa* marble that are part of the original temple to Ceres. This portrait of the Virgin is in two parts. The bust, carved of brown wood, is the work of Montano d'Arezzo and was completed about 1340. The head was brought from Constantinople by Catherine, wife of Philip d'Anjou, the titular emperor of that city. Legend holds that this painted head was the work of St. Luke in Antioch.[10] Swinburne takes issue with the legendary origin of the head:[11]

This image is of gigantic or heroic proportion, and passes for the work of St. Luke the Evangelist, though the very size is an argument against its being a portrait from the life, had we even the slightest reason to believe he ever handled the pencil. There are in Italy and elsewhere some dozens of black, ugly Madonnas, which all pass for the work of his hands, and as such are revered.

Swinburne goes on to explain that there was a painter in Constantinople called "Holy" Luke because of his piety and because of his exemplary life devoted to painting representations of the Virgin. His work was later attributed to St. Luke, since no one knew of another saint or painter by that name. Swinburne casts doubt on the idea that St. Luke was ever an artist.[12]

Catholic sources, for the most part, have denied the possible connection between the black madonnas and the Roman Ceres. Nevertheless, it was St.

Augustine who noted that the Virgin Mary represents the Earth and that Jesus is of the earth born. Archbishop John Hamilton in his Scot's Catechism (1552) states ". . . (these statues) darkened into something not far from idolatry . . . when . . . one image of the Virgin (generally a black or ugly one) was regarded . . . as more powerful for the help of suppliants. . . ." A Mrs. Jameson, writing in the 1890s on the Legends of the Madonna, remarks:[13]

Because some of the Greek pictures and carved images have become black through extreme age, it was argued by certain devout writers that the Virgin herself must have been of very dark complexion; and in favor of this idea, they quoted from the canticles, "I am black, but comely, O ye daughters of Jerusalem."[14] But others say her complexion became black only through her sojourn in Egypt. At all events, though the blackness of these antique images were supposed to enhance their sanctity, it has never been imitated in the fine arts. . . .

As we have previously noted, although some of the black madonnas are black because of age, this mechanistic explanation fails to account for all of them. It is at this point that we suggest our hypothesis: The black madonnas are Christian borrowings from earlier pagan art forms which depicted Ceres, Demeter, or Isis as black in the color characteristic of these goddesses of the earth. Along this line, in 1355 a prior at the Monastery of Châlis in France, named Guillaume de Deguilleville, noted that Mary represents the earth, which is the body and darkness;[15] hence, Mary being of the earth, can rightfully act as celestial attorney for all earthly sinners.

Experts on medieval art forms have demonstrated the influence of classical mythology on the paintings of the Middle Ages. It is entirely possible that medieval painters borrowed from classical mythology, dropped the original forms, and related them to the Virgin Mary.[16] However, in this paper we are concerned with some statues which seemingly predate the period of the Middle Ages. We are probably dealing with more direct forms of culture borrowing, possibly as part of direct culture contact.

We will reiterate that all the black madonnas are *powerful* madonnas, that is, miracle workers. (However, not all miracle-working madonnas are black.) They are implored for intercession in the various problems of fertility. The degree of adorational fervor accorded these images far exceeds that attached to other representations of the Virgin. Hence, we are equating their blackness with their power.

Students of mythology have long pointed out that "black" could be regarded as associated with the earth. Carl G. Jung has equated "black" with the fertility powers of the earth, with the power of death, and with a fear of the power of darkness. Although we do not claim that any such necessary and inherent relationship would obtain in all parts of the earth, this association can be demonstrated easily for the cultures involved in our thesis.

Prolonged close culture contact between groups in a relatively restricted geographical area invariably results in an exchange of culture elements. Over long periods of time continuing contacts between two diverse cultures will bring forth a fusion of elements to result in a new pattern which is a melting, or merger, of both forms. This mode of culture change is called *diffusion,* that is, cultural transmission.[17]

Cultural change, by definition, is a dynamic process. The ongoing process of transmission of cultural elements is called *acculturation*. Not all elements of a culture are easily or readily verbalized and transmitted. The physical or outward form of the element tends to be more readily transmissible. The borrowing group may often-times adopt the outward form and adapt their own meanings to the form. Reinterpretation of borrowed elements occurs in all realms of culture, including religion. Cultural elements which are borrowed, or syncretized, by a religion are thought to be part of the original belief system by the adherents to that faith. These reinterpretations are made in terms of the prevailing pattern of culture within that society.

Anthropology is replete with examples of syncretism and reinterpretation as parts of the general process of acculturation. The development of Hinduism is one of the classic examples of syncretism in supernaturalism. Equally illustrative and analogous to our topic is the almost endless and intricate modification of various Egyptian deities in the early dynastic periods. When the capital of Egypt was moved to Thebes, Amon, who was the local god of the city, merged with Rē, the national sun god, to become Amon-Rē.[18] Changes in the culture of any society are always influenced by the pre-existing customs and institutions of that society. This is not to say that displacements never occur, or that innovations never obliterate older patterns of behavior.[19] For the most part, however, mankind is not easily detached from the patterned customs and beliefs which have fastened themselves securely upon human beings. The adoption of new beliefs is facilitated when beliefs can be equated in some fashion with older and compatible experiences.

It is in this light that we offer our hypothesis that these madonnas exemplify a reinterpretation of pagan customs, and that they have functioned as aids in the preservation of cultural continuity in the transition from pagan beliefs to Roman Catholicism.

Notes

1. The madonnas in this third category are found in such diverse locations as: Altötting, Bavaria, Germany (Our Lady of Altötting); Atocha, Spain (Our Lady of Atocha); Czestochowa, Upper Silesia, Poland (Our Lady of Czestochowa); Montserrat, Catalonia, Spain (La Santa Imagen, Our Lady of Montserrat); Einsiedeln, Switzerland (Our Lady of Hermits); Chartres, France (Notre Dame du Pilier, La Vierge Noire); Tindari, Sicily (Madonna di Tindaro); Enna, or Castrogiovanni, Sicily (La Madonna della Grazia); Lucera, Puglia, Italy (Madonna della Spiga); Potenza, Basilicata, Italy

(Santa Maria di Vigianno); Manfredonia, Puglia, Italy (Santa Maria di Siponto); Monte Vergine, Avellino, Italy (La Madonna di Constantinopoli).

2. Lechler, G. Personal communication.

3. Scheyer, E. Personal communication.

4. Sladen, D., *Sicily* (New York: Dutton, 1907), pp. 315–24.

5. Paton, W. A. *Picturesque Sicily* (New York: Harper and Brothers, 1897), pp. 250–51, 252–53.

6. Corrado, G. Lucera, *Nella Storia della Patria* (Lucera: Tipografia Scepi, 1937), pp. 1–38.

7. Jung, C. G., and Karenyi, K., *Essays on a Science of Mythology* (New York: Pantheon, Bollingen Series, 1949), *passim*.

8. Hare, A. J. C., *Cities of Southern Italy and Sicily* (New York: Routledge and Company, 1905), p. 286.

9. Swinburne, H., *Travels in the Two Sicilies* (London: Emsley, 1783), Vol. I, p. 121.

10. Ayscough, J., *Saints and Places* (New York: Benziger, 1912), p. 348.

11. Swinburne, H., *op. cit.*, Vol. I, 123.

12. Other black madonna statues and paintings attributed to "St. Luke" are found in: Bari, Italy (Sta. Maria di Constantinopoli, Church of St. Sabino); Brno, Czechoslovakia (Die Schwarze Muttergottes); Custonaci, Sicily; Loreto, Italy (Chiesa della Casa Santa); Messina, Sicily (Madonna della Lettera, Cathedral la Matrice); Rome, Italy (Borghese Chapel, Chiesa di Sta. Maria Maggiore); and Tenos, Greece (Church of St. Evangelistria).

13. Jameson, Mrs., *Legends of the Madonna* (New York: Houghton Mifflin and Company, 1890), p. 63.

14. The canticles (Song of Songs) refers not to the Virgin but to a conversation between King Solomon and his black Queen. The intent of the original Hebrew version clearly sets forth the relationship between the two lovers.

15. Jung, C. G., *Psychology and Religion* (New Haven: Yale University Press, 1938), 83ff., 126, quoting Abbé Joseph Delacotte, *Guillaume de Deguilleville, Trois Romans-Poèmes du XIVe Siècle* (Paris, 1932).

16. Panofsky E., and Saxl, F., *Metropolitan Museum Studies*, 4, (New York: Metropolitan Museum of Art, 1933), p. 228–80.

17. Herskovits, Melville J., *Man and His Works* (New York: A. A. Knopf., 1948), p. 523ff.

18. For a discussion of this kind of gradual modification of deities, see H. Frankfort *et al.*, *The Intellectual Adventure of Ancient Man* (Chicago: The University of Chicago Press, 1946), pp. 31–121.

19. A recent work discusses this process in detail. See L. S. B. Leakey, *Mau Mau and the Kikuyu* (London: Methuen Company, 1953), pp. 78–85, 112.

Joshua Trachtenberg   THE ATTACK UPON USURY

THE USURER was one of the most thoroughly despised and hated members of
the medieval community. At best he was a necessary evil, tolerated by the
state because the gentry required his services—and exercised sufficient power
to scale down their debts by the method of force and expropriation, as well
as of repayment. But to the masses he was a wholly unmitigated evil. In an
economy of rudimentary capitalism, when trade was insecure and investments
often went into unproductive enterprise such as war or castle-building, the
high rates which the usurer had to charge were an intolerable burden upon
the peasantry and emerging burgher class in the towns, incapable of turning
over their capital rapidly enough to meet such rates or of using as a regular
technique the *force majeure* available to kings and nobles.

But credit was essential to the expanding economy that was a major
product of the First Crusade, and through a combination of circumstances
it became the uneasy lot of many Jews to find their economic energies limited
to this field. The extinction of the comparatively large-scale Jewish trade
with the Orient after the Crusade left them no other economic function, since
agriculture and handicrafts were virtually closed to them—though occasional
individuals or small communities continued in these pursuits, particularly in
certain specialized crafts. The Church, while prohibiting Christian usury and
thus restricting effective competition, acknowledged the right of Jews to engage in it, so that for a very short time they enjoyed an advantageous position
as moneylenders. An incidental urge in that direction was contributed by the
insecurity of Jewish life. Faced with the perennial threat of expulsion and
massacre, it was advantageous for them to keep their possessions in a fluid
state, easily negotiable and transportable. But perhaps the most telling circumstance lay in the discovery that Jewish moneylending had its fiscal uses:
rulers directly fostered it in order to be able to exact a steady flow of tribute,
while the constant extortions to which they were subjected obliged Jews to
keep a fund of ready cash on hand.[1]

Here was a vicious circle from which there was no escape for the Jew.
Society conspired to make him a usurer—and usury exposed him to the
cupidity of feudal overlords and to the embittered hatred of the people. So
long as he was a source of profit, the state protected him, in a measure. But
when Christian competition began to press him hard, as it did in the thir-

Reprinted with permission from *The Devil and the Jews: The Medieval Conception of the
Jew and Its Relation to Modern Anti-Semitism,* by Joshua Trachtenberg (New Haven: Yale
University Press, 1943), Chapter XIII. Paperback edition published by Meridian Books, The
World Publishing Company, and The Jewish Publication Society of America, 1961.

teenth century when Christians realized that easy profits were to be made from moneylending, and when non-Jewish commercial activity increased to such an extent that the Jew no longer counted for much in the field, his importance as a source of governmental revenue vanished. The state's investment in the protection of the Jew no longer paid and was therefore hastily withdrawn. He was mulcted of what little he still possessed and unceremoniously shown the gate. During the thirteenth and fourteenth centuries a number of major expulsions took place in England and on the Continent (the first, in England, in 1290) wholly for reasons affecting the royal exchequer.

"The traditional conception of usury as a Jewish monopoly is a myth."[2] This is the opinion of the leading authorities on the subject. The church's proscription was ineffectual in deterring Christians from entering this lucrative field. The Church actually concentrated its attack even more against Christian usury than against Jewish. Nor was the Jewish moneylender the sole victim of popular resentment, by any means; the Lombards and Cahorsins, and the priests too, when they engaged in usury, as they often did more or less surreptitiously, felt the wrath of their debtors in no uncertain terms. "It is a well-established fact," as Baron points out, "that the Christian Lombards and Cahorsins frequently suffered expulsion with the Jews; indeed in England and France they usually were expelled before the Jews."[3]

Yet, "though medieval testimony is amusingly unanimous in preferring them [Jewish usurers] to their Christian competitors," their brief concentration in this trade permanently fixed its stigma upon them. In the twelfth century the words Jew and usurer had become almost synonymous; Berthold of Regensburg, one of the most representative preachers of the thirteenth century, used the word usurer invariably to identify the Jew.[4] Thus the Jew was obliged to bear the brunt of popular feeling against the moneylender from the outset, and long after his short-lived prominence in the field had been preempted by others, he still remained *the* usurer in the mass memory and had to suffer for the sins of his successors. Even when Christian usurers were under attack, the Jews could not escape, for they provided the universal standard for odious comparison: the harshest criticism of Christian usurers (and it was made often) was that they were "worse than Jews." Christian usury itself was blamed on them, since "were there but Jews enough, Christians would not have to become usurers"![5] So powerful was, and for that matter still is, the hold of a myth that never had more than a meager basis in fact.

The popular hatred of usurers received the strongest support from the policy of the Church, for Catholicism regarded usury as a grievous sin, more on dogmatic grounds (based on the biblical prohibition)[6] than on social ones: a sin against the Church of Jesus, and therefore against the human race it sought to save. The inevitable increase of Christian moneylending forced the Church to adopt a firm stand.

Usury became a serious matter, the subject of frequent Church and civil legislation, in the twelfth century, and was promptly classed as a crime with sorcery, incendiarism, homicide, sacrilege, and fornication. Pope Alexander III, in 1179, decreed the excommunication of all manifest usurers, and the state soon followed with enactments confiscating the property of usurers who died unrepentant.

But these were feeble measures to counteract the pressing economic need that the moneylender filled, and the Church vainly piled obloquy upon threat until but one final step remained: in 1257 Alexander IV issued a bull officially identifying usury with heresy and placing it under the tender jurisdiction of the Inquisition; and the Council of Vienna in 1311 confirmed this position. The association was not in itself, however, new. In Toulouse as early as 1209 a group had been founded "to drive out heretics and to combat usurers." Matthew Paris spoke of Milan as "a home of all heretics—Paterines, Luciferians, Publicans, Albigenses, and usurers." Pope and council, therefore, merely added formal assent to a verdict already popularly held. The fact that some of the medieval heretical sects were extensively engaged in usury lent added color to the association and made it all the easier to identify the two.[7]

The taint of heresy thus adhered the more strongly to the Jewish people, whose early prominence in the profession singled them out as prime offenders, and at the same time endowed moneylending with a peculiarly heretical odor, especially since the Church expressly and vehemently forbade Christians to engage in it. The relationship between heresy, usury, and the Jewish people was so fundamental to the medieval mind that Bernard of Clairvaux, in appealing to King Louis VII to prevent Jews from exacting what he considered excessive rates of interest from those who took the Cross on the Second Crusade, could make the astounding comment: "I keep silence on the point that we regret to see Christian usurers judaizing worse than Jews, if indeed it is fit to call them Christians and not rather baptized Jews"! Just as heretics were often labeled "Jews" and "Judaizing" was the commonest charge against them, so Christian moneylenders were as frequently condemned for the same crime.[8]

The Jew-heresy-usury equation became a medieval cliché; not even the terminology suffered change. Christian moneylenders were forced to hear themselves slandered as "those other Jews, called Christians," or simply *Kristen-Juden;* in the fifteenth century Christian usury became known in Germany as the *Judenspiess,* the "Jews' spear."[9] At a time when Jews as such had been unknown in England for several centuries, Sir Francis Bacon recommended in his essay "Of Usury" (1612) that all usurers "should have tawny orange bonnets, because they do Judaize."[10]

It was the Jew's fate that the Church should begin an intensive campaign against usury at the very time when almost no other economic function was open to him, and during the very period marked by the successive superstitious accusations. When the Inquisition took usurers under its wing it expressly included Jews in this category, branding them not as common miscreants but as heretics. ("Jews shall desist from usury, blasphemy, and magic," ran the characteristic trinitarian formula.)[11] And when the heresy iron branded usurers with the mark of Satan, it was believed to grace the Jewish usurer more fittingly than all others.

"In almost every city, town and village of France the ingrained malice of the devil has firmly established synagogues [sic] of usurers and extortioners, commonly called communes; and these diabolical institutions, forbidden by ecclesiastical constitutions, are completely wrecking the ecclesiastical system of jurisdiction," wrote the Council of Paris in 1212,[12] by which time the field had been virtually preempted by Christian sinners. Medieval pulpiteers castigated moneylenders in the most uncompromising terms. "Unnatural monsters," they were called. "God created farmers, priests, and soldiers," thundered the preachers and popular rhymsters in almost identical terms, whether in France, Germany or England, "but this fourth category [usurers] was invented by the devil himself." Above the entrance to the church of Notre Dame at Dijon there was, in 1240, a sculptured figure of a usurer between the claws of a demon.[13]

The usurer as Satan's creature could be none other than the Jew, presented over and over in the plays, the legends, the poetry, the sermons, which were the sole intellectual food of the masses, as the immortal type of the usurer. That this was an inevitable conclusion we may well surmise from the vivid portrait of the Jew already familiar to medieval Christians. And the extant source material offers ample proof that the relation between Jewish usury and Satan's anti-Christian venom was not overlooked.

In the Passion plays, Judas, often represented as the tool of the devil, plays the typical role of usurer associated in the medieval mind with the Jew. Egged on by demons, he drives a hard bargain, smirking and whining while he cunningly tries to outwit his confederate in crime. After Caiaphas slowly counts out his thirty *pfennigs* hire for betraying Jesus, Judas raises every possible objection to the coins: "this penny is red, this one is sick, this one is broken, this one has a hole in it, this one is improperly stamped, this is too black, look at the long crack in this one, here's one that's dull," etc.[14] And Judas haggles and complains and can hardly be satisfied, while the audience howls with glee and malice at this clever take-off on the devilish Jewish moneylender of its own acquaintance. "The devil's dogs," Hugo von Trimberg, the fourteenth-century minnesinger, calls the Jews, attacking them particularly for their trade in money. A number of medieval tales present the devil as a partner (and not a silent partner, either) in the Jew's usury.[15]

Artists also did not hesitate to portray the devil as an actual participant in Jewish financial operations. The title page of a sixteenth-century diatribe against Jewish usury and wealth depicts three devil-Jews, complete with horns, tails, claws—and Jew badge. A copperplate, dated about 1600, shows the devil sharing in the profits of Jewish moneylending. A seventeenth-century cartoon directed against coin-clipping, portrays a group of Jews engaged in various financial transactions, with the devil prominently represented among them in full Jewish garb, including the Jew badge, like all the rest. The medieval *Arbogastkirche* at Ruffach, in Alsace, has a statue of the devil in company with a Jew tightly grasping a bulging moneybag.[16]

Luther spoke to a responsive and understanding audience when he lashed out, with rabble-rousing accusations and vituperation, against Jewish usury, and concluded with savage irony: "Should the devil not laugh and dance, when he enjoys among us Christians such a fine Paradise, when he, through the Jews, his saints, devours our substance, and in return fills our mouths and nostrils with his effrontery, and mocks and curses God and man, in the bargain?"[17] Devil, Jew, usurer, and heretic have become one and the same creature.

Notes

1. In Angevin England, for example, in the latter half of the twelfth century, when there were about two thousand Jews among the total population of some one and a half million, the Jews were obliged to account annually for one-twelfth of the total royal income (about £ 3.000 out of £ 35.000); in 1187, through fines, fees, tallages, special imposts, etc., the royal exchequer derived £ 60.000 from the Jews, as against another £ 70.000 from all the rest of England! Jacobs, from whom these figures are derived —see Joseph Jacobs, *The Jews of Angevin England* (New York: Putnam, 1893), pp. xviiiff. and p. 382—puts the matter quite justly: "They acted the part of the sponge for the Royal Treasury," he says; "they gathered up all the floating money of the country, to be squeezed from time to time into the king's treasure chest. . . . The king was thus . . . the sleeping-partner in all the Jewish usury, and may be regarded as the arch-usurer of the country." Moreover, the king's right to confiscate the estates of Jewish usurers, prescribed by canon law, immeasurably strengthened his political power over the barons and clergy whose debts would ultimately fall into his hands. See also the very interesting defense of Jewish usury by King Ladislaus of Bohemia in Gottlieb Bondy and Franz Dworsky, *Geschichte der Juden in Boehmen, Maehren und Schlesien* (Prague: J. Bondy, 1906), I, pp. 173ff.

2. James Parkes, "Christian Influence on the Status of the Jews in Europe," *Historia Judaica*, I (1938–39), p. 37; cf. also James Parkes, *The Jew in the Medieval Community* (London: Soncino Press, 1938), Chaps. VIII and IX.

3. Salo W. Baron, *A Social and Religious History of the Jews* (New York: Columbia University Press, 1937), III, p. 107; see also Cecil Roth, "The

Most Persecuted People?" *Menorah Journal,* XX (New York, 1932), 136–147.

4. Cf. J. Aronius, *Regesten zur Geschichte der Juden im fränkischen und deutschen Reiche* (Berlin: L. Simion, 1902), p. 319.

5. Moritz Güdemann, *Geschichte des Erziehungswesens und der Cultur der abendländischen Juden waehrend des Mittelalters und der neueren Zeit* (Vienna: A. Hölder, 1880–88), III, pp. 182ff.; Ludwig Geiger, "Die Juden und die deutsche Literatur des 16. Jahrhunderts," *Zeitschrift fuer die Geschichte der Juden* (1888), II, 348, III, 297; Johannes Pauli, *Schimpf und Ernst,* ed. by Johannes Bolte (Berlin: H. Stubenrauch, 1924), No. 192.

6. Ex. 22, 25, Deut. 23, 19, enforced by the supposed direct prohibition of the Gospel, Luke 6. 35: *Mutuum date, nihil sperantes* (Vulgate), "Lend, hoping for nothing again" (A.V.), but now translated (R.V.): "Lend, never despairing." "Usury," of course meant lending on interest in general, no matter what the rate.

7. James Parkes, *op. cit.,* II, pp. 283ff., 288f; Louis I. Newman, *Jewish Influences on Christian Reform Movements* (New York: Columbia University Press, 1925), pp. 194ff., 197ff. On the general subject, see F. Schaub, *Der Kampf gegen den Zinswucher, ungerechten Preis und unlauteren Handel* (Freiburg: Herder, 1905).

8. Georg Caro, *Sozial- und Wirtschaftsgeschichte der Juden im Mittelalter und in der Neuzeit* (Frankfurt a.M.: J. Kaufmann, 1924), I, p. 223; Newman, *op. cit.,* p. 197.

9. Sebastian Brant, *Das Narrenschiff,* ed. by Karl Goedecke (Leipzig: F. A. Brockhaus, 1872), pp. 148, 188; Hans Wilhelm Kirchhof, *Wendunmuth,* ed. by Hermann Oesterley (Tuebingen: Lit. Ver. in Stuttgart, 1869), V, p. 131; Güdemann, *op. cit.,* III, pp. 192, 276.

10. Montague F. Modder, *The Jew in the Literature of England to the End of the Nineteenth Century* (Philadelphia: Jewish Publication Society of America, 1939), p. 33.

11. Cf. the decree of Louis IX, the saint, 1254 in Heinrich Grätz, *Geschichte der Juden,* 3rd ed. (Leipzig: O. Leiner, 1878–1897), VII, p. 410, and of the Council of Beziers the following year in Solomon Grayzel, *The Church and the Jews in the XIII Century* (Philadelphia: The Dropsie College for Hebrew and Cognate Learning, 1933), p. 336ff.

12. James Parkes, *op. cit.,* II, p. 284.

13. G. R. Owst, *Literature and Pulpit in Medieval England* (Cambridge: University Press, 1933), p. 554 and n. 1; Güdemann, *op. cit.,* III, p. 189; Lecoy de la Marche, *La Chaire française au moyen âge* (Paris: Didier, 1868), p. 116ff., 416ff.; Thomas F. Crane, *The Exempla or Illustrative Stories from the Sermones Vulgares of Jacques de Vitry* (London: D. Nutt, 1890), Nos. 168ff.

14. Oskar Frankl, *De Jude in den deutschen Dichtungen des 15., 16. und 17., Jahrhunderts* (Maehrisch Ostrau: R. Papauschek, 1905), p. 88ff.

15. Güdemann, *op. cit.,* III, pp. 188, 191; Charles Lenient, *La Satire en France au moyen âge,* 3rd. ed. (Paris: Hachette, 1883), pp. 182, 185. Johann Jacob Schudt, *Jüdische Merckwürdigkeiten* (Frankfurt & Leipzig, 1714–18), I, p. 258, ascribes to Edwin Sandys the statement that in Italy, on being baptized, Jews were required to foreswear the devil and all his works, including usury.

16. Eduard Fuchs, *Die Juden in der Karikatur: ein Beitrag zur Kulturgeschichte*
(Munich: A. Langen, 1921), p. 13; Georg Liebe, *Das Judentum in der
deutschen Vergangenheit* (Leipzig: E. Diederichs, 1903), pp. 18, 37, 69.
17. Martin Luther, "Von den Juden und ihren Lügen," *Werke* (Weimar: H.
Böhlau, 1921), LIII, p. 521.

Norman Birnbaum   THE ZWINGLIAN REFORMATION
IN ZÜRICH

I. The Problem

THE ECCLESIASTICAL and theological distinctiveness of the Zwinglian Reformation in Zürich (1519–31) has been recognized;[1] its historical significance
requires further discussion.[2] Zwingli developed his conception of the Evangelical faith and church in partial opposition to Luther and in conflict with
the extremely articulate Zürich Anabaptists. By 1524, the Zürich church was
influencing all of south German Protestantism;[3] its influence later extended
to Calvin's Geneva[4] and to Anglicanism and Puritanism.[5] For our understanding of the Reformation, however, the importance of Zwinglianism is larger
than the question of the direct influences it exerted. The Zürich Reformation
poses, in small but critical compass, a sociological problem touched upon by
much of the historiography of the Reformation: the question of the relationship between capitalism and early Protestantism.

Zwinglianism, with its radically anti-sacramental doctrines, its emphasis
on community participation in Church government, and above all in its
ethical attitude to the profane world, anticipated those Calvinist doctrines
described by Max Weber as indispensable to the emergence of that complex
of anxieties, aspirations and ideas he termed the capitalistic spirit.[6] This is
not the place to reiterate the controversy over Weber's thesis. Weber renounced
the substitution, in his words, of a one-sided idealistic interpretation of history
for an equally one-sided materialistic one. And, it will be recalled, he dealt
primarily with seventeenth-century variants of Calvinism. The Zürich Reformation allows us, however, to see some of the components of Calvinism

This is an abridged version of a paper originally published in *Past and Present*, No. 15 (April
1959) and, with some corrections kindly suggested by Dr. Werner Schnyder, in *Archives de
Sociologie des Religions*, No. 8 (July–December, 1959). The author is indebted to the American
Philosophical Society, the Central Research Fund of the University of London, and the Social
Science Research Council for grants-in-aid to these researches. He also wishes to thank Professor
Joseph Lortz for having introduced him to Reformation studies, and Dr. Paul Guyer for placing
at his disposal the list of members of the Zürich City Council, 1515–40.

in statu nascendi. An investigation of its social context may allow us to consider anew the connection between capitalism and Protestantism.

It is usually held that the republicanism of the Swiss cities shaped the special characteristics of Swiss Protestantism in general and of the Zürich Reformation in particular.[7] This view raises more questions than it answers. The Swiss cities differed; some were more, some less, oligarchic. In Zürich violent political struggles throughout the latter half of the fifteenth century placed the artisanry in opposition to the patriciate.[8] There, as elsewhere, republican institutions were *loci* of social conflict. The conflict between artisanry and patriciate in Zürich was, however, not simple. Divisions within each of the groups made for a complex and changing set of political alignments, and the relationship between town and country was an added complication. Rather than considering the general characteristics of the society in which the Zwinglian Reformation occurred, then, we should do well to relate it to the specific pattern of social conflict of which it was both the expression and the partial resolution.

II. Zurich's Social Structure on the Eve of the Reformation[9]

Zürich was in this period not simply a city but a city-state with a large rural population. Of a total population of 60,000, 50,000 lived in the countryside, 5,000 in Winterthur and Stein am Rhein, and only 5,000 in Zürich itself.[10] The state's rural territory influenced its political characteristics. The peasantry provided military manpower and the city had direct access to its own food supplies. Rural offices and holdings were available to the city's notables. The artisanate and the merchants had, then, to contend with a patrician elite with military skills indispensable to the state and economically based on the countryside. The peasants, meanwhile, were, despite a certain local autonomy, governed by a City Council on which they were unrepresented. These were the strata whose political alliances and conflicts were involved in the Reformation.

The Constitution of 1498, in force in 1517, ended a period of conflict provoked by the attempt of a group of newly wealthy guild masters to monopolize power. Constitutionally, the artisan guilds dominated the City Council. It did not follow that the artisans did so, since the politically important guildsmen were usually the wealthy masters. Indeed, the latter joined the remaining patricians (once their opponents) in the army and in state posts. The fact that the male citizenry of the city numbered 923 in 1529, and that there were two hundred places on the Large and Small components of the City Council did *not,* then, mean that two of every nine citizens participated in government. This discrepancy between theoretical possibility and factual limitation may have been a political irritant, the more so because in a small society politics were necessarily exceedingly visible.

In the latter half of the fifteenth century, Zürich's economy underwent some striking vicissitudes.[11] A lost war, in 1496, deprived the city of much of its population and wealth; the textile industry contracted. By 1500, Zürich's wealth came primarily from trade: ore from northeast Switzerland was exchanged for salt, grain, and manufactures obtained elsewhere. Additionally, however, cotton wool was produced for export; weaponsmiths were important. Of 435 foreigners naturalized between 1500 and 1530, at least 232 were artisans—a hint of industrial development.

Zürich's economy had two additional components. The direct exploitation of the countryside by the city was especially advantageous to the urban elite which administered church lands, represented the state in its rural jurisdictions, had income from peasant mortgages, or owned Church tithes. The elite, further, profited from foreign wars—either as private military entrepreneurs or as officers in the state's forces. The supply of military forces to foreign powers, either by private enterprise or by state treaties, was another source of Zürich's wealth. Foreign payments to Zürich notables, not alone for services rendered but for services anticipated, were economically important; they also constituted a political issue of the first order.[12]

Zürich at first sight did not appear to be a center of the new capitalism. There were no great local banks, manufactures had not produced an industrial proletariat, and merchants did not operate on a large scale. The contrast with great centers of capitalism like Augsburg was striking. Rural revenues and the income from mercenary and state service satisfied many whose energy and position might elsewhere have impelled them into economic entrepreneurship. Yet we may consider Zürich neither backward nor provincial. The ore trade, the smithies, and textiles were local footholds of the new capitalism. Moreover, the radical discontinuities in the city's economic and political history before and around 1500 hindered the fixation of traditional economic values in important sectors of the populace. Augsburg, too, had had a rapid and discontinuous development; perhaps the two cities were not as dissimilar as initial appearances suggest.

The Zürich elite in our period was divided between *rentiers* of the old patriciate and new men—some still active in trade—who remained in the artisan guilds. These *parvenus,* however, ended the old families' monopoly of military leadership and state office. The conflict between these two groups was of some importance to the Zürich Reformation. The artisanate was in turn divided between those in traditional crafts and trades (barrelmakers and bakers, for instance) and those in the newer or technically developed occupations (printers and smiths, for example.) Precisely in these, however, the average artisan could accumulate the capital necessary for independence only with great difficulty. To the artisanate's distrust of the patriciate was added, therefore, its resentment of the newly wealthy. The latter were, however, part of the workaday world; the artisans did join them, initially, in the struggle over the Church.

III. The Reformation in Zurich[13]

Zwingli came to Zürich in 1519, at the age of 35, and as an Erasmian; a former chaplain with the Swiss in Italy, he rated mercenary service as an expression of all the flaws of Swiss society. Moreover, like many ordinary citizens of Zürich, he was against the acceptance of foreign favors generally. He thought a moral regeneration possible within a reformed Papal Catholicism and it was only in 1520–21 that he arrived at an essentially Protestant position.[14] Reliance on man's unaided will was blasphemous; sin was justified (that is, overcome) only by faith in God's mercy. Christ embodied that mercy, the sole record of which was Scripture. Only the Word had authority and the Word mentioned neither Pope nor Catholic hierarchy. Zwingli's transformation from an Erasmian to an Evangelical, to use the contemporary term, was clearly facilitated by Luther's early teachings and activity—but the consensus of recent scholarship is that he was a good deal more independent of Wittenberg than is commonly supposed.

Zwingli, a gifted preacher, had been brought to Zürich by the elite but quickly won a following among the common folk. Preaching directly from the Bible, he denounced abuses in Church and society. A variety of social and religious discontents crystallized in a wave of enthusiasm for the Evangile. The local clergy, mercilessly attacked, cried heresy. The Erasmian Bishop of Constance, at first conciliatory, became increasingly hostile. Rome kept silent until it had hired Zürich troops in 1521, only to embarrass the local Catholics by refusing to pay for them.

The Catholic campaign against Luther, as well as these local pressures, convinced Zwingli that reform within the received structure of Catholicism was impossible. Popular Evangelicism, manipulated by Zwingli, was a constant source of pressure on the City Council, which in any case included a pronouncedly Protestant faction. In the years 1521–23, the state broke with episcopal and Roman authority. In a disputation in 1523, Zwingli argued his Sixty-Seven Theses against episcopal representatives. Christ was the sole head of the Church; local congregations had the right of ecclesiastical self-government; Catholic ritualism offended the faith, which alone was Christian; the distinction between priest and layman was null and void; secular authority was legitimate only if based on scripture. The City Council endorsed Zwingli's Theses, an implicit contradiction which was to cause explicit conflict among the Zürich Protestants: Zwingli had promulgated a new Christian freedom and, just as promptly, bound himself to another authority. In fact, he resigned his Episcopal commission in 1522, only to accept a preaching office from the Council.

The break with Rome having occurred, the inner structure of Zürich Protestantism and its implications for the larger life of the society had to be decided. A radical group used Zwingli's own Biblicism against him. The immediate abolition of the mass was demanded, iconoclasm made its appearance, congregational autonomy of the state was sought, and conventicles for prayer and study began to form. Six rural communes demanded the abolition of tithes as unscriptural. Zwingli utilized some of this radical pressure against a recalcitrant Council, but his recourse to political authority meant that, in contradiction to his earlier congregationalist views, he was bound to develop the theory and practice of the State Church. Zwingli argued that the State's intervention in the Church entailed its recognition of the truth and not promulgation of it. Further, the State acted on behalf of the entire local community of Christians. Indeed, Zwingli's conflict with the conventicles and the early Zürich Anabaptists led him to see advantages in strict ecclesiastical discipline; he went so far as to declare that the "evil spirited and ignorant" community needed overseers.[15]

Zwingli's conflict with the Anabaptists involved the entire doctrine of the Church.[16] Zwingli, unlike Luther, held that infant baptism was a symbolic transaction by which parents and community pledged to raise the child as a Christian. He saw in the Biblicist literalism and separatist convictions of the Anabaptists a danger to the Christian community and the social order. In 1525, the Council prescribed infant baptism and proceeded to terrible punishments for the Anabaptists.

These decrees were part of a larger system of Church government developed between 1524 and 1528. Church property was confiscated for welfare purposes and administered by the state. New schools prepared candidates for what was now termed the preaching office. The clergy was organized into a Synod under state supervision. Most important was a Marriage Court, established in 1525 and converted in 1526 into a Morals Court.[17] A model for similar institutions elsewhere, notably in Geneva, this instrument of ecclesiastical discipline was used for political purposes. Its members (four laymen and two pastors) could cite miscreants before the Council, which itself reserved the right of excommunication. The Council controlled the Court, but Zwingli and his supporters by 1525 controlled the Council; through the Court, they sought to terrorize their opponents. The Court, despite Zwingli's retreat from his early Biblicism, attested his idea of a sanctified community militantly committed to the Evangelical life. Aware of the contradictions between a State Church and Evangelical Freedom, Zwingli sought to overcome these in the Evangelical State.

The contrast with the Lutheran Territorial Churches was striking. Church reorganization in Saxony did not begin until 1527 and the Lutheran cities rarely experienced this sort of stringent discipline.[18] The sacramental controversy, meanwhile, pointed to the dogmatic differences between Zwingli and

Luther.[19] Zwingli's ritual reforms were founded on his denial of scriptural warrant for the efficacy of the sacraments; the Spirit spoke only to the Spirit, and the sole purpose of public worship was the preaching of the Word. Luther's theology of the sacraments was more equivocal; he retained Baptism and the Eucharist but held them objectively effective only with faith. Zwingli rejected the Real Presence in the Eucharist; his symbolic interpretation of the rite struck Luther as blasphemy.

The sacramental controversy prevented a political-military union of Swiss and south German Protestantism with the Lutheran northern German cities and principalities.[20] Zwingli, through his refusal to compromise, contributed to Zürich's political isolation; he himself fell in battle.

IV. Social Conflict and Reformation

In Zürich, as elsewhere, the beginnings of the Reformation divided the populace; the social correlates of the division, although regular, were not altogether neat.[21] Many of the political oligarchy were enthusiastic Evangelicals. Initially, the Reformation opposed a united front of artisans and merchants—behind Zwingli—to a considerable part of the patricians. The leadership of this initially united Evangelical movement was a new and energetic group of oligarchs who had prospered in crafts and trade—particularly in the economically and technically new activities connected with the recent upturn in the city's fortunes. Generational succession was also relevant: in 1524 two new and young mayors, pronounced Protestants, replaced elder men.

The social composition of the opposition was peculiar.[22] There were patrician rentiers and mercenaries although, of course, not all mercenaries were patricians. There were, however, also certain retailers, second-hand dealers, and oil vendors. Butchers and millers, perhaps anxious about strained trade relations with the rural Catholic cantons, were in the opposition. The artisan and kleinbürgerliche opposition in general was concentrated in the more traditional and local trades, which perhaps inhibited the development of new spiritual perspectives.

These divisions were visible in the ecclesiastical politics of the City Council. Resistance to or lack of enthusiasm for the Reformation was at first concentrated in the oligarchical Small Council. In 1524, the more determinedly Protestant Large Council itself assumed the right to judge doctrine. The Council as a whole often moved more slowly than the Evangelicals wished, and Zwingli often had to agitate public opinion from the pulpit to stir the Council to action. In 1526 he obtained the prosecution and condemnation of those in receipt of foreign pensions. In 1528 a purge of Catholics, ostensibly the high point of his political influence, actually marked its turning point.

The purge followed guild elections whose results displeased Zwingli, but following the purge there was an ostentatious Catholic display during the

New Year's dinners at the guild halls. The Council refused to impose punishments but issued a general warning and instituted compulsory Church attendance.[23] A decree in 1530 complained of neglect of Church attendance, full taverns during Divine Service, the jeering of preachers.[24] The guilds, however, were left to impose punishments on those found guilty by the Morals Court. This concession to democratic theory in fact pointed to popular resistance to the increasingly rigorous theocratic discipline of the new state.

The purge was followed, in 1529, by a constitutional revision which deprived the patrician Konstaffel guild of its special political privileges. The new Zwinglian elite consolidated its hold on the state, not least in the administration of Church property, not unaccompanied by scandal. Reliable Zwinglians replaced the patricians as senior officers in the army.[25] The financial burdens of service on the average citizen were, however, increased. Zwingli's aggressive foreign policies met such resistance that in 1529 and 1531 he threatened resignation. Popular coolness to the new elite was expressed by a contemporary: "My Lords burned the wooden images but they took the golden ones and stole away with them in their pockets, and many became evangelical only to obtain office."[26] The moral impulses reflected in and generated by the Reformation among the artisanry remained unsatisfied; they subsided, or turned elsewhere.

The assumption of an automatic association between theological and social radicalism, in Zürich as elsewhere, has been disproved.[27] True, radical social demands during the Reformation were often based on a literal Biblicism found among the Anabaptists. That Biblicism, however, did not automatically produce social revolutionary doctrines. Some of the Zürich Anabaptists were quietist and the mutual aid they practiced was not a communist political program, but a practical imitation of early Christian models. Urban Anabaptism in Zürich began, at least, among dissenting educated laymen who held Zwingli insufficiently true to his own biblical principles.[28] Zürich lacked an industrial proletariat and the artisanate did enjoy a certain political participation. At any rate, in Zürich extreme social conflict seemed to occur chiefly in the countryside.[29] As early as 1523, Zwingli distinguished between Divine and Human Justice—in response to the peasant demand for the abolition of tithes in the name of the Evangile, which he repudiated.[30] Zwingli by no means reacted as violently to peasant demands as did Luther, and did propose a concrete program of reforms for the Zürich countryside. The reforms were never carried out (we may recall that the new as well as the old elite of the city drew income from rural rents) and the discontents remained. Their activation cannot be attributed to Anabaptist agitation; indeed, some scholars suggest that Anabaptist successes in the countryside followed (and were due to) the frustration of the peasants' social protest.[31]

The Zürich Reformation, then, mastered more easily than elsewhere the double challenge of social and theological radicalism. Zwingli's rejection of a

Biblicist social radicalism, and his hostility to the Anabaptists, were understandable. Taken separately, each was a threat to his version of the Christian
polity in Zürich; together, they might have overwhelmed it. Yet Zwingli's
rejection of each was a response to the dominant social and political pressure
on him.

The Zürich Reformation was the occasion, indeed the vehicle, for the
replacement of one political elite by another; the merchants and master artisans, some of them entrepreneurs, displaced the patriciate. This, however,
was the latent consequence of the new doctrine in Zürich. Was there, however, something *intrinsic* about it that illuminates its origins?

The Zwinglian view of the Church reflected the self-respect of educated,
or at least literate, burghers, alienated from a corrupt and profane Church,
which combined the arrogant remoteness of bureaucratic rule with the gra-
tuitous insolence of nepotism. Unbeholden to the aristocratic powers of late
medieval society, these self-confident city-dwellers had their own vivid political traditions, which rendered ever more repugnant a hierarchical theory of
church government. The theologians' demonstration of the latter's want of
scriptural legitimation made possible the break with Rome. Scriptural authority
(as interpreted by the doctrine of salvation through faith) gave every man
direct access to God. The symbolic interpretation of the sacraments was a
blow at the priestly estate and as such was welcome to many in late medieval
society. The peasantry, who frequently encountered Churchmen as rural ex-
ploiters, found it easy to accept Evangelical doctrine. The active Zürich
Protestants, however, were recruited from those who dealt with the new
technical processes in the economy, mastering materials or commanding
rather abstract economic forces. They distrusted an earthly representation of
divine processes. They were not forerunners of theological liberalism: the
ultimate mystery remained, but it was banished from ordinary sense
experience.

Zwinglianism's social ethic was developed in the highly visible circumstances of the city state whose citizens sought new moral standards—to judge
others and to justify themselves. Ritual practice, then, could not exhaust their
demands on the Christian life. The Zwinglian ethical imperatives united a
number of groups against those aspects of the existing order which they all
opposed; it was incapable, in the end, of resolving the conflicts among them—
or it was applied to the advantage of the most powerful elements in the
Zwinglian Church.

The new Church in Zürich not only reflected but altered the balance of
forces in Zürich society. The divisions within the latter made religiously
legitimated social dissent potentially dangerous; a disciplined State Church
had to be constructed. Its masters were the new men seeking control of the
state. The Morals Court, devised for individual discipline, became a political

instrument. The Biblical promise of Zwingli's early teaching was unfulfilled and Evangelical freedom remained a vision pursued in despair by the persecuted Anabaptist conventicles. Meanwhile, sacrifices were demanded of the ordinary artisan and peasant and a stringent outer discipline imposed upon them.

V. Conclusion

What does this analysis of the Zürich Reformation imply about the relationship of capitalism to Protestantism? Weber asserted that the "typical bearers of the capitalistic ethic and the Calvinistic Church" were those petty and middle *bourgeoisie* who had become entrepreneurs.[32] Weber was primarily interested in the seventeenth century, but the sixteenth-century antecedents of this type were surely the dominant element among the Zürich Zwinglians. Weber also asserted that Calvinistic Protestantism was an indispensable prerequisite for the development of a capitalistic work ethic. But Zürich in the early sixteenth century was *not* a prominent center of the developing capitalism of the period. We know that later its Protestant population, admittedly swelled by Protestant refugees from the Ticino, was conspicuously ingenious at technical innovation and successful in accumulation. We also know that, typically, at the beginning of the century, members of the Zürich elite abandoned economic pursuits for state service and adopted a patrician style of life. At first glance, then, the Reformation in Zürich seemed to have been followed (in a situation of historical indeterminacy) by the development of capitalistic attitudes in the populace.

No such simple formulation is legitimate. The very indeterminacy of the historical situation in Reformation Zürich allows another interpretation. Many capitalistic characteristics were already present: for example, mercantile accumulation and technically advanced production. That Zürich was not a capitalist metropolis like the Fuggers' Augsburg may have been an advantage: the great monopolies were missing and the newer economic patterns could crystallize locally without the restraints and encrustations of the transitional forms of the late medieval economy. Urban Zürich's relatively small size and the state's struggle for autonomy amid the convulsions of late medieval society likewise may have been advantageous. Zürich had experienced a very rapid rate of social change. Many of its members had participated in the recasting of their own traditions; the vested values and ideologies which elsewhere hindered change were missing or weak. Consequently, the breakthrough of a radically new religious system was more possible in these circumstances than elsewhere. The potentialities for the development of both capitalism and Zwinglianism were simultaneously present in the city. If Zwinglianism was the road toward capitalism for Zürich, it was taken because the route in any case already led in that direction.

Notes

1. There has been something of a renaissance in Zwingli studies recently: see R. Pfister, "Die Zwingli Forschung seit 1945," *Archiv für Reformationsgeschichte*, XLVIII (1957), 230–40.

2. Ernst Troeltsch, "Die Soziallehren der christlichen Kirchen u. Gruppen," *Ges. Schriften*, I (Tübingen, 1919) hardly mentions it; Max Weber dismissed it as of but transitory historical importance, in "Die protestantische Ethik u. d. Geist des Kapitalismus," *Ges. Aufsatze z. Religions-soziologie*, I (Tübingen, 1920), p. 84. With his usual perspicacity, Professor Tawney has seen that it cannot be dismissed so lightly; see *Religion and the Rise of Capitalism* (Pelican Edition, London: 1938), pp. 104 and 114–15. The brilliant essay by Franz Borkenau, "On Lutheranism," *Horizon*, III (1944), pp. 162–76, ought also to be mentioned in this connection.

3. W. Kohler, "Zwingli u. Luther," I, *Quellen u. Forschungen z. Reformationsgeschichte*, VI, Leipzig, 1924 and II, *QFRG*, VII, Gütersloh, 1953, deals with the political and ecclesiastical ramifications in this area of the sacramental controversy. His "Zürcher Ehegericht u. Genfer Konsistorium," I–II, *Quellen u. Abhandlungen z. Schweizerischen Reformationsgeschichte, VII, X*, Leipzig, 1924–42, depicts the influence of the Zürich Church on the organization of the neighboring ones.

4. Köhler, "Zürcher Ehegericht," etc. and J. McNeil, *The History and Character of Calvinism* (New York, 1954).

5. H. Kressner, "Schweizer Ursprunge des anglikanischen Staatskirchentums," *Schriften des Vereins f. Reformationsgeschichte*, CLXX, Gütersloh, 1953; C. H. Garret, *The Marian Exiles* (Cambridge, 1938).

6. Weber, *op. cit.*

7. L. v. Ranke, *Deutsche Geschichte im Zeitalter d. Reformation* (edited by P. Joachimsen), III (München, 1925), pp. 43ff.; L. v. Muralt, "Die Reformation," *Historia Mundi*, III (Bern, 1957), p. 69; G. Rupp, "The Reformation in Zürich, Strassburg and Geneva," *Cambridge Modern History*, III, 1957, pp. 96–7. Rupp does suggest that the cities differed from one another socially.

8. K. Dandliker, *Geschichte d. Stadt u. d. Kantons Zürich*, I, Zürich, 1908; L. v. Muralt, "Stadtgemeinde u. Reformation i. d. Schweiz," *Z. f. Schweizerische Geschichte*, X (1930), pp. 349–84; P. Guyer, *Verfassungszustände d. Stadt Zürich im 16., 17., 18. Jh.*, Zürich, 1943 and *Die soziale Schichtung d. Bürgerschaft Zürichs v. Ausgang des Mittelalters bis 1798*, Zürich, 1952. I have found both of Guyer's works invaluable in preparing this essay.

9. This section of the essay rests on the sources cited in notes 8 and 10 to 14.

10. W. Schnyder "Die Bevölkerung d. Stadt u. Landschaft Zürich vom 14. bis 17. Jh.," *Schweizer Studien z. Geschichtswissenschaft*, XIV, 1, Zürich, 1925. The statistical data in this section come from Schnyder's admirable work.

11. J. Maliniak, "Die Entstehung d. Export-Industrie u. des Unternehmerstandes i. Zürich i. XVI. u. XVII. Jh.," *Zürcher Volkswirtschaftliche Studien*, II (Zürich, 1913); P. Keller, "Grundzüge einer Zürcher Wirtschaftsgeschichte," *Zürichs Volksund Staatswirtschaft* (Zürcher Volkswirtschaftliche Gesellschaft: Zürich, 1928), pp. 113–151; H. Amman, "Untersuchungen über d. Wirtschaftsstellung Zürichs im ausgehenden Mittelalter," *Z. f. Schweizerische Geschichte*, XXIX (1949), pp. 305–56.

12. G. Gerig, "Reisläufer u. Pensionsherren in Zürich, 1519–32," *Schweizer Studien z. Geschichtswissenschaft, N.F., XII* (Zürich, 1947). This is a most useful source for the entire mercenary problem in the Reformation period.

13. For this section, I have used the literature cited by Pfister in his bibliographical essay (Note 1.) See especially, O. Farner, *Huldrych Zwingli,* I–II–III (Zürich, 1943–46–54) and J. V. M. Pollet, "Zwinglianisme," *Dictionnaire de Theologie Catholique,* XV (1950), pp. 3745–3927.

14. A. Rich, "Die Anfänge der Theologie Huldrych Zwinglis," *Quellen u. Abhandlungen z. Geschichte d. schweizerischen Protestantismus,* VI (Zürich, 1949).

15. Cited by R. Ley, "Kirchenzucht bei Zwingli," *Quellen u. Abhandlungen z. Geschichte de. schweizerischen Protestantismus,* II (Zürich, 1948), p. 60. See also the earlier work by P. Meyer, *Zwinglis Soziallehren* (Linz, 1921), p. 79.

16. The significance of this controversy has been emphasized by F. Littel, *The Anabaptist View of the Church* (Philadelphia: 1952), which analyzes recent research into the early Anabaptists in a most illuminating way. A second, revised edition has been published (Boston, 1958); I have used the first edition.

17. Köhler, "Zürcher Ehegericht," etc.

18. C. A. H. Burkhardt, *Geschichte d. dt. Kirchen-und Schulvisitationen im Zeitalter d. Reformation,* I (Leipzig, 1879).

19. W. Köhler, "Zwingli u. Luther," etc.

20. H. V. Schubert, *Bekenntnisbildung u. Religionspolitik* (Gotha, 1910).

21. I have used a variety of sources for this section, among them: E. Egli. *Actensammlung z. Geschichte d. Zürcher Reformation i. den Jahren 1519–1533* (Zürich, 1879) and the informative essay by L. Wirz, "Zürcher Familienschicksale im Zeitalter Zwinglis," *Zwingliana,* VI (1938), pp. 194–222, 242–271, 470–499, 537–574. I have made a list of the most prominent lay Zwinglians from the following: the authors of a 1523 pamphlet defending Zwingli against attacks from Constance, those delegated by the City Council to confer with Zwingli on the proposal to establish a Marriage Court, and those delegated to confer with him on the pensions issue in 1526, those expelled from the Council after the defeat of 1531 as warmongers (i.e., active supporters of Zwingli's political policies), those who served as lay members of the Marriage Court (later, the Morals Court), and those who became administrators of the secularized *Grossmünsterstift* (Cathedral Endowment). This gives us thirty-nine names. There were seven apiece from the Tailors' Guild and the Meise, five from the Saffran Guild and four from the Smiths'. The Tailors' Guild, of course, included textile merchants; the Meise, wine dealers, painters and glaziers; the Saffran, merchants; the Smiths', all who worked with metal. The Secret Council when it worked most closely with Zwingli included a goldsmith, a blacksmith, a tanner, a merchant, a carpenter, and a glazier. The leading Zwinglians, it would seem, were from the city's mercantile and artisan elite and in striking measure came from those trades and crafts in which economic and technical change was most pronounced.

22. Gerig's monograph, cited above, was very useful in identifying the lay opposition. I have compiled a list of twenty-eight opposition leaders from those who led the pro-French party in Zürich, 1521–2, those accused as recipients of pensions in 1526, those expelled from the Small Council in the purge of

1528, those who ate fish ostentatiously at the Friday New Year's Day dinners, 1529, those relieved of their military posts in 1529, and those cited before the Council by the Morals Court in 1530, allegedly for helping an adulterer to escape but in fact on account of their general opposition to Zwingli. Eleven of the twenty-eight came from the patrician Konstaffel and the only other noteworthy concentration was in the Kambel guild of retailers, second-hand dealers, and oil vendors.

23. See the discussion of this episode in Gerig, *op. cit.*, pp. 73–8.
24. Egli, *op. cit.*, No. 1656, gives the full text.
25. The military reorganization, and its political causes and consequences are discussed in R. Braun, "Z. Militärpolitik Zürichs im Zeitalter d. Kappeler Kriege," *Zwingliana*, X, 1958, pp. 537–73.
26. Quoted by R. Staehlin, *H. Zwingli*, II (Basel, 1897), p. 480.
27. See Littel, *op. cit.*, and P. Peachey, *Die sociale Herkunft d. Schweizer Täufer i. d. Reformationszeit* (Karlsruhe, 1954).
28. Peachey's figures, *op. cit.*, show that the early urban Anabaptists in Zürich included five priests, nine other educated men, five nobles and but seven ordinary citizens.
29. See W. Classen, "Schweizer Bauernpolitik i. Zeitalter Zwinglis," *Ergänzungshefte z. Zeitschr. f. Sozial-und Wirtschaftsgeschichte*, IV (Weimar, 1899); L. v. Muralt, "Jorg Berger," *Festgabe Hermann Escher* (Zürich, 1927), pp. 98–126; H. Nabholz, "Z. Frage nach d. Ursachen d. Bauernkrieges, 1525," *Gedächtnisschrift f. G. v. Below* (Stuttgart, 1928), pp. 221–253; O. Vasella, "Bauerntum u. Reformation i. d. Eidgenossenschaft," *Hist. Jahrbuch*, LXXVI (1957), pp. 47–63. Vasella shows that the opposition of the peasants to their political overlords was associated elsewhere in Switzerland with an antagonism between Catholic peasants and Protestant city-states— above all in Bern. He notes that many peasant communes insisted on retaining the mass but rejected tithes.
30. H. Zwingli, "Von göttlicher u. menschlicher Gerechtigkeit," *H. Zwinglis sämtliche Werke*, II, *Corpus Reformatorum*, LXXIX.
31. L. v. Muralt, "Jorg Berger," etc., and Peachey, *op. cit.*, pp. 50ff.
32. Weber, *op. cit.*, p. 50. For another attempt at a sociological interpretation of some aspects of Zwinglianism, see H. Koditz, "Die gesellschaftlichen Ursachen d. Scheiterns d. Marburger Religionsgespäräche v. 1. bis Oktober, 1529," *Z. f. Geschichtswissenschaft*, II (1954), pp. 37–70. See also the very good article by G. Fuchs, "Karlstadt's radikal-reformistisches Wirken u. Stellung zwischen Münzer u. Luther," *Wiss. Z. d. Martin Luthers Universität Halle-Wittenberg*, III (1954), pp. 523–51.

3. Enterprise, Labor, and Social Change

The papers in this section deal with problems of social change in connection with the growth of business and industry in the modern world. Two of these, namely those by Sylvia L. Thrupp and William Petersen, tangentially also refer to the role of the family in the new situation. Sylvia L. Thrupp proves, chiefly from genealogical materials, that the medieval merchants of London were less oriented toward participating in the government of the city than their continental counterparts and that the outlet for their energies, if it was not trade, was likely to be the acquisition of landed estates. William Petersen analyzes the available data underlying the demographic transition in the Netherlands and concludes that present theory concerning fertility trends in a western society undergoing modernization needs revision. In Thrupp's paper, the structural difference between England and continental Europe becomes visible; Petersen's paper is important because historical demography has been neglected in the past both by historians and sociologists—by historians because they are not trained to use demographic data, by sociologists because they tend to regard demographic data as "pre-sociological."

The papers by Reinhard Bendix and Rupert B. Vance both investigate the historical roots of contemporary industrial systems. In Russia, we are confronted not only with an autocratic system of government which is reflected in industry, but also with an attitude of the workers which refuses to accept the fact that the absolute power of the Tsars was necessarily and irrevocably employed in favor of the employers and could not as well be enlisted on the workers' side. Little imagination is needed to understand why Tsarism toppled when this expectation was finally frustrated and why Tsarist domination was then superseded by the equally autocratic system imposed by the Communist Party. The new system, built on the old, clearly and unmistakably used governmental power for the purposes of proletarian rule. Social change is implicit here, but in the example taken from Anglo-Saxon society it is the main topic of investigation. Rupert B. Vance traces the change in value systems which accompanies the structural transformation from manor and guild economy to modern industry and reveals the contradictions in which these systems become involved. The sequence is dialectical in nature: from the thesis of a locally enmeshed system of security through the antithesis of unchecked adjustment the synthesis of social security in a free society is ultimately reached. Liberalism and conservatism are thus transcended by a higher unity and the historical basis for the emergence of the welfare state is epitomized in a few bold strokes.

Vance applies an analysis of English economic history to American
social security legislation, but William Miller is entirely concerned with
the American scene. In addition, his piece represents a growing literature
on business history which has become indispensable for the sociological
analysis of American society. This literature cannot be quoted here *in
extenso;* it must suffice merely to point to some of the other papers in
William H. Miller's book, *Men in Business,*[1] such as Robert K. Lamb,
"The Entrepreneur and the Community," referring to the early history of
industrial communities in New England, Frances W. Gregory, "The
American Industrial Elite in the 1870's—Their Social Origins," and David
S. Landes, "Bankers and Pashas—International Finance in Egypt in the
1860s." Among these, William Miller's piece is notable for its use of
ideal-typical procedure, in this case based on Max Weber's concept of
bureaucracy. With that concept as a basic reference point, Miller shows
that in the first decades of the twentieth century leadership in industry was
assumed by a new elite of salaried men, who had neither risen from the
ranks nor distinguished themselves by risk-taking, nor excelled in technical
training or expertise—as both popular myth and the writings of serious
historians, like the Beards, have made us believe. But he also shows that in
actual operation bureaucracy need not function according to the ideal-
typical model of purposive rationality, since "knowing the ropes" in
informal relations frequently appears more conducive to advancement than
legal-administrative or any other kind of competence. It should be added
that Miller uses both personal documents and quantitative data—a
combination which earlier American historians seem to have largely
neglected.

Note

1. William H. Miller (ed.), *Men in Business—Essays in the History of
Entrepreneurship* (Cambridge: Harvard University Press, 1952, and New
York: Harper Torchbooks, 1962).

Sylvia L. Thrupp   MERCHANTS IN MEDIEVAL LONDON:

PATTERNS IN FAMILY HISTORY

HEAVY ODDS AGAINST THE SURVIVAL of male heirs do not preclude the chance
favoring of individual families for successive generations. Despite the continued need of new recruits, the merchant class at all times contained a small
core of families that had behind them a long tradition of London life.

Some of these had worked their way up from the lesser companies. Of four

Reprinted with permission from *The Merchant Class of Medieval London,* by Sylvia L.
Thrupp (Ann Arbor: The University of Michigan Press, 1963).

generations of Dogets who continued in the wine trade, the first was represented by a taverner who died in 1282 leaving two sons, the other three by vintners, the last of whom died childless in 1403; two more vintners of the name, who lived to 1456, may represent a fifth generation, descended from the taverner's other son. Both branches were attached to the parish of St. Leonard's, Eastcheap, held property in that neighborhood, and left their monuments and inscriptions in the church. One of the sons of Gilbert Prince, a fourteenth-century painter who invested in trade, became a mercer and left a son who became a tailor. Many sons of workers in the base metals became goldsmiths, and a number of vintners and grocers came from families in the lesser victualing trades. Behind the ambitious parents who thus enabled their sons to push upward there may in turn have been several generations of London shopkeeping.[1]

Other families make their first appearance in city records with the transactions of some fourteenth-century merchant, whose sons and nephews and grandsons and grandnephews kept the name and the business alive throughout all the worst periods of plague. A single branch of the Elsyng family covered a span of some hundred and twenty years as well-to-do mercers. Although the first who appears, William, devoted a substantial sum to founding a hospital for the blind, his son was prosperous enough to add to the endowment; the grandson, Thomas, followed the lead of his guardian, Jordan de Elsyng, mercer, in buying country property but was living in London when he made his will and died, childless, in 1431. The son and grandson of Richard Odyham, grocer and chamberlain, succeeded him in his company, and there were three generations of Claverings in the drapers' company in one direct line. Such a record was rare enough to justify a certain pride. The grandson of the first Clavering, dying childless in 1421, ordered his descent, with his father's arms and a plea for prayers, to be embroidered on white vestments for his parish church. The most remarkable record yet discovered is that of the Gisors, presumed to be of Italian origin, who had settled in London by the beginning of the thirteenth century. Owing to the chance survival of five brothers in the generation immediately preceding the Black Death, they were still represented by at least one line in the sixteenth-century city. Yet, on the whole, astonishingly few names recur in company membership lists: of ninety-seven on the mercer's list for 1347, for example, only eleven recur between 1392 and 1420. It is true that sons did not have to join the same company as their fathers or even, unfortunately for the researcher, necessarily bear the same surname, names derived from trades sometimes alternating, in a disconcerting way, with place names. Nevertheless, the percentage of the members of the greater companies who represented a third generation of successful trade in London can never have been very large.

The slackening of political ambition on the part of the older city families was a very marked feature of the fifteenth century. In part this may have been due to lingering fears of family compacts in the court of aldermen, in part to the greater wealth and the valuable business connections of new immigrants from provincial centers of trade and industry. In a sample of twelve aldermen serving early in the century, four can be identified as sons of London merchants; among thirty-seven serving after 1450 only two were sons of Londoners.[2] Another element in the situation was the fascination that the legal profession was coming to hold for wealthy citizens' sons. The elder son in the fourth generation of the Coventry family, which had migrated originally from Coventry and had bought its way from the pinners' company up to the ranks of the mercers, in 1432 entered Gray's Inn. A little earlier the grandson of William Wodehouse, alderman, defied his guardians by marrying outside the merchant class at the age of fourteen and began legal studies; he was perhaps urged on by an aunt who had married a successful lawyer. In two other instances merchants are known to have encouraged grandsons, who were their sole surviving heirs, to take up the study of law. In some families one branch might take to the law and another remain in trade. In the Costantyn family, for example, three generations of drapers and aldermen were succeeded by a well-to-do citizen esquire whose second son, in the fifteenth century, became a fellow of Gray's Inn. The branch that remained in trade was exceptional among the older merchant families in achieving re-entry of the court of aldermen, a contemporary of the lawyer, either his brother or a nephew, serving in it for six years. The alderman's son became a grocer but passed also as a gentleman and esquire of Kent. The lawyer's sons may have remained more loyal to the family's urban traditions than the merchant's. The eldest inherited ancestral property in London, the second was apprenticed to a draper, and the third was educated to be a priest.[3]

Occasionally Londoners' sons struck out into business in the provinces.[4] More often, especially in time of trade depression or if for any other reason they found business distasteful, they turned their back on it and settled on family property in the country. The move may not always have been of their own volition. A merchant's last resource in dealing with a wayward son who ran into debt was probably to follow the example of an early fifteenth-century draper who paid the youth's debts, bought his wedding clothes, married him, and stocked one hundred and ninety acres of land for him at Fulbourne, in Middlesex.[5] There were others who moved out to small country properties in happier but equally unambitious fashion, with the intention of eking out their living by London rents. This arrangement did not always satisfy the next generation, yet, if the heirs wished to go back to the city, they would find that the family had lost caste there by its spell of obscurity. Two of the Hardels, one of the old governing families, abandoned trade in this way early in the fourteenth century to live quietly in Surrey and Essex. Later both estates fell to a single heir who took up citizenship in the lowly company of the tapicers.[6] The Sely family underwent a similar experience. John Sely, skinner, successor to four generations of distingushed members of that company, at the end of the fourteenth century settled in Wiltshire, where the family had perhaps originated. There he brought up two illegitimate sons, who went off to Buckinghamshire, one as a tailor, one as a mere husbandman. His only legitimate son returned to London but had to be content with taking up citizenship through the brewers instead of through the skinners.

The sons of city magnates who had been able to build up country estates comparable in value with those of important local landowners were in a very different situation. By settling down on their manors they stood to gain in status, not to lose, for the head of the family was before long likely to be drawn into the influential circle that controlled the administration of the county. The strategic steps that assured a son's entry into the leisured landowning class required a patient watching of the land and marriage markets and were probably all more or less motivated by social ambition. An extreme instance in point is that of a member of the grocers' company, under Richard II, who acquired land in Essex held in chief by service at the king's coronation; although he was not allowed to perform this service in person, he retained the property, bought an heiress' marriage for his son, and settled him there. By his time a number of London families had established a senior branch on estates near by, junior branches continuing in trade in the city. Even so tenaciously urban a family as the Gisors had by the early years of the century planted a line at "Gesoresplace" at Edmonton. In the same period the Swanslands put out two country branches, one at Harefield in Middlesex and one which held the manor of North Mymmes, on the border of Hertfordshire, for four generations. The last heir let this manor pass into the possession of Thomas Knolles, grocer. Knolles, securely seated in the court of aldermen for over forty years, was in no mind to leave the city or to see his wholesale business abandoned. He placed an agent in charge of the manor and cannily bred both his sons to trade, keeping the elder in London, sending the younger to Bristol. Not until the third generation, in this case, did the heir retire to the country and move into the squirearchy. If the hold on civic honors had been less firm, the move might not have been so long deferred. Sometimes the rise was more impatient and ostentatious. One of the most decorative pictures of an esquire of the reign of Edward IV is to be found at Staundon, in Hertfordshire, on the monumental brass of John Felde, showing him with long, curled hair, in conventionally designed heraldic dress. Yet only a few years before his death Felde had been associated with his father, a former alderman, in the wholesale business of a stockfishmonger and wool merchant.

Very often the evolution from merchant to gentleman was but a small step, signifying merely the knitting-up of family traditions that had been temporarily broken or the assimilating of younger sons into ways of living long customary with the senior line. Many fifteenth-century families, for example, the

Lovelaces of Kent and the Babhams of Cookham, put only a single member into trade in London, a younger son, whose eldest son in turn reverted to the country gentleman's life.

All the seemingly disparate elements within the merchant class were linked together by a complex pattern of intermarriage, which grew up and was maintained the more readily from the circumstance that many of the families dying out in the male line survived through daughters. These London women, remaining for the most part attached to city property and city ways and marrying within their class, must have contributed immeasurably to the stability of its culture. Another circumstance tending toward the same result was the fact that, when sons failed to grow up, their places were often filled by nephews or cousins or by the children of friends in the provinces who were taken in tutelage as apprentices. Country immigrants therefore did not necessarily represent so much alien raw material to be assimilated only through the process of education offered in apprenticeship but often fitted in a most welcome and intimate way into some family situation.

The types of citizen family history that have been illustrated here could without a doubt be duplicated from the archives of any medieval city comparable in size with London. Everywhere in Europe the same underlying conditions of fertility and mortality made for fluidity in the composition of the upper urban classes. Yet Caxton, returning from abroad, became aware of some lack of depth in London culture, and it struck him as peculiarly English. As regards the longevity of patrician families on the Continent, his imagination may have outrun his powers of critical observation. He may have been misled, as local patriots with whom he talked about the history of Bruges may have been, by mere coincidences of name, or he may have been thinking of instances in which great families had contrived to prolong their lives, when sons failed, by the adoption of heirs. This practice had never taken root in London. The Faringdon family, in the early fourteenth century, offers almost the only certain example of it. But the question immediately arises and surely occurred to Caxton: Why had the practice of adoption, on failure of heirs, not become customary in London: Why was there so little pride in preserving a long record of high family status in the city?

The question calls for more careful statement and much longer consideration than can be given it here. But the answer would probably lie in the circumstances that conditioned citizens' opportunities for careers. In the great Continental cities patrician groups held aloof from active participation in trade, concentrating on government and finance. In London the work of government was limited and specialization in finance was slow to develop. In consequence young men of ambition who did not care for trade looked elsewhere for careers, and those who were merely restless sought the only other life they knew that was easy of access, life on the land.

Notes

1. On the Doget, Brill, Coventry, Constantyn, Wodehouse families, see Appendix to Sylvia L. Thrupp's *The Merchant Class of Medieval London, op. cit.,* pp. 321–396; on the Elsyngs, Princes, Odyhams, Claverings, and John Wiltshire, see List of Abbreviations, XI–XIII, where sources are quoted.

2. Of forty-two aldermen in the first half of the fourteenth century, thirteen had certainly been sons of London merchants and nineteen more probably so; of twenty-five in the latter part of the century, six can be identified as sons of Londoners, and five more were related to citizen families.

3. On the purchase by Coventry and his sons of membership in the mercers see Wardens' Accounts, fol. 39v. The grandson of William Michell, grocer, member of parliament for the city in 1415, was intended to study law.

4. For a case of a grocer's son going to Bristol see Knolles, Appen. A. Case of a goldsmith's son setting up his trade in Maidstone (Westminster Abbey Muniments, 5206 [1491]).

5. The only surviving son of John Olyver, who made three marriages (*Calendar of Plea and Memoranda Rolls,* IV, 6–7). The deeds enrolled in the husting court records contain many references to merchants' sons and grandsons in country places, without specifying their occupation; e.g., cases in Suffolk, Surrey, and Oxfordshire (Hustings Rolls of Wills and Deeds, 133/30, 138/40, 159/52). Case of an ironmonger's son settling in Glaston, Somerset, shown by wills of John and Stephen Lane (Prerogative Court of Canterbury, Godyn, 31; P.C.C., Vox 23; Letter Books of the City of London, fol. 101*b*).

6. This heir was William, great-grandson of Robert Hardel, alderman. His father had appointed a tapicer as his guardian (Calendar of Wills Proved and Enrolled in the Court of Hastings, I, 429). Details of his descent and property in London and Surrey in Escheat Rolls, *m. 67d,* and Westminster Abbey Muniments, 1907, 1908.

William Petersen   THE DEMOGRAPHIC TRANSITION IN
THE NETHERLANDS

OFFHAND ONE MIGHT SUPPOSE that demography ought to be one of the happiest meeting-grounds of sociologists and historians. Studying the population of any society is typically begun with a social analysis—comparing the fertility, say, of one class with that of another. And in this case such an analysis is

The research for this study was done in Holland under a grant from the National Science Foundation. An earlier version was read by G. A. Kooy, E. W. Hofstee, T. van den Brink, F. Kool, and John T. Krause. I am most grateful for their criticisms. The paper was read at the annual meeting of the American Sociological Association, September, 1959 and is reprinted from *American Sociological Review,* Vol. 25, No. 3, June, 1960, with the permission of the author and the American Sociological Association.

much less likely to be static than is usual in other branches of sociology, for both the flow of life from one generation to the next and the succession of censuses suggest, and sometimes demand, a historical framework. Actually, however, demography has not benefited from very much interpenetration of the two disciplines. Most of the historians seriously concerned with population have concentrated on the period before the advent of reliable statistics, and their demographic expertise has not ordinarily been at a high level. And sociologists have usually been content with that roughest and most simplistic of models, the theory of the demographic transition, the bare bones of which have all too seldom been rounded out with historical detail.

This at least was the situation until rather recently. But the last decade or so has seen a relatively large number of excellent studies, which in sum may eventually revise our ideas of population trends in the early modern period. Perhaps the most important change being made in the conception of the demographic transition is in the refinement of the original thesis that it applies equally well to all countries undergoing modernization. It has by now become obvious that there are more differences than similarities in the population development of, say, nineteenth century England and twentieth century India. Several writers have suggested that among Western cultures overseas countries like the United States and the British dominions, whose empty lands were filled in large part by immigration, constitute a special subclass. Even population growth in so homogeneous a culture area as Western Europe has differed significantly from one country to another, and in order to obtain a true picture of its demographic past it will be necessary to undertake many more national or even local historical studies and at some future time to synthesize them into a more complex, but more accurate, overall model.

In this paper I wish to bring to the attention of their English-speaking colleagues some of the interesting and important work that Dutch sociologists and historians have been doing in population analysis, and to suggest a few of the general theoretical implications of their findings. That the population history of the Netherlands is anomalous is of course well known, but some of its specific features seem also to be variations on Western themes. If the relation between population growth and modernization is to be better understood, we must learn how to maintain a delicate balance between the specific facts of the historian and the generalizing function of the sociologist.

Population Growth

In the theory of the demographic transition, one postulate is that the population growth was wholly a natural increase; and before we apply this theory to any specific historical case we must ask whether the net migration actually was insignificant. This was the case in the Netherlands during the nineteenth and twentieth centuries, to the extent that one can tell from the inadequate statistics.[1] But what of earlier centuries? When the Republic of the United Netherlands was established in the sixteenth century, it became a haven for refugees from Catholic Europe, first of all Calvinists from the reconquered Spanish Netherlands (now Belgium) and Jews from Spain itself, later French Protestants and East European Jews. No accurate record was kept of this immigration,[2] nor of the emigration that partly balanced it. That the Spanish Jews and Huguenots had a great impact on Dutch commerce and industry is not a good clue to their numbers, particularly when these are to be taken as a percentage of the national population rather than of the relatively few towns where the immigrants mainly settled. Whether the zero net migration that the model demands was true of the Netherlands is not known, but it is reasonable to assume that it was.

Estimating internal migration is no less difficult, and the problem cannot be wholly bypassed. The best of the early data refer principally to the urban population, and in order to use them for our purpose we must try to distinguish between the natural increase of the towns and the net migration to them. During the three centuries or so preceding the first national census, the towns' population increased greatly,[3] but certain of the data suggest that this was the consequence mainly of large in-migration.[4]

Sometimes it is possible to check this impression by relating the population growth of the towns to that of the countryside by the use of provincial censuses. In the case of Holland Province, for example, we can compare the urban and rural sectors in 1622.[5] and in 1795, as shown in Table 1.[6] The

Table 1—Population of Holland Province, 1622 and 1795

	Towns	Countryside	Total
1622	397,882	269,698	667,580
1795	518,561	258,561	776,566
Per cent increase	+30	−5	+16

increase of 16 per cent over 175 years means an average of less than 0.1 per cent per year, but this figure can be accepted only with three reservations: (1) If we substitute for the two actual census counts the larger figures including underenumeration as estimated by Van Dillen, the increase would be by 25 rather than 16 per cent. (2) The calculation of the trend between the two censuses by simple subtraction blurs the fact that the growth curve for both towns and countryside rose during the seventeenth and early eighteenth centuries and fell off sharply from about 1750. (3) Neither the towns nor especially the rural regions of Holland Province were typical of the Netherlands as a whole.

This last point is worth explaining. In their generalizing function, sociologists tend to structure any analysis of town and country in the early modern period into a fairly rigid functional division between agricultural and non-agricultural localities, and thus between *Gemeinschaft* and *Gesellschaft*. The historical example of Holland Province suggests that in any particular case this can be a gross oversimplification. Its rural economy, according to De Vooys, included the following quite heterogeneous and sometimes dynamic elements: (1) *Agriculture.* In some areas this sector of the economy and the population based on it were relatively static. But in the so-called Westland— the strip along the coast south from The Hague, which to this day is the center of commercial horticulture—the intensification of agriculture afforded a base for population increase during the seventeenth and eighteenth centuries. (2) *Peat-cutting.* With the depletion of peat bogs in South Holland, peat workers were replaced by a smaller number of agriculturists, resulting in a population loss in this region. (3) *"Suburban" commerce and handicrafts,* particularly in the environs of Amsterdam and Rotterdam. Here the population fluctuated together with that of the cities. (4) *Fishermen and marine workers* living in both coastal and inland villages north of the IJ River. The virtual disappearance of their means of subsistence resulted in a considerable out-migration and decline in population in the second half of the eighteenth century.

That the urban population of Holland Province increased by thirty per cent over the designated period while the rural population fell off by five per cent was undoubtedly due in large part to migration, both between these sectors and from other provinces to Holland's cities. But in view of the atypical features of Holland Province, it is well to check this conclusion with data from Overijssel, a generally agricultural province with some early industry. In Table 2 the population growth of this province is shown separately for the three largest towns and, below, for the smaller towns and the countryside of the three socio-economic areas of Salland, Twente, and Vollenhove.[7] Note that before the nineteenth century the rate of increase in the three large towns was well below the average for the whole province, and that, by and large, the growth curves of the small towns and the countryside tended to move together. These figures suggest that rural-urban migration was not so important a factor in urban growth as in Holland Province, and perhaps Overijssel was more

Table 2—Regional Population Increase in Overijssel, 1675–1849

| | PER CENT INCREASE IN POPULATION | | | |
	1675–1723	1723–1764	1748–1795	1795–1849
Overijssel	37.6	35.9	9.5	60.4
Three largest towns				
(Zwolle, Deventer, Kampen)	20.7	15.8	3.1	65.8
Other towns in				
Salland	44.1	36.6	12.4	24.3
Twente	33.4	74.9	7.0	58.2
Vollenhove	37.5	4.0	13.4	60.3
Countryside of				
Salland	31.1	34.9	17.1	69.0
Twente	72.5	58.1	8.4	42.0
Vollenhove	41.6	24.6	9.7	75.7

representative of the country as a whole. It may be indicative that for the period since 1795, the growth curves of this province and of the Netherlands are almost identical.[8]

According to the estimate of Slicher van Bath, the population of Overijssel at the specified dates was as follows:

1475	52,660	Earliest estimate possible; not reliable.
1675	70,678	Earliest fairly reliable estimate.
1795	134,104	First national census.
1840	197,694	First reliable national census.
1957	748,337	A recent estimate from population registers.

This steady and increasingly rapid growth does not include short-term fluctuations. A more detailed analysis[9] permits the population increase from 1675 to 1930 to be divided into four periods, with the average annual rates of growth as follows:

75 years (1675–1748)—0.75 to 1.0 per cent.
60 years (1748–1811)—zero to 0.5 per cent.
80 years (1811–1889)—almost 1.0 per cent.
40 years (1889–1930)—1.3 rising to 1.7 per cent.

Do these data take us back to the hypothetical Stage I of the demographic transition? The so-called static population characteristic of this stage typically fluctuates around a horizontal mean, and it would seem that this cycle is to be seen in Overijssel between 1675 and 1811. The average growth during this period, however, was not zero; this suggests that these 136 years constitute rather a transition from Stage I to Stage II. If the upswing from 1675 to 1748 was faster than that of an ordinary Stage I cycle, as may well have been the case, this was presumably because the premodern prosperity was enhanced by the new factors that eventually would effect a steady increase in numbers. In the second half of the eighteenth century, a time of economic depression, the population growth slowed down and for the leanest thirty years was not much more than zero. Here again we can reasonably hypothesize that the figures reflect two overlapping curves—a decrease in population that would have resulted from a Stage I depression, cancelled by Stage II factors favoring population increase.

It seems reasonable, lacking precise data, to apply this scheme to the population history of the whole country. According to one estimate—or better, guess—the number of inhabitants of the present area of the Netherlands in 1540 was 882,400.[10] To specify this figure to the nearest hundred is certainly unwarranted, but it may well be correct to the nearest hundred thousand. From the middle of the sixteenth to the middle of the eighteenth century, then, the population probably grew from less than a million to something over two million, and during the second half of the eighteenth century it probably remained nearly static. The growth since the date of the first national census, as shown in Table 3, falls within Stage II of the demographic transition, and even within the early phase of this stage, before the long-run growth rate has begun to decline. From 1795 to 1870 the annual increase averaged about 0.75 per cent, and since 1870 it has been around 1.25 per cent. In the Netherlands, there is not only no indication of the "incipient decline" in population

Table 3—Population Growth in the Netherlands, 1795–1958

Year*	Population (–000)	Per Cent Average Annual Increase During Preceding Period
1795	2,097	—
1829	2,613	0.72
1839	2,861	0.91
1849	3,057	0.67
1859	3,309	0.80
1869	3,580	0.79
1879	4,013	1.14
1889	4,511	1.18
1899	5,104	1.24
1909	5,858	1.39
1920	6,865	1.45
1930	7,935	1.46
1940	8,923	1.18
1950	10,200	1.35
1958	11,278	1.25

* As of December 31 of the designated year, except for 1849 (November 19) and 1869 (December 1). Figures from 1795 to 1930 are from the census; thereafter from the population registers.

characteristic of Stage III but hardly any sign of an incipient deceleration of the present rapid rate of growth.

That the population increase characteristic of modern times began in the seventeenth century or earlier is in accord with the usual macroscopic estimates. Both Willcox and Carr-Saunders took 1650 as their starting date and posited a subsequent continuous growth both of the world's population and, more specifically, of Europe's.[11] In a historical analysis of one particular country's population, however, the probability that the increase in numbers began so early requires reexamination of the usual thesis that its cause was wholly, or almost wholly, the decline in mortality.

Mortality

One can trace the course of Holland's mortality by fairly reliable statistics only since the middle of the nineteenth century. Attempts have been made to devise estimates from burial records of earlier centuries, but the data are so poor that they cannot yield even satisfactory local rates. In a recent article, De Haas has compiled from a number of contemporary sources the expectation of life at various ages from 1825 to date.[12] In Amsterdam, expectation of

Table 4—Crude Death Rates in the Netherlands, 1850–1957

	Decennial Average	RANGE OF ANNUAL RATES FROM LOW TO HIGH	
		National	Provincial
1850–59	25.5	22.3–31.0	17.7–40.4
1860–69	24.9	22.9–28.7	17.7–39.8
1870–79	24.4	22.2–28.4	18.0–39.0
1880–89	21.3	19.7–23.6	16.5–26.4
1890–99	18.7	16.9–21.0	13.8–18.9
1900–09	15.6	13.7–17.9	12.6–16.6
1910–19	13.5	12.3–17.5	11.2–20.0
1920–29	10.6	9.6–12.3	8.9–14.8
1930–39	8.8	8.4– 9.6	6.8–11.0
1940–49	9.9	8.1–15.3	7.0–17.6
1950–57	7.55	7.3– 7.8	6.6– 9.0*

* This is the range of what might be termed the normal death rate. In the new province of the Northeast Polder, with an almost total absence of elderly people, the death rate was only 1.7 in 1951. In Zeeland in 1953, after the main dikes broke and several of the large islands were flooded, the death rate rose to 11.4.

life at birth rose slowly from about thirty-five years in 1825 to about thirty-eight years in 1845. For the whole of the country, this index was about thirty-eight years in 1845 and only forty years in 1875; but from that date on the rise has been much faster and, apart from World War II, without interruption.

As Table 4 shows, the remarkable decline in the Dutch death rate over the past century has been, more precisely, only since around 1880.[13] The thirty years preceding that date saw little change, either in the decennial averages or in the extremes of the considerable variation from year to year and from one province to another. The same trend can be noted in infant and child mortality, which in this period constituted a large fraction of the general death rate.[14] The reasons for the decline from the relatively high plateau on which the death rate rested in the middle of the last century are, of course, no mystery. Both specific cures for various diseases and highly significant improvements in the environment began to be developed with accelerating speed in the last decades of the nineteenth century. That is to say, the application of the most efficient means of death control effected not a transition from a static to a growing population, but the quickening of the rate of growth from 0.75 to 1.25 per cent per year that, as we have noted, also took place in the 1870s.

Was the considerable population growth before the introduction of modern medicine and public health also the consequence, either wholly or mainly, of a prior decline in mortality? And, if so, how can we account for this fall in the death rate? While it is not possible to answer these questions directly from mortality statistics, at least plausible hypotheses can be suggested from known institutional changes and their probable effect on the death rate.

The conclusions that McKeown and Brown reached in their important paper on mortality in eighteenth century England are relevant also to other

European countries of that period.[15] They divided the possible causes of a reduction in mortality into three broad classes, as follows:

(1) Specific preventive or curative therapy. In the Netherlands as in England, most treatments of the various important causes of death can be discounted for the period earlier than the middle of the nineteenth century. It is a moot question whether fever hospitals, for example, helped restrict contagion by the semi-quarantine they imposed or raised the death rate by the fact that virtually all persons who entered them would be infected.[16] So long as bleeding was the first treatment for illness, the contribution that physicians made to their patients' health was minimal; so long as something like half of surgical patients died of infection, it can be questioned whether surgeons saved more patients than they killed. "It might safely be said," McKeown and Brown conclude, "that specific medical treatment had no useful effects at all, were it not for some doubt about the results of the use of mercury in syphilis, iron in anaemia, cinchona in malaria, and inoculation against smallpox."

(2) A change in the balance between the virulence of the infective organism and the resistance of the host. In specific instances—for example, the transformation of scarlet fever from a frequently fatal disease to a relatively trivial complaint—this was problably the decisive factor. The general effect of such changes on the long-term trend in the death rate, however, was probably slight.

(3) Improvements in the environment. By the partial elimination of the other two classes, this would seem to be the major cause of any important decline in mortality before about 1850. It is difficult to analyze these improvements, not only because data of all kinds are less numerous and less accurate before that date, and because the relation between environmental changes and presumably consequent declines in mortality are typically vague, but because it is hardly possible to speak of "improvements" in Dutch living conditions during the century from 1750 to 1850.

It was during this period, a hundred years of almost unrelieved economic depression, that the first systematic studies were made relating mortality in the Netherlands to the environment. As early as 1770, the Academy of Sciences was sufficiently interested in this relation to offer a prize for the best answer to the question, "What human diseases derive from this country's physical conditions?," and the competition stimulated a larger number of persons to statistical research.[17] They and their counterparts in other countries laid a necessary base for the rapid advances in understanding during the past century.

There is very little in these early statistical studies to suggest a rise in the standard of living. Take the matter of food supply, one of the more important environmental influences on mortality. The Netherlands of the seventeenth century was ahead of the rest of Western Europe in its agricultural techniques.

In the eighteenth century, thus, the first stimulus to the transformation of the English countryside—improved drainage and fertilizers, new crops, better breeding of farm animals—was an imitation of Holland. There can be little doubt that in both seventeenth-century Holland and eighteenth-century England the better and more varied diet of the populace resulted in better health. But for the latter decades of the eighteenth century and the first half of the nineteenth, the Dutch data recount mostly inadequacy, often misery. In the 1840s, when the potato blight spreading across Europe invaded the Dutch fields, the endemic deficiency developed into a near-famine. "Food consumption, at least in the cities, was just as low as in Ireland."[18]

The variation in infant mortality can also be explained in part by diet. In some regions and among the upper classes generally, babies were breast-fed. But where mothers had to work, they fed their infants on bread soaked in water with a bit of milk or even gin. When the babies cried, they were given a piece of rag in which a piece of chewed bread with sugar had been tied. "This murderous thing," as De Vooys terms it, went by a variety of local names, but everywhere it was more infectious than nutritious.

Living conditions of the poor, particularly in the cities, were deplorable. Often a family of eight shared one bed. Almost one-tenth of the population of Amsterdam lived in damp cellars. According to various urban samples, infant mortality ranged from one-third to one-half. The correlation between size of township and the rate of infant mortality was positive until the 1880s; with the more rapid improvement of urban health facilities the correlation was reversed during the following twenty years.[19]

One reason for the high rates of urban mortality, both infant and general, is that many Dutch cities are in Holland Province, most of which is below sea level. This fact was certainly relevant to their state of health before the full development of modern engineering. The average death rates for 1841–1860 ranged from above thirty-two per thousand population in the low-lying townships of Holland Province and Zeeland, to below twenty-two per thousand in the high-lying townships in the East. The segregation of sewage from drinking water was especially difficult in the western provinces, and there were recurrent outbreaks of cholera until the 1860s. What was termed "swamp fever" (*moeraskoorts*) was actually a group of diseases, which each year ran through a seasonal cycle—influenza and malaria in the spring; in June and July diarrhea among infants, often linked to typhus or bacterial dysentery, whose incidence increased in the fall; and at the end of the year the various respiratory diseases. The drinking water in Zeeland was particularly poisonous: on one occasion in the 1780s, of 1,040 Swiss troops stationed in Sluis, only twelve or thirteen could stand on their feet after just one month.[20]

In short, there is good circumstantial, though not decisive statistical, evidence to support the thesis that, at least for some social classes and regions, the death rate rose from the average of, say, 1650–1750 to that of 1750–

1850. So long as public-health measures were relatively primitive, the congestion of the cities increased the danger of contagion, and under such circumstances the growth of cities would tend to increase mortality. There was probably also a decline in the living standards and especially the diet of the mass of the people. Extant accounts of seventeenth-century food habits are concerned principally with the well stocked tables of the bourgeoisie, but in this relatively prosperous period even the poor probably ate better than their more numerous counterparts in the 1820s and 1830s, certainly better than in the 1840s.

If there was any decline in general mortality, then, it was probably quite small. Was it great enough to account for the increase in population—taking only the period measured by national censuses—from roughly 2.1 million in 1795 to almost 3.1 million in 1850? Or is there not a *prima facie* case here for the probability that fertility rose?

Fertility

In the conventional model of the demographic transition, it is assumed that Stages I and II were characterized by a more or less constant fertility at close to the physiological maximum. The population growth during Stage II —the consequence thus, wholly or almost wholly, of the fall in mortality— pushed parents to adopt the small-family system, which was based on a new rationalist attitude toward conception and the various contraceptive means invented or popularized during the nineteenth century.

While this model has a certain rough validity, there is little evidence on the face of it to support some of the details. Reproduction up to the physiological maximum is not the typical practice among either primitive peoples or preindustrial civilizations. Conscious family limitation did not have to wait for mechanical and chemical contraceptives; it can be effected by coitus interruptus, abortion, or infanticide—methods as old as human history.[21] The average size of the family, moreover, depends not merely on the parents' will but on the variety of cultural, religious, and magical norms governing the age at marriage, the proportion of adults that marry, the remarriage of widows, the frequency of marital intercourse, and the like.

The conscious regulation of family size in late medieval and early modern Europe was in part accomplished by coitus interruptus, in part by abortion and infanticide.[22] A more significant check to fertility, however, had been gradually inculcated: the principle that a man might not marry until his living was assured.[23] In some cases, this norm was spelled out in detailed regulations of particular institutions. In other cases, it was strong enough to govern family formation without being specified in written laws. The principal check to unlimited procreation in the Dutch countryside of several centuries ago, the joint household, is a good example of the second type.

In the Netherlands as in all Germanic countries, the sib remained an important legal body until the late Middle Ages.[24] And in many parts of the Dutch countryside, the extended family functions still today as a meaningful organization. Until rather recently a discussion of it could have been based on nothing more than the impressionist writings of folklorists, plus a few incidental jottings by social scientists; but since the war the three-generation household has suddenly become a "social problem," to be studied by social workers, churches, and government agencies. This new interest has culminated in Kooy's excellent sociological analysis,[25] based in part on a questionnaire survey of the Achterhoek (literally, "back corner"), an agrarian region in the province of Gelderland. But this study is also relevant to other areas where a strong organization of the extended family still persists, and to a historical analysis of the Dutch countryside as a whole.

In its typical form, the joint household can be described as follows.[26] One of the sons (or where there are no sons, one of the daughters) is designated as the sole heir to the family farm, either explicitly in a legal document or implicitly by the tradition that all accept. When he marries, his bride comes to live under his parents' roof. In principle, the heir's brothers and sisters leave the farm; in practice, they often remain, unmarried uncles and aunts with a status between that of family members and servants. Variation in the present-day expression of this tradition is illustrated in Table 5.[27] The normal household consists of two families of successive generations (lines 1 and 2, plus some other families, probably, in which both grandparents had died).

Table 5—Percentage Distribution in Patterns of Joint Residence in Two Regions of the Achterhoek

	Graafschap	Lijmers
1. Two families of successive generations	49.9	38.6
2. Family with one grandparent	27.5	27.0
3. Family with an unmarried uncle or aunt	8.6	18.2
4. Two families of the same generation	0.1	0.4
5. Family with a more distant relative	4.2	7.4
6. All other patterns	9.7	8.4
	100.0	100.0
	(3,918)	(740)

Attached to this nucleus, however, there may be an unmarried sibling of the heir or his wife (line 3), or a more distant relative (line 5), or servant or farm-worker, also unmarried (line 6). Note how seldom the property is shared by two families of the same generation (line 4). The restriction that this system imposes on fertility is patent. The main desideratum, that from generation to generation the farm remain undivided in the same family, is safeguarded, but to this principle is sacrificed the normal family life of a considerable proportion of the adult population.

Because of their frustration, this pattern has been inherently unstable under modern conditions. Whenever a change in circumstances makes it possible, the unmarried hangers-on of these joint households rush to set up their own homes and establish their own families. Thus, several times in Holland's recent history there has been an explosive rise in the fertility of certain areas or certain social classes:

(a) The extension of arable land by reclamation has had the paradoxical effect of aggravating population pressure. For the settlers on the polders being built out of the former Zuider Zee are mostly younger sons of farmers, many of whom in their prior status would have been unable to marry. And in the new settlements, in part because of the preponderance of young adults, the birth rate has on occasion been more than seventy per thousand population![28]

(b) During the last quarter of the nineteenth century artificial fertilizers were introduced in the sandy regions of the East and South, and the greatly improved productivity of the soil made it possible to divide up family farms into viable units of smaller acreage. For two or three generations, it was possible in this way for a much larger proportion of young adults to marry and procreate. And today these regions generally have the highest fertility rates in the country, for it has been difficult both to reestablish the traditional pattern of family limitation by the nonmarriage of some adults, and to overcome the opposition of the various churches to family limitation by the use of contraceptives.[29]

(c) The joint household and the limitation on human fertility that it implies disappeared earlier where agriculture was based on the naturally more fertile clay soil. This process has been analyzed in detail by Hofstee, particularly for the Oldambt, a region in northeast Groningen. Until the eighteenth century, the farm laborers there lived almost as members of the farmer's family, sleeping in the same house, eating at the same table, working together during the day, talking over common interests in the evening. From about 1775 on, this patriarchal relation began to disappear, to be supplanted eventually by a sharp class differentiation. The well-to-do landowners underwent an *embourgeoisement* that transformed them from traditional peasants into modern farmers. Even earlier than in the cities, they adopted a small-family system by which the relation between the land and the number of landowners was kept almost constant. The farm workers, converted into a landless proletariat, were released from the institutional and moral inhibitions to procreation implicit in the old system. In the century following 1775, their number in the province of Groningen increased four times.[30]

(d) If the fertility of agricultural workers increased when they became a *rural* proletariat, should this not have taken place also when they moved to the towns and were there released from the same checks to procreation? That urban fertility in the Netherlands was higher than that in the countryside until about seventy-five years ago has long been an established fact, but its implications have seldom been explored until a recent paper by Hofstee.[31] In order to supplement the existent compilations of township data, Hofstee compiled from provincial and township archives his own breakdown for 1850–1880, and thus obtained a valuable new base for analyzing fertility during this transitional period. Average birth rates for 1851–1855 showed a regional patterning almost precisely the opposite of that to be seen today. The highest birth rates at that time—thirty-five per thousand or more—were in the agricultural provinces with a clay soil (Zeeland, Friesland, and Groningen) and the country's urban center (North and South Holland). Birth rates in specific cities varied somewhat, but in general they were close to the level of the surrounding countryside. This differentiation is not due, as one might suspect, to a difference in age structure; it holds also when the fertility is compared by other measures.

At one time the three-generation household was standard in the Dutch countryside, and something like it seems to have existed also in the cities.[32] In both cases, the principal check to fertility was by the relatively high proportion of the population that remained single. It is reasonable to suppose that the same forces that prevented the marriage of some tended to postpone that of the others. However, the secular trend in the median age at marriage cannot be realistically discussed in statistical terms, for the following reasons:

(1) Data are completely lacking for the earlier period.[33]

(2) As is well known, in societies where the postponement of marriage constitutes an important method of family limitation, the age generally rises and falls according to economic conditions.[34] Given the poor statistics, it is therefore still more difficult to discern a possible long-term trend underlying these fluctuations.

(3) In any case, the trend in the median age at marriage of the whole population, if it were possible to establish it for the early modern period, would not reveal the changes presumably taking place in several of the social classes.

Even so, although the point cannot be statistically documented, it is reasonable to assume that the same institutional changes that permitted a larger number to marry also tended to reduce the age at marriage.[35]

With respect to fertility, a more important consequence of the breakdown of the moral and institutional norms inherent in the joint household was the probable rise in illegitimacy. Like all Germanic countries, the Netherlands has inherited a tradition of "window wooing."[36] By this folk norm, premarital intercourse is usual, and marriage does not take place until the bride is pregnant. According to a government survey made just before World War II, the percentage of forced marriages in the Netherlands ranged from just over thirteen in large towns to sixteen in villages.[37] In a number of areas, generally quite fundamentalist in religion, the custom is still more prevalent.[38] It is something of a misnomer, however, to call these "forced marriages," a term that suggests a more or less random liaison. With respect to both the timing and the mate chosen, these are usually planned, or at least half-planned, conceptions; and so long as the village's social control is unbroken, marriage follows them almost inevitably. Yet this is a system that all but invites dalliance once the control is released—and in the nineteenth century the urban illegitimacy rates were generally high.[39]

Conclusions

In the theory of the demographic transition, the population growth of an area undergoing modernization is divided into three stages: (1) a more or less static population at high levels of fertility and mortality; (2) a period of constant fertility and falling mortality, with a consequent rapid increase in population; (3) a more or less static population at more efficient levels of birth and death control. It is generally believed that the population of the Western world has increased continuously from 1650 on, at the latest. The decline in mortality that is used in the model to explain this growth cannot be documented for anything like so long a period. In the Netherlands, as generally in the Western world, the most dramatic rise in life expectation dates from the last quarter of the nineteenth century, and for the prior several hundred years the presumed fall in mortality can neither be proved from the statistics nor even—for a substantial portion of this period—plausibly related to institutional changes.

The unlikelihood of a decline in mortality is increased when we examine more closely the other half of the balance—the assumption that fertility remained more or less constant at a high level until it began to fall with the advent of the modern small-family system. It is strange that this thesis has not been challenged more often. It is not even in accord with the established statistical record of the nineteenth century. Because of the accident that the high point in the British birth rate coincided with the Bradlaugh-Besant trial, most demographers know that in that country there had been an upward trend prior to that date. But something of the same pattern can be seen in the course of the fertility of most other West European countries. The French pattern of a steady decline in natality since the beginning of reliable records, which has often been taken as the model with which to analyze the fertility of the Western world, seems rather to be an exception.[40]

For the early modern period a statistical analysis must be based on data poor enough to make it suspect, but the hypothesis that there was a rise in fertility is strongly reinforced by what we know of the institutional changes that accompanied modernization. The Middle Ages bequeathed to the present-day Western world a social system with built-in guards against excessive procreation. Whatever their form, these were expressions of the principle that a man might not marry and beget offspring until he had established an appropriate place for himself which would enable him to carry out his family responsibilities. Perhaps the most precise form of this type of institutional check was contained in the regulations of the English guilds, which prohibited marriage during a long apprenticeship and made it difficult for a period thereafter.[41] In the Netherlands (apparently as in most other Continental countries), the control by the guilds was less rigid, but there too one function of the apprenticeship system was to prescribe, or at least to facilitate, this norm of responsible parenthood.

At any time prior to the most recent past, however, the vast majority of all populations lived in the country, and for a long-term analysis the rural institutions governing fertility demand the most attention. In the Netherlands this institution was the joint household.[42] In principle, in each generation only one person on each farm married and had children. The household also furnished a function and a home, however, for the unmarried. Whether as uncles or aunts to the farm owner's children, or as more distant relatives, or as servants and farm workers, these had a place as meaningful parts of an economic and social unit. The limitation to fertility in the joint household was efficient, but it was dependent on the maintenance of the institutional forms. As the joint household began to disintegrate, in part because in modern times the nuclear family has been more strongly emphasized, or because the unmarried hangers-on found an opportunity to escape from what they began to perceive as sexual and social frustration, it was inevitable that fertility should rise. And this rise can be demonstrated in a number of particular instances.

Generalizing from the Dutch case, we can posit the following hypothesis in place of the present theory concerning fertility trends in a Western country undergoing modernization.[43] In the *traditional family,* typical of the preindustrial period, the postponement of marriage, plus the nonmarriage of a portion of the population, constituted an onerous but efficient means of holding fertility in check. In the *proletarian family,* typical of the mass of either rural or urban workers released from the prior institutional and normative restrictions, there was no effective bar either to early marriage or to procreation. Indeed, social control was often barely strong enough to compel marriage once a child had been conceived. In the *rational family* type, which arose first among the middle classes during the nineteenth century and then gradually spread to the rest of society, a sense of parental responsibility reappeared, and with it a limitation of family size. The average age at marriage rose again, and later the same end was achieved with less privation by the use of contraceptives. Thus, in order to trace the changes in the fertility of any country, we would need statistical data on completed family size *by social class* from the seventeenth century at latest. By this time the disintegration of institutional checks to fertility, the development of new means of death control, and the resultant increase in population were all under way. These data will never become available. But such statistical records as we do have, at least in the Dutch case, support the thesis that the population growth characteristic of the modern West must be explained as the consequence of both a rise in fertility and fall in mortality.

Notes

1. See William Petersen, *Planned Migration: The Social Determinants of the Dutch-Canadian Movement* (Berkeley: University of California Press, 1955), Chapter 3.

2. For example, Amsterdam maintained a "dénombrement de tous les Protestants réfugiés" from 1681 to 1684, but discontinued it just before the revocation of the Edict of Nantes and the consequent much larger migration. During these three to four years, almost 2,000 persons were listed. See the discussion in J. G. van Dillen, "Omvang en samenstelling van de bevolking van Amsterdam in de 17e en 18e eeuw," *Bijdragen en Mededelingen der Dialecten-Commissie van de Koninklijke Nederlandse Akademie van Wetenschappen te Amsterdam*, XIV, *Bevolking en taal van Amsterdam in het verleden* (Amsterdam: Noord-Hollandsche Uitgevers Maatschappij, 1954), pp. 1–24. During the eighteenth century, many of the Sephardic (so-called "Portuguese") Jews left Holland, and were replaced by Ashkenazi Jews from Germany and Lithuania; see Ernst Baasch, *Holländische Wirtschaftsgeschichte* (Jena: Gustav Fischer, 1927), pp. 251–252.

3. Around 1500, which is almost as far back as the first records will take us, the largest city, Utrecht, had fewer than 20,000 inhabitants. Five or six others —in order of size, Leiden, Delft, Haarlem, Amsterdam, Gouda, and Dordrecht—had more than 10,000 each, and a half dozen others something under this figure. About 1550, Amsterdam and Utrecht each had about 35,000, four other cities about 20,000, eight others between 12,000 and 15,000. Shortly after 1600, Amsterdam had over 100,000 and was the largest city in the Low Countries, Leiden and Haarlem were almost half as large, three other towns had more than 20,000 each, four others more than 15,000. In the late seventeenth and eighteenth centuries, the urban growth was slower, and in some regions there was even a considerable decline from about 1750 on. See Roger Mols, *Introduction à la démographie historique des villes d'Europe du XIVe au XVIIIe siècle* (Gembloux: Duculot, 1954–1955), 2, pp. 520–523; Leonie van Nierop, *De bevolkingsbeweging der Nederlandsche stad* (Amsterdam: Binger, 1905); W. S. Unger, "De oudste Nederlandsche bevolkingsstatistiek," *Economist*, 62 (1913), pp. 745–764; Van Nierop, "De aanvang der Nederlandsche demographie," *Economisch-Historisch Jaarboek*, 5 (1919), pp. 192–208.

4. Of the men inscribed in Amsterdam's marriage registers, for instance, 51 per cent were born outside the city during the first quarter of the eighteenth century, 55 per cent in 1750, 60 per cent in 1791 (*ibid.*). These very high proportions cannot be taken, however, as in-migration rates. The migrants were undoubtedly mostly young adults and thus disproportionately represented among bridegrooms, and whatever out-migration from the city took place usually escaped being recorded. In any case, Amsterdam was not typical of Dutch cities, nor is it today. See also Van Nierop, "Het zielental

van Amsterdam in het midden van de achttiende eeuw," *Amstelodamum*, 38 (1951), pp. 151–154, where data of the same type are used to argue that the city's natural increase during the eighteenth century was nil, so that both the growth and the later decline were the consequence of migration.

5. The census of 1622 was taken to prepare for the levy of a special head tax, and earlier analysts have for this reason rejected it out of hand. But Van Dillen, who has made the most detailed study of this count, believes that the underenumeration typical of fiscal censuses was less serious than in most others, because in this case the administration was exceptionally efficient. The province was divided into twenty-three localities, each under a special commissioner who directed the precinct officials in the towns and the sheriffs in the countryside, and both of these latter groups were required to take a special oath of office. Moreover, even at this early date, the tax was a progressive one, adjusted to both the payer's income and the size of his family. See J. G. van Dillen, "Summiere staat van de in 1622 in de Provincie Holland gehouden volkstelling," *Economisch-Historisch Jaarboek*, 21 (1940), pp. 167–189.

6. A. C. de Vooys, "De bevolkingsspreiding op het Hollandse platteland in 1622 en 1795," *Tijdschrift van het Koninklijk Nederlandsch Aardrijkskundig Genootschap*, 70 (1953), pp. 316–330.

7. B. H. Slicher van Bath, *Een samenleving onder spanning: Geschiedenis van het platteland in Overijssel* (Assen: Van Gorcum, 1957), pp. 70–71. The overlap of sixteen years between columns 2 and 3 is intentional: it is not possible to fix precisely the date when the retardation in population growth began. The early population figures in this work are based on the plausible manipulation of a wide variety of local statistics. While the methodology is an interesting topic in itself, to discuss it here would take us too far afield.

8. See the graph in *ibid.*, p. 81.

9. *Ibid.*, p. 56.

10. J. C. Ramaer, "De middelpunten van bewoning in Nederland voorheen en thans," *Tijdschrift van het Koninklijk Nederlandsch Aardrijkskundig Genootschap*, 38 (1921), pp. 1–38, 174–214. The estimate was based on counts of the number of *dwellings* in various towns and in the whole of Holland Province, but more than half of the total constitutes the unmeasured rural sector of the other provinces.

11. Both sets of figures are given in United Nations, *The Determinants and Consequences of Population Trends* (New York, 1953), p. 11.

12. H. K. de Haas, "De bevolkingsgrooten gedurende de laatste eeuw," *Nederlandsch Tijdschrift voor Geneeskunde*, 94 (July 8, 1950), pp. 1972–1977. For the period 1825–1845, the calculation is based on Lobatto's study of the population of Amsterdam, which undoubtedly differed somewhat from the rest of the country in its mortality.

13. The figures are calculated from the convenient compilation in A. Polman, *Ontwikkeling en huidige stand van de sterfte in Nederland en België* (The Hague: Vereniging voor Demografie, 1951).

14. Infant mortality fluctuated around an almost constant mean from 1840 to 1880, and the age-specific rates for children and adolescents began to fall only in the 1870s. For a good discussion illustrated by a striking graph, see J. H. de Haas. "Van strijd tegen sterfte naar strijd voor gezondheid," *Wentenschap en Samenleving*, 13 (May, 1959), pp. 59–63.

15. Thomas McKeown and R. G. Brown, "Medical Evidence Related to English Population Changes in the Eighteenth Century," *Population Studies,* 9 (November, 1955), pp. 119–141.

16. Indeed, the hospital that Herman Boerhave (1668–1738) established in Leiden set a new standard for cleanliness and care of patients, but however important it was as a training center, the fact that it had fewer than two dozen beds tells how little effect it can have had on the conquest of the mortality of that time.

17. See Van Nierop, "De aanvang," *op. cit.* An interesting commentary on these works is given in two articles by A. C. de Vooys: "De opkomst van de medische geografie in Nederland," *Geografisch Tijdschrift,* 4 (1951), pp. 1–8; "Een regionale statistiek uit het begin der 19e eeuw," *ibid.,* 1 (1948), pp. 110–114.

18. I. J. Brugmans, *De arbeidende klasse in Nederland in de 19e eeuw (1813–1879),* The Hague: Nijhoff, 1925, p. 155. See also A. C. de Vooys, "De sterfte in Nederland in het midden der 19e eeuw: Een demogeografische studie," *Tijdschrift van het Koninklijk Nederlandsch Aardrijkskundig Genootschap,* 68 (1951), pp. 233–271; P. Geyl, *Geschiedenis van de Nederlandse stam (1751–1798),* Amsterdam: Wereld-Bibliotheek, 1959, 3, pp. 59–61 and *passim.*

19. Centraal Bureau voor de Statistiek, *Sterfte van kinderen beneden het jaar in elke gemeente van Nederland,* The Hague, 1910.

20. Callenfels, as cited in De Vooys, "De sterfte in Nederland," *op. cit.*

21. Compare A. M. Carr-Saunders, *The Population Problem: A Study in Human Evolution* (Oxford: Clarendon Press, 1922). The thesis of this interesting work, that the conscious restriction of fertility is characteristic of all cultures, is documented in a long bibliographical appendix in which references to ethnological works are classified under R (prolonged restriction of intercourse), A (abortion), and I (infanticide).

22. The opposition of the Catholic Church to these latter practices was vehement and specific enough to suggest that they were common. Five means of controlling family size were specifically forbidden—inducing sterility by drugs or incantations, aborting the fetus by violent exercise, killing the infant at birth, refusing to nurse one's child, and accidentally sleeping on it. See J. C. Russell, *British Medieval Population* (Albuquerque: University of New Mexico Press, 1948), p. 160. As late as the seventeenth century, when Vincent de Paul established the charitable order associated with his name, one impetus to his act was to furnish foundling hospitals as a functional substitute for the continuing high rate of infanticide.

23. This process in England is suggested by the etymology of the two words, *husband* and *anlepiman.* The word *husband* derives from two words meaning "house" and "dwell," and its original meaning (still preserved in *husbandman* and *husbandry*) was a householder, a man who had a home. The Middle English word for a single man was *anlepiman* ("only man"). These two terms, one referring to property and the other to marital status, gradually became associated as opposites, *anlepiman* coming to mean a man who had no living and therefore could not marry, and *husband* a man who was able to care for a family and therefore could get (or, eventually, was) married. See George C. Homans, *English Villagers of the Thirteenth Century* (Cambridge: Harvard University Press, 1941), Chapter 10.

24. See, e.g., G. A. Kooy, *Het veranderned gezin in Nederland: Een sociaal-*

historische studie (Leerdam: Ter Haar & Schuijt, 1957), Chapter 3 and especially p. 41.

25. G. A. Kooy, *De oude samenleving op het nieuwe platteland: Een studie over de familiehuishouding in de agrarische Achter-hoek* (Assen: Van Gorcum, 1959).

26. *Ibid.*, pp. 35–36.

27. Calculated from Table VI, *ibid.*, p. 33. This pattern was influenced in this case by a severe housing shortage, the consequence in part of war damage.

28. This situation is discussed at greater length in Petersen, *op. cit.*, pp. 103–108. See also Sjoerd Groenman, "L'asséchement du Zuiderzée et le problème de la population aux Pays Bas," *Population,* 7 (October-December, 1952), pp. 661–674; "Zuiderzee gronden en sanering van de kleine boerenbedrijven," *Landbouwkundig Tijdschrift,* 64 (January, 1952), pp. 5–14.

29. This relation between soil type and human fertility patterns has been analyzed by E. W. Hofstee in "De landbouw en de migratie," *Economisch-Statistische Berichten,* 35 (December 20, 1950), pp. 1024–1026; "De functie van de internationale migratie," *Tijdschrift voor Economische en Sociale Geografie,* 15 (January-February, 1949), pp. 10–22.

30. See E. W. Hofstee, *Het Oldambt: Een sociografie* (Groningen: Wolters, 1937), pp. 193–235. Of the several articles in which the theme of this work is analyzed more intensively, the most recent is "De ontwikkeling van de huwelijksvruchtbaarheid in het Oldambt in de periode 1880–1950," in J. Brummelkamp *et al.*, editors, *De wereld der mensen* (Groningen: Wolters, 1955), pp. 295–353. This is a report of the marital fertility of the total sample of first marriages in three townships of the Oldambt, with a detailed analysis of differentiation by social class and religion. Among the well-to-do farmers, the completed fertility fell from below four children in the last decades of the nineteenth century to about 2.5 in marriages contracted around 1910, and it has remained at approximately this level. Among agricultural workers, completed family size began at approximately six children around 1880, then fell with varying speeds according to the religious denomination. Among the small local businessmen, the trend in family size has been less clearly defined, but in general this group stands intermediate between farmers and agricultural workers.

31. E. W. Hofstee, "Regionale verscheidenheid in de ontwikkeling van het aantal geboorten in Nederland in de 2e helft van de 19e eeuw," Koninklijke Nederlandse Akademie van Wetenschappen, *Akademie-dagen,* 7 (1954), pp. 59–106. A typical instance of a certain blindness usual in earlier analyses can be seen in a paper by the highly competent demographer and former director of the Central Bureau of Statistics, H. W. Methorst. In an article published in 1913 he compared the trend in birth rates in townships with more than and fewer than 20,000 inhabitants—a rough but sufficiently accurate differentiation between "urban" and "rural." According to his data, the urban birth rate was higher until 1890, the two were almost identical at the end of the 1890's, and only in the twentieth century was the urban birth rate lower. Yet his analysis is limited to a discussion of the very latest trend. See H. W. Methorst, "Nederlandsche bevolkingsstatistiek," *Economist,* 62 (1913), pp. 126–154, 250–259, 367–400.

32. So long as apprenticeship entailed living in the master craftsman's home-workshop, which was passed on from father to one son, the similarities with the system in the countryside were clear, though the number of persons

affected was of course smaller. Some of the heterogeneity supposedly typical of urban life can be discerned in Dutch cities, but until well into the modern period the guilds—or at least the style of economic organization that they represented—remained one important factor. They were in decline in the eighteenth century, but toward its end there were still 51 trade and craft guilds in Amsterdam, for example. Guilds were formally abolished during the French occupation, but remnants of the system persisted into the 19th century. See Cornelius Wiskerke, *De afschaffing der gilden in Nederland* (Amsterdam: Paris, 1938); A. J. M. Brouwer Ancher, *De gilden* (The Hague: Loman & Funke, 1895).

33. The degree to which this is the case can be illustrated by an article by van Nierop that, with painstaking effort, has winnowed every bit of information from the marriage records in Amsterdam for the last decades of the 16th century. As is generally the case until national compilations of civil records began in the middle of the last century, direct data on age at marriage were scarce and deficient in the Amsterdam records, and a number of complicating factors made it difficult even to estimate the trend. See Leonie van Nierop, "De bruidegoms van Amsterdam van 1578 tot 1601," *Tijdschrift voor Geschiedenis,* 48 (1933), pp. 337–359; 49 (1934), pp. 136–160; 52 (1937), pp. 144–162.

34. This was true of the Netherlands until about 1870, although apparently less so than of some other countries. See J. H. van Zanten and T. van den Brink, *Population Phenomena in Amsterdam in Comparison with Other Big Towns,* Statistical Communication No. 103a (Amsterdam: Municipal Bureau of Statistics, 1939), pp. 4–39.

35. In contrast to rural Ireland, there is apparently no impetus to the early marriage of the heir. In Ireland the young man takes over the management of the farm when he gets married, but in the Netherlands one of the frequent sources of friction noted in recent publications is that, on the contrary, even responsible family men are still given no voice in running the property. In some areas—for example, the bulb-growing region in Holland Province—fathers try to keep all their sons single as long as possible, paying them small wages for long hours of work. See, e.g., I. Gadourek, *A Dutch Community: Social and Cultural Structure and Process in a Bulb-Growing Region in the Netherlands,* Netherlands Institute of Preventive Medicine, Publication XXX (Leiden: Stenfert Kroese, 1956), pp. 173–174. The effect of this practice on fertility is ambivalent, however, for while marriage is postponed, each horticulturist has an economic incentive to have many sons, which reinforces his traditional, often Catholic, morality.

36. This is the literal translation of "venster vrijen," one of the terms by which the custom is designated in Dutch. Most books on the family written in English pass lightly over this important element of the West European cultural tradition. The best general account is by a Swede: K. R. V. Wikman, *Die Einleitung der Ehe: Eine vergleichende ethno-soziologische Untersuchung über die Vorstufe der Ehe in den Sitten des schwedischen Volkstums,* Acta Academiae Aboensis, Humaniora XI.1 (Abo: Abo Akademi, 1937). As *"fensterln"* the custom is well known in Bavaria and Austria. [Ed. note.]

37. Kooy, *Het veranderend gezin . . ., op. cit.,* p. 146.

38. In the village of Staphorst, for example, of the eighty-seven first births in 1937–1938, thirty-four were within seven months of the marriage ceremony. In the 1920s, a number of ministers cooperated in a determined effort to

stamp out the practice and fulminated from their pulpits against the young people who spent Saturday night in sin and then came to church on Sunday morning. Finally they succeeded—but only in having the traditional night for "window wooing" changed to Friday. See Sjoerd Groenman, *Staphorst: Sociografie van een gesloten gemeenschap* (Meppel: Stenvert, 1948) [?], pp. 96, 153ff.

39. In Amsterdam, for example, almost one out of every five births was illegitimate for the period 1811–1824, the earliest for which this information is available, and the percentage remained high until the last quarter of the century. See "Statistiek der bevolking van Amsterdam tot 1921," *Mededeelingen van het Bureau van Statistiek der Gemeente Amsterdam,* 67, 1923.

40. See, e.g., Gerhard Mackenroth, *Bevölkerungslehre: Theorie, Soziologie und Statistik der Bevölkerung* (Berlin: Springer, 1953), pp. 122–134. This section is divided into two parts, the first on the general development of fertility in Northwest and Central Europe, the second on the reasons for the exceptional development in France.

41. "Apprenticeship in its fully grown Elizabethan form requires that those learning any trade then practiced in England should serve an apprenticeship for seven years or until he was twenty-four years of age, with the possible exception of agriculture in which it was sufficient that he should attain the age of twenty-one if the parties had been unable to agree on twenty-four. It is clear that these provisions were looked upon quite as much as a check on the exuberance of youth as essential for the technical education of the country." G. Talbot Griffith, *Population Problems of the Age of Malthus* (Cambridge: Cambridge University Press, 1926), p. 112.

42. In their excellent analysis of the interrelation among social structures, family type, and fertility, Davis and Blake argue, on the contrary, that a joint household favors high fertility. This is indeed the case in classical China and India, the examples they use to illustrate their thesis. In such a household, marriage and procreation are feasible as soon as they are physiologically possible, for the supervision of household affairs does not depend on the social maturity of each individual couple. See Kingsley Davis and Judith Blake, "Social Structure and Fertility: An Analytical Framework," *Economic Development and Cultural Change,* 4 (April, 1956), pp. 211–235. Krause is presently analyzing the relation between the joint household and fertility in eighteenth-century England.

43. The following discussion derives largely from Hofstee, "Regionale verscheidenheid," *op. cit.* Hofstee acknowledges a debt to Mackenroth (*op. cit.,* p. 474), who in turn notes that a germ of the hypothesis is to be found in Malthus.

Reinhard Bendix   THE IDEOLOGY OF THE

                                     MASTERS IN RUSSIA

IN EIGHTEENTH-CENTURY RUSSIA the Tsars retained their autocratic supremacy despite the increasing authority of the landed aristocracy and despite its
absolute power over the serfs. By using the premises of autocratic rule for
its own ends, the popular protest of the masses had a similar political effect.
I shall turn now to a consideration of the ideologies which emerged from these
social and political relations among the Tsar, the aristocracy, and the serfs,
and which had a direct effect upon the relations between employers and
workers. These considerations will carry us well into the nineteenth century,
for the class relations and ideologies which had come to prevail during the
eighteenth century remained relatively unaffected by the political developments up to the emancipation of the serfs in 1861.

Toward the end of the eighteenth century, different types of economic
enterprises existed side by side. Enterprises of the state were either managed
by officials of the government or leased to private entrepreneurs. Manufacturing enterprises and the so-called mountain works were located on the landed
estates of the aristocracy. And commercial or industrial enterprises were in
the hands of foreign or native merchants and manufacturers. The agents and
owners who managed these enterprises exercised their power over the serfs
and the free laborers on the assumption that nothing but ill will and laziness
could be expected of them. Work, they believed, was the result of fear, and
punishments must be cruel and frequent, or else fear, and hence the stimulus
to labor, would diminish. Of course, there were exceptions; wherever the exercise of power over subordinates is absolute and arbitrary, it can be benevolent as well as tyrannical. And it may be that the chances for benevolence
were greater among those managers whose wealth and social position were
very secure, and consequently relieved them of all pressures which in others
would aggravate their exercise of power. Among the landowners the chances
for a benevolent treatment of the peasant serfs increased also, wherever such
treatment would enhance the commercial and productive enterprises among
the serfs and hence accrue to the benefit of the masters. Such due allowances
should certainly be made, but they merely take account of individual idiosyn-
crasies. The chances for moral conduct in the mass are probably greatest

Reprinted with permission from *Work and Authority in Industry: Ideologies of Management in the Course of Industrialization,* by Reinhard Bendix (New York: John Wiley and Sons,
1956).

when they are favored by the general conditions of a social order, and such conditions did not exist in eighteenth- and nineteenth-century Russia.

Several documents illustrate the prevailing ideologies of the masters. In 1717 Peter the Great ordered the translation of a German manual entitled *The True Mirror of Youth or Instructions in Etiquette*. Along with illuminating instructions on how to behave in public, the young nobleman was advised how he should treat his servants. He should converse in a foreign language so as to distinguish himself from "various numskulls" and to prevent servants from understanding what he said. He should not speak with servants more than was necessary. And he should not trust them, for they distort what they hear and they divulge secrets.

> He who keeps good discipline in his household is served well and respectfully, for the slaves are by nature impolite, stubborn, and shameless. Therefore, it is necessary to break their spirit and to humiliate them.[1]

These instructions referred originally to the treatment of domestic servants. But the Russian translation referred instead to "slaves." Its popularity suggests that the Russian readers perceived little or no difference between unruly domestic "slaves" and the mass of peasant serfs. The whole approach implied a sense of rank-order, which was expressed with classic simplicity over a hundred years later in the address of an aristocratic landowner to his peasants.

> I am your master, and my master is the Emperor. The Emperor can issue his commands to me, and I must obey him; but he issues no commands to you. I am the Emperor upon my estate; I am your God in this world, and I have to answer for you to the God above.[2]

The implications of this ideology for the relation between the employer and his workmen are revealed in a report by John Perry, an English engineer who had been engaged by Peter the Great to act as supervisor of canal construction and of other projects. Perry observed that peasant serfs who were skilled craftsmen would anxiously hide their ability at all times. It was apparent that they anticipated an even more intensified exploitation by their masters, if their ability became known. In Perry's judgment, the major obstacle to improvement was the practice of demanding work without wages.

> . . . this being the custom of Russia, when I have made my utmost application for the encouragement of some few persons who have been really ingenious, that they might have but a copeck a day reward allow'd them to animate the rest, I have received for answer, particularly by my lord Apraxin . . . that there was no such precedent for the giving of money out of the Czar's treasure for men to do their duty for which they were sent; but in the place of it they had batoags that grew in Russia, and if they did not do their work, when requir'd, they must be beaten to it.[3]

A similar attitude is revealed by a set of instructions which a landowner, Count P. A. Rumiantsev, gave to his estate steward in 1751. The Count was a military man who conceived of the household order on his estate after the manner of a commander in the army. Serfs were to receive the most severe penalties for every misdemeanor. Petty theft, for example, was to be punished by loss of property, flagellation with whips, and consignment to the army, penalties which the legal code reserved for such crimes as brigandage or arson. For insulting a master the serfs were to be beaten with rods until the insulted person was satisfied, aside from a fine of two rubles to the master.[4] General practices such as the trade in serfs and the frequent disregard of court jurisdiction in criminal cases or special evils such as the breakup of peasant families went unchecked.

Such absolute power of the masters over their serfs was interpreted as a principle of government which supported the established social order. Consequently, proposed reforms concerning the serfs were persistently rejected on the ground that nothing should be done to interfere with the power of the landowners. According to one critic, a grant of rights to the peasants would only mean that the landowners might violate the law, a contingency that could be avoided, obviously, if no rights were granted.[5] Even masters who had committed crimes against their serfs, like murder or rape, were immune from prosecution, though such crimes were legally prohibited. The law forbade the serfs to enter complaints against their masters, and the police officials, who were ordered to uphold the law, would not proceed against members of the aristocracy. It is significant that the serfs had only one right which limited the power of their masters, and that right was a duty. The serfs were obliged to bring complaints against their masters in case the latter had committed crimes against the state.[6] Hence, the subjugation of the serfs was limited by the interests of the state. Yet, many actions of the masters interfered with these interests, even if they did not constitute crimes against the state. And the simultaneous effort of the Tsars to safeguard these interests *and* to support the preeminent position of the aristocracy led to an ambivalent approach to the governmental control of labor relations.

A Senate investigation of privately owned mountain works under Catherine II illustrates the dilemma.[7] According to an official memorandum, the major task was to bring the peasants "into the usual slavish obedience." Where disturbances continued, a manifesto of the Empress was to be read to the peasants, according to which "those who oppose our authority resist God." Such declarations and the presence of military forces were frequently insufficient, however, and the ideology of leading Tsarist officials is revealed in their "solution" of the recurrent difficulties in the mountain works. In her Manifesto Catherine II revealed herself as the protector of all her subjects.

Our just and merciful intention is to correct the simple and those who have fallen into error, to defend those against whom offenses have been committed, and to avoid direct aggression against the peasants by administering the works to their advantage, paying them according to their labor, or allowing them to go from the works as may be found more advantageous for their own welfare and for the safety of the works.

In her instructions, however, the Empress directed Prince Vyazemsky to punish the peasants for their insubordination, and then to inquire into their grievances. If owners or their managers were found to be at fault, then these individuals should be punished also. Punishment of individuals in the highest ranks was reserved for the Empress. Moreover, the instructions added the observation that owners or managers should not be punished except in the most extreme cases, because otherwise the peasants might become too proud. And if their offenses were relatively minor, then punishment should be administered in secret, so that "the simple people might not be given a motive to step out of servility."[8] Apparently, the need of the government to correct the abuses of the owners was checked at every point by the fear that the "insolence of the peasants" would gain the upper hand.

Since the government was unable and unwilling to penalize highly placed persons, it tended to avoid the issue by entrusting the management of mountain works to its own officials. In the period from 1762 to 1796 the number of serfs in the mountain works of the Treasury increased almost three times, while in the privately owned works it increased only by a little more than one-half.[9] The reason for this discrepancy was that the government found itself unable to transfer these works to private ownership despite the fact that whole villages would be ascribed to the new owner and all necessary equipment would be furnished as well. Apparently, the aristocratic landowners who were so favored either shunned the obligation to make payments and deliveries to the government or they failed to meet these obligations through the inefficiency of their agents. Thus, when Count Shuvalov died, two of his mountain works owed the Treasury 600,000 rubles, and the government resumed operation in an attempt to obtain partial payment of the arrears which had accumulated.[10] The need of the government to receive deliveries from these enterprises, however, was only one of the reasons why most of them remained under the management of officials.

An equally important reason was the fact that the treatment of the ascribed workers deteriorated seriously when these mountain works were transferred from the Treasury into the hands of private owners. Such transfers were accompanied by drastic reduction in wages, by the employment of artisans who had been exempt from such service, by the prohibition of work outside the enterprise which had been permitted before by payment in kind rather than money, by arbitrary removal over great distances, and many others.[11] Of course, the government officials who managed the mountain works of the Treasury probably were as inefficient and corrupt as the agents of private owners. And government officials as well as private agents conceived of the peasant serfs as chattels to be exploited for the benefit of the owner, whether he was the Tsar or a private landlord. The difference between these two groups was therefore by no means clear-cut, but it was significant none-theless. The private owner of a mine or his agent could be single-minded in the exploitation of his serfs, because he could always count upon the aid of the military authorities to protect life and property against uprisings of the peasant serfs. Government officials, however, were responsible themselves for the success or failure of their management. Their somewhat greater leniency may have been due, therefore, to the recognition that the brutal treatment of serfs led time and again to disturbances the government was called upon to suppress.

If the government continued for the most part to have its own officials manage the mountain works because it could not control the actions of the landed aristocracy, the same reasoning did not apply to the enterprises of merchants and manufacturers. The supervision of these "possessional factories" may be contrasted, therefore, with the virtual absence of supervision with regard to the aristocratic owners of mountain works. Owners of "possessional" enterprises were not permitted to dissolve them, or to sell the ascribed workers without also selling the enterprise, or to transfer these workers to a different enterprise, or to change the organization of production, or to limit output. No change of ownership was permitted without prior authorization by the government. The workers who had been ascribed to the enterprise were to be paid a "sufficient" wage, though the government granted the owners the right to determine the wage rate and the length of the working day. Workers were also given official permission to petition against the regulations of the owners. The government reserved the right to dispossess the owner of a "possessional factory," for example, when he discontinued production. And the government threatened to emancipate the workers if the owner employed the workers as domestic servants rather than in production.[12] This public regulation of the employment relationship had the same purpose as the public management of the mountain works: to safeguard the production of goods needed by the government. And it simply reflected the weak position of middle-class entrepreneurs that the government sought to regulate their power over the workers but made no comparable attempt to regulate the landowners' power over their serfs.[13]

To be sure, these regulations were frequently not enforced, and the employers acted as if their powers over the workers were the same as those of the landowners. But the assumption that the government would determine the organization of labor and of production had far-reaching consequences even if opinions concerning this role of the government varied widely. In 1818, officials of the Ministry of the Interior stated that the unrest of workers in the "possessional" enterprises was due to the failure of the government to regulate

. . . the reciprocal relations and duties of owners and workers. Wages still depend upon the arbitrary decisions of the owner, who naturally proceeds in a selfish manner, since he is not obliged to give an accounting to the government. . . .

By the same token the workers are lazy, which in turn leads to penalties and corporal punishment, and that gives them the excuse to address wailing protests to the government.

Only a thoroughgoing regulation of all the "possessional" enterprises would put an end to this. Yet, the same Ministry was of a different opinion eight years later (1826). By then the regulation of the largest "possessional" enterprises had been attempted in view of the interminable complaints by owners about workers and by workers about owners. This had not solved the problem, however, for aside from the specific problems involved there was this basic difficulty:

> The factory regulations set down how the owner should use his workers; hence the latter have an excuse to think of themselves as independent and to resist their master as soon as he undertakes anything at all. . . . The workers imagine that they are not obliged to produce for their master unless this is stipulated in the regulation. Hence, the authority of the owner is held by them in little esteem.[14]

Thus, the officials would vacillate between the attempt to regulate everything and the recognition that regulations produced more problems than they solved. And this vacillation was necessarily increased by employers who wanted the government to aid their exploitation of the work force and by aristocratic spokesmen who would criticize the conduct of these employers and represent themselves (on these occasions) as paternalistic protectors of the serfs.[15]

Such varied opinions were necessarily reflected in the actual regulation of the employment relationship. Officials of the central government tended to favor the middle-class entrepreneur, since deliveries to the government depended upon the continuity of production. Local administrators, on the other hand, were concerned with maintaining peace and order, aside from their general antagonism to middle-class employers, and they would at times placate the workers by listening to their complaints.[16] Thus, self-interest and expediency governed the actions of those concerned with the relations between employers and workers. Yet such considerations led to consequences which transcended expediency. Employers, officials, and landowners were unanimous in the belief that "it is necessary to break the spirit [of the workers] and to humiliate them." But the conflict of interest among them prevented a clearcut approach to factory regulation, which alternated rather between attempts to supervise the employers as well as the workers in response to the complaints from both sides and efforts to ensure the complete subordination of the workers to their employers. The resulting uncertainty of the masters encouraged among the workers the familiar idea, compounded of expediency and sincere conviction, that their cruel suffering was the work of officials who abused their authority. The workers believed above all that the supreme authority of the Tsar gave the government the power and the responsibility to right their wrongs, while it gave the people the right to petition the Tsar. Thus, the ideologies of the masters not only committed the government to certain lines of action, but also gave rise to expectations among the masses. It will be useful to examine the resulting interaction of officials, employers, and workers, for their conflicting beliefs established the basic pattern of labor management in the more developed industry of the later nineteenth century.

On the basis of files in the Ministry of Finance, Tugan-Baranowski surveyed the history of unrest in twenty-three "possessional" enterprises, and his findings, which cover the period from the 1790s to the 1840s, give an insight into the practical implications of the ideologies I have discussed. Low wages were the most frequent source of unrest, especially where free workers were employed also, since the latter earned often twice as much as the "possessional" workers. Complaints were frequent also with reference to the penalties and deductions which were imposed by the employers. In other cases unrest was occasioned by the work conditions imposed on children or on the aged and infirm, such as a fifteen- to seventeen-hour day in the winter. Again, some of the very old workers were simply deprived of all wages. There were complaints about cruel mistreatment, complaints against the military recruitment of workers in lieu of the serfs belonging to the employer, against the sale of workers' families to estate owners, against the use of land belonging to the workers in the interest of the employers, against the employment of workers on other tasks than factory labor, against the refusal to issue passports[17] to workers, against prohibiting women to marry persons outside the factory's work force, and so on. The long list reflects typical complaints of workers in the early phases of industrialization as well as the peculiar problems arising from the use of forced labor in the Russian factories of the late eighteenth and early nineteenth centuries.[18]

It is of interest to see how the Tsarist government handled these recurrent complaints, and in the case of several factories Tugan-Baranowski presents case histories of "labor relations" for a fifty-year period. One of these concerns the "possessional" enterprise of Osokin in Kazan, in which a total of 1,400 ascribed workers were employed. A schematic tabulation of this case history provides us with a summary view of the interaction among officials, employers, and workers, even though the case involved "possessional" workers only.[19] In the overwhelming majority of instances the authorities sided with the employers, and met the protest of the workers with dire warnings and severe punishments. In a few cases the government recognized the justice of a complaint against the employer. But more important than the partiality of the officials was the *assumption of employers and workers alike that the government and even the Tsar personally would determine their rights and obligations.* Hence, employers looked to the authorities for support in their dealings with recalcitrant workers, while the workers appealed to the same authorities to hear their grievances and protect them against abuse and exploitation.

Efforts by the authorities to stabilize the relations between employers and workers by comprehensive regulations (e.g., the rules established in 1818) were of no avail. By these rules the authorities sought to secure for the employer his absolute power over the workers. And since they identified his power with the security of the established order, they would consistently refuse the petitions of the workers and indeed deny them the right of petition. Yet, this position of the government was inherently unstable. By its comprehensive regulation of the relations between employers and workers the government asserted its ultimate authority over both groups, and then it proceeded to to use this authority to grant complete powers to the employers and deny all rights to the workers. Both of these actions had their rationale. The Tsarist government was in the hands of aristocrats, who could never consent to grant to a middle-class employer the same absolute power which they regarded as an exclusive prerogative of the aristocracy; hence, the employer's actions had to be regulated. The same officials were also concerned with safeguarding the established order: hence, the employer must have complete authority over his workers and all petitions against him must be denied. It is not surprising that the workers in effect utilized this inherent contradiction. They would accept the autocratic supremacy of the Tsar and seek to enlist it on behalf of a control over the employers. The government could not explicitly reject this demand; it could only declare that it was the Tsar's arbitrary will to give absolute power to the employer. But by their astonishing perseverance in the face of all methods of oppression, the workers helped to establish, albeit unwittingly and in the long run, that it was impossible for the Tsar to assert his absolute authority and to divest himself of it at one and the same time. This "limitation" of autocratic power had a profound impact upon the relations between employers and workers, for eventually it compelled the Tsarist government to extend rather than restrict its regulation of manufacturing enterprises.

Notes

1. Quoted in George V. Plekhanov, *A History of Russian Social Thought* (Vol. 16 of transl. into English of Foreign Social Science Monographs; New York, Columbia University, mimeo., 1938), p. 21; see also pp. 18–22, in addition to V. O. Kluchevsky, *A History of Russia* (New York: E. P. Dutton and Company, 1912), Vol. IV, pp. 259–60.
2. Cited in Baron von Haxthausen, *The Russian Empire, Its People, Institutions, and Resources* (London: Chapman and Hall, 1856), Vol. I, p. 335.
3. John Perry, "The State of Russia," in Peter Putnam, ed., *Seven Britons in Imperial Russia* (Princeton: Princeton University Press, 1952), p. 61. Apraxin was an admiral in the Russian navy under Peter the Great.
4. See Kluchevsky, *op. cit.*, Vol. V, pp. 82–83, where this and other examples are cited.
5. See J. Engelmann, *Die Leibeigenschaft* (Leipzig: Duncker & Humblot, 1884), pp. 134–51.

6. *Ibid.*, pp. 155–56. It is in keeping with the character of autocratic rule that the one right of the serfs was officially regarded as a duty, while the "rights" of the aristocracy were, in fact, privileges inasmuch as they were subject to an arbitrary revocation by the Tsar.

7. Like others, this investigation, in 1762, was initiated as a result of local uprisings and numerous petitions. Of course, the distinction between petitions and uprisings often depended on how officials chose to regard the petitions submitted to them.

8. Quotations from the Manifesto and the instructions in James Mavor, *An Economic History of Russia* (New York: E. P. Dutton and Company, 1914), I, pp. 454–55. It may be added that some managers and clerks of the mountain works were actually punished, though superior officials were not. Vyazemsky was also reluctant to find those responsible for the deaths of peasants from beating. Cf. *ibid.*, Vol. I, p. 461. The investigation of Prince Vyazemsky was greeted by the peasants in the expectation that finally the Empress herself had decided to right all wrongs. When their previous condition was confirmed by the highest authority instead, the peasants became ready to join Pugachev. See *ibid.*, pp. 464–65.

9. The figures are respectively: from 99,000 to 241,000 and from 43,000 to 71,000. See Mavor, *op. cit.*, Vol. I, pp. 441, 493, cited on p. 144, n. 53.

10. And this action led in turn to disturbances among the peasants, who claimed that an edict of the government had limited their period of service, and that they were consequently free to leave. Of course, no such edict existed, but the resumption of government operations sufficed for rumors to start. See *ibid.*, Vol. I, pp. 473–74.

11. *Ibid.*, Vol. I, p. 495. Other examples are given on the following pages.

12. These details are given in M. Tugan-Baranowski, *Geschichte der russischen Fabrik* (Berlin: Emil Felber, 1900), pp. 130–31. The official sanction of the right to petition was formally revoked in 1767 with reference to aristocratic landowners, but not with regard to middle-class entrepreneurs; however, petitions continued to be submitted regardless of whether they were allowed or prohibited.

13. *Ibid.*, p. 29. While the entrepreneurs had been permitted in 1736 to discipline the ascribed workers by corporal punishment, all further penalties were to be administered by governmental authorities to whom "delinquent" workers were to be handed over by their employers.

14. Quoted in Tugan-Baranowski, *op. cit.*, 137–40.

15. The details of this controversy are given in *ibid.*, pp. 190–95, 198–201.

16. *Ibid.*, p. 194.

17. Instituted by the Tsarist government in an effort to regulate internal migration and to ensure the collection of taxes.

18. *Ibid.*, pp. 159–62.

19. I treat this case history as representative for these reasons. It is one of several contained in Tugan-Baranowski, and all of these tell the same story. Also, it gives the same picture as the material on privately owned mountain works, to which reference has been made, if allowance is made for the difference of rural and urban location and the consequent differences in the labor problem. It is further in keeping with the logic of the situation arising from the relations among officials, employers, aristocratic landowners, and workers, which have been analyzed.

Rupert B. Vance   SECURITY AND ADJUSTMENT: THE
RETURN TO THE LARGER
COMMUNITY

ADJUSTMENT RATHER THAN SECURITY, we are occasionally told, should be
the keynote of public policy. Social security is a static concept, one that
encounters the risk of failure whenever it attempts to use the social surplus
to underwrite inefficient economic arrangements. On the other hand, adjustment, however drastic, is regarded as more dynamic in that it impels men to
seek the remedy for their own undesirable situations. Thus, an overall program of social security might use the insuring capacity of the economy to hold
people in stranded communities and overcrowded occupations. Social adjustment forces upon each individual the necessity of a decision as to whether
he shall change his occupation or migrate to an area in command of greater
resources.

It is not the intention of this paper to defend social security by a frontal
attack on the theory of social adjustment. The concept of adjustment has too
large and respectable a place in the history of economic and social theory for
such summary treatment. In mechanics, adjustment means realignment of
parts to promote better functioning of the whole. In biology the term in its
wider usage has come to denote that adaptation of organisms to the environment and each other that comprises the subject matter of ecology—a usage
that has been accepted by sociology and extended to social and psychological
relationships. In economics the wider meaning is mechanistic, corresponding
to the analysis of economic equilibrium. In this discussion, however, we are
not concerned with specific questions of the market, of supply and demand
and price relationships, but simply with the adjustment of individuals to a
changing institutional order. It is, of course, in the institutional phases of
economics that we should expect the discipline to develop a doctrine closely
related to the theory of social adjustment.

Adjustment is a process; security is a status—the goal, whether attained
or not, of the process of adjustment. It is the thesis of this paper, however,
that social security, instead of representing a new goal made possible by the

Read before the Eighth Annual Meeting of the Southern Sociological Society in Atlanta,
Georgia, March 31, 1944. The first draft of this paper, a memorandum to the Social Security
Board to which the author was then consultant, was written at the suggestion of Walton Hale
Hamilton, then Director of the Bureau of Research and Statistics for the Board. It was published,
in a revised form, in *Social Forces*, Vol. 22, No. 4 (May 1944), pp. 363–370, and is reprinted
here with the permission of the author and of *Social Forces*.

economic surplus afforded by modern industrialism, represents the return to an accepted value developed in the local community. In the feudal manor and the guild system, society was regarded as a human community, not as an impersonal mechanism, continually adjusting and readjusting. This earlier concept of security, all the more remarkable in that it was attained at the low level of customary status in a niggardly domestic economy, conforms to what we know of security in primitive society.

England's Road to Social Security[1] in her experience with the break up of the manor and the guilds, the development of the Poor Law System, the emergence of the Industrial Revolution, and the final enactment of social insurance well shows the nature of this transition. To trace the running fight between the values of security and adjustment in this transition from the community of status to impersonal society would no doubt demand that we telescope a half century of history.

Break Up of the Manor

The opening of the sixteenth century found England on the verge of the agrarian revolution, the break up of the manor. Perfected under feudalism and introduced into England by William the Conqueror, this system of landholding had developed two main classes: the landholders and the servile laborers. The feudal manor was a unit of government as well as of tillage, having as responsible head the lord of the manor. Theoretically the lord had the disposal of the land and its tenants; actually the manor was, as the Hammonds have pointed out, essentially a cooperative agricultural community in which custom and tradition regulated even the methods of agriculture. As a social system the manor provided security; but as an economic organization its usages and customs restricted efficiency, for they hindered adjustments to change.[2]

Men belonged to the land and in a measure land belonged by tradition to the serfs who tilled it. The servile laborers also belonged to a community and the community belonged to them in the sense that it functioned in their behalf. Under the system of feudal land tenure the obligation of the serf to work on the manor implied his right to maintenance. The worker did not merely receive a day's pay for a day's work; he was reasonably sure of a lifetime of economic support in return for the services of his working life on the manor. Mass poverty was great, but there were no wandering poor; the hazards of war, pestilence, and recurring scarcity were present, but in this community it remained true that, as long as there was security for one, there was a measure of economic security for all. There was no unemployment and the helpless aged were not thrown out to starve.

This social order was broken down by the transition to pecuniary standards. Commerce in agricultural products replaced subsistence agriculture. The prestige of the lord, as it came to pass, was no longer determined by the numbers of his retainers but by the amount of his income. Lords with armies of retainers were already "land poor" when the profit from sheep farming came to outweigh the returns that might be secured from working the servile population under the self-sufficing nonpecuniary economy of the manor.

The wool trade, the introduction of large scale sheep farming, and the enclosure movement displaced thousands. It resulted, write the Webbs, "in the rise in England of the Tudor Kings of a new class of men, the 'poor' who had no claim on the manor or on any feudal superior for subsistence."[3] The classic statement of this case has been made by the Hammonds: "The enclosures created a new organization of classes. The peasant with rights and a status, with a share in the fortunes and government of his village, standing in rags but standing on his feet, makes way for the laborer with no corporate rights to defend, no property to cherish, no ambition to pursue, bent beneath the fear of his masters and the weight of a future without hope."[4] The transition from a community of status to adjustment in an impersonal society was under way.

The movement was more than a transition from a subsistence to a commercial agriculture; it was aided and abetted by other factors. Men were detached from their anchorage to place and custom by the demands of kings and nobles for recruits for their armies. When the armies were disbanded many of these recruits became wandering vagrants. The recurring epidemics of plagues, culminating in the Black Death, limited the supply of laborers and soldiers and created demands that tore men from their accustomed place and occupation. Needs existed in the growth of towns for manual workers in trade and manufactures. With the expansion of commerce and industry the rulers of England, write the Webbs, connived at the escape of people out of serfdom, since the hired man proved the superior in efficiency to the bondsman in agriculture, in war and in industry.[5]

Sir F. M. Eden in 1797 pointed out that the uprooting of a great body of people continually in a state of destitution coincided with the creation of a numerous class dependent for livelihood entirely on being hired for day labor at wages. In a passage that deserves quoting at length he wrote:

When the nation consisted principally of the two classes of landholders and servile cultivators, the latter had, at least in ordinary times, a fund to which they could resort for maintenance; and although they could not acquire property, they were, in general, certain of food because it was the obvious interest of those who could command their services to provide for their support. A West Indian island, perhaps, is a picture of the condition of the agricultural class in this country soon after the conquest. The proprietor of a sugar plantation . . . is bound to feed the Negroes belonging to his establishment, whether they are disabled by sickness, accident, or old age. . . . The capital stock of Yorkshire is perhaps ten times as great as that of the Island of Jamaica; and the number of those who, in that part of England, have no visible means of support and subsist entirely on charity, I doubt not exceeds those in Jamaica of a similar description, in as great a proportion. Rousseau justly inquires, "Why is it that in a thriving city the poor are so miserable, whilst such extreme distress is hardly ever experienced in those countries where there are no instances of extreme wealth?"[6]

The loss of security for the working class was not regretted on every side. The Webbs feel that the multiplication of poverty was not regarded with entire disfavor by the rulers of England. "Everyone but an idiot," wrote Arthur Young,[7] "knows that the lower classes must be kept poor or they will never be industrious." The author of the *Fable of the Bees* drew a moral to the same effect. "The poor," he wrote, "have nothing to stir them to labor, but their wants, which it is wisdom to relieve but folly to cure." Wrote the inventor of the modern police system, "Without a large proportion of poverty, there could be no riches, since riches are the offsprings of labor while labor can only result from a state of poverty."[8]

The Poor Laws

With free laborers accordingly came the destitute and with the destitute came that remarkable development of the English Poor Laws, directed against the displaced farmers which the law came to call "sturdy beggars." In the history of the Poor Laws, say the Webbs, we have a history of the relations between what Disraeli termed, "The two nations over which the kings and queens of England ruled, namely, the rich and the poor."[9] For our purposes it is not necessary to trace this history in detail. The earliest group of laws relating to the poor, the Statute of Laborers, contained methods of thrusting the free laborer back into the social status (at least) of the serfdom from which he had escaped. The earliest law for relief of the poor, found in the statutes of Henry VIII in 1531 was significantly entitled: "How Aged, Poor, and Impotent Persons Compelled to Live by Alms Shall Be Ordered." It did no more than direct that the justices shall give the impotent poor licenses to beg and see that each is assigned a defined district.[10]

In the main, however, the penal statutes threatened dire punishment to sturdy beggars, sought to make labor compulsory, and disciplined those who were without work. The point can well be made in the early period that, instead of moving into the free play of social adjustment, the displaced laborer escaped one level of social control only to fall into another. "As his plight grew worse," write the Hammonds, "game laws, vagrancy laws, and settlement laws were drawn more tightly around the laborer's life and liberty. He became a kind of public serf at the disposal of the parish overseer, maintaining himself by poaching and stealing when his allowance no longer kept him."[11] With thousands of unemployed roaming the country the various penalties proved impossible to enforce. Repression was attended with attempted generosity, and laws for the ordering of the poor came to be subjected to abuses from both sides.

It is interesting to note that even the much abused Law of Settlement and Removal (13 and 14 Charles II, 1662) with its succeeding legislation grew out of the accepted doctrine that every person, serf or freedman, was a member of some local community to which he owed obligation, and from which he was entitled to expect some measure of protection and, when in need, some undefined support. Out of such a wholesome basis in the local community's responsibility for the security of its members, grew the whole system whereby officials shunted the poor from parish to parish in the effort to escape responsibility.

The case for a national instead of a local interest in the dependent is shown by the social effect of giving parishes the legal right to remove certain classes who were likely to become public charges. One device of the overseers to prevent the increase of their chargeable poor was to hinder the marriage of poor persons by encouraging the destruction of cottages. The result of this action to restrict the marriage of the poor was to encourage the growth of bastardy. Bastardy, as such it may be remarked in passing, was not an offense against the laws of England, but for the poor to have illegitimate children was an offense against the Poor Law since it was likely to raise the parish rates. Illegitimate children became burdens on the parish and a succession of laws were passed with the view of forcing parents to provide for support of their illegitimate offspring.

The procedure, after 1733, was to take the oath of the woman before a Justice as to the father of her child and to arrest the man, who was then forced to give security for its support. Many opportunities for abuse existed. Pregnant women were sent back to place of settlement in time for delivery, for bastards took the settlement of the parish where they were born. If possible, her own parish likewise turned the unfortunate mother adrift and every other parish hounded her out. If parishes failed to rid themselves of such women before delivery, an affiliation order was served on the putative father. There followed the imprisonment of the reputed fathers, the forced marrying between parents, or the punishment of women. The whole attitude toward the question was absolutely nonmoral, yet the stringency failed to suppress bastardy. The whole procedure serves to show the effect of leaving the administration of poor laws to small local units.[12]

The effect of confining responsibility to the local community was to prevent the free play of adjustment within the larger society. Thus the Act of Settlement penalized the development of the country by depriving the laborer of any incentive to look for work outside his parish and by terrifying him with the harsh provisions of the vagrancy laws. It also brutalized the administration of the act. Dorothy Marshall concludes: "To have bullied the helpless, corrupted the children, and polluted the moral life of the countryside—such were the consequences of leaving to the parish a problem which it had neither the wit nor the will to solve."[13]

Nevertheless, the point can be made that however crudely the poor laws were administered, they admitted a social responsibility for insecurity. In their ineffectual way, they functioned and were intended to function as a cushion for poverty and a safety valve for a sorely tried social order. They erred greatly on the side of local responsibility, but they looked back to a time when the local community had functioned under such responsibility. While they served as a poor substitute for any approach to security, it can be pointed out that their replacement by modern social insurance was the completion of a logical evolution.

The Community of Custom in Industry

So far we have neglected a most important aspect of this transition, the medieval organization of industry and trade. In the merchant guilds and the craft guilds a community of status and security had grown up. The guilds represented a system of customary regulation by small producers' associations based on the relative economic independence of local areas. Merchant guilds developed first, but by the middle of the twelfth century the organization of artisans into publically regulated occupational associations was normal and universal throughout the towns and cities of Western Europe.

"In England the early boroughs were communities that had secured their exemption from the obligations of the manor; within their walls the guilds helped to control industry and commerce, just as outside their walls the manor court helped to control agriculture."[14] These associations of producers, as the Hammonds point out, differed in power, character, history, and length of life, "for the guilds did not cover all industrial life, just as the common field communities did not cover the whole field of agriculture."[15]

The development of the craft guild to the height of its power in the fifteenth and sixteenth centuries is explained, says Henri Pirenne, as the result of two principles acting simultaneously: voluntary association and legal authority. "These two original contradictory tendencies merge at the moment when the authorities recognized the workers' associations as compulsory in reserving to their members the right to devote themselves to a particular branch of industry."[16] The establishment of just prices, the expulsion of those who dealt in short weights and shoddy materials, the establishment of group monopoly over local trade and production—in short, the whole system of customary regulation in the interest of group security came out of this combination of voluntary association and legal power.

Throughout its history the system was an evolving institution. It changed and finally disintegrated because of internal struggle for power within the guilds and the transition from domestic to world markets without. Internally the guilds moved from their original arrangement for the joint control of handicraft industry by a large number of small masters to a hierarchal structure with the principal power concentrated in the hands of a few.

This came about partly because of a great differentiation in function. The craft guilds represented interests and functions that were combined in the fourteenth century but quite separate by the seventeenth. The medieval craftsman as Unwin showed in his *Industrial Organization in the Sixteenth and Seventeenth Centuries* was at once a workman, a foreman supervising his journeymen and apprentices, an employer undertaking responsibilities and supplying capital for materials, food, and wages, a merchant buying something and a shopkeeper selling something. By the end of the seventeenth century he had split up into no less than six different persons: the large merchant, the shopkeeper, the merchant employer, the large master, the small master, and the journeyman.

By the fifteenth century it had become more and more difficult for the small master to keep a status in the guild or for the apprentice to attain it. Devices of all kinds were adopted to limit influence and effective membership to the richer craftsmen. Thus the Guild Merchant of Newcastle excluded anyone with "blue nails" since this indicated that he worked with his own hands at dyeing.[17] Although they still retained their monopoly in the seventeenth and well into the eighteenth century, the craft guilds were in a process of dissolution throughout this period because of the extension of domestic manufactures and the introduction of new industries organized on a more modern basis.

Because their surviving practices impeded the process of adjustment the early contribution of the guilds to the security of craftsmen was not highly regarded by the leaders of the Enlightenment in England. It is the conclusion of Henri Pirenne, however, that the guild system must be recognized as the only source of protection to the worker before the development of social legislation in the nineteenth century. "At the height of its development," he writes, "the institution assured the craftsman an existence as satisfactory from the economic as from the social point of view."[18] It is true that attempts to trace the origin of the labor union movement to the guilds have failed, but the similarity of function is striking. Like the guilds, modern union organization depends on the combination of voluntary association with legal authority and, like the guilds, these organizations are accused of developing policies of restriction and monopoly in the attempt to preserve the security of their members.

At first the transition from the local community was in the direction of social control on a wider basis. The place of the guilds as they lost their efficiency and power was taken in part by the national government. The first impulse of the government was to reform the guilds and adapt them to new needs. Thus the acts of 1531 and 1536 tried to protect apprentices from the disqualifying practices that had been introduced and forbade guild officers to require an oath from journeymen that they would not set up for themselves.[19]

By the time of Elizabeth, the State was trying to do for industry what the guilds had done when they were effective organs. Thus wherever industry had formerly been regulated by guilds of producers receiving their authority from the city, it was now regulated by the Crown and Parliament which bestowed patents and privileges on bodies or companies that represented particular interests in a trade. Thus these companies turned into privileged bodies bent on monopoly, and, as the Industrial Revolution gathered strength, the experiment in regulation was followed by that strong reaction against State authority over industry which finally culminated in the victory of the classic plea for liberalism and laissez-faire in Adam Smith's *Wealth of Nations* (1776).

Even as the Industrial Revolution loomed, earlier trends survived in laws protecting the security of the craftsman in his craft. Many of these regulations supported minimum wages, others attempted to restrict the trend toward mechanization. Among the many laws regulating the ancient woolen industry was one prohibiting use of a machine known as the "gig mill" for raising the nap on fibers in the cloth. The difficulties facing the attempt to underwrite security by outlawing technological change can be indicated by the fact that this law tended to become a dead letter because of the doubt that the gig mill used in the eighteenth century was the machine that Parliament had forbidden in the sixteenth. In the long struggle over the transition, the men were constantly prosecuting or threatening to prosecute masters for the infringement of these and similar acts. For several years in succession Parliament suspended these laws but finally the masters gained the day and in 1809 Parliament repealed them.

Throughout this whole period of social change, the workmen and the peasants, write the Hammonds, would have refused to admit that they were merely defending obstructive survivals from the past. "They saw leaders of the State defending property in land and capital with great zeal and they felt that their own property was equally entitled to the protection of the law."[20] Thus, the cotton weaver wrote in a petition manifesto in 1823:

> The weavers' qualifications may be considered as his property and support. It is a real property to him as buildings and lands are to others. Like them his qualifications cost time, application, and money. There is no point of view (except visible and tangible) wherein they differ.[21]

"Parliament may be tender of property," said the peasant in a case put to Arthur Young, "all I know is that I had a cow and an act of Parliament has taken it from me."[22]

The Industrial Revolution

In the background was the emerging Industrial Revolution. The old industrial order, wrote Arnold Toynbee, was suddenly "broken in pieces by the mighty blows of the steam engine and the power loom." Actually it is doubtful that we should apply the term "Revolution" to a movement which as

Herbert Henton[23] writes had been 150 years in the making and 150 years in the completion. Toynbee saw 1760 as the eve of the Industrial Revolution, but Unwin felt that in 1760 "the Revolution had been in preparation for two centuries."

In terms that apply equally well to earlier conditions, Arnold Toynbee wrote of conditions preceding the Industrial Revolution in England: "Though there were periods of keen distress, there was no such thing as long-continued widespread depression of trade. Overproduction was impossible when the producer lived next door to the consumer and knew his wants as well as the country shoemaker of today knows the number of pairs of boots that are wanted in his village." The market was almost as narrow as the local community. Toynbee writes: "The majority of employers were small masters, in ideas and habits but little removed from the workmen out of whose rank they had risen, and to whose rank they might return once more. Few there were that did not work with their own hands and many taught trade to their apprentices."

"Between men living in such close and continuous relations the bonds were naturally very intimate." His master knew his affairs, his particular wants, his resources, the number of his children. If the weaver were sick the master lent him money; if trade were slack, he kept him on at a loss. "Masters and men," said an employer, "were in general so joined together in sentiment, and if I may be permitted to use the term, in love with each other that they did not wish to be separated if they could help it." It was not uncommon for workers to be employed by some master for forty years. "It seldom happened," said a weaver, "that the small clothiers change their men except in case of sickness and death." A workman would live and die on the spot where he was born, and the same family would remain for generations working for the same employer's family in the village. The master busied himself with the welfare of the workmen.[24]

The rights granted laborers, however, were not enforceable. They were customary and personal, the outcome of a primary group relationship that was often granted but could not be demanded. Along with this relationship went laws against combination and conspiracy on the part of laborers. "We have," wrote Adam Smith, "no acts of Parliament against combining to lower the price of work but many against combining to raise it." Thus, points out Toynbee, a breach of contract on the part of the employer was a civil offense; on the part of the laborer, a crime. Organizations of employers were encouraged, but the organization of workers could be, and was, dealt with under the law of conspiracy. "The workman," he concludes, "half way between a serf and a citizen, was treated with kindness by those who injured him; he was protected, depressed and dependent."

In the pages of the Hammonds, Toynbee, and others the transition to insecurity was no less marked. Population "was torn up by the roots," like industry, the population "was dragged from cottages in distant villages into factories and cities," to become a collection of hands, "the living tools of whom the employer knew less than he did of his steam engine."[25]

As specialization increased, so the thesis runs, the laborer's claim on his community for security and his power to create work for himself decreased. When with simple tools he could still create goods, to find someone to buy those goods was not easy. The specialization of the market was already creating the wholesale and the retail merchant in their more modern form. The introduction of machinery means specialization of function in production, and now the worker could no longer create goods with the tools of the master craftsman. The new tools were in a factory and his access to that factory depended on whether the owner needed him. The owner needed him only when the state of trade was such that his labor would return a profit.

The particular system of industrial relationships which grew up in England during this long transition came to be rationalized in a system of politico-economic and legal individualism dignified under the term of "economic law." The "dismal science" of economics rationalized the mobility, the poverty, and the insecurity of the worker in terms of a laissez-faire order perfectly adjusted to the maximization of production. Even the liberalism of the day "regarded society as existing to enforce respect for rights that man brought with him into society; not as a community whose members and classes served different purposes and stood in some organic relation to one another."[26] This type of reasoning culminated in a theory of wages of which the Hammonds write: "The first discovery, following Adam Smith, that the state could not really protect the workman, was followed by another, even more interesting, that the employer could not really injure him." The recompense of labor was fixed by natural laws, and no human effort could alter it.

The ultimate beneficence of this system attained classical statement in that passage in which Adam Smith compared competition to the invisible hand of Providence. "As every individual," wrote Smith, ". . . endeavors as much as he can to employ his capital in the support of domestic industry and so direct that industry that its product may be of the greatest value, every individual necessarily labors to render the annual revenue of the society as great as he can. He is led as by an invisible hand to promote an end which was no part of his intention."[27]

In a particular period in the evolution of institutions the prevailing arrangements were seen in terms of universal economic laws, as cosmic as the physicist's law of matter. This law determined that men everywhere should gain their subsistence in a certain way and under certain conditions. To oppose the working of economic law was worse than futile, to use the economic surplus to underwrite a minimum of social security would not only cancel the gains of technology; it would tear asunder the very mechanism by which the social and economic order functioned. And Herbert Spencer, having developed an analysis of human society as a functioning organism of interrelated members, threw the whole weight of his authority behind this dogma without realizing the contradiction involved.

Conclusion

In so far as we can draw inferences about social values and theories from a survey of this type, it is not our contention that the doctrine of social adjustment has no future; it is rather the conclusion that the doctrine of security has a past—a past which to sociological analysis appears quite respectable. The crux of the argument with which economists may be concerned—and doubtless rightly so—is whether the underwriting of a minimum degree of security against the risks of unemployment and old age tends to break down the whole process of adjustment. Obviously modern nations in their enactment of social insurance—from the first legislation of 1870 in the Germany of Bismarck to our Social Security Act of 1935—have made the political decision that it does not.

Our tradition of security had its origins in the organization of the local community—communities that in agriculture and industry were synonymous with the arrangements of feudalism and the guilds. In the transition to modern industrialism the worker initially moved from a reasonable expectation of security from unemployment and a dependent old age to a not unreasonable expectation of insecurity.

This transition from the community of custom to impersonal society in the Tönnies' sense involved the change from a doctrine of security and status to one of adjustment to an impersonal economic and social order. The risks facing the workers were thus the consequences of an industrial transition from which the state and society as a whole have benefited. Their insecurity, moreover, was rationalized in a doctrine of adjustment which by the very nature of the transition included the values of individualism and liberalism. Actually, society, before the process of industrialization got under way, existed under one form of social control; it floundered for a time in the trough of adjustment; and it is now returning to another system of control. Today it is recognized that in the attempt to mitigate these risks only the great power of the modern state can succeed to the place once held by the local community.

Security, most historians would conclude, is not one of the historic rights of Englishmen. The rights of Englishmen owed much to the historic achievements of liberalism but neither the men of the Enlightenment nor the leaders in the movement for individual freedom were predisposed to see either formal or informal values in the older communities. It was the claim of liberal leaders that they overthrew the survivals of serfdom as well as the monopolies and restrictions inherited from the guilds. We rightly honor the triumph of liberalism, but in seeking to give men an abstract freedom these movements ignored earlier community values.

In America we had no comparable background, and for a long time our unappropriated resources made the problem of security seem so remote that there was no established right of the poor to relief such as had come to prevail in England. Thus it was a moot question whether our national constitution, written at the height of the struggle for personal and political freedom, embodied the dogma of a perfectly adjusting laissez-faire order. Witness the oft-quoted protest of Mr. Justice Holmes to the effect that it was not the intent of the Fourteenth Amendment to enact Mr. Herbert Spencer's *Social Statics* as the basic law of the land.

For a long time it seemed that under this philosophy our responsibile and propertied classes, unlike those of England, would continue to hold the attitude that virtually all regulatory and protective legislation could be nullified on constitutional grounds. This essentially false dilemma of freedom and security operated to delay America's achievement of social security behind that of most countries in Western civilization.

Actually the passing of the old individualism was assured as soon as those below the middle classes were granted sufficient public education to realize that for the vast majority, wage labor was not a temporary stage on the road to place and power.[28] The laborer's next lesson was to learn the relative inability of wage labor under successive depressions to furnish him steady employment, security, and comfort for old age at the status to which he had perforce resigned himself. The change in our society may be marked as the precise date at which the American Federation of Labor officially decided that the term social insurance was not synonymous with the "dole."

The demand for social security in our day is the resultant of a relatively high degree of personal and political freedom, on the one hand, and a growing consciousness of dependence on the social and economic order as a going concern on the other. The legal rationalization by which this change was incorporated in the American constitutional system is emblazoned in the luminous prose of Mr. Justice Cardozo in the historic decision which validated the Social Security Act under the terms of the general welfare clause. It is hardly to be imagined that we shall ever reverse this step.

Notes

1. By Karl de Schweinitz (Philadelphia: University of Pennsylvania Press, 1943).
2. J. L. and Barbara Hammond, *The Rise of Modern Industy* (New York: Harcourt, Brace & Co., 1937), pp. 81–84. See also the excellent summary of this work in Floyd N. House, *Range of Social Theory* (New York: Henry Holt, 1929), pp. 422–34.
3. Sidney and Beatrice Webb, *English Poor Law History,* 2 vols. (1929), Part I, pp. 44–46.

4. J. L. and Barbara Hammond, *The Village Laborer, 1766–1832* (London: Longmans, Green & Co., 1920), p. 103.
5. The Webbs, *op. cit.*
6. Sir F. M. Eden, *State of the Poor* (1797), I, pp. 58–59.
7. Arthur Young, *Tour Through the East of England* (1771), IV, p. 361.
8. Patrick Colquhoun, *A Treatise on Indigence* (1806), pp. 7–9.
9. The Webbs, *op. cit.*, I, p. 6.
10. The Webbs, *op. cit.*, I, pp. 44–45.
11. The Hammonds, *Rise of Modern Industry*, p. 96.
12. Dorothy Marshall, *The English Poor in the 18th Century: A Study in Social and Administrative History* (London: G. Routledge & Sons, 1926), pp. 206–224.
13. *Ibid.*, p. 224.
14. The Hammonds, *Rise of Modern Industry*, p. 103.
15. The Hammonds, *op. cit.*, p. 98.
16. Henri Pirenne, "Guilds," *Encyclopaedia of the Social Sciences*, VII, p. 211.
17. R. H. Gretten, *The English Middle Class* (London: G. Bell & Sons, 1917), p. 65.
18. Henri Pirenne, *op. cit.*, p. 214.
19. The Hammonds, *op. cit.*, p. 101.
20. The Hammonds, *Rise of Modern Industry*, p. 108.
21. The Hammonds, *The Town Laborer, 1766–1832* (London: Longmans, Green & Co., 1917), p. 300.
22. The Hammonds, *Village Laborer*, p. 59.
23. "Industrial Revolution," *Encyclopaedia of the Social Sciences*, VIII, p. 5. An article critical of Toynbee's interpretation.
24. Arnold Toynbee, *Lectures on the Industrial Revolution* (new ed., London: Longmans, Green & Co., 1908), pp. 179–88.
25. Arnold Toynbee, *Lectures on the Industrial Revolution*, passim.
26. The Hammonds, *Rise of Industry*, p. 214.
27. Adam Smith, *The Wealth of Nations* (London, 1904 edition), p. 421.
28. See W. B. Catlin, *Labor Problems*, p. 17.

William Miller   THE BUSINESS ELITE IN BUSINESS
BUREAUCRACIES: CAREERS OF
TOP EXECUTIVES IN THE EARLY
TWENTIETH CENTURY

I

BY 1902, WHEN THE MORGAN SPOKESMAN, George F. Baer, made his prideful remark about how "God, in his infinite wisdom," had "given control of the property interests of the country" to "the Christian men" who then managed them,[1] many of these Christians had already learned that what God might give, men might take away. Among them, indeed, was Baer himself whose career as Morgan's "confidential legal advisor,"[2] though it had brought him to the head of numerous great enterprises, resembled a new type in American business life. Louis D. Brandeis said in the 1890s, "I would rather have clients than be somebody's lawyer," and to a considerable degree he satisfied his preference.[3] Baer's career, as was especially plain during the coal strike which was the occasion of his Calvinistic utterance, was more like that of a trained professional no longer free to have clients or to reject them, but tied to the service of a single business interest that could move him about like an ordinary employee.

Even more representative of this type of "captive" professional—for these men engaged in fewer independent ventures than Baer—were such company lawyers as Vanderbilt's Chauncey M. Depew, Huntington's Charles H. Tweed, Harriman's Robert S. Lovett, each at some time president or board chairman of one or more of his sponsor's firms and always on call to the great man himself. Properly classified here too are the counterparts of company lawyers in the "law factory" of a Paul D. Cravath, George W. Wickersham, or William N. Cromwell, which by the end of the nineteenth century had become "virtually an annex to some group of financial promoters, manipulators, or industrialists."[4] Of Cravath, his associate Robert T. Swaine tells this story:

Early one morning when he had not yet arrived at the office, [Otto] Kahn [of Kuhn, Loeb] wanted to see him in a great hurry. One of the younger associates sought to locate Cravath by telephone, but in vain; going downstairs at

52 William Street to tell Kahn of the futility of his efforts, he met Cravath coming in the door and rushed up with: "I've been looking all over for you; Mr. Kahn wants to see you at once." Cravath broke into a broad smile: "You make me feel just like my father did when he used to say to me: 'Paul, come to the woodshed.' "[5]

This new ubiquitousness of lawyers at big businessmen's elbows, not to say under their thumbs, reflects an epochal change in the structure of American big business enterprises and in their relation to their employees and to society at large. First among the railroads, but by the turn of the century in many other lines as well, the characteristic big business firm had become a big bureaucracy. Functions at each level of operation, supervision, and policy making had become more or less strict and specific, channels of authority and communication had been set up, and hierarchies of ascent had become articulated. Lifetime, salaried careers thus had become attainable, leading all the way to the top, albeit, as Max Weber has pointed out, "the bureaucratic official" is always "appointed by a superior authority"[6]—a higher functionary, a college of cardinals, a board of directors, the "organization" itself.

In such bureaucracies, ideally, as Weber said, "control" is exercised "on the basis of knowledge"; the "development of bureaucracy . . . tends to eliminate . . . the occupation of offices on an honorary basis or as an avocation by virtue of wealth."[7] The upshot, however, is not "democratization" but rather the rise of a new elite: "The most decisive thing here . . . is the *leveling of the governed* in opposition to the ruling and bureaucratically articulated group, which in turn may occupy a quite autocratic position."[8] This new elite, in Weber's terms, may "increase its power by the knowledge growing out of experience in the service."[9] To become even more firmly seated it may enlist expert technicians not the least useful of whom were those qualified to serve as intermediaries with the leveled populace. Knowledgeable lawyers, expert in their own field, also fitted this second role. Trained in advocacy and persuasion as well as in the law, they were among the first professional lobbyists and public relations men as well as the first formally certified business experts. Their new importance by the turn of the century reflects the growth of bureaucratic managements typically in need of help in navigating legal and political labyrinths and in conciliating public groups often made hostile by the results.[10]

II

That men risen to power as bureaucrats or as their professional adjuncts had not wholly superseded independent entrepreneurs in the key positions in the American economy by 1900 is indicated by the histories of some of the leaders who were still at the head of great business enterprises. Of 185 men so placed in the decade 1901–1910, 14 per cent either started the firms through the development of which, by expansion or more commonly by merger, they had attained their peak positions,[11] or bought these firms or high places in them with resources accumulated in independent ventures. Hugh J. Chisholm of the International Paper Company, Anthony N. Brady of the Brooklyn Rapid Transit Company, and Frederick Ayer of American Woolen, were such men. So, too, though each ultimately paid for his independence by being squeezed out of his own firm, were John C. Osgood, one of the organizers of the Colorado Fuel and Iron Company; Frederick A. Heinze, founder of the United Copper Company; and George Westinghouse, founder of the Electric and Manufacturing Company which still bears his name.

Twenty-seven per cent of these 185 business leaders, moreover, and certainly not the least able ones, may be said to have inherited their high positions. This suggests that while kinship ties may have become more honored in the breach in the transfer of business power, and inherited wealth and tradition less convincing than "self-help" and bureaucratic "rationality" as legitimations of such power, dynasties still could be established and maintained.[12] Most of the men in this group had taken over their father's, father-in-law's, or uncle's firms. Others had used their continuing connection with such firms or funds available through them to gain key positions in major outside companies. In the latter class, typically, are sons, sons-in-law, and nephews of great merchants or private bankers—James Stillman and August Belmont in New York, Gordon Abbott in Boston, Henry A. Blair and Henry G. Foreman in Chicago. Among the more direct heirs, besides bankers like J. P. Morgan, Henry Lee Higginson, or Frank E. Peabody, are Daniel Guggenheim in copper, Henry O. Havemeyer in sugar, Morgan G. Bulkeley in life insurance, Cornelius K. G. Billings in Chicago utilities. Even railroad presidents George Jay Gould and Louis W. Hill may be included here, each having reached the top of his father's highly bureaucratized company by a route so direct as to leave him virtually unaware of the articulated channels through which henceforth he was expected to work.

All the rest of these 185 leaders, however, except for the 12 per cent who were lawyers,[13] climbed the bureaucratic ladder, not infrequently, of course, after their family status, education, and other social endowments helped them get the proper start. These bureaucrats make up 47 per cent of the whole group. Typical is Charles S. Mellen, who at the age of eighteen began as a clerk in the cashier's office of the Northern New Hampshire Railroad. From here he "rose in his profession," as his biographer puts it, "through successive positions on the Central Vermont" and other roads.[14] After a novitiate of almost a quarter of a century, during which he never forsook railroading, he became second vice-president of the New York, New Haven and Hartford. In 1897, Mellen was made president of the Northern Pacific, only to be moved seven years later back to the New Haven also as president. After a stormy decade, he was ousted in 1913.

Scarcely any of these bureaucrats ever satisfied the urge, if indeed they ever had it,[15] to launch a company of their own, "to plunge into and toss upon the waves of human affairs," as Carnegie said, "without a life-preserver in the shape of a salary."[16] More than 80 per cent of them never headed an enterprise—never were sole owner, partner, president, or chairman—before attaining the eminent office that makes them of interest here. That is not to say that their ascent, once auspiciously under way, was unfaltering or automatic. Nor does it compromise the designation of their careers as bureaucratic to point out that many of them, like many lawyers, became the favorites—with all the hazards of that predicament—of men of more elevated rank.[17]

Jesse T. Welborn, for example, had "advanced through regular stages"[18] in the Colorado Fuel and Iron Company from bookkeeper to vice-president in charge of sales and traffic, when in 1907 the Rockefellers, who a few years earlier had acquired the company, made him president. James T. Harahan had risen "through successive stages"[19] in railroading from clerk on the Boston and Providence to second vice-president of the Illinois Central, when Harriman in 1906 ousted president Stuyvesant Fish of the latter road and put Harahan in his place. Mellen himself, who soon after becoming president of the New Haven was regarded as "The Railroad Lord of New England,"[20] once said of his experiences there, "I suppose that there is more or less prejudice against me because I wear the Morgan collar, but I am proud of it." After Morgan's death in 1913, Mellen said: "I took orders from J. P. Morgan, Sr. I did as I was told. . . . So far as I was concerned, the handwriting was on the wall the moment the old man breathed his last."[21]

The distribution by career types of the 185 business leaders of the decade 1901–1910 is summarized in the accompanying table.

Table 1—American Business Leaders by Type of Career

Type of Career	Number	Per Cent
Professional (Lawyers only)	23	12
Independent Entrepreneur	25	14
Family	51	27
Bureaucratic	86	47
Total cases	185	100

III

That this early in the twentieth century almost half of the leaders in American business were men who had been salaried officeholders virtually their entire business lives is remarkable enough. Such men, predominant in railroads, were also most numerous in nearly every major business field, while independent entrepreneurs were fewest in every field but one.

The whole group, nevertheless, remains representative of what appears to have been a transition period not simply in the form of the typical big business career but in the environment that made new careers possible and in the sanctions that eventually made them preferred. Earlier, so great a proportion of American business leaders could not have been subordinates, of however high rank, for so long a term; the rarity before the last quarter of the nineteenth century of companies in which hierarchical careers could be followed makes this certain. Today, on the other hand, the number of great hierarchical organizations and the scope of their activities make it almost as certain that

Table 2—American Business Leaders by Type of Career and Business Field

Type of Career*	Manufacturing and Mining	Railroads	Public Utilities	Commercial Banking	Life Insurance	Investment Banking
	%	%	%	%	%	%
Independent	24	8	12	29	0	0
Family	42	8	40	18	43	89
Bureaucratic	34	84	48	53	57	11
Total cases (= 100%)	55	49	25	17	7	9

* Lawyers are omitted from this and subsequent tables.

the proportion of bureaucrats among business leaders has become far larger than ever before, and that the proportion of great independent entrepreneurs has fallen.

That the latter trend was well under way before the turn of the century is suggested not only by the small representation of independent entrepreneurs among the men studied but also by the distribution of these men by period of

Table 3—American Business Leaders by Type of Career and Date of Birth

Type of Career	Before 1841	1841–1850	1851–1860	After 1860
	%	%	%	%
Independent	26	19	11	8
Family	22	24	42	36
Bureaucratic	52	57	47	56
Total cases (= 100%)	23	59	55	25

birth. Considerably more than half of those born before 1840 were to become bureaucrats and this proportion remained more or less unchanged for those born later. The percentage of independent entrepreneurs, however, dropped from 26 to 8, even though such entrepreneurs tended to attain their peak offices at a relatively early age.

How much further this percentage has dropped, how indeed it has tended to disappear, is suggested by a study of presidents of big corporations today.

Of 159 such presidents, only four—a scant 2.5 per cent—"started out as self-employed. Just one of these four was able to boost his company to national significance and remain president—the other three men shortly sought employment with established concerns.[22]

"Starting your own company," says the report of this recent study, "is one way to be president," but "the evidence shows that engineers and lawyers have a much better chance to become president of a successful firm." So great, indeed, is the current demand for such professionals that young men now study law or engineering often with no idea of independent practice and many forego practice altogether and start immediately in administrative posts. In the middle of the nineteenth century, however, such opportunities were rare and in any case grasping them would have been frowned upon.

IV

Though increasingly honorific, bureaucratic business careers have continued since the time of Schwab and Corey to involve able young men in conflicts between their personal aspirations and the health of their firms. This is partly due to the persistence of the self-help ideology which shames men with slogans such as "always a yes man, never a boss"; and partly to the separation of ownership and management which Weber presented as an ideal of bureaucratic organization but which, given American traditions, has only heightened the war between the self-help ideology and the realities of bureaucratic life.[23]

Largely for these reasons the old difficulty of maintaining the allegiance of able executives has had to be constantly fought. Even as late as 1947, *Nation's Business,* the organ of the United States Chamber of Commerce, featured an article on this theme. To the uncertain though highly placed and highly paid hero of the piece who one day asked himself, "Am I a failure? Where did I make the wrong turn? Did I sacrifice my independence for security? Wouldn't I have done better if I had gone into business for myself?" this article replied: "You're happy with your work and richer than you know."[24] Such pronouncements have served less as balm to disenchanted bureaucrats than as symptoms of their ambivalent position. A striking instance of how this ambivalence might disrupt an organization was the split, early in 1950, between Charles Luckman and Lever Brothers, the American company of Unilever, Ltd., of which Luckman was president. "On the record," said *Business Week* at the time, "shifts in Lever personnel since Luckman took over have been broad and frequent. This is apparently what caused Unilever to lay down its ultimatum for a wider management base. To nail down strategic executive posts and prevent turnover, Unilever had a plan for a wider participation in authority and earnings. Luckman wouldn't buy it, and that was the end."[25]

The persistence, nevertheless, with which most American firms have attacked this problem and the means they have employed—liberal executive bonus plans, broader participation of administrators in ownership, and especially noncontributory pensions for management—have added to the seriousness of another and I think even more fateful source of trouble. That is not so much the problem of bridging the conflict of loyalties in able bureaucrats as of disencumbering the bureaucracy itself of incompetents, often risen to key positions, who have proved altogether too loyal. I say more fateful, for this newer problem, especially, mirrors a characteristically closed economy in which huge enterprises are astride the major avenues of opportunity. Top management in such enterprises often appears unable to avoid promoting faithful or friendly men who themselves have no way to go but up. Such men, in turn, even when endowed with exceptional talent for bureaucratic ascent, often prove to be cliquish and otherwise irresponsible as top executives. In emergencies they and their cabals may pull their big firms down, and with them in most recent times the whole rigid system.[26]

The problem of what to do with such men, who nowadays are sometimes raised to board chairman, may already be noted in the transition period around the turn of the century when such chairmanships first were becoming fashionable. Then as now it had become apparent that for many men—for independent entrepreneurs drawn into the bureaucratic vortex as well as for true blue bureaucrats themselves—the greater their business success, the greater their personal insecurity; the higher their ascent, the nearer their approach to failure. How often this paradoxical history marked the careers principally of former independent entrepreneurs is evident from the series of cases in Arthur S. Dewing's *Corporate Promotions and Reorganizations,* written at the end of this epoch.[27] How general it was up and down the line of the emergent bureaucratic organizations is equally evident from Frederick W. Taylor's classic *Principles of Scientific Management,* issued at about the same time.[28]

This situation heightens interest in the general question not only of the structure of big business careers in this transition period but also of the means by which such careers were attained—by the most able big businessmen as well as by others who also rose to the top.

V

For some of the men studied here, an answer to this question is comparatively easily arrived at, though it may itself raise other more difficult questions. Henry H. Rogers, for example, one of the older and most independent of these men, was perhaps more richly endowed than many of his contemporaries with what Peter Cooper once called the "knack for contriving."[29] (Why this was so is one of those more difficult points.) His innovations in oil refining and pipe-line transportation probably gave the early impetus to his ascent. Yet

Rogers, by his own description, was also "a gambler" often out to "have a little fun" and "always for fighting." "Once when Rogers had A. C. Burrage [a copper magnate] at the foot of the table with four other guests, one of the guests said to Mr. Rogers: 'How can you tolerate that Mr. Burrage opposite to you at the table?' Rogers said: 'I am enjoying it immensely. I was thinking all the time how he would look after I plucked him.' " "Almost the whole story of his gas interests," says one of Rogers' biographers, "was one of warfare, as was his connection with copper." John D. Rockefeller once said that "in working with so many partners," among them Rogers, "the conservative ones are apt to be in the majority, and this is no doubt a desirable thing when the mere momentum of a large concern is certain to carry it forward."[30] But that was hardly Rogers' view; he abhorred partners and involved the Standard Oil Company in the copper business and other speculations against the wishes of Rockefeller himself.[31] One of Rogers' last enterprises—which probably speeded his death—was the construction, virtually with no outside financial assistance, of the 443-mile, $40,000,000 Virginia Railway tying the rich coal fields of West Virginia to the port of Norfolk.[32]

Equally simple in its way, though different enough to be instructive, is the story of another of these men, Conrad H. Matthiessen, in his own view like Rogers a self-made man. In 1897, at the age of thirty-two—precocious, surely, by this time—Matthiessen became the first president of the "glucose trust," just organized as the Glucose Sugar Refining Company. The following year he was reported to have received the then extraordinary annual salary of $75,000, three times that of the president of the United States.

My success, as you call it [Matthiessen told reporters], is due to hard work and that alone . . . I started at the bottom. [Then he said] My father was president of the old Chicago Sugar Refining Company [the keystone of the new "trust"] and when I came West [from Yale] he put me in as a workman at $1.50 a day . . . I was gradually promoted and in 1890 [just four years out of college] the management of the company was given to me.[33]

Even where other types of careers may be as clearly outlined as those of Rogers (independent) and Matthiessen (family-made), reasons for the successive steps in them may often be more difficult to expose. This is especially true of careers which were largely hierarchical.

In owner-manager and family firms, the individual and the enterprise almost always must rise and fall together. The ups and downs of both, in turn, are largely ascribable to their adaptability—itself often a matter of the personality of the controlling entrepreneur—in meeting objective economic changes such as those affecting the market for commodities or capital, the techniques of production, the size and quality of the labor force, and so forth. Moreover, the competition among such firms and hence among the individuals whose fates are so closely tied to them is largely for advantage in regard to these objective factors. The course of bureaucratic firms and the competition, where it exists, among them, are also affected by changes in their relation to these factors. But the fate of *individual* bureaucrats and hence the competition for preferment *within* the bureaucracy—the firm in Kenneth Burke's terms, becoming less the "agency" and more the "scene" of the drama[34]—appear to involve in addition a host of other variables.

Among bureaucrats, for example, an individual's success, as defined by his progress up the ladder, may conceivably have been won despite a concomitant decline in his firm's position, or, indeed, because of it, such a decline sometimes causing a shuffle in management that results in extraordinarily rapid advancement for whole teams of executives. The careers of many railroad men, risen to the presidency of their firms in this transitional period while the firms were clearly on the way to receivership, are striking examples of this. Similarly, an individual bureaucrat's failure—failure meaning that ascent ceased below the ladder's top—may have occurred while his hierarchical firm, even largely through his efforts, was itself riding a wave of prosperity and unprecedented growth. Certain popular preconceptions about the history of American business leadership, moreover, can now be systematically cleared away and some outward characteristics, at least, of bureaucratic as of other types of careers presented so as to prepare the ground for more penetrating work.

One of these preconceptions, expressed most felicitously, perhaps, by Charles and Mary Beard and given currency by the legitimation implicit in it, is that until late in the nineteenth century, "the government of American railroads and staple industries, with exceptions of course," had been in the hands of "men who had grown up in the roundhouses and the mills through all the technical processes."[35] But who were these men? The merchants and traders who governed the early textile establishments? Surely not. The industrialists and financiers, then, who governed the early railroad companies? Obviously not these either. Indeed, for a considerable part of the nineteenth century and for most of the industries then pursued, it is relevant to ask what were "all the technical processes"? "Tinkering" aside as a lifelong avocation, what technical processes were there, the mystery of which required an apprenticeship of more than a few years?

Among the men in the present study, moreover, whose careers on the whole did coincide with a vast and complex technological development, the Beards' "exceptions" outnumber those who started in mill or roundhouse by almost three to one, and of the latter more than half were out of the shop by the age of twenty-five. Mine, to be sure, are largely men of a later period than the Beards refer to; of the few among them, nevertheless, who did start in a shop of some sort, the smallest proportion (though only scarcely smaller than their representation in the whole group) is that of independent entrepreneurs. And these, on the average, are the oldest men in my selection and the ones whose careers were in the oldest tradition. Were professionally trained engi-

neers not counted in the technical group but in the managerial one to which
most of them quickly moved, the proportion of shop-trained independent
entrepreneurs would be significantly smaller still, while that of independent
entrepreneurs in the "managerial and clerical" category would be significantly
increased.[36]

Table 4—American Business Leaders by Type of Career and Type of First Regular Job*

Type of Career	Managerial and Clerical	Technical and Manual
	%	%
Independent	18	13
Family	33	15
Bureaucratic	49	72
Total cases (= 100 per cent)	109	39

* First business, professional or other job (except work on family's farm) after leaving school or, in very
few cases, the Union or Confederate army. In "Managerial and Clerical" are included officers, general
managers, superintendents, and the like; and clerks, bookkeepers, telegraphers, and similar office workers.
In "Technical and Manual" are hourly workers of various degrees of skill, and draftsmen, engineers, sur-
veyors, and other trained technicians.

The largest cluster by far of those who did start in mill or roundhouse,
and one much greater than would be expected by their representation in the
whole group, is that of bureaucrats—as the table shows. This is especially
striking in view of the fact that the Beards introduce their proposition about
nineteenth-century men with technical "know how" mainly to decry the
latter's loss of place to adventurers with less legitimate claims to power—a
second untenable preconception. "By the end of the century," they write,
"captains of industry were as a rule no longer evolved by natural selection;
they were chosen by the dominant bankers."[37] But what sort of men did the
bankers choose? The Beards only answer by innuendo; yet if by "natural
selection" they mean long exposure and successful adaptation to conditions of
work, the "bankers' men" and the other bureaucrats fit the case much better
than the lamented nineteenth-century captains. This is true even if shop work,
as the Beards imply, were the only honest kind of preparation for business
leadership. It is all the more true if other categories of experience are
admitted, as they must be.

Were this not the case, of course, my designation of these newer types
of executives as "bureaucrats" would be less justified. To see how well justified it is, take first the question of the number of industries in which these
men worked before attaining their peak positions. As the next table shows,
relatively few in the whole group jumped from industry to industry. But in
this category the independent entrepreneurs are to be found much *more*
frequently, the so-called bureaucrats considerably *less* frequently than in any
other. Scarcely any of the independent entrepreneurs, on the other hand,
remained in the industry in which they started. Among the men who never

forsook this industry those I call bureaucrats are relatively more numerous than anywhere else.

Table 5—American Business Leaders by Type of Career and Number of Industries Worked In

Type of Career	One Industry	Two Industries	Three or More Industries
	%	%	%
Independent	4	17	32
Family	38	31	22
Bureaucratic	58	52	46
Total cases (= 100 per cent)	66	59	37

Take next the ages at which these men entered the industry in which they attained their peak position, to remain in it. Table 6 only confirms what Table 5 suggests: as the entering age groups gets older, the greater is their representation of independent entrepreneurs; as they get younger, the greater is their representation of bureaucrats.

Table 6—American Business Leaders by Type of Career and Age on Entering Listed Industry

Type of Career	Under 20	20–25	26–39	40 and Over
	%	%	%	%
Independent	4	10	28	28
Family	29	32	30	36
Bureaucratic	67	58	42	36
Total cases (= 100 per cent)	52	38	33	34

The relatively greater experience of the newer men—the bureaucrats—in their particular industries is made most abundantly clear by Table 7, which is concerned with the years spent by these men in their industries before attaining the peak job in them.

The idea of an almost frictionless mobility of labor and capital—of great freedom in jumping from one industry to another—was one of the pillars of nineteenth-century economic theory, just as the warm sanction for risk taking was one of the factors that operated to make the theory seem representative of life. Walter Bagehot's statement of this idea in 1879 may be cited: "The first assumption I shall take is that labour and capital circulate readily within the limits of a nation from employment to employment, leaving that in which remuneration is smaller and going to that in which it is greater."[38]

Bagehot felt that "no assumption can be better founded" than this. He was aware of the problem of inexperience but brushed it aside.

In modern England [he wrote, and he could even more appropriately have spoken of the United States] there is a great speculative fund which is always ready to go into anything which promises high profits. The largest part of this is composed of the savings of men of business . . . who have made money rapidly, and who fancy that the skill and knowledge of a special trade which have enabled them to do so will also enable them to judge of risks, and measure contingencies out of that trade.[39]

Table 7—American Business Leaders by Type of Career and Years in Listed Industry Before Attaining Listed Job*

Type of Career	Under 20 Years	20–29 Years	30 or More Years
	%	%	%
Independent	24	12	4
Family	38	32	14
Bureaucratic	38	56	82
Total cases (= 100 per cent)	58	43	44

* Board chairmen are not included in this table.

Evidence already presented attests to the strength of Bagehot's dictum, as it applies to the men in the older, independent group. Typically, these men ranged from their specialty; their listed industry was but one of many they engaged in, they entered it comparatively late in life, and they entered it at or near the top.

The striking thing about the experience of the great proportion of the rest of these men is the degree to which it was white collar in character. This is especially noteworthy in view of the universal neglect by historians of the development of the business office and of the preconception implicit in this neglect, that modern technology is possible without modern administration.[40]

In white-collar work, especially in the whole range of the executive hierarchy, there are few if any adequate standards of efficiency, few if any accurate measurements of performance. In ascent through white-collar channels, therefore, much more than through others, the display and manipulation of personal factors is most important. "Ability" is likely to be judged, as in the cited instance of Edward T. Jeffrey, by the capacity to be congenial with colleagues, compatible with superiors. Barnard writes of this situation: " 'Learning the ropes' in most organizations is chiefly learning who's who, what's what, why's why of its informal society." Yet this process, he adds, often results in "excessive compatibility . . . 'single track minds' and excessively crystallized attitudes and in the destruction of personal responsibility."[41]

Perhaps it was a view of this crippling effect of bureaucratic life and a determination to escape it that impelled Henry H. Rogers and Henry M. Flagler, individualists caught for a time in the Standard Oil Company in this transition period, to undertake their own great private enterprises—Rogers with his $40 million railroad already described; Flagler with his $30 to $40 million development of Florida.[42]

But even such Paul Bunyanesque ventures were unavailable to salaried bureaucrats and their professional retainers to whom, as Andrew W. Mellon [the financier and former U.S. Secretary of the Treasury] said, "the fortune generally comes when it is too late for us to enjoy it."[43] Nor was the spirit likely to move them, even had they the required capital. For early in this century, as the press and politics of the time make abundantly clear, the condition was already growing which *Fortune* in 1950 described in its full development:

The businessman used to get satisfaction out of being the man on the hill, the patron of the arts, the payer of the church mortgage—and did not everyone agree that it was right and proper that he be entrusted with the destiny of the country? Now, satirized in countless novels, politically a prophet without honor, he is stripped of the former dignities and of much of the old feeling of moral contribution.[44]

Notes

1. *Dictionary of American Biography,* essay on Baer.
2. As he described himself in *Who's Who in America.*
3. Alpheus T. Mason, *Brandeis* (New York: The Viking Press, 1946), p. 86.
4. Adolph A. Berle, Jr., "Modern Legal Profession," in *Encyclopedia of the Social Sciences,* IX, 341. See also John R. Dos Passos, *The American Lawyer* (New York: Banks Law Publishing Co., 1907); Robert T. Swaine, *The Cravath Firm,* 3 vols. (New York: Privately printed, 1946, 1948); and J. Willard Hurst, *The Growth of American Law* (Boston: Little, Brown and Co., 1950), Chap. xiii.
5. Swaine, *Cravath Firm,* II, 127.
6. H. H. Gerth and C. Wright Mills, Trans. and eds., *From Max Weber* (New York: Oxford University Press, 1946), p. 200.
7. Talcott Parsons, Trans. and ed., *Max Weber: The Theory of Social and Economic Organization* (New York: Oxford University Press, 1947), pp. 339, 340. This, of course, need not mean that those with wealth could not also acquire the requisite knowledge.
8. Gerth and Mills, *From Max Weber,* p. 226 (italics Weber's). On the extent to which big business in most recent times takes this "leveling of the governed" for granted, see "Is Anybody Listening?" *Fortune,* September 1950.
9. Parsons, *Max Weber,* p. 339. Weber also says in this connection: "Every bureaucracy seeks to increase the superiority of the professionally informed by keeping their knowledge and intentions secret. Bureaucratic administration always tends to be an administration of 'secret sessions': in so far as it can, it hides its knowledge and action from criticism." (Gerth and Mills, *From Max Weber,* p. 233.)
10. The persistence of "anti-trust" agitation as a political topic in the United States is one index of the need to conciliate the public. At the time of the passage of the Sherman Act of 1890, conservative Republican Senator Orville Platt said: "The conduct of the Senate . . . has not been in the line of honest preparation of a bill to prohibit and punish trusts . . . the whole effort has been to get some bill headed: 'A Bill to Punish Trusts' with which to go to the country." It was this Act of which Mr.

Dooley said at the time of the formation of the United States Steel Corporation in 1901: "What looks like a stone wall to a layman is a triumphal
arch to a corporation lawyer." On the Interstate Commerce Act of 1887,
Senator Nelson W. Aldrich said the Act was "a delusion and a sham . . .
an empty menace to great interests, made to answer the clamor of the
ignorant and the unreasoning." Quoted from Thomas C. Cochran and
William Miller, *The Age of Enterprise* (New York: The Macmillan Co.,
1942), pp. 171–172. On more recent times see J. K. Galbraith, "Monopoly
and Concentration of Economic Power," in Howard S. Ellis, ed., *A Survey
of Contemporary Economics* (Philadelphia: The Blakiston Co., 1948), pp.
115–124.

11. Here and elsewhere, "peak" or "listed" position, company, or industry refers
to the presidency, chairmanship, or partnership which made men eligible
for this study.

12. On the importance of businessmen's dynastic aspirations, see Joseph A.
Schumpeter, *Capitalism, Socialism and Democracy* (New York: Harper
& Brothers, 1942), pp. 156ff.

13. Since all the men studied were selected because of their *business* positions,
the group of lawyers includes only those who actually were president or
board chairman of business corporations in 1901–1910. No regular members of "law factories" are included. Thus the group is not representative
in size or composition of the whole class of business or corporation
lawyers. Since this is so and since even most of the lawyers included here
had professional rather than distinctly business careers, little more will
be said of them. A study of professional careers in the business community
is reserved for another occasion.

14. *Dictionary of American Biography,* essay on Mellon.

15. Eight of these men who themselves never started a business were part of
a large panel of outstanding men in all fields who in 1902 were asked if
they would advise "a young man of experience and ability, at a fair
salary, to go into business for himself." One of the eight gave no answer.
The remaining seven said "yes" even if it was "upon borrowed capital";
see Nathaniel C. Fowler, Jr., *The Boy: How to Help Him Succeed* (Boston:
Oakwood Publishing Co., 1902), pp. 167ff.

16. Andrew Carnegie, *The Empire of Business* (New York: Doubleday, Page &
Co., 1902), p. 190.

17. It may be true, as Robert K. Merton says in summarizing Weber's theory,
that "bureaucracy maximizes vocational security." Robert K. Merton,
Social Theory and Social Structure (New York: The Free Press, 1949),
p. 152. But in business, at least, this is relatively certain only in comparison
to the "vocational security" of the ordinary worker. It has yet to be shown
that the bureaucrat, even on the highest level, is more secure than the
great "captain of industry," for example, either in his hold on his status
or in the psychological attributes of it. Even while the bureaucrat may
be supposed, in Weber's terms, to be "set for a *career* . . . in which *tenure
for life* is presupposed," Weber notes that "this is not recognized as the
official's right to the possession of the office." (Gerth and Mills, *From
Max Weber,* pp. 202, 203; italics Weber's.) I am aware that this com-
plicates the ideal bureaucratic picture with "patrimonial" factors; but
it seems that in business at least the hierarchical nature of ascent may
not be altogether divorced from the patrimonial aspects of tenure. Indeed,

it may well be that the higher a bureaucrat goes the more dependent is his tenure on patrimonial factors.

18. Will C. Ferril (ed.), *Sketches of Colorado* (Denver: Western Press Bureau Co., 1911), p. 179.

19. Independent, 61:1491 (December 20, 1906).

20. *World Today,* 13:829 (August 1907).

21. Clarence W. Barron, *More They Told Barron* (New York: Harper & Brothers, 1931), pp. 153, 168.

22. "More Facts About Presidents," in *The Corporate Director* (November 1950). Virtually all of these presidents were of firms large enough to be listed on the New York Stock Exchange.

23. See Parsons, *Max Weber,* p. 331. For an illuminating account of the nature of this "war" in a man who eventually became president of the New Jersey Bell Telephone Company and one of the most enlightening writers on bureaucracy in business, see Chester I. Barnard, "Collectivism and Individualism in Industrial Management," an address delivered in 1934 at the Fourth Annual Economic Conference for Engineers at the Stevens Institute of Technology Engineering Camp, and printed by the Institute.

24. *Nation's Business* (October 1947), pp. 40ff.

25. *Business Week* (January 28, 1950), p. 21.

26. See Chester I. Barnard, *The Functions of the Executive* (Cambridge: Harvard University Press, 1938), pp. 224–225 and Chap. xvii, esp. pp. 272, 278; Talcott Parsons, "The Professions and Social Structure," in Talcott Parsons, *Essays in Sociological Theory Pure and Applied* (New York: The Free Press, 1949), p. 198; and Schumpeter, *Capitalism, Socialism and Democracy, passim.*

27. Arthur S. Dewing, *Corporate Promotions and Organizations* (Cambridge: Harvard University Press, 1951); see especially Chap. xxi, 558–560. See also Frederick W. Taylor, "Shop Management," first published in 1903 and reprinted with other works of Taylor's in *Scientific Management* (New York: Harper & Brothers, 1947), see pp. 17, 18.

28. Frederick W. Taylor, *Principles of Scientific Management* (New York: Harper & Brothers, 1911). See especially Chap. 2 where the prevailing system of "initiative and incentive" is contrasted with Taylor's "scientific management." In the former, in the vernacular of our own time, management did not manage, but left the initiative and planning of production to the worker.

29. Edward C. Mack, *Peter Cooper* (New York: Duell, Sloan and Pearce, 1949), p. 109.

30. These quotations are from John T. Flynn, *God's Gold* (New York: Harcourt, Brace & Co., 1932), p. 336; Matthew Josephson, *The Robber Barons* (New York: Harcourt, Brace & Co., 1934), p. 338; Barron, *More They Told Barron,* p. 77; *Dictionary of American Biography,* essay on Rogers; John D. Rockefeller, *Random Reminiscences of Men and Events* (New York: Doubleday, Page & Co., 1909), p. 6.

31. Cf. note 27, above. Of Archbold, who succeeded Rockefeller when Rogers wanted that role for himself, Nevins writes: "Never as cautious as Rockefeller, he had learned from him that in a multitude of councillors there is wisdom; he believed in a large executive committee, and insisted that it hold daily meetings to present a variety of points of view . . . He reserved his judgment until the end, and usually based it upon a consensus of opinion" (Nevins, *Rockefeller,* II, 433).

32. *Dictionary of American Biography*, essay on Rogers; Nevins, *Rockefeller*, II, 436. On Rogers generally, see Barron, *More They Told Barron*, pp. 76, 89.

33. *New York World*, March 27, 1898; and from an unidentified newsclip in the *New York Times* "morgue" but obviously from the same period and probably based on the same interview as that reported in the *World*. For the large holdings of the Matthiessen family, see Dewing, *Corporate Promotions*, Chap. iv.

34. Kenneth Burke, *The Grammar of Motives* (New York: Prentice-Hall, 1945). This entire work is given to an elaboration of the interrelations of Burke's "pentad"—act, scene, agent, agency, purpose.

35. Charles A. and Mary R. Beard, *The Rise of American Civilization* (New York: The Macmillan Co., 1930, 2 Vols. in one), II, 196.

36. With the engineers included in the "managerial" class, the proportion of independent entrepreneurs in that class is 20 per cent, and in the "technical" class, 5 per cent.

37. Beard, *Rise of American Civilization*, II, 196.

38. Walter Bagehot, *Economic Studies* (New York: Longmans, Green and Co., 1902; first ed., 1879), p. 28.

39. Bagehot, p. 61.

40. One of the earliest systematic books on the administration of the office is J. William Schulze, *The American Office* (New York: Key Publishing Co., 1913). The importance of office work in successful management was emphasized as early as the 1850s by Henry V. Poor. Frederick W. Taylor put good office administration at the core of business success. See "Shop Management" (1903) in *Scientific Management*, as cited, especially pp. 61ff., and 121f.

41. Barnard, *Functions of the Executive*, pp. 121, 225.

42. Sidney W. Martin, *Florida's Flagler* (Athens: University of Georgia Press, 1949), is largely devoted to this. See also Nevins, *Rockefeller*, II, 435.

43. Letter of Mellon's in files of James T. White and Co., November 23, 1912.

44. "Is Anybody Listening?" *Fortune* (September 1950), p. 178.

4. Political Behavior and Social Structure

In the field of political behavior in its relation to the social structure, the data used and the methods employed are of particular importance. Both Rudolf Heberle and Lee Benson use quantitative data conjointly with other sources. In addition, Heberle employs the ecological approach in order to make the *Gemeinschaft-Gesellschaft* continuum concretely intelligible, while Benson avails himself of the insights made possible by *reference group theory* for the purpose of developing analytical categories of American voting behavior. One must remember that a number of authors concerned with the rise of Nazism have used vague theories of individual or national character as an explanatory principle, or else, that they have resorted to postulating an undifferentiated economic chain of causation. In contradistiction, Heberle concludes that social determinants, such as a marginal position in the class structure and a correlated inclination toward political protest movements, predisposed the middle classes of the rural society in Schleswig-Holstein toward the rising Nazi movement. In a comparable argument, Benson disproves, at least insofar as the State of New York is concerned, the contention that Jacksonian democracy was identical with political progressivism and that it was an expression of the interests of certain economically defined classes in the population. His contention is that "directed approaches should be employed in historiography to support those that are predominantly 'intuitive' in nature." He suggests that such factors as past issues which have been kept alive, inherited role conceptions that cannot be dislodged, and positive as well as negative reference orientations (often of religio-ethnic connotation) are the decisive motivational elements that ought to guide research into American voting behavior. One must beware, however, of the inference, not directly promoted by either Heberle or Benson, that research on voting behavior can go far to reveal causative factors in political decision-making. In this regard, historically oriented studies of communal power structures, such as the one by Robert A. Dahl on New Haven,[1] may serve as a needed complement.

Comparable to Heberle, ecological approaches are also employed in the papers by H. W. Gilmore and Walter Firey on New Orleans and Boston, respectively. Both differ from classical ecological theories of the growth of cities in their emphasis on the historically conditioned differential symbolic value of certain locations and neighborhoods within a city. But there the comparison ends. H. W. Gilmore merely describes a historical case while Firey uses history to argue against "orthodox" ecological theory. Gilmore shows the interplay between river location, ridge and swampland, on the one hand, and Creole, American and Negro settlement patterns on the other, in order to demonstrate the unique features in New Orleans' development as compared with the development typically found elsewhere in American cities. Firey describes old Boston, especially the Beacon Hill area, accurately and vividly and stresses symbolic values as against a purely competitive valuation in order to disprove the validity of the ecological theories of Burgess and Hoyt, but he disregards the proposition that in ideal-typical procedure no given case must entirely agree with the theoretical model. He provides his own answer, though, when he refers to "lags" in ecological succession; in the meantime, urban renewal projects have penetrated the very heart of old Boston and have brought the city in line with widely observed trends. One thing is true, however: the Burgess and Hoyt theories must be regarded as historical theories, that is, as providing models for city growth in an industrial society only. They are not applicable to all times and places.

The two pieces by E. Digby Baltzell and by Wilbert E. Moore and Robin M. Williams deal with stratification theory in a historical context;

across the distance of, ages and continents, they are comparable to the paper by Tung-tsu Ch'u (Section I). There is a difference, however: the paper by Baltzell on the Social Register refers only to the American upper classes while the paper by Moore and Williams unfolds a panorama of the entire stratification system of the *ante-bellum* South. The Baltzell paper is paradigmatic for what a historically oriented sociology can do, not only because it is based on historical data, but also because it describes the process of social change which transformed small-town upper-uppers into denizens of the Philadelphia main line and which is transforming these again into members of the national upper class in an associational society. At the same time, the thesis of Baltzell's story is developed from the data themselves, not conceived independently and then superimposed upon the data.

The Moore and Williams paper takes its point of departure from a more clearly stated theoretical orientation and professes interest in the data chiefly from the point of view of their serviceability for the construction of a general theory of social systems. We have mentioned earlier that it must remain in doubt whether such a desired general theory can ever go beyond the comparative evaluation of divergent as well as convergent data; but it is certain that the Moore and Williams analysis does go a long way to show both what structural-functional theory can do for the understanding of historical situations and what historical data can do for the refinement of the theory. That the analysis of the system of stratification in the *ante-bellum* South contributes to the better understanding of contemporary race relations is merely a by-product.[2]

There are various reasons for the decision to conclude this section with an excerpt from Americo Castro's fascinating book on "The Structure of Spanish History." First, here is an attempt to analyze the meaning and cultural content of a social structure, not only social structure as such; this attempt goes beyond the concern for both "system" and "change." Castro investigates the vital components of a system and the continuity that is maintained in change. Further, Spain is for the western world what Japan is for the Orient—the exception that confirms the rule. If the sociological problem posed by Japan is to explain the development of modern capitalism in a non-western society, then the corresponding problem in Spain is to derive the absence of the capitalistic spirit, which is typical of the West, from the specific amalgam which is Spanish history. This, then, invites comparison with England, on the one hand, and with the unfolding of Hispanic modes of life in the Americas, on the other. The contrast of this Hispanic development with the development of Anglo-Saxon institutions in the American environment must be grasped, if one is to ponder the possible efficacy of the *Aleanza para Progreso*.

Notes

1. Robert A. Dahl, *Who Governs? Democracy and Power in an American City* (New Haven and London: Yale University Press, 1961).
2. Compare Rudolf Heberle, "The Changing Social Stratification of the South," *Social Forces,* 38, 1 (October 1959), pp. 42–50. The Moore-Williams

paper is focused on the interconnectedness of phenomena, the Heberle paper on quantitative and qualitative change. The Moore-Williams paper is valuable as a point of departure, a first step. The Heberle paper is nearer the complexities of actual development, and hence is theoretically more eclectic.

Rudolf Heberle   A REGIONAL BACKGROUND

FOR NAZISM

THE POLITICAL CHOICES of rural people, especially of farmers, are determined less by ideologies and general political ideals than by the weighing of concrete advantages and disadvantages to be expected from the rule of one or the other party. The readiness of the farmer to support any particular government depends largely on the expectation that the government's policy will produce tangible results for agriculture. The more commercialized the farming in a given region, the more will the farmers' prosperity depend on oscillations of the market prices of staple products. In other words, the more commercialized and the more specialized the farming in a region, the more the political attitude of the farmers will be influenced by the vagaries of business cycles and of structural changes in the general economic system of the country.

On the other hand, everybody familiar with party constellations in the United States will know that such sensitivity can be modified by the firmness of regional political traditions. In a region where a broad and influential local class has for a long time been leading in certain political parties, any new party will find it difficult to win support in this class and to break its influence on or control over the other classes in the region.

But where such leadership has been lacking and where a class hitherto not vocal in political life is coming of age, there the chances for a new political movement to win adherents will be more favorable.

We shall now consider the development in each of the three major zones in Schleswig-Holstein separately.

The *marshes* are the most commercialized agricultural region. The fertile coastal lowlands of Dithmarschen and Eiderstedt especially have a tradition of more than two centuries of commercial farming. Labor relations in the coastal marshes have long since been known for their contractual character and for their lack of community spirit. The deep cleavage between rich and poor,

Reprinted with the permission of the author and the Louisiana State University Press, from Rudolf Heberle, *From Democracy to Nazism: A Regional Case Study on Political Parties in Germany* (Baton Rouge: Louisiana State University Press, 1945), 100–111.

between farmer and cottager or laborer, is emphasized by the settlement pattern: the farmers live on single farmsteads with spacious buildings in the midst of their fields and pastures; the poor, the working class people in villages and in small line-settlements along the sea dikes and the edge of the sandy and moory *Geest*.

Similar conditions are found in the Elbmarshes; but farming here is more diversified, and the wealthy farmers are perhaps more tradition-bound than those in Eiderstedt and Dithmarschen. However, the segregation of the rural social classes and the dependence on markets are the same.

The particular nature of marsh farming, which requires little continuous work on the part of the farmowners, made them available for public offices, and even permitted some of them to practice the legal profession or to engage in business activities. Thus the wealthy among the farmers constitute an old political ruling class.

Dithmarschen, however, is not entirely marsh; about half of its area lies on the *Geest*. The *Geest* people were until recently much poorer than the marsh farmers and did not play any leading role in the public life of the region. Economically, the two parts are closely interrelated, because the *Geest* farmers raise the cattle which are bought by the marsh farmers for fattening on their rich pastures. The same interdependence of marsh and *Geest* and the same social distinctions exist farther north in North Friesland (Kreis Husum and Kreis Sued-Tondern).

Before 1918 the rich marsh farmers were traditionally attached to the *Nationalliberale* or to the *Freikonservative* party, while the smaller farmers, the middle classes in the small towns and also the working class people adhered to the *Freisinnige* or the Progressive party.

The elections for the National Constitutional Assembly in 1919 resulted in a very strong majority in favor of the new regime; in the rural marsh communities of Eiderstedt and Dithmarschen 83.4 per cent of the vote was cast for the DDP, *Landespartei,* SPD, and USPD. About half of these went to the two Marxist parties, a clear indication of the intensity of class cleavage.

While the Marxist parties held their strength fairly well from 1920 on (receiving between 30 per cent and 37 per cent of the votes in the rural communities of the marsh areas in Eiderstedt and Dithmarschen together, and between 34 per cent and 44 per cent in the marshes of Dithmarschen alone) the Liberal parties declined sharply and gave way to the Conservatives, who in turn lost the top rank to the Nazis.

The decline of the Liberal parties in the rural marsh communities of Dithmarschen and Eiderstedt from 46.5 per cent of the vote in 1919 to 9.2 per cent in 1930 signifies a complete change in the political attitude of the marsh farmers.

On the other hand, it is interesting and highly significant that since 1928 the NSDAP scored considerably less in the marshes of Dithmarschen than on the *Geest*. Also, the *proportion* of the total vote for the non-Marxist or "middle class" parties which went to the Nazis was on the whole smaller in the marshes of Dithmarschen than on the *Geest*, although in some earlier elections the relation had been the reverse.

Table 1—Radicalization of "Middle Class" Parties in Rural Communities of Dithmarschen by Subregions

	PERCENTAGE OF MIDDLE CLASS PARTY VOTES CAST FOR NSDAP		PERCENTAGE OF TOTAL VOTE CAST FOR MIDDLE CLASS PARTIES	
	Marsh	Geest	Marsh	Geest
1924 I	10.2	7.0	69.4	84.9
1924 II	5.5	3.6	68.7	85.8
1928	16.1	41.1	63.3	82.4
1930	66.5	67.4	63.6	82.0
1932	87.1	92.1	69.0	87.7

The marsh showed thus less solidarity of political opinion than the *Geest*, but on the other hand also a slightly greater stability of political opinion.

Dithmarschen and the Steinburg and Pinneberg Kreise which comprise most of the Elbmarshes were early strongholds of the organized NSDAP. However, it is significant that the communities in which the Nazis had strong organizations were located either on the *Geest* or in the border zone between marsh and *Geest* and not in the marsh proper.

Nevertheless, the radicalization both of the labor class and of the farmers in the marshes remains remarkable. An explanation may be attempted in terms of increasing economic insecurity rather than of actual suffering from the agricultural depression. The marsh farmer has always been inclined to incur great speculative risks: cattle grazing and cabbage farming involve a gambling element—the enormous gains of one year may be cancelled by the losses of the next; sometimes the entire market value of the farm may be earned by a single good crop, while the heavy demand for short term credit may plunge the farmer deeply into debt in the next year. During the period of cheap bank loans after the First World War, many of the marsh farmers had incurred heavy debts, and not always for production purposes. When the markets collapsed and credit became difficult to obtain—that is, from 1929 on—these farmers found themselves in a very critical financial situation.

In the Elbmarshes the decline of horse breeding (because of motorization and reduction of army demands) and of certain rural industries (the raising and processing of willows for basket-making) as well as the repeated crises in the hog fattening industry in 1926–1927 and 1929–1930, accounted for rising discontent with the existing political conditions among the farmers, large and small. This paved the way for the Nazis.

On the other hand, the Marxist parties obtained support not only from the workers and artisans in the small coastal towns but also from the fisher-men who were quite severely hit by the depression, and therefore began more than ever to feel their dependence on the canning companies as employers and creditors. A similar radicalization of fishermen was observed on the east coast, on the island of Maasholm.

The *eastern hill zone* comprises two different types of subregions: Angeln, the Isle of Fehmarn and the Probstei (a group of villages in the northern tip of the Ploen Kreis) are farmers' districts, while the rest is characterized by the prevalence of large estates. These estates dominate especially in the Ploen and Oldenburg Kreise. Agriculture in the entire region is well diversified, except for Fehmarn, where barley and wheat are the predominating crops. Angeln has an especially well-balanced system of family farming, with grain production, dairying, cattle and horse breeding and hog raising well integrated.

The social stratification in Angeln was more complex than in the coastal marshes: While the big farmers constituted the leading and ruling class, there was a substantial class of smaller farmers and cottagers, sometimes settled in small communities which are old offshoots of the original villages; finally there was a class of day-laborers and of hired hands. Labor relations were stable, with a residue of patriarchalism. In spite of distinct stratification neighborhood relations were strong and well institutionalized. The class struc-ture of Fehmarn was more like that in the marshes.

Until 1919 the large estates in east Holstein resembled in social structure those on Mecklenburg and other regions east of the Elbe. However, the con-centration of farming operations in the hands of the landlord had not been as far advanced as in those other regions. There existed a cooperation between the main estate with its cottagers and wage laborers and the often quite well-to-do tenant farmers in the villages, most of whom had held the same farm through many generations.[1] Land reform legislation after 1919 resulted in the transformation of tenants into owners on the former tenant land of the estates and in the resettlement of some of the former cottagers with public financial support.[2]

Thus, while the old upper classes of estate owners and big farmers were, thanks to their diversified economy, fairly safe against the vicissitudes of the postwar agricultural cycles, there had come into existence a layer of new pro-prietors of small, and often too small, farms who were committed to fixed interest and annuity payments to public finance institutions—a situation which became quite threatening when agricultural prices began to drop in the late twenties and credit became more difficult to obtain.

Politically, east Holstein before 1918 had been dominated by the owners of estates. These adhered to the Conservative or *Freikonservative* party, while the Social Democrats and the Progressives competed for the vote of the agricultural laborers, the small farmers and the tenants, and also the lower middle class in the small towns. The control of the landlords over the villages, however, constituted a severe handicap for the democratic parties.

After the revolution of 1918, the discontent with the politically obsolete system of tenancy resulted in strong majorities for the Socialist and Democratic parties. Very soon, however, the Conservatives (DNVP) became the leading "middle class" party in east Holstein, strongly opposed by the combined Marxist parties. When finally, in 1930 and 1932, the Conservatives gave way to the Nazis, the latter obtained their strongest successes in the farmers' areas of east Holstein and not in the areas of large estates, where both the Marxists and the Conservatives preserved their strength somewhat better.[3] (Table 2.)

Angeln was before 1918 politically dominated by an upper class of rich and often well-educated farmers who, not being quite so conservative as the large landlords, adhered to the *Nationalliberale* or to the *Freikonservative*

Table 2—Election Results in Rural Communities in the Eastern Hill Zone

Type of Community	NSDAP		DNVP		SPD and KPD	
	1932	1930	1932	1930	1932	1930
Estates—prevalent						
Kreis Oldenburg	41.4	16.0	11.0	18.6	45.0	49.6
Kreis ploen	45.3	18.8	9.8	15.3	42.4	46.5
Farmers' villages						
Isle of Fehmarn	47.0	23.9	8.6	16.7	41.8	44.3
Kreis Oldenburg	52.0	25.5	9.3	19.0	36.4	41.6
Kreis Ploen	52.2	23.9	10.9	16.7	33.9	36.1
Probstei	59.5	38.0	11.8	17.4	26.0	29.7
Kreis Eckernfoerde (mixed)	60.1	22.2	9.2	11.3	28.2	31.4
Angeln (farmers)	70.8	24.6	10.5	7.0	12.5	15.0

party. In 1919 the *Landespartei,* political creation of the *Bauernverein* which had many members among the smaller farmers in Angeln, emerged as the leading party, with 35.5 per cent of the total vote. The DDP was second with 27.9 per cent, and the DVP obtained 8 per cent—the three liberal parties together 71.4 per cent, or as much as the NSDAP scored in 1932. By 1924 the Conservatives had become the strongest party, with 43 per cent, which was about the average for Schleswig-Holstein. The Marxist parties were weak throughout the entire period but formed a rather firm block of about 3,500 votes. The important feature of the political development in Angeln and the factor which retarded the rise of the NSDAP was the strong position of the right-wing Liberals, the DVP. This party, successor to the *Nationalliberale Partei,* obtained in 1928 and 1930 almost twice as large a percentage of all votes as in the average of Schleswig-Holstein. Another factor which retarded the penetration by the Nazis was the strength of the *Landvolkpartei* in 1930.

A firm political tradition, a definite social stratification, and at the same time a well-developed agricultural ladder which facilitated social climbing, a well-balanced agriculture and a sound farm-credit situation, together with the moderate temper and the religiousness of the Anglian, may account for the tardiness of the region in giving in to the oncoming wave of Nazism. Even in 1933 the party organization was reported to be much weaker in Angeln than in most other sections of Schleswig-Holstein. However, the high degree of political solidarity which distinguishes family farm areas from areas of large estates made it possible for the NSDAP to obtain in Angeln in 1932 the highest percentages of the total vote in the entire hill zone.[4]

Of all three major zones, the *Geest* showed the greatest instability of political opinion. Here, on the sandy and moory soils, the tradition of past poverty lingered on, and the standards of living of the rural people were still decidedly simpler than in the other two regions. Also, the *Geest* farmer was less commercially minded, less given to risky business transactions than the marsh farmer. On the other hand, agriculture was not so well balanced on the *Geest* as in Angeln or Ostholstein; the preponderance of animal husbandry made the *Geest* farmer dependent on the demand, by the grazing farmers in the marshes, for young cattle (*Magervieh*), that is, ultimately on the beef cattle market in Hamburg or the Rhineland, and also on the hog market with its well-known cycles. This was especially true of the northern *Geest* while in the south, in the hinterland of the metropolitan cities of Hamburg, Kiel, and Luebeck, milk production and truck farming were more developed and furnished a fairly steady cash income. Needs for production credit were generally less than in other zones.

The social structure of the *Geest* villages was less complex than the village structure in the other zones; there were very few large estates; and, since most of the farms are small enough to be operated by the family and a few hired servants and occasional day laborers, there existed in these villages no broad class of agricultural laborers. The few small cottagers were usually accepted as part of the village community. Differences in wealth were not emphasized as status distinctions. Neighborhood relations were strong, and there was no spatial segregation of rich and poor. Thus, the *Geest* villages presented a much higher degree of community solidarity than any of the other zones.

However, until 1918 the *Geest* had been lacking political leadership, nor had the *Geest* farmers participated in the rural political leadership of the region which rested with the marsh farmers or the eastern landlords (*Gutsbesitzer*), none of whom accepted even the well-to-do *Geest* farmers as their social equals. Although the *Geest* people had never known serfdom, there was no old tradition of self-government as in the marshes. The prevailing political tendency before 1918 had been that typical of the "small" people in Schleswig-Holstein—Progressive Liberalism. About 1918 there emerged on the *Geest* an organization of farmers which later on formed the foundation of the short-lived *Landespartei*—for the first time a movement of *Geest* farmers, led by men of their own group.

It seems very likely that this lack of an old, experienced political leadership, together with the relative absence of class antagonism and class distinctions in the *Geest* villages, accounts for the completeness of political shifts in this zone. The social structure prevented the development of a strong bloc of Marxist voters in most of the rural *Geest* villages, except in some rural industrial communities,[5] and this weakness of the Marxist parties gave the Nazis a much wider margin than in the other zones. The strongly developed sense of community solidarity made it easier to swing the vote of an entire village towards a new party, than in the marshes where a more developed individualism and sharper class distinctions operated as retarding factors.

We may then, in concluding our regional survey, state tentatively that, while the decline of liberalism and the growth of the counter-revolutionary parties were conditioned by the general factor of economic distress, the subregional differentials between the strength of the various parties were primarily determined by the social structure of the communities rather than directly by economic factors.

Notes

1. Either as *Zeitpaechter* (long-term tenants) or *Erbpaechter* (hereditary tenants). These forms of tenancy were the substitutes for serfdom which had been abolished at the end of the eighteenth century, that is, much earlier than in Prussia.
2. Resettlement activity in Schleswig-Holstein was strong; from 1919 to 1935 (that is, chiefly until 1932) more than the acreage which the province was legally required to make available (103.4 per cent) for resettlement purposes was actually made available, and 5,899 new and 1,542 "Anlieger" farms were established. (*Statistisches Jahrbuch fuer das Deutsche Reich, 1936*, p. 82.)
3. While the relative resistance of the landed aristocracy to Nazism is being emphasized here, it should not be forgotten that the Conservative landowners did nothing to prevent the rise to power of the Nazis and that they lent them their support in various ways.
4. A particularly striking case of farmers-village solidarity was revealed in Schwackendorf, a village in Angeln. Here almost the entire population voted NSDAP in 1932, while in the neighboring village of Gelting the Nazis obtained only sightly more than half of the votes. Local informants stated that in Schwackendorf the leading farmers had agreed among themselves to join the NSDAP in a body. The important point is that this action was taken primarily because the farmers wanted to maintain the political unanimity of the village, out of a spirit of neighborliness. Gelting on the other hand comprises an estate, belonging to a Catholic family; consequently both the Socialists and the "other parties" (including the Center party) remained here relatively strong.

	Schwackendorf	Gelting
Total Number of Voters in 1932	180	325
SPD and KPD	3.9%	18.8%
DNVP	0.6	13.5
Other parties	1.1	12.0
NSDAP	94.4	55.7
Total	100.0	100.0

5. A good illustration of the relation between social structure and political con-
stellation is offered by the two industrial villages of Muensterdorf and
Laegerdorf on a *Geest* "island" south of Itzehoe (Kreis Steinburg). Since
the comparison of these villages is suited to convey an idea of the way
in which the regional analysis was pursued into local detail (in the original
study), the findings may be briefly presented as an example. Both are
former farmers' villages whose population at the time of the investigation
consisted largely of workers in the near-by stone quarries and a cement
factory in Laegerdorf. (P. Hermberg, *Die Bevoelkerung des Kirchspiels
Muensterdorf* [Dissertation, Kiel, 1913].) A third village on this *Geest*
"island," Daegeling, was still predominantly an agricultural village. While
in Daegeling the relation between "labor" and "middle class" votes in 1919
was almost 50:50, the two industrial villages had very considerable majorities of the Marxist parties. This relation had not been changed in 1932
in Muensterdorf and Laegerdorf; however, within the "middle class" bloc
a considerable shift toward the Nazis had taken place, and in Laegerdorf
the radicalization of the labor vote was noteworthy. This difference in
the political attitude of the labor class in the two villages may be explained
mainly by the much higher degree of migratory mobility among the
workers in Laegerdorf; for, a high turnover in the labor force makes
union organization difficult and therefore impedes effective organization
of a labor party that, like the SPD, is based on labor unions. In Daegeling,
where the Marxists obtained almost 50 per cent of the vote in 1919, a
complete reversal occurred: the middle parties were wiped out by 1932
and the Nazis dominated the community with 79 per cent of the vote
against 20 per cent Marxists.

PERCENTAGE OF VALID VOTES CAST FOR SPECIFIED PARTIES

	SPD	KPD or USPD	Marxists	DDP	Landespartei	Right DNVP, DVP, etc.	NSDAP	Other Parties
Muensterdorf								
1919	70.8	0.2	71.0	17.3	0.8	10.7	—	0.2
1932	53.5	13.8	67.3	1.3	—	3.0	26.9	1.5
Laegerdorf								
1919	76.6	0.9	77.5	17.4	—	4.6	—	0.5
1932	26.8	43.7	70.5	0.8	—	2.6	24.0	2.1
Daegeling								
1919	x	x	49.5	15.9	18.7	15.9	—	—
1932	x	x	20.1	0.9	—	—	78.7	0.8

Lee Benson   A TENTATIVE CLASSIFICATION FOR
                              AMERICAN VOTING BEHAVIOR

HISTORIANS WHO ARE SKEPTICAL of the value of scientific procedures when
applied to refractory human beings in nonlaboratory or nonexperimental
situations, may ask: Why bother with devising an abstract classification system? Why not concentrate upon finding out the actual determinants of voting
behavior in specific situations?

In my opinion, a clear, logical system of categories helps to alert historians
to the *possible* determinants of human behavior in specific situations. It is
axiomatic that before decisions are made about the relative importance of any
determinant, the range of determinants that may have operated in a given
election should be considered. The record demonstrates that the axiom has
not always been recognized. For example, I believe that lack of a comprehensive classification system has significantly contributed to the long dominance
of economic determinism in American political historiography.

If we look only for "economic factors," we are likely either to find *only*
economic factors or *no* economic factors at work. Collecting only certain
limited types of economic data, we ignore the possibility that other determinants may have modified or counterbalanced the impact of economic factors.
It seems reasonable to assume, therefore, that a comprehensive classification
system can serve to guide us, and help to guard us, against such errors of
omission.[1]

A set of comprehensive, clearly-defined categories serves as more than a
check list. By providing a framework for ordering data in some systematic
and logical fashion, it brings into focus relationships among empirical data that
are not readily apparent.[2] Thus insights derived from seeing how one determinant influences voting behavior can illumine other determinants that have
much the same effect. Conversely, recognizing the uniformities that link a
number of determinants points up sharper distinctions among them and leads
to fuller understanding of how they individually influence behavior.

At this early stage of development, the main function of the theory may
well be to widen the frames of reference of American historians. Two quotations from editorials by Horace Greeley transform the vagueness of a "wide
range of factors" into a more concrete, vivid image of Americans behaving
politically. The first quotation calls attention to a subtle process by which

group voting patterns, originally shaped by a "political" issue (defined later), tend to be perpetuated after the resolution, or disappearance, of the conflict: "In Connecticut a good deal of sectarian bitterness exists and thousands of Episcopalians, Methodists, Universalists, etc., who would be Whigs almost anywhere else, usually vote Loco-Foco [Democratic] in Connecticut, primarily from hostility to the 'Standing Order of Orthodox Congregationalists,' who formerly were favored by law in Connecticut [disestablishment took place in 1818], who are still by far the most numerous denomination there, and who are somehow mixed up in the popular sentiments of the other sects with the Whig party; so that while an 'Orthodox' citizen votes as *Political considerations* [italics added] impel him to do, a citizen of another church or no church is strongly drawn toward the support of the opposite party by considerations which have properly nothing to do with Politics. This side-current may not always be perceptible even to those drawn by it, but it is none the less potent for that; and we believe that not less than an eighth of the votes cast against the Whig party are influenced by variance of religious creed from the church with which the Whig party is in that State popularly identified."[3]

Systematically analyzed, the process described by Greeley falls into three stages. During the first stage, an issue (here church-state relations) generates intense conflicts until it is resolved by some government action, or until the issue ceases to command attention and disappears from the political arena. In the second stage, antagonisms aroused by the original conflict remain acute and influence voting behavior through the formation of what sociologists call "negative reference groups." That is, certain voters continue to range themselves against each other, even though the original political conflict is no longer an active issue (for example, Connecticut Episcopalians "vote against" Congregationalists after as well as before disestablishment). In the final stage, sufficient time elapses so that neither the original conflict nor the subsequent political antagonisms stemming from it are perceptible to contemporaries. Nevertheless, both factors continue to influence voting behavior in the form of *political roles* traditionally played by members of certain groups (for example, Connecticut Episcopalians vote Democratic because members of that group "always have").

A consideration not mentioned by Greeley deserves emphasis. During any one of the three stages described above, the emergence of another political issue that is related to the original conflict, or that pits the same antagonists against each other, reinforces established group voting patterns and makes them more visible to contemporaries. And, though not as directly, much the same results are produced by antagonisms originating outside the political sphere (for example, Episcopalian and Congregational denominational rivalries).

The next quotation is from an editorial by Greeley which also observed that voting behavior was determined by factors other than views of politico-economic issues. If a "real" political issue, such as the tariff, were forcefully presented to the workers in any machine shop or shoe factory in the Union, Greeley insisted, three-fourths would vote Whig: "But the very shop wherein fifteen out of twenty workmen would be with us on the Tariff issue fairly made and fully considered, will often give a majority *against* us in the absence of such discussion. Jones hates the Whigs, because Esq. Simpson is a leading Whig, and feels too big to speak to common people. Marks has been trained to believe that the Whigs were Tories in the Revolution and starved his father in the Jersey prisonship; so he is bound to hit them again at each election. Smithers is for a Tariff himself, but his father before him was a Democrat, and he isn't going to turn his coat. Smolker don't object to anything his Whig shop mates propose; but he is a Foreigner and thinks the Whigs hate foreigners, so he feels bound to go against them. Pitkin is a heretic in religion and most of the leading Whigs he knows are Orthodox; and he can't stand Orthodoxy anyhow you can fix it. And so, for one or another of a hundred reasons, *equally frivolous or irrelevant* [italics added] voters are piled up against us not for anything we as a party affirm or propose, but because of considerations as foreign from the real issues of the canvass as is the subjugation of Japan."[4]

We discern three categories of voting determinants. In the quotation above, Greeley emphasized men's conscious motives. But, as the earlier quotation shows, he recognized that voting determinants operating on less conscious levels are no less potent. For our present purposes, the accuracy of Greeley's specific observation is immaterial. But his editorials illustrate how we can classify the determinants of American voting behavior under three main headings or categories. In time, I believe, they can be developed to form an inclusive classification system; and dependent upon the specific elections and groups analyzed, we can devise subcategories for each of these three main categories:

1. *Pursuit of political goals by individuals or groups.* For example, the disestablishment of the "Standing Order of Orthodox Congregationalists" in Connecticut; the establishment of a protective tariff.

2. *Individual or group fulfillment of political roles.* For example, "Smithers is for a Tariff himself, but his father before him was a Democrat, and he isn't going to turn his coat"; Connecticut Episcopalians continuing long after 1818 to vote against the "Congregational Party."

3. *Negative or positive orientation to reference individuals or groups.* For example, "Jones hates the Whigs because Esq. Simpson is a leading Whig, and feels too big to speak to common people"; "Marks has been trained to believe that the Whigs were Tories in the Revolution and starved his father in the Jersey prisonship; so he is bound to hit them again at each Election." (The quotation would have exemplified positive orientation had it read: "Jones *likes* the Whigs because Esq. Simpson is an admirable man and he is a leading Whig.")

As is true of any classification system, these categories are doubtless easier to distinguish analytically than empirically. But surely significant differences exist and can be recognized among these three types of alleged behavior: (a) Connecticut Episcopalians voting before 1818 to abolish a State Congregational Church; (b) men voting Democratic because their fathers voted Democratic and they weren't going to "turn their coats"; (c) men voting Democratic because they substituted the Whigs for the Tories who had maltreated their fathers.

1. *Pursuit of Political Goals.* If, for our present purposes, we assume that Greeley accurately observed voting patterns, then a clear-cut political issue originally determined the voting behavior of Connecticut Episcopalians. They used political means to get the state to take "political action" which they regarded as beneficial to them, or to the community at large, or to both. Political actions are broadly defined here to include actions taken by any state agency in respect to laws, policies, rulings, government personnel, and government structure. Sometimes voters' choices (including no choices) are determined by their opinions of party positions on specified political actions, or a general, more vaguely-defined program of action; at other times, they are determined by the belief that the candidates of one party will carry out desired political actions either more effectively or more faithfully than will the candidates of another party. Whether the desired political actions represent grand "disinterested" measures, petty "selfish favors," or appointment of members of a particular group to a particular office, all behavior determined by such considerations is assigned to the category, "pursuit of political goals." Concrete examples may clarify the discussion and indicate how subdivisions can help differentiate voting behavior within the same main category.

According to this classification system, passage of a high tariff law and appointment or election of an Irish Catholic to high office are both defined as political goals. Desire for a high tariff exemplifies an economic goal, desire for appointment of an Irish Catholic exemplifies a status goal (that is, attainment of a political objective that would give members of certain groups greater power to command respect or deference from other members of the community or society). Though their motives differ significantly, men who pursue either one of those goals are seeking to get the state to take some action, or are approving some action the state has taken. In other words, their common desire for state action determines and links the behavior of men who pursue the different kinds of economic and status goals described above. (Of course, men can also pursue "nonpolitical" economic and status goals, that is, goals that do not require state action.)

For our present purposes, it is irrelevant whether voters are consciously aware that they are seeking political goals or whether historians can empirically distinguish among degrees of conscious awareness. The point is that, logically at least, a category can be created to encompass all voting behavior designed to produce specified state actions. By definition, therefore, voting behavior determined by other considerations is assigned to one of our remaining two categories.

2. *Fulfillment of Political Roles.* As the Greeley quotations pungently suggest, men knew and used the concept of social role long before social scientists invented the term. In this context, brief definition and exposition convey its central premise and indicate its usefulness to a theory of American voting behavior: "The ways of behaving which are expected of any individual who occupies a certain position constitute the [social] *role* . . . associated with that position."[5]

Individuals occupy many positions, however, and the great majority of them do not usually carry expectations of prescribed *partisan* political behavior (for example, males, husbands, adults). Moreover, role definitions vary, at least in the United States, and positions expected to produce certain ways of behaving politically at one time and place do not necessarily carry the same expectations at other times and places. In short, occupancy of a certain position constitutes a "political role" only when it is associated with clearly defined and recognized ways of behavior. Such roles, I contend, are unlikely to be deduced theoretically by analysts and must be discovered empirically.

In Greeley's description, Smithers' father was a Democrat in an era when sons were expected to vote for their fathers' parties. Thus, despite his agreement with the Whigs on a "real" political issue (tariff), he voted Democratic. Otherwise he would have regarded himself and have been regarded by others as "turn[ing] his coat," that is, not fulfilling his political role. It is worth noting that Smithers could conceivably have favored a protective tariff strongly enough to disregard the pressures exerted upon him by his political role. That he did not do so indicates, therefore, the relative importance he attached to his political role and to his political goal.

Establishing the category "fulfillment of political roles" makes it easier to discover in voting behavior essential similarities which might otherwise appear disparate. Men may vote in a particular fashion because they are their fathers' sons, because they are members of certain ethnic, religious or socioeconomic groups, because they reside in certain areas or political units, because they belong to and are loyal to a certain political party. Whatever the surface differences, at least two significant uniformities characterize the voting behavior that fulfills political roles. It is determined primarily by membership in a certain group or occupancy of a certain position and by adherence to tradition or habit rather than by a desire to have the state take certain actions or follow a less precisely defined general course of action.

Inconveniently for a fool-proof classification of voting behavior, men's motives in real life are less neatly compartmented and less easily distinguished than we should like. But lines of demarcation are universal problems for analysts. Whatever phenomena or objects are classified, whatever kind of system is used, borderline cases always cause trouble and blurring always occurs as one moves away from the extremes. Though historians can never dispense with judgment in classifying determinants of voting behavior, the argument here is that agreement is not always impossible. For example, significant differences clearly distinguish these phenomena: (1) Connecticut Episcopalians using political means to rid themselves of politically-established disabilities; (2) the same men voting for one party because their group has traditionally done so.

In both of these hypothetical cases, membership in a religious group determined how men voted. But in the first case, to attain their objective some specific state action was necessary. In the second it was not; they may well have voted for the traditional party of their group even though they preferred the program of the opposing party and thought its candidates were better qualified. Thus it seems reasonable and possible to differentiate between the pursuit of political goals and the fulfillment of political roles.

3. *Orientation to Reference Groups and Individuals.* Like the type of voting behavior assigned to the category "fulfillment of political roles," the type assigned to our third category is not primarily determined by a desire for specific state action. But it differs from the second type of behavior in a crucial respect: it designates men who behave according to patterns set by *groups to which they do not belong, or by certain individuals whose patterns influence them in determining their own.* The difference between those two categories is perhaps best suggested by quoting Robert K. Merton on the difference between "social role" and "reference group" theories: "That men act in a social frame of reference yielded by the groups of which they are a part is a notion undoubtedly ancient and probably sound. Were this alone the concern of reference group theory, it would merely be a new term for an old focus in sociology, which has always been centered on the group determination of behavior. There is, however, the further fact that men frequently orient themselves to groups *other than their own* in shaping their behavior and evaluations. . . ."

"In general, then, reference group theory aims to systematize the determinants and consequences of those processes of evaluation and self-appraisal in which the individual takes the values or standards of other individuals and groups as a comparative frame of reference."[6]

Unlike Smithers, whose vote was determined by his political role, Marks voted Democratic because he identified the Whigs with the Tories and wanted "to hit them [Tories] again at each Election." In Merton's terms, the Tories represented for Marks a negative reference group. Thus his behavior fundamentally resembles that of Jones who voted against the Whigs because he identified them with the arrogant Esquire Simpson whom *he* wanted "to hit again at each Election." But we surely are justified in saying that the behavior of Smithers, Marks, and Jones differed from that of Connecticut Episcopalians who voted to achieve disestablishment, or from that of iron manufacturers in Essex County, New York, who voted to secure a high protective tariff.

In an attempt to distinguish between such varied types of voting behavior, some political analysts have classified men as acting rationally and irrationally. In my opinion, such categories have value connotations that make them necessarily subjective and drastically limit their usefulness. That contemporaries and later historians have sometimes stigmatized men's behavior as irrational because it was designed to achieve objectives that *they* regarded as undesirable is not news. And that historians with different frames of reference frequently disagree about the rationality of exactly the same behavior is not news either. Why then employ categories more likely to compound than to reduce confusion?

4. *Combinations of Determinants.* It is worth repeating that the three main categories sketched above are more easily established analytically than demonstrated empirically. It is also worth noting that I do not regard monistic explanations of voting behavior as credible, whether the "single factor" is ascribed to all men or to specific individuals and groups. "No man," Coleridge observed, "does anything from a single motive." Thus the problem of interpreting voting behavior at a given time and place is always to decide which *combination of determinants* influenced voters identified by some attribute, or set of attributes. Under certain conditions, and in certain cases, it may be possible to give particularly heavy weight to one determinant or factor. But such assessments are not monistic. They recognize that other determinants contribute to the same result, although to a lesser degree.

Notes

1. I have developed this argument at greater length in an essay called "A Critique of Beard and His Critics." See *Turner and Beard, American Historical Writing Reconsidered* (New York: The Free Press of Glencoe, 1960).
2. For the advantages of qualitative classification systems, see Paul F. Lazarsfeld and Allen H. Barton, "Qualitative Measurements in the Social Sciences: Classification, Typologies, and Indices," in Daniel Lerner and Harold Lasswell, eds., *The Policy Sciences* (Stanford, Cal.: Stanford University Press, 1951), 155–182.
3. *New York Tribune* (w.), March 22, 1851, p. 5. Although unsigned, the editorials quoted here have all the hallmarks of Greeley's style and I am reasonably certain that he wrote them. But the points made in the text do not depend upon correct identification of the editorial's author.
4. *Ibid.,* September 11, 1852, p. 2.
5. Theodore M. Newcomb, *Social Psychology* (New York: Dryden Press, 1956), 280. In discussing and using the social role concept, I have considerably benefited from reading the relevant chapters in this text on social psychology.
6. Robert K. Merton, *Social Theory and Social Structure* (New York: The Free Press, 1957), 234. American historians in particular, I believe, would benefit heavily from the two chapters dealing with reference group theory. *Ibid.,* pp. 225–386.

H. W. Gilmore   THE OLD NEW ORLEANS AND THE
                     NEW: A CASE FOR ECOLOGY

NEW ORLEANS is sufficiently different from the general run of American cities
to make it an interesting laboratory for studying ecological principles evolved
on the basis of data from other cities. Its topography, on casual observation,
appears to be rather similar to that of Chicago or of any number of plains
cities. Yet in certain respects its topography is very different, and uniquely, it
has been changed fundamentally during the history of the city. In its population history it has shown evidence of the processes of accommodation and
assimilation of minority groups characteristic of other cities, plus long standing
patterns of accommodation of racial groups which assimilated very slowly or
not at all. As a result of these complex factors, ecological maps of New Orleans look like a crazy-quilt to sociologists acquainted with the ecology of conventional American cities. Actually, however, the city is not without an
ecological pattern and this pattern is not difficult to see once the city's topography and history of ethnic groups are understood.

As was said above, the topography of the city is in some respects typical
but in other respects it is unique. The city is located on a strip of land roughly
five to seven miles wide between Lake Pontchartrain on the north and the
Mississippi River on the south. Though eighty miles from the gulf, this land,
like all land in the area, was built up by a long process of sedimentation.
Therefore, in contrast to inland areas, the higher land is found along streams,
or where streams once existed, while the lowest land is found farther away
from streams. Thus, while the land may appear to be perfectly flat, a contour
map shows that the land ranges from fifteen feet above to two feet below mean
gulf level.

The highest land in the city is found along the river and ranges from five
to fifteen feet above mean gulf level. Passing north from the river, the altitude
declines to two feet below gulf level. The low area, however, is transversed
by "ridges" where bayous are or have been. Thus there is Metairie Ridge, two
feet above sea level running east and west almost parallel with the river and
about half way between the river and the lake. There is also a ridge about two
feet above gulf level, running north-south from the end of Bayou St. John to
the river, passing the lower end of the French Quarter. We will call this
Esplanade Ridge. This ridge divides the city into what may be conceived as

Reprinted with the permission of the American Sociological Association from the *American
Sociological Review*, Vol. IX, No. 4 (August 1944), pp. 385–394.

two saucers sitting edge to edge, the other edges being formed by Metairie Ridge and the high land along the river. Each saucer is two feet below sea level at its center and is from two to fifteen feet above sea level at its periphery. Until relatively modern times the centers of these saucers were swamps and habitation was feasible only along the rims of the saucers. It is in terms, therefore, of the struggle of the nationality groups for residential space around the edges of the saucers that the ecology of the city is to be understood.

Creole New Orleans

New Orleans, of course, was settled by the French. Presumably the particular site was selected because they wanted an inland water route to the gulf coast of the present state of Mississippi where they already had a settlement at Biloxi. Such a route was available through Bayou St. John, Lake Pontchartrain and a series of lakes and bayous which link this lake to the gulf. A short and easy portage between the river and Bayou St. John was provided by Esplanade Ridge which was already in use for this purpose by the Indians when the French explorations and settlement were made. The settlement originated at the junction of Esplanade Ridge and the River and as it expanded it did so mostly to the west where the land was higher than it was to the east. This is the area that is now known as the French Quarter.

Like the settlers in most colonies, the early French settlers of New Orleans were a rather motley lot. They came from various walks of life and various stations in France and probably are not to be considered as coming primarily from any particular social element of the homeland. After a period of frontier hardship, however, they began to be moulded into a quite distinctive and homogeneous group. The French government followed a very liberal policy of land grants to individuals with the result that most of the early settlers became big land holders. This policy was continued by the Spanish government when this territory passed into the hands of that nation. Thus under both France and Spain, there was a tendency for government officials and military personnel sent out to the colony to acquire sizeable land holdings usually without having to purchase them. On these holdings the French-established plantations worked with slave labor and rapidly attained prosperity on this basis. Most of them, however, continued to live in the city, particularly during the winter and if they lived on their plantations at all they did so in the summer. Their city life was based almost as much on slave labor and the labor of free Negroes as was their plantation life. Thus at the time of the Louisiana Purchase there were twice as many Negroes as whites in the city. As time went on these French plantation owners came to refer to themselves as Creoles and they will be so referred to in the remainder of this paper. The

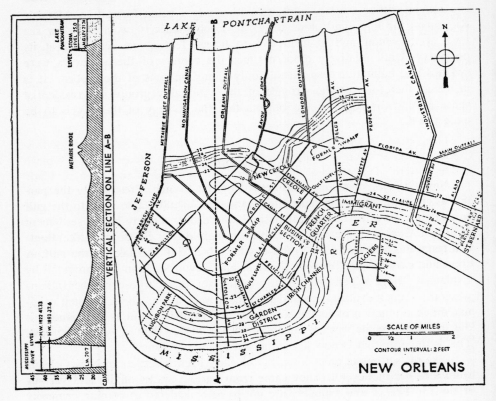

CHART I
Residential Areas
(Adapted from drawing by H. W. Gilmore)

term itself does not refer to land ownership but merely to unmixed descendants of French or Spanish settlers.

This prosperous, land-endowed group, plentifully supplied with colored labor, and gathering in the city for a winter of leisure, made a very favorable situation for an elegant social life. The city being also the colonial capital made this almost inevitable. Such a development seems to have taken place in a large way from 1743 when the great marquis, Pierre Francois de Riguod, Marquis de Vaudreuil, came as governor of Louisiana. He and his wife were accustomed to life in the royal courts of Europe and apparently sought with considerable success to set up a similarly pretentious society in New Orleans. Once established, this pattern was continued by succeeding governors, French and Spanish, with the exception of a brief period under General ("Bloody") O'Reilly who was sent by Spain to suppress a revolt against Spanish rule.

Spanish rule does not seem to have altered the situation in any significant way. The Spanish made no attempt to colonize New Orleans or Louisiana. They did make a half-hearted attempt to teach Spanish in the colony but it attained very indifferent success. For the most part, Spanish officials and military men seem to have found the Creole social life much to their taste and to have been accepted by the Creoles into that social life. Thus they came nearer being assimilated by the Creoles than the reverse. In reality many of them did marry Creoles and others received land grants, established plantations and became part of the Creole aristocracy.

Thus, prior to the Louisiana Purchase, the city was dominated by this Creole landed aristocracy centered around the colonial capital. It was a typical Estate pattern. The emphasis was on inherited wealth in the form of land. There was a law of primogeniture with the surplus sons placed in professions or the government service and stress was laid on social life or leisure time pursuits instead of occupational attainment.

The following description by a French traveler, C. C. Robin, of a reception given in 1803 may give a glimpse of the life of these Creoles prior to the Louisiana Purchase:

The Louisiana Ladies appeared there with a magnificence that was astonishing in such a colony, and that magnificence could be compared with what is most brilliant in our principal towns in France. The stature of the ladies, generally tall, and their fair complexion, which was set off to advantage by their light dresses adorned with flowers and rich embroideries, gave a fairy-like appearance to these festivities. The last one, especially, astonished me by its magnificence. After the tea, the concert, the dances, the guests descended at midnight into a hall where, on a table of sixty to eighty covers, rose from the midst of rocks the temple of Good Faith, surrounded with columns and surmounted by a dove; underneath was the statue of the allegorical goddess. But further, outside of that hall, the brilliance of the lights attracted the guests under an immense gallery closed by awnings. Forty to fifty dishes, served in different styles, were offered to the choice of four or five hundred guests who were assembled in little groups.[1]

In addition to the Creoles and the Negroes, there were other nationality groups in the city prior to the nineteenth century. A number of Germans had come to the Louisiana territory during the John Law boom in the 1720s and after unsuccessful attempts at settlement on the Arkansas River had settled in the vicinity of New Orleans. Also, French immigrants came from Santo Domingo as a result of slave uprisings and from France as a result of the French Revolution during the latter part of the eighteenth and early part of the nineteenth century. Most of these groups were unable to get large land grants and hence did not become plantation owners. In large part they seem to have become dairymen and truck gardeners though many of them also became artisans. There were also, of course, some representatives of numerous other nationalities but they can be ignored in an ecological study.

With this information before us, let us try to get a picture of the city at the time of the Louisiana Purchase in 1803. It contained a population of only 8,475 (census of 1805) and covered a correspondingly small area. The heart of the city was what is now known as the French Quarter, bounded by Canal Street, Rampart Street, Esplanade Avenue and the River. In this area were the government buildings, what business there was and the homes of the Creoles. The slaves were housed on the premises of their owners so far as possible. Since most of the Negroes, whether free or slave, were employed in service around the homes of the Creoles, and hours were long and travel was by foot, the Creoles desired them to live close to their homes. Thus those who could not be quartered on the premises formed a residential fringe around the Creole section. Outside this Negro zone was the immigrant truck gardening and dairying zone, the latter using land which was too swampy for residence or cultivation but usable as pasture. On the high land adjacent to the river and east of the city this trucking zone expanded into a considerable area. Outside of this area were plantations wherever the land was high enough to permit cultivation. Thus there were plantations along Bayou St. John and along the river on both sides of the city.

Creole-American Conflict

Up to the time of the Louisiana Purchase the infiltration of Americans into New Orleans had been small. They came in and out with the shipping and there were some permanent residents but in some degree immigration of Americans had been held back by unfavorable Spanish laws. With the Louisiana Purchase, however, the dam was breached and the tide began to flow. Thus within the five year period from 1805–1810 there was a 125 per cent increase in the white population of the city, and a large part of this increase undoubtedly was American.

These incoming Americans were a sharp contrast to the polished, wealthy Creoles with their elegant social life. While as a group the Americans who came to New Orleans were perhaps not as crude as the American frontiersman in the open country, certainly they had among them many who were just that crude. In fact the river men who floated down the Mississippi on barges and were known locally as the Kentucks were just as crude and rough and ready as the frontiersmen in any part of the country. Thus, in New Orleans, the spreading American frontier ran into a culture which, on a basis of manners and fine appearance at least, was superior to its own; the only case of its kind in American history.

The difference in degree of cultural refinement, however, was not the only difference between the Creoles and the Americans. The Creoles, it will be remembered, laid stress on family tradition, hereditary wealth, leisure and social position. The American, on the other hand, had as his sun god the self-made man. The individual who had been born free and equal, had through his own initiative, industry and thrift gained wealth or success, was the man to be worshiped whether he was the son of a prince, a millionaire, a beggar, a criminal or a simple frontier woodchopper. Thus the two had basically different social philosophies as well as social systems; neither understood the philosophy of the other and neither was much impressed if he did understand. Also the fact that the Creoles were Catholic whereas most of the Americans were Protestant did little to foster mutual affection. Language differences of course increased these tensions, and furthermore, the question which language would be the official language, was an issue of serious moment.

On the basis of their culture, their wealth and their numbers in a more normal situation, the Americans might have been expected to have assumed the role of a minority group but, as usual, New Orleans was not a normal situation. The Americans were representatives of the nation which had just purchased Louisiana and now controlled the government and they were in no psychological mood to be a minority group. Nor was the government in any mood to insist on their playing a minority role. Thus from the beginning, to the tune of much conflict, overt and covert, with the Creoles, they were forced by the factors of the situation into a position somewhat better than that of a minority group.

The course of events brought a rapid improvement in their situation. The passage of the Louisiana Territory into the hands of the United States ended all barriers to commerce on the Mississippi River and brought a rapid commercial development in New Orleans. The Creoles with their philosophy of hereditary wealth and leisurely social life, had never had much taste for the make or break drive for efficiency characteristic of the commercial world and they did not take to it now. Since most of the tillable land was already held by the Creoles, most of the Americans had little chance of establishing themselves as landlords. In any event, the uncertainties, the big stakes and the competition of the business world, had a natural appeal to the worshipers of the self-made man, and they rapidly took over the competitive area as their special domain.

Thus the port figures for the first six months of 1803 show that the shipping was already largely in American hands even before the Louisiana Purchase. Of the 153 cargo ships entering the Mississippi during that period 93 were American, 58 were Spanish and only 2 were French.[2] Similarly, Vincent Nolte who visited New Orleans in 1806, three years after the Purchase, informs us that the mercantile system was made up of four or five French establishments founded during the French rule, three Scotch counting-houses, one German concern and eight or ten commission houses lately opened by young American merchants from New York, Philadelphia and Baltimore.[3]

This near-monopoly on the thriving commerce of the port city rapidly brought prosperity to the Americans and along with it brought a rapid increase in their numbers. With their nationality status thus backed by wealth and numbers, the Americans increasingly challenged the Creoles for the leadership role, culture or no culture, and the struggle between the two groups grew in severity and bitterness.

Ecology of the Old New Orleans

This struggle made inevitable an ecological separation of the two groups. The first Americans did live and have their business in the French Quarter but the crowded conditions in addition to the Creole-American struggle brought growing pressure for them to go elsewhere. Being so heavily engaged in commerce, it was imperative that they stay on the high land along the river but the fact that they moved west instead of east of the French Quarter was perhaps the result of the Marigny affair.

About 1822 two Americans, James H. Caldwell and Samuel J. Peters, planning to develop a succession of warehouses and cotton presses and other important enterprises (hotel, gas works and water works, etc.), approached Bernard de Marigny with a proposition to buy the whole of his extensive property along the Elysian Field Section. The Creole was extremely unwilling to deal with the Americans, whom he disliked intensely, but was finally persuaded to do so, for a stipulated sum. When the necessary legal documents had been drawn up to conclude the sale, Mrs. Marigny failed to appear at the notary's office. Her signature was necessary to ratify the sale and Marigny used her absence as an excuse to prevent the sale. Infuriated, Mr. Peters is said to have cried out to the Creole: "I shall live, by God, to see the day when rank grass shall choke up the streets of your old faubourg."
. . . Outraged but not discouraged, the two pioneers transferred their interests above Canal Street. They felt that the Americans would be glad to congregate there since they would be separate from those whom they regarded as their oppressors. With the assistance of other local American capitalists a considerable part of the holdings of Jean Gravier was purchased.[4]

Whether or not this event is a full explanation, at any rate from about this time on an American section did grow rapidly to the west of the French Quarter. Into this section moved both American residents and American business. This movement was particularly rapid in the early thirties and a survey made by a local newspaper in 1834 showed that about three-fifths of the "merchants," two-fifths of the "retailers" and four-fifths of the "brokers" were by that time in the American section.[5] Thus the city quickly evolved a pattern with the business section around Canal Street as the center, the Creole section to the east and the American residential section to the west of this. Each of these residential areas had Negro slaves living on the premises and a horseshoe-shaped fringe of Negro residences around it with the open side of the horseshoe being towards the business section. Outside of this was the trucking-dairying zone.

The strife which produced this residential segregation was manifest in a severe degree in political circles. The Creoles, considering themselves the settlers of Louisiana, felt the government belonged to them, and the Americans, considering that they had purchased Louisiana, felt the government was theirs. The Creoles had been accustomed to use government positions to support their sons who could not inherit land under primogeniture, and the Americans had no inclination to use tax funds to support Creole families. In contrast, the Americans wanted the government to build all sorts of facilities which would be of aid to commerce, and the Creoles were not interested in being taxed to bring prosperity to the Americans. These differences were so great that as the two factions attained near equality numerically and financially one government could no longer contain them. Thus in 1836 New Orleans was divided into three municipalities, having one mayor but for all practical purposes having separate governments. In the center was the Creole city bounded on the east by Esplanade Avenue and on the west by Canal Street. To the east of it was the immigrant truck-gardening city and to the west of the Creole section was the American municipality. In all three cases the river was the southern boundary and the lake was the northern boundary.

This separation of the city into three municipalities practically established Canal Street and Esplanade Avenue as national boundary lines. It became a matter of honor and of loyalty to one's cause to live on the proper side of these streets; those who moved into enemy territory were viewed askance if not actually as deserters. And after more than a century these definitions have by no means disappeared.

With this division the American municipality launched an almost extravagant program of public improvements. Old wharves were improved and new ones were built, streets were paved, public schools were developed and public buildings were constructed. Accompanying this was a growing prosperity and a rapid inflow of white population. Thus the white population in the whole city (three municipalities combined) increased from 21,281 in 1830, to 59,519 in 1840, and 91,431 in 1850. Meanwhile there were no more Negroes in the city at the end of this period than at the beginning.

A significant part of this influx of white population was Irish workmen. The growth in commerce and shipping brought laboring jobs and the public works program of the American municipality meant the need for many workmen. To meet these needs there was virtually no local labor supply. There were not enough free Negroes, slaves were too expensive, and the immigrants were happily employed in their crafts and agricultural pursuits. As a result, outside laborers were brought in and these for the most part were Irish immigrants.

This growth in population with the influx of a new immigrant element brought an expansion and reshuffling of the residential areas in the American section. With their mounting wealth the American elements were in a position to move farther out and build themselves new homes. South was the river, north were the swamps, and to the east were the business section and Creole land. Their logical move, therefore, was toward the strip of higher land adjacent to the river, and this move they made, developing a pretentious residential section with large homes and spacious grounds. This section has since been known as the Garden District. At the time it was built, it equaled or surpassed anything the Creoles possessed either in the city or on their plantations, and doubtless served to give the Americans a psychological compensation for their lack of "culture" and family background as compared with the Creoles.

This move of the Americans meant that the Negro residential fringe and the truck-gardening zone had to be invaded and pushed out farther. It was the beginning of a process which continued up to relatively recent times both in the Creole and American sections. While in both cases the invasion did take place, the succession was not completed, particularly with reference to the Negro residences, for in all of the older sections of the city today there are scattered small groups of Negro residences which are remnants of a once solid Negro residential zone. Also, in moving out, the Americans deserted their old residences. Since the Irish were working for the Americans, they were not welcomed in other sections of the city, and being laborers, they needed no land to cultivate. Thus they were glad enough to get the discarded residences and New Orleans gave birth to what has since been known as the Irish Channel.

As the city grew, the Creole area, being adjacent to the central business section, tended to deteriorate and this, with a natural increase in Creole population, created pressure for that group to move out also. If the Americans had their fate sealed as to where they might move, so also did the Creoles. To move east meant crossing the national boundary line of Esplanade Avenue and invading the immigrant truck gardening section and this would violate their pride and honor. To the west was Canal Street, the central business section and the unthinkable American section. Their only recourse was to move out Esplanade Ridge to Bayou St. John, and here today New Orleans has lovely old homes which are a product of this period. The migration process in this area was similar to that in the American section with some significant differences. The invasion process was about the same but the tendency of the Creoles to stay in the French Quarter in spite of deterioration was much greater. Thus there resulted an extraordinarily large number of what in other cities would be called marooned families, and there are in that area today many homes which are still owned and occupied by descendants of the families who originally built them.

Due to administrative and financial difficulties, the three municipalities were recombined into one in 1855, but by that time the ecological pattern was firmly fixed. Esplanade Avenue and Canal Street were made and the Creole section limited to Esplanade Ridge while the American section was confined to its ridge west of the city.

The strips of habitable land on these ridges were rather narrow and any tendency of these residential areas to widen was quickly checked by the swamps or the river. Therefore, expansion could only take place by building farther and farther out along these ridges. Such building, however, meant greater and greater distances from the central business section, and greater distance meant serious inconvenience when travel was by walking, bicycle or horse and buggy. In the American section, where the growth had been the greatest, the distances became so great as practically to approach the toleration point. Thus further expansion was made with a minimum of land and a minimum of added distance. This was done by making the yards inconveniently small and building the houses close together. Economically, of course, this was reflected in very high land values.

The immigrant truck-gardening section to the east of the city seems to have had, by comparison, relatively few growing pains. Being engaged in agriculture, the residents were not densely settled and, as the city developed, the population turned more and more to nonagricultural occupations. There was little accretion to this area by migration, and the rate of natural increase was not enough to take up for residential uses the land which was thrown out of cultivation. Thus while other sections were crying for land, this section had land to spare. As a result, land in this section became a quicksand for real estate speculators who knew land but did not know New Orleans. For the same reason there was a plentiful supply of land on that side of town for military uses during the First and Second World Wars.

Thus up to the early part of this century the basic ecological pattern of the city was T-shaped. The T was formed by the intersection of Esplanade Ridge and the ridge running along the river. The French Quarter (original French settlement) was approximately at the intersection of this T. The immigrant truck-gardening area was at the east end of the cross bar and on the west end were the central business section, the Irish Channel and the Garden District (American section), respectively. The newer Creole area was on the leg of the T, Esplanade Ridge, running vertically to the river. All of these were long narrow rectangular shaped areas, strung out along the top of the ridges, flanked on both sides by the swamps or the river. The American section and the Creole area were fringed by horseshoe shaped residential areas for Negroes and outside of these was a truck-gardening and dairying zone. The latter used land which was dry enough to cultivate or pasture but too low for residential use.

The New Ecology

During the present century several developments have been taking place which have been materially altering this ecological pattern. About 1910 the city began to attain success in a long effort at artificial drainage of surface water. The city had early used canals and drainage ditches to hasten the flow of water from the ridges to the swamps. Then in the latter part of the last century it tried canals with windmill powered pumps to drain lower sections. These pumps were found inadequate and in 1903 they were replaced by electric-powered centrifugal pumps. These were an improvement but still did not have the capacity necessary for a city with the heavy rainfall which New Orleans has. Finally in 1917 a large screw type of electric pump, something like a ship's propeller installed in a large pipe, was developed and this proved adequate to the task. With these pump developments went a gradual improvement in surface and underground drainage facilities. From small beginnings this system was thus expanded until today it has a pumping capacity of 16½ billion gallons per day (24 hours), enough water to cover eighty square miles of land one foot deep. As a result, the water level was gradually lowered until by the 1930s all of the former swamp areas were as effectively drained as the higher areas.

The development of this drainage system ecologically had the effect of changing the topography of the city. In virtually no place in the city is the change of altitude sudden enough that there is any visible difference between high land and low land. With drainage, therefore, the land, for ecological purposes, is perfectly flat and as far as topography is concerned it is all equally desirable for building purposes. Hence the barrier which the swamps had formerly been to residential expansion was now removed and the residential areas began to respond accordingly. The American section most strikingly turned squarely north away from the river and directly toward the center of a former swamp. Thus during the past two decades, census tracts which are in this former swamp area, show population increases of from 700 to 1400 per cent. The Creole section correspondingly, spread out in both directions from the Bayou St. John area, though the population pressure here was not nearly so great as in the American section.

About the time these drainage developments were taking place, transportation developments were in process which also had marked effects on the ecological pattern. So far as this city is concerned probably the most important transportation development was the street car. Like other social developments, this one cannot be very specifically dated. Horse-drawn cars and steam "dummies," of course, date well back into the past century. The successful electric car was not developed until about 1885 and its effect on the ecology of the city was not very evident until well into the present century. While the street car aided greatly in relieving pressures in the American and Creole sections, probably its most pronounced effect was on the Negro residential fringe. With the street car available it was no longer necessary for the Negroes to live so close to where they worked. In other words, the electric street car made the Negro residential fringe obsolete. As a result, this fringe began to disappear. In its stead, large Negro residential areas began to develop back toward the central business section in the formerly swamp areas between the white residential sections. This concentration has in turn attracted to these areas schools and other facilities for Negroes which are an incentive for more Negroes to move there.

The automobile which had such profound effects on most American cities had a relatively small effect on New Orleans. It augmented the effect of the streetcar in a number of ways but since it was not commonly used by Negroes and other poor elements in the population, it created no new trends related to these residential areas. The only part of the city where there was sufficient residential pressure to make a demand for residential suburbs was the American side of the city, and here the outlying areas were so swampy that this was impractical. There did develop on the west end of Metairie Ridge over in an adjoining parish a suburb known as Metairie. However, the 1940 census still showed New Orleans as ranking among the lowest cities in the country in the proportion of its population living in the metropolitan area outside the official city.

In general, the drainage system, the street car and the automobile combined, have created a tendency for New Orleans to shift from its former ecological pattern to a zone system similar to that recognized in other cities. However, this pattern is by no means yet completed and it seems likely it will not soon be completed. Vast areas of the city are still socially taboo to large elements of the population and these do not conform to a symmetrical zone pattern. In addition, on the American side of the city, the drainage did not provide enough land to bring the price of building lots down to what would be considered elsewhere as "reasonable." Therefore, building new homes is still expensive and as a result old ones are not recklessly discarded. Consequently the "nice" old residential areas do not deteriorate except under the greatest of duress. And by the time the natural pressures for deterioration have become sufficiently great these areas have accumulated enough tradition to make them antiques. Thus the French Quarter is now protected by special legislation designed to prevent invasion and deterioration. Under this protection it has actually been undergoing a restoration with middle and upper class Americans moving in. Correspondingly the Garden District has tenaciously remained respectable. The 1940 rent map shows that this district is still one of the high rent areas of the city. Very high order rooming houses are about the only degradation it has yet suffered and to date it has not needed special legislation to protect it. However, should that necessity come, its antiquity is such that it will doubtless be museumized in the legislative halls.

In summary, the ecological pattern of New Orleans up to the present century was primarily the result of its topography. This pattern was set by the ridges and limited by the swamps and the river. In the historical process, sections of these ridges were occupied by the different nationality groups and came to be considered their special domain. Due to the ethnic conflicts and status differences between these nationality groups the social definitions of these areas became very strong and highly emotionalized. As a result of the division of the city into three municipalities in 1836 Canal Street became the accepted boundary line between the American section and the Creole section and Esplanade Avenue became the dividing line between the Creole area and the immigrant area. With the development of the drainage system during the present century the swamps disappeared and this land became as well drained as the ridges. Therefore, with the land being so nearly flat, today there is no visible difference between the low land and the high. Thus, for all practical purposes, topography as an ecological factor has disappeared except for outer limits set by the Mississippi River, Lake Pontchartrain and outlying swamps. In this situation the ecological pattern is tending to respond to modern transportation facilities and develop in the direction of a symmetrical zone pattern. The social definitions of the different areas carried over from the previous era, however, are proving very strong and resistant to change. This resistance is further increased by the fact that suitable land is not available for developing extensive suburbs which would make inevitable the deterioration of the old areas. Therefore, the old areas tend to be preserved and occupied by the same groups as formerly and, wherever necessary, protective legislation is provided to facilitate this preservation.

Notes

1. Fortier, Alcée, *History of Louisiana* (New York: Goupil Co. of Paris, 1904), II. pp. 240–241. Nellie Warner Price, "Le Spectacle de la Rue St. Pierre," *Louisiana Historical Quarterly* I, p. 218.
2. *Annals of Congress, Seventh Congress—Second Session*, Washington, 1851, p. 1525.
3. *Biographical and Historical Memories of Louisiana*, Chicago, 1892, I. p. 30.
4. Klein, Selma L., Social Interaction of the Creoles and Anglo-Americans in New Orleans, 1803–1860, M.A. Thesis, Department of Sociology, Tulane University, 1940, pp. 35–36.
5. *The Bee*, May 29, 1935.

Walter Firey   HISTORICAL DIFFERENTIATION AND
SUCCESSION OF LAND USES IN
BOSTON

The arrangement of materials in this chapter has been governed by two main problems: (1) Does the territorial migration of any particular type of social system, say upper class families, follow along a single sector as argued by Homer Hoyt or expand by gradual concentric spreading as suggested by Ernest W. Burgess, or does it proceed in a wholly different way? (2) Does the territorial distribution at a given time of any particular class of social systems resemble a concentric or sector pattern? If the Burgess or Hoyt theories are valid, we may expect to find territorial arrangements which conform to a concentric or sector pattern, or both. Any significant departure in actual land use from such idealized patterns will call into question the explanatory adequacy of the Burgess and Hoyt theories.[1]

We are dealing here primarily with the historical differentiation and succession of land uses in Boston, not with the present arrangement of these land uses. Perhaps the most obvious fact about Boston's spatial development is that land uses have become increasingly differentiated, with the result that homogeneous areas, each put to a different use, have gradually emerged. Pioneer Boston had but a rudimentary spatial differentiation, the principal one being that between the storekeepers and townspeople who lived right in the heart of the settlement at what is now the head of State street, and the majority of the settlers, who were distributed along the shoreline north and south of this center.[2] Dock square, as the town's landing place, became the main produce market. Here the fish and corn markets were located and here imports were received and stored. On nearby State street there were established retail shops, a merchants' exchange, a postoffice, and the town house.[3] Extending away from this center, but avoiding the steep slopes of Beacon Hill, Copp's Hill, and Fort Hill which lay to the interior, the bulk of the settlers located their homesteads. These homesteads were scattered about more or less indiscriminately, and there was very little territorial differentiation in terms of affluence or prestige.

But after 1685, with the change from a colonial to a crown government, there arrived in Boston a new and more class conscious group of people. The

English governor, his officials and assistants, as well as shrewd enterpreneurs seeking wealth and prominence, all introduced a class differentiation into colonial Boston which showed itself in a corresponding spatial differentiation of residences. With the erection of the governor's mansion on Charter street the North End became the "court end" of town and a number of fashionable families located there. North square, then known as Clark's square, became the social center of Boston and nearby were built Christ Church and the Old North Church to serve the well-to-do English families residing nearby.[4] Other prominent families located toward the northern ends of what are now Washington and Tremont streets and at Pemberton square. But the area below here was "so near the extreme south end of the town as to be socially out of the world."[5]

What little industry there was in colonial Boston was centered mainly around the Mill Pond—a body of tide water situated in the vicinity of present day North Station. Here was a lumber mill, a grain mill, a chocolate mill, and some distilleries.[6] Shipyards were located at the base of Copp's Hill in the North End, and in Charlestown.[7] Beyond the settlement lay the "fields," some owned by the town and some by a few men some of whose names even now survive in the Boston aristocracy—Phillips, Leverett, Russell, Staniford, Chambers, Lynde, and Allen. The Common was at this time a cow pasture and waste land.[8]

This early differentiation of land uses is of course too vague to warrant its being compared with the concentric sector patterns outlined in the idealized descriptive schemes. It is enough now to appreciate the role of volition that was manifest in the development of a distinct fashionable residential district in the North End. This spatial differentiation, corresponding to and symbolizing a new class differentiation, is only too clearly the expression of a cultural factor, namely, the rise of a governing and mercantile class out of a hitherto democratic community of pioneer settlers. Let us see, however, if the later differentiation of spatial areas in early Boston proceeded along the simple sector or concentric lines described by Hoyt and Burgess.

The first definite shift of the preferred residential districts occurred in the middle 1700s with the gradual development of the western part of the town. By 1740 a few fine mansions were located on Cotton Hill, one of the three peaks that then comprised Beacon Hill. Bowling Green, now known as Bowdoin square, likewise became a favorite residential neighborhood and was destined to remain so for nearly a century.[9] Another fashionable area appeared at the opposite end of town from the North End and from the Beacon Hill-Bowdoin square vicinity, for by 1780 there was a pronounced shift of the elite to the Fort Hill and Pearl street districts near the present South Station. Other streets lying to the south end of town also became lined with expensive mansions—particularly Summer, Winter, Franklin, and High streets.[10] Of course this new southward movement was not as yet at the expense of the other aristocratic areas, with the result that by 1780 there were fully three fashionable residential areas: the North End, the Beacon Hill-Bowdoin square area, and the Fort Hill and Pearl street vicinity, all lying on opposite sides of the business center. Lower class districts apparently occupied the back streets and interstitial areas although very little descriptive material is available on that point until the post-Revolutionary period.

Thus, at the time of the Revolution the upper class residential districts had become well differentiated into definite preferred areas. The sequence of their development had been roughly from north to west and then from west to south, following no consistent sector outward and expanding in no peripheral concentric fashion. Moreover, when viewed statically, the arrangement of these residential districts conformed to no concentric or sector pattern. Upper class homes were located on three different sides of the commercial portion of the city and were of varying proximities to this center. The Fort Hill and Pearl street vicinity was close to the commercial center and lay to the south; the North End was likewise close to the center and lay to the north; Beacon Hill was then remote and lay to the west. To look for simple patterns of land use in this arrangement seems rather futile. Let us, however, defer our full judgment of the idealized descriptive schemes until later, for we shall presently encounter data that will render the problem a little less simple than it now appears.

With the outbreak of the Revolution Boston suffered an enormous loss of population. Most of the crown officials and a large share of the upper classes in general had left the town with the British evacuation. In their place there appeared a new class of commercial people who came into Boston to capitalize on the economic possibilities opening up as a result of the Revolution.[11] These changes in the class composition of the community were accompanied by certain shifts in the spatial distribution of upper class families. These shifts were all at the expense of the North End. The new aristocracy which had been bred by the Revolution desired more palatial homes than were available in the North End. That district had become well built up with dwellings, generally small, close together, and ill suited to the tastes of the time. Consequently the nouveaus looked elsewhere for their residences and those of the old aristocracy who came back to Boston generally did not return to their former homes in the North End. Gradually the district became occupied by skilled workers and small entrepreneurs. A few "substantial families" did remain until as late as 1840, particularly along Sheafe street with its old rear gardens.[12] But the early transformation of North street, then close to the waterfront, into an area of ill repute catering to the demands of sailors and other transients, gradually destroyed the entire area's reputability.[13] Over the course of time the North End became a definitely lower class district and with the advent of the Irish in the 1850s it was established as a distinctly immigrant community.

It was to the then rural and out-of-the-way Beacon Hill district that upper class families turned after the Revolution. Apart from a few mansions located on Cotton Hill this vicinity had so far undergone but little settlement.[14] But with the construction of the New State House on Beacon street, in 1795, the Beacon Hill area acquired a high degree of desirability.[15] Hancock, himself a nouveau, soon afterwards built his gubernatorial mansion on Beacon street and thereby furthered the new movement of upper class families toward the Hill. It will pay us to look at this development in a little detail, for the case brings into somewhat clearer focus the real scope of volition in spatial adaptation, as against the inevitability that is postulated by the idealized descriptive schemes.

The development of Beacon Hill as a fashionable residential district, far from being inevitable, was to a considerable extent the result of deliberate promotion. Of course, no one is now in a position to say whether or not the fashionable character of the Hill might have been acquired in the absence of the promotion. We can only demonstrate that the actual laying out and settling of the Hill was brought about by men who deliberately planned the neighborhood as a fashionable residential district. The construction of the New State House came at a propitious time, when upper class people, many of recently acquired wealth, were seeking a "proper" place in which to live. The New State House apparently lent an appropriate distinction to the Beacon Hill vicinity. In 1795, the very year of the State House's construction, a syndicate known as the Mount Vernon Proprietors was organized for the purpose of buying up land on Beacon Hill and laying out an appropriate arrangement of streets and lots.[16] The members of this syndicate, consisting of Jonathan Mason, Harrison Gray Otis, and Charles Bulfinch, were all socially prominent, and Mason and Otis themselves built mansions on the Hill for their families. Thus, a proper character to the Hill was set. To further establish the fashionable character of the projected district an elaborate plan was drawn up by Withington, calling for residences all of strictly mansion type, each surrounded by large estates, and with streets so designed as to minimize north-south traffic.[17] This latter feature had a purpose rather obvious to one who knows modern Beacon Hill, for then as now the northern slope of the Hill was occupied by lower class families. The Mount Vernon Proprietors wished to ensure the upper class character of the southern slope and achieved this through minimizing north-south movement and through stipulating a certain standard of mansion construction, thereby restricting that slope to families of some means.

The whole venture was speculative and in the opinion of some writers was by no means foreordained to success. The first advertisements pointing out the desirability of the Hill appeared in the *Columbian Centinel* of August 3, 1796, but it was not until 1802, following the erection of Otis' and Mason's own mansions, that other wealthy people began moving to the neighborhood.[18]

A wave of financial prosperity, by expanding the fortunes of many families, further aided the syndicate and after the turn of the century the Hill underwent a rapid settlement.[19] Mount Vernon, Chestnut, and Walnut streets were the first to develop, but by 1804 the higher portions of the Hill, on Pinckney and Myrtle streets, likewise became occupied by upper class families.[20] The subsequent history of Beacon Hill is largely one of alternate expansion and neglect, correlating with the successive waves of prosperity and depression affecting the American economy. From 1814 to 1820 the Hill lost many of its families following the ruin inflicted upon wealthy people by the federal embargo against foreign trade. After 1820 the Hill underwent another burst of building, only to be checked by the 1829 panic which ruined many Boston families. In the 1830s residential development was resumed only to be again interrupted by the 1837 panic.[21] But by this time the Hill had been substantially built up and its later fluctuations in residential occupancy attended other causes. None of these fluctuations at any time jeopardized the status of Beacon Hill as a fashionable residential neighborhood, though significant recessions and revivals have taken place that will engage us at the proper place.

It is interesting to realize that the entire development of Beacon Hill proper was, from its very beginning, directly contiguous to an area containing, as one writer of the nineteenth century put it, "the most miserable huts in the city."[22] This area, occupying the north slope of the Hill, is more generally referred to as part of the West End. From the time of the Revolution down to the present day this slope has been occupied by lower class families and has been but little influenced by its direct contiguity with the fashionable south slope, Beacon Hill proper. After 1789, when Massachusetts legally abolished slavery within the state, a large Negro population appeared in Boston and gradually took over the cheap dwellings around the north end of Joy street and the adjoining portion of Cambridge street, from there spreading over the entire north slope.[23] Here the Negroes lived in extreme poverty and disorganization. The area was notorious for its disreputable houses, its vice, and its riots. An entry in the police reports for July 14, 1826 reads: "—July 14. A riot on Negro Hill; several houses pulled down."[24] By the time of the Civil War this slope had become a sanctuary for escaped slaves and a terminus of the "underground railway."[25] Further toward the Charles River a population of skilled workers and seamen was more predominant. However, toward the 1870s and 1880s the north slope underwent a new development. By this time thousands of immigrants from southern and eastern Europe were seeking cheap quarters in Boston and real estate speculators were quick to see their opportunity. In a relatively short span of time the old wooden shacks and single family dwellings were razed and in their place arose the solid brick fronts of tenements lining the streets up and down the steep hillside.[26] Into these new quarters moved the Irish and, more extensively, the Jewish immigrants from Russia and Poland. It is these latter, interspersed with some Italians, who now dominate the north slope of Beacon hill.

Thus within the Beacon Hill area, considered as a geographical unit, there have been, for a century and a half, two contiguous areas sharply set off from one another in terms of prestige value and class status, each maintaining its "reputation" through all the vicissitudes that have accompanied Boston's growth. The reasons for this "persistence of reputation" will engage us more fully at a later point. Our principal concern now is in the general arrangement of land uses, particularly as they pertain to the hypotheses of the idealized descriptive schemes. Certainly the sharp demarcation of Beacon Hill into an upper class area and a lower class area presents a phenomenon that does not fit in very well with the Burgess-Hoyt theories. By itself, to be sure, it is not a refutation of those theories but, when added to other evidence, its implications become fairly significant. For one thing, both sides of the Hill lie within the same concentric zone—the "area of transition" in Burgess' terminology. Yet their ecological characteristics are vastly different. For another thing, even if we drew sectors in such a way as to put the south side of the Hill, Beacon Hill proper, into one sector and the north side into another sector, the pattern would hardly reconcile with the Hoyt hypothesis that adjoining sectors represent a gradation rather than a contrast; in our case the two sides of the Hill are actually polar opposites, whether viewed in terms of rent, housing standards, or the class status of occupants. It is quite evident that further factors have to be invoked if we are to explain this spatially objectified class differentiation which is so sharply delineated within the Beacon Hill vicinity.

Behind the State House, on Hancock, Temple, and Bowdoin streets were additional upper class families—this in spite of the northerly exposure of the position. To the north of here, in the West End proper, lived families of apparently middle class status, occupying Chambers, Staniford, Lynde, and Leverett streets. Allen and McLean streets, also in the West End, seem to have enjoyed a somewhat more exclusive character than the adjoining streets.[27] However the West End did not endure long as a middle class district. Gradually it lost its families, and the dwellings were taken over by landladies who rented out rooms to single men employed in the city. This rooming-house phase of the West End's history was terminated at the same time that the lower class north slope of Beacon Hill underwent its architectural transformation, and for the same reason. The influx of immigrants during the last quarter of the nineteenth century made tenements a more profitable real estate venture than rooming houses. As a result the West End was converted into a tenement quarter and has remained one to the present time.

There is one additional development in the western portion of Boston that merits attention. As early as 1811 extensive topographical alterations had been made on Beacon Hill in the form of reducing its summit to the level of the

State House foundation.[28] The operation was so successful, from the real estate standpoint, that it was applied in 1835 to the complete obliteration of Cotton Hill, one of the old summits of Beacon Hill. The promoter of this venture, Patrick Jackson, then proceeded to develop the area now known as Pemberton square into a magnificent residential neighborhood. Expensive mansions were built, grounds were terraced, and by the late 1830s Pemberton square constituted one of the exclusive residential quarters of Boston.[29]

A recapitulation of the upper class portions of Boston as they were distributed in the late 1830s reveals no real sector or concentric pattern at all. To the west and northwest lay Beacon Hill, Pemberton square, Bowdoin square, and Temple place. Slightly to the south was Tremont street (between West street and Boylston street). Then, to the south and southeast were Fort Hill and the adjoining portions of Pearl and Franklin streets.[30] The upper class districts thus embraced fully two points of the compass, only the northeast and east being unrepresented owing to the deterioration of the North End and the existence of the harbor on the east. The discovery of any sector of upper class residential distribution from such an arrangement appears to be quite impossible. Perhaps the concentric hypothesis may make some sort of case for itself, in view of the fact that all of the districts in question lay within rough walking distance of the city's business center.[31] It should, however, be borne in mind that within this very same radius were located a middle class district in the West End and the working class districts in the North End and on the northern slope of Beacon Hill. Surely to point out an equidistance of upper class districts from the city center can have little explanatory value when middle and lower class areas lie in the very same concentric band. To avoid any unfairness in our criticism it is only right to point out that Burgess himself acknowledges certain variations within his concentric zones, as his own Chicago data clearly indicate. Our only purpose is to raise a question as to the explanatory adequacy of any theory which so idealizes land use patterns as to assign to a given zone social systems of very different and indeed sharply contrasting character. It seems as though such a procedure explains what least needs explaining and leaves unexplained that which most requires explanation. Some issue might be raised as to possible "lags" in natural succession which have enabled us to include as upper class neighborhoods areas that were presently fated to decay, thereby making an unfair case for ourselves. It is true that some of the districts noted above did later deteriorate in prestige value. Indeed, all but one of them was eventually displaced by other land uses so that only Beacon Hill survived as a fashionable residential quarter. However, there is certainly nothing wrong in selecting a given moment in history, as we have done with the late 1830s, and observing how at that time social systems of a given character (upper class families) were spatially distributed. Land uses are always changing; no one can say which are "lags" and which are not. If the Burgess-Hoyt theories are to claim any validity they must have a reasonable descriptive accuracy for any given period of land use history.[32]

Notes

1. Ernest W. Burgess, "The Growth of the City," in Robert E. Park, *et al.*, eds., *The City* (Chicago: The University of Chicago Press, 1925), pp. 47–62. Homer Hoyt, *The Structure and Growth of Residential Neighborhoods in American Cities* (Washington: Federal Housing Administration, 1939).
2. Justin Winsor, *The Memorial History of Boston* (Boston: J. R. Osgood, 1880–81), I, 531.
3. *Ibid.*, I, 539.
4. *Ibid.*, I, 550; Robert A. Woods, *Americans in Process* (Boston: Houghton Mifflin, 1930), pp. 19–24.
5. Winsor, *op. cit.*, I, 543.
6. *Ibid.*, II, 447; IV, 79.
7. *Ibid.*, II, 443; and Woods, *Americans in Process*, p. 27.
8. Winsor, *op. cit.*, I, 533–537, 552; and Woods, *Americans in Process*, pp. 21–22.
9. Woods, *Americans in Process*, p. 28.
10. Winsor, *op. cit.*, II, 513; IV, 63–64; and Thomas W. Tucker, *Bannisters Lane 1708–1899* (Boston: Houghton Mifflin, 1899), p. 16.
11. Woods, *Americans in Process*, p. 32; and Charles Phillips Huse, *The Financial History of Boston* (Cambridge: Harvard University Press, 1916), p. 3–4.
12. Woods, *Americans in Process*, pp. 33–34.
13. *Loc. cit.;* and T. R. Sullivan, *Boston New and Old* (Boston: Houghton Mifflin, 1912), p. 19.
14. Abbie Farwell Brown, *The Lights of Beacon Hill* (Boston, 1922), p. 8.
15. Robert Means Lawrence, *Old Park Street and its Vicinity* (Boston: Houghton Mifflin, 1922), p. 13; and Allen Chamberlain, *Beacon Hill, its Ancient Pastures and Early Mansions* (Boston: Houghton Mifflin, 1925), pp. 5–6.
16. Chamberlain, "The Beacon Hill of the Forefathers," in *Old Days on Beacon Hill, 1824–1924,* issued by the Women's Municipal League (Boston, 1924), pp. 6–9, 18.
17. Chamberlain, *Beacon Hill, Its Ancient Pastures and Early Mansions*, pp. 45–46.
18. *Ibid.*, pp. 45–46.
19. *Ibid.*, pp. 61–62.
20. Woods, *Americans in Process*, p. 33.
21. Chamberlain, *Beacon Hill, Its Ancient Pastures and Early Mansions*, pp. 45–46.
22. Cited in "A Century Ago: 60,000 Citizens, Cobbled Streets," *Boston Transcript*, July 24, 1930.
23. Cited in "A Century Ago: 60,000 Citizens, Cobbled Streets," *Boston Transcript*, July 24, 1930; and Woods, *Americans in Process*, p. 37; and J. Ross McKeever, "The Beacon Hill District" (M.S.), Master's Thesis, Massachusetts Institute of Technology, 1935, p. 22.
24. Cited in William Marshall Warren, "Beacon Hill and Boston University," *Bostonia, the Boston University Alumni Magazine*, 4: 3–21 (November, 1930), p. 8.

25. McKeever, *op. cit.*, p. 22.
26. Chamberlain, *Beacon Hill, Its Ancient Pastures and Early Mansions*, pp. 42–43.
27. Woods, *Americans in Process*, pp. 36–37.
28. William W. Wheildon, *Sentry, or Beacon Hill; the Beacon and the Monument of 1635 and 1790* (Concord, 1877), pp. 96–97.
29. Alexander S. Porter, "Changes of Values in Real Estate in Boston the Past One Hundred Years," *Collections of the Bostonian Society*, I, 57–74 (1888), p. 67; Chamberlain, *Beacon Hill, Its Ancient Pastures and Early Mansions*, p. 32.
30. Cited in "A Century Ago: 60,000 Citizens, Cobbled Streets," *Boston Transcript*, July 24, 1930.
31. By this time Beacon Hill was less isolated than it had been in 1796 when first opened for development. Business itself had migrated in a southerly and westerly direction, as will be shown later, and the intervening areas had become fully settled, so that Beacon Hill was no longer a remote rural district.
32. However, compare pp. 10–11 and pp. 119–120 in this volume, for an ideal-typical interpretation of ecological theories [Eds.].

E. Digby Baltzell   THE SOCIAL REGISTER: A NATIONAL
UPPER-CLASS INDEX

IN ANY COMPLEX CIVILIZATION, social and economic power tends to gravitate toward the large metropolis; and centralization is especially characteristic of modern American society where the national corporation, mass producing for a nationwide market, has steadily absorbed or replaced the local firm. In their analysis of the first successful labor strike in *Yankee City's* long history, which occurred in 1935, Warner and Low carefully document this modern pattern of centralization:

Big City capitalism had superseded small town capitalism in the vertical structure of corporate enterprise which had extended on beyond Yankee City to the great metropolis. At the time of the strike the local men, although born and reared in Yankee City, were little more than the factory managers for the Big City capitalists since they occupied inferior positions in this vastly extended vertical structure. They were not in a position to take leadership; they were not in a position of great power where they were free to make the decisions which always characterized the lives of Choate, Weatherby, and Pierce.[1]

Choate, Weatherby, and Pierce, highly respected upper-class leaders in a departed era of local autonomy and local pride, "had long since taken up their

E. Digby Baltzell, *Philadelphia Gentlemen: The Making of a National Upper Class* (New York: The Free Press of Glencoe, 1958), pp. 16–24.

residence in the Elm Hill Cemetery" in *Yankee City*. By 1930 the local shoe factory was owned and controlled by a New York corporation which operated a number of factories as well as a chain of 110 shoe stores in 56 cities: "even the name of Yankee City is not known to those whose financial power often controls decisions of the utmost importance for the town."[2]

All over America, as the members of small town elites become less and less important in each decade of the twentieth century, the more enterprising (and socially ambitious) members of the local upper classes moved to the large city. Many descendants of former coal barons in Scranton, Hazelton, or Wilkes-Barre lived along Philadelphia's Main Line in 1940.

At the same time that the large cities were absorbing members of many small town elites and upper classes, a national, inter-city, metropolitan upper class was becoming a reality in America: for the first time, in the last part of the nineteenth and early twentieth centuries, the New England boarding schools and the fashionable eastern universities provided the sons of the new and old rich from many cities with a common experience and a set of sub-culture standards.

The *Social Register* became an index of this new, inter-city upper class which emerged in the last part of the nineteenth century in America; moreover, in certain of the older metropolitan areas in 1940, the members of this new upper class were, in turn, also members of the contemporary elite, those listed in *Who's Who in America*. In other words, this chapter will serve to place the more detailed study of the upper class and the elite in Philadelphia within a national, rather than local, context, both historically and structurally.

It must be understood that human society is a historical process wherein each generation sifts to the top particular individual types—warriors, prophets, priests, merchants, bankers, or bureaucrats—whose talents are needed in any given period; these individuals, in turn, and within limits, make the decisions which shape the course of history. Thus Brooks Adams saw the history of England as partly reflected in the circulation of elites, wherein the feudal warrior, whose power lay in men and spears, was replaced during the Reformation by the large landowners who ruled England from the time of Henry VIII to the Revolution of 1688; the rising merchant adventurers who finally won their rights in 1688 were soon replaced by the manufacturing men such as Watt and Boulton whose talents led them to power after the Industrial Revolution. And, finally, from the time of the defeat of that symbol of martial power on the hill at Waterloo, both the manufacturing and landowning elites were dominated by, and often in debt to, the money power of Lombard Street.[3] The English upper class, often called an aristocracy, centers in a group of families who are descendants of those successful individuals of the remote and recent past, and is of course alloyed with those new men with a talent for power in the modern bureaucratic period.

As in England, America has produced a procession of successful men who have risen to positions of wealth and power, and whose children and grand-children have been brought up in a more or less money-insulated world, often called polite society. In each generation, however, the old-money world has remained aloof from the larger and more opulent world of the newly rich.

All families are equally old. Thousands of Americans apparently boast of the sacred blood of *Mayflower* passengers, and all of us go back to Adam and Eve! In the limited social class sense, "old families" are those whose ancestors were affluent in an earlier day than their "new family" emulators. Within America's Eastern upper class, for example, the "old families" are certainly not *Mayflower* descendants; rather they are the descendants of eighteenth and early nineteenth century merchants and manufacturers. Inherited wealth is always and everywhere the basis of gentility. "All through Boston history," writes Cleveland Amory, "when a family loses its financial stability, it has a way of beginning to disappear."[4]

After the Civil War, America's eastern seaboard, provincial and familial aristocracies were eventually replaced by an exclusive and competitive asso-ciational plutocracy, rooted in the "Gilded Age" and continuing to the present day. As with so much else in American life, the 1880s witnessed a turning point in the structure of the upper class. Edith Wharton portrays this transitional period in three novels—*The Age of Innocence, The House of Mirth,* and *The Custom of the Country.* The first novel, which opens "on a January evening in the early seventies," presents a small, intimate, and formal "Society" which is soon to surrender to the assault of the *parvenu* described in the other two novels.

After 1880, New York became the center of upper-class social life in America. For one thing, new fortunes of undreamed-of proportions were founded in this period. According to Charles A. Beard, while there were only three millionaires in the United States in 1861, thirty-six years later there were at least thirty-eight hundred.[5] From all parts of the American continent, barons of drygoods, utilities, coal, oil, and railroads moved their wives and families to the great metropolis, built ostentatious Victorian mansions, entertained on the grand scale, and, where possible, moved into "Society." Even their literary hero, Mark Twain, a self-made man from Missouri, was "a candidate for gentility."[6]

At first there was the usual resistance to accepting these new rich families. But "by one process or another amalgamation was effected and new varnish softened by the must of age. As the landed gentlemen of England had on various occasions saved their houses from decay by discreet jointures with mercantile families, so many of the established families in Boston, New York, Philadelphia, and Baltimore escaped the humiliation of poverty by judicious selections from the onrushing plutocracy."[7]

In the year 1887, amidst this incredible "Gilded Age," the *Social Register* was copyrighted by the Social Register Association; the first volume appeared for New York City in 1888.[8] There were less than two thousand families listed in this "record of society, comprising an accurate and careful list of its members, with their addresses, many of the maiden names of the married women, the club addresses of the men, officers of the leading clubs and social organizations, opera box holders, and other useful social information."[9] America's associational aristocracy was born with the advent of the *Social Register*. "Here at last," wrote Dixon Wecter, in his *Saga of American Society,* "unencumbered with advertisements of dressmakers and wine merchants, enhanced by large, clear type and a pleasant binding of orange and black—which if anything suggested the colors of America's most elegant university—was a convenient listing of one's friends and potential friends. It was an immediate triumph."[10]

The New York *Social Register* was soon followed by volumes for Boston and Philadelphia in 1890, Baltimore in 1892, Chicago in 1893, Washington, D.C. in 1900, St. Louis and Buffalo in 1903, Pittsburgh in 1904, San Francisco in 1906, and Cleveland and Cincinnati-Dayton in 1910. Volumes for all these twelve cities have been issued yearly down to the present and in substantially the same form as the original New York *Social Register*. Other volumes were issued for Providence, R.I. (1905–1926), Minneapolis-St. Paul (1907–1927), Seattle-Portland (1914–1921), Pasadena-Los Angeles (1914–1926), Detroit (1918–1927), and Richmond-Charleston-Savannah-Atlanta (1905–1927) but were discontinued because of lack of interest.[11]

It is interesting that the *Social Register* is privately owned and lists social status, as it were, for a profit. The *Social Register* is issued annually in November and is sent to all families listed within its pages. The annual charge for a subscription ranges from five to ten dollars per city volume. Potential members must make application and include written references from present members; the only exceptions are to be found in Washington, D.C., where the President, the Vice-President, the Supreme Court, the cabinet, various members of the diplomatic corps, and all United States Senators (not Representatives) are listed automatically. This last point is indicative of stratification in a bureaucratic social structure where, like in the military services, social class follows functional position; the senator, like the naval officer, is automatically a "gentleman."[12]

What is the relationship between the families listed in the *Social Register* and the captains of industry and finance who came to power in the "Gilded Age"? In his *Lords of Creation,* Frederick Lewis Allen shows how ten ideal-typical examples of the American financial elite at the turn of the century alloyed their gold with the American upper classes. Of interest here is the fact that, of these ten men—J. Pierpont Morgan, George F. Baker, James Stillman, Edward H. Harriman, John D. Rockefeller, William Rockefeller, Henry Huddleston Rogers, William K. Vanderbilt, James R. Keen, and Jacob H. Schiff—all save the last were listed in the *Social Register* as of 1905. Allen notes that the exclusion of Schiff was "presumably due to the fact that he was a Jew, and the Jews constituted a group somewhat apart; the fashionable clubs were almost exclusively gentile; and the *Social Register* was virtually a gentile register."[13] As it illustrates the dynamics of upper-class formation in America, it is of interest to observe that Jacob Schiff's grandson, who married George F. Baker's granddaughter, was listed in both the *Social Register* and *Who's Who* as of 1940.

Ferdinand Lundberg's *America's 60 Families* is a study of America's wealthiest families, the majority of whose fortunes were made between the Civil War and World War I.[14] Of these sixty consanguine family units, well over three-fourths have traceable descendants (the same given and surnames as the family founder) who are listed in the 1940 *Social Register*. These descendants are married one with another as well as with those of less spectacular wealth but higher social position: in the twentieth century, for instance, "blood" has been nicely alloyed with "gold" as Biddles, Roosevelts, and Peabodys have married Du Ponts, Dukes, or Fields.

Finally, Gustavus Myers' *History of the Great American Fortunes* is a useful volume for validating the *Social Register* as an index of an American upper class.[15] This well-known book is a study of the men who amassed great fortunes in America from colonial times to the present (1936). The names of these wealthy family-founders (taken from the index of Myers' book) have been carefully checked against the names of the families listed in the twelve *Social Registers* in 1940. Table 1 is a listing of the famous family-founders in Myers' book whose descendants are listed in the contemporary *Social Register*.

The distinguished historian, Samuel Eliot Morison, once facetiously remarked that he attached great significance to the fact that the founding of the Brookline Country Club, in a Boston suburb, in 1882, coincided with the closing of the frontier in America. Certainly, the closing of the frontier (1890), the formation of the United States Steel Company (1901), the founding of Groton School (1884), the opening of the new "millionaires' country club" at Tuxedo Park, New York (1885), the rule of Mrs. Astor and Ward McAlister (1880's and 1890's), the Bradley Martin ball (at the cost of $369,200 in 1897), and the first issue of the *Social Register* (1888) were important, and interdependent, variables in a social situation which foreshadowed a centralized America in the middle of the twentieth century.

A centralized elite and upper class quite naturally follows from a centralized economy. From the beginning, provincial aristocracies of birth and breeding have been characteristic of all the older eastern cities in America. *The Social Register,* on the other hand, was born in an age of centralization and lists a new, associational, inter-city, aristocracy. For the first time, upper-class associations other than the family played an important role in socializing the young. The New England boarding school and the fashionable Eastern university became upper-class surrogate families on almost a national scale. J. P. Morgan, the symbol of economic centralization in America, for example,

Table 1—Deceased Elite Individuals in American Economic Life with Descendants who Are Listed in the 1940 Social Register; the Names Are Taken from the Index of History of the Great American Fortunes, by Gustavus Myers

Deceased-Elite Individual	Period When Wealth Was Acquired	Occupation: Or the Way in Which Wealth Was Acquired*
Elite Individuals with Descendants Listed in the Philadelphia Social Register **in 1940**		
Baer, George F.	Late 19th Century	Railroads
Biddle, Nicholas	18th–19th Century	Finance
Cassatt, A. J.	Late 19th Century	Railroads
Cope, Thomas Pym	18th–19th Century	Merchant
Dolan, Thomas	Late 19th Century	Utilities
Drexel, Anthony	Late 19th Century	Finance
DuPont, Coleman	20th Century	Chemistry
Elkins, William L.	Late 19th Century	Utilities
Hopkins, Johns	Early 19th Century	Railroads
Knox, Philander	Late 19th Century	Law
Penrose, Boies	20th Century	Politics
Ridgway, Jacob	18th–19th Century	Merchant
Scott, Thomas	Late 19th Century	Railroads
Wanamaker, John	Late 19th Century	Merchant
Widener, P. A. B.	Late 19th Century	Utilities
Elite Individuals with Descendants Listed in the Boston Social Register **in 1940**		
Adams, Charles F	Late 19th Century	Railroads†
Aldrich, Nelson	Late 19th Century	Finance
Ames, Oakes	Late 19th Century	Railroads
Brooks, Peter C.	18th–19th Century	Merchant
Cabot, George	18th–19th Century	Merchant
Derby, Elias	18th–19th Century	Merchant
Peabody, Joseph	18th–19th Century	Merchant
Perkins, Thomas	18th–19th Century	Merchant
Thorndike, Israel	18th–19th Century	Merchant
Elite Individuals with Descendants Listed in the Chicago Social Register **in 1940**		
Armour, J. Ogden	Late 19th Century	Manufacturing
Field, Marshall	Late 19th Century	Merchant
Leiter, Marshall	Late 19th Century	Merchant
McCormick, Cyrus	Late 19th Century	Manufacturing
Palmer, Potter	Late 19th Century	Merchant
Patterson, Joseph M.	Late 19th Century	Publisher
Elite Individuals with Descendants Listed in the New York Social Register **in 1940**		
Astor, J. J.	Early 19th Century	Furs, Land
Baker, George F.	Late 19th Century	Finance
Beekman, Henry	18th–19th Century	Land
Belmont, August	Late 19th Century	Finance, Utilities
Blair, John I.	Late 19th Century	Railroads
Brevoort, Henry	18th–19th Century	Land
Brown, Alexander	Late 19th Century	Finance
Carnegie, Andrew	Late 19th Century	Manufacturing
Choate, Joseph	Late 19th Century	Law

Clews, Henry	Late 19th Century	Finance
Cravath, Paul D.	Late 19th Century	Law
Cromwell, W. Nelson	Late 19th Century	Law
Dodge, Cleveland	Late 19th Century	Copper
Duke, James B.	20th Century	Cigarettes
Flagler, H. M.	Late 19th Century	Oil
Ford, Henry	20th Century	Autos
Goelet, Peter	18th Century	Land
Gould, Jay	Late 19th Century	Railroads
Griswold family	18th–19th Century	Merchants
Harriman, E. H.	Late 19th Century	Railroads
Havemeyer, H. O.	Late 19th Century	Sugar
Hill, J. J.	Late 19th Century	Railroads
James, D. Willis	Late 19th Century	Copper
Ledyard, L. Cass	Late 19th Century	Law
Lee, Ivy	20th Century	Public Relations
Livingston, Robert	18th Century	Land
Lorillard, Pierre	Early 19th Century	Snuff, Land
Morgan, J. P.	Late 19th Century	Finance
Payne, O. H.	Late 19th Century	Oil
Perkins, George	Late 19th Century	Finance, Insurance
Phelps, John T.	Late 19th Century	Copper
Phillips, Adolphus	18th–19th Century	Merchant
Rhinelander, William C.	18th–19th Century	Land
Rockefeller, John D.	Late 19th Century	Oil
Rogers, H. H.	Late 19th Century	Oil, Finance
Roosevelt, James	18th–19th Century	Land
Ryan, T. Fortune	Late 19th Century	Utilities
Schermerhorn, Peter	18th Century	Land
Schiff, Jacob	Late 19th Century	Finance
Schley, Grant B.	Late 19th Century	Finance
Schuyler, Peter	18th–19th Century	Land
Stettinius, Edward	Late 19th Century	Matches, Finance
Stillman, James	Late 19th Century	Finance
Stokes, Thomas	Late 19th Century	Copper
Taylor, Moses	Early 19th Century	Railroads, Finance
Vanderbilt, Cornelius	Early 19th Century	Shipping, Railroads
Van Rensselaer, K.	18th Century	Land
Villard, Henry	Late 19th Century	Railroads
Whitney, William C.	Late 19th Century	Utilities

Elite Individuals with Descendants Listed
in the Baltimore, Cincinnati, Pittsburgh,
San Francisco, St. Louis, or Washington
Social Registers in 1940

Crocker, Charles	Early 19th Century	Railroads
Elkins, Stephen B.	Late 19th Century	Land
Frick, Henry Clay	Late 19th Century	Manufacturing
Garrett, John W.	Early 19th Century	Railroads
Longworth, Nicholas	18th–19th Century	Land
Mellon, Andrew	20th Century	Finance, Manufacturing
Mills, D. O.	Early 19th Century	Finance
Pulitzer, Joseph	Late 19th Century	Publisher

* The occupations listed are of necessity limited to the principal field of endeavor. There was much overlapping. While "land" is listed for only a few individuals, almost all of the great fortunes in this country profited from the ownership of urban real estate. Finally, several lawyers and politicians are listed because these men were prominent in their day and were listed in the index of Myers' book.

† While Charles Francis Adams (Jr.) was a prominent railroad executive, he was a man of inherited wealth. When Charles Francis Adams I, the father of Henry, Charles, and Brooks, married the daughter of Peter Chardon Brooks, one of Boston's first millionaire merchants, the Adams family became wealthy for the first time.

joined his contemporaries as trustees and benefactors of these exclusive educational associations, where they all, in turn, sent their sons to be educated together. Of the eighty-seven family-founders listed in Table 1, no less than sixty-five had one or more descendants who had attended either Groton, St. Mark's, or St. Paul's schools in the period between 1890 and 1940.

Groton, which opened its doors in 1884 with the elder Morgan as an original trustee, was founded by Endicott Peabody, whose ancestors were great Salem merchants.[16] In the twentieth century its role as an upper-class family-surrogate on almost a national (and international) scale is indicated by the fact that its 192 boarding students in 1940 were residents of fifteen states, the District of Columbia, Bermuda, Brazil, China, England, Hungary, Ireland, and Venezuela.[17]

These boarding schools not only bring together the sons of the "old" and "new" rich from Boston, New York, and Philadelphia to be socialized in one homogeneous atmosphere (the school family); they also serve to drain off the sons of the local, small-town upper classes all over America. Thus in *Yankee City* a young lady of the "upper-upper" class, according to an observer in the Warner team, confessed that she could not find a suitable marriage mate because "all the young men have left."[18] She goes on to describe how her brother, a graduate of St. Paul's and Harvard, had recently taken a job in a large New York law firm and was engaged to marry a New York girl, "a sister of one of his classmates at St. Paul's."[19]

In the middle of the twentieth century, symbols of membership in exclusive associations have replaced the family *arms* of an earlier day. The school, or college club, "tie" or "hatband" is now, as we have said, a status symbol recognized within the upper classes in all cities. Although it has received little attention thus far from sociologists, this change to a uniform national upper-class structure parallels the well-documented trend towards a centralized economy.

Notes

1. W. Lloyd Warner and J. O. Low, *The Social System of the Modern Factory* (New Haven: Yale University Press, 1947), p. 153.
2. *Ibid.,* p. 156.
3. Brooks Adams, *The Law of Civilization and Decay* (New York: The Macmillan Company, 1896), pp. 186ff.
4. Cleveland Amory, *The Proper Bostonians* (New York: E. P. Dutton and Co., Inc., 1947), pp. 39–40.
5. Charles A. Beard and Mary R. Beard, *The Rise of American Civilization* (New York: The Macmillan Company, 1937), Vol. II, pp. 383–84.
6. See Van Wyck Brooks, *The Ordeal of Mark Twain* (New York: E. P. Dutton and Co., Inc., 1920), Chapter V.
7. Charles A. Beard and Mary R. Beard, *op. cit.,* Vol. II, p. 388.
8. *Social Register* (New York: The Social Register Association, 1888).
9. *Ibid.,* preface.

10. Dixon Wecter, *The Saga of American Society* (New York: Charles Scribner's Sons, 1937), p. 233.

11. This information was obtained by checking the volumes of the *Social Register* in the stacks of the Library of Congress. In 1937, according to Dixon Wecter, about 10 per cent of the total copies of the *Social Register* sold in that year went to commercial firms, *ibid.*, p. 235.

12. *Ibid.*, pp. 232–36.

    Herbert Spencer saw "progress" in terms of the movement of society from the militant-military to the industrial type of social structure. In the modern state where social and functional classes merge in one all-inclusive bureaucratic hierarchy, Spencer's ideal-typical militant social structure may well be a cogent description of the "Brave New World." See Herbert Spencer, *The Principles of Sociology* (New York: D. Appleton and Company, 1896), Vol. II, Chapter XVII.

13. Frederick Lewis Allen, *The Lords of Creation* (New York: Harper and Brothers, 1935), pp. 98–99.

14. Ferdinand Lundberg, *America's 60 Families* (New York: Vanguard Press, 1937).

15. Gustavus Myers, *History of the Great American Fortunes* (New York: The Modern Library, 1937).

16. Frank D. Ashburn, *Peabody of Groton* (New York: Coward McCann, Inc., 1944), p. 5.

17. *Independent Schools,* Meriden, Conn., 1943.

18. W. Lloyd Warner and Paul S. Lunt, *The Social Life of a Modern Community* (New Haven: Yale University Press, 1941), p. 136.

19. *Ibid.*, p. 135.

Wilbert E. Moore and
Robin M. Williams

STRATIFICATION IN THE ANTE-BELLUM SOUTH

RENEWED INTEREST among sociologists in well-documented historical materials as a basis for comparative study of social systems has recently turned attention to the backgrounds of the American treatment of the Negro during the period of slavery. Such materials, however, can be of maximum utility to the science only through careful and systematic analysis in terms of basic elements and relationships as a foundation for general theory. The present paper attempts to present the principal features of the social structure of the ante-bellum South, particularly as exemplified in the system of social stratification, in such a way that the broader implications of the various more or less well known descriptive data may be seen. Formal structures and concrete

Reprinted with the permission of the authors and the American Sociological Association from the *American Sociological Review*, Vol. VII, No. 3 (July 1942), pp. 343–351.

social relationships thus become meaningful, not as isolated events or aspects of "culture," but as related features of a complex social system. It may thus be possible, not only to provide examination and verification of available data, but to relate these data to the broader outlines of the society.

Classes in the Dominant Caste. The pattern of social stratification in the ante-bellum South was fairly complex and by no means constant in time and space. Nevertheless, constant points of reference in social valuation are observable and it was about these well-understood criteria of rank and status that the major lines of demarcation are discernible. The slavery system, and the caste system which partially parallelled it, was the most common and the most certain fixed point of orientation in the stratification system. This becomes even more significant when it is recognized that, despite the general impression to the contrary, slaveholding was in no statistical sense typical of Southern whites. For the South as a whole, during the period for which census data are available, the slaveholders constituted only 35.3 per cent of the total free population in 1790 and this had declined to 26.1 per cent in 1860. All those immediately connected with the slavery system (combined slave and slaveholding population) formed only 57 per cent of the entire population in 1790 and precisely one half (50 per cent) in 1860.[1] However, the significance of the plantation organization and of the slavery system was not dependent on numerical weight in a statistical computation.

Aside from the direct economic function of the plantation as a prime example of commercial large-scale production of staple agricultural commodities and the manifest importance of the planter as a social type, there is the tremendously revealing fact of the dominance of the planter and plantation as an ideal and as a goal of aspiration. The cue to understanding one of the main elements of social stratification in this society is given by the high prestige accorded to slave ownership and the possession of a landed estate. The evidence is substantial that the planter-pattern stood as an *end* or standard of achievement and that the attainment of such a status was typically an effective desire among a large portion of the white population.[2]

To a very large degree, therefore, class status among the white population was determined by the nature of the relation to the slavery system. Among slaveholders, status was largely relative to the number of slaves held. Among nonslaveholders, the immediacy of relationship or closeness of approximation to the goal of slaveholding was the primary relevant consideration. Other criteria of valuation were by no means irrelevant. However, aside from making possible distinctions among those of roughly the same social class, the importance of family connections, personal qualities, and achievements tended to correspond to the central importance of the relation to the slavery system.

The principal social classes among the whites of the ante-bellum South have been described fairly completely in the literature and need be men-

tioned only briefly here. The "aristocracy" included owners of large plantations with many slaves as well as some of the wealthy urban "factors" and
merchants and those in the learned professions—groups closely associated
with the planters and dependent upon their dominance for social status.[3]
The upper middle class included small planters, commercial farmers, lesser
merchants and professionals. Because of their position as slaveholders or
their close relationship with slaveholders and general acceptance as social
equals, those of the upper middle class were valued members of Southern
society.[4]

Slightly lower in the scale of stratification than those of the upper middle
class but partially merging into it, were the independent nonslaveholding
farmers (yeomen) who were not to be accounted equals of the slaveholding
classes but yet who remained respectable and respected members of the
community. Also, members of what may be called the lower-middle class
were independent white artisans, and to a certain extent the independent
as economically.[5]
"highlanders" who were separated from the slavery system spatially as well

At the very bottom of the social scale of the dominant caste were the
"poor whites," a narrower term than nonslaveholding whites. The "poor
whites" were not a large group numerically and were largely separated from
the plantation-slavery system geographically.[6] Since this lowest white class
was of particular significance in relation to the integration of the entire class
and caste system of stratification, it will be more fully discussed below.

In a slightly anomalous position in the class structure were those two
necessary but overtly despised groups whose social status was not commensurate with their economic standing, the slavetraders and the overseers.
The former group was avowedly universally despised by defenders of the
slavery system, yet they served a necessary function in providing utility in
slave property and as agents in maintaining the fluidity of the slave market.
A number of "reasons" for despisal of the slavetrader were usually given,
chiefly in terms of undesirable traits of character. All were supposed to be
dishonest, unscrupulous, greedy, ill-bred, and immoral. Bancroft has shown
that this was by no means universally true but that the stereotype remained.[7]
It may be suggested that there was a value conflict involved in fixing the
status of the trader. The trade in slaves was definitely a "sore spot"[8] in the
"peculiar institution." The Southerner felt a distinct conflict between certain
elements of the Christian ethic and the behavior involved in the slave trade
—a conflict which was intensified by the attempt of outside groups to impose
this ethic in all strictness on the South. Now the slave trader represented the
antithesis of the modifying and justifying aspects of the system; he was a
constant reminder of the moral conflict inherent in the system, between the
demands of the market and the dicta of sacredness of the family and of individual personality.

Although it may be said cynically that the slavetrader bought and sold slaves and the slaveholder sold and bought them, the latter could "justify" his buying and selling in terms of hard necessity, reuniting slave families, or disposing of an unmanageable slave. The trader was openly concerned only with the market but his function as a scapegoat for various guilt feelings connected with the slavery system should not be overlooked.

Analogous in many respects to the slavetrader was the overseer. Like the former, the overseer's connection with slavery was, by virtue of his position, primarily or exclusively an economic one. He was hired and fired according to his economic efficiency as judged primarily by his ability to direct the labor force in the production of a satisfactory profit for the slaveholder. He it was who had the chief immediate responsibility for the sheerly exploitative aspects of the use of slave labor.[9]

The crucial character of the status of the trader and overseer for the institutional support of the total system of stratification may be seen in the fact that their valuation was *not* commensurate with either their authority or economic position nor of course with their usefulness or the character of their segmental social (economic) relationships with the upper classes.

The Caste Barrier and the Negro. Between the whites and Negroes there was truly a great gulf fixed. That gulf consisted of the "caste line." The dominance of the whites did not rest solely on their legal ownership of slaves, for not all whites, or even a majority, were slaveholders. Likewise, the subservience of the Negro was not exclusively and immediately due to the slavery relationship for although a majority of Negroes were slaves many were freemen. Negroes were not only subject to slave law but also to "caste law," that is, to special disabilities attaching to them as Negroes, regardless of their legal status as slaves or freemen.[10] The caste relationship then was wider than the slavery relationship and the features of the former were not exclusively dependent upon the latter.[11] As indicated by Warner not only does a caste arrangement involve unequal division of privileges, duties, obligations, and opportunities among the various social strata but also prohibits marriage between members of distinct strata and allows no opportunity for rising or falling across the caste boundaries.[12]

Although the possibility or impossibility of legitimate intermarriage is probably crucial in a caste system, other elements which distinguish it from other types of social stratification may be noted. In a caste system, the criteria of membership are clearly and rigorously defined. This membership is determined by birth and this is partial explanation for the prohibition upon caste intermarriage. That is, socially sanctioned marriage normally implies the subsequent class equality of the marriage partners and the legitimization of the offspring. Permission of intercaste marriage would thus make the child's status indeterminate.[13] This, of course, does not carry over to the intercaste sexual unions since these remain unofficial and imply no further

social bonds. Moreover, the children of such unions are by definition illegitimate and can lay no claim to higher caste status than that of the parent
belonging to the lower caste. In the Negro-white caste system, this rule
was related to the legal rule concerning the hereditary character of slavery—
the child followed the condition of the mother. The normal intercaste union
was, and has remained, the white male and the Negro female.[14] How extensive such unions were during the slavery period is difficult to determine, but
the fairly large number of "Negroes" who were mulattoes and lighter testifies that they were not rare.[15] The sexual exploitation of female slaves and
other Negroes by masters or members of the dominant caste was a further
symbol of at least semilegitimate authority.

Of particular interest in the relation of a caste structure to the general
institutional order and value system regarding slavery is that individual
qualities, worth, achievement, and so on, are irrelevant to caste status.
Caste divisions may thus cut across differential valuation on these other
bases. Of basic importance in maintaining a caste system, particularly if it
is not uniformly accepted by those whose status suffers thereby, is *visibility*.
Since this is social categorization[16] *par excellence,* there must be some
external symbol for fixing the caste status of any individual whose social
background is unknown. The importance of the visibility of the Negro—the
pigmentation of his skin—was notable in the early transition from indentured servitude to slavery.[17] Moreover, the presumption of occupational
status (slavery) arising from skin color was basic to the legal conception of
slavery.[18]

It is only in reference to the caste system, and the barrier of the "color"
(or caste) line that the legal and more informal disabilities placed upon free
Negroes can be understood. A "race" question was involved.[19] In general,
therefore, the Negro belonged to an inferior caste (demonstrated by his
complexion and enforced by law and custom), and then was presumed to be
a slave, but might be free. Although the caste system was in general more inclusive than the slavery system, it was in some cases slightly less inclusive.
Those cases were the slaves who were visibly white by inspection and had
the presumption of freedom in their favor but who had inherited slavery
from a Negro maternal ancestor.

Without attempting to distinguish gradations of slaves, Figure 1 illustrates the relationship between class, legal, and caste lines. Below the caste
line there was only slightly less variability than above it. The free Negro
varied in occupation and economic well-being from fairly prosperous artisans and independent farmers to a status equivalent (except for the caste
line!) to the poorest of the poor whites.[20] Below the legal line, gradations did
not end for there were social classes among the slaves.

Those at the "top of the bottom" in the Southern social structure—the
free Negroes—were generally conceded to be a serious threat to the main-

tenance of that structure.[21] The reasons given for this situation were ordinarily in terms of their sympathy for the slaves, the likelihood of their inciting revolts, and their economic inadequacy. The free Negro was not allowed to vote, was subject along with the slave to the severity of the slave codes, and was considered a constant menace to the slavery system. Toward the end of the period, it was almost impossible to emancipate slaves by will, deed of gift, or any other common method; manumission required a special act of the state legislature. The available evidence by no means bears out the contention that free Negroes in general actively interfered with the slavery system or became any greater burden on the community than other classes with limited economic opportunities. Why then fear the free Negro and prohibit the manumission of slaves? As Dumond has remarked, "The mere act of emancipation was looked upon as an implied censure of slavery. . . ."[22] Likewise, whatever the "real" danger of free Negroes in the population, their symbolic danger cannot be denied. The whole tenor of the development of the legal status of slavery was the attempt to fix slavery as a status properly attaching to the Negro.[23] In other words, the racial justification of slavery and the doctrine of the presumption of slavery arising

FIGURE I

Diagrammatic Representation of Class, Legal, and Caste Lines
in the Ante-Bellum South

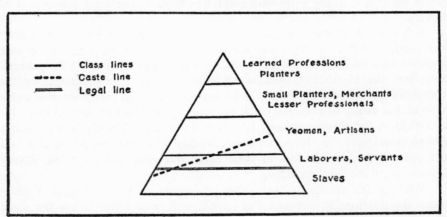

This figure modifies Warner's scheme in that the caste line cuts across *both* the legal line and the class lines. It is recognized that any two-dimensional diagram does not permit accurate "location" of certain specific groups, e.g., slave-traders.

from color may be said to have been attempts to make the caste line and the slavery line parallel, if not indistinguishable, for those of the subordinate group. The mere presence of free Negroes was a denial that slavery followed naturally and inevitably from Negro ancestry. The manumission of Negroes moreover, was a notable example of the intrusion of personalistic factors into a stereotyped and categorized situation. It was evidence of the possibility of an extension downward, in a diluted form, of the values of the dominant caste in respect to individual achievement[24] and the value of liberty, and an indication of some possibility of the slave's legitimately aspiring to those culture goals.

Below the free Negroes in the scale of stratification was the majority of the black population, the slaves. The latter might, however, be superior in economic position to the former, since slaves had a fairly large degree of economic security and varying degrees of comfort. The "freedom" of the free Negro was so little greater than that of the slave that it may often have been a poor bargain. Especially was this the case in the later slavery period with the increasing restrictions upon free Negroes and the prevalence of caste, rather than slave, law. Near the end of the slavery period a number of states passed enabling acts to allow free Negroes voluntarily to enter slavery.[25] There is no evidence, however, of any considerable movement to trade even so limited (but official) liberty for slavery.

Even the slaves were by no means without class distinctions. The most clear-cut of these was that obtaining between house servants and field hands. The former, together with some artisans, formed the "aristocracy" of the slaves by virtue of their better treatment, closer contact with the life and symbols of status of the whites, and greater economic and social security.[26]

Class distinctions might be multiplied beyond that between house servants and field hands, but with less certainty. Within the general slavery system, the status of slaves was partially determined by their occupational rank and market value but also by a sort of reflected status according to the social class of the master.[27] The relation of slaves to the slavery system was thus by no means identical and their interest in its preservation varied.

White Support of Caste and Slavery. The slaves and free Negroes below the caste line were not the only groups in the population which occupied inferior positions because of the peculiar orientation of social stratification about the slavery system. The relationship of nonslaveholders, often erroneously lumped together as "poor whites," to the slavery system is also of importance in any adequate appraisal of the social order and its elements of stability and instability. It was noted above that a majority of the dominant caste did not own slaves. Many of these nonslaveholders belonged to the lower middle class and only those at the bottom of the scale of stratification (that is, above the caste line) could be called "poor whites." Yet many of the others, although not strictly "poor whites," were poor white people and suffered both economically and socially from their subordinate position.

The key to the understanding of the support of the slavery system by nonslaveholders, particularly the poor whites for whom there was no honorable employment,[28] is to be found in the caste structure associated with slavery. So long as the Negro remained a slave, the poor white by definition remained superior, even though his economic position was no better or manifestly inferior. Nonslaveholders of all classes were continually held in line by the politically dominant class by emphasis upon caste rather than class. By the existence of a subordinate and servile caste, all whites became members of the dominant "class."[29] A further consideration was, however, involved in the support of slavery within the caste structure. The Negro, belonging to an inferior caste, *and as a slave,* did not compete so much in the *immediate* sense with white labor. The free Negro, although still a member of an inferior caste, was necessarily in a situation of competition with the poorer whites. It is typical of caste organization that the occupation of the lower or lowest caste becomes stigmatized and for an upper caste member to be forced into that type of employment is considered as completely degrading. This is one clear basis for the opposition of laboring whites to the freeing of slaves from rough agricultural labor. White artisans were continually protesting against the intrusion of free Negroes (against whose intrusion they were moderately successful) and slaves into skilled labor.[30]

Slavery was interpreted by the nonslaveholding whites as essential for maintaining their superiority over the Negro both in the occupational world and in the broader scheme of stratification. Even the limited occupational sphere allowed the Negroes, however, largely closed those types of employment to the whites because of the association between occupation and caste. The unskilled laborer, the true "poor white," had no place open to him. Slavery and the caste system gave him a social position above that of the Negro, but took away any means of economic advancement or other competitive means for the achievement of the symbols of status in the white society.[31] The "peculiar" stratification system took precedence over economic and class interests.

Thus, the entire complex of differential valuations supported the cleavages existing in the population of the ante-bellum South, yet included elements of instability as a system of social stratification. The principal bases of differential valuation applicable to the whites were officially, but not uniformly in fact, denied to the Negroes. The free Negro was real and symbolic evidence of that indeterminacy. Even among the dominant caste, various modes of relationship to the slavery system took precedence over other normally effective criteria of status, particularly in the case of the traders and overseers. The stratification was no less real because of these elements of instability but the areas of uncertainty and conflict in social relationships indicate the difficulties attendant upon the attempted fusion of several systems of relative valuation.

Notes

1. Based on a table compiled by L. C. Gray, *History of Agriculture in the Southern United States to 1860,* vol. I: 482, Table 7 (Washington, D.C., 1933). Original data from census sources.

2. Edgar T. Thompson, "The Planter in the Pattern of Race Relations in the South," *Social Forces,* 19: 249–252 (December 1940).
   Although the extent and ease of class mobility is not of immediate concern here, it may be noted that toward the end of the slavery period class lines tended to "freeze." This was undoubtedly associated with an increasing concentration of slaveholding. In general, the Old South approached an "estate" society (*cf.* Max Weber, *Wirtschaft und Gesellschaft,* 177–180 *et passim,* Tübingen: J. C. B. Mohr, 1925) at top and bottom of the social scale with rather free movement in the intermediate gradations. The tendency toward rigidification was perhaps most apparent in the Southwest, where change from an open-class system to a fairly rigid "estate" society was rapid. *Cf.* R. W. Shugg, *Origins of Class Struggle in Louisiana,* 32–33, 79–83, 114–116 (Baton Rouge: University of Louisiana Press, 1939).

3. In addition to Thompson, *loc. cit.,* *cf.* L. C. Gray, *op. cit.,* vol. I: 492–497; D. R. Hundley, *Social Relations in Our Southern States,* chaps. I and IV (New York, 1860).

4. *Cf.* L. C. Gray, *op. cit.,* vol. I: 488–492, 498–500; Hundley, *op. cit.,* chaps. I and II.

5. Concerning the yeomen, see Hundley, *op. cit.,* chap. V; U. B. Phillips, *Life and Labor in the Old South,* chap. XVII (Boston: Little, Brown & Co., 1929). Concerning white artisans, see L. C. Gray, *op. cit.,* vol. I: 500–501; Phillips, *Plantation and Frontier,* vol. II: 347–349 (Cleveland, 1910). "Highlanders" are briefly described in Gray, *op. cit.,* vol. I: 487–488.

6. There was in the South a partial geographical basis for class distinctions. Although lack of space prohibits any extended discussion, it may be pointed out that in general, because of the plantation system and the competitive advantage of that system, there was a general tendency for social classes to be divided (very roughly) according to land configuration. *Cf.* Shugg, *op. cit.,* chap. I.

7. Frederic Bancroft, *Slave-Trading in the Old South,* 365–381 (Baltimore: G. H. Furst, 1934). *Cf.* Hundley, *op. cit.,* 139–146. The low valuation of the status may of course have provided a negative selective factor and thus have reinforced the stereotype by giving it some validity.

8. *Cf.* L. C. Gray, *op. cit.,* vol. I: 521.

9. *Cf.* L. C. Gray, *op. cit.,* vol. I: 501–503. Hundley (*op. cit.,* 203–206) strangely enough partially defends the overseer because of the difficulty of his position. Phillips, *Life and Labor in the Old South,* chap. XV, devotes an interesting chapter to a number of plantation overseers and illustrates their various types. His *Plantation and Frontier,* vol. I:323–338, contains documents relating to the problems of overseers.

10. *Cf.* Wilbert E. Moore, "Slave Law and the Social Structure," *Journal of Negro History,* 26: 188–190, April 1941.

11. Dollard is thus clearly mistaken when he speaks of the Negro-white caste system as a postwar development and as a substitute for the slavery system.

Cf. John Dollard, *Caste and Class in a Southern Town,* 62–63 (New Haven: Yale University Press, 1937).

12. *Cf.* W. Lloyd Warner, "American Caste and Class," *American Journal of Sociology,* 42: 234–237, September 1936; W. Lloyd Warner and Allison Davis, "A Comparative Study of American Caste," in Edgar T. Thompson, ed., *Race Relations and the Race Problem,* 219–245 (Durham, N.C.: Duke University Press, 1939).

13. For a fuller discussion of the functional necessity of caste endogamy in a racial caste system, see Kingsley Davis, "Intermarriage in Caste Societies," *American Anthropologist,* 43: 378–379, 386–390, July–September, 1941.

14. As Dollard and others have pointed out, this is associated with the ideal of the patriarchal family, chivalry, and the double standard. *Cf.* Dollard, *op. cit., passim.*

15. *Cf.* E. B. Reuter, *The Mulatto in the United States,* 105–126 (Boston: Richard G. Badger, 1918).

16. That is, removal of a segment of the population from the sphere of application of the general criteria of relative valuation, and fixing its status on quite different grounds.

17. Moore, *loc. cit.,* 171–184.

18. *Ibid.,* 187–191. Although the criterion of visibility would not seem to apply in the caste system of India, often taken as a type case, the "visibility" is none the less real but is of a slightly different sort. The Indian caste system is primarily a social structure oriented around relatively immobile village communities where the caste status is known because the caste of the parents is known. There is, in addition, evidence of at least a rough color gradation from the upper to the lower castes. Visibility, as a means of subjugation and control, decreases in importance with the increased institutionalization (and consequent general acceptance) of the system of stratification.

19. Avery Craven, *The Repressible Conflict, 1830–1861,* 59 (Baton Rouge: University of Louisiana Press, 1939). Pitirim A. Sorokin, *Social and Cultural Dynamics,* vol. III: 37 (New York: American Book Co., 1937–41), has noted the widespread incidence in such systems of ideologies of race and blood purity, "chosen people" and the like. Reference should also be made to the same author's *Social Mobility,* 133–163, 381–382 (New York: Harper, 1927).

20. An interesting list of the gainful occupations of free Negroes of Richmond County, Georgia, in 1819 is presented in Phillips, *Plantation and Frontier,* vol. II: 143–147.

21. For further discussion of the problems of the free Negro in the South, and the legislative and customary restrictions upon his activities, *cf.* B. W. Doyle, *The Etiquette of Race Relations in the South,* 7 and Chap. VII (Chicago: University of Chicago Press, 1937); L. C. Gray, *op. cit.,* vol. I: 522–528; U. B. Phillips, *Plantation and Frontier,* vol. I: 141–164, *Documents: 1649–1863* (Cleveland: A. H. Clark, 1909); *idem., American Negro Slavery,* chap. XXI (New York: D. Appleton, 1918).

22. D. L. Dumond, *Antislavery Origins of the Civil War in the United States,* 13 (Ann Arbor: University of Michigan Press, 1939). *Cf.* Charles S. Sydnor, "The Free Negro in Mississippi before the Civil War," *American Historical Review,* 32: 769–788, July 1927.

23. *Cf.* Moore, *loc. cit.*

24. Manumission was ordinarily effected because of "meritorious services" by the slave.

25. *Cf.* Moore, *loc. cit.*, 194 n.

26. *Cf.* Gray, *op. cit.*, vol. I: 520–521; Ophelia Settle, "Social Attitudes during the Slave Regime: Household Servants versus Field Hands," *Publ. Amer. Sociol. Soc.*, vol. 28(2), May 1934.

27. Further discussion of social classes among the slaves may be found in Phillips, *Life and Labor in the Old South*, 206–207; Doyle, *op. cit.*, 72–78.

28. *Cf.* W. O. Brown, "Role of the Poor White in Race Contacts of the South," *Social Forces*, 19: 258–268, December 1940; Paul H. Buck, "The Poor Whites of the Ante-Bellum South," *American Historical Review*, 31: 41–54, October 1935. Buck, *loc. cit.*, 46–47, notes that the poor whites were not so much exploited as superfluous.
    Despite the low valuation of the position of overseer in the general scheme, this status was regarded as a fortunate advancement by the poor white. *Cf.* L. C. Gray, *op. cit.*, vol. I: 486. Undoubtedly it was the power and the authority of the position of the overseer, together with the opportunity afforded for assertion of superiority and the discharge of aggressions and frustrations, which made the position attractive to the lowest white class.

29. An excellent presentation of the way in which white class conflicts were minimized, in fact practically avoided, by emphasis upon common white superiority, is to be found in Shugg, *Origins of Class Struggle in Louisiana*, 1–195. *Cf.* Hundley, *op. cit.*, 273–274. The theory of the two-class (caste) society, with no essential distinctions within the dominant class, was well developed in pro-slavery thought. *Cf.* William Sumner Jenkins, *Pro-Slavery Thought in the Old South*, 285–290 (Chapel Hill: University of North Carolina Press, 1935).

30. Typical public protests are quoted in Phillips, *Plantation and Frontier*, vol. II: 360–368. *Cf.* Shugg, *op. cit.*, 119–120 *et passim.;* Sterling D. Spero and Abram L. Harris, *The Black Worker*, chap. I (New York: Columbia University Press, 1931).

31. *Cf.* Buck, *loc. cit.* Recognition of the economic implications of slavery was not completely lacking among those in such a position. Shugg has found evidence of much latent, and some overt, resistance to slavery by the white laborers in Louisiana; *op. cit.*, 120, 145–146, 172, 174. Lack of education and of property qualifications for voting kept down any effective opposition. The most famous appeal to the poor whites on economic grounds by one of their number was Hinton R. Helper's *The Impending Crisis of the South* (New York, 1857). This book was distributed as Republican campaign literature in 1860.

Américo Castro   HIDALGUISMO: THE SENSE OF
                                   NOBILITY

THE FIRST THING to surprise the observer is that as early as the fifteenth
century the Castilians should have felt the necessity of characterizing Spain.
They had no doubt reached the conviction that they had rounded the cape of
uncertainty in their struggle with Islam, and that a splendor-filled future was
approaching. But precisely at the same time the Castilians who spoke for
Spain began to be preoccupied not only with the form of their existence but
also with what they had to do in order to exist. What surprised me first of
all was that in 1459 the well-known humanist Alonso de Palencia should say
that Spain was "a province that is not inclined to take rational points of
view," and this he said in a book significantly entitled *Perfection of Military
Triumph*.[1] But much earlier, in 1434, Don Alonso de Cartagena, Bishop of
Burgos, had pronounced a famous discourse before the Council of Basel
justifying the precedence of Castile with respect to England. His petition
brings us the first description of the characteristic features of Spain. As is
well known, Don Alonso was a new Christian, or convert, and the son of
another illustrious convert, Don Pablo de Santa Maria, who had occupied
a very high position among the Spanish Jews, and in the Church he attained
a rank of equal eminence. Without entering now into the complexity of that
fact, let us note that Don Alonso, great jurist that he was, argued like a good
diplomat filled with patriotic fervor: for centuries the Spanish Jews had stood
out as excellent ambassadors of the Christian and Moslem kings. Let no one
believe that the Bishop of Burgos recited an insincere speech to his Basel
audience. His words were an overflow of Hispanic awareness, and the preferences and contempt expressed in them are the very ones that were characteristically Spanish then and for long afterwards: "Spaniards are not wont to
prize great wealth, but rather, virtue; nor do they measure a man's honor by
the store of his money but rather by the quality of his beautiful deeds; where-
fore riches are not to be argued in this matter (as the English argued them);
for if we should mete out the precedences according to riches, Cosimo de
Medici, or some other very rich merchant, mayhap would come before some
duke."[2]

The spirit of nobility, united with a scorn for commercial activities,
already marks the abyss that will separate Spain from capitalist Europe:

Reprinted with permission from *The Structure of Spanish History* by Américo Castro (Princeton, N.J.: Princeton University Press, 1954).

so far as this Jewish arch-Spaniard ecclesiastic was concerned, Cosimo de Medici was but a contemptible merchant. No visible trace of insecurity exists in this expression of awareness of what it means to be a Spaniard: "The kings of Spain—among which the principal and first and greatest one is the King of Castile and Leon—have never been subject to the Emperor; for this singularity do the kings of Spain have, that they have never been subject to the Holy Roman Empire, nor to any other, but rather have they won and raised up their kingdoms out of the jaws of their enemies" (p. 214), a very acute observation the meaning of which will later become apparent. "In the time of the Goths, many of the princes of Spain were called emperors" (p. 215). Actually, however, Leon and Castile—as it will be seen—were only nominally a continuation of the Visigothic kingdom; for their spiritual strength and their political titles, including the imperial ones, had their foundations in the city of Santiago, the resting place of St. James the Apostle, which was for those monarchs what Rome was to the Holy Roman Empire. For Don Alonso de Cartagena the strength of Castile was grounded less on material realities than on the spiritual and transcendent virtue of the monarchy; otherwise it would not have occurred to him to bring up as a great Spanish merit, and against England, that "the Castilians and Galicians and Biscayans are different nations, and they use completely different languages" (p. 350). In this statement is implicit the idea that was to be expressed a century later by Gonzalo Fernández de Oviedo, to wit, that the only thing that harmonized the discordant variety of the Hispanic peoples was the fact that they were subjects of the king of Spain. Moreover, in the words of the Bishop of Burgos can be traced already the future imperial policy of Charles V, a policy aimed at the spreading of a belief rather than at the establishment of a system of human interests: "The lord and king of England, although he makes war, yet does not make that *divine* war . . . for it is neither against the infidels nor for the glorification of the Catholic faith, nor for the *extension of the boundaries of Christianity, but rather is it made for other interests*" (p. 353).[3] Belief is thus a firm base upon which rises the collective life; its efficacy in the struggle against the infidel brought riches and power, reflected in turn in the spectacular prestige of the monarchy and its surrounding aureole of nobility: "I say nothing here concerning the beauty and grandeur of his court, for, to speak reverently and without offense of all the princes, I could say that in that part of the world known to us, except that it be for the tumult and movement of warfare, there is no prince's court so much visited and so full of so many prelates and counts and barons and other noblemen, and of such a throng of townspeople, as is the royal court of Castile" (p. 351). The court was like a temple to which one repaired in order to obtain earthly benefits just as one visited the house of God to win heavenly favors; the transcendent powers under which the Spaniard found refuge showed their visible form in the nobility and the priesthood. Reflecting such splendors, the Bishop of Burgos succeeded in persuading the Council of Basel to recognize the precedence of Castile with respect to England.

Against the Castilians, the English argued that their own land was richer and more productive, and to this the Bishop answered: "I did not wish to argue the abundance of land, because it seemed to me a *base argument,* for it is not of peasants but of very noble kings that we are speaking; honor comes not from the abundance of the field but from the virtue of man" (p. 533). It is not easy for Don Alonso to descend to the plane of material things, but since the English wish it, he adduces "the vineyards and olive groves, of which there is a great abundance in the kingdom of Castile, and which have been exiled forever from the kingdom of England. . . . And all nations know the esteem which, among all the things that belong to the abundance of the earth, is enjoyed by wine and olive oil. If they should speak of those skilled in the making of cloths, I would perhaps grant them something, for there are in our land no weavers who can make cloth so fine as London scarlet; but even that product which we call *grana* (Kermes dye), from which the scarlet receives the sweetness of its odor and the flame of its color, has its birth in the kingdom of Castile, whence it is carried to England. . . . I might speak of metals, but in my judgment such a base and earthly argument is not proper to such an exalted subject" (pp. 533–534). In the last analysis, riches are something secondary, a possession which "abets in the exercise of virtue, but they are not to be adduced as a principal thing;" in any case, Castile is rich, perhaps in excess, since some fear lest "such an abundance of riches as there is today in Castile may do some harm to virtue." So that nothing may be lacking in this first and most faithful picture of the Hispanic soul—drawn by a Jew, it must not be forgotten—Don Alonso ends his harangue—for it is more this than an argument—with a gesture of supreme arrogance: "I shall bring no other evidence save this embassy, for from a poor kingdom such ambassadors do not usually come forth" (p. 536).

The foregoing remarks will gain strength from a summary examination of the Spaniard's sense of nobility. The Hispano-Christian entered his history with the dangerous feeling that it was possible for him, in one burst of energy, to scale its greatest heights. As early as the year 1000 A.D., the Castilian was beginning to think that he could really "take" the Moor, and that fabulous Cordova was within the reach of his sword. The conquests of Toledo and Valencia (although the latter conquest was temporary) provided an eleventh-century confirmation of his feeling of superiority, based on an awareness of his "intrinsic value." The Archpriest of Hita was later to say: "It is by serving well that Spanish knights win victories." To serve well as a knight was in fact a supreme aspiration. A person's value depended upon the vigor of his conduct in this regard. This attitude predisposed the Hispano-Christian to adopt whatever might reinforce it, even to the point of raiding the spiritual camp of the enemy. Thus he was ready to adopt Arabic ways of expressing personal value (*fijodalgo*), or what there was good in Arabic actions (*fazañas*). *Fazaña*, "feat, prowess," originally "model of goodness, generous act," comes from the Arabic *hasanah* (good act, generosity).[4]

Fijodalgo and *fazaña* are clear evidence of the impression of superiority which the Moslem left with the Hispano-Christian a thousand years ago. Then, the Christian's feeling of superiority grew stronger and stronger. This must be the point of departure for understanding the inordinate urge to nobility and the sense of caste that took possession of the Hispano-Christian. I shall begin by citing texts that will put us in contact with the living reality of history. In a proclamation made in Valencia in 1410 against blasphemers who "soiled their lips and tongues by speaking ill of God and the Virgin Mary," plebeians were condemned to be publicly flogged and pilloried; "but if it be a *person of honor who does not work with his hands,* let him pay as a penalty fifty gold *maravedis*."[5] An abstract conception of history would treat such an idea as a "theme" or "commonplace," and would relate it to Plato's contempt for physical labor and his low regard for crafts, which reappears in the Middle Ages: "Opus humanum, quod natura non est, sed imitatur naturam, mechanichum, i.e., adulterinum vocatur."[6] But what good would it do here to compose a study of the contempt for manual labor through the ages? We are actually faced with a kind of people who composed their existence out of the vital "impossibility" of working at tasks deemed not honorable. "You have always kept me busy with the base things of your mechanical job," says the soul to the body in the *Diálogos de la fantástica filosofía de los tres en uno*.[7] The author could and may have taken his idea from a repertory of medieval commonplaces, but in its historical context the idea has a peculiarly Spanish meaning, for it implies that great value is attached to that which was not mechanical work, that is, the *intrinsic value* of the person.[8]

That value was not only a matter of high spirit, courage, or *brio,* predicated as attributes of the person. It was the very substance of the person, that which made him whole, all of a piece.[9] The Spaniard has been the only example in Western history of a man whose purpose in life is founded on the idea that the only calling worthy of a man is to be a man, and nothing more. When Pedro Crespo entrusts his son to the general, Don Lope de Figueroa, he reasons thus: "What would he do here with me but idle his time away in a life of profligacy? Let him go and serve the king."[10] Pedro Crespo, a successful peasant, feels that the value of his prosperity lies not in the fact that his life has been materially productive but in the fact that his wealth will assure his son a career in the ennobling service of the king.

No other European country so stigmatized manual labor, which was not accorded legal dignity until the reign of Charles III in the eighteenth century, in the course of the invasion of rationalist ideas from foreign lands, an invasion which affected only the epidermis of Spanish life. But it is also certain that belief in intrinsic value was continually shaken by the worry of those who found themselves locked up in their consciousness of caste as well as by the similar worry of those who realized the grave dangers of Spanish exclusivism. Pedro Fernández de Navarrete writes: "This court has been filled with many other persons of low degree: lackeys, coachmen, saddle boys, water-carriers, wafer peddlers, porters. . . . The harm that comes from the fact that these people are leaving the work in the fields undone need not be emphasized." The porter is singled out for special censure: "With the introduction of this not very ancient occupation, it has begun to be the custom that, if a servant buys a *real's* worth of fruit, he must give half to the porter who carries it, an extravagance tolerated only at the court of Spain."[11] This criticism is closely connected with another: "No sooner has a merchant or a worker or a peasant enough to buy a government pension worth 500 ducats a year than he buys with this income a pension for his eldest son, where-upon not only this son but all his brothers become ashamed to occupy themselves at the humble tasks with which that money was originally earned," for "those who are not nobles aspire to make themselves nobles, and those who are aspire to rise to higher places still" (ed.cit., pp. 473, 475).

In 1541 there were already in Castile and Leon 781,582 tax-paying commoners and 108,358 hidalgos; that is, 13 per cent of the families in the kingdom paid no taxes and performed no work of any kind,[12] and they lived like a closed caste. It was observed, however, that it was not possible "to preserve in good condition a republic that consists entirely of nobles, for, to assure mutual assistance between citizens, it is necessary to have a head to rule, priests to pray, counselors to counsel, judges to judge, noblemen to give orders, soldiers to defend, farmers to till, tradesmen to do business, and artisans to take care of mechanical matters."[13] The last two classes of activity had been precisely the ones that had belonged to the Moors and Jews.

When the Spaniards got to the Indies, they implanted and perpetuated their way of life there. In 1590 the inhabitants of Buenos Aires wrote to Philip II in desperation, complaining of the poverty of the Argentine land (which for the English Puritans would have been a paradise), because it is not the land which makes the man but the reverse, even though the importance of natural conditions and the historical moment are not to be denied. In Argentina there was no gold or silver, nor were there native cities, as there were in Mexico and Peru, and the Spaniard, incapable of creating things, did not know what to do: "We are so poor and needy that we could not be more in want, in proof of which, *we do our plowing and digging with our hands.* . . . Such is the need from which the settlers suffer that *their own women and children bring their drinking water from the river.* . . . Spanish women, noble and of high quality, because of their great poverty *carry their drinking water* on their own shoulders." The superior of the

Franciscan convent who was the author of this letter, sorrowfully confirms that "the people do their own work and [take care] of their cattle *with their own hands,* for I have seen it happen thus, and it is a pitiable state of affairs; the people wait on themselves as if it were the tiniest village in Spain."[14]

I know no document more significant, especially for making understandable the history of Hispano-America and the contrasts it presents with the rest of America. The Spaniard moved into the region of the Plata in the sixteenth century just as in the tenth and eleventh he had spread down over the south of the Iberian Peninsula, with the object of gaining honor and maintaining seigniory for himself. Since there were neither Moors nor Jews to do the work in Buenos Aires, and since the Indians quickly fled out into the pampa, what was eventually to become the Argentina we know today remained in rather a wretched condition until about a century ago. Houses in Buenos Aires were straw-covered adobe huts, for this was the only kind of masonry the conquistador knew how to obtain without his wealth and his vassals to carry out his orders. As late as 1852, the future city was a pest-ridden village: "the skeletons of oxen and horses lay about in the mud in the middle of the street; even in front of the doors of some of the houses you could see the putrefied remains of animals."[15]

But at the same time people in America and Europe were already familiar with *Facundo,* a brilliant historico-critical picture of Argentine life by Sarmiento, for to produce such a work of personal integration and expression there was no need of debasing manual labor. But work with the hands was precisely what Sarmiento was later to propose as the remedy for his country's ills, a program similar to that proposed in Spain by the licentiate Fernández de Navarrete in 1626; bring people in from the outside, make others work, give foreigners special privileges, let them "make the rivers navigable and dig ditches for irrigation. . . . The children of these foreigners would, in the second generation, be Spaniards who would fill out the population of Spain, which is the object toward which this discourse is directed" (p. 478). He went so far as to advocate the importance of Negroes "to improve some of the many mines that Spain possesses." These Negroes would, "by the second or third generation be white; if they were not, it would make no difference, since they were apt at manual labor and the cultivation of the soil" (482). Fernández de Navarrete foresaw what was to happen in Brazil.

At first glance, Fernández de Navarrete's program looks like an attempt to correct the course of Hispanic history. More closely examined, it turns out to be the contrary. His negative criticism and lamentations over the poverty and depopulation of the land could have been the utterances of any representative of the "Enlightenment," with the sole difference that the author did not in the least suspect that the lack of things, the sense of emptiness, belonged to the very direction of Spanish life. The proposed solutions were of a mechanical nature, requiring the addition of an element rather than the funda-

mental changing of any existing element in Spanish life, that is, they called for
the addition of people to do what the Moors and Jews had long been doing
without any thought that the dominant caste would cease to be what it was.
That it was the working castes that were missed is clearly seen in this statement
of utopian and nostalgic longing: "I am persuaded that if, before the Moors
and Jews had reached the state of desperation that brought them into such bad
odor, a way had been found to admit them to certain honors, to avoid keeping them under the brand and stigma of infamy, it would have been possible
for them to enter *through the door of honor* into the temple of virtue and into
the bosom and obedience of the Catholic Church" (p. 466). This is in agreement with the ideas of Duarte Gómez referred to earlier (see Chapter 14).
Fernández de Navarrete's ignorance of his own history and the rationalistic
naïveté of the statement are obvious. He was also dreaming of a unique
utopian caste, without realizing that if the Moors and Jews should have
attained an awareness of their "intrinsic value," they would have ceased to do
the work whose lack was now ruining Spain.

In fine, this excellent treatise is discreet throughout and is full of the
anguish of a person who sees clearly what the situation is and would like
it to be different.[16] But Fernández de Navarrete is like the madman in the
asylum (*Don Quixote*, II, 1) who, just after he was adjudged sane and was
about to leave, said to one of his fellow inmates: "If that man is Jupiter and
won't rain, I, who am Neptune, . . . shall rain whenever I feel like it." According to Fernández de Navarrete's advice to the king, the pursuit of letters
"usually engenders a certain melancholy that weakens the spirit by opposing
the cheerful impulsiveness with which dangerous adventures are undertaken
when reflection does not cause them to lag. And that is why the goddess of
knowledge was called 'Minerva, *quasi minuens nervos*' [!], for the peoples
that indulge excessively in the pleasure of learning easily forget the practice
of arms. Spain has examples enough of this, *for as long as the ejection from
Spain of the Saracens' heavy yoke lasted, she was raw and lacking in letters,*
and to remedy this the universities and schools were founded by the kings" (p.
542)—as a foreign importation, it might be added.

Similar observations might be made about the writings of Diego de
Saavedra Fajardo, Spain's representative at the preparatory conference for the
Peace of Westphalia (1648) and a man widely read, widely traveled, and
well-versed in foreign languages. He too laments the harm and poverty suffered by his country, and we might expect to find in him an advocate of
Europeanization ready to shatter the forms of traditional Spanish life. But
nothing of the kind. When the time comes to face the decisive issues, Don
Diego feels like a Spaniard of the tenth century. His world is the world
of belief: "Don Juan de Austria commanded his banners to be embroidered
with the cross and this motto: 'With these arms I have conquered the Turks;
with them I expect to conquer the heretics! . . . I avail myself of them and

of the standard of Constantine to signify to the princes the confidence with which they should raise the banner of religion against their enemies. . . .' Heavenly spirits will attend this banner; *two riding on white horses* were seen fighting in the vanguard when King Ramiro II conquered the Moors near Simancas. . . . At the battle of Mérida in the time of King Alonso IX there appeared that divine lightning bolt, Santiago, the son of thunder, the patron of Spain leading the squadrons with his blood-stained sword."[17]

This belief, genuinely Spanish, was the sap and bark of the tree of Spanish life. Those who have been part of it include Quevedo, Gracián, and all those who have expressed something of what they have felt about themselves and Spain. Belief, not thought,[18] intrinsic value, the sense of nobility, the spirit of caste, one and the same thing—the triple-stranded contexture of Christians, Moors, and Jews, 900 years old.

Notes

1. Américo Castro, *Aspectos del vivir hispánico* (Aspects of Hispanic Existence), Cruz del Sur, Santiago de Chile, 1949, p. 21.
2. Discurso pronunciado por don Alonso de Cartagena en el Concilio de Basilea acerca del derecho de precedencia del Rey de Castilla sobre el rey de Inglaterra" (Discourse pronounced by Don Alonso de Cartagena at the Council of Basel, Concerning the Right of Precedence of the King of Castile over the King of England), in the journal *La Ciudad de Dios,* 1894, xxxv, 122–542.
3. See also, *ibid.,* p. 526. There are other curious observations on England: "Even though it may be a noteworthy island (for it is called *Anglia* which some say means 'more vainglorious of money'), there are not in it so many provinces nor such broad ones" (p. 349). I know no basis for Don Alonso's curious semantic interpretation of Anglia, but the legend of "English gold" is, for that matter, quite ancient.
4. J. Corominas, *Vox Romanica,* 1949, x. 67–72.
5. F. Danvila, in the *Boletin de la Academia de la Historia,* 1886, viii, 388.
6. Hugo of Saint Victor, in *Patrologia,* Vol. 176, col. 747 (quoted by E. R. Curtius, in the *Zeitschrift für romanische Philologie,* LVIII, 23).
7. By Don Francisco Miranda Villafañe, Salamanca, 1583, fol. 21r.
8. Don Artal de Alagón, Count of Sástago, wrote: "I am not trying to condemn all combat between individuals or to discourage men from preserving their honor and standing up for the honor of God and of themselves in the way that one should . . .; rather I would want to encourage them and give them enthusiasm for these purposes, such enthusiasm, I understand, being more necessary than cooling their blood, which is already so cold that it is pitiful to see how *intrinsic value* has grown weak in those men in whom it should be strongest" (*Concordia de las leyes divinas y humanas,* Madrid, 1593, fol. 126r).
9. This is something different from the "moral integrity" which preserves intact the moral principles on which conduct is based. The idea of "wholeness" refers to something which implies active fortitude and courage and which leaves aside everything else.

10. Calderón, *El alcalde de Zalamea,* ii, 11. 765–768.
11. "Conservación de monarquias," 1626, discourse xxvi (in the *Biblioteca de Autores Españoles,* xxv (504b).
12. "Relación de los vecinos no pecheros que hay en las 18 provincias del reino para el repartimiento del servicio de 1541, y de los hidalgos que se presupone podrá haber en cada una de las dichas provincias," in *Colección de documentos inéditos para la historia de España,* 1848, xiii, 521–528.
13. Fernández de Navarette, *Conservación de monarquías,* ed. cit., p. 472.
14. Emilio A. Coni, *Agricultura, comercio e industria coloniales,* Buenos Aires, 1941, p. 15.
15. Rafael Alberto Arrieta, *Centuria porteña,* Buenos Aires, 1944, p. 37.
16. The work even proposes the creation of shipbuilding schools, "through which Spain would be freed from dependence on the help of foreigners, who, because they are foreign and without obligations or pledges of faith or love, are apt to undertake any kind of treason" (p. 542). It is incredible (although readily explicable) that the work of Fernández de Navarette has not been published, with a sound historical commentary, to serve as basic instruction for all those who have to do with the government of the Hispano-Portuguese peoples, who are all alike in this respect. In the twentieth century (just as in the seventeenth or in the twelfth), no Hispano-Portuguese country is capable of building its own ships without foreign help.
17. *Idea de un príncipe politico-cristiano, representada en cien empresas,* xxvi.
18. It was natural that foreigners should think of Spain as a strange and incomprehensible country. Voltaire could not understand, of course, how a Spanish ambassador in London could have taken for fools two English scholars who asked his aid for a scientific expedition (probably to some of the mountains of America). The ambassador "*les prit pour des fous: lui seul était peu sage.*" (Epistle LV, De l'usage de la science dans les princes.)

5. The Arts, Literature, and Science

There are many ways in which the sociology of the arts and of literature stands in need of a historical perspective. The arts in the widest sense are the symbolic expression of a culture; and cultural changes, therefore, are reflected in changing architectural, pictorial, musical and literary styles. Jacob Burckhardt and his student, the art historian Heinrich Woelfflin, were sensitive to interrelations of this kind.[1] But styles are not always unique cultural phenomena, as for instance the Greek or Gothic modes of seeing; styles may be indicative of recurrent types of social organization, like the music written for a ruler's court or the songs which articulate the longings of an oppressed population. If one starts at the other end, one becomes aware, as Florian Znaniecki did, of the social roles of artists, scholars, and scientists.[2] A comparative evaluation of these roles will ascertain what may be universal and lasting in them and what remains subject to historical change. As far as science is concerned, the problem is still more historical in character. The arts are ubiquitous, but science is very much a product of the western world and, in particular, seems inseparable from the socio-economic style of modern capitalism or perhaps, in a wider sense, of industrial society. More specifically, it is likely that a correlation can be established between the Protestant Ethic and the spirit of modern science. This point, following the theoretical formulations and historical researches of Alfred and Max Weber,[3] has been brought to the attention of sociologists by Robert K. Merton.[4]

It is, of course, not possible to illustrate these and all other conceivable approaches in a general volume such as this. We open the section with a broadly suggestive essay, "Class Systems and the Arts," by Adolph S. Tomars, which is based on Robert M. MacIver's distinction between corporative and competitive class systems. In the examples chosen from Greek, medieval, and modern art, the author does not intend to deny the individuality of any given piece of art; he merely draws attention to the fact that the artist, because of his great sensitivity, expresses with particular forcefulness the subtle shifts in meaning which are inherent in changing social situations. In the end, the question is posed whether a "principled sacred society," such as one or the other of the modern totalitarian systems, will not return art from its highly competitive present state to the rigidity of corporate expression.

Herbert Moller's paper, "The Social Causation of the Courtly Love Complex," is more specific. The world of the troubadors, if viewed purely artistically, may seem remote, but it becomes vibrantly alive, if one considers the variety of human conditions which it reflects. It is a world in change, a world in turmoil, filled with unstable and emergent relations between the sexes and the social classes, and replete with vague strivings and deep frustrations. Special attention should be given to the Notes in this essay which refer to a wide variety of literary sources, among them the works of Marc Bloch. In the text itself, Moller follows Bloch's lead when he points out that the validation of a hypothesis in socio-historical research must be sought by means of a comparison of cultural complexes. The wider the variety of historical situations, the more favorable are the laboratory conditions, the greater the chances for a synthesis which is generalizing and individualizing at the same time. It is the merit of a young journal, *Comparative Studies in Society and History,* from which Moller's piece is taken, to have impressed this principle upon scholars in the related but separated departments of the social and historical sciences.

The papers by Ernest Manheim and Joseph Ben-David conclude this section. Manheim's piece, "The Communicator and His Audience," points to the possibilities of historically oriented public opinion research and perhaps, beyond this, to the possibilities of comparative research in the entire field of collective behavior and social movements. Another example of research in this area is E. Herbert Norman's "Mass Hysteria in Japan,"[5] which vividly depicts a state of collective unrest, antecedent to revolutionary change.

Manheim's paper deals with publics rather than with crowds, that is, with an ongoing discussion, not with a sudden outburst. But a situation of uneasiness and unrest is present also in this instance, resulting, however, not in the overthrow of an existing order, but in social indecision. (Cf. Alvin Boskoff's paper in Section II). The literary expression in this context is merely a camouflage. In addition to its theoretical significance the paper is a contribution to the historical psychology of the German socio-political illness. In Ben-David's paper, on the other hand, the corresponding virtues of the unsettled condition of modern Germany become apparent. What was paralyzing indecision in the political realm became stimulating competition in science. A similarly stimulating competitive situation has been present in America, but under different social and political circumstances. Ben-David's paper is suggestive of a wide variety of further researches about the relations between science and society.

Notes

1. Jacob Burckhardt, *The Civilization of the Renaissance in Italy* (New York: Harper Torchbooks, 1958); Heinrich Woelfflin, *Principles of Art History: The Problem of the Development of Style in Later Art* (London G. Bell & Sons, Ltd., 1932).
2. Florian Znaniecki, *The Social Role of the Man of Knowledge* (New York: Columbia University Press, 1940).
3. Alfred Weber, *Fundamentals of Culture Sociology: Social Process, Civilizational Process and Culture-movement,* transl. G. H. Weltner and C. F. Hirshman (New York: Works Progress Administration and Columbia University, 1939); Max Weber, *The Protestant Ethic and the Spirit of Capitalism,* transl. Talcott Parsons (New York: Charles Scribner's Sons, 1958).
4. Robert K. Merton, *Social Theory and Social Structure,* Part IV (New York: The Free Press, 1957).
5. E. Herbert Norman, "Mass Hysteria in Japan," *Far Eastern Survey,* 14 Jan. 17, 1945, pp. 65–70.

Adolph S. Tomars   CLASS SYSTEMS AND THE ARTS

SOCIOLOGICALLY CONSIDERED, the arts are a set of social institutions among the other institutions within a social structure. As such, they must be affected by the nature of the social structure of the society in which they exist. The sociology of art, then, requires an examination of the effect of major structural variables upon the function, subject matter, and style of art.

In the following material the variable within the total social structure that

Condensed and adapted with the permission of the author from A. S. Tomars, *Introduction to the Sociology of Art,* privately printed, Mexico City, 1940 (also Columbia University Ph.D. Dissertation, 1941), Chaps. VII–IX, pp. 141–219.

is examined for its effect upon art is the class structure, i.e., the nature of the structure of social classes and the basis of the class system. The conceptual formulations are derived from the analysis provided by R. M. MacIver, especially from his distinction between corporate and competitive class systems and the corresponding forms of class consciousness.[1]

Corporate class consciousness is class feeling which unites the members of a group possessing the same status; in which individuals, aware of sharing a particular status with others, feel this awareness as a bond of unity and solidarity with other members of their class. Its necessary condition is the presence of rigid and impassable class barriers; its characteristics are established class customs, firm class traditions, and strong class solidarity. Corporate class consciousness is most likely to be found in a stable society with a class system deeply rooted in the mores, and where status is determined by birth.

Competitive class consciousness is revealed in the attempt of individuals to emulate or outrival the status of others, where members of the group sharing the same status regard each other as competitors. Here, awareness of status leads not to class solidarity but to individual competition for status. The necessary condition of competitive class consciousness is sufficient vertical mobility to make status change a reality for some, a goal for others.

Class groups exert an important influence upon the function, subject matter, and style of art. The nature of this influence varies with the nature of the class system, the basis of status within it, its relative rigidity or mobility, and the predominance of the corporate or competitive type of class consciousness. The basic art institutions are communal but the social classes within the community impress their customs and institutions upon the communal art. Where the classes are rigidly separated, this differential influence may transform the communal art institutions into forms so diverse as to allow us to speak of distinct class forms of art.

By the cross-sectional comparative method, it is possible to find many illustrations from different societies and epochs of the ways in which class customs and institutions affect art; and where parallels emerge, generalizations can be formulated as hypotheses. A more clear-cut basis for any broad generalization is afforded by the longitudinal method of tracing the effect of a major change in the class structure upon changes in the arts. Parallels thus obtained are likely to yield fundamental generalizations and a high probability of causal relationship in the variables examined.

Twice in the history of the western world a class system has gone through the process of change from a rigid, stable, corporate type based upon birth to a mobile competitive type based upon moneyed wealth as a society became highly urbanized. One case was the change of Greek society from the Hellenic city-state to the urban Hellenistic civilization (Roman society underwent a parallel development, eventually merging into the Hellenistic society). The other was the shift from the feudal society of medieval western Europe to the modern European-American pattern.

The history of Greek art affords a particularly illuminating case study. According to W. Deonna,[2] Hellenic art down to the close of the fifth century B.C. had as its basic function the glorification of the city-state community and the provision of votive offerings to the divinities that personified it. Its ideal human personification was in the citizen of good birth, the male citizen-soldier-athlete, the type idealized in the youthful ephebic ideal. In Athens and elsewhere, gymnastic training was a civil obligation for the younger men of good families and expressly forbidden to lower ranks, such as slaves. This upper class ephebic ideal made the nude male the dominant subject matter of the representational arts. The conventionalized and idealized type of the *ephebus* (even the bearded mature man was represented with the body of a young athlete) conditioned the stylistic treatment of old age, of women and of children which avoided any realistic representation of natural characteristics. All upper class human representation was assimilated to this conventionalized ephebic type. Children, when used as subjects, were presented as miniature athletes; women were either not shown undraped or else as robust, virile featured, well muscled, and athletic.

The hierarchy of ranks in both human and superhuman society was carefully distinguished, as Deonna shows, by stylistic differentials of treatment. The nonhuman status system extended from the gods, heroes and heroicized dead to the inferior mythological ranks of Satyrs, Centaurs, Sileni, Titans, and Antaeus. The human system was headed by the elite of citizens of good birth, descending to lesser citizens, tradesmen, slaves, and barbarians.

"Noble and dignified attitudes are reserved for the gods, for the dead and . . . the living of high birth."[3] They are seated majestically or stand erect in the conventional frontal pose. If shown in athletic or warlike action the pose is harmonious, calm and balanced. Even when wounded or dying, the pose and face remain dignified and restrained, serene in suffering. The lower orders are shown in careless, sprawling postures, crouching, lying on their stomachs, crossing their legs, or gesticulating violently, faces contorted with pain or anger —realistically.

Superior beings are given the perfect musculature of the athlete. The bodies of slaves, barbarians, satyrs and sileni may be coarse, obese, ill-shapen. For the elite, the conventionalized ideal-type shows hair and beard always neat and, in the fifth century, the idealized straight "Hellenic profile." The lower orders may be shown with tousled hair and realistic stubby noses, hideous or comic in visage. Greek realistic art begins in the treatment of the lower ranks; for the high born a rigid conventionalized style is prescribed.

Instead of deriving this convention of classic Greek art from an imputed Greek esthetic theory of artistic harmony and restraint, as some older art critics such as G. E. Lessing (in his *Laokoon*) have done, it would be more to the point to consider the Greek concept of artistic fitness as deriving from the social concept of the ideal man, a concept in turn dictated by the aristocratic type in the Greek class system.

As Deonna concludes: "Greek art is aristocratic. It never sought to give a complete picture of the social complex and did not interest itself to the same extent in the various classes. . . . It glorified Greeks of good birth and the gods conceived in their likeness and for them it sought the most beautiful and noble types. The lower orders might hold the curious regard of the ceramist . . . in high art the common people merely accompanied their masters and in the classic period are never treated for their own sake.[4]

The general characteristics of the function, subject matter, and style of Greek art in the period of a stable, corporate class system can be summed up. The function of art was the glorification of the civic community and its gods. Art was primarily didactic rather than esthetic, an instrument for the teaching of civic patriotism and religious devotion. This function dictated its subject matter, the representation of superior beings, human and superhuman. On the human level, the civic ideals were embodied in the upper class elite as the exemplars of the community. Function and subject matter in turn dictated a nonrealistic style embodying conventionalized types. The analagous characteristics could be shown to permeate the nonrepresentational arts, as literature, drama and music.

An analysis of medieval art, again in a period of a stable corporate class system, would yield the same generalized characteristics, despite the cultural variations of another era and region, the major variations being the unity of the feudal system instead of the city-state, the existence of an organized church interwoven with the feudal structure, and the presence of a clerical class, its upper hierarchy interlocked with the feudal aristocracy.

We return to Greek society as the type-case. From the fourth century B.C., the social structure undergoes a great transformation as a result of intense urbanization with its attendant commercialization and secularization. The traditional politico-religious unity and the corresponding status system are undermined. Three sociological features characterize the social change: the disintegration of civic community solidarity leading to individualism, a shift in the basis of the class system from birth to wealth, and a change from corporate to competitive class consciousness. Again, the effects upon art have been well described by Deonna, richly documented by reference to specific works of art.

Political power . . . formerly in the hands of the citizens . . . was now concentrated in . . . one absolute ruler. A brilliant court gave the tone to the rest of society. Art ceased to serve the city . . . and placed herself at the disposal of kings and princes. The prince was glorified by his images and the recital of his exploits . . . Thanks to Alexander . . . who united diverse races, a cosmopolitan era began . . . Art gradually acquired that international character which was its hall-mark during the Hellenistic period.

In the cities of independent Greece a man had to be a citizen . . . before he could attain any influence . . . Now a man's origin mattered little . . . Adventurers and parvenus began to play an important part. Social distinctions which the artist had once conveyed by so many subtle shades grew less discernible. . . . The gods themselves did not scruple to take the . . . familiar attitudes once reserved for the lower orders . . . The high born Greek no longer monopolized attention . . . the world of small folk was opened to the artists . . . realism, which had been confined to the lower order, now invades the whole of art.

Individualism, which had been seeking to break its chains . . . since the fourth century, now triumphs. The Greek no longer takes an active part in . . . government . . . and concentrates on his private affairs. Artists and savants confine themselves to their arts and sciences . . . The artist puts himself at the service of private persons. Hence the individualistic character of art . . . Forms of literature develop which answer these new tendencies . . . biographies become numerous . . . Portraits become numerous, in every genre there is insistence on the characteristic detail which differentiates the models and on the divergences in age, sex, race or environment. The art of the fifth century tended to bring all ages of life to the ephebic ideal—children, old men . . . women . . . Now that realism has asserted itself, not only does art become interested . . . in women, whose specific features it observes, but . . . seeks to characterize the various ages . . . in Hellenistic art children and old men take on the appearance proper to them.

. . . The rich made a display of their wealth . . . Woman played a great part in this elegant and refined civilization . . . The cult of Woman dates from the Hellenistic period . . . Olympus did not escape this altered Greek mentality. To the grave and austere divinities of the fifth century, men now preferred the gods of the senses and passions. Aphrodite, Eros, Dionysius . . . Satyrs . . . Maenads —subjects which permitted of the sensuous appeal of the bodies of women and *ephebi* being emphasized . . . Aphrodite is a mortal woman, more courtesan than goddess . . . Hellenistic society was voluptuous . . . Instead of making their women and children virile, as in the fifth century, artists now make their young gods effeminate and bestow on them a soft and sensitive beauty.

The secularization of art increases from the fourth century . . . skepticism grew . . . Myths increasingly became for the artists themes to stimulate their virtuosity . . . In older times art chose subjects to be understood by all. Now . . . it essays to be personal and original. There comes a break between the people and art which is now become the domain of the elite.

Incomprehensible to the public at large . . . art, which has broken its ties with the national life . . . loses its didactic character . . . It seeks above all to please by its beauty, to stimulate the esthetic sense . . . The artist has become independent . . . more concerned with producing a personal piece of work than in docilely following a tradition . . . The position of the artist begins to grow in dignity with the fourth century, and in the Hellenistic period . . . becomes higher still. Extravagant prices are paid for his work.

The close relation between the utilitarian and the beautiful is slackened. From the end of the fifth century . . . works that are beautiful are distinguished from those merely useful. This dissociation is still more clear in the Hellenistic period

. . . that elegant, voluptuous . . . and learned society which no longer saw beauty in the exact conformity of form with ideal, but in form alone . . . The artists often find their ideal in skilled technique independent of the subject represented or its utility . . . The theory of art for art's sake is not a modern one, it was born in the Hellenistic period.[5]

The tendencies to realism were no longer checked by the necessity of adherence to a conventionalized type and the emergence of a mobile class system brought all classes into view as artistic subject matter. The new individualism and the function of art to serve individuals reinforces realism in the form of the portrait. Luxurious aesthetic cultivation combined with the new realism and individualism brought an emphasis on novelty and complexity with the use of even formerly sacred material as opportunity for aesthetic virtuosity in treatment.

Fine art and the successful artists now soared high above crafts and craftsmen. Increasing divorce from the utilitarian functions inherent in a prescribed subject matter created a tendency away from stress on subject to stress on formal qualities leading to aesthetic autonomy and the rise of the doctrine of art for art's sake. Again, these characteristics can be shown to have their analogues in the literary, dramatic and performing arts.

The same general characteristics emerge from an examination of the other analogous case in western history—the transformation of the medieval corporate type feudal system into the modern competitive type commercial and industrial class structure. The same social and historical forces were at work as a rising money economy replaced birth by wealth as the chief determinant of status. Again, we find rationalism undermining the religious basis of feudalism, individualism breaking the barriers of caste. We see secularization and growing complexity leading art from emphasis on subject matter to stress on form. The general effects on art are revealed again in the trends to realism, individualism and purism.

The focus of these changes was, as in Greece, the growing city, the center of communication, where the interrelated forces of moneyed wealth, economic individualism, rationalism and purism gather their strength. Modern European art, as distinct from medieval art, arose in the wealthy trading cities of Italy and Flanders. Associated with this art were the new urban competitive classes based upon wealth, the burghers, whose rise broke the feudal system and whose upper ranks merged with or displaced the former noble elite. In this sense, modern European art may properly be designated as bourgeois art.[6]

Because urban society is far more complex than the nonurban, the competitive class system requires more analysis to discern its manifold factors. The corporate class system is characterized by custom, the competitive system by fashion. Corporate classes have their distinctive group customs which change but slowly. Thus there are scarcely any peasant or aristocratic fashions. Fashion is only fully developed in a competitive class structure and plays an important functional role in such a system through the operation of the "fashion pyramid." A simplified model of the process may be described as follows:

Competitive classes do have distinctive customs but individual members of each class seek to raise their status by taking over the customs of the class above them, thus identifying themselves with a reference group of a higher order. Customs thus move down the status ladder. The elite seeks especially to distinguish itself from the rest, and, since the lower classes continually tend to take over more and more of its customs, it becomes necessary to adopt new modes of expression, which must be sharply distinguishable from the old ones. The new customs are again copied by the lower classes and when they no longer serve to distinguish the elite, they must be changed again, often reverting to customs similar to the original ones. The total process takes on the nature of a series of waves emanating from the topmost strata. This constant changing of customs in oscillating cycles constitutes fashion and becomes a necessary element in the preservation of a competitive status system. The needs of an expanding commercial and productive system intensify the fashion process and artificially stimulate the cycle to an ever faster tempo.[7]

The reigning fashion is superior because: (1) it is practiced by the superior class, (2) it is the newest, superseding what has become *passé*, (3) it is rare, restricted to the few, and not yet the possession of the many, (4) it is likely to be expensive, indicative of superiority in wealth. Different forms of art and aesthetic taste are indicators of leisure, wealth and social superiority. Hence the art customs of the elite, even more than their other customs, are drawn into the cycle of fashion. The work of a particular writer, painter or composer may be in *vogue* a few years or even a single season and then dropped. The celebrity of one year is eclipsed by a new celebrity. The unknown artist can always hope to become a "discovery." Art fads succeed each other in rapid succession.

The criteria of fashion superiority are novelty, rarity, and expensiveness. When art becomes part of the fashion process these criteria also become criteria of beauty. Thus a competitive class system influences art by introducing its own standards of judgment. Since novelty is the essence of fashion, the superiority of a new fashion carries with it the ridicule of the outmoded fashion. Thus in art the reigning fashion is always beautiful, the preceding fashion ugly and ridiculous. A genuinely old fashion is far enough removed from the process of social rivalry to be quaint or beautiful and may return as the latest fashion. The principle that the sharpest revulsion is against the preceding fashion holds whether the cycle moves in seasons, generations or periods. Shakespeare and Bach were eclipsed in the succeeding periods, to return later; the Renaissance found Gothic art ugly; the nineteen twenties derided everything Victorian, but by the forties Victorian artists and writers were once again held in respect.

The search for novelty may take many forms. It may lead across class lines in taking up art forms from the lower classes, as a self-conscious enthusiasm over folk songs, rural handicrafts, workers' ballads—a kind of aesthetic "slumming"; across time, in seeking art forms of the past for discovery and revival, as Italian primitives, medieval Gothic, colonial handicrafts; or across space, selecting foreign arts as fashionable to the deprecation of native products. Novelty may also be sought in any unique characteristics of the subject or style of a work of art or in the personality of the artist. A banned book, a painting of bizarre style or subject, the work of an artist who "went native," a Negro art singer, a child prodigy, a one-arm pianist—any of these may become a sensation for a time because of a spectacular element of novelty.

The criteria of rarity and expensiveness are of necessity correlated since what is rare and sought after will be costly. Since expensiveness is itself a mark of superiority in a competitive class system based upon moneyed wealth, a high price for a work of art or a high fee for a performer becomes a sign of artistic worth.[8] Costliness becomes a standard entering into judgments of art, setting up what Veblen called "pecuniary canons of taste." The word "cheap" becomes the most derogatory epithet in art.[9]

Interwoven with the total fashion process is the upper-class luxury of collecting, a characteristic of a competitive elite. To be fashionable and status-enhancing, the class of objects collected must be nonutilitarian, rare and expensive. Collecting has no necessary connection with art, but fine art works are peculiarly well fitted for collecting because they are nonutilitarian, contain many rarities and are expensive, with the additional advantage of cultural value and the prestige of implied aesthetic cultivation. The various ways in which the values of collecting effect and even supplant aesthetic values have been well pointed out by Charles Lalo, who, though not a sociologist, came very close to a sociological interpretation of art history.[10]

One important effect stems from the fact that, in collecting, the rarer the specimen the greater its value. The peak of value lies in the sole existing specimen, hence the great value and prestige of the "original" work. Although masked by various pseudo-aesthetic explanations, the superiority of the original over the copy derives basically from considerations of rarity. In corporate class systems without the collecting spirit, artists themselves hardly troubled over the distinction between original and copy. Medieval composers used the same tunes repeatedly, Hellenic and medieval artists made numerous copies of the same work, a tradition so strong that even as late as Titian and Rubens, we find these artists making several copies of their works, or having them copied by pupils and signing them (with some retouching) without any sense of loss of integrity. By the eighteenth century this was no longer permissible. Under a competitive class system, wealthy collectors in imperial Rome paid large sums for old Greek originals, as collectors did again in the West from the Renaissance to the present. In both periods the faking of originals became a lucrative business.

Another important effect of the collecting spirit in a competitive elite is the tremendous aesthetic prestige of the art of the past. The *parvenu,* unsure of his own taste, seeks the certainty of tradition and collects works of long established reputation. Works of the past are also more likely to be rare. Living artists are still producing, and both the artistic repute and the rarity of their works are uncertain. Finally, the art of the past is old enough to be removed from the cycle of fashion to achieve "classic" status. Quite different is the behavior of the competitive elite toward an immediately preceding art which has gone out of fashion, or the attitude of a stable corporate elite toward its ancient art. As Lalo points out, *parvenus* have antique or imitation Louis XVI furniture as a mark of good taste; the remnants of the titled aristocracy have genuine Louis XVI furniture as heirlooms, a sign of ancient lineage; the aristocrats of Louis XVI's day had it because it was the fashionable style.

Fashionable collecting also has great impact upon contemporary art, affecting its subject matter and style. The most basic criterion of collecting is rarity. Rarity is found not only in the uniqueness of a specimen, but also in uniqueness of style and subject. With old masters of established reputation rarity is assured by the paucity of original works. With contemporary artists such rarity is in the future and problematic, but the rarity of uniqueness can be achieved by work that is "different" and personal, rare not by being *the* original specimen but in being *an* original specimen.

Thus the collecting criterion of rarity reinforces the fashion criterion of novelty in making for individualism in art. The demand for a personal and individual style and manner creates a multitude of artistic styles, schools, experiments and movements as, in recent Western painting—impressionism, expressionism, cubism, futurism, neoclassicism, dadaism, surrealism, abstractionism—and analogous successions and proliferations in the other arts. Artists may become so much a part of this process that an artist may found a new and original style only to desert it, once it is taken up, for a new and different one. These values enter into the standards of aesthetic taste and judgment to the extent that craftsmanship may be wholly subordinated to originality.

All of these effects are best seen in works of art capable of physical ownership and possession. However, their analogues can be demonstrated in the literary, musical and performing arts where they reveal themselves in the collection of aesthetic experiences and expressions of taste. For example, in the theater, the counterpart of possession of the original work is attendance at the "first night," the social prestige of which is not derived from any artistic superiority of the première. Similarly, in music the abrupt stylistic changes of a Stravinsky are the counterparts of the successive styles of a Picasso.

It should be emphasized that in tracing these competitive class influences upon art, no judgment is implied as to the aesthetic worth of the art so influenced. Judgments of aesthetic value are not the concern of the social scientist. What is being pointed out is: (1) that under a competitive class system, fashion influences art by setting conditions under which an artist or art work may or may not obtain a hearing, or, having been brought to light, may or may not enjoy popularity; and (2) that the standards of fashion imperceptibly enter into and become a part of aesthetic standards and thus influence aesthetic judgment. Art critics and art historians may regard such values as extrinsic and nonaesthetic; the sociologist merely points out their intrinsic interconnection with aesthetic values and their sources in the changing social structure.

Insofar as it is possible to generalize from the two cases in western history of a change from a corporate to a competitive class structure, what is the broadest hypothesis that can be formulated expressing the effect of such a change upon art? Stated in its most summary form, it would be that the shift to a competitive class system influences art in the direction of realism, individualism and purism.

Two of these terms—realism and purism—represent opposing tendencies. Realism emphasizes subject matter and thereby the nonaesthetic social functions of art from which subject matter is derived; it develops a naturalistic style for the faithful portrayal of the subject. Its aesthetic doctrine becomes "art as imitation of life." Purism moves away from stress on subject matter to emphasis on stylistic and formal values and the development of autonomous aesthetic canons. The function of art becomes the provision of purely aesthetic experience and the corollary doctrine is "art for art's sake." Underlying both is the tendency of individualism, which throws its weight now in the one direction, now in the other.

If we may generalize from Greece and Western Europe, the effect of the change from a corporate to a competitive system is, in its first phase, to influence art in the direction of individualism and realism and, in its later phase, toward individualism and purism.

The factors, positive and negative, that make for realism in the earlier phase of a competitive system may be summed up: (1) dissolution of the values upholding the corporate system frees art from religious and caste symbols that bind it to a rigidly conventionalized style and releases the tendency to realism those restraints had held in check; (2) rise of a mobile individualistic class system releases art from the aristocratic and religious restrictions of a limited subject matter so that the whole of nature and society becomes open to realistic treatment in all its diversity; (3) a rationalistic, secularized outlook and the development of the scientific temper encourages the search for more accurate portrayal of man and nature; (4) the new function of art—to glorify individuals in a competitive, individualistic system rather than to portray idealized social types—stimulates realistic representation; (5) because realistic subject matter is individual and novel by its own distinctive character, as the portrait is uniquely original by its portrayal of a unique individual, the extension of subject matter to all specific aspects of the life of man and nature opens up a vast field for the exercise of the novelty and uniqueness in art that individualism calls forth. Individualism thus becomes a powerful force making for realism.

Again, if the observable trends in Greece and Western Europe represent a general process, we find that as a society becomes more highly urbanized and the competitive system more highly developed, individualism now shifts its weight away from realism in art and in the direction of purism. Once more both positive and negative factors making for purism may be summarized:

1. With increasing development of realistic art a saturation point is reached, as the possibilities for individuality through unique and novel subject matter are exploited to the point of exhaustion and technical standardization. Even portrait technique becomes so standardized that any number of properly trained craftsmen can produce an accurate portrayal. At this point novelty and originality become difficult to achieve through subject matter; individuality must be sought in formal technical and stylistic qualities beyond the technique of realistic representation.

2. The fact that fine art is an upper class function of cultivated leisure and diversion shifts emphasis from realistic subject matter to the free exploitation of pleasingly decorative formal patterns and to stimulating aesthetic experience.

3. As technical proficiency in representation becomes widespread, there is increasing need to differentiate further the fine art of the cultivated classes from ordinary art. The artist needs again to distinguish himself from the mere craftsman, and the patron to distinguish purely aesthetic qualities, appreciated by the cultivated few, from the realistic art understood by the many. The artist's exploration of radical new technical and formal possibilities thus proceeds unchecked. He is freed not only from the earlier conventions of social symbolism, but now also from the conventions of realistic technique and fidelity to subject matter. He becomes a law unto himself, responsible only to art as he conceives it and as others may be induced to accept it.

4. The extension of subject matter and technique made possible by realism and the further differentiation of fine art from craftsmanship gives rise to new formal values. Recognition that even the most faithful realism implies some selection raises problems of the nature and aims of artistic selection and sets up ideals of what constitutes the aesthetic *per se*. This serious preoccupation with the autonomous values of art and the possibilities of their realization provides a major impetus to purism. In this sense, purism and the idea of art for art's sake are results of the increasingly complex development of art in a complex urbanized society.

The rise of the competitive class system disrupted the old religio-communal solidarity of the city-state and of feudalism, but the equilibrium of society was maintained by other forms of solidarity. In the West, as the older class structure disintegrated into competitive individualism, there arose a new and more inclusive form of social cohesion. The inclusive national community must be understood as a counter-weight to these divisive forces by imposing a broader, but looser, form of social integration.

A final consideration of the possible future course of history raises the question: could this integrative force become so strong as to restore the old type of close-knit social solidarity? In recent Western history, several totalitarian states have attempted to envelop all aspects of life in one comprehensive unity through the religio-ideological doctrines of fascism and communism. In all of them an official national art has appeared, didactic in nature, dealing with idealized types and group symbols. The fascist societies were short-lived, the communist totalitarian state system is still growing. Should this or a similar type of solidarity increase and spread in the West the consequences for art would be tremendous. It would mean the return to a nonindividualistic art expressing a unified synthesis of social values and doctrines which would be imposed.

Notes

1. R. M. MacIver, *Society, Its Structure and Changes* (New York: Long and Smith, 1931), Chap. V; also R. M. MacIver and C. Page, *Society, An Introductory Analysis* (New York: Rinehart, 1949), Chap. XIV.
2. A. de Ridder and W. Deonna, *Art in Greece* (New York: A. A. Knopf, 1927).
3. de Ridder and Deonna, *op. cit.*, p. 81ff.
4. *Ibid.*
5. de Ridder and Deonna, *op. cit.*, p. 110ff.
6. Some of the above conclusions are paralleled in the interpretation of art history made in P. Sorokin, *Social and Cultural Dynamics,* Vol. 1 (New York: American Book Company, 1937). However, they are not analyzed sociologically as consequences of urbanization and a changing class structure but considered as part of a general philosophy of history whereby urbanization and all its concomitants are seen as expressions of an immanent principle of eternal fluctuation between two kinds of civilization whose polar types are defined as "ideational" and "sensate."
7. On the social-psychological theory of fashion, cf. Herbert Blumer, "Collective Behavior" in Alfred McLung Lee (ed.), *Principles of Sociology* (New York: Barnes & Noble, 1955), pp. 216–218, and Neil J. Smelser, *Theory of Collective Behavior* (New York: The Free Press of Glencoe, 1963), pp. 172–73, 207–208 [Eds.].
8. Compare the worshipful reaction of the public to the acquisition by the Metropolitan Museum of Art in New York of Rembrandt's "Aristotle Contemplating the Bust of Homer." The price paid for this painting was $2,300,000.
9. T. Veblen, *The Theory of the Leisure Class* (New York: Vanguard Press, 1927), Chap. VI.
10. Lalo, *L'art et la vie sociale* (Paris: Dion, 1921), Chap. 2.

Herbert Moller   THE SOCIAL CAUSATION OF THE
                     COURTLY LOVE COMPLEX

I

How TO ACCOUNT for the courtly love complex of the troubadours and minnesingers has been an unsolved puzzle ever since the romanticists discovered
it as a scholarly problem. For about three generations, in the twelfth and
thirteenth centuries, Provençal and German lyrical poetry was preoccupied
with a strangely uneven love pattern. In the classic version of this poetry, the
male lover presents himself as engrossed in a yearning desire for the love of
an exceedingly beautiful and perfect woman whose strange emotional aloof-
ness and high social status make her appear hopelessly distant. But the
frustrated and sorrowful lover cannot overcome his fascination and renders
faithful "love service" to this "high-minded" and exacting lady who recipro-
cates in a surprising manner: She does not grant him the amorous "reward"
which he craves, but she gives him what immeasurably increases his "worth":
She rewards him with approval and reassurance. The great lady accepts him as
being worthy of her attention, but only at the price of behavioral restraint and
refinement of manners, that is, at the price of *courtois* behavior. As the contemporaries put it, *courtoisie* is the result of courtly love.

It is now generally accepted that courtly poetry did not describe contemporary ways of courting and love-making. Its nonrealistic nature, however, does not indicate that it was intrinsically meaningless, as some modern
authors have concluded. Even though the poems, as a rule, did not realistically
portray any personal love experiences of the troubadours, and even though
these lyrics were highly patterned according to literary conventions, some, and
especially the greater, poets showed an unmistakable and deep emotional involvement and furthermore a strong sense of moral and cultural responsibility
which is evidenced, for instance, by the earnest disagreements between
Walther von der Vogelweide and Wolfram von Eschenbach regarding the concepts of courtly love and chivalry. Courtly lyrics clearly provided more than
mere entertainment, since they did not offer simple fantasies of erotic wish-
fulfillment, as did the contemporary *pastourelle* which described the easy success of a knight with a shepherdess. The fantasy content of the courtly
love complex was not altogether pleasurable: To crave against hope for the

Abridged and reprinted with the permission of the author and the publisher from *Comparative
Studies in Society and History*, Vol. I. No. 2 (January 1959), pp. 137–163.

possession of an inaccessible woman, who usually was understood to be already married, to suffer agonizing fears of rejection, and to gain the coveted approval of a protecting figure only at the cost of self-denial and frustration.

Any discussion of the social causation of the courtly love complex has to take into account the abiding interest of the public in this poetry. It was not read in privacy but presented at social gatherings. The majority of the troubadours and minnesingers and all of the performing *jongleurs* were poor and had to cater to the tastes of their audiences; even great noblemen, however, composed love songs in order to win the applause of noble society. Courtly poetry, in connection with courtly behavior and attitudes, became an intrinsic part of the value system of the new noble *genre de vie* in the "second feudal age." The courtly love complex no doubt has to be investigated in a sociocultural context rather than by analyzing individual poets, and the problem arises: Why did this configuration of specific anxieties and wishful fantasies appeal to a socially significant number of men of the secular upper classes? And what is the solution to the much debated question of the social background of troubadour poetry and *Minnesang?*

The major reason why the psychological meaning and the social basis of courtly love and *courtoisie* have never been satisfactorily explained lies in the dominance of the "philology of influences," which narrowed down the field of investigated reality to intercultural comparisons of ideas and poetical forms. This line of research with its quest for thematic similarities and chronological priorities is theoretically related to the sterile associationist psychology of the later nineteenth century and, while it gives the illusion of being free from any psychological and sociological presuppositions, it actually is built upon the assumption that imitation is the sole motive force in human history, interrupted only in rare moments by the appearance of unaccountable innovation. This type of comparative history, instead of aiming at discovering causations or dynamic interrelations, limits itself to the observation of surface similarities. The diffusion of culture traits, however, is never automatic but selective.[1] Numerous—virtually innumerable—features are at any time available to be borrowed, but only a very few are chosen and assimilated; and for any adoption as for any rejection there must be accountable reality factors.

In the search for a specific social causation, the first step is the formation of a hypothesis which advances one factor or a combination of factors as the causative agent. In the social sciences, it is usually plausibility or empathetic insight into the situation which accounts for the formation of a hypothesis. The validation of the hypothesis, which in the natural sciences is obtained by experimentation with isolated factors, must be made in historical research by a comparison of cultural complexes. In either case certain correlations are being tested. The infinite variety of historical situations, far from making objective history-writing impossible, as the relativistic school has concluded, actually can have the same use for the historian as a vast laboratory has for those scientists who can isolate factors at will. As courtly poetry originated and flourished only during a certain period, in certain geographic areas, and in certain social strata, it will have to be shown that the hypothetic cause or combination of causational factors also was limited to the same time, areas, and social classes. A more or less perfect fit will spell the difference between verification or falsification of an otherwise merely plausible hypothesis.

In order to detect the specific condition out of which the composition of love lyrics and the public interest in them developed, we have to look for factors which reached their greatest force in Muslim Spain in the eleventh century, in southwestern France in the twelfth century, and in southern Germany in the later twelfth and early thirteenth centuries. In each of these three areas we may expect, and to a certain extent can prove, the existence of an earlier period during which the social and emotional conditions were present, but during which the preoccupation with love lyrics had not yet crystallized into written literary productions or rather had not yet received the social recognition which was the prerequisite for being committed to writing.

II

Hispano-Arabic love poetry with features foreshadowing the later troubadour lyrics is known to have been produced since about A.D. 820. The poetic forms known as *muwaššaha* and *zaǧal* reportedly were invented in Spain at the end of the ninth century. Andalusian love poetry reached its greatest height in the eleventh century. In or about 1022, Ibn Hazm wrote *The Dove's Neck-Ring* which in scope, realism, and beauty is vastly superior to *The Art of Courtly Love,* a stilted command performance, composed more than a century and a half later.

As to the factor of causation, it appears that in Muslim Spain the inordinate preoccupation with uncontrollable eroticism, of which Ibn Hazm and other contemporary authors give many indications,[2] was conditioned by a chronic shortage of women. Among the Arabs of the Near East there was an older poetical tradition of frustrated and excessively sentimental love which appears to have been connected with the deprivations resulting from female infanticide and the increasing monopolization of women by the wealthy and the powerful in a polygynous society.[3] For Muslim Spain, there is ample proof that a high sex ratio, that is, a surplus of men over women, was created in the marriageable adult population by almost continuous migration into the peninsula. The invasion of Spain in 711–712 brought approximately 30,000 soldiers, both Arabs and Berbers. Thereafter, Arabs came only as individual immigrants, but Berbers continued to arrive in large numbers; the great majority of them, as in most migrations of this type, were young males. The hoarding of women in harems increased the imbalance of the sexes in the unattached population. Both Arabs and Berbers married native Spanish women, as there was no prejudice against racial and religious intermarriage.[4]

After 974, Berbers were brought into the country especially as mercenaries. Al-Mansur drew on the Maghrib, even including Ifrikya, i.e., modern Tunis, as an inexhaustible reserve of military manpower. After Al-Mansur's death in 1002, the mass influx of Berbers continued and led to an internal struggle and finally to the decomposition of the khalifate of Cordova in 1031 and the weakening of the Hispano-Arab elements over against the Berbers. Eleventh-century Spain exerted a strong pull on the surrounding populations, as it was a wealthy country and offered many openings for soldiers, intellectuals, and others at the courts of the petty kings. Northwestern Africa, however, was an overpopulated area with more or less continuous migrations northward. This northward push took on catastrophic proportions, when the nomadic Sanhaja tribes of the Sahara desert built an empire, were reinforced by Berbers from the Maghrib, and conquered the Spanish peninsula (1086–1106). Significantly, Ali, the son and successor of the great conquerer Yusuf ibn Tashfin, had a Spanish-Christian mother. For Muslim Spain there is thus a clear-cut parallelism between the incidence of amorous poetry and a high sex ratio owing to the masculinization of the population through sex-selective immigration.

III

The lyrics of the troubadours and minnesingers, it will be remembered, have aptly been called "courtly," because they were definitely class poetry. Although in later centuries *courtois* behavior patterns and attitudes of "romantic" love were adopted by one social class after another, they were originally restricted to the nobility and knighthood;[5] in fact, they served these people to define themselves as socially superior. In connection with this social limitation of courtly poetry, the emphasis on education and moral uplift was incomparably stronger in the courtly culture area than in Muslim Spain, and tied up with it was the behavioral ideal of *courtoisie* (*cortezia; höfischeit*). Whatever the specific causative agents that were operative in the formation of the courtly love complex, they must have been conterminous with the social confines of the secular upper classes and also, of course, with the chronological and geographical limits of courtly love attitudes.

Chronologically, troubadour poetry was restricted to the twelfth and early thirteenth centuries, probably with some preliterary beginnings in the eleventh century, at least in southwestern France. Duke William IX of Aquitaine (1071–1127) was the first whose poems were transmitted to posterity; but the fact that of his eleven poems only four are of the tender genre and that he obviously did not write these poems out of inner necessity—in addition to the fact that he wrote them in the dialect of the Limousin instead of that of his native Poitou—make it likely that he used the pattern of a poetry which was already well developed at this time. Thus it may have begun at some time in the eleventh century; it reached its apogee between 1150 and 1210, and rapidly lost its vitality thereafter. Geographically, troubadour love poetry originated and experienced its vital flowering in Aquitaine, more exactly from the southern part of the Limousin and Perigord southward to Gascony, and in the county of Toulouse. From this nuclear area it radiated with diminished strength northward to Poitou, southwestward to Aragon, and eastward to Auvergne, Languedoc, and western Provence. In the Rhone valley it found reception only in the last third of the twelfth century.

The only other area where courtly poetry was cultivated with such force and originality as to indicate emotional involvement was southern Germany. According to Heinrich von Melk, the praise of women was already a typical trait of German knighthood in his day, about 1160.[6] The first courtly poems which, in the 1180's, were committed to writing and considered worthy of preservation were the work not of professional entertainers or of the numerous knights, but of several noblemen of high lineage. Among those who wrote love poems around 1180 was Henry VI of Hohenstaufen.[7] As in southwestern France, a personage of a great ruling house was among the first whose poems were preserved, but his models are unknown, though there was apparently an earlier tradition. In Swabia, Minnesang was produced to the middle of the thirteenth century. In Bavaria and Austria, it came to an end about twenty years earlier, when the moods of hopeless passion and plaintive yearning were no longer appreciated. About 1250, Tannhäuser was a representative of the new attitudes of the south German nobility: courtoisie and knightly ideals were still valued highly as distinguishing marks of upper-class behavior, but love service in adoration of an unapproachable and demanding lady was rejected as whimsical. Poems were still written in the traditional manner, but they were artifacts devoid of emotional content.[8]

The regional limits of German Minnesang are most important from the comparative point of view. Only the southern half of Germany produced courtly lyrics: the southwest corner of the Empire, Alsace and eastern Switzerland, the Rhine down to Worms, Rhenish Franconia and Swabia; farther east, Bavaria, Austria, Tirol, Styria, and Carinthia.[9] Northern Germany, on the other hand, had no courtly poetry. The only Dutch poet who wrote courtly love poems in his native Low Franconian dialect was Heinrich von Veldeke. He introduced Minnesang concepts to his compatriots, but without any noticeable success; he did not find followers in his homeland.[10] Central Germany was intermediate between cultural extremes. There, lyrical love poetry was dependent on the courts of landgrave Hermann of Thuringia and his father-in-law, margrave Dietrich of Meissen, who attracted several outstanding poets to this region. But the mental climate differed greatly from that in the south. When Walther von der Vogelweide came to Wartburg, he became keenly aware of the gap separating the literature which was appreciated in Thuringia from the expectations of his south German "courtly" public. He later ironically called the Thuringian knights "proud heroes" (*stolze helde*) which implied that their style of life was that of oldfashioned warriors and not sufficiently tempered by the influence of courtly love and courtliness. In this dissonant meeting of two subcultures, Wolfram von Eschenbach, a Bavarian, who made his permanent home in Thuringia, defended the attitudes and tastes of the central German nobility and rejected the ladies' service of the minnesingers.[11] Wolfram, the greatest of the central German poets, was the first to let courtly and marital affections merge.

Central German conditions resembled those of northeastern France where troubadours were attracted by Eleanor of Aquitaine and her daughters and where courtly poetry was cultivated by some of the so-called *trouvères* from about 1170. Chrétien de Troyes, the outstanding poet of this area, played a role similar to that of Wolfram in Germany, in that his works translated the one-sidedness of southern *fin' amors* into attitudes of mutuality of sentiment.[12] The court circles of some of the northern French dynasts became receptive to southern amatory conventions only in the last third of the twelfth century. For generations thereafter courtly poetry was produced in the north but, except in a very few individual cases, it remained uninspired and insincere. It owed its beginnings to the predilections of southern princesses, especially Marie of Champagne, and only to a minor extent can it be assumed that the stress on tenderness in amatory literature jibed with a real change in attitudes and coincided with a greater need for restraint in the later feudal period. The stronger motivation for the borrowing of southern material was its high prestige value among the nobility who appreciated cultural refinement as an expression of social exclusiveness. In northern France, more than anywhere else in Europe, the clergy as well as the bourgeoisie of the twelfth and thirteenth centuries indulged in a rough and unbridled antifeminism, and even among the minor country nobles the doctrines of chivalry and the corresponding poetry had scarcely any success.[13] By contrast, the greater nobles, ambitious knights, and self-conscious courtiers were intent on distinguishing themselves from the rest of the population and adopted from the south the new style of personality cultivation. Finally, from the middle of the thirteenth century, noble dilettantes all over Western civilization—from Silesia to Sicily, and from Spain to Cyprus and Constantinople—wrote stilted courtly poetry, and the nobility everywhere adopted the corresponding behavior pattern. Thus it came to pass, through the overwhelming formative power of northern French culture, that a ritualized public adoration of ladies in combination with servant-like actions toward them—such as granting ladies precedence, picking up their things, performing all kinds of small personal services, etc.—became a badge of social superiority for men.[14] The problem of this essay, however, is not the later functioning of *courtoisie* as a stereotyped pattern of upper-class behavior, but rather the origin of the courtly love complex in that period and those regions where it had intrinsic strength as a live emotional reaction to the given situation, that is, in southwestern France and southern Germany.

IV

What were the conditions that set off the southwest of France from the north and east, and southern from northern Germany? What specific regional factors were operative in producing the mental climate for the courtly love complex? It is the contention of this essay that the numerical increase of the nobility and knighthood provided the background for the courtly mentality, through a web of causation which will now have to be clarified.

It is well known that between the eleventh and the thirteenth centuries a minor nobility was formed in most areas of western Civilization which finally merged with the high nobility and to a considerable extent even replaced it. For about two hundred years, while Western society went through fundamental structural changes, there arose a need for a larger secular upper class of heavily armed knights and lay administrative personnel; during this period the nobility was an open class, both legally and in reality. This development, however, was greatly modified by regional diversities. Where the political powers could cooperate with the burghers and draw on their accumulating wealth, or where cities became more or less independent administrative units, it became possible to build up centralized administrations with paid officials and paid soldiers. The highest political functions, as a rule, remained reserved to the nobility, and this nobility, especially the princes, became even more powerful than they had been before; but their numbers did not grow significantly, since they delegated intermediate power increasingly and preferably to non-nobles. These economically most advanced areas were, first, Italy, and secondly, the Low Countries, including Flanders, with a wide arc of surrounding regions: Southeastern England, Normandy, the Ile-de-France, Champagne, Westfalia, and Saxony. In these areas the courtly love complex had no native strength and was accepted only in its later conventionalized forms.

The process of the restocking of the nobility is most clearly traceable in Germany, as German feudal law was extremely heedful of class distinctions. For several generations it preserved the term *ministeriales* for persons of unfree origin who filled important positions and were entrusted with power over men, but who had not acquired noble status, even after they had become socially acceptable to the old nobility and sometimes superior to many a minor nobleman in wealth and power. Conrad II (1024–1039) was the first German emperor to organize *servitores* of his royal domain into an executive staff of officials, to equip others as knights, and to legalize them as a juridical class. In the twelfth century, and particularly in the latter half, the number of imperial *ministeriales* grew, but also bishops, abbots, dukes, counts, and lesser barons surrounded themselves with *ministeriales* of their own. Intricate differences of juridical conditions and social distinctions developed within this class. At the top were those families who had transmitted their fiefs through a succession of generations and who in some territories had shaken off their servile condition. Others were well established but remained under certain restrictions recalling their servile status. There was a large contingent who were not born into this class, but were personally appointed and given a fief consisting of land or rent; they might serve the emperor, a great lord, or a minor baron, which again made a great difference in their status; there also were men who were not enfeoffed but rather were highly trained mercenaries on horseback, castle guards, or men seeking services in some other capacity, as for instance, a minnesinger such as Walther von der Vogelweide. Below these, there were aspirants to knighthood, teenagers serving their way up, lightly armed soldiers on horseback, and plain hangers-on and entertainers. While the number of old baronial families was steadily dwindling in Germany, the class of the *ministeriales* increased so that in the twelfth and thirteenth centuries they vastly outnumbered the old nobles. When thousands of men had become knights whose parents or grandparents had been serfs, the avenues of advance became clogged; and from the end of the twelfth century the dynasts increasingly resisted further upward mobility.[15]

The spectacular growth of the upper class proceeded with great regional differences which were due not so much to any special laws or the absence of laws, but to the existence of different social needs and opportunities. The rise into the knighthood, ministeriality, and nobility was strongest in the areas where *Minnesang* flourished, that is, first in the area organized by the Hohenstaufen: Alsace, Swabia, parts of Bavaria and of east central Germany; and secondly, in Austria and the other southeast German border regions.[16] The *ministeriales* were the basis of Hohenstaufen policy, including their Italian imperialism, while the Welf party in northern Germany relied on a few wealthy cities as the centers of their power.[17] The decisive reason for this disparity of social structures and political organizations was economic. Northern Germany, from the lower Rhine area through Westfalia and Saxony to Lübeck, was part of the newly emerging north European economic boom area and excelled in trade and in textile and mining industries. Southern Germany, however, remained comparatively backward during the twelfth century; its towns were small; the great days of the Upper German cities, Augsburg, Nuremberg, and others, were not to come before the fifteenth century.[18] The Hohenstaufen were aware of the potential role of the cities for the building of a modern state; indeed, they made use of, and fostered, the humble towns existing in their areas. Yet since they failed to control effectively the wealthy north Italian communes, which alone could have given them the wherewithal for setting up a centralized government,[19] feudal conditions were given a new lease on life. The Hohenstaufen and other dynasts in southern Germany had to use feudal *ministeriales* for the organization of government.[20] During the great period of castle construction from the eleventh to the thirteenth centuries, by far the largest number of castles were built, by secular and ecclesiastical lords, in southern and particularly in southwestern Germany which in the twelfth century formed the center of the Hohenstaufens' expansionist policy. The new contingents of knights, who were needed to man the castles and to secure the imperial communication system, and the administrative *ministeriales* were often promoted from lower social ranks or were moved in, usually from more northern locations.[21] A comparable need for castle guards, administrators, and judges existed in southeastern Germany and accounts for the remarkable increase of *ministeriales* and *milites* in Bavaria, Tirol, Austria, Carinthia, and Styria. Here even more than in the German southwest, nobles and *ministeriales* were to a considerable extent recruited from more northerly regions.[22]

Very different conditions prevailed in northern Germany (the lower Rhine area, Westfalia, Saxony), with its rapidly advancing urban economy, its spectacular conquest of the eastern and northern European markets, and its eastern colonization. Here, the upper classes played a different role than did those of the economically backward and of necessity feudal south; and ultimately this contrast accounts for the differences in mental climate and literary tastes.

Corresponding socioeconomic disparities existed in France. Northeastern France and Flanders were important parts of the new prosperous northern industrial and trading area. The entire region from Anjou to Flanders was brought under the effective rule of a few dynasts who reduced the role of the feudal nobility and increasingly relied on salaried administrators, hired knights, and mercenaries.[23] The term *ministeriales* occurred in France, but only in its original meaning, denoting servile agents of feudal lords or court officers; these people never developed into a separate juridical class.[24] There were, to be sure, opportunities to rise into the higher ranks of feudal society, particularly for serf-knights and unfree *sergents* who did military service on horseback; but most of these persons were absorbed into the nobility as early as the eleventh century without leaving any traces of their earlier condition. The northern French nobility tended to become a closed class during the eleventh century.

It has often been tacitly assumed that the given social and cultural areas of the European Middle Ages coincide with the political boundaries of the modern nation-states. Regarding the secular upper classes and their social mobility in the twelfth century, the natural units for comparison are not France and Germany, but northern France, the Low Countries, and northern Germany on the one hand and southern France and southern Germany on the other.[25] In contrast to the north of France, the south was politically an area which had become decentralized in the course of the eleventh century. Outside their hereditary patrimony in Poitou, the dukes of Aquitaine had barely a nominal suzerainty over the vast area extending from the Loire to the Pyrenees, and from the Cevennes to the Atlantic coast. Likewise the counts of Toulouse, who until 1167 also held Languedoc, were weak overlords over a chaotic congeries of lordships whose numerous barons were resisting any central control and were fighting each other in local wars. The unification of Aquitaine by the Angevin administration became effective only in the thirteenth century, and that of Toulouse only after the Albigensian wars had decimated the nobility and brought southward the nobles of the north including the Capetians themselves.[26] In the southwest of France, numerous castles were built during the eleventh and twelfth centuries which were controlled not by a few dynasts but by a large number of self-styled "princes," counts, viscounts, barons, and seigneurs. At the same time the Templars and Hospitalers built fortified monasteries, the *commanderies*. In this area the density of castles was no doubt higher than in any other part of France; most of them were built in isolation from other settlements, and each castle required its contingent of knights.[27] In southern France as in southern Germany, aspirations for upward social mobility were predominantly focused on noble or at least knightly status. Mercantile and urban expansion was rapid only in Provence and along the coast of Languedoc, that is in those eastern parts of southern France where troubadour poetry did not flourish.

As a result of these conditions, the southern nobility was an open class well into the thirteenth century, when nobles and prelates were still knighting at will any person they wished. There also were numerous adventurers who threaded their way into the knightly class by serving as soldiers and who then pretended to be noble. In Aquitaine, the nobility employed large numbers of castle guards (*milites castri*), both knights and auxiliary soldiers, and mercenary knights who received a fief (*milites casati*). Their status apparently was similar to that of the German *ministeriales,* even though probably the majority of them were not of servile but of free origin. The recruitment of a large number of knights and the multiplication of fiefs (*casamenta*) created an anarchic type of feudalism, similar to that of Swabia before it was consolidated by the Hohenstaufen. While the *milites castri* usually belonged to well-established native families, the *casati* were soldiers of fortune, frequently the sons or grandsons of rustics or of obscure origin. There is documentary evidence for the servile extraction of some of them, but many, especially those who came from distant baronies, escaped all investigations and with good luck became the ancestors of noble families. In addition to the fully armed knights, many administrative agents such as the *prévots, viguiers, juges, bailes,* and *forestiers* aspired to noble status and in the course of several generations, in the eleventh and twelfth centuries, often achieved it.[28] The regional disparities in the condition of the secular upper classes are reflected in their contrasting attitudes toward emigration. The north had a spectacular surplus of knights and nobles who sought chances for advancement abroad, whereas the southern regions offered opportunities close at hand.

In sum, while in southwestern France and in southern Germany there were rising opportunities for knights and *ministeriales* and a subsequent enlargement of the nobility, in northern France, Flanders, and northern Germany such opportunities existed for comparatively fewer persons in the eleventh century and rapidly diminished thereafter.

V

So far only a geographical coincidence has been established between a certain social structure and the prevalence of the courtly love complex. The connection between the two becomes more plausible in the field of marital conditions, selective mating, and amorous adventures. The continual rise of men to the lower nobility, to the *ministeriales,* and to the knights, and the existence of numerous aspirants of knighthood involved an extremely high sex ratio in the secular upper classes. Every castle also had its "bachelor" knights, boys of fourteen to twenty-one years of age, beginning their training for knight's service, or sometimes older men belonging to the lowest rank of the knights. From the latter half of the eleventh to the early thirteenth centuries these *baccalarii, simples chevaliers, Knappen,* etc., became extremely numerous.[29]

This high sex ratio became magnified and socially important in connection with the consequences of marriage for status and property. Even if we make the unlikely assumption that not more noble women than men entered monastic institutions, the shortage of marriageable women which existed in the lower stratum of the upper class affected also the old nobility. It was imperative for a nobleman, or a knight, or even a young aspirant to the knighthood to avoid a misalliance, lest he jeopardize his status or his chances for promotion and the status and inheritance of his children. In this fluid situation, when the nobility was not yet a closed class, public opinion and usage insisted that a marriage to a woman of lower social status necessarily depressed the status of the issue from this union. A nobleman's right of inheritance could be dependent on his mother's being a *nobilis.*[30] The more immediate danger of hypogamy, however, threatened the man himself. A *ministerialis* or a knight who married an *ancilla* could many years later get into serious trouble.[31]

Yet for these same social climbers it was highly desirable to marry women of a superior status than their own, and they often succeeded in doing so. All over feudal Europe, marriage to a woman of superior social status, even if it did not bring any immediate material or legal benefits, usually introduced a man to higher social circles and opened up greater economic opportunities; sometimes it even led to his official change of status. The higher up on the social ladder were the people with whom he associated, professionally and convivially, the higher was a man's prestige within his own group. This factor is largely accountable for the high prestige of the *ministeriales* of the Empire and of the Church. There was no one below princely rank who was not aware of this. Serf-knights who married a free woman found it easier to gain their freedom; or, since there were no written genealogies, they could more easily bluff their way into noble society, if they had the funds for living a noble life.[32] In Germany, with its emphasis on neat class labels, the tendency of men to marry upward is particularly noticeable. Imperial *ministeriales* of well established and respected families are known to have married daughters of dynasts; daughters of the lower nobility did not disdain unions with *ministeriales* of more modest position. Such alliances were extremely frequent, and there is no German noble family tree without them; they did not affect the legal status of the parental house of the daughters and were often economically advantageous. As a consequence there resulted a strange discrepancy: women could easily marry beneath their status, while men, as a rule, could approach only daughters of their peers or superiors with the intention of marriage.[33] To sum up, the surplus of men in the secular upper classes of the twelfth and thirteenth centuries, which was due to upward social mobility and to migration to certain southern regions of the Continent, was aggravated by the preference of males for hypergamy and avoidance of hypogamy. The usual state of things in Western civilization, where men in large proportion have been wont to marry "simple girls," thus was reversed during this period. The upper nobility lost a number of their daughters to the lower nobility and *ministeriales;* these classes in turn lost some of their daughters to the urban aristocracies and also, usually for economic reasons, to the wealthier strata of the peasantry.

The imbalance of the sex ratio in combination with the desire for social ascent through marriage and the dread of losing status produced a situation which explains certain semi-realistic features of troubadour poetry. It is not known how frequently great feudal ladies allowed this poetry to be used for the gratification of their own vanity. Reimar von Hagenau said of the ladies of court society: "They enjoy being constantly wooed, and yet it is so gratifying to them to deny."[34] Many of the poets voiced disappointment and even disgust with the meager results of their efforts and broke off their tenuous love relationships.

VI

The imbalance of the sex ratio was part and parcel of the changing social structure; correspondingly, the symbolic contents of courtly poetry expressed not only amatory discontent and hopes of marrying upward, but it also reflected the strains and stresses of the whole life situation of the knightly class. The nobilities of southwestern France and southern Germany had not yet withdrawn into caste-like exclusiveness; they did not base their claims to privilege solely on birth, as they were still an open class and were in fact growing by an influx from lower strata. The avenues of personal advancement led predominantly through service in the military and administrative upper class. But there were signs of overcrowding. To be knighted, to receive a fief, to get positions of command over men, these and other forms of personal advance were contingent upon arduous service and upon being found useful and pleasing to a representative of the old nobility or higher clergy. Complaints were frequently voiced that the rich and powerful lords had become stingy, and that there was less joy in the world than there had been in the olden days.[35]

Several historians of literature have emphasized the large number of dependent knights and outright upstarts among the troubadours and minnesingers; and a few have in a somewhat narrow manner explained the note of insecurity pervading their lyrics as the mere result of the social distance between the lover and his highborn lady. This line of thought soon ran into difficulties when it was realized that the lyrics, as a rule, do not describe any real love affairs. There seemed to be only one explanation left, namely, to interpret the erotic praise of ladies as nothing but calculated flattery by the poets in order to gain material advantages. This interpretation is incompatible with a number of facts. First, almost all power positions of feudal society, even in southern France, were in the hands of men who, as husbands, would not have tolerated the sexual allusions of troubadour lyrics, sung in public to the accompaniment of music, if they had referred to their own wives. Second, this utilitarian hypothesis cannot explain the deep sense of moral and cultural responsibility which animated all the great troubadours and minnesingers; they were not just flattering some great ladies in the expectation of gifts. Third, it cannot explain the genuine interest of the male public who, after all, supported this type of poetry for about three generations. No interpretation can succeed which does not take the nonrealistic meaning of this poetry into account. The unconscious symbolic significance of the lowly poet's aspiration should be seen in the desire for approval by an unquestioned authority figure who is able not only to judge the knight, but also to raise his self-respect, even despite his shortcomings and in the face of all rivals and detractors. There is no doubt that these acceptance anxieties were felt more keenly by the rising elements and by the lower echelons of the military and administrative upper class. In the south of France and Germany, most of the preserved poetry did in fact originate in these classes.[36]

It is a fact, however, that in the "second feudal age," even the nobles of ancient lineage, once the unchallenged monopolists of wealth and power, were faced with the task of redefining their existence in a changing world. The rise of monarchies, the reform of the Church, the wealth of some townspeople and even of peasants, the new prestige of knowledge, and the increasing importance of public opinion—these and related factors raised a morale problem for the nobility as a whole. The need to justify the claim to social superiority to themselves as well as to the rest of the population was felt by the nobility all over western Europe, though it was most acute in those areas where the nobility, in one form or another, was an open class. In former times, wealth or birth had made the nobleman; in the twelfth century, there appeared the additional requirement of a certain style of life, and grudgingly it was even admitted that "good character in overwhelming quantity" was a substitute for birth and wealth. Andreas Campellanus observed: "Men of the higher nobility are bound to have more noble manners than other men, and they do more harm to their reputations by a little boorishness . . . than men of low birth."[37] If Charlemagne could have eight wives in succession and an uncounted number of concubines on the side without the least injury to his reputation, in the age of Philip Augustus this was no longer possible even for a king. Courtliness provided a guide in the transition to new demands on civilized behavior. In this general cultural transformation, the troubadours with their emphasis on restraint served as morale officers who verbalized what the conditions required. A prime example is the conversion of the troubadour Jaufré Rudel from sensual to restrained or pure love; it is significant that this man was not a lowly knight, but a representative of the great nobility of ancient lineage. One night, he reports, when he visited a lady, he was discovered in the act of satisfying his desires and was trounced and humiliated. The public disgrace and the sneers preyed upon him until, with the good counsel of friends, he finally managed to regain his self-respect.

For now I know assuredly that he is wise who defers and he is mad who is too precipitate . . . I have outstripped that anguish and never do I wish to return to it.[38]

He had gained self-respect through renunciation of immediate gratification, and he called on his fellow troubadours to broadcast the message of dignity through restraint (*mezura; mâze*). And this was, indeed, one of the main functions of the troubadours and minnesingers. Just as in private life "one should point out his mistakes and weaknesses to a friend,"[39] so in his literary activities the poet should elaborate the new noble values and rules of chivalrous behavior.

Many modern authors have realized that courtly poetry expresses something beyond its overt contents—an attitude towards man and the world. The great troubadours and minnesingers themselves conceived it as basically an ethical or, at the least, a morale-building complex. The symbolism of courtly love has apparently different layers of meaning, the common element of which is an anxiety regarding acceptance, which is assuaged by self-improvement and devoted service. The range of this symbolism extends from the field of love and marital prospects to that of professional advancement; above all it refers to the deep human need of being accepted in congenial circles, that is in this case, in courtly society; and approval by courtly society implies the privilege of considering oneself superior.

When the troubadours and minnesingers expatiated upon their "pure love" of a great lady, they created a twilight zone between fantasy and reality in which the process of symbolization became operative. Here the hopes, strivings, and insecurities of contemporary reality evoked images connected with deeper, more elementary needs of proving oneself worthy of being loved and being singled out for a special share of approval. The poems verbalized anxieties of rejection and at the same time helped to allay these anxieties. What would have been painful to discuss as personal problems, could be worked through in a communal fantasy centering on the image of a woman who was able to grant acceptance in privileged society, self-assurance, and a feeling of personal worth in a world of changing values.

Notes

1. Robert H. Lowie, *An Introduction to Cultural Anthropology,* enlarged ed. (New York: Rinehart, 1940), p. 374.
2. Ibn Hazm, *A Book Containing the Risâla Known as the Dove's Neck-Ring about Love and Lovers,* tr. A. R. Nykl (Paris: Geuthner, 1931), pp. 99, 395–396, and *passim.* See also Lawrence Ecker, *Arabischer, provenzalischer und deutscher Minnesang* (Bern and Leipzig: Haupt, 1934), pp. 130–134.
3. Gustave E. von Grunebaum, *Medieval Islam* (Chicago: the University of Chicago Press, 1946), pp. 311–312, 316–317; Ecker, *Minnesang,* pp. 2, 113; Margaret Smith, *Râbi'a the Mystic and Her Fellow-Saints in Islam* (Cambridge: Cambridge University Press, 1928), pp. 111, 124–127.
4. Henri Terrasse, *Histoire du Maroc des origines à l'etablissement du Protectorat français* (Casablanca: Ed. Atlantides, 1949), I, pp. 150–151; E. Lévi-Provencal, *Histoire de l' Espagne musulmane* (Paris: Maisonneuve, 1953), III, pp. 167–172, 399–401; Henri Pérès, *La poesie andalouse en arabe classique au XIe siècle* (Paris: Librairie d'Amerique et d'Orient, 1937), pp. 253–254, 258–260, 283; Philip K. Hitti, *History of the Arabs,* 3rd ed. (London: Macmillan, 1943), p. 544.
5. Alfred Jeanroy, *La poésie lyrique des troubadours* (Toulouse: Privat, 1934), I, pp. 80–81.
6. K. Voretzsch, *Einführung in das Studium der altfranzösischen Literatur,* 3rd ed. (Halle: Niemeyer, 1925), p. 346; P. Kluckhohn, "Ministerialität und Ritterdichtung," *Zeitsch. f. deutsches Altertum u. dt. Literatur,* LII (1910), pp. 139–140; Hermann Schneider, *Heldendichtung, Geistlichendichtung, Ritterdichtung* (Heidelberg: Winter, 1943), pp. 439–440. For conclusive evidence regarding Provençal and French inspiration of specific German *Minnelieder,* István Frank, *Trouvères et Minnesänger* (Saarbrücken: West-Ost-Verlag, 1952).
7. Schneider, *Heldendichtung,* p. 436; J. Nadler, *Literaturgeschichte der deutschen Stämme und Landschaften* (Regensburg: Habbel, 1923–24), I, pp. 115–117.
8. Fritz Schmitt and G. Fricke, *Deutsche Literaturgeschichte in Tabellen* (Bonn:

Athenäum, 1949), I, p. 87; Margarete Lang, *Tannhäuser* (Liepzig: Weber, 1936), pp. 101–103, 138, 141; Nadler, *Literaturgeschichte,* I, pp. 141, 148.

9. J. Nadler, "Die Literaturkarte," *Euphorion,* XXX (1929), pp. 9–10; Friedrich Vogt, *Geschichte der mittelhochdeutschen Literatur,* I (Berlin and Leipzig: de Gruyter, 1922), pp. 142–143, 147, 170; Schmitt and Fricke, *Literaturgesch.,* I, pp. 81–87, 94, 96; Schneider, *Heldendichtung,* pp. 427, 499–505; Nadler, *Literaturgeschichte,* I, pp. 115–117, 120; K. Weller, *Geschichte des schwäbischen Stammes* (München: Oldenburg, 1944), pp. 343, 413; S. Singer, *Die mittelalterliche Literatur der deutschen Schweiz* (Frauenfeld: Huber, 1930), pp. 142–160, 183–184; Switzerland is overrepresented because it was there that the largest anthology was compiled. E. Thurnher, *Wort und Wesen in Südtirol* (Innsbruck: Verlagsanstalt, 1947), pp. 94–105.

10. Nadler, *Literaturgeschichte,* II, p. 58. The eastern areas which were settled by Germans during the twelfth century produced no literature in this period except some religious verse. Veldeke was a conscious imitator of the new foreign poetry and used the courtly clichés with his tongue in his cheek; Schneider, *Heldendichtung,* pp. 438–439; K. Korn, *Studien über 'Freude und Trûren' bei mittelhochdeutschen Dichtern* (Leipzig: Weber, 1932), pp. 28–29; J. v. Dam in *Deutsche Literatur des Mittelalters, Verfasserlexikon* ed. W. Stammler, II (Berlin and Leipzig: de Gruyter, 1936), p. 359.

11. Konrad Burdach, *Vorspiel* (Halle: Niemeyer, 1925), I, pp. 381–388.

12. Chrétien was pressed by Marie de Champagne to comply with the troubadour love pattern; his hesitations apparently prevented him from completing his *Chevalier de la charette.* Parry, "Introduction" to Andreas Capellanus, *The Art of Courtly Love,* ed. J. J. Parry (New York: Columbia University Press, 1941), pp. 14–15; Sidney Painter, *French Chivalry* (Baltimore: Johns Hopkins University Press, 1940), Chap. IV, in addition to his interesting interpretation of Andreas' *Art of Courtly Love;* Voretzsch, *Einführung,* pp. 271–297; Jeanroy, *Poésie,* I, p. 274; J. Misrahi in *Romance Philology,* IV (1951), p. 352.

13. Jeanroy, *Poésie,* I, pp. 250–252, 273; August Wulff, *Die frauenfeindlichen Dichtungen in den romanischen Literaturen des Mittlelalters* (Halle: Niemeyer, 1914). The third book of Andreas' *Art of Courtly Love* gives the antifeminist argumentation of his day. R. L. Kilgour, *The Decline of Chivalry* (Cambridge: Harvard, 1937), pp. 111–116.

14. Marc Bloch, *La société féodale,* 2 vols. (Paris: Michel, 1939–1940), I, pp. 35–44. On the diffusion of *courtoisie,* G. Braun, "Der Einfluss des südfranzösischen Minnesangs und Ritterwesens auf die nordfranzösische Sprache," *Romanische Forschungen,* XLIII (1929), pp. 1–160; F. Brunot, *Histoire de la langue française des origines à 1900* (Paris: Colin, n.d.), I, pp. 389–391; Painter, *French Chivalry,* pp. 133, 137–139; L. Olschki, *Die romanischen Literaturen des Mittelalters* (Wildpark-Potsdam: Athenaion, 1928), pp. 101, 213, 220–222; J. Huizinga, *The Waning of the Middle Ages* (London: St. Martin's Press, 1924), Chaps. VIII and IX, where he comments: "The same circles who showed so much shamelessness in sexual relations professed to venerate the ideal of courtly love."

15. Bloch, *Société, passim;* K. Bosl, *Die Reichsministerialität der Salier und Staufer,* 2 vols. (Stuttgart: Hiersemann, 1950–1951); E. Molitor, *Der Stand der Ministerialen* (Breslau: Marcus, 1912); F. L. Ganshof, *Étude*

sur les ministeriales en Flandre et en Lotharingie (Bruxelles: Lamertin, 1926); Paul Kluckhohn, *Die Ministerialität in Südostdeutschland vom 10. bis zum Ende des 13. Jahrhunderts* (Weimar: Bohlau, 1910); P. Dollinger, *L'évolution des classes rurales en Bavière depuis la fin de l'époque carolingienne jusqu'au milieu du XIIIe siècle* (Paris: Belles Lettres, 1949); E. Otto, "Von der Abschliessung des Ritterstandes," *Hist. Zeitsch.*, CLXII (1940), pp. 19–40; P. Schmitthenner, "Lehnskriegswesen und Söldnertum im abendländischen Imperium des Mittelalters," *Hist. Zeitsch.*, CL (1934), pp. 229–267; P. Guilhiermoz, *Essai sur l'origine de la noblesse en France au moyen âge* (Paris: A. Picard, 1902), pp. 460–461, quotes several documented cases of fugitive serfs who succeeded in being dubbed knights. J. Bühler, *Die Kultur des Mittelalters* (Leipzig: Kröner, 1931), p. 102, estimates that there were finally about a hundred *ministeriales* for one old aristocratic family.

16. Geographical statistics on the differential distribution of *ministeriales* are not available. The distribution of imperial *ministeriales*, exclusively, has been recorded by Bosl, *Reichsministerialität*, in seven valuable maps. For Alsace, *ibid.*, I, pp. 190, 214.

17. K. W. Nitzsch, *Ministerialität und Bürgertum im 11. Jahrhundert* (Leipzig: Teubner, 1859), pp. 356–357; Fedor Schneider, *Mittelalter* (Leipzig and Wien: Deuticke, 1929), pp. 366–367.

18. F. Rörig, *Die europäische Stadt und die Kultur des Bürgertums im Mittelalter* (Göttingen: Vandenhoeck & Ruprecht, 1955), pp. 16–22; M. Postan, "The Trade of Medieval Europe: The North," *Cambridge Economic History of Europe*, II, ed. M. Postan and E. E. Rich (Cambridge: Cambridge University Press, 1952), pp. 160, 184–190; R. S. Lopez, "The Trade of Medieval Europe: The South," *ibid.*, pp. 292, 319, 349. On the slow development of towns in southeast Germany, also Dollinger, *Classes rurales*, pp. 491–492; Kluckhohn, *Ministerialität*, p. 97; H. Teske, *Thomasin von Zerclaere* (Heidelberg: Winter, 1933), p. 4; H. J. Seeger, *Westfalen's Handel und Gewerbe vom 9. bis zum Beginn des 14. Jahrhunderts* (Berlin: Curtius, 1926), pp. 95–130.

19. G. Deibel, "Die finanzielle Bedeutung Reichs-Italiens für die staufischen Herrscher des 12. Jahrhunderts," *Zeitsch. d. Savigny-Stiftung f. Rechtsgesch., Germ. Abt.*, LIV (1934), pp. 134–177.

20. Bosl, *Reichsministerialität*, I, p. 140; II, pp. 493–494, 600–601.

21. W. Hotz, *Staufische Reichsburgen am Mittelrhein* (Berlin: Stilke, 1937), pp. 5–6; K. Weller, *Geschichte des schwäbischen Stammes* (München: Oldenburg, 1944), pp. 262–263, 267, 333, 401; Nadler, *Literaturgeschichte*, I, pp. 120–121, 128; Nitzsch, *Ministerialität*, p. 324; P. Schmitthenner, *Das freie Söldnertum im abendländischen Imperium des Mittelalters* (München: Oldenburg, 1934), pp. 5–7, 27, 77–78, 80–81, 88.

22. E. Keyser, *Bevölkerungsgeschichte Deutschlands* (Leipzig: Hirzel, 1938), p. 166; R. Kötzschke and W. Ebert, *Geschichte der ostdeutschen Kolonisation* (Leipzig: Bibliograph. Institut, 1937), p. 56; Teske, *Thomasin*, pp. 5–7, 9, 11, and n. 25.

23. Postan, "Trade," pp. 181–184; Ch. Petit-Dutaillis, *The Feudal Monarchy in France and England from the Tenth to the Thirteenth Century* (London: Kegan Paul, 1936), *passim;* H. Mitteis, *Der Staat des Hohen Mittelalters*, 3rd ed. (Weimar: Böhlau, 1948), pp. 240–242, 339, 342.

24. Petit-Dataillis, *Feudal Monarchy*, p. 235; Ganshof, *Ministeriales*, pp. 69,

338; F. Thibault, "La condition des personnes en France," *Rev. Hist. de droit*, 4e ser., XII (1933), p. 699; Marc Bloch, "Un problème d'histoire comparée; La ministérialité en France et en Allemagne," *Rev. hist. de droit*, 4e ser., VII (1928), p. 50.

25. This dichotomy is, of course, a simplification. As Ganshof, *Ministeriales*, pp. 81–161, 203, 229, 251, 304–334, 377, points out, there were regions which presented an intermediate picture, namely Brabant, Liège, Namur, and Hainault. Economically retarded Burgundy, to mention another area, could neither be centralized by its dukes before the end of the twelfth century, nor could the nobility improve their political and economic situation. Cf. Jean Richard, *Les ducs de Bourgogne et la formation du duché du XIe au XIVe siècle* (Dijon: Bernigaud et Privat, 1954), pp. 132–135, 260–266, 517, 520. G. Duby, *La société aux XIe et XIIe siècles dans la region mâconnaise* (Paris: Colin, 1953), pp. 241–243, 381–396, 411–421, 636, 642, has shown for southern Burgundy that, from the tenth to the twelfth century, the nobility and the knighthood shrank to almost half of their original numbers.

26. J. Boussard, *Le gouvernment d'Henri II Plantagenêt* (Paris: D'Argences, 1956), pp. 113–155; Petit-Dataillis, *Feudal Monarchy*, pp. 169–173; G. Tenant de la Tour, *L'homme et la terre de Charlemagne à Saint Louis* (Paris: Desclée de Brouwer, 1943), pp. 282, 586–595; P. Feuchère, "Essai sur l'évolution territoriale des principautés françaises (X-XIIe siècles)," *Moyen Age*, LVIII (1952), pp. 95–96; E. C. Lodge, *Gascony under English Rule* (London: Methuen, 1926), pp. 12–13; J. Brutails, *Étude sur la condition des populations rurales en Roussillon au moyen âge* (Paris: Imprimerie nationale, 1901), pp. 286–287; J. H. Mundy, *Liberty and Political Power in Toulouse 1050–1230* (New York: Columbia University Press, 1954), pp. 21–23.

27. P. Ourliac, "Les villages de la région toulousaine au XIIe siècle," *Annales, E. S. C.*, IV (1949), pp. 272, 275, 277; P. Deffontaines, *Les hommes et leurs travaux dans les pays de la moyenne Garonne* (Lille: S.I.L.I.C., 1932), p. 159; Lodge, *Gascony*, p. 11; Marc Ballot, "Histoire du Limousin," *Visages du Limousin et de la Marche*, ed. A. Perpillon *et al.* (Paris: Ed. Horizons de France, 1950), p. 60; S. Painter, "Castellans of the Plain of Poitou in the Eleventh and Twelfth Centuries," *Speculum*, XXXI (1956), pp. 243–257.

28. Bloch, *Société*, II, pp. 63–64; R. Boutruche, *La crise d'une société: Seigneurs et paysans du Bordelais pendant la Guerre de Cent Ans* (Paris: Belles Lettres, 1947), p. 82; L.-J.-B. Bérenger-Feraud, *Les Provençaux à travers les âges* (Paris: Leroux, 1900), pp. 265–272; Tenant de la Tour, *L'homme*, pp. 291–294, 399–408, 462, 474–475, 516–535, 653–654; Brutails, *Roussillon*, p. 198; Lodge, *Gascony*, pp. 193, 204–205.

29. F. Fellinger, *Das Kind in der altfranzösischen Literatur* (Göttingen: Vandenhoeck and Ruprecht, 1908), pp. 18–19; P. Guilhiermoz, *Essai sur l'origine de la noblesse en France au moyen âge* (Paris: A Picard, 1902), pp. 170, 245–246 n. 8, 250. Occasionally there were married "bachelors."

30. Bosl, *Reichsministerialität*, I, p. 108, and Heinrich Freiherr von Minnigerode, *Ebenburt und Echtheit: Untersuchungen zur Lehre von der adeligen Heiratsebenburt vor dem 13. Jahrhundert* (Heidelberg: Winter, 1912), pp. 44, 45, 53, 58; both with evidence predominantly from southern Germany.

31. Bosl, *Reichsministerialität*, I, pp. 108–110; August Freiherr von Fürth, *Die Ministerialen* (Koln: Bachem, 1836), pp. 303–305, 342; Kluckhohn, *Ministerialität*, p. 138.

32. Ganshof, *Ministeriales*, pp. 172, 243; Bloch, "Ministerialité," pp. 81–83; G. Waitz, *Deutsche Verfassungsgeschichte*, V, 2nd ed. (Berlin, 1893), p. 356; Fürth, *Ministerialen*, p. 150; E. C. Lodge, "Serfdom in the Bordelais," *Eng. Hist. Rev.*, XVIII (1903), p. 429.

33. Bosl, *Reichsministerialität* I, pp. 67–70, 77–78, 80, 86, 138–139; II, pp. 604–607; Aloys Schulte, "Die Standesverhältnisse der Minnesänger," *Zeitsch. f. deutsches Altertum u. dt. Literatur*, XXXIX (1895), pp. 198–203; Aloys Schulte, *Der Adel und die deutsche Kirche im Mittelalter* (Stuttgart, Encke, 1910), pp. 23–27, 296, 326; Kluckhohn, *Ministerialität*, pp. 83–84, quotes four cases of *ministeriales* marrying daughters of princes and counts, and the marriage of the divorced wife of emperor Frederick Barbarossa to a *ministerialis, i.e.,* legally a serf-knight. Fürth, *Ministerialen,* pp. 296–298.

34. Reinmar in *Minnesang's Frühling,* ed. C. von Kraus (30th ed., Zürich: Hirzel, 1950), 171: 11–12: See also Bernard de Ventadour, *Seine Lieder,* ed C. Appel (Halle: Niemeyer, 1915), no. 43: 25–32; Giraut de Bornelh, no. 25: 92–95; no. 51: 16–30; no. 52: 45–55.

35. E.g., Giraut de Bornelh, *Sämtliche Lieder,* ed. A. Kolsen (Halle: Niemeyer, 1910), no. 48: 55–60, and *passim.*

36. W. Powell Jones, "The Jongleur Troubadours of Provence," *PMLA,* XLVI (1931), pp. 307ff; Jeanroy, *Poésie,* I, pp. 92–94, 133–134. By contrast, in northern France all the *trouvères* belonged to the nobility with the sole exception of Chrétien de Troyes; *ibid.,* I, p. 273.

37. Andreas Capellanus,*Courtly Love,* pp. 53–54, 93, 120. In the same vein, Thomasin von Zirclaria, *Der Wälsche Gast,* ed. H. Rückert, lines 1593–1606; and Freidank, 54:6, "He who is virtuous is wellborn." On *morum probitas* and the nobility of the heart, E. Wechssler, *Das Kulturproblem des Minnesangs* (Halle: Niemeyer, 1909), I, pp. 52–54. The dependence of true nobility on behavior was denied again when the noble class considered itself closed; it was debated anew in the fifteenth and sixteenth centuries, e.g., by Castiglione.

38. *Les chansons de Jaufré Rudel,* ed. A. Jeanroy, 2nd ed. (Paris, 1924), no. 4: 12–21, as trans. and interpreted by A. J. Denomy, "Fin' Amors: The Pure Love of the Troubadours, Its Amorality and Possible Source," *Mediaeval Studies, VII* (L945), pp. 161–163.

39. Giuraut de Bornelh, no. 37: 1–9; also no. 58: 36–37; no. 76: 41–48, the poet as a moral guide.

Ernest Manheim   THE COMMUNICATOR AND HIS
AUDIENCE: LIBERALS AND
TRADITIONALISTS IN
EIGHTEENTH-CENTURY
GERMANY

HISTORIANS AT TIMES BORROW WORDS from meteorologists, particularly when they describe new currents of thought whose diffusion is unexplained. In such cases historians like to speak of ideas which are in the air, a changing political atmosphere, or a new climate of opinion. Metaphors of this type point to increasingly frequent utterances which are germane in content but not traceable to a single source—a mass organization, the press, or a public authority. Undoubtedly, such atmospheric processes ushered in the Reformation, the national revolutions of Europe, and the recent Hungarian, Turkish, and Korean revolts. How is the student of communications to account for such an osmosis of ideas?

It is one of the aims of the present case study to replace these metaphors by a description of the underlying communication processes. The subject of the case history is the early beginnings of what may be termed with some license illiberal and conservative foci of opinion in Germany between the late seventeenth and the early nineteenth century.

The student of public opinion may ask why one should study communications in a historical setting and from secondary sources when the subject is open to controlled observation in the contemporary scene and to manipulation under experimentally contrived conditions. The objection to the historical detour is valid when it is taken as a substitute for more rigidly controlled types of investigation, that is, when it is possible to abstract from the real life process a laboratory scale model which is structurally representative of the original phenomenon. That is not always feasible. Nor, as a rule, can the field observer gain access to the type of pertinent detail which the historian gathers from the consecutive accounts of a host of "insiders" and witnesses. Some crucial processes of unquestioned relevance to the social scientist exceed the time span available to the field observer; their exploration requires the use of secondary sources. Whether they are recent or of an older vintage has relatively little bearing on their reliability. Obviously, the testimony assembled

Revised version of a paper presented at the Annual Meeting of the American Sociological Association, Seattle, Washington, August 1958.

from the record of antecedent observation lacks the precision which the contemporary field investigator can achieve. Precision is the hallmark of the advanced or concluding stages of research. Should the lack of precision in the earlier stages be a reason for not beginning an inquiry?

This introduction to the following case study seeks to elaborate some working concepts which bear on communication theory and provide the focus for the historical description. We take our point of departure from three basic categories of communication: the communicator, the conveyed message, and the audience. Some audiences are limited in scope, while the term "public" will be reserved to unrestricted audiences. A club meeting or a classroom constitute limited audiences, while the newspaper, the radio and television address themselves to publics. One must assume that an effective communication —one which elicits the intended audience response—establishes a compatible relationship between these three categories. A given audience is receptive to a limited variety of messages and responds only to particular communicators, and, likewise, a given speaker is capable or willing to convey only certain types of messages.

The expression "communicator" is not used here in a narrow, technical sense. For the present purpose, he is not merely the person who speaks in a meeting hall or writes for the press, but he is also the agent who entertains the ideas which reach the meeting hall or the reader. Thus, the communicator, as the term is understood here, plays two combined roles: he conceives, supports, or advocates certain ideas; and he conveys them to others. Although individuals may perform these roles, as a rule it is groups or collectivities which entertain and convey, or urge the spread of, ideas of public significance.

Once the communicator is conceived as a *corporate actor,* an additional category enters the set of variables which define the communication process: the consensus of the communicating group. The message which a goal-seeking group conveys to outsiders embodies some part of its consensus—views or understandings which the members share and exchange through interlocking channels, provided that such internal channels are available. Membership meetings, periodical questionnaires, and office correspondence may provide the opportunity for discovering or reaching the necessary working agreements which maintain a group as a corporate agent.

Functioning groups, however, do not always possess internal channels. Political mass parties largely use the same public channels for both internal and external communications, and they usually depend for their daily action consensus on the same utterances which they address to the public. The effectiveness of these public utterances depends not only on the responsiveness of their external audience but also on the internal requirements for creating or sustaining the needed action consensus of the mass party. In the absence of a differentiated network of communication, the same message must satisfy three conditions: be consistent with the goals of the communicator, maintain the cohesiveness of his group, and bring forth the intended external responses. The relationship between the internal and external effects of communications will be of particular interest in the present study.

The two distinct functions of corporate communications are not always apparent. The problem of bi-functionality in communications arises when the internal and external requirements of effectiveness become discrepant, when for example the message designed to achieve an external goal prevents or weakens the action consensus necessary to pursue it, or when the message is internally effective but arouses external resistance. One of the current occasions for such a discrepancy is the propaganda campaign which accompanies the armament race of antagonistic powers. Each power seeks to strengthen its combat morale and state of preparedness as well as to create a relaxed climate of opinion abroad, using for both efforts largely the same public media. The inevitable feedback which takes place when the media convey both types of propaganda to either side reduces its effectiveness to the extent to which it must pass through the unrestricted channels accessible to both sides.

Bi-functionality is a recurrent problem of modern social and political movements whose aims provoke resistance or repressive force and are, therefore, partially withheld from communication. The anticipation of resistance may affect the conduct of promotional activities in a variety of ways. Three of these are of interest in this study.

One leads to the creation of a chain of small, primary-group-type organizations which circulate internal messages but do not engage in propaganda activities. The principal aim of the internal communications is to maintain the corporate consensus of the members. The continuous flow of messages is "self-directed," since fraternal organizations do not address external audiences and the members exercise the active and passive functions of communication interchangeably. Some of these organizations are the products of defeat or accommodation to the pressure of external circumstances—persecution, repression or permanent lack of response. Once a movement renounces its external aims and adopts internal ones instead, it rarely reverts to the previous, activistic type. Such movements tend to retain their sectarian character as long as they confine themselves to internal communications among the intitiates. Intimate associations which permanently accept such a state of self-containment take on the characteristics of a ritualistic fraternity: a closely knit group which makes the maintenance and cultivation of some esoteric understandings its principal agenda.

A second mode of adaptation to external resistance affects not only the communication channels of promotional associations but also their action consensus. Goal-seeking groups which expand to the point of having to use unrestricted media for both internal and external communications tend to modify and adapt their consensus to the receptivity of the audiences with which they seek rapport. Internal adaptations usually accompany a shifting focus of promotional activity from one audience to another. The successive platforms of parliamentary parties, for example, reflect periodical changes in the composition of the crucial, uncommitted segment of the voters. This internal metamorphosis is particularly notable when a sectarian or fraternal movement relinquishes its esoteric structure and begins to advance its goals through public media. Likewise, pressure groups which evolve from restricted coteries of like-intentioned individuals usually pass through such organizational and ideological adaptations.

Militant parties organized for the conquest of power reveal a third mode of adaptation to conflict. It incorporates essential elements of both the sectarian form of grouping in small, ideologically resistant cells and the versatile mass party. The communist and fascist parties and the embattled nationalistic movements of nineteenth-century Europe and twentieth-century Asia and Africa have combined these two organizational features into complex structures with differentiated channels of communication.

The active and goal conscious nucleus from which these mass organizations evolve continues as a closely knit aggregation whose action consensus depends only on restricted, internally circulating messages. The mass propaganda is conducted through a diversified network adapted to the varying susceptibilities of mass audiences. The external network is of two types. The unrestricted channels serve to convey propaganda to the public at large, while the appeal to special audiences passes through restricted channels. Such restricted, but externally used media of persuasion may become available through the infiltration of opinion-forming organizations which control or influence people of some common center of identification. The purpose of infiltration is to obtain control of the channels and accepted public image of the captive organizations and, through these, gain access to their constituencies.

In summary, understanding of the contents of communications requires familiarity with their effects on the communicator and his audience. The nature of this circular relationship varies with the structure of the goal seeking group. Some respond to an expected external resistance through an internal accommodation, while others pursue the identical goals through divided channels and tactically diversified messages. The internalization of goal directed activities within ritualistic groups marks the third type of response to resistance. The following historical sketch offers indications of how such diverse systems of communication can effect public opinion.[1]

The seventeenth and eighteenth centuries were a period of centralization and absolutism in Germany. The rulers of the German states, particularly Prussia, eliminated the traditional privileges of the urban middle classes and the landed nobility. Urban self-government largely disappeared as most cities became districts of the royal administration, while at the same time the landed estates lost their control over taxation and the appointment of officials. The *diets* went out of existence or became rubber stamps. Last, but not least, the country nobleman, notably in Prussia, lost his ancient privilege of direct communication with the king and his counsellors. With the centralization of the state, public communication became a state function, except for specially licensed publications.

During this period fraternal organizations of various types formed in increasing numbers. Their activities were of a ritualistic sort. The local chapters were small, restricted to like-minded persons, and they devoted themselves to the practice of communication skills and the creation of channels for the dissemination of ideas which nowadays one would associate with the middle classes.

These organizations divide themselves into three types. The so called *Language Societies*[2] were the first to spread throughout Germany; their activities cover nearly two hundred years, beginning with the early seventeenth century. The societies sought to popularize the vernacular, in place of the courtly French and official Latin; and, with an equal devotion, they cultivated the paradigms of self-control, moderation in consumption, and unpretentious bearing in social intercourse. The local groups assumed symbolic names, such as the "Fruitbearing Society" (*Fruchtbringende Gesellschaft*), "The Shepherd Society," "The Elb Swan Society," and "The Laureated Pigeon Society." They provided a continuing meeting place for people of varied ranks and stations. Nobles and commoners, lawyers and officials, poets and army officers freely mingled at the ceremonial sessions of these fraternities. Membership was of two classes. The active members formed the inner fraternity, the *"Collegium fratrum,"* consisting of six to twelve persons, while the visiting members were more numerous. All members used a *nom de plume* as if to stress the primacy of ideas and literary skills over rank and title.

Several decades later in origin are the "Moral Societies," "Patriotic Societies," and "German Societies."[3] The names designate different organizations, but they are of a similar type. They, too, took up German as a subject of ceremonial exercises, but in matters of moral philosophy and social values they were more articulate than the Language societies. The most frequently mentioned themes of literary exercises were forthrightness, altruism, intellectual self-reliance, critical reasoning, and the use of dialect-free German speech. The printed bylaws make a point of impressing on the members the things to be avoided at meetings, namely quarrelling, tardiness, loud talk during a lecture, and discourteous behavior. Obviously, these fraternities provided for many the first opportunity for social intercourse beyond the circle of relatives and business associates. The meetings served as "practice" sessions in the newly acquired organizational skills and the art of dealing with people.

The third and last type of organization to emerge was the *Masonic Orders*.[4] Their corporate views are akin to those of the Moral and Patriotic

Societies, but the Masons were more anxious to avoid solicitation and propaganda among outsiders. The lodges confined themselves to the ceremonial exercise of such virtues as trustworthiness in private and business dealings, altruism, the practice of fraternal equality within the conclaves, the recognition of merit over and above inherited rank, and moderation. The membership was more diverse than that of the societies mentioned previously. For instance, among the 128 masonic officers listed in a contemporary publication 57 were officials, 22 army officers, 13 academicians, 12 merchants and bankers, 8 churchmen in leading positions, 4 ministers, 6 physicians, and 36 noblemen.

Within a few decades after their adoption in Germany, the masonic orders formed a wide network of intercommunicating chapters. Their social influence became marked and their effect on public life came to be more than merely atmospheric. This was the result of the great diversity of their membership, which included persons of note. The masonic radius of effectiveness was further enhanced by the practice of mutual patronage among members, the cultivation of contacts between lodges, and the numerous affiliations between individual masons or whole chapters with writers' leagues, literary clubs, book clubs, and libraries. A good portion of German humanistic literature and of the Storm and Stress movement is traceable to persons with masonic affiliations.

The organizations sketched so far consisted of small, autonomous chapters in which congenial individuals met for ceremonial exercises in some area of common interest. Although they all cultivated some social paradigm and certain images of the right society, they confined themselves to the secluded practice of these paradigms. Nevertheless, the rapid spread of these fraternities and their success in drawing socially prominent persons into their ranks gave the associations a controlling influence over the media of communication available to the middle and upper-middle classes of Germany. In fact, the only private channels to the public were creations of these fraternal organizations. They, moreover, adopted the practice of holding occasional open sessions which invited outsiders could attend. During the last few decades of the eighteenth century these open meetings became accessible not only to invited guests but to anybody who paid an admission fee. Public concerts seem to have evolved from similar customs. The "Patriotic Societies for the Exercise of Music" expanded their closed music conclaves into periodic public performances with entrance charges. Thus, the esoteric societies began to create their own public through both the meeting hall and the press.

Quite characteristic is the development of a series of periodicals sponsored and controlled largely by the Moral and Patriotic Societies and the Freemasons.[5] *The Moral Weeklies* were often the mouthpieces of the masonic chapters in Germany as well as in Switzerland and England. These journals were essentially published conversations and so labeled. Their literary form was the "fragment," as if to hint at the continuing ceremonial conversation from which the published pieces were excerpted. The essays were to rally likeminded readers rather than to persuade and convert indifferent outsiders.[6]

One can hardly overestimate the diffusion of the Moral Weeklies during their peak years, from 1720 to 1765. They were published in repeated editions and frequently reprinted.[7] Each copy circulated among friends and relatives, and each issue was read and discussed in a series of reading clubs formed for the purpose of assimilating the current number of a Moral Weekly.[8] The available source material warrants the conclusion that the ceremonial fraternities of the eighteenth century created channels through which they reached and swayed the preponderant part of the middle classes in favor of views of which Enlightenment, Humanism, and Liberalism formed the principal components.

However, during the second part of the eighteenth century a new class of organization emerged which, too, made its imprint on the German public.

While the masonic fraternities provided a common meeting place for elements of the middle classes and the powerful civil service, with some effects on the public orientation of both, the landed estates lost their previous contacts with the king, cabinet, and civil service, at a time when the nobility also lost much of its economic and administrative prerogatives. Three noblemen, Baron von der Marwitz, Count Finckenstein, and Major von Selrakowsky, attempted to reopen the lost channels to the king, by sending a petition to Frederick II directly, rather than through the prescribed chain of bureaus. The petitioners were arrested and sent to prison. They learned their lesson.

The disaffected peers found themselves deprived of their privileged avenue for reaching and swaying the king and the cabinet bureaucracy. The prescribed official channels were largely controlled by commoners, many of them trained lawyers, who were sympathetic to the rationalists and in closer touch with the middle class elite than the Junkers. The Enlightenment, which the king and his civil service embraced, became the symbol of the forces which brought about the isolation of the land-owning aristocarcy. The masonic lodges did, however, open up new avenues to the cabinet and council: the king himself and some of his councillors were practicing masons. This avenue was discovered and used successfully.

During the last four decades of the eighteenth century a host of masonic organizations of a new type emerged.[9] Some called themselves the "genuine" and "original" orders; other took on fanciful names, such as the "Clerici," the "Order of Strict Observance," the "Knights Templars," the "Order of the Devout," the "Order of Jonathan and David," the "Rosicrucians," and the like. They differed in organization and symbolism from the masonic, patriotic, and moral fraternities in several regards. They imposed on the customary three masonic grades of apprentice, journeyman, and master, a number of additional ranks with medieval designations, such as *Novice, Armiger, Socius,*

Eques, Eques Professus, and *Clericus.* In control of the hierarchy was a secret council, sometimes titled *Superiores Ignoti,* or the Invisible Superiors. The officials received ecclesiastic or feudal titles, such as *Magister Provincials, Subprior, Chancellor,* and *Commendator Domus.* The medieval knights orders provided the nomenclature for the geographic divisions of the orders; the terms were *Province, Prefecture, Commenda, Prepositura,* and *Comtura.* In place of the masonic aprons medieval costumes were introduced, complete with robes bearing the Knights Templars' cross, scarlet coats, sky blue vests, sashes, and medals. Some orders took up the practice of the secret arts, notably alchemy, spiritism, and the search for the *primae materiae,* the basic matter of all things. Even a new, "qualitative" natural science was on the agenda of some chapters. According to contemporary sources, these societies were partly the products of infiltration into the original masonic lodges, and partly satellite formations which adopted the masonic form but followed the directives of the traditionalists.

The pseudo-masonic societies became the gathering places of noblemen, elements of the church orthodoxy, and a steadily growing number of commoners in positions of influence. A membership roll of the "Order of the Strict Observance," founded by a Baron von Hund, lists 244 persons of the upper nobility, including 22 dukes, 2 princes, 126 counts and marquises, 438 persons of the lower nobility, and an equally large group of untitled persons in administrative positions, a number of writers, and some professors.[10] At last, an organizational contact with the upper echelons of the civil service was established. For a considerable period of the reign of King William II of Prussia Rosicrucians controlled key positions in the cabinet and in the church consistory. The king himself and several of his cabinet ministers were practicing Rosicrucians and engaged in the search for the *primae materiae* under the supervision of their fraternal seniors. This affiliation marks the beginning of a period of tight censorship imposed in Prussia on the publications of the rationalists and a campaign for the elimination of their influence from the schools, the church, and the administration.

The point of view which some of the better known of these societies cultivated opposed almost all the tenets of the Enlightenment: the thesis of the perfectibility of man, intellectual self-reliance, critical reasoning, and faith in the rational solution of human problems. Contemporary documents reveal a new emphasis on the doctrine of hereditary sin and the dualism of good and evil conceived as forces of separate existence. Man's evil nature, it is emphasized, calls for stern secular authority. Evil is not merely the product of ignorance or insufficient opportunity but an innate force. The seductive theories about human nature are designed to relax the vigilance of the legitimate authorities and to undermine the moral order. To the popular thesis of freedom of thought the theory of a qualified public was opposed. Such a public must not be the marketplace for the circulation of mere opinions but a forum for the expression of affirmative ideas. Conformity to established truths must be the precondition of public expression, not the freedom to err. True enlightenment is the premise and not the upshot of free discussion.

The relative success of the pseudo-masonic organizations in counteracting the influence of Enlightenment and Liberalism on the court and bureaucracy was accompanied by attempts to reach the public through a popular press. The better part of the unofficial press, however, functioned as a public extension of the esoteric exercises of the masons and the Moral Societies. To use a comparable public medium meant addressing a new audience with which rapport could only be established through a new universe of discourse, new concepts, and a new language. The men who spearheaded the conservative opposition were not in a favorable position for performing such an intellectual transmutation. In its first, private form, traditionalism was not an articulate school of thought but a personal exchange of complaints among peers about particular encroachments and breaches of custom. Such complaints had little meaning for middle and upper-middle class readers who had more to expect of change than of tradition. By upbringing and habit, the disaffected Prussian landowner was not adept in the craft of the professional writer, whose daily bread depends on his success in keeping *en rapport* with the reading public. To make the conservative appeal relevant to the literate masses, it was necessary to broaden its ideological basis and adapt it to the vocabulary and sensitivities of strata with which the traditionalists were not in touch.

The needed transformation of the conservative ideology was the achievement of socially mobile and marginal individuals who were conversant with more than one class, were not committed to any one point of view, and could write effectively. Most of these writers were sons of ministers, craftsmen, and petty officials. Early in their professional careers they came in close contact with individuals of inherited rank and position. This took place mostly in the pseudo-masonic organizations or in the position of a private secretary or house tutor at the country seat of the patron. Writers of such background initiated the first phase of literary romanticism. It was of the cloak and dagger variety, but it appealed to the very real claustrophobia of the restive small town reader. This literature raised his horizon and transported him into exotic lands and earlier epochs of history.

Gradually, an idealized image of the past and its survivals emerged as the motive of early romantic fiction. It was a literature in which the present was seen as a state of decay rather than as a formative period of growth. The ruins of castles became the shrines of a glory that was no more, and the manor and village appeared as islands of vitality which had resisted the forces of dissolution. At the turn of the century the romantic movement made its entry into the field of political literature and for several decades furnished the conceptual reservoir of restoration and conservatism. Its political imagery transcended the narrow class basis of the original coteries of the traditionalists; it was no longer the plea of a small, isolated group of land owners for the restoration of their rights but the rallying call of a movement which did have a certain appeal to the civil service and the academic clientele. The original thesis of man's inherited evil nature gave way to an organismic theory of the state, elaborated in terms which Enlightenment and Liberalism had made popular previously.

The change which took place illustrates an interesting aspect of communication worthy of attention: when an action group broadens its ranks and adopts new media of communication in order to address new audiences, it tends to evolve new conceptions of itself and to rethink its aims. As the traditionalists learned to speak not only to one another but also to new and larger segments of the public they began to communicate different views and to learn to accept those different views. Once the traditionalist movement outgrew the limitations of the private coterie and the ritualistic society of both the independent and satellite type, it began to align itself with strata far removed from those which initiated the conservative rally. The romantic ideology marks the first appeal that reached an internal as well as an external audience through identical public channels. For a considerable period this appeal effectively performed both internal and external functions, and crystallized opinion in favor of the traditionalist point of view. It may well be that in the period of 1925–1933 a similar transformation took place when the restoration platform of the small, isolated, and stationary German-Nationalist Party of the Weimar Republic gave way to the popular mass propaganda of the Nazi movement.

Stirrings similar to the pseudo-masonic activities of the traditionalists made their appearance at the other extreme of the political gamut. During the last three decades of the eighteenth century secret societies sprang up on the pattern of the pseudo-masonic orders, for the distinct purpose of spreading democratic or republican views. The *Evergeten* and the largest of these secret societies, the *Illuminati,* had practically the same structure as their pseudo-masonic counterparts.[11] The lower ranks were constituted in the usual masonic style and served as screening organs for members found suited for the camouflaged activities of the inner council. They, too, made inroads into the civil service, schools, courts, churches, libraries, and reading clubs. The *Illuminati* infiltrated both the masonic lodges and the pseudo-masonic chapters of the traditionalists. To attract unsuspecting members, the *Illuminati* adopted some of their opponents' practices, including the cult of secrets, mysticism and medievalism, but in their hands these devices proved less effective, since in the end such attractions worked more to the advantage of the romantic movement than in favor of the rationalists.

Until the turn of the century the lodges and sodalities formed the principal channels for the private pursuit of political ends. As a consequence, the fraternal organizations became the battleground of the rival forces for control of the available organs of public opinion. This explains the seeming paradox that the diverse currents of public opinion took shape in the meetings of small, esoteric societies rather in the arena of public discussion.

If the foregoing analysis is correct, the conclusion seems inescapable that the various forms of eighteenth century German liberalism and traditionalism are not merely reflections of the social experiences of different strata or elaborations of political themes. They are aspects of a political controversy between communicators who appealed to varied audiences.

Notes

The following references represent a selection of the historical sources and secondary presentations used for the preceding essay.

1. Ernest Manheim, *Die Träger der öffentlichen Meinung* (Brünn, Prag, Leipzig, 1933).

2. Anonymous, *Der neusprossende teutsche Palmbaum, oder ausführlicher Bericht von der Hochlöblichen Fruchtbringenden Gesellschaft* (Weimar, 1688), pp. 24f, 34, 68, 85, 143, 449.
Anonymous, *Historische Nachricht von dem löblichen Hirten—und Blumenorden an der Pegnitz* (Nürnberg, 1744), pp. 50f, 55, 63.
Journal von und für Deutschland, 1784, No. 9, p. 148ff.
Anonymous, *Der Teutsche Palmbaum: Das ist, Lobschrift von der Hochlöblichen Fruchtbringenden Gesellschaft* (Nürnberg, 1647), pp. 77, 143.
O. Denk, *Furst Ludwig zu Anhalt Cöthen und der erste deutsche Sprachverein*, 1917, pp. 51, 59.
L. Keller, Akademien, *Logen und Kammern des XVII und XVIII Jahrhunderts* (Jena, 1912), p. 8ff.
W. Begemann, *Die Fruchtbringende Gesellschaft und J. V. Andreä* (Berlin, 1911); *Der Orden der Unzertrennlichen des XVIII. und die Fruchtbringende Gesellschaft des XVII Jahrhunderts* (Berlin, 1911).

3. Sicul, *Annalium Lipsiensum* (Leipzig, 1730), pp. 30, 43f, 51, 959.
Anonymous, *Beyträge zur Historie der Gelährtheit* (Hamburg, 1748).
Anonymous, *Nachrichten von der erneuerten Deutschen Gesellschaft in Leipzig* (Leipzig, 1727), p. 15.
Vetter (ed.), *Chronik der Gesellschaft der Maler in Zürich* (Diss. Zürich, 1895).
Christian Haymann, *Kurzgefasste Geschichte der vornehmsten Gesellschaften der Gelehrten* (Leipzig, 1743).
Anonymous, *Der Deutschen Gesellschaft in Leipzig Nachrichten und Anmerkungen*, 1. Stuck (Leipzig, n.d.), p. 93, 151.
Witkovski, "Die Deutsche Gesellschaft in Leipzig," *Minerva*, Aug. 1927, pp. 165ff.
B. Stuberl, *Die Deutsche Gesellschaft in Leipzig von ihrem Entstehen bis zur Gegenwart*, Mitteilungen der Deutschen Gesellschaft, VI (Leipzig, 1877).
Eugen Wolff, "Die Deutschen Gesellschaften zu Erlangen und Altorf im XVIII Jh,." *Monatshefte der Comenius Gesellschaft*, VIII, 1899.
Christian Petersen, "Die Teutsch-übende Gesellschaft in Hamburg," *Zeitschr. d. Hamburgischen Geschichtsvereins*, 1847, vol. 2, p. 535.

P. Otto, "Die Deutsche Gesellschaft in Göttingen 1738–58," *Forschungen z. neueren Literaturgeschichte,* VII (München, 1898), pp. 13, 49.

Joh. Dierauer, *Die Toggenburger Moralische Gesellschaft* (St. Gallen, 1912).

Bodmer, *Die Gesellschaft der Maler in Zürich und ihre Diskurse* (Diss. Zürich 1895), pp. 38ff.

4. Kleinschmidt (ed.), *Des Verbesserten Konstitutionenbuchs der alten ehrwürdigen Bruderschaft der Freimaurer zweiter Teil* (Frankfurt, 1784), pp. 91ff.

Anonymous, *Über den Zweck des Freymaurerordens,* Germania, 1781, p. 193.

Anonymous, *Der Flammende Stern oder die Gesellschaft der Freimaurer von allen Seiten betrachtet* (Berlin, 1779), I, p. 201; II. pp. 37, 47ff.

Anonymous, *Saint-Nicaise oder eine Sammlung merkwürdiger maurerischer Briefe,* n.p., 1786, pp. 12, 100, 106f.

J. Stuve, *Kleine Schriften gemeinnützigen Inhaltes,* 1794, II. p. 94ff.

Anonymous, *Die preussischen Staaten vor und seit dem 16 November,* 1797, vol. I., p. 177.

Anonymous, *Gesammelte Freymaurer Reden von einem Mitgliede der Mutterloge zu Berlin* (Berlin, 1777), pp. 34ff, 43.

Maier, *Über Jesuiten, Freymaurer und deutsche Rosenkreutzer* (Leipzig, 1781), pp. 84ff, 344ff.

Reinhard Morgenstern (pseudonym), *Der Weisheit Morgenröte,* 1786, p. 159ff.

Anonymous, *Der neu aufgesteckte Brennende Leuchter,* n.d., pp. 177, 181, 195.

Wolfstieg, *Ursprung und Entwicklung der Freimaurerei* (Berlin, 1920), III, p. 178.

Ad. Bartels, *Freimaurerei und deutsche Literatur* (München, 1929).

H. Grantzow, "Geschichte des Göttinger und Vossischen Musenalmanachs," *Berliner Beitr. z. germanischen u. romanischen Philologie,* XXXV (Berlin, 1909).

Flohr, *Geschichte der Grossen Loge von Preussen,* gen. Royal York, I. (Berlin, 1898), p. 98.

5. R. Ischer and J. G. Altmann, *Die Deutsche Gesellschaft und die Moralischen Wochenschriften in Bern* (Bern, 1902).

Der Hamburger Patriot, Jan., Aug., Oct., 1824.

Die Vernünftigen Tadlerinnen, 1726, No. 17.

Der Eremit, No. 8, 9, Leipzig, Oct. 1768, Febr. 1769.

Der Patriot, Aug. 1724, No. 31, Feb. 1725, No. 59.

Emil Umbach, *Die deutschen moralischen Wochenschriften und der Spectator* (Diss. Strassburg, 1911), pp. 86ff.

L. Keller, *Die deutschen Gesellschaften und die Moralischen Wochenschriften,* 1900.

6. *Der Helvetische Patriot,* 1755, I.

Der Leipziger Spectateur (Leipzig, 1723), p. 4f.

Die Discourse der Mahlern, new ed. by Th. Vetter, 1891, pp. 6f, 21, 45ff, 65.

7. J. Kirchner, Die *Grundlagen des deutschen Zeitschriftenwesens* (Leipzig, 1928), I. p. 54ff.

8. *Der Patriot,* Febr. 15, 1725, No. 59.

9. H. v. Ecker v. Eckhofen, *Der Rosenkreuzer in seiner Blösse* (Amsterdam, 1782).

A. F. Cranz, *Stein des Anstosses und Fels des Ärgernisses*, Teutschland, 1780.

B. J. Schloss v. Löwenfeld, *Der im Lichte der Wahrheit strahlende Rosenkreuzer* (Leipzig, 1782).

Karl H. L. v. Plumenock, *Geoffenbarter Einfluss in das allgemeine Wohl der echten Freimaurerei* (Amsterdam, 1777).

Anonymous, *Vorläufige Darstellung des heutigen Jesuitismus, der Rosenkreuzerei* (Frankfurt, 1786).

S. L. de Marees, *Neue Briefe zur Verteidigung der evangelischen Christen*, No. I. (Leipzig, 1781), p. 7.

H. D. Hermes, *Die Lehre der heiligen Schrift*, Breslau, 177, p. xxv.

E. A. v. Gochhausen, *Enthüllung des Systems der Weltbürger-Republik*, 1786, pp. 363, 367ff, 432; *Was trägt am meissten zu den Revolutionen itziger Zeiten bey?* (München, 1791), pp. 38, 41.

C. F. Bahrdt, *Geschichte und Tagebuch meines Gefängnisses nebst geheimen Urkunden u. Aufschlüsse über Deutsche Union* (Berlin, 1790), p. 184.

H. v. Ecker v. Eckhofen, *Freimaurerische Versammlungsreden der Gold- und Rosenkreuzer des alten Systems* (Amsterdam, 1779).

C. Engel, *Geschichte des Illuminatenordens* (Berlin, 1960), pp. 92, 95, 106, 110f.; *Der Freimaurer-Konvent zu Altenberga* (Leipzig, 1914).

Schiffmann, *Die Entstehung der Rittergrade in der Freimaurerei um die Mitte XVIII Jh-s.* (Leipzig, n.d.).

L. Lang, *Aus dem Ordensleben des XVIII Jh-s.* (Heilbronn, 1929).

K. H. Sack, "Zur Geschichte des geistlichen Ministers Wöllner," *Zeitschr. f. histor. Theologie*, 1862.

F. J. Schneider, *Die Freimaurerei und ihr Einfluss auf die geistige Kultur in Deutschland am Ende des XVIII Jh-s.* (Prague, 1909).

Marianne Holmann, *Der Trivialroman d. XVII Jh-s.*, German. Studien, 33 (Berlin, 1923).

10. R. Taute, *Der Wilhelmsbader Konvent* (Berlin, 1908), p. 23.

11. Anonymous, *Die neuesten Arbeiten des Spartacus und Philo in dem Illuminatenorden*, 1793, pp. 26, 38ff, 50, 76f, 103, 137ff, 142f.

Anonymous, *Wie ist es möglich geworden, Aufklärung und Aufklärer verhasst zu machen?* (Auf der Insel Felsenburg, 1789), pp. 40f.

Fessler, *Actenmässige Aufschlüsse über den Bund der Evergeten in Schlesien* (Freiberg, 1804), pp. 27, 31, 54, 101f, 106.

Anonymous, *Über Geheime Gesellschaften zu populärer Aufklärung, von einem Protestanten* (Schweinfurth, 1786), pp. 5, 78.

Anonymous, *Über Aufklärung und die Beförderungsmitteln derselben, von einer Gesellschaft* (Leipzig, 1789), pp. 50, 206f.

Joseph Ben-David   SCIENTIFIC PRODUCTIVITY AND
ACADEMIC ORGANIZATION IN
NINETEENTH-CENTURY
MEDICINE

THE PURPOSE OF THIS PAPER is to describe and explain differences as well as fluctuations in the productivity of the medical sciences in Germany, France, Britain, and the United States, from 1800 to about the time of World War I. Scientific productivity as defined here does not comprise any evaluation of the greatness or depth of various scientific ideas, or of the "efficiency" of scientific production as measured by some input-output ratio. It refers only to two gross quantities: the number of scientific discoveries (including scientifically important technical inventions), and the numbers of people making such discoveries. Provided that these numbers are not a fixed proportion of the general population or some other general quantity, they are a measure of the active interest in science existing in a society at a certain time.

The two suggested indexes of productivity—the numbers of discoveries and of discoverers—have not precisely the same meaning and there are obvious objections to both. It can be argued that since scientific discoveries are disparate units of unequal significance, it is meaningless to count them.[1] The first part of the claim is true, but not the deduction from it. It has been shown time and again that "great" discoveries had been preceded by intensive activity manifested in numerous "small" discoveries, often leading to the simultaneous finding of the final solution by more than one person.[2] Similarly, one of the signs of a great discovery is that it leads to a greater number of smaller discoveries based on the newly discovered principle.[3] Therefore, viewing science as a flow of constant activity, great discoveries appear as waves built up gradually by the ant-like work of predecessors, leading first to an upsurge of activity by followers and disciples and then diminishing into routine when the potentialities of the great idea have been exhausted. Thus there is no need to

Reprinted with the permission of the author and the American Sociological Association from the *American Sociological Review,* Vol. 25, No. 6 (December 1960), pp. 828–843.

A preliminary draft of this paper was written while the author was a fellow at the Center for Advanced Study in the Behavioral Sciences, Stanford, California. He is indebted to Harry Alpert, S. N. Eisenstadt, Jacob Katz, Morris Janowitz, Robert K. Merton, D. Patinkin, Dr. George G. Reader, and the late Dr. J. Seide for comments on the manuscript or discussion of its subject matter, and to A. Zloczower for his help with the research.

weight the individual discoveries. The weighting is done automatically by the clustering of discoveries around the significant event. This is not to deny that there are lone discoveries, neither expected beforehand nor understood after they are made. For the historian who sits in judgment of individual greatness and stupidity, these are important events that prove the absurdity of our method of counting. But if one's purpose is to gauge the extent to which various social systems induce people to scientific productivity, then the relatively negligible weight accorded to the lone discovery is a good index of the relative lack of inducement to engage in research in that society.

The use of the number of discoverers as an index of scientific activity can be justified by similar reasoning. Such men as Newton, Lavoisier, and Einstein did not spring up in scientific deserts but in environments of intensive scientific interest, and their work inspired disciples and followers. So we can expect a general correspondence between this index and the previous one. Yet, there are numerous problems involved in the use of this index. In principle, the same numbers of discoveries can be made by quite different numbers of people, so that there may be no relationship between the two counts. In fact, however, the variation is quite limited, because the accomplishment of even a single scientific discovery demands as a rule considerable investment of time and training: one can assume that discoveries will be made by persons with special characteristics ("discoverers") and not randomly, either by them or others. Thus we take this figure, too, as a good index of the social inducement to engage in research. No more than general correspondence between the two sets of data is expected, however, because, first, there may be variations due to institutional circumstances in the length of the creative period of discoverers, and in the chances of "outsiders" for making discoveries; and, second, even if these things were constant, the shape of the two curves would still differ because each discovery is a single event counted only once, at the time of its occurrence, while discoverers must be counted over a period of time or at an arbitrarily fixed point of time (such as their age at the beginning of the professional career). For these reasons we expect this second index to correspond with the first only in registering relatively long-term and gross changes. But in such details as the exact time of the changes and short term fluctuations no correspondence between the two indices can be expected.

A second problem requiring preliminary clarification is the definition of medical sciences. We have adopted the criteria of our sources, which include all discoveries that eventually became part of the medical tradition. Undoubtedly this implies the inclusion of some nonmedical discoveries and discoverers; therefore, from the viewpoint of the history of scientific ideas, this may not be too meaningful a category. However, in a study of scientific activity one needs data reflecting activity in more or less homogeneous institutional frameworks, irrespective of whether they do or do not relate to a logically coherent system of ideas. On this score, medicine in the nineteenth century seems to be a good choice. Through most of the century it was closely interwoven with the natural sciences. It had been the first profession based on the study of natural sciences, and medical faculties were the first university departments to teach them. For many years the only large-scale and permanent organizations where research was systematically conducted were the teaching hospitals. Also, the art of the apothecary and the science of chemistry were often connected until the early nineteenth century. Thus the sciences associated with medicine have formed a complex of scientific activity which has been related to well defined social structures since the eighteenth century, whereas most of the basic sciences were the professional concern of only a few individuals in any country well into the second half of the nineteenth century. The medical sciences, therefore, appear to be well suited for discerning the effect of structural changes upon scientific creativity during the period under consideration.

The Questions to Be Explained

Table 1 is based on a count of medical discoveries made in the countries here surveyed from 1800 to 1926, according to a "Chronology of Medicine and Public Hygiene."[4] The data reveal two different trends.

Table 1—Number of Discoveries in the Medical Sciences by Nations, 1800–1926

Year	U.S.A.	England	France	Germany	Other	Unknown	Total
1800–09	2	8	9	5	2	1	27
1810–19	3	14	19	6	2	3	47
1820–29	1	12	26	12	5	1	57
1830–39	4	20	18	25	3	1	71
1840–49	6	14	13	28	7	—	68
1850–59	7	12	11	32	4	3	69
1860–69	5	5	10	33	7	2	62
1870–79	5	7	7	37	6	1	63
1880–89	18	12	19	74	19	5	147
1890–99	26	13	18	44	24	11	136
1900–09	28	18	13	61	20	8	148
1910–19	40	13	8	20	11	7	99
1920–26	27	3	3	7	2	2	44

Source: see footnote 4.

First, between 1810 and 1819 a rise in the number of discoveries in France and Britain begins, followed in Germany in the next decade. By 1840, the rise has passed its peak in France and Britain and a decline sets in lasting until the 1870s. Second, an upsurge starts simultaneously in all these three nations and in the United States in 1880. These parallel movements reflect the story of the convergence of chemical, anatomical, physiological, and pathological discoveries in the first half of the nineteenth century, and the spate of bacteriological and surgical innovations which followed the work of Pasteur, Lister, and Koch in the last quarter of the century. Both waves show only that certain fruitful ideas had been simultaneously, or nearly simultaneously, exploited in Western European countries beginning from the early nineteenth century, and in the United States as well from the end of the century. Apart from indicating that scientific communication among these countries was well established by that time and that therefore the phenomena reflect the course of scientific ideas, they call for no sociological explanation. What needs to be explained is the conspicuous change in the relative shares of the countries during this period. French supremacy in the beginning of the century with Britain a close second gave way to an overwhelming preponderance of German discoveries through the second half of the last century. The American share was rapidly increasing from the 1880s and became the largest by 1910–1919. Since this was the time of World War I, comparison with the European countries may seem of doubtful validity; but the relative decline of the European countries started prior to the war and lasted well into the twenties, so that it should not be attributed entirely to the war.

A significant aspect of this change of relative positions is that it is connected with an atypical growth in the curve of discoveries in the country which is gaining the largest share. Thus the number of German discoveries continually increases through the middle of the nineteenth century in a period of decline in France and Britain. A similar deviation marks the change in the relative position of the United States at the beginning of the twentieth century.

A similar pattern marks the number of discoverers. Table 2 shows the "productivity" of the various countries in terms of scientists.[5] France and Britain, with the largest numbers at the beginning of the century, fall behind Germany starting about 1835. While the number of German scientists entering upon their careers increases regularly, with only one considerable drop until 1885–1890, there are fluctuations and a generally downward slope in France and England through the middle of the century. The American trend, like the German, shows much less fluctuation. Thus, with respect to major trends, the two indexes validate each other.[6]

Two questions emerge: What explains the change of scientific leadership from France to Germany to the United States? And what explains the "deviant" nature of the development in Germany during the middle and in the United States toward the end of the nineteenth century, as manifested in (1) the continuous rise in the number of discoveries during periods of relatively low creativity in the other countries; and (2) the relatively smaller fluctuations in the number of people embarking upon scientific careers in these two countries compared with the others?

Table 2—Discoverers in the Medical Sciences at the Age of Entering Their Professions (Age 25) in Various Countries, 1800–1910

Year	U.S.A.	England	France	Germany	Other
1800	1	7	8	7	4
1805	1	8	5	8	2
1810	3	11	6	6	2
1815	2	12	12	7	3
1820	3	11	23	18	2
1825	2	17	15	18	6
1830	8	12	25	10	6
1835	11	13	26	29	7
1840	5	24	22	35	12
1845	5	14	13	33	5
1850	10	18	21	37	10
1855	15	16	20	49	27
1860	16	23	13	61	23
1865	25	15	36	71	26
1870	25	15	31	83	41
1875	40	31	23	84	46
1880	48	17	40	75	50
1885	52	16	34	97	52
1890	43	11	23	74	41
1895	47	9	27	78	29
1900	32	9	17	53	30
1905	28	4	4	34	25
1910	23	6	7	23	18

Source: *Dorland's Medical Dictionary* (20th ed.).

Hypothesis: The Organizational Factor

Neither the changes in scientific leadership nor the deviant nature of the German and American developments can be manifestations of differences in the scientific ideas in the various countries. This could be the case only if international communication had been deficient, so that new ideas in one country would have no effect upon the work of scientists in the others. This was by no means the case, as demonstrated by the parallel upward movements of the curves of discoveries in all the countries in periods of crucial scientific advance. Independently from this fact, whatever barriers to scientific communication had existed between France and Germany during the first decades of the nineteenth century had disappeared by the beginning of the fourth decade. By about the same time, the British too, established contacts with continental science, from which they had become isolated during the eighteenth century, as did the Americans.[7] Therefore nothing immanent to science as a body of ideas explains the observed differences and changes. The explanation has to be sought in external circumstances.

Among the possible external causes there are some general and obvious ones, such as population growth and the growth of national income. A few unrefined attempts to assess the population factor suggested that this is not a promising line of approach. The introduction of this factor does flatten out the curves somewhat, but does not eliminate the characteristic waves of development, and it hardly affects the changes in the relative position of the nations.[8]

Nor do differences in national or personal income seem to be relevant. The indexes of national income in all the countries here surveyed show a fairly gradual and constant rise through the whole period without such ups and downs and such extensive changes in the relative positions of the countries as indicated by our data. Moreover, the United States and Britain were the richest of these countries, at least since the middle of the nineteenth century (and no doubt earlier in the case of Britain). Yet, as to medical discoveries, these countries were relatively backward during much of the period.[9] None of these factors, therefore, seems to be directly and consistently related to the differences in the growth of discoveries in the various nations.

Thus, it is assumed that the conditions determining the differences are to be sought in the *organization* of science. But this is a complex phenomenon: we still must seek the particular organizational factor which reasonably answers our questions. It is proposed to isolate this factor by comparing the main aspects of the organization of science in France and Germany during the first half and the middle of the nineteenth century and those same aspects in Britain and the United States during the three decades preceding World War I. This particular pairing is selected because France and Germany maintained a publicly supported network of scientific instruction and research from the early nineteenth century, while Britain and the United States did not begin to develop their systems until the second half of the century. There were short-lived experiments in Britain during the first half of the century, but these were overshadowed by the archaic nature of the most important universities. If it is possible to isolate a theoretically relevant condition common to the organization of science in Germany and the United States, but absent in France and Britain, that condition may reasonably be taken as the cause of the observed differences.

France and Germany

Three conditions are mentioned in the literature in explanation of German scientific superiority in the nineteenth century: (1) the relative excellence of laboratory and hospital facilities for research and the faster recognition of the importance of new fields of research, especially physiology; (2) the clear recognition of the aim of the university as a seat of original research, and efficient organizational devices to achieve that aim, such as far-reaching academic self-government, the freedom of the teacher regarding the content of his courses, the freedom of the student in the choice of his courses and his teachers (including easy transfer from one university to another), the requirement of submitting theses based on research for attainment of academic degrees, and, above all, the institution of *Habilitation*, that is, the submission of a high level scientific work based on original research as a precondition of academic appointment; (3) the existence of a large number of academic institutions which made possible the mobility of teachers and students, and resulted in an atmosphere of scientific competition that did not exist elsewhere.[10] The superiority of the German scientific facilities from about the middle of the century is an undeniable fact. But instead of explaining the differences in creativity, it is itself a phenomenon that needs explanation.

The pioneering country in the establishment of modern scientific facilities was France. Founded in 1794, the Polytechnique had been the model academic organization in the natural sciences. Among other new features, it possessed the first academic research laboratories (in chemistry). The physiological laboratory at the Collège de France, where Magendie and Claude Bernard conducted their studies, was considered most inadequate by the middle of the nineteenth century. Yet it was there that modern experimental physiology began. The idea of studying illness as a natural phenomenon, not necessarily for the sake of cure, was first conceived in Paris, and the beginnings of systematic clinical research in medicine were made in the hospitals of that city.[11]

Until the 1830s German medical research and natural science research in general was backward compared with the French, and probably with the British too. The famous network of modern German universities already existed from the time when, following tentative beginnings at Halle, Goettingen and Jena, the University of Berlin was established in 1809.[12] But the universities, rather than promoting, retarded the development of empirical science. They regarded philosophy as the queen of sciences, and usually disparaged empirical research. The biological sciences in particular were under the sway of *Naturphilosophie,* which stimulated much imaginative writing but little research.[13]

Only around 1830 did this atmosphere change under foreign influence. Liebig, who had studied in Paris, established in 1825 the first chemical laboratory at the small university of Giessen. A few years later Johannes Mueller, the central figure of German physiology, abandoned his early attachment to *Naturphilosophie* and became converted to the empirical method by studying the works of the Swedish chemist, Berzelius. About the same time the Vienna school of clinicians adopted the methods of investigation initiated by the Paris clinicians, and various learned journals began to propagate the new scientific approach in the medical sciences.[14]

Thus the French showed at least as much understanding of the value and the needs of scientific research as the Germans. It should not be assumed that this understanding suddenly declined around the middle of the century. The influentials of French science at that time, such as Dumas, and later Pasteur,

Claude Bernard, and Victor Duruy, were certainly not less enlightened and brilliant than their German counterparts. In fact, they may have been more sympathetic to the needs of scientific research than German academic policy makers, since obscurantism was rather prevalent within both the faculties of the German universities and the governmental offices in charge of higher education.[15] The greater expansion of German scientific facilities and the prompter recognition of new fields are therefore as much in need of explanation as the continuous growth in German discoveries.

The second condition—the presumably peculiar values and organization of the German university—is also a very doubtful explanation. The idea of academic freedom notwithstanding, atheists, Jews, and socialists were often kept out of academic careers in Germany. Academic self-government was not necessarily enlightened: liberal scientists in the 1840s regarded it as an essentially retrograde arrangement. In fact, some of the most beneficial academic decisions—with relation to the growth of science—were taken by civil servants, most notably Friedrich Althoff, who interfered with academic self-government. Even the *Habilitations-Schriften* were often rather mediocre pieces of research, and there was nothing in the constitution of the universities efficiently to prevent mediocre professors from confirming inferior theses.[16]

At the same time, the ideas as well as some of the arrangements said to be characteristic of the German universities also existed in France. Freedom of teaching already formed the core of the tradition at the Collège de France before the Revolution and was carried further than in the German universities. The ideals of pure research were formulated in French scientific ideology at least as clearly as in German and they were practiced and encouraged in a great many ways.[17] There is no proof that the lack of the paraphernalia of academic self-government interfered with the research of French scientists more than in Germany. It is true that, compared with the *Habilitation,* the French *aggrégation* and the system of open examinations seem to be inefficient ways of selecting people for academic careers. But there is little evidence that this irrelevant hurdle actually prevented potentially creative people from entering scientific careers. Moreover, there were other means, such as numerous prizes and public honors, which encouraged original research in France.[18]

Decentralization has been written about much less than the first two conditions, partly because it was an unintended circumstance, and partly because its effect upon research is less immediately evident. The decentralization of the German academic system was the result of the political dismemberment of the German-speaking people. There were nineteen independent universities in Germany proper, maintained by the princes of the numerous small states constituting Germany in the eighteenth and early nineteenth centuries, as well as German language universities in Switzerland, Austria (including the Czech provinces), and Dorpat in the Baltic Sea Provinces of Russia.[19] At the same time the French boasted a unified academic system, most of it situated in

Paris. Although some of the features of this centralization introduced by Napoleon were deplored, the central administration of science and academic institutions generally was considered to be desirable by French politicians of science.[20]

Nevertheless, decentralization seems to have been the decisive factor in determining the differences in the scientific creativity of the two countries. It gave rise to academic competition, and competition forced upon the individual institutions decisions which would not have been made otherwise, or at least not made at that time. In all areas crucial to the development of the medical sciences German policies turned out to be in the long run more farsighted and bold than French policies, although the first initiative was often taken by the French. What, then, was the actual competition and how did it influence the decisions about the crucial problems of academic policy?

The Crucial Decisions

Given the situation of the medical sciences (and perhaps of the sciences in general) at the beginning of the last century, the problem faced by the French and the German systems (and not confronted by Britain and the United States until later) was to find adequate criteria for the evaluation and support of science. The governments, and increasingly the people too (especially in France), believed in the value and usefulness of science. Academies, universities, and other institutions were set up everywhere, or rejuvenated where they existed before, in order to promote research and to disseminate knowledge. One of the aims of these institutions was to enable a selected few scientists, who had already proved their greatness, to devote all of their time to financially supported scientific research. But it was not intended to create in these institutions academic careers which one entered as in any other profession. The large majority of the scientists had independent means or a lucrative profession (very often medical practice, even in sciences not connected with medicine), and pursued their scientific interest in their free time, often at a considerable personal cost. This idealistic pattern seemed to fit perfectly that sacred pursuit of truth which was science. Academic appointments therefore were regarded as honors rather than careers, and turning science into an occupation would have seemed something like a sacrilege.

A corollary, in this amateur stage of science, was the absence of specialization. The great names of the early nineteenth century were those of generalists who were creative in more than one field. And the new scientific disciplines developed from their work. While it was increasingly believed that the new disciplines required specialists, the fact that they were opened up by generalists seemed to indicate that specialization was not really necessary. Moreover, there persisted the reluctance to abandon the conception of general science which explains to the adept all the secrets of nature. Thus there was considerable disinclination to substitute for the *savant* such narrow specialists as chemists, physiologists, and the like. And there was even more reluctance to redefine such a traditionally unified field as medicine into a number of sub-specialties.

The second problem was the development of criteria for the support of research. Today it is still difficult to decide what constitutes adequate and sufficient support of research, but at least budgets can be drawn for determined purposes. At that time even this was impossible, since research was an unpredictable, erratic process, and important discoveries were made as often outside as inside the laboratories.

Finally, there was the question of training scientists. Until the second half and particularly the last quarter of the nineteenth century, science had few practical applications. Most of it was pure science, benefitting no practice. Under these circumstances, to train every medical student, would-be chemist, and engineer in scientific research was about as justified as it would be today to teach every concertgoer advanced musical composition.[21]

These problems existed in both countries and were approached in France and Germany with the same concepts. Yet, to repeat, the long-term decisions made in France concerning all three problems were the opposite of those made in Germany.

Scientific careers and specialization.—The creation of regular careers in science and the recognition of specialized disciplines were closely connected problems. Both may be illustrated with the case of physiology, the most decisive science for the development of medicine in the nineteenth century.

As a systematic discipline, physiology emerged at the beginning of that century. François Magendie, considered to be the founder of experimental physiology, was professor of medicine. He established the new specialty and could follow it undisturbed (though practically unsupported) at the Collège de France, because of the full degree of academic freedom prevailing in that institution. But his disciple, Claude Bernard, who became the most outstanding representative of the new field around the middle of the century, for many years had to use his private laboratory and private means to pursue his research. At last, against the opposition of those who regarded the new discipline as merely a branch of anatomy, a special chair was created for Bernard at the Sorbonne in 1854. Soon thereafter he also fell heir to Magendie's chair at the Collège de France and held both appointments until 1868; he then transferred his work to the Museum of Natural History, relinquishing the post at the Sorbonne to his disciple, Paul Bert.

The recognition of the discipline of physiology, however, did not create opportunities for purely scientific careers in the traditional field of medicine. In this connection, the only change was that after the retirement of the chair's incumbent a single successor would have to be found. This was not a prospect on the basis of which one could realistically take up research as a career.

Therefore, potential scientists first had to build up a practice, and engaged in research as a part-time activity.[22]

Thus, the academic career changed very little in France through the nineteenth century. Appointments were made from an undifferentiated group of practitioners—amateur scientists—and usually at a fairly advanced age. Even academically successful persons did not become full-time scientists before they reached their forties or fifties, and since the chair to be vacated was not known they had to maintain as broad interests and activities as possible. But in the second half of the century there was increasingly less chance for nonspecialists to make important discoveries. French scientific productivity therefore declined even in fields pioneered by Frenchmen. Whenever a discipline reached the stage of development where its efficient pursuit required specialists, there was little chance that the French system would produce such scientists.[23]

Physiology as a science was received with more sympathy in Germany than in France, but its recognition as an academic specialty there also ran into difficulties. The man who did most for the introduction of the discipline to Germany, Johannes Mueller, was a generalist who taught, in addition to physiology, anatomy, ophthalmology, and surgery.[24] His eventual successor in Berlin, Du Bois-Reymond, had been refused one professorial chair after another because he was considered a mere specialist.[25] The early creation of a separate chair in physiology (for Purkinje in Breslau, 1839) had no general effect, and for some years physiology and anatomy continued to be taught by the same person in all other German universities. But pressure for the separation of the disciplines by the younger generation of scientists continued, and those with some bargaining power raised the demand when they were offered university chairs. Thus, when Carl Ludwig was offered a professorship at Zürich in 1849, he accepted it only on the condition that a separate teacher be appointed for anatomy;[26] thereafter the recognition of the new discipline proceeded rapidly. No university could afford to neglect the new field, so that by 1864 there were already fifteen full professors of physiology in Germany and several others in the wider system of German-language universities.[27] The separation of physiology from anatomy at this stage became the official policy of university administration. In some cases, where traditionally-minded incumbents were reluctant to abandon one of the disciplines, the separation was forced upon them by administrative pressure.[28]

All of this led to a complete transformation of the scientific career in Germany. In spite of the strictures against narrowness and of the continuing lipservice paid to the image of the scientist who works because of devotion, science became a specialized and regularized occupation. As we have seen, success, fame, or even sheer enterprise had a good chance for reward. Once a new fruitful field was recognized in one university, strong pressures led other universities to follow suit, thereby creating more opportunities for those willing to work in the new field. Therefore, it was possible—and for the very able also worthwhile—to concentrate after graduation on one well defined and promising field of research with the definite aim of a scientific career. Not only was it unnecessary first to build up a practice and to retain as general an interest as possible, but if one had taken such a course his academic prospects would have been negligible in competition with the full-time specialists. Thus specialized science became a career, and the amateur general scientist disappeared in Germany.[29] This difference in career possibilities, not the distinction between *Habilitation* and *aggrégation,* explains the greater research orientation of German than of French science.

The same mechanisms which explain the development of scientific roles also explain the development of facilities for research, and the introduction of scientific methods into the training of physicians. The creation of new facilities was part and parcel of the bargaining between universities and scientists. Facilities (laboratories, assistants, and so on) were offered to attract desirable candidates or to prevent scientists from moving elsewhere. The extension of facilities made possible, and to some extent made necessary, the training of a growing number of persons capable of doing research. Since not all such individuals could be given academic appointments in the basic medical sciences or otherwise, they used their research skills and interests to transform clinical medicine into an exact science. These processes and their results may be briefly illustrated.

Research facilities.—As has been pointed out, the French were the first to establish modern institutions for scientific training and research. But the facilities and arrangements established in France about 1800, considered to be ideal for their time, were hardly extended or changed until World War I or later. The Pasteur Institute, established in 1888, was the first independent research institute of the world. Again, it remained the only one in its field in France at least until World War I.[30]

Thus in France a new type of organization was apt to remain a single show-piece for 50 years, while in Germany such novelties became routine features of the organization of research in a much shorter time. By the 1840s there were apparently more and better chemical laboratories in Germany than in France, and by the sixties the contrast was extreme. At a time when it was an achievement for Pasteur to obtain any (and most inadequate) laboratory facilities, the Prussian government built new laboratories at Bonn and Berlin (the Bonn laboratory, for example, could accommodate more than 60 students) equipped with the most up-to-date facilities, and the older ones probably were also more adequate than anything that existed elsewhere. And there were good laboratories at other universities in Germany.[31]

Scientific training.—The differences in the development of medical training were no less conspicuous. The fact that until about the 1880s all the great advances in the basic medical sciences contributed little to the cure of illness largely explains the persistent and overwhelming emphasis on the practical art of medicine rather than on its few scientific bases in the training of the student-physician. Indeed, apprenticeship and bedside demonstrations were the most important parts of medical training in France, England, and the United States.[32]

Only in Germany did the training of the doctor become a privilege of scientists. By the 1860s even clinical chairs were given exclusively to people with attainment in research rather than to outstanding practitioners. And from the middle of the century, even public hospitals were increasingly staffed by doctors both interested and trained in research. Thus much earlier than elsewhere (possibly prematurely), medicine in Germany became an applied science.[33] As a result, when the great opportunities for clinical research arose, following the discovery of the bacteriological causation of illness and the perfection of anesthesia and aseptic surgery, there were in Germany enough doctors trained in research to take full advantage of the opportunity, and to transform public (even non-teaching) hospitals into veritable institutions of applied medical science.[34]

Britain and the United States

The similarities, differences, and differential effects observed in the cases of France and Germany were, in essentials, repeated in the cases of Britain and the United States.

From the middle of the nineteenth century, British—and soon after, American educators—scientists, and administrators displayed increasing interest in the organization of science in Germany. Scientists and intellectuals who visited Germany returned home enthusiastic about German academic life, and soon German university training became a standard preparation for scientific careers among British scientists.[35]

Consequently British universities, though retaining certain traditions, introduced measures to bring themselves in line with German standards and practices. Oxford and Cambridge, which until the 1860s were training centers primarily for the rich and the clergy, began to emerge as institutions of empirical science and positive scholarship pursued in an atmosphere of academic freedom and autonomy. The newer University of London and the universities in the provinces imitated the German pattern even more closely and were imbued, from the beginning, with the spirit of empirical science.

The rapid growth of the modern academic system also began in the United States in the 1860s. The Land Grant Act passed in 1862 and other circumstances brought about a large increase in the number of American colleges and universities between the sixties and the eighties.[36] In the present context, the most important events were the rise of the graduate schools in the seventies, and in the following decade the establishment of Johns Hopkins Medical

School which was directly influenced by the German example.[37] Eventually older institutions, such as Harvard, also abandoned certain traditions derived from pre-nineteenth century England and adopted new methods in imitation of the Germans.[38]

In this development of a system of up-to-date institutions for medical research and training Britain had most of the advantages over the United States, similar to those possessed by France over Germany at the beginning of the century. The British began the adoption of the German patterns earlier, and they began from a higher level than did the Americans.[39] Nevertheless, while the effect of the academic reform on British science was slow and partial, in America it produced a conspicuous rise in scientific creativity.

That the social mechanisms at work in these cases were similar to those involved in our first pair of comparisons can be illustrated best by the organization of clinical research and the creation of clinical chairs. Attempts to copy the Germans by making hospital departments into virtual research establishments and filling the clinical chairs according to criteria of scientific achievement ran into serious opposition in both countries. They seemed like an infringement on the rights of the profession, whose members had run the teaching hospitals independently of the universities, and it also seemed to be endangering the charitable purpose of the hospitals. Therefore, when Oxford and Cambridge decided to overhaul their medical training programs along German lines, they confined themselves to the basic departments and sent their students to continue their clinical studies in the hospital medical schools of London. This division was a decision in favor of preserving the traditions of the professional fraternities attached to the various public hospitals and of the philanthropic bodies which governed these hospitals. Of course, it could also have been justified by the aim to keep apart pure research and professional practice.[40] However, *a priori* reasons for incorporating the teaching hospitals in the universities and staffing them on the basis of attainments in research might have been advanced. As shown above, this was one of the problems which could not at that time be decided on *a priori* logical grounds; only future experience could indicate the effective choice.

The conditions for acquiring the needed experience existed in England, since there were approximations of a proper university hospital and university clinical departments in the London University College Medical School (founded as early as 1836), and similar opportunities arose when the provincial universities were established.[41] Yet, instead of representing competing alternatives, none of these departments ventured further than the model established by the Oxford-Cambridge-London triangle; that is, their clinical departments were run by local practitioners as practical training centers rather than being organized as university departments engaged in research and staffed by persons selected on the basis of scientific eminence. This was quite different from the situation in Germany, where, for example, the little University of

Giessen successfully pioneered in establishing its chemical laboratory, imitated later by universities of much greater prestige. It also differed from the innovation of the Johns Hopkins Medical School, where a full-scale medical faculty that included basic as well as clinical departments was established—a pattern that was followed by other universities and led to a rapid transformation of American medicine reminiscent of German, notwithstanding the strength of a professional and philanthropic tradition similar to that of Britain.[42]

All this shows unequivocally that the British system was not competitive. Yet seemingly it was decentralized, since universities and public hospitals were private institutions financed and governed in a variety of ways, as in the United States. In fact, however, Britain also had a centralized system, though centralized in a somewhat different way than that of the French. The provincial universities did not begin to confer degrees until 1880 (with the exception of Durham, established in 1831) and their status, as well as the status of London University, never reached that of the two ancient universities. The system was totally overshadowed by the Oxford-Cambridge duopoly, which, in spite of differences in matters of religion and politics, represented basically similar educational philosophies and academic policies.[43] The special position of these two institutions was maintained in large part by their unwritten exclusive right of educating the political, administrative, ecclesiastical, and professional elite of the nation. In the case of medicine, the two universities were, as we have seen, connected with the leading medical corporations of London, whose members traditionally received their pre-professional education in "Oxbridge." Thus the centralization of academic life, which in France was the result of administrative design, was achieved in England through the more subtle functions of a class system, in which academic institutions like people "were kept in their place" through internalized traditions and networks of semi-formalized bonds among persons, groups, and independent organizations. The United States, however, provides a case similar to the German, where competition within a decentralized system encouraged the establishment of specialized research roles and facilities.

Conclusion

The continuous growth in the curves of German discoveries during the middle decades of the nineteenth century and in the American curves starting from the 1880s is thus attributed to the extent to which these societies exploited, through enterprise and organizational measures, the possibilities inherent in the state of science. They were quicker than France and Britain in the recognition of new disciplines, the creation of specialized scientific jobs and facilities for research, and the introduction of large-scale systematic training for research. They were also quicker to abandon traditional notions which had lost their usefulness. None of these conditions alone could have sustained scientific growth for a long period of time. It was no coincidence, however, that they went together, since a common underlying factor, competition, determined the crucial decisions concerning all of these conditions in the two decentralized systems. Successful scientists were rewarded with university chairs and facilities. Their success encouraged others to take up science and, incidentally, transformed the pursuit of science into a regular professional career; it created pressure for further expansion of facilities and training, and exposed the inadequacies of out-of-date traditions.

This interpretation of the curve of scientific discoveries, according to which their growth was due to increased opportunities for entering research careers (and not, for example, to better selection of scientists), is also consistent with the differences between the countries shown in the second index based on the numbers of discoverers. As pointed out earlier, beginning in 1835 in Germany and in 1860 in the United States, the growth in the numbers of those entering upon scientific careers became continuous, while in France and Britain there were fluctuations over the whole period. Continuous growth represents a situation in which research becomes a regular career; fluctuations, a situation in which research to a large extent is a spontaneous activity engaged in by people as the spirit moves them.

Finally, nothing has been said about the conditions that maintain scientific competition. Political decentralization gave rise to competition in Germany, and political decentralization enhanced by private financing and administration of higher education led to competition in the United States. It is not argued, however, that competition is the only possible outcome of any state of decentralization, or that competition, once established, is self-maintaining. Decentralization may lead to collusion or mutual isolation, as well as to competition; and competition may be replaced by either of these alternatives. Determination of the general conditions that ensure competition, therefore, is another problem, which needs further study.

Notes

1. The method is applied and discussed by T. J. Rainoff, "Wave-like Fluctuations of Creative Productivity in the Development of West-European Physics in the Eighteenth and Nineteenth Centuries," *Isis*, 12 (1929), pp. 291–292. See also S. C. Gilfillan, *The Sociology of Invention* (Chicago: Follet, 1935), pp. 29–32; Joseph Schneider, "The Cultural Situation as a Condition for the Achievement of Fame," *American Sociological Review*, 2 (August, 1937), pp. 480–491; Frank R. Cowell, *History, Civilization and Culture: An Introduction to the Historical and Social Philosophy of Pitirim A. Sorokin* (London: Black, 1952), pp. 90–106; and especially the methodological comments of Robert K. Merton, "Fluctuations in the Rate of Industrial Invention," *The Quarterly Journal of Economics*, 59 (May, 1935), p. 456.
2. *Cf.* William F. Ogburn, *Social Change* (New York: Huebsch, 1922), pp. 90–

122; Bernhard J. Stern, *Society and Medical Progress* (Princeton: Princeton University Press, 1941), pp. 41–44.

3. Merton, *op. cit.,* pp. 464–465.

4. Published in F. H. Garrison, *An Introduction to the History of Medicine,* 4th edition (Philadelphia and London: Saunders, 1929).

5. Based on W. A. Newman Dorland, *The American Illustrated Medical Dictionary,* 20th edition (Philadelphia and London: Saunders, 1946).

6. The pattern which emerges from these indexes parallels the qualitative descriptions of up-to-date histories of medicine and science. See, e.g., Arturo Castiglioni, *A History of Medicine* (New York: A. A. Knopf, 1947); Richard H. Shryock, *The Development of Modern Medicine* (New York: A. A. Knopf, 1947); H. T. Pledge, *Science Since 1500* (London: Philosophical Library, 1940). Rather than simply referring to such sources, I prefer to present the numerical indexes in detail for two reasons: (1) They contain some information not sufficiently emphasized—or even blurred—in those sources. Thus the small amount of medical research in Britain is blurred in the qualitative descriptions by the dazzling brilliance of England's few scientist-intellectuals and by the glamor of the British medical profession. Also, the different patterns of growth of scientific personnel (discoverers) is a subject not sufficiently emphasized in the histories of medical science. (2) What is called here scientific productivity is only one aspect of the development of science; in terms of the interrelationships of scientific ideas it is perhaps a peripheral one. Since traditionally the history of science is an history of ideas, even the few historians interested in such sociological phenomena as differences in the scientific development of various countries are not very explicit about the bases of their judgments, nor do they sufficiently differentiate between the various aspects of science as a social activity. It is important, therefore, to present explicitly the quantitative basis of the historians' judgment and clearly delimit the particular aspect of scientific activity dealt with here from others.

7. *Cf.* Shryock, *op. cit.,* pp. 193–196; Paul Diepgen, *Geschichte der Medizin* (Berlin: Gruyter, 1955), Vol. II/1, pp. 204–207; Charles Newman, *The Evolution of Medical Education in the Nineteenth Century* (London: Oxford University Press, 1957), pp. 265–269.

8. The sources used for population data were *La Population Française: Rapport du Haut Comité Consultatif de la Population et de la Famille* (Paris: Presses Universitaires de France, 1955), p. 19; Michel Huber, Henri Bunle, et Fernand Boverat, *La Population de la France* (Paris: Librairie Hachette, 1943), p. 19; W. S. and E. S. Woytinsky, *World Population and Production* (New York: Twentieth Century Fund, 1953).

9. For national income data, see, e.g., Colin Clark, *The Conditions of Economic Progress,* 2nd edition (London: Macmillan, 1951).

10. *Cf.* Abraham Flexner, *Universities: American, English, German* (Oxford: Oxford University Press, 1930), pp. 317–327; Donald S. L. Cardwell, *The Organization of Science in England* (London: Heinemann, 1957), pp. 22–25; H. E. Guerlac, "Science and French National Strength" in E. M. Earle, editor, *Modern France* (Princeton: Princeton University Press, 1951), pp. 85–88.

11. *Cf.* Shryock, *op. cit.,* pp. 70–71, 151–169; Newman, *op. cit.,* p. 48; Guerlac, *op. cit.,* pp. 81–105.

12. *Cf.* Flexner, *op. cit.,* pp. 311–315; R. H. Samuel and R. Hinton Thomas,

Education and Society in Modern Germany (London: Routledge & Kegan Paul, 1949), pp. 111–113; Jacob Barion, *Universitas und Universitaet* (Bonn: Rörscheid, 1954), pp. 14–20.

13. *Cf.* Shryock, *op. cit.,* pp. 192–201; Diepgen, *op. cit.,* Vol. II/1, pp. 23–28.

14. *Cf.* Cardwell, *op. cit.,* pp. 22–25; Shryock, *op. cit.,* pp. 188, 195; Garrison, *op. cit.,* pp. 451–452.

15. See Guerlac, *op. cit.,* pp. 85–88 on France. On the relative backwardness of German academic administration, see Ervin H. Ackerknecht, *Rudolf Virchow: Doctor, Statesman, Anthropologist* (Madison: University of Wisconsin Press, 1953), pp. 139–140; Samuel and Thomas, *op. cit.,* pp. 114–130; Max Weber, *Jugendbriefe* (Tübingen: Mohr, n.d.), pp. 151–152. In order to realize the amount of obscurantism and intolerance in German universities at the time it is useful to read the otherwise shallow work of Richard Graf du Moulin Eckart, *Geschichte der deutschen Universitaeten* (Stuttgart: Enke, 1929).

16. *Cf.* Flexner, *op. cit.,* pp. 317–327; Samuel and Thomas, *loc. cit.*

17. See Claude Bernard, *Morceaux Choisis, dirigé et préfacé* par Jean Rostand (Paris: Gallimard, 1938), pp. 16–18, for one of the most beautiful descriptions of the traditions of the freedom of teaching and research as it was practiced at the Collège de France. See also Ernest Lavissé, *Histoire de France* (Paris: Librairie Hachette, n.d.), Vol. IX/1, p. 301, on the pioneering beginnings of the teaching of pure sciences in the same institution in the 1770s and 1780s.

18. For a good description of how the French system of examinations actually worked, see René Leriche, *Am Ende meines Lebens* (Bern und Stuttgart: Huber, 1957), pp. 53–55. Leriche, like others, attributes the lack of originality of French medicine to the examinations. But his own account shows that the problem was rather the lack of career opportunities for young medical scientists (*ibid.,* p. 34).

19. With the addition of Strassburg in 1872 there were 20 universities in Germany. *Cf.* Christian v. Ferber, *Die Entwicklung des Lehrkörpers der deutschen Universitaeten und Hochschulen* 1964–1954, Vol. III of Helmuth Plessner, editor, *Untersuchungen sur Lage der deutschen Hochschullehrer* (Göttingen: Vandenhoeck & Ruprecht, 1956), pp. 37–38. The German-language universities of Switzerland were Zürich, Bern, and Basel; and of Austria, Vienna, Prague, Graz, and Innsbruck.

20. *Cf.* Guerlac, *op. cit.,* pp. 87–88.

21. On the state of science in the early nineteenth century, see Pledge, *op. cit.,* pp. 115–151. On scientists in the same period, see Elie Halévy. *History of England in 1815* (London: Pelican, 1938), Vol. 2, pp. 187–200; René J. Dubos, *Louis Pasteur: Franc-tireur de la science* (Paris: Presses Universitaires de France, 1955), pp. 3–4; and Diepgen, *op. cit.,* Vol. II/1, pp. 2–5, 66–69, 152–153.

22. *Cf.* Bernard, *op. cit.,* pp. 154–157, 263–285; J. M. D. Olmsted, *Claude Bernard: Physiologist* (New York: Harper, 1938), pp. 51–89. For the situation at the beginning of the twentieth century, see Edouard Rist, *25 Portraits des médicins français, 1900–1950* (Paris: Masson, 1955), pp. 29–40.

23. See Rist, *op. cit.,* pp. 97–104, on the career of S. A. Sicard, who seems to have been a relatively lucky and successful scientist. When at the age of 51 he was appointed as professor he had to abandon his life-long interest and

research in neurology because the vacant chair was designated for internal pathology, and course preparation in the new field required great effort.

24. *Cf.* K. E. Rothschuh, *Geschichte der Physiologie* (Berlin-Göttingen-Heidelberg: Springer, 1953), pp. 93, 112–118.

25. George Rosen and Beate Caspari-Rosen, *400 Years of a Doctor's Life* (New York: Schuman, 1947), pp. 248–250; Ernst Gagliardi, Hans Nabholz and Jean Strohl, *Die Universitaet Zürich und ihre Vorlaeufer 1833–1933* (Zürich: Erziehungsdirektion, 1938), pp. 548–549.

26. *Ibid.*, pp. 539–548. Virchow, who was also offered the chair, refused to accept it on the ground that he wished a chair for pathological anatomy exclusively (without teaching responsibilities in either surgical anatomy or physiology). In Ludwig's time the nominal unity of physiology and anatomy was still maintained, the separate teacher in anatomy was only an extraordinary professor. But when Ludwig left Zürich in 1855 and the position was offered to Koelliker, the chairs were finally separated upon the latter's suggestion (although Koelliker himself refused the job). For similar instances of creating new specialties at the same university in order to attract or retain teachers, see *ibid.*, pp. 562, 879.

27. *Cf.* Von Ferber, *op. cit.*, p. 204.

28. For example, Valentin in Bern, in 1865; see Bruno Kisch, *Forgotten Leaders in Modern Medicine* (Philadelphia: American Philosophical Society, 1954), pp. 174–175.

29. Max Weber, writing in 1918, regarded science as a most risky career; see his "Science as a Vocation," in H. H. Gerth and C. Wright Mills, *From Max Weber: Essays in Sociology* (London: Oxford University Press, 1947), pp. 132–134. But, it should be realized that Weber was referring to a crisis situation in an already established discipline; the circumstances were much more hopeful in the middle of the nineteenth century. Of those who took their *Habilitation* between 1850 and 1859, 85 per cent received full-time academic appointments, while for those who recieved their *Habilitation* between 1900 and 1909 only 62 per cent received such posts. The corresponding proportions in medicine are 84 and 48 per cent, respectively. (This does not necessarily mean a relatively greater decline of research opportunities in medicine, because there were good research opportunities outside the universities in public hospitals.) See Von Ferber, *op. cit.*, pp. 81–82, for the statistical data; and Adolf Struempell, *Aus dem Leben eines deutschen Klinikers* (Leipzig: Vogel, 1925), on the *Habilitation* as a preparation for a hospital career.

30. The ideal arrangements of French medical schools in 1798 are noted in Newman, *op. cit.*, p. 48. Concerning the quite different picture presented by French academic medicine early in this century, see Abraham Flexner, *Medical Education in Europe* (New York: The Carnegie Foundation for the Advancement of Teaching, 1912), pp. 221–223; and Leriche, *op. cit.*, p. 34. On the Pasteur Institute, see Guerlac, *op. cit.*, p. 88.

31. *Cf.* Cardwell, *op. cit.*, p. 80; and Dubos, *op. cit.*, pp. 34, 78–79.

32. *Cf.* Diepgen, *op. cit.*, Vol. II/1, pp. 212–214; Vol. II/2, pp. 154–155, 286–288; Abraham Flexner, *Medical Education: A Comparative Study* (New York: Macmillan, 1925), pp. 211–212, 241, 248.

33. Diepgen, *op. cit.*, Vol. II/1, pp. 152–153. See also Theodore Billroth, *loc. cit.*; Bernhard Naunyn, *Erinnerungen, Gedanken und Meinungen* (Munich: Bergmann, 1925), pp. 375–376.

34. There was a parallel development in chemistry. There too the availability of relatively large numbers of trained chemists afforded Germany the opportunity to build up within a short time a chemical industry based on applied science, after the discovery of the aniline dyes made the practical application of science a permanent possibility; *cf.* Cardwell, *op. cit.*, pp. 134–137, 186–187.

35. *Ibid.*, p. 50.

36. *Ibid.*, p. 80.

37. *Cf.* Flexner, *Universities . . . , op. cit.*, p. 73; and Abraham Flexner, *I Remember* (New York: Simon and Schuster, 1940), pp. 63–64.

38. *Cf.* Edward D. Churchill, *To Work in the Vineyards of Surgery: The Reminiscences of J. Collins Warren (1842–1927)* (Cambridge: Harvard University Press), pp. 193–197, 257–271.

39. *Cf.* Newman, *op. cit.*, pp. 269, 276; Cardwell, *op. cit.*, pp. 46–51, 80, 103–107, 110–114, 118–119, 134–137, and *passim.* Flexner, *Universities . . . , op. cit.*, pp. 46–65; Richard H. Shryock, *American Medical Research: Past and Present* (New York: New York Academy of Medicine, 1947), pp. 106–108, 118–119.

40. *Cf.* "The First Hundred Years: Notes on the History of the Association," extracts from Ernest M. Little, "History of the Association," *British Medical Journal*, 1932, 1, pp. 672–676; A. M. Carr-Saunders and P. A. Wilson, *The Professions* (Oxford: Clarendon Press, 1933), p. 87; Flexner, *Medical Education . . . , op. cit.*, p. 28; Newman, *op. cit.*, pp. 49–50, 133 ff.

41. *Cf.* Flexner, *Universities . . . , op. cit.*, pp. 242–244.

42. *Cf.* Donald H. Fleming, *William Welch and the Rise of Modern Medicine* (Boston: Little, Brown, 1954), pp. 173 ff. On competition in American academic life in general, see Logan Wilson, *The Academic Man* (London: Oxford University Press, 1942), pp. 157–174, 186–191, 195–214; and Theodore Caplow and Reece J. McGee, *The Academic Marketplace* (New York: Basic Books, 1958).

43. *Cf.* Flexner, *Universities . . . , op. cit.*, p. 249; Bruce Truscot, *Red Brick University* (Harmondsworth: Penguin Books, 1951), pp. 19–29. See also R. K. Kelsall, *Higher Civil Servants in Britain* (London: Routledge & Kegan Paul), 1956, p. 137, on the preservation of the educational duopoly in another field; as late as 1950, 47.3 per cent of British civil servants in the ranks of Assistant Secretary and above had attended Oxford or Cambridge.

Werner J. Cahnman THE RISE OF CIVILIZATION AS A
PARADIGM OF SOCIAL CHANGE

THE SUM TOTAL of man's history cannot be encompassed by a single theory, sociological or otherwise, nor is it likely that all data of history will be of equal value to sociologists. But, as change and transformation are inseparable from any consideration of human affairs, it appears that among sociological concerns social change theory stands most in need of historical materials and, in turn, is best fitted to illuminate the course of history. The aim of the following deliberations, therefore, is to offer a theoretical framework, based on historical evidence, which may be put to use in analyzing social change. To this end, the concepts of culture and civilization are examined and the transition from tribalism to urbanism (that is, from a monocultural to a multicultural social system) is set up as a paradigm for the processes of social change. In doing this, the intention is not to reduce social change to urbanization, but rather to isolate the sociological element which makes for social change within the supersession of a familial by a territorial society, wherever it occurs. The inquiry is structural in character, but the social-psychological consequences will also be indicated.

Definitions of Society, Culture and Civilization

Throughout the paper, the concept of society is taken for granted, but the differentiation between society and culture is not pursued. Conceptually, to be sure, it is possible to keep social and cultural systems apart, but to what extent this dichotomy can be brought to bear on a research situation is dubious. For instance, the norms which govern social relationships also refer to a way of life which is shared and transmitted, and therefore is cultural in character. The problem becomes further entangled if we consider change. If one takes as an example the transformation of the cult of the goddess of fertility into the adoration of the "black Madonna," as analyzed by Moss and Cappannari,[1] he can argue that the form of worship of the Italian peasant has remained unaltered while the meaning attached to this formal organization,

---

This paper is an enlarged and revised edition of a paper, "Culture, Civilization, and Social Change," published in *The Sociological Quarterly,* Vol. III, No. 2 (April 1962), pp. 93–106.

or his "world view," including the sacred artifacts which symbolize the "world view," have undergone a radical change. But he can also argue that regularities in behavior and the values inherent in them have persisted and that only the form of worship has been refashioned. In historical analysis the argument is irrelevant because, as Toynbee asserts, it is impossible, in analyzing societies and cultures in practice, "to study either apart from the other."[2] Going a step further, Sorokin has drawn attention to the fact that social and cultural systems, or the social and cultural aspects of systems, change together, even if no mechanical or precise synchronicity is implied.[3] In other words, social and cultural systems, whatever else they may be, are indistinguishable under the aspect of change. Neither do forms of interaction change without changing their meaning, nor can values change without changing in some degree the patterns of interaction in which they are expressed. However, compared with civilization, culture appears as a distinct stage in societal development.

Our departure from the concept of culture is provoked by the fact that the unanimity regarding this concept is among the most remarkable convergences in modern sociological and anthropological theory. Ever since Tylor's definition, almost a century ago, that "culture, or civilization, is that complex whole which includes knowledge, belief, art, law, morals, custom, and any other capabilities and habits acquired by man as a member of society," innumerable definitions of culture have been formulated, but they all seem to be aimed at the same thing. According to Kroeber and Kluckhohn's compilations in "Culture—A Critical Review of Concepts and Definitions," there seems to be a slight shift over the decades from a historical to a psychological emphasis, but there is continuing consensus that culture is a group product, that it refers to a social heritage and a patterned system, that it embraces a totality of ways and modes of behavior, that it includes values and artifacts, that it involves learning processes, and that it results in the adjustment of the individual to the group as well as in the reflection of the group in the individual.[4]

In other words, culture is seen as the motivating force, or the "meaning," behind the network of formal relationships which we call society. In this sense, the concept of "culture" appears to be closely related to other overall concepts in social science, such as Durkheim's "*conscience sociale*" or Sumner's "folkways and mores." Like the air we breathe, culture is presumed to be everywhere. Whatever we think and say and do is the container, with culture the content. Culture, in this view, is the "superorganic" aspect of life itself.

But is this a workable proposition? To be sure, the very inclusiveness and all-pervasiveness of the concept of culture makes for its fundamentality and wide application in the social sciences, but it would seem to impair its usefulness as a theoretical tool. If concepts are to serve the purpose of isolating and thereby recognizing traits and aspects within the universal context of life as it is being lived in the uninterrupted flow of reality, then a concept which comprises a totality of phenomena must of necessity come very near to defying its purpose. The concept of "culture" may be compared to the concepts of "space" and "time," adding, as it were, a social-psychological aspect to the geographical and historical aspects of human existence and development. Like "space" and "time," culture is a mode of seeing phenomena and a means of ordering them, but it must be capable of subdivision and confrontation with related concepts to retain its usefulness for analysis. The only subdivision which is generally accepted—the one between one culture and another —falls short of this requirement because it is based on the assumption that cultures are unique wholes even to the point of being incomprehensible to each other. Hence, one culture may replace another or borrow traits from another, but, regarding their being suffused with "culture" rather than "a culture," they are all alike. Within the concept of culture, then, we can account for growth and accretion, but not for the transformation of interpersonal relations, that is, for the essence of social change.

Contrary to the concept of culture, the concept of civilization has had an uncertain and confused history.[5] The term "civilization" first appears in the Dictionary of the *Académie Française* in 1798 and since has been widely accepted, but in a variety of loosely interconnected connotations. Civilization has been considered as a *synonym* of culture, as a selected *part* of culture, and as a kind or *phase* of culture. We will briefly review these three varieties before we present our own analysis.

1. The consideration of civilization as a synonym of culture is most common. Webster's Dictionary defines civilization in terms of culture and culture in terms of civilization. Some anthropologists, for instance Sapir and Goldenweiser, have used culture and civilization interchangeably. Tylor, in the above-quoted sentence and elsewhere, wavered between culture and civilization, but finally chose the former as less burdened with the connotation of a high degree of advancement.[6] This decision makes sense from the point of view of the anthropologist whose chief interest is in the analysis of preliterate societies, but it is likely to make less sense for those social scientists who are concerned with advanced societies. Nevertheless, a sociologist like William Graham Sumner shows the same wavering attitude. In *Folkways,* to be sure, Sumner uses civilization rather than culture, but in Sumner and Keller's joint work, *The Science of Society,* we find "the sum of men's adjustment to their life conditions" defined as "culture or civilization."[7] All this amounts to an imprecise use of language which we will try to avoid.

2. More specific are those authors who see in civilization a selected part of culture, coexistent with other parts. Not satisfied with leaving undecided the problem of how to relate culture and civilization to each other, they construe these two terms as complementary and contrasting elements within a larger societal complex. However, there is a wide divergence with regard to what is considered culture and what civilization. Early American sociologists, such as Albion Small and Lester Ward, defined culture in reference to material prod-

ucts and technology or, in Albion Small's words, "the control of nature by science and art," while civilization was thought of as implying a high and ennobling degree of socialization and "the increased control of the elementary human impulses by society."[8] The derivation of culture from cultivation, as in "agriculture," and Samuel Johnson's device of "civility" rather than "civilization" shines through here.

Later American writers have attached the labels differently. Ralph Linton looks upon civilization as comprising the sum total of human "means" and upon culture as the "collectivity of human ends."[9] Similarly, MacIver and Merton confront civilization as the "impersonal" and "objective" and culture as the "personal" and "subjective" element in social life.[10] In doing so, they have adopted the position of Alfred Weber, who in his "culture-sociology" defined civilization as utilitarian and materialistic in content and transferable and cumulative in nature. By way of contrast, culture is superstructural, ideational, unique, and creative. Both are associated with social process, which reveals itself in the network of interpersonal relations; all three movements, or processes, are considered as ever-present components in the experience of mankind.[11]

3. The notion which pervades a vast body of writing in the social sciences, that civilization is a kind, or phase, of culture, is not necessarily incompatible with the view that both are selected parts of culture, that is, divergent conceptualizations of one or the other aspect of the same societal system. *Gemeinschaft* may coexist with *Gesellschaft* (Toennies), customary usage with codified law (Savigny), familistic relations with contractual relations (Sorokin), folk culture with urban civilization (Redfield), folkways with stateways (Odum). But Toennies—to mention only the most influential of these authors —in establishing the dichotomy of *Gemeinschaft* and *Gesellschaft* meant to say that *Gemeinschaft* was not only different from *Gesellschaft,* but also older and nearer to the mainsprings of human nature. In other words, primary relations are established first in societal as well as in personal development and they remain a constituent element in later stages, when mechanization and segmental contacts take command. With still another group of authors, such as Brooks Adams and Oswald Spengler, the secondary and sequential nature of civilization is more clearly established, and the value accent on civilization becomes emphatically negative. Only slightly divergent here and there, both Adams and Spengler agree that from early "culture" to late "civilization" the *locus* of domination shifts from village to town and then to city, and the dominant institution from the religious to the military and finally to the commercial sector. The end is decadence and death.[12] A similarly romantic world view has been expressed by Howard Odum in defense of his native South[13] and by Lewis Mumford with regard to the rise and fall of Megalopolis.[14]

It is intriguing to note that with evolutionary theorists, especially Herbert Spencer, the sequence from military to industrial society is maintained, but with the value emphasis reversed: what is "decadence" for romanticists, denotes "progress" for evolutionists. However, Spencer's scheme of unilinear evolution, which took change for granted, did not enable him to grasp the structural differentiation which is implicit in civilization. This is in contrast to the latter-day evolutionism of MacIver, who assimilated the structural elements in the theories of Toennies, Durkheim, Alfred and Max Weber, but not without introducing a significant shift in meaning. In Alfred Weber's scheme— the most pertinent in the present context—the historical distinction between culture and civilization, which looms so large in romantic thought, is abolished, but the romanticists' value accent on "culture" is retained. MacIver, on the other hand, restored the sequential aspects of the terms "culture" and "civilization," but neutralized the value accent on "culture." This occurred almost inadvertently, as is usually the case when traits are borrowed from one culture area to another.

As one scans the MacIver and Page volume, *Society,* it would seem as if the thinking of the authors had undergone a subtle process of transformation from Book II, which deals with the major forms of social structure, to Book III, which is concerned with social change. In Book II, civilization represents utilitarianism, culture immediacy. By civilization is meant "the whole mechanism and organization which man has devised in his endeavor to control the conditions of his life"; by culture is meant "the expression of our nature in our modes of living and thinking, in our everyday intercourse, in art, in literature, in religion, in recreation and enjoyment."[15] The two orders are seen as interactive, so that particular artifacts may combine cultural and technological aspects. They are regarded as distinct but interpenetrating orders of society.

In Book III the *leitmotif* is maintained, but in the very last pages of the last chapter, as in an afterthought, the tune is ever so subtly changed. Going beyond Durkheim's emphasis on the lesser role of the division of labor in primitive as compared with civilized life, MacIver and Page maintain that the very distinction between the cultural and the utilitarian elements was scarcely discernible in primitive society. This phenomenon, called "primitive fusion," amounts to saying that primitive society is largely homogeneous in character, that it is based on undifferentiated solidarity and that it spells *Gemeinschaft* in the sense which Toennies gave to the term, that is, that it denotes a type of social organization which springs from the fundamental character of man as embedded in blood ties and familial bonds. In other words, primitive fusion refers to that unified system of values and material as well as behavioral manifestations of values which is called "culture." In contradistinction, advanced society, according to MacIver and Page, results from the breakup of the primitive fusion; it transcends the familial, or cultural, community and encompasses a multiplicity of values and manifestations of values, i.e., cultures rather than culture.[16] The implication is that a technological civilization permeates all cultural communities within an advanced society. It would seem preferable to say that *the multiplicity of values in and of itself represents civilization and that the processes which transform a monocultural into a multicultural system bespeak social change.*

Civilization as a Culture of Cultures

The anthropologist Philip Bagby proposes that we take our cue from etymology and define civilization as "the kind of culture found in cities."[17] But the philosopher Morris R. Cohen takes a further step when he says that "literally, the term 'civilization' means the *making* of cities, or of city-life," thus implying the element of change and designating the city as the locale of change.[18] Morris R. Cohen's definition at once raises the question as to the stuff cities are made of and the nature of the non-city-like society which preceded the rise of civilizations. The answer is that prior to the emergence of cities social structure was chiefly, if not exclusively, determined by kinship. For long periods of time, man was a roving hunter, a food collector, a herdsman and finally—at least in the ancient Near East and in China—a settled agriculturist before he became a town dweller; yet, while a profound difference in social organization exists between wandering nomads and sedentary villagers or, as V. Gordon Childe calls them, food gatherers and food producers, the important point in the present context is that they resemble each other insofar as their social organization is based on the sentiment of kinship.[19]

Possibly, because of the burdensomeness of children to nomadic hunters and herders as compared to their usefulness in gardens and fields, the importance of the total clan looms larger among food gatherers than among food producers. But it would be a mistake to assume that the fixation of villagers to a particular locality is contradictory to the kinship principle. Actually, in a neolithic peasant village, as in all peasant villages, kinsmen and neighbors are identical. There is nobody else around in the first place, but the idea that one could experience a bond of loyalty with people of different blood lines merely because one shares with them a common habitat is utterly foreign to tribal societies even in those places where people of divers ancestry are settled side by side. When wandering nomads first provided a permanent and collective abode for their revered forebears in a ceremonial city of the dead and then settled in the vicinity of the caves and graveyards, they reinforced blood ties; they did not break the magic bond.[20] It is only in the city that size of population and the concomitant division of labor proceed to a point where proximity, or habitat, supersedes kinship as the focal point in social organization. The urban revolution gives birth to civilization.[21]

The Emergence of the City. How did the city come about? Following Mumford, the change was initiated when neolithic villagers, descending from the dry uplands to the river bottoms along the banks of the Euphrates and Tigris, or those already settled here and there amidst the swampy waste, mingled with clans of palaeolithic hunters who acted as guides, protectors and taskmasters.[22] However, according to other authors, such as Childe, Frankfort, and Turner,[23] such an initial stratification of rulers and ruled may be viewed either as a precondition or as a consequence or urbanization, but not as its sufficient cause. These authors emphasize that cities emerge when a technological complex creates an economic surplus.[24] The technological complex which makes its appearance between the years 6000 and 3000 B.C. consists in the knowledge of harnessing the force of oxen and of winds, the invention of the plow, the wheeled cart and the sailboat, the discovery of the physical property of metals and the chemical processes involved in smelting copper ores, and in the first steps toward working out an accurate solar calendar.[25] The most conspicuous economic surplus was achieved in the river valleys and by means of irrigation; the yields of wheat and barley were multiplied many times over. But even here, the surplus produced in a single village was not sufficient to maintain the specialists who practiced the new skills. They broke away and turned into itinerant workers, loosely organized into craft clans, occupational castes and even guilds, which means that they became strangers to the sacred round of village activities. Society had to be reorganized to accommodate an increasingly indispensable segment of the population.[26] The agent of reorganization was the city; here was the "dividing line" between a simple, traditional culture and a complex civilization.

Cities are instrumentalities of social change, but change is brought about by external contact. At later stages, that is, in more inclusive societies, change may be occasioned by contacts from within, by means of a growth of population which, through closer settlement and improved communication, leads to increased social density, meaning an intensified division of labor. But initially, cities are meeting places of a variety of clans and specialists and consequently combinations of various ethnic, linguistic and other kinds of groups and subgroups. They are hardly ever "orthogenic" in character; to their heterogenic origin and heterogeneous composition forces from without add a further impetus.[27] As the ancient philosophers pointed out long ago, the "cake of custom" is broken by the confrontation of homegrown virtues, which are forever yielding, with disturbing mores introduced by strangers. The creation of an exchangeable surplus promotes commerce with distant areas from which, in turn, raw materials and luxury products are imported. This applies especially to ancient Mesopotamia. According to Childe and Frankfort, imports of building materials and metals were a necessity on the alluvial plains while, at the same time, transport was facilitated because of the availability of waterways.[28] In the ancient Orient, as elsewhere, merchants, craftsmen, and their escorts travel along accessible trade routes and conquests add forced labor and foreign wives—and with them race mixture—to the elements making for widening contacts and profound transformations.

If historical change is not immanent, it is likewise not technological. In Braidwood's words, "the great change between pre-civilization and civilized human life came in realms of culture other than the technological and economic," that is, in the realm of the social, of new institutions, new modes of thought, new loyalties.[29] It came through social action and through man, the actor. The role of material innovations is acknowledged, but what counts are merchants, not ships, craftsmen, not tools, conquerors, not armaments. Inventions are relevant inasmuch as they open new horizons, promote new contacts, introduce new varieties of contact. This is especially true concerning the inventions of writing and money. The introduction of abstract symbols for communication and exchange is a symbol in itself for the supersession of the concrete and immediate relationships which permeate the familial society by the more generalized and remote relationships which are the hallmark of civilization. Writing and money are twins; they stand for the transition from quality to quantity, from simple coordination to complex unity.[30] The city is the place where these contact situations occur. Once they are institutionalized, "a certain degree of cultural tolerance" is achieved which makes further adjustments comparatively easy.[31]

The King's City and the Citizen's City. V. Gordon Childe's ten "criteria for cities" imply a more inclusive organization of society as a result of interaction.[32] Outwardly, according to Childe, a city can be recognized because it is larger and more densely populated than other settlements, but this is already the result of effective accumulation by primary producers and the presence of specialists. Those not engaged in food production are supported by the surplus accumulated in the temple or royal granary, with the resulting social power expressed in monumental buildings and other artistic creations, and made effective in systems of recording and writing and the calendrical and mathematical sciences which are their corollaries. Other parts of the surplus are used for the importation of raw materials. Consequently, the city is described as "a community to which a craftsman could belong politically as well as economically" because, in addition to gaining access to raw materials, he was "guaranteed security in a state organization based on residence rather than kinship." In terms of a theory of social change, Childe's summary amounts to saying that customary relations among blood-brothers were not immediately superseded by competitive relations in the market place (as is implied in the theoretical views about the growth of cities of Robert E. Park and his students at the University of Chicago), but by a society under the aegis of kingship. Initially, there was no free market, no independent entrepreneurship.[33] As Alfred Weber has suggested, the totemistic magic of the substratum of cultivators became subordinated to the rational bureaucracy of the rulers. The hunter-ruler, established as priest-king, organized, commissioned, protected, rewarded and punished. The cultivators were taxed, the specialists employed.[34] The King's city, or the city-state, became centered around the fortified temple compound as an all-encompassing symbol.

The transformation entailed in this development is momentous. It enables us to understand what is "social" in social change. That everything changes is an old insight. Climatic conditions or other aspects of the geographic environment may change. Technologies may change, that is, inventions may be introduced. Property relations may change, either in response to geographic or technological changes or in response to political upheavals, such as war or conquest. Ideologies may change as a result of these transformations, or else, changes in idea systems, especially notions of a religious nature, may of themselves bring about profound transformations in other spheres of life. But all these aspects of change are incomplete from a sociological point of view because they do not lay bare the processes through which social change is enacted. *Change, to be social, must connote a significant variation from accustomed patterns of interaction and the generation of new loyalties resulting from new contacts.* This is precisely what occurs when families, clans and tribes, for whatever reasons, draw together and swear a solemn oath of allegiance over a burning fire upon a newly erected altar to a god who is to be the guarantor of peace among them and the protector of them all, the god of the city. This ceremony symbolizes the absorption of older and narrower loyalties into more inclusive patterns of association. Fustel de Coulanges relates that each kinship group retained its house-god, as it were, but added to it the overarching bond of citizenship.[35]

In this context, it matters little whether the citizen's city was already foreshadowed in the King's city, especially in Mesopotamia—as Frankfort maintains[36]—or whether its growth occurred in Greece and Rome, or whether it was fully developed only in the European Middle Ages. Historically speaking, a good case can be made for either contention. Personal rule was never abolished east of Athens, and even Roman citizenship excluded slaves. But personal rule as well as self-rule by an independent citizenry is territorially organized and rationally motivated. The Kings of Erech or Lagash, and later the rulers of Akkad, Assyria, and Babylonia, represented everybody within their domain, irrespective of clannish affiliation.[37] In Athens and Rome the traditional organization founded on birth (*ethnos*) in the course of time was replaced by a new order, based either on locality (*demos,* from which the term democracy is derived) or on social class, defined by property criteria.[38] And because the transmission of customary wisdom from one generation to another does not serve where social integration must proceed beyond the affirmation of blood ties, rational (that is, codified) law first complements and then supplants sacred usage. This means that social imitation, instead of being directed toward the ancestors and the continuation of a hallowed past, receives a momentum which may throw it even beyond legality in the direction of the imitation of creative ("charismatic") personalities who show the way into the future.[39] The "disenchantment" of the world which this process entails and the subsequent rationalization of all social processes may then awaken a craving for unrestricted and unconditional leadership. But this is a late development, typical of mass societies.

The analysis of the emergent city confirms our initial contention. The unqualified concept of culture is an inadequate tool for the understanding of social change because it fails to account for the difference between a unified simple culture and that complex interpenetration of cultures which is called a civilization. As clans associate with each other in cities, more than a mere change from one culture to another takes place. The word civilization, says Morris R. Cohen, embodies "our highest attainments and sets them apart from the attainments of more primitive peoples.[40] The difference is due to federation and fusion on a large scale. What we have in mind is not "primitive fusion," but the merger of traits and interests in a complex society. Thus, Mediterranean civilization represents a merger of Greek, Latin, and Germanic with Phoenician, Hebraic, and Arabic elements, upon all of which Christianity and Islam were superimposed. Within this edifice, a variety of old regionalisms were preserved and new ones established. However, political unity is merely a reminiscence in the area between Gibraltar and the Turkish Straits. Nearer home, American society is held together by a political union, shot through, however, with divergencies of race, creed, section, ethnicity, socio-economic class, party allegiance, and other subdivisions. Moreover, American civilization combines culture traits which originated in many parts of the world.[41]

In brief, whether in the Sumerian and Akkadian city-states of Mesopotamia, or in Rome with its hospitable Pantheon, or in teeming contemporary America, civilization must be understood as a vastly heterogeneous culture of cultures—from the point of view of pre-urbanites a new departure in history. Terms like "diffusion," "borrowing," even "acculturation," do not seem to be sufficient to describe what is happening. More adequate is Godfrey and Monica Wilson's designation of a fragmentation or expansion of an existing society, that is, a diminution or an increase in *scale,* as the mark of change and of societies which are "wide scale" as "civilized."[42] To summarize: *Isolated tribal and local cultures, held together by blood ties and grouped around a single configuration of traits, are one thing; a complex civilization, comprising a multitude of interlocking associations, is another*. Its emergence marks a change *of* a system, not only *within* a system.[43]

Federation, Fusion, and Anomie

Rome and America. It is not enough to say that change arises from contact and that it involves an increase or decrease in scale. Historically both these aspects are closely connected, and their combination requires a further departure. In the ancient Mediterranean world, according to Fustel De Coulanges, the confederation of two or more tribes or clans into a city would have foundered on the fact that a stranger would have been excluded from the participating groups because he prayed to other gods. A new worship had to be proclaimed, a new moral order established. "The tribes that united to form a city," says Fustel de Coulanges, "never failed to light a sacred fire, and to adopt a common religion."[44] Romulus is reported to have done this when he founded Rome.[45] In addition, each of the men of Alba who were co-founders with Romulus, contributed a clod of earth from ancestral soil; as these clods mingled, sanction was given to a new societal unit. We call this the process of *federation,* as distinct from the process of *fusion* which is like-wise observed in cities and, generally, in complex civilizations. It so happens that Rome offers an example for both. While the citizen's city was founded on the Palatine, an asylum was created at the foot of Capitoline hill and to it came, to quote Livy, "a heterogeneous crowd of people from neighboring regions, a confused mixture of free men and slaves, all seeking novelty. . . ."[46] Fusion and confusion are seen here closely related, with the sequence working either way. An atomized mass of footloose people cannot be federated, it can only be fused; at the same time, the merger of disparate parts that are bound to each other by material interests rather than by shared moral values, may be-come another source of confusion. *In the latter case, the citizen's city is trans-formed into the anomic city.*

In Rome, the heterogeneous plebs was fused into an independent societal unit by the institution of the tribuneship, then federated with the Patrician clans who had formed a "city," that is, their own federation previously; after a struggle lasting four centuries, Patricians and Plebeians coalesced in the period of the late Republic. When the fusionist process was completed, the first mass society in history had come into existence. Imperial Rome has been described as a melting pot where all comers were subjected to processes of assimilation while "the Roman proper was submerged . . . by the multitude of provincials bringing with them from every corner of the universe their speech, their manners, their customs, and their superstitions."[47] The common denominator was lost and disintegration grew apace. As we observe the emergence of civilization in Mesopotamia, so do we recognize in Rome the processes of federation, fusion and anomie which—potentially and actually—are present in every civilization.

Although space does not permit elaboration, a brief comparative glance at some major efforts directed at the analysis of our own society may be in order. In America, the fusionist "melting pot" philosophy has been challenged by various theories of pluralism.[48] In addition, recent urban studies have shown that kinship ties continue to be a potent factor among 73 to 84 per cent of low as well as high class populations in Detroit, Los Angeles, San Francisco and New Haven.[49] But this does not imply that individuation, even disintegra-tion, and the concomitant as well as consequent sway of the mass media are not potent factors in the situation. Louis Wirth's famous definition of a city as "a relatively large, dense, and permanent settlement of socially hetero-geneous individuals"—with emphasis on *individuals*—retains validity, but it is obvious that it refers chiefly to the anomic city.[50] Wirth's definition is based on Robert E. Park's concept of civilization as a symbiotic or associational relationship, predominantly economic and political in character, and devoid of the "moral order" which permeates small groups with a homogeneous cultural content. People of divergent cultures, Park maintains, coexist in cities, but in moral isolation.[51] Robert C. Angell, on the other hand, goes beyond Park and Wirth insofar as his theory of moral integration in large cities searches for the citizen's city behind the veil of the anomic city.[52] In finding moral integration impaired by ethnic, especially racial, heterogeneity and by a pronounced degree of social mobility, Angell's analysis, although referring only to American cities, is consistent with the recorded experience from earlier civilizations.

Expansion of Urbanism. The American city must be seen as a variant of old world patterns. In the European middle ages, the process of transculturation, which had begun in antiquity, was resumed and carried further.[53] Compared with African tribesmen or with the pre-Columbian Indians of America, the peasantry of medieval Europe was merely a loosely organized mass of poor people scattered over the countryside. Those who escaped from manorial bonds carried no supernatural obligations with them; footloose individuals could repair to a city, join in voluntary associations with others with whom they had nothing in common but their trade, and thus establish a community based predominantly on economic interests.[54] Subsequently, the expansion of foreign trade fostered industrial development and the rise of the middle classes in nation-states and empires, until the market-place society, in ever widening circles, engulfed the familial society everywhere. The city grew out of bounds, not only to become "urban region" and "megalopolis," but to fill out the whole expanse of advanced societies. In the United States of today, people may live in dense or scattered settlements ecologically, but they are all urbanites sociologically. In terms of ecology, the modern city may be losing its "external and formal structure," but in terms of social organization "the new community represented by the nation" is nothing but a continuation of the city on a vastly enlarged scale.[55] The same is true in terms of historical development. Although not unchecked and even reversed at times, a powerful trend runs from homogeneous to complex, from communal to associational, from clan to city, and from there to the society of the industrialized nation-state. The urban middle classes are the banner-bearers of nationalism as well as the exponents of rationalism. Wherever social change is cast in this mold, a society is exposed to the danger of over-extension and anomie. But where this danger is avoided, the varied cultural heritage carried by migrants from small places to metropolitan areas is not simply superseded and cast aside, but becomes part and parcel of a new and inclusive civilization.

African Laboratory. If we compare the oldest cities in the western world, those in the ancient Near East and in the Mediterranean region, with the newest cities that have emerged in our time, the cities of Africa, the historical model which the older cities provide, will have to be modified. Two considerations apply to a comparative evaluation of this kind. The oldest cities provide us with mute archaeological evidence, that is, with the material manifestations of a civilization rather than with living evidence; even where scanty literary documentation exists, conclusions referring to human interaction are reached chiefly by inference. By contrast, a multitude of actions can be observed and analyzed on the contemporary scene. Further, the more we proceed in history, the more do we have to reckon with "combined development." The theory of combined development states that a backward country, in assimilating the material and intellectual achievements of advanced countries, does not necessarily reproduce all the stages of their past. It may pass over intermediate steps and combine them in one large step.[56] The vast laboratory of social change which is modern Africa is a case in point. If one reviews the literature on detribalization, urbanization and social change in Africa, a number of seemingly contradictory trends may be ascertained.[57]

1. The African city, like any other city, creates a society on a larger scale, initiating contacts with strangers, developing marginal individuals, and resulting in a wide network of human relations. The division of labor in commercial, industrial, and administrative activities makes for new experience and offers an "opportunity to choose" (Balandier). Money becomes a measurement of value. Tribal controls and customary behavior are weakened by the very fact of translocation, but also because isolated migrants or small family groups, not entire tribal units, enter the city. Especially in mining towns, for instance in the Rhodesian copper belt, where the sex ratio is high and up to 70 per cent or more of the labor force is nonpermanent (Mitchell), social disorganization, as measured by a high incidence of illegitimacy, disease, alcoholism, petty quarrelling and serious crime, is rampant. The coincidence of high mobility, low status and excessive segmentality, if accompanied by attrition in kinship contacts, may result in anomie.[58] In some places, rootlessness and frustration are indicated by the prevalence of magic practices and messianic cults.

2. Elsewhere, especially in the cities of West Africa, where there is less coming and going but hardly less heterogeneity than in some of the urban areas of central and East Africa, a reintegrative challenge to disintegration is more readily at hand. In these cities, work-groups, cliques and gangs may be fashioned into occupational and recreational associations, which under favorable circumstances grow into sport clubs, craft guilds and labor unions. Also, Islam seems to be a reintegrative force of this kind. In these instances, new lines of responsibility and loyalty, replacing lineage connections, are in evidence (Balandier, Banton, Forde, Little). There are instances of intertribal marriages in the higher strata and of intermingling leading to marital unions of some duration in the lower strata, but this does not appear to be a frequent occurrence. On the whole, "coexistence" rather than "mixing" is the rule (Forde, Comhaire, and *Introduction to Urbanization in Tropical Africa*, I).

3. There are indications that tribal divisions are being replaced by economic divisions, but the formation of voluntary associations, which is part of the replacement, does not necessarily imply intertribal fusion. Where membership in associations is restricted to people of one tribe or where particular tribes

specialize in particular occupations, the resulting social structure remains implicitly dominated by kinship (Balandier, Banton). In all these instances, while the chieftain's or the elder's authority, as measured by such indices as lack of residential propinquity, severance of personal relationships and independent source of income, is weakened (Hellman), ethnic cohesion is almost always maintained, and is frequently strengthened.

4. Even where migration to urban areas has been on an individual basis, secondary kin groups in the form of extended families have emerged as a potent structural element in the life of urban natives in Africa (Comhaire, Marris). In such widely scattered places as Timbuctoo in Mali, Lagos in Nigeria, Brazzaville, Leopoldville, Stanleyville in the Congo, kinsmen tend to live as close to each other as possible, visit each other, take counsel with each other, and extend aid and assistance to those among them who are in need. A "skeleton structure" deriving from the tribal system remains operative even in the disruptive environment of a South African slum (Hellman).

5. Beyond the kin groups, larger ethnic units are making their appearance. As a rule, the laboring population is composed of individuals from many tribes and localities, but a tribe native to the region where the city is located usually prevails numerically and dominates politically. The dominant tribe may combine sub-tribes into a larger ethnic group, as is the case with the Bakongos in Leopoldville, or it may assimilate isolated members of minority tribes, especially young males, into its lower strata, as is the case with the Ganda and Soga in Kampala, Uganda (Comhaire, C. and R. Sofer). In other instances, a *lingua franca* provides a loose bond, for instance the Bemba language in the Rhodesian copper belt (Powdermaker). The process is comparable to the emergence of an Italian-American group in American cities where there had been merely village compatriots or, at best, men with provincial loyalties previously.

6. Modern African cities contain large and heterogeneous racial and ethnic groupings side by side. In East and Central African cities, one finds Europeans as technicians and administrators, East Indians and Greeks as traders, and a fluctuating mass of African laborers of various backgrounds (Denis, C. and R. Sofer, Southall, Gutkind). In West Africa, Libanese and Haussa act as intermediaries, while educated Africans have taken possession of the administrative apparatus. Some of these elites are detribalized or even racially mixed, as the "Creoles" in Sierra Leone (Banton). In Portuguese Africa, the dividing line runs between *assimilados* and *indigenos* (Duffy). Everywhere, races and ethnic groups are residentially segregated, but in the Union of South Africa, Bantus, "Coloureds," East Indians, Boers and people of British descent are kept apart not only by custom but—as far as non-whites are concerned—also by law. In South Africa, African and "European" populations do not even dwell together within the limits of the same city.

In comparison with the cities of antiquity and the European cities of the middle ages, African cities are distinguished by the fact that no sacred fire is kindled, no common allegiance generated. The pluralism of family groups and ethnic units is not transcended; the citizen's city is conspicuous by its absence. The reason is that urbanization in Africa, instead of being an independent process, is coincidental with industrialization and the formation of nation-states.[59] This is what is indicated by the term "combined development." The processes of federation and fusion take place on a more inclusive level. Some African nations, such as Morocco, Nigeria, Kenya, possibly the Congo, are being initiated by federated tribes, but this is not the whole story. Initially, the Moroccan nation, as one of its contemporary spokesmen, Allal El Fassi, asserts, may have been the outgrowth of a federation of Arabic-speaking and Berber-speaking tribes, but more recently the process of unification has been borne along by Arabized townspeople whose tribal affiliations were blurred.[60] Elsewhere in Africa, especially in Ghana, reluctant tribes are immediately forced into a national mold. In most instances, fusion does not so much follow federation, but takes place simultaneously with it, or even without it. In all instances, the new moral order is nation-wide, if not continent-wide, in scope. Consequently, if anomie is to be avoided, an African civilization must be expected to emerge.

Civilization and the Moral Order

The African development, which we have compared with a model of the city of antiquity, is in itself paradigmatic inasfar as it exemplifies the forces of disintegration and reintegration which are present in a changing society. This introduces a social-psychological consideration into what has been, on the whole, a structural treatment of the topic. The transition from a mono-cultural to a multicultural society, as well as any kind of secondary change within a civilization, is marked by unrest. Accelerated mobility, the mixture of racial and ethnic strains, and the rapid succession of fads and fashions once the cultural anchors are lifted bring about a confusion of values and a desire to reestablish a sense of direction. At first, when previously shared norms are challenged and break down as a consequence of their encounter with conflicting norms, diffuse mass behavior takes the place of the corroded moral order. But when new ideologies rise to cope with the situation, a new moral order is born with them.[61] Thus, the city of antiquity, founded upon an altar of altars and grouped around a temple compound, brought forth its own moral order, encompassing the more circumscribed normative systems which it superseded. Amidst violent dissensions, it created its own loyalty. The same is true of the guild-dominated medieval city in which new attachments, transcending and even supplanting feudal and ecclesiastical bonds, were forged. Later, nation-states and their nationalisms outgrew regional and other specialized allegiances, as the history of England, France and the United States and many other countries amply demonstrates. In our time, the "two nations" of the rich and the poor, over whom the King of England ruled earlier in the nineteenth century, are about to be reconciled in a new industrial society.[62]

It may be of interest to return to Robert E. Park at this point. Not unlike the nineteenth-century pessimists, he regards civilization as corrosive of the moral order. In many of his writings, Park emphasizes that the territorially organized society of cities, nation-states and empires, centering around the "market place," is held together by material interests while moral cohesion, typified by familial bonds, is formed inside, not between, small groups, or folk-societies. Luckily at variance with this position, Park adopts another point of view in his paper on "The Nature of Race Relations."[63] He points out there that, although people in the modern world "are no longer bound and united as people once were by familial and tribal ties," they are, nevertheless, "profoundly affected by sentiments of nationality," and he adds that most of our racial conflicts are conflicts of "we" groups and "they" groups which are, however, "integral parts of a great cosmopolitan and free society." In these words, the sequential concept of civilization is upheld and the possibility of a moral order in large-scale civilizations acknowledged.

In conclusion, we would like to reiterate that the rise of cities, and generally of inclusive civilizations, provides a historically ascertainable paradigm of social change. *The concept of civilization is crucial because a multicultural civilizational system represents a different principle of social organization than a monocultural tribal system: a monocultural society consists of multipurpose kinship roles, a multicultural society consists of differentiated economic roles.* At the same time, we must go beyond MacIver and Park in emphasizing that civilization connotes more than a technological accumulation or a symbiotic relationship. For example, an Andaman Islander or a Marquesan may have his "basic personality" defined exclusively by the fact that he was brought up as an Andaman Islander or a Marquesan, but a New Yorker's "basic personality," if such a thing exists, is not so easily circumscribed. He has a great many ingredients "bred" into him and much depends on what combination of components he represents. On the other hand, a metropolitan city, such as New York, includes not only Tammany Hall and the Stock Exchange, the St. Patrick's Day Parade and the United Jewish Appeal, the Abyssinian Baptist Church and the West Side Tennis Club, but adds to these segmental institutions others, like schools and courts, and a value system and behavior pattern which are common to all. *A unifying moral order is not incompatible with cultural diversity.*

However, a question mark hangs over any kind of change and transformation in human affairs. The moral order of a city or a nation grows more slowly than the specialized institutions which compose and guarantee the coexistence of its constituent parts. This lag between the growth of institutions and their integration into an inclusive moral order is the true "cultural lag." Unfortunately, while we have not yet mastered the task of the moral integration of our cities, we are faced with the same problem on a grander scale, as we change from a national to a world order. The very probability that Dante's vision (in *De Monarchia*) of civilization as *humana civilitas* may be approaching realization, makes us aware of the limitations interposed by human nature. The technological and symbiotic aspects of a world order are all around us, but the normative aspects, that is, the morality without which coexistence does not work, are but feebly indicated. To reconcile the discrepancy, one must know that those who live through a period of change are always at midpoint and uncertain about the way ahead. But, if analogies serve, the alternative is clear that an emerging civilization must generate its own moral order or fail to survive.

Notes

1. Leonard W. Moss and Stephen C. Capannari, *The Black Madonna—An Example of Culture Borrowing*, in this volume.
2. Arnold J. Toynbee, *A Study of History—Reconsiderations*, Vol. XII (London: Oxford University Press, 1961), 273.
3. Pitirim A. Sorokin, *Social and Cultural Dynamics* (New York: American Book Co., 1937), Vol. I, 376–77; cf. Florian Znaniecki, *Cultural Sciences* (Urbana, Ill.: University of Illinois Press, 1952), 398.
4. A. L. Kroeber and Clyde Kluckhohn, "Culture: A Critical Review of Concepts and Definitions," *Papers of the Peabody Museum of American Archaeology and Ethnology* (Cambridge, Mass.: Harvard University), Vol. 47 (1952), No. 1, 43ff.
5. The pertinent literature is critically reviewed by Kenneth V. Lottick, "Some Distinctions between Culture and Civilization as displayed in Sociological Literature," *Social Forces*, Vol. 28, No. 3 (March 1950), 240–250.
6. A. L. Kroeber and Clyde Kluckhohn, *op. cit.*, 147.
7. *Ibid.*, 55.
8. *Ibid.*, 13.
9. Ralph Linton (ed.), *The Science of Man in the World Crisis* (New York: Columbia University Press, 1945), 78.
10. Robert M. MacIver and Charles H. Page, *Society: An Introductory Analysis* (New York: Rinehart, 1949), Chaps. 20–29; Robert M. MacIver, *Social Causation* (Boston: Ginn & Co., 1942), 172ff., 281–282, 284; Robert K. Merton, "Civilization and Culture," *Sociology and Social Research*, 21 (Nov.–Dec. 1936), 103–113.
11. Alfred Weber, *Fundamentals of Culture-Sociology: Social Process, Civilization Process and Culture-Movement*, tr. by G. H. Weltner and C. F. Hirshman (New York: WPA and Columbia University, 1939), 1.
12. Cf. Alvin Boskoff, "Social Change: Major Problems in the Emergence of Theoretical and Research Foci," in Howard Becker and Alvin Boskoff (eds.), *Modern Sociological Theory in Continuity and Change* (New York: Dryden Press, 1957), 281–83.
13. Howard W. Odum, *Understanding Society: The Principles of Dynamic Sociology* (New York: Macmillan, 1947), 261, 281–87. In a later paper, "Folk Sociology as a Subject Field for the Historical Study of the Total Human Society and the Empirical Study of Group Behavior," *Social Forces*, Vol. 31, No. 3 (March 1953), 193–223, Odum defines civilization, somewhat ambiguously, as an "advanced state of culture." But in the earlier work he

says clearly that "modern society has too much civilization and not enough culture" and that "civilization as an end destroys society."

14. Lewis Mumford, *The City in History* (New York: Harcourt, Brace & World Inc., 1961), Chap. 17. However, Mumford recognizes the presence of regenerative forces in metropolitan civilization.

15. MacIver and Page, *op. cit.,* 498–99.

16. *Ibid.,* 630ff.

17. Philip Bagby, *Culture and History: Prolegomena to the Comparative Study of Civilizations* (London: Longmans, Green, 1958), 162–63.

18. Morris R. Cohen, *The Meaning of Human History,* quoted acc. to Ralph Marcus, "Notes on Civilization in Historical Perspective," in Salo W. Baron, Ernest Nagel, and Koppel P. Pinson (eds.), *Freedom and Reason: Studies in Philosophy and Jewish Culture in Memory of Morris R. Cohen* (New York: The Free Press, 1951), 185–186.

19. Robert Redfield, *The Primitive World and its Transformation* (Ithaca, N.Y.: Great Seal Books of Cornell University, 1957), 10, referring to V. Gordon Childe. Among sociologists, Childe's position has been most emphatically accepted by William F. Ogburn and Meyer F. Nimkoff in *Sociology* (Boston: Houghton Mifflin, 3rd ed., 1958), 652.

20. Lewis Mumford, *op. cit.,* 6ff.

21. V. Gordon Childe, *Man Makes Himself* (New York: Mentor Books, 1958), Chap. 7.

22. Lewis Mumford, *op. cit.,* 25ff.; cf. V. Gordon Childe, *op. cit.,* 85.

23. V. Gordon Childe, *Man Makes Himself, op. cit.; What Happened in History* (Hammondsworth: Penguin Books, 1942); "The Birth of Civilization," *Past and Present,* No. 2 (1952); "The Urban Revolution," *Town Planning Review,* Vol. XXI, No. 1 (April 1950); "Civilizations, Cities and Towns," *Antiquity,* Vol. XXI, No. 121 (March 1957); Henri Frankfort, *Kingship and the Gods: A Study of Ancient Near East Religion as the Integration of Society and Nature* (Chicago: University of Chicago Press, 1948); *The Birth of Civilization in the Near East* (New York: Doubleday Anchor Books, 1956); "Town Planning in Mesopotamia," *Town Planning Review,* Vol. XXI, No. 2 (July 1950); Ralph Turner, *The Great Classical Traditions,* Vol. I, *The Ancient Cities,* Vol. II, *The Classical Empires* (New York: McGraw-Hill, 1941); cf. Carl H. Kraeling and Robert M. Adams (eds.), *City Invincible: A Symposium on Urbanization and Cultural Development in the Ancient Near East* (Chicago: University of Chicago Press, 1958), Robert J. Braidwood, *The Near East and the Foundations for Civilization* (Eugene, Oregon: Oregon State System of Higher Education, 1952); and Robert J. Braidwood and Gordon R. Willey (eds.), *Courses toward Urban Life: Archaeological Considerations of Some Cultural Alternates* (Chicago: Aldine Publishing Co., 1962). The date at which the first walled urban settlements appear may perhaps have to be updated, as a result of Kathleen Kenyon's excavations in Jericho. Compare Kathleen Kenyon, *Digging up Jericho: The Results of the Jericho Excavations* (New York: F. Praeger, 1957), as well as her paper, "Jericho and its Setting in Near Eastern History," *Antiquity,* Vol. XXX (1956), and the controversy published in subsequent issues of the same journal.

24. A good sociological summary of the argument is contained in Paul Meadows, "The City, Technology and History," *Social Forces,* Vol. 36, No. 2 (Dec. 1957), 141–147. However, Robert M. Adams, in Carl H. Kraeling and Robert M. Adams, *op. cit.,* 28–30—doubts the "social surplus" theory and

stresses instead the "complementarity of resources" which prevailed in the lower Euphrates and Tigris valley and led to the establishment of distributive institutions in cities.

25. V. Gordon Childe, *Man Makes Himself, op. cit.,* 187.

26. V. Gordon Childe, "The Urban Revolution" in *Town Planning Review* (1950), *op. cit.* Especially the occupation of smith is surrounded by a particular "mystique"; at the same time, as a metallurgical expert, the smith is everywhere in demand.

27. Robert Redfield and Milton B. Singer, "The Cultural Role of Cities," first published in *Economic Development and Social Change,* Vol. 3, No. 1 (1954), 53–73; here quoted from *Man in India,* Vol. 36, No. 3 (July–Sept. 1956), 161–194, Redfield and Singer's argument is contradictory on more than one count. The authors separate the technical from the moral order, but fuse culture and civilization; they speak of "orthogenic" and "heterogenic" "roles" of cities, when these terms actually refer to origin; they blur the difference between "orthogenic" and "heterogenic," on the one hand, and "homogeneous" and heterogeneous," on the other; they fail to show how orthogenic—and homogeneous—cities are at all possible. They may have had in mind autochthonous cities, founded by natives of a region, and cities founded by conquerors or invaders.

28. V. Gordon Childe, *Man Makes Himself, op. cit.,* 115; *What Happened in History, op. cit.,* 96; Henri Frankfort, *The Birth of Civilization in the Near East, op. cit.,* 74 et passim. It should be added that "commerce" and semimilitary expeditions were closely related.

29. Robert J. Braidwood (1958), *op. cit.,* 42.

30. Georg Simmel, *Philosophie des Geldes, Gesammelte Werke,* Vol. 1 (Berlin: Duncker and Humblot, 1958), 190, 290–291, 384. Cf. Ignace J. Gelb, *A Study of Writing* (Chicago: University of Chicago Press, 1952) and Richard Thurnwald, *Black and White in Africa: The Fabric of a New Civilization* (London: G. Routledge & Sons, 1935), 370 et passim. Thurnwald refers to the supersession of clan and family bonds by individualistic behavior patterns through the medium of money.

31. Cf. Robert C. Angell, *Free Society and Moral Crisis* (Ann Arbor: University of Michigan Press, 1958), 150.

32. *Town Planning Review* (1950), *op. cit.;* cf. *What Happened in History, op. cit.,* 91.

33. Karl Polanyi, Konrad Arensberg, Harry W. Pearson, *Trade and Market in the Early Empires: Economics in History and Theory* (New York: The Free Press, 1957), esp. 12ff. and 30ff. However, initial "spurts of commercial activity," based on individual enterprise, are acknowledged by the authors.

34. Alfred Weber, *Kulturgeschichte als Kultursoziologie* (Munich: R. Piper & Co., 1950), 51ff.

35. N. D. Fustel de Coulanges, *The Ancient City: A Study of the Religion, Laws and Institutions of Ancient Greece and Rome* (Garden City, N.Y.: Doubleday & Co., 1956), Book III.

36. Henri Frankfort, *The Birth of Civilization in the Near East, op. cit.,* 77; cf. Thorkild Jacobsen, "Primitive Democracy in Ancient Mesopotamia," *Journal of Near Eastern Studies,* III (Chicago, 1943), 159–72, and A. L. Oppenheim, "Nature of Civilization in Mesopotamia," in Polanyi and Arensberg, *op. cit.,* 30ff.

37. Ignace J. Gelb, "The Function of Language in the Cultural Expansion of Mesopotamian Society," in Carl H. Kraeling and Robert M. Adams, *op.*

cit., 315–328. Gelb stresses the role of a *lingua franca* in the growth of civilizations and empires in the ancient Near East.

38. Jean Comhaire and Werner J. Cahnman, *How Cities Grew* (Madison, N.J.: The Florham Park Press, 1959), 4–6.

39. Robert Redfield, *The Primitive World and its Transformations* (Ithaca, N.Y.: Great Seal Books of Cornell University, 1957), 55, 112, 113, 119, 120, 136. Cf. Arnold J. Toynbee, *op. cit.*, 274. One can say that education in primitive societies stresses continuity while education in multicultural civilizations tends to add education for change.

40. Morris R. Cohen, *op. cit.* Cohen's statement agrees with the definition advanced by Carl Brinckman in "Civilization," *Encyclopedia of the Social Sciences*, 3, 525–529.

41. A. L. Kroeber, "Structure, Function and Pattern in Biology and Anthropology," *The Nature of Culture* (Chicago: University of Chicago Press, 1952), 93. It should be added that Kroeber belongs to those authors who use the terms "culture" and "civilization" interchangeably.

42. Godfrey and Monica Wilson, *The Analysis of Social Change: Based on Observations in Central Africa* (Cambridge: University Press, 1945), 43–44, 59.

43. Cf. Talcott Parsons, *The Social System* (New York: The Free Press, 1951), 486.

44. Fustel de Coulanges, *op. cit.*, 127.

45. *Ibid.*, 134ff.

46. Livy I, 8, 6 quoted acc. to Raymond Bloch, *The Origins of Rome* (London: Thames and Hudson, 1960), 52.

47. Jerôme Carcopino, *Daily Life in Ancient Rome: The People and the City at the Height of the Empire* (New Haven: Yale University Press, 1955), 55–56.

48. The most sophisticated of these theories of pluralism is contained in Horace M. Kallen, *Cultural Pluralism and the American Idea* (Philadelphia: University of Pennsylvania Press, 1956).

49. Morris Axelrod, "Urban Structure and Social Participation," *American Sociological Review*, Vol. 21, No. 1 (Feb. 1956), 13–18; Scott Greer, "Urbanism Reconsidered," *American Sociological Review*, Vol. 21, No. 1 (Feb. 1956), 19–24; Wendell Bell and Marion D. Boat, "Urban Neighborhoods and Informal Social Relations," *American Journal of Sociology*, Vol. 62, No. 4 (January 1957), 391–398; Marvin B. Sussman, "The Help Pattern in the Middle Class Family," *American Sociological Review*, Vol. 18, No. 1 (Feb. 1953), 22–27.

50. Louis Wirth, "Urbanism as a Way of Life," in Paul K. Hatt and Albert J. Reiss, Jr. (eds.), *Cities and Society* (New York: The Free Press, 1957), 46–63; reprinted from the *American Journal of Sociology*, Vol. 44 (July 1938).

51. Everett C. Hughes, et al. (eds.), *The Collected Papers of Robert Ezra Park* (New York: The Free Press, 1952–55), Vol. I, *Race and Culture:* "The Problem of Cultural Differences," 3–14; "Culture and Civilization," 15–23; "Reflections on Communications and Culture," 36–52; Vol. II, *Human Communities:* "The City and Civilization," 128–44; Vol. III, *Society:* "Modern Society," 321–42. Park's concept of civilization, although not clearly formulated, is essentially sequential in nature.

52. Robert C. Angell, "The Moral Integration of American Cities," *American Journal of Sociology*, Vol. LVII, No. 1, Part 2 (July 1951).

53. The term "transculturation" was first used by Fernando Ortiz, *Cuban Counterpoint: Tobacco and Sugar,* transl. by Harriet de Onis (New York: A. A. Knopf, 1947).

54. Henri Pirenne, *Medieval Cities* (New York: Doubleday Anchor Books, n.d.), 86, 87, 94, 153ff. *Medieval Cities* was originally translated in 1925 and published by the Princeton University Press.

55. Don Martindale, "Prefatory Remarks: The Theory of the City," in Max Weber, *The City,* transl. by Don Martindale and Gertrud Neuwirth (New York: The Free Press, 1958), 62. Max Weber uses a twofold model of the citizen's city—the Greek *polis* and the commercial city of the high middle ages. He does not analyze the modern city because urbanism and nationalism become indistinguishable after the seventeenth century.

56. Leon Trotsky, *The Russian Revolution,* selected ed. by F. W. Dupee (Garden City, N.Y.: Doubleday Anchor Books, 1959), Chap. I. The theory of combined development was devised by Trotsky in order to explain why a proletarian revolution does not have to wait for the rise of a mature "bourgeois society"; one may add that it is applicable to underdeveloped areas without a political (Marxist) purpose to justify it.

57. There is a considerable literature pertaining to urbanization and social change in Africa. Compare especially:

Georges Balandier, *Sociologie des Brazzaville Noires* (Paris: Cahiers de la Fondation Nationale des Sciences Politiques, 1955).

Michael Banton, *A Study of Tribal Life in Freetown* (London: Oxford University Press, 1957).

K. A. Busia, *Report on a Social Survey of Secondi-Takoradi* (London and Accra: Crown Agents for the Colonies, on behalf of the Government of the Gold Coast, 1950).

Jean L. Comhaire, "Economic Change and the Extended Family," *Annals of the American Academy of Political and Social Science,* Vol. 305 (May 1956), 45–52.

Jean L. Comhaire, "Some Aspects of Urbanization in the Belgian Congo," *American Journal of Sociology,* Vol. LXII, No. 1 (July 1956), 8–13.

Jacques Denis, *Le Phenomène urbain en Afrique Centrale* (Bruxelles: Academie Royale des Sciences Colonialles, 1959).

James Duffy, *Portuguese Africa* (Cambridge: Harvard University Press, 1959).

Walter Elkan, *Migrants and Proletarians. Urban Labour in the Economic Development of Uganda* (London: Oxford University Press, 1960).

Daryll Forde (ed.), *Social Implications of Industrialization and Urbanization in Africa South of the Sahara* (Paris: Tensions and Technology Series, UNESCO 1956): Georges Balandier, "Urbanism in West and Central Africa: The Scope and Aims of Research," 495–509.

Daryll Forde, "Social Aspects of Urbanization and Industrialization in Africa: A General Overview," *ibid.,* 11–52.

Ellen Hellman, "The Development of Social Groupings among Urban Africans in the Union of South Africa," *ibid.,* 724–743.

G. Malengreau, "Observations on the Orientation of Sociological Researches in African Urban Centers, with Reference to the Situation in the Belgian Congo," *ibid.,* 724–743.

Meran McCulloch, "Survey of Recent and Current Field Studies on the Social Effects of Economic Development in Inter-tropical Africa," *ibid.,* 624–537.

P. Mercier, "An Experimental Investigation into Occupational and Social Categories in Dakar," *ibid.,* 510–523.

J. C. Mitchell, "Urbanization, Detribalization and Stabilization in Southern Africa," *ibid.,* 693–724.

V. G. Pons, "The Changing Significance of Ethnic Affiliation and Westernization in the African Settlement Patterns in Stanleyville," *ibid.,* 638–669.

C. Sofer, "Urban Social Structure and Working Group Behavior in Jinja, Uganda," *ibid.,* 590–612.

C. Sofer, "Adaptation Problems of Africans in an Early Phase of Industrialization at Jinja, Uganda," *ibid.,* 613–623.

A. W. Southall, "Determinants of the Social Structure of African Urban Populations, with Special Reference to Kampala, Uganda," *ibid.,* 557–578.

Max Gluckman, *Custom and Conflict in Africa* (New York: The Free Press, 1955).

Germand Grévisse, *La Centre extra-coutumier d'Elisabethville* (Bruxelles: Institut royal colonial belge, 1951).

Peter W. Gutkind, "Congestion and Overcrowding: An African Urban Problem," *Human Organization,* Vol. 19, No. 3 (Fall 1960).

Ellen Hellman, *Rooiyard: A Sociological Survey of an Urban Native Slumyard* (Capetown and Livingstone: Rhodes-Livingstone Papers, No. 13), 1948.

Melville J. Herskovits, *The Human Factor in Changing Africa* (New York: A. A. Knopf, 1962), 259–297.

Guy Hunter, *The New Societies of Tropical Africa* (London: Oxford University Press, 1962).

Jean-Paul Lebeuf, "Centres Urbains d'Afrique Equatoriale Française," *Africa,* Vol. XXIII, No. 1, (Oct. 1953), 285–297.

Kenneth L. Little, "The Study of Social Change in British West Africa," *Africa,* Vol. XXIII (Jan. 1953), 274–284.

Kenneth L. Little, "The Role of Voluntary Associations in West African Urbanization," *American Anthropologist,* Vol. 59, No. 4 (Aug. 1957), 579–596.

Kenneth L. Little, "A Study of Modern Social Change in a West African Community," in Morton H. Fried, *Readings in Anthropology, Linguistics and Archeology,* Vol. II (New York: Thomas Y. Crowell, 1959), 379–380.

Kenneth L. Little, "The West African Town: Its Social Basis," *Diogenes,* No. 29 (Spring 1960), 16–31.

P. C. Lloyd, "The Yoruba Town Today," *American Sociological Review,* Vol. 7, No. 1, 1959.

P. C. Lloyd, "Craft Organization in Yoruba Towns," *Africa,* Vol. XXIII, No. 1 (Jan. 1953), 30–44.

Peter Marris, "Slum Clearance and Family Life in Lagos," *Human Organization,* Vol. 19, No. 3 (Fall 1960), 123–128.

David F. McCall, "Dynamics of Urbanization in Africa," in Simon and Phoebe Ottenberg (eds.), *Cultures and Societies of Africa* (New York: Random House, 1960), 522–535.

Horace Miner, *The Primitive City of Timbuctoo* (Princeton: Princeton University Press, 1953).

Hortense Powdermaker, *Coppertown—Changing Africa* (New York and Evanston: Harper and Row, 1962).

Audrey I. Richards, *Economic Development and Tribal Change* (Cambridge: East African Institute of Political Research, 1954).

Hugh H. Smythe, "Social Change in Africa," *American Journal of Economics and Sociology,* Vol. 19 (January 1960), 193–206.

Cyrill and Rhona Sofer, *Jinja Transformed: A Social Survey of a Multiracial Township* (Kampala, Uganda: East African Institute of Social Research, 1955).

A. W. Southall and P. C. W. Gutkind, *Townsmen in the Making: Kampala and its Suburbs* (Kampala, Uganda: East African Institute of Social Research, 1957).

"Leopoldville and Lagos: Comparative Study of Urban Conditions in 1960," *U.N. Economic Bulletin for Africa,* Vol. 1, No. 2 (Addis Ababa, U.N. Economic Comm. for Africa, June 1961), 50–65.

Introduction to the Problems of Urbanization in Tropical Africa, I, II (Addis Ababa: U.N. Economic Comm. for Africa, April-May 1962), *passim.*

58. A. W. Southall, *The Theory of Urban Sociology,* an address given before a conference held at the East African Institute of Social Research, Kampala, Uganda, January, 1957 (mimeo.).

59. A. W. Southall, *op. cit.,* Southall's theory refers to urban regions in an industrial society, that is, to a late stage in urban development. It is lacking historical perspective. But it must be taken into consideration that the theory was conceived in Africa where urbanization and industrialization tend to coincide.

60. Allal El-Fassi, "La Nation Marocaine," *Études Mediterranéens,* 1957, No. 1, 21–25.

61. The process has been described and analyzed in Herbert Blumer, "Collective Behavior," A. M. Lee (ed.), *Principles of Sociology* (New York: Barnes and Noble, 1951), 165–222. In his monograph on the British Cotton Industry, Neil J. Smelser develops a seven-step "sequence of structural differentiation" which bears close similarity to Blumer's sequence from the breakdown of an established order through various stages and manifestations of collective behavior and social movements to a "new order of life." Smelser, using different terminology, proceeds from "dissatisfaction" through "new ideas" to the routinization of the "usual patterns of performance." However, Blumer moves from experience to theory while Smelser descends to the data from a theoretical *a priori.* At any rate, Smelser's theory would seem to be social-psychological rather than structural in nature. Cf. Neil J. Smelser, *Social Change in the Industrial Revolution: An Application of Theory to the British Cotton Industry* (Chicago: The University of Chicago Press, 1959), 15–16.

62. T. S. Ashton, *The Industrial Revolution, 1760–1830* (London: Oxford University Press, 1948); Karl Polanyi, *The Great Transformation* (Boston: Beacon Press, 1957); Reinhard Bendix, *Work and Authority in Industry: Ideologies of Management in the Course of Industrialization* (New York: Wiley & Sons, 1956); Neil J. Smelser, *op. cit.*

63. Robert E. Park, *Collected Papers, op. cit.,* Vol. I, 81–116.

Werner J. Cahnman   SOCIOLOGY AND HISTORY:
and Alvin Boskoff   REVIEW AND OUTLOOK

THE CONSCIENTIOUS READER may wish to pause and reflect upon the meaning of the preceding discussions and selections, and he may wonder how he can utilize what he has learned. If he seeks to compare the viewpoint of this volume with his previous understanding of historical works and sociological writings, he may conclude that these two sources are quite different in intent and execution. In some respects, the impression will not be entirely incorrect because the thinking of many of us is compartmentalized: history here, sociology there. This is what the division of labor seems to demand and what academic tradition most assuredly upholds. But we believe that the ways in which history and sociology are similar and complementary are as significant as the avowed differences, and that the specialized scholar ought to pause occasionally and look about to see whether his strivings and findings are in line with the general concerns of mankind. We will emphasize these points once more by drawing attention to the widely diversified research literature which, to one degree or another, is sociological in concept and historical in execution. Since we cannot hope to be exhaustive, we will restrict ourselves to classics in the field of research, which may serve as examples, and to the pertinent literature which we have consulted and which may not have been quoted elsewhere in this volume. We hope thereby to facilitate some practical uses and applications of the insights gained in the preceding pages.

Classic Examples

In retrospect, writers who have used a sociological approach to historical materials—whether these scholars can be called sociologists or historians—seem to be commonly concerned with one or more of two or three basic problems. One such focus has been the understanding of the emergence and development of specific societies, particularly those undergoing the demographic, economic, and social transformations of urbanization. Historians of renown—such as Coulanges, Glotz, Pirenne, Maunier, Maitland, Stephenson, and Bloch[1]—focused on the classical or the medieval period of European history for clues to causal conditions and characteristic structural adaptations to social change, especially to urbanization. In this country, Adna F. Weber's pioneering study, although historical only in a restricted sense, deserves particular mention.[2] More recently, American historians have pursued problems comparable to those of the European authors in the analysis of typical developmental sequences during the eighteenth and nineteenth centuries, chiefly (but not exclusively) for a limited number of eastern and Ohio Valley cities.[3]

But this general orientation has also been applied to a number of *contemporary* urban areas by sociologists, social anthropologists, historians, social geographers, and political scientists. Using such sources as newspapers, census materials, memoirs, and public records, these students of the phenomena of urbanism and industrialism have traced community development (1) through historical analyses of political, economic, and other institutions and in many cases through (2) detailed investigation of trends in stratification and the power structure. The Lynds' two studies of "Middletown" are still unequalled for perceptive blending of various types of information and for the resultant cohesive picture of an urban community over a forty-five year span.[4] By comparing six major areas of life in Muncie, Indiana, in 1890, 1924, and 1935, the Lynds accomplished their avowed purpose; namely, to study the effects of industrialization on community life, in a way which has not been surpassed by later efforts. On the other hand, an equally famous study of the much older community of Newburyport, Massachusetts—"Yankee City"— has fallen short of fruitful contribution to our knowledge because the authors "decided to use no previous summaries of data collected by anyone else (maps, handbooks, histories, etc.) until . . . [they] had formed . . . [their] own opinion of the city."[5] As a result, Warner and his associates had to accept uncritically the judgments of the people of Yankee City about their town, thereby confounding appearance and reality.[6]

A full listing of historically oriented community studies is of course beyond our scope.[7] However, mention should be made of Liston Pope's perspicacious account of the social history of Gastonia and its relation to violence in the 1920s; Horace Miner's and Everett C. Hughes' studies of French Canadian communities in transition; Elin Anderson's detailed survey of ethnic and class relations in Burlington, Vermont; and Pauline Young's study of the development of a sectarian enclave in Los Angeles. In addition, useful case studies may be found in Firey's historically oriented description of selected Boston neighborhoods, Lowry Nelson's analysis of change in the Mormon community, Whyte's account of an Italian-American "street corner society," Blanchard's comprehensive historical-ecological survey of Grenoble, Roger Le Tourneau's multifaceted case study of Fez in Morocco, Margaret Stacey's study of economic and stratificational changes in Banbury, and Robert Dahl's recent meticulous review of changes in the community power structure of New Haven.[8] Briefer research reports, like those on New Orleans (Gilmore), La Paz (Leonard), Guatemala City (Caplow), Birmingham and Lyons (Asa Briggs), the pre-industrial Chinese city (Eberhard), the city in economically advanced areas (Lampard), and others are too numerous to be exhaustively recorded.[9] But Pinkney's paper "Urban Studies and the Historian," referring to nineteenth-century Paris, ought to be especially mentioned because it points to the rich mine of data on urban processes which still lies unused.[10]

A highly complex field of investigation is encountered in the area of culture case studies. Here, the skills of the historian and the sociologist are demanded in equal measure because the implications of studies of this kind carry the researcher beyond the uniqueness of the case under investigation. Advisedly, we speak of "implications" rather than "conclusions" because the idiographic case can be enlarged into a nomothetic statement only in a tentative manner. The principles underlying culture case studies have been formulated by Howard Becker,[11] but the masters of factual analysis are Jacob Burckhardt, Johan Huizinga, Max Weber, Alexis de Tocqueville, James B. Bryce, Gilberto Freyre, Fernando Ortiz, and Americo Castro;[12] others, like Toynbee, the Beards, Potter, Brogan, Riesman, Madariaga, and Wittfogel may likewise be mentioned.[13] Jacob Burckhardt clearly states that his intention is neither that of the recording chronologist nor of the philosopher of history whose mind is fixed upon stages of progress; he looks at "the recurrent, the constant, the typical" as something which can be accepted and understood.[14] Consequently, as Benjamin Nelson has shown, Burckhardt does not tell the *story* of the fourteenth, fifteenth, and sixteenth centuries in Italy; he speaks about states of mind and underlying motivational patterns, emphasizing the emergence of the unbridled individual as the main theme of the period. The situation is unique, but the implications can be observed in many areas of modern life.

The theme which is posed by *The Civilization of the Renaissance in Italy* is taken up, although somewhat inconclusively, by Johan Huizinga's *Waning of the Middle Ages* and, focusing on the conscience of a Christian, in Max Weber's oft-quoted monograph on the Protestant ethic. In a way, all of Max Weber's writings are the fragments of a culture case study which encompasses the entirety of Western civilization under a specific principle of organization. In the field of American studies, Tocqueville, in the Preface to the second volume of *Democracy in America,* recognizes the existence of a great many causes for the emergence of "inclinations and ideas" in the area of his investigation, but confesses that he has concentrated on a single causative factor of wide applicability, when he endeavored to show how far such "inclinations and ideas" (institutions, in modern parlance) "are affected by the equality of men's conditions."[15] Similarly, Gilberto Freyre has interpreted Brazilian society in the light of the single "synthetic principle" of cultural fusion and racial amalgamation. A related theme appears in Americo Castro's analysis of the structure of Spanish history. However, one misses a unifying theme in Max Lerner's *America as a Civilization.*[16]

A third general type of investigation in which sociological and historical orientations are fruitfully combined concerns the description and analysis of the emergence of institutional patterns and especially of interactions between major institutions in given societies. Frequently, this interest has been expressed in studies of the relation between economic and political systems, religious and political or economic systems, and religious and scientific patterns. The effective link between the sociological and historical approaches in such studies seems to have been a concern for *changes* in the interaction of institutions and the *consequences* of such changes for the operation of specific societies.[17]

The classic instances of this combined orientation would include Maine's treatise on *Ancient Law,* Coulanges' analysis of the religious roots of *The Ancient City,* Pirenne's various works on the social and economic history of West European towns and nations, Max Weber's studies of rural and urban social structures and his unfinished comparative study of religion and socio-economic structure, Bloch's careful analyses of medieval France, Boutruche's comparative evaluation of master-servant and lord-vassal relationship, and Rostovtzeff's richly documented histories of the Roman Empire and the Hellenistic world.[18] The comparative studies in cultures and civilizations, edited by Robert Redfield and Milton Singer, as well as related studies, chiefly on the societies of China and of Islam, might be added.[19] However, one of the most fruitful applications of this approach has been the study of origins and development of "modern" capitalism in England, Norway, France, Germany, Switzerland, Italy, and Japan. In addition to the earlier work of Weber, Sombart, Strieder, and others on this score, we should mention the contributions of Tawney. Sée, Fanfani, M. and R. Wax, Pernoud, Lestocquoy, Nelson, Birnbaum, Merton, Lockwood, and Jacobs.[20]

Other important instances of the study of institutional change and concomitant problems cover a wide range of subject matter and geographic settings. Special mention must be made of the classic work, *The Polish Peasant in Europe and America,* by W. I. Thomas and Florian Znaniecki.[21] This work employed the family history and the personal history approach, through such media as letters and autobiographies—both as illustrations of, and foundation for, analyses of social and personal disorganization processes, of personality types, and of the effects of migration on family structure. It should be noted that these subsequently neglected sources are chiefly of a genealogical nature. If data of this kind were systematically gathered, the study of migrations and of social mobility would acquire historical depth.

There are a number of challenging comparative studies of revolutions—especially those by Lyford Edwards, Crane Brinton, and Hannah Arendt—which seek to discover meaningful similarities in the revolutionary process from relevant historical materials.[22] A comparison of these studies is of particular interest because Edwards uses the data of history as examples for sociological processes while Brinton uses sociological categories to analyze the meaning of historical events. Hannah Arendt is in a category by herself. Consciously or not, these studies are indebted to the older works of Brooks Adams and Sorokin, as well as to Tocqueville's masterly analysis of the causes of the French Revolution.[23] In addition, despite the critical reactions they have received, Turner and Webb have made significant efforts to clarify the emergence and transformation of specifically American political and economic institutions as adjustments to "frontier" situations.[24] The arguments of both these authors are environmental in nature, but in contrast to Turner's thesis, which now appears vague and insufficiently supported by evidence, Webb's derivation of social change in the Great Plains from the introduction of the Colt revolver and the barbed wire fence would seem to retain its illuminating character. Referring to a related frontier situation, S. D. Clark has provided several valuable analyses of Canadian history, with particular attention to religious and political developments.[25] Lipset's study of the emergence of the Cooperative Commonwealth Federation in Canada and Elizabeth Nottingham's account of frontier Methodism are likewise relevant.[26]

There are many other studies of the causes, processes, and consequences of institutional change. The importance of invasions, migrations, and the translocation of peoples has been stressed, as far as the world of antiquity is concerned, by Bury and Teggart, with regard to slavery by Wyndham and Williams, and with regard to American immigration problems—such as the adaption of immigrants, the emergence of nativism and the activities of the Immigration Restriction League—by Marcus Lee Hansen, Oscar Handlin, John Higham, and Barbara Miller Salomon.[27] John A. Hawgood's account of the history of German-Americanism has dramatic quality while the partly controversial, partly complementary studies of institutional development among American Negroes by Frazier and Herskovits derive their fascination from the psychological and political significance of the scholarly argument.[28] Without attempting to offer a definitive listing, we might further refer to Selma Stern's and Neil J. Smelser's respective accounts of the processes of social change in absolutistic German principalities and in industrial Lancashire, Elinor Barber's and Helen Merrell Lynd's expositions of social stratification and ideological transformation in eighteenth-century France and nineteenth-century England, E. K. Francis' analysis of the evolution of monastic organization and of the utopian quest of the Mennonites, and Stanley M. Elkins' review of the institutional and intellectual aspects of slavery.[29]

In reviewing the selections in this volume and the literature which has been cited in the past few pages, we are struck by a generally unrecognized fact: the relative ease with which historians and sociologists have been able to employ one another's concepts, data, theories, and general methods. In some instances, this appears to have occurred without conscious intent; in many cases, however, the crossing of disciplinary lines has been premeditated and carefully prepared. Despite the barriers of academic labels and philosophical or epistemological polarization, working historians and sociologists, as well as other social scientists, seem to accomplish in practice what the guardians of disciplinary identity assert is either impossible or dangerous. Indeed, this volume is testimony to that accomplishment. Perhaps it is fair to conclude that "history"—conceived as the accumulated products of human behavior over ascertainable periods of time—is so pervasive and significant for human beings that its study cannot be adequately pursued by any *one* academic specialty.

But what, in retrospect, has facilitated the substantial interchange that is variously reflected in these pages? Although some historians and sociologists prefer to follow their own bent, there seems to be an underlying concern for *process* in both fields. This inevitably requires concern for time and sequence, for basic attention to both description and explanation of continuity and change.[30] Furthermore, neither the historian nor the sociologist, whatever his specific problem, can long postpone thought and investigation of the *relation* between continuity and change. Changes in technology, in the structure of the family and of leadership, even changes in religious expression can become a vehicle for the continuation of deeply anchored values and goals, by means of "antagonistic acculturation" or otherwise.[31] Examples are the emergence of modern Japan after 1868, of modern Turkey after 1908 (or 1920), and of the Zionist movement in Judaism.[32] In a general way, one may say that we are confronted with continuity *in* change, as in a fast-flowing river which stays within its banks today and floods the countryside tomorrow, but still "keeps rolling along."

In practice, scholars in both fields have not approached this complex problem in anything but a tentative and incomplete manner. Consequently, data with a time perspective (either in the contemporary or distant past) are inherently attractive and necessary for sociologists. In the same way, the recurrent search for means of *establishing* continuity in data and clearly ascertainable variations or changes in specific institutions appears to result in the implicit or explicit use of sociological concepts and generalizations by historians.[33]

Yet, as the papers in Part I of this volume indicate, the analysis of continuity and change has been marked by considerable variety and hotly opinionated controversy, out of which arose the conviction that the all-encompassing generalizations of previous theorists must be complemented, if not replaced, by a usable common repertory of limited generalizations—limited in time, space, and conceptualization. It is our belief that the impressive *corpus* of past and present interchange between sociologists and historians on this level has served not only as a critical mirror in which the imperfections of both were reflected, but may also serve as a basis for the more modest and responsible theories of societal operation and change that students of human affairs so clearly need.

Agenda for Investigation

Both historians and sociologists affirm the significance of origins, antecedents, and past events. The fact that human beings often refuse to learn from experience is a melancholy footnote to repeated mistakes and persistent social problems. But we have attempted to indicate here that sociologists and historians have had considerable success in combining their orientations for the elucidation of specific problems. This provides a good base for *future* interchange. Let us therefore try to suggest an informal agenda for subsequent investigations in the interest of continuity and more fruitful results. These suggestions are addressed primarily to sociologists, but may prove stimulating also to historians.

1. *Community*. Despite the efforts of the past fifty years, we still have not adequately investigated more than a few dozen communities. In particular, we need comprehensive analyses of varied types, periods, and geographic locations, with special attention to the proximate origins of urban communities of various sizes, the factors crucial to each stage or phase of development, the nature and changes in community power structure and decision-making, and the network of relations with other communities and more comprehensive "national" structures. Some past efforts that might serve as an orientation are the works of the Lynds, Ware, Dahl, Miller, Homans, Baron, among others.[34]

2. *Political dynamics*. The undisputed importance of political *organization* has often postponed adequate concern for the details of the *processes* by which political structure is sustained, replenished, and changed. Several critical problems require more study of historical data from many societies, especially in the recent past. First, what have been the specific sources, material or otherwise, of the emergence and the decline of contending groups (elites, factions, cliques, parties)?[35] Second, what devices have been used, with varying degrees of success, in attaining and maintaining power and the support of significant groups, both in democratic and autocratic societies (e.g. material benefit, personal appeal, racial and other demagoguery, threats and coercion, bribery, pressure politics, but also mass media like newspapers and magazines, cartoons and caricatures, radio and television)?[36] Third, what are the crucial psychological, cultural, and demographic dimensions in voting behavior for national and local elections?[37] What changes in the relative weight of these dimensions can be discovered—and what conditions help to account for such shifts? Finally, what seem to be the major factors in political decision-making with respect to important economic, military, and "social" issues?[38]

3. *Stratification and social mobility*. The renewed interest during the past twenty-five years in social classes and their effects on social behavior has been largely expressed in descriptive and predominantly static studies. Some notable exceptions to this trend have been the emerging concern for mobility as indicated by occupational or educational advancement.[39] However, these studies have likewise been descriptive and concerned with gross statistical categories. Consequently, there is a vast gap in our knowledge on the following points. What are the changing sources of status and power for given communities, nations, and periods? Precisely how do families at given levels

and in various periods assign status and class "culture" to their offspring? What are the details of "style of life" that correspond to, or fail to be consonant with, the ubiquitous occupational index of status?[40] What explains differentials in mobility aspirations within and between status categories? What has been the role of intermarriage between status levels as a channel of mobility? Under what conditions do families rise and under what conditions do they remain on the same level or sink in status? What are the probable mechanisms of social mobility, as derived from careful analysis of the social careers of "mobile" persons and families? Finally, what are the conditions which help account for differentials in relations between status levels (e.g., cooperation, rivalry, conflict, insulation)?

4. *Social movements, public opinion, and mass communications.* The study of social movements, including revolutionary upheavals, touches upon a vital aspect of the present world situation, but the rising interest in movements as a vehicle of social change, to be sociologically relevant, must rest on a historical and comparative basis.[41] Among the many problems that are awaiting investigation in this context, reference is made here to but one, namely, the relation between the structural components of a situation of unrest and the emergence of leadership. Do circumstances bring forth the leader or does the leader direct circumstances?[42] But even if leadership looms larger than is commonly assumed among social scientists, the fact remains that the discovery of the emergence and proliferation of publics represents a delayed recognition of the importance of mass influence mechanisms and the less than perfect domination of an entire population by one or more elites. It is no longer possible to make accurate estimates of what numbers of people think (or thought) by referring to their political or religious leaders, their employers, or social superiors. Consequently, to assess the supportive, negative, or neutral attitudes and values of a community or nation at a given period, sociologists must use functional equivalents of the opinion poll and the sample survey. For earlier historical periods, we can obtain clues to attitudes and values of various social categories by analyzing popular literature and its distribution (e.g., where best-sellers, advertisements, newspapers, pamphlets, etc. are available), as well as cartoons, caricatures, wood-cuts, and letters.[43] Increasingly, too, opinion polls are acquiring a "historical" dimension, since we now have data on some issues for a twenty-year span. It remains dubious whether and to what extent, even by appropriate questions, sample surveys can furnish *post festum* information, not only on opinions but also on the influences that tend to produce persistence or change in opinions. But where historical processes, as well as past opinions about them, are sufficiently documented, the contrast between these known data and the "myths" which have grown around them may open up a new field of inquiry which will be largely social-psychological in nature. Finally, where the myth is known but factual information is lacking, as is the case in pre-literate societies, the social-psychological record of the impression which an event made on past

generations (saga, legend) serves as the sole basis for historical reconstruction.[44]

5. *Sociology of knowledge, religion, art, and science.* One of the continually fascinating problems with which the social scientist is faced is understanding the creation of new and competing ideational systems. In general, this demands attention to several component problems: *identification* of coherent ideational systems; the *connection* of such systems with persons representing specific social categories (socio-economic classes, status groups, etc.); *explaining* the significance of cultural creations for these categories and not for other social categories; and the *process of diffusing* ideational systems (and their objectification) to larger circles and publics. Since the intellectual, or ideational, heritage of Western civilization is extremely rich, there are numerous opportunities to analyze the processes by which specific philosophies, ideologies, art forms, and social innovations attain prominence and even enduring consequences. Limiting ourselves arbitrarily to American society, sociologists might meaningfully examine or re-examine the development of humanitarianism, pragmatism, "progressive education," the labor and agrarian movements from 1870 to the present, the shifts in religious, musical, and theatrical performance,[45] the divergent attitudes among physicians (e.g., faculties of medical schools vs. practitioners) on social issues, the sources of isolationism and interventionism following World War I, and changes in the orientations of the social sciences themselves.[46] By widening the range of such investigations, sociologists will be able to develop somewhat more differentiated theories concerning the reciprocal relations between ideas and social structure, and hopefully will also be able to specify the conditions under which aspects of social structure "produce" ideas, and vice versa.[47] The whole area of institutional change is a closely related problem.

6. *Sociology of business and industry.* Sociology has perhaps more affinity to economic history than to any other branch of historical scholarship. This is well documented by the work of older scholars, from Marx and Schmoller to Bloch and Clapham, but among contemporary sociologists perhaps only Benjamin Nelson, Leland Jenks, and Sigmund Diamond have made significant contributions.[48] These contributions refer not only to the structural position of business in medieval and modern society but also to the image of the businessman and the evaluation of his activities. More work along this line will be welcome. However, considering the focal role of business and industry in our society, we also need sociologically oriented studies of the development of the internal structure of economic institutions (enterprises, industries, business associations), of the relations between the representatives of capital, management and labor, and of the influence which individual businessmen as well as organized industry and labor exert, or have exerted, in communal endeavor and in the affairs of municipal, state, and federal governments.[49] Finally, the history of leisure and its relation to work and social class should prove to be of interest to social scientists.[50]

7. *Demography*. Continued failures in the past to arrive at universal laws of a demographic nature have brought home the lesson that varying rates of population change depend on distinctive types of causal factors which operate differently in different social contexts and historical epochs.[51] Consequently, demographers develop a strong interest in historical materials concerned with population size, composition, natural increase and decrease, and migration. This interest can express itself in various ways. Faced with the limitations or the unavailability of official statistics, the demographer can use a variety of clues from historical sources to construct the demographic outline of a given period.[52] In addition, demographers are increasingly interested in the *relation* between such demographic items as fertility rates, death rates, migration streams, and the like and the relevant values and attitudes of given populations as a means of studying the processes by which demographic trends are either maintained or transformed.[53] But the demographer also concludes from known demographic data to the structure of the society which is under investigation. For instance, a careful demographic analysis of the Roman Empire, medieval Europe, or the American colonies—to take but a few instances —can furnish important clues concerning the strains and opportunities directly or indirectly expressed in the social and cultural products of an era. An example is Herbert Moller's analysis of the romantic love complex in this volume, pp. 484–502.

8. *Race and ethnic relations*. There has been an understandable, but not always defensible, tendency to focus on contemporary, and even exclusively American, dimensions of race and ethnic relations and problems. For instance, the various race relations "cycles" (actually sequences) have reference to the history of transatlantic and transpacific migration during the nineteenth and twentieth centuries, but are hardly applicable to those contact situations at various times and places that result in expulsion, population transfer and exchange, and genocide.[54] About this, American Indians have a tale to tell, but so have Jews, Armenians, Greeks, the Moors of Spain, French settlers in North Africa, the Bushmen and the Bantu in South Africa, and the Slavic and Germanic populations of Eastern Europe. Possibly, the entire nature of race and ethnic relations has changed with the passing of colonialism on the one hand and the rise of nationalism on the other.[55] The important difference between migrant superordination and native subordination versus migrant subordination and native superordination has recently been elucidated, but in a wider sense the relation between social structure and attitudes of a racial nature awaits further comparative analysis.[56] Under what circumstances does social structure determine attitudes, under what circumstances is legislation effective, and under what circumstances is the ideological or emotional factor the independent variable?[57] The processes by which ethnic differences are converted into class distinctions have been classically formulated, but they are hardly sufficiently substantiated by research.[58] The American Negro bears testimony to the reverse process, whereby a status gap is rationalized into an

immutable racial trait. Further, we are lacking a comparative analysis of the conditions under which two or more ethnically different populations may coexist as equals, as in Switzerland and Canada, and those where either separation or amalgamation will be the result. These are but a few questions among many.

As we pause at this point, we are aware that we have raised more questions than we could ever have hoped to answer, not only in this last chapter but throughout the book. This is perhaps inevitable if one attempts to outline an area of interest that, although old in fact, appears new in the way in which it has been formulated and consciously appraised. We are sure that alternative formulations and appraisals are possible, but we trust that we have opened a vista, aroused curiosity, and stimulated thought. The remainder must be left to fruitful controversy and diversified research.

Notes

1. Fustel de Coulanges, *The Ancient City* (New York: Doubleday Anchor Books, 1956); Gustave Glotz, *The Greek City and Its Institutions* (New York: A. A. Knopf, 1930); Henri Pirenne, *Medieval Cities* (New York: Doubleday Anchor Books, n.d.): René Maunier, *L'Origine et la fonction économique des villes* (Paris: Girard et Brière, 1910); Frederick William Maitland, *Township and Borough* (Cambridge: Cambridge University Press, 1898); Carl Stephenson, *Borough and Town* (Cambridge: The Medieval Academy of America, 1933); Marc Bloch, *La France sous les derniers Capétiens 1223–1328* (Paris: Colin, 1958). See also Alfred F. Havighurst, *The Pirenne Thesis: Analysis, Criticism and Revision* (Boston: Heath, 1958), and Karl H. Kraeling and Robert M. Adams, eds., *City Invincible: A Symposium on Urbanization and Cultural Development in the Ancient Near East* (Chicago: The University of Chicago Press, 1960).
2. Adna F. Weber, *The Growth of Cities in the Nineteenth Century* (New York: Macmillan, 1899).
3. Carl Bridenbaugh, *Cities in the Wilderness* (New York: Ronald Press, 1938); Carl Bridenbaugh, *Cities in Revolt* (New York: A. A. Knopf, 1945); Richard C. Wade, *The Urban Frontier* (Cambridge: Harvard University Press, 1959); Leon S. Marshall, "The English and American City of the Nineteenth Century," *Western Pennsylvania Historical Magazine*, XX (1937), 169–180; Merle Curti, *et al.*, *The Making of an American Community: A Case History of Democracy in a Frontier Country* (Stanford: Stanford University Press, 1959). Blake McKelvey, *The Urbanization of America: 1860–1915* (New Brunswick, N.J.: Rutgers University Press, 1963).
4. Robert S. Lynd and Helen M. Lynd, *Middletown* (New York: Harcourt, Brace, 1929); Robert S. Lynd and Helen M. Lynd, *Middletown in Transition* (New York: Harcourt, Brace, 1939).
5. W. Lloyd Warner and Paul S. Lunt, *The Social Life of a Modern Community* (New Haven: Yale University Press, 1941), p. 40.
6. W. Lloyd Warner and Paul S. Lunt, *op. cit.;* W. Lloyd Warner and Paul S. Lunt, *The Status System of a Modern Community* (New Haven: Yale University Press, 1942); W. Lloyd Warner and J. O. Low, *The Social*

System of the Modern Factory (New Haven: Yale University Press, 1947). For some representative critiques, see C. Wright Mills, review of *The Social Life of a Modern Community*, in the *American Sociological Review*, 7 (April 1942), 263–271; Ruth R. Kornhauser, "The Warner Approach to Social Stratification," in Reinhard Bendix and Seymour M. Lipset, eds., *Class, Status and Power* (New York: The Free Press of Glencoe, 1953); Oscar Handlin, review of *The Social Life of a Modern Community*, in *New England Quarterly*, 15 (September 1942), 454–457; Oscar Handlin, review of *The Social System of the Modern Factory*, in *Journal of Economic History*, 7 (November 1947), 275–277.

7. An appraisal of some of the American community studies may be found in Maurice R. Stein, *The Eclipse of Community: An Interpretation of American Studies* (Princeton: Princeton University Press, 1960).

8. Liston Pope, *Millhands and Preachers* (New Haven: Yale University Press, 1942); Horace Miner, *St. Denis* (Chicago: The University of Chicago Press, 1939); Everett C. Hughes, *French Canada in Transition* (Chicago: The University of Chicago Press, 1943); Elin Anderson, *We Americans* (Cambridge: Harvard University Press, 1939); Pauline V. Young, *The Pilgrims of Russian Town* (Chicago: The University of Chicago Press, 1932); Walter Firey, *Land Use in Central Boston* (Cambridge: Harvard University Press, 1947); Lowry Nelson, *The Mormon Village* (Salt Lake City: University of Utah Press, 1952); William F. Whyte, *Street Corner Society* (Chicago: The University of Chicago Press, 1943); Raoul Blanchard, *Grenoble* (Grenoble: Editions Didier et Richard, 3rd ed., 1935); Roger Le Tourneau, *Fès avant le protectorat: étude économique et sociale d'une ville de l'occident musulman* (Casablanca: Societé marocaine de librairie et d'édition, 1949); Roger Le Tourneau, *Fez in the Age of the Marinides*, translation by B. A. Clement (Norman: University of Oklahoma Press, 1961); Margaret Stacey, *Tradition and Change* (Oxford: Oxford University Press, 1960); Robert A. Dahl, *Who Governs?* (New Haven: Yale University Press, 1962). See also Sam B. Warner, Jr., *Streetcar Suburbs* (Cambridge: Harvard University Press, 1962).

9. Harry W. Gilmore, "The Old New Orleans and the New," *American Sociological Review*, 9 (August 1944), 385–394; Olen E. Leonard, "La Paz, Bolivia: Its Population and Growth," *American Sociological Review*, 13 (August 1944), 448–454; Theodore Caplow, "The Social Ecology of Guatemala City," *Social Forces*, 28 (December 1949), 113–133; Asa Briggs, "Social Structure and Politics in Birmingham and Lyons, 1825–1848," *British Journal of Sociology*, 1 (March 1950), 67–80; Wolfram Eberhard, "Data on the Structure of the Chinese City in the Pre-Industrial Period," *Economic Development and Cultural Change*, IV, 3 (April 1956), 253–268; Eric E. Lampard, "The History of Cities in the Economically Advanced Areas," *Ibid.*, III, 2 (January 1955).

10. David H. Pinkney, "Urban Studies and the Historian," *Social Forces*, 28 (May 1950), 423–429.

11. Howard Becker, "Culture Case Study and Greek History," *American Sociological Review*, 23, No. 5 (October 1958), 489–503.

12. Jacob Burckhardt, *Die Kultur der Renaissance in Italien*, 14th ed., by Walter Goetz (Leipzig: Alfred Kröner, 1925); the latest English translation is *The Civilization of the Renaissance in Italy*, 2 vols., ed. by Benjamin Nelson and Charles Trinkaus (New York: Harper Torchbook Series, 1958); Johan Huizinga, *The Waning of the Middle Ages: A Study of the Forms of Life,*

Thought and Art in France and The Netherlands in the XIV and XV Centuries, translated by F. Hopman (London: E. Arnold, 1937); Max Weber, *The Protestant Ethic and the Spirit of Capitalism,* translated by Talcott Parsons (London: G. Allen and Unwin, 1930); Alexis de Tocqueville, *Democracy in America,* ed. by Philipps Bradley, 2 vols. (New York: A. A. Knopf, 1945; Vintage Books, 1958); James B. Bryce, *The American Commonwealth,* 2 vols. (First ed. New York: Macmillan, 1888; the numerous subsequent editions were also published by Macmillan); Gilberto Freyre, *The Masters and the Slaves: A Study of the Development of Brazilian Civilization* (New York: A. A. Knopf, 1946); Fernando Ortiz *Cuban Counterpoint: Tobacco and Sugar* (New York: A. A. Knopf, 1947); Américo Castro, *The Structure of Spanish History* (Princeton: Princeton University Press, 1954); see also Albert Salomon, "Tocqueville 1959," *Social Research,* 26, No. 4 (Winter 1959), 449–470; Alfred von Martin, *Sociology of the Renaissance,* translated by W. L. Luetkens (London: Kegan, Paul, Trench, Trubner & Co., 1944) and Gilberto Freyre, *The Mansions and the Shanties* (New York: A. A. Knopf, 1963).

13. Arnold J. Toynbee, *Hellenism: The History of a Civilization* (New York: Oxford University Press, 1959); Charles A. and Mary R. Beard, *The Rise of American Civilization,* revised ed. (New York: Macmillan, 1947); David Potter, *People of Plenty: Economic Abundance and the American Character* (Chicago: The University of Chicago Press, 1954); D. W. Brogan, *The American Character* (New York: Vintage Books, 1956); David Riesman, *The Lonely Crowd: A Study of the Changing American Character* (New Haven: Yale University Press, 1950); Salvador de Madariaga, *Englishmen, Frenchmen, Spaniards: An Essay in Comparative Psychology* (London: Oxford University Press, 1928); K. A. Wittfogel, *Oriental Despotism: A Comparative Study of Social Power* (New Haven: Yale University Press, 1957).

14. Jacob Burckhardt, *Weltgeschichtliche Betrachtungen,* ed. by Rudolf Marx (Leipzig: Alfred Kröner, n.d.), 6; transl., *Reflections on History* (London: G. Allen and Unwin, 1943).

15. Alexis de Tocqueville, *op. cit.,* II, Author's Preface, v, vi.

16. Max Lerner, *America as a Civilization: Life and Thought in the United States Today* (New York: Simon & Schuster, 1957).

17. Warren B. Walsh, *Perspectives and Patterns: Discourses on History* (Syracuse: Syracuse University Press, 1962), pp. 108–119; H. P. R. Finberg, ed., *Approaches to History: A Symposium* (London: Routledge and Kegan Paul, 1962), pp. 17–82; Barrington Moore, Jr., *Political Power and Social Theory* (Cambridge: Harvard University Press, 1958), pp. 123–149.

18. Henry S. Maine, *Ancient Law: Its Connection with the Early History of Society and Its Relation to Modern Ideas* (1st American ed. from 2nd London ed., New York: C. Scribner's, 1864); Fustel de Coulanges, *op. cit.;* Henri Pirenne, *Les Villes et les institutions urbaines,* 2 vols. (Paris: Alcan, 1939); Henri Pirenne, *Economic and Social History of Medieval Europe* (New York: Harcourt, Brace, 1937); Max Weber, *Law and Economy in Society,* ed. by Max Rheinstein (Cambridge: Harvard University Press, 1954); H. H. Gerth and C. Wright Mills (eds.), *From Max Weber: Essays in Sociology* (New York: Oxford University Press, 1946), Parts 3, 4; Max Weber, *The City,* transl. and ed. by Don Martindale and Gertrud Neuwirth (New York: The Free Press of Glencoe, 1958); Max Weber, *Die Römische Agrargeschichte in ihrer Bedeutung für das Staats-und Privatrecht* (Stutt-

gart: F. Enke, 1891); Max Weber, "Die sozialen Gruende des Untergangs der antiken Kultur," in *Gesammelte Aufsaetze zur Sozial-und Wirtschaftsgeschichte* (Tuebingen: I. C. B. Mohr, 1924), pp. 289–311; Marc Bloch, *Les caractères originaux de l'histoire rurale française* (Paris: Colin, 1931); Marc Bloch, *La France sous les derniers capétiens, op. cit.;* Robert Boutruche, *Seigneurie et féodalité* (Paris: Aubier, 1959); Michael I. Rostovtzeff, *Social and Economic History of the Roman Empire* (Oxford: The Clarendon Press, 1926), 2 vols.; Michael I. Rostovtzeff, *Social and Economic History of the Hellenistic World* (Oxford: The Clarendon Press, 1941), 3 vols.; C. Delisle Burns, *The First Europe* (London: Allen and Unwin, 1947).

19. Gustave E. von Grunebaum, ed., *Islamic Studies and Cultural Research* (Comparative Studies in Cultures and Civilizations, ed. by Robert Redfield and Milton Singer; The American Anthropological Association, Vol. 56, No. 2, part 2, Memoir No. 76, April 1954); Gustave E. von Grunebaum, *Unity and Variety in Moslem Civilization* (Comparative Studies; Chicago: The University of Chicago Press, 1957); Gustave E. von Grunebaum, *Medieval Islam: A Study in Cultural Orientation* (Chicago: The University of Chicago Press, 1945); Gustave E. von Grunebaum, *Islam: Essays in the Nature and Growth of a Cultural Tradition* (London: Routledge and Kegan Paul, 1955, Barnes & Noble, 1961); H. A. R. Gibb and Harold Bowen, *Islamic Society and The West: A Study of the Impact of Western Civilization on Moslem Culture in the Near East*, 2 vols. (London and New York: Oxford University Press, 1950); Reuben Levy, *The Social Structure of Islam*, 2nd ed. of *The Sociology of Islam* (Cambridge: The University Press, 1957); E. A. Kracke, *Civil Service in Early Sung China* (Cambridge: Harvard University Press, 1953); Marion J. Levy, *The Family Revolution in Modern China* (Cambridge: Harvard University Press, 1949); Y. C. Wang, "Intellectuals and Society in China 1860–1959," *Comparative Studies in Society and History*, Vol. III, 4 (July 1961), 395–426; Ralph Pieris, *Sinhalese Social Organization: The Kandyan Period* (Colombo: The Ceylon University Press Board, 1956).

20. R. H. Tawney, *Religion and the Rise of Capitalism* (New York: Harcourt, Brace, 1926); Henri E. Sée, *Modern Capitalism: Its Origins and Evolution* (London: N. Douglas, 1928); Murray and Rosalie Wax, "The Vikings and the Rise of Capitalism," *American Journal of Sociology*, 61 (July 1955), 1–10; Amintore Fanfani, *Catholicism, Protestantism, and Capitalism* (New York: Sheed and Ward, 1955 ed.); Régine Pernoud, *Les Origines de la bourgeoisie* (Paris: Presses Universitaires de France, 1947); J. Lestocquoy, *Les Villes de Flandre et d'Italie* (Paris: Presses Universitaires de France, 1952); Benjamin N. Nelson, "The Usurer and the Merchant Prince: Italian Businessmen and the Ecclesiastical Law of Restitution," *Journal of Economic History*, VII (May 1947), 109–122; Norman Birnbaum, "Social Structure and the German Reformation" (Unpublished Ph.D. thesis, Harvard University, 1958); Norman Birnbaum, "The Zwinglian Reformation in Zurich" *Past and Present*, No. 15 (April 1959) and *Archives de Sociologie des Religions*, No. 8 (July-December 1959), abridged version in this volume; Robert K. Merton, "Science, Technology and Society in Seventeenth Century England, *Osiris*, 4 (1938), 360–597; William W. Lockwood, *The Economic Development of Japan* (Princeton: Princeton University Press, 1954); Norman Jacobs, *The Origins of Modern Capitalism in Eastern Asia* (Hong Kong: Hong Kong University Press, 1958).

21. W. I. Thomas and Florian Znaniecki, *The Polish Peasant in Europe and America,* 5 vols. (Chicago: The University of Chicago Press, 1918–20); cf. Louis Gottschalk, Clyde Kluckhohn, Robert C. Angell, *The Use of Personal Documents in History, Anthropology and Sociology* (New York: Social Science Research Council, 1945).

22. Lyford Edwards, *The Natural History of Revolution* (Chicago: The University of Chicago Press, 1927); Crane Brinton, *Anatomy of Revolution* (New York: Norton, 1938); Hannah Arendt, *On Revolution* (New York: The Viking Press, 1963); cf. Sigmund Neumann, "The Structure and Strategy of Revolution, 1848–1948," *Journal of Politics,* 11 (1949), 532–544; Rex Hopper, "The Revolutionary Process," *Social Forces,* 28 (May 1950), 70–79; James C. Davies, "Toward a Theory of Revolution," *American Sociological Review,* 27 (February 1962); for a specific aspect of the revolutionary process, see George Rudé, *The Crowd in the French Revolution* (New York: Oxford University Press, 1949).

23. Brooks Adams, *The Theory of Social Revolution* (New York: Macmillan, 1914); Pitirim A. Sorokin, *The Sociology of Revolution* (Philadelphia: J. B. Lippincott, 1925); Alexis de Tocqueville, *The Old Regime and the Revolution,* transl. by John Bonner (New York: Harper, 1956).

24. Frederick J. Turner, *The Frontier in American History* (New York: Holt, 1920); Frederick J. Turner, *The Significance of Sections in American History* (New York: Holt, 1932); Walter P. Webb, *The Great Plains* (Boston: Ginn & Co., 1931); Walter P. Webb, *The Great Frontier* (Boston: Houghton Mifflin, 1952). See also the critical discussions in Fred A. Shannon, *An Appraisal of Walter Prescott Webb's "The Great Plains"* (New York: Social Science Research Council, 1940, Bulletin 46); Lee Benson, *Turner and Beard* (New York: The Free Press of Glencoe, 1960); James C. Malin, "Mobility and History," *Agricultural History,* XVII (1943); David Potter, *op. cit.,* 142–165. Walter P. Webb has applied the "frontier" concept to the entire history of the expansion of Europe in *The Great Frontier;* Werner J. Cahnman and A. N. J. den Hollander have applied the same concept to the East-West conflict in "Frontiers between East and West in Europe," *The Geographical Review,* 39 (December 1949), 605–624, and to Danubian Europe in "The Great Hungarian Plains: A European Frontier Area," *Comparative Studies in Society and History,* III, 1, 2 (October 1960, January 1961), 74–88, 155–169.

25. See the following works of S. D. Clark: *Church and Sect in Canada* (Toronto: University of Toronto Press, 1948); *Movements of Political Protest in Canada 1640–1840* (Toronto: University of Toronto Press, 1959); *The Developing Canadian Community* (Toronto: University of Toronto Press, 1962).

26. Seymour M. Lipset, *Agrarian Socialism* (Berkeley: University of California Press, 1950); Elizabeth K. Nottingham, *Methodism and the Frontier: Indiana Proving Ground* (New York: Columbia University Press, 1941).

27. J. B. Bury, *The Invasion of Europe by the Barbarians* (London: Macmillan, 1928); Frederick J. Teggart, *Rome and China: A Study of Correlations in Historical Events* (Berkeley: University of California Press, 1939); Hugh H. Wyndham, *The Atlantic and Slavery* (London: Oxford University Press, 1935); Hugh H. Wyndham, *The Atlantic and Emancipation* (London: Oxford University Press, 1937); Eric Williams, *Capitalism and Slavery* (Chapel Hill: University of North Carolina Press, 1944); Marcus Lee Hansen, *The Atlantic Migration, 1606–1860: A History of the Con-*

tinuing Settlement of the United States (Cambridge: Harvard University Press, 1940); Marcus Lee Hansen, *The Immigrant in American History* (Cambridge: Harvard University Press, 1940); Oscar Handlin, *The Uprooted* (Boston: Little, Brown, 1951); Oscar Handlin, *The Newcomers* (Cambridge: Harvard University Press, 1959); John Higham, *Strangers in the Land: Patterns of American Nativism, 1860–1925* (New Brunswick: Rutgers University Press, 1955); Barbara Miller Salomon, *Ancestors and Immigrants: A Changing New England Tradition* (Cambridge: Harvard University Press, 1956).

28. John A. Hawgood, *The Tragedy of German America: The Germans in the United States during the Nineteenth Century and After* (New York: Putnam, 1940); E. Franklin Frazier, *The Negro Family in the United States* (New York: Dryden Press, 1948); E. Franklin Frazier, *The Negro in the United States* (New York: Macmillan, 1949); E. Franklin Frazier, "A Comparison of Negro-White Relations in Brazil and in the United States," *Transactions of the New York Academy of Sciences,* Series 2, VI, 251–269; Melville J. Herskovits, *The Myth of the Negro Past* (New York: Harper, 1941); Melville J. Herskovits, *Rebel Destiny* (New York: McGraw-Hill, 1934). Cf. Lorenzo D. Turner, *Africanisms in the Gullah-Dialect* (Chicago: The University of Chicago Press, 1949).

29. Selma Stern, *The Court Jew: A Contribution to the History of the Period of Absolutism in Central Europe,* transl. by Ralph Weiman (Philadelphia: The Jewish Publication Society of America, 1950); Neil J. Smelser, *Social Change in the Industrial Revolution: An Application of Theory to the British Cotton Industry* (London: Routledge and Kegan Paul, 1959); Elinor G. Barber, *The Bourgeoisie in Eighteenth Century France* (Princeton: Princeton University Press, 1955); Helen Merrell Lynd, *England in the Eighteen-Eighties: Toward a Social Basis for Freedom* (New York: Oxford University Press, 1955); E. K. Francis, "Toward a Typology of Religious Orders," *American Journal of Sociology,* LV, 5 (March 1950), 437–449; E. K. Francis, *In Search of Utopia: The Mennonites in Manitoba* (New York: The Free Press of Glencoe, 1955); Stanley E. Elkins, *Slavery: A Problem in American Institutional and Intellectual Life* (Chicago: The University of Chicago Press, 1959).

30. Committee on Historiography, *The Social Sciences in Historical Study* (New York: Social Science Research Council, 1954, Bulletin 64), Chap. 5; Seymour M. Lipset, "A Sociologist Looks at History," *Pacific Sociological Review,* 1 (Spring 1958), 13–17.

31. George Devereux and Edwin M. Loeb, "Antagonistic Acculturation," *American Sociological Review,* 8 (April 1943), 133–147.

32. Robert N. Bellah, "Religious Aspects of Modernization in Turkey and Japan," *American Journal of Sociology,* 64, 1–5; Ben Halpern, *The Idea of a Jewish State* (Cambridge: Harvard University Press, 1961).

33. *The Social Sciences in Historical Study,* Chaps. 3, 4; Lee Benson, "Research Problems in American Political Historiography," in Mirra Komarovsky, ed., *Common Frontiers of the Social Sciences* (New York: The Free Press of Glencoe, 1957), pp. 113–182.

34. Lynd and Lynd, *Middletown in Transition;* Dahl, *op. cit.;* Caroline Ware, ed., *The Cultural Approach to History* (New York: Columbia University Press, 1940), pp. 140–161, 228–242; William Miller, ed., *Men in Business* (New York: Harper Torchbook, 1962), Chap. 4; George C. Homans, *English Villagers of the Thirteenth Century* (New York: Russell

& Russell, 1961; 1st ed. 1941); Salo W. Baron, *The Jewish Community,* 3 vols. (Philadelphia: The Jewish Publication Society, 1942).

35. See Seymour M. Lipset, *et al., Union Democracy* (New York: The Free Press of Glencoe, 1956); Jackson Turner Main, *The Antifederalists: Critics of the Constitution 1781–1788* (Chapel Hill: University of North Carolina Press, 1961); D. Brunton and D. H. Pennington, *Members of the Long Parliament* (Cambridge: Harvard University Press, 1954); André Siegfried, *Tableau politique de la France de l'ouest sous la Troisième République* (Paris: Alcan and Colin, 1913); Richard Hofstadter, *The Age of Reform: From Bryan to F.D.R.* (New York: A. A. Knopf, 1955); V. O. Key, *Southern Politics in State and Nation* (New York: A. A. Knopf, 1949); Alexander Heard, *A Two-Party South?* (Chapel Hill: University of North Carolina Press, 1952); Samuel Lubell, *The Future of American Politics,* 2nd ed. (New York: Doubleday Anchor, 1956).

36. S. N. Eisenstadt, *The Political Systems of Empires: The Rise and Fall of the Historical Bureaucratic Societies* (New York: The Free Press of Glencoe, 1963); Hans Rosenberg, *Bureaucracy, Aristocracy and Autocracy: The Prussian Experience 1660–1815* (Cambridge: Harvard University Press, 1958); Hannah Arendt, *The Origins of Totalitarianism* (New York: Harcourt, Brace, 1951); C. Vann Woodward, *Reunion and Reaction: The Compromise of 1877 and the End of Reconstruction,* 2nd rev. ed. (New York: Doubleday Anchor, 1956); Wolfram Eberhard, *Conquerors and Rulers: Social Forces in Medieval China* (Leiden: Brill, 1952); E. Kracke, Jr., "Family vs. Merit in Chinese Civil Service Examinations under the Empire," *Harvard Journal of Asiatic Studies,* X, 2 (September 1947), 103–123; Robert C. Marsh, "Bureaucratic Constraints on Nepotism in the Ching Period," *Journal of Asian Studies* (February 1960), 117–133.

37. Lee Benson, "Research Problems," *loc. cit.;* Rudolf Heberle, *From Democracy to Nazism: A Regional Case Study on Political Parties in Germany* (Baton Rouge: Louisiana State University Press, 1945).

38. Richard C. Snyder, ed., *Foreign Policy Decision-Making* (New York: The Free Press of Glencoe, 1962).

39. D. V. Glass, ed., *Social Mobility in Britain* (London: Routledge and Kegan Paul, 1954); Natalie Rogoff, *Recent Trends in Occupational Mobility* (New York: The Free Press of Glencoe, 1953); A. B. Hollingshead, "Trends in Social Stratification: A Case Study," *American Sociological Review,* 17 (December 1952), 679–686; Pitirim A. Sorokin, *Social Mobility* (New York: Harper, 1927); Roger W. Shugg, *Origins of Class Struggle in Louisiana: A Social History of White Farmers and Laborers during Slavery and After, 1840–1875* (Baton Rouge: Louisiana State University Press, 1939); Robert M. Marsh, *The Mandarins: The Circulation of Elites in China 1600–1900* (New York: The Free Press of Glencoe, 1961); Ping-ti Ho, *The Ladder of Success in Imperial China: Aspects of Social Mobility, 1368–1911* (New York: Columbia University Press, 1962).

40. Svend Ranulf, *Moral Indignation and Middle Class Psychology* (Copenhagen: Levin and Munksgaard, 1938); Asa Briggs and John Saville, eds., "The Language of 'Class' in Early Nineteenth-Century England," *Essays in Labor History* (New York: St. Martin's Press, 1960), pp. 43–73; Lawrence Stone, "Marriage among the English Nobility in the Sixteenth and Seventeenth Centuries," *Comparative Studies in Society and History,* III, 2 (January 1961), 182–206; Cleveland Amory, *The Proper Bostonianʳ* (Boston: E. P. Dutton, 1947).

41. The account that comes nearest to this requirement is Rudolf Heberle's *Social Movements: An Introduction to Political Sociology* (New York: Appleton Century-Crofts, 1951).

42. Among many controversial accounts, the following are outstanding: Georges Sorel, *Reflections on Violence,* transl. by T. E. Hulme and J. Roth (New York: The Free Press of Glencoe, 1950) and Sidney Hook, *The Hero in History: A Study in Limitation and Possibility* (New York: The John Day Co., 1943). Cf. Henry Peyre, "The Influence of Eighteenth Century Ideas on the French Revolution," *Journal of the History of Ideas,* 10 (1949), 63–87; Hans Gerth, "The Nazi Party: Its Leadership and Composition," *American Journal of Sociology,* 45 (1940), 517–541; Walter Z. Laqueur, *Young Germany: A History of the German Youth Movement* (New York: Basic Books, 1962).

43. Leo Lowenthal, "Biographies in Popular Magazines," in Paul Lazarsfeld and Frank Stanton, eds., *Communications Research 1948–49* (New York: Harper, 1949); Leo Lowenthal and Marjorie Fiske, "The Debate Over Art and Popular Culture in Eighteenth Century England," in Komarovsky, *op. cit.,* pp. 33–112; Leo Lowenthal, *Literature, Popular Culture and Society* (Englewood Cliffs, N.J.: Prentice-Hall, 1961); M. Dorothy George, *English Political Caricature,* 2 vols. (Oxford: The Clarendon Press, 1959); Grete de Francesca, *The Power of the Charlatan* (New Haven: Yale University Press, 1939); Aytoun Ellis, *The Penny Universities: A History of the Coffee-Houses* (London: Secker and Warburg, 1956); Shelby T. McClay, *The Humanitarian Movement in Eighteenth Century France* (Louisville: University of Kentucky Press, 1957); Eleanor Flexner, *Century of Struggle: The Women's Rights Movement in the United States* (Cambridge: Harvard University Press, 1959); Hans Speier, "Historical Development of Public Opinion," *American Journal of Sociology,* 55 (January 1950) 376–388; Robert T. Bowers, "Opinion Research and Historical Interpretation of Elections," *Public Opinion Quarterly,* 12 (Fall 1948), 457–458.

44. Martin Buber, *Moses* (Oxford & London: East and West Library, 1956), pp. 13–19.

45. Among the few accounts that can be mentioned are: C. Wright Mills, *A Sociological Account of Some Aspects of Pragmatism* (unpublished Ph.D. thesis, University of Wisconsin, 1942); J. Brooks, *American Syndicalism: The I.W.W.* (New York: Macmillan, 1913); S. Perlman, *A History of Trade Unionism in the United States* (New York: Macmillan, 1937); Carl C. Taylor, *The Farmer's Movement* (American Book Company, 1952); Alvin Boskoff, Agrarian Ideology and the Farm Bloc (unpublished M.A. thesis, Columbia University, 1948); Arnold Hauser, *The Social History of Art,* 4 vols. (New York: Vintage Books, 1957, 1959); John Mueller, *The American Symphony: A Social History of Musical Taste* (Bloomington: Indiana University Press, 1951); Lloyd Morris, *Incredible New York: Highlights and Lowlights of the Last 100 Years* (New York: Random House, 1951); Adolph Tomars, *The Performing Arts in New York, 1880–1915: A Cultural and Biographical Study* (New York: forthcoming); Margaret Just Butcher and Allan Leroy Locke, *The Negro in American Culture* (New York: A. A. Knopf, 1956); D. C. Holton, *Modern Japan and Shinto Nationalism: A Study of Present-Day Trends in Japanese Religion* (Chicago: The University of Chicago Press, 1947); H. Richard Niebuhr, *The Social Sources of Denominationalism* (New

York: Holt, 1929); Benjamin E. Mays and J. W. Nicholson, *The Negro's Church* (New York: Institute of Social and Religious Research, 1933); A. H. Fausset, *Black Gods of the Metropolis* (Philadelphia: University of Pennsylvania Press, 1944); Marshall Sklare, *Conservative Judaism: An American Religious Movement* (New York: The Free Press of Glencoe, 1955); Nicholas Tavuchis, *Pastors and Immigrants: The Role of a Religious Elite in the Absorption of Norwegian Immigrants* (The Hague: Martinus Nijhoff, 1963); Thomas F. O'Dea, *The Mormons* (Chicago: The University of Chicago Press, 1957); James H. Barnett, *The American Christmas: A Study in National Culture* (New York: Macmillan, 1954); James H. Barnett, "The Easter Festival: A Study in Cultural Change," *American Sociological Review*, 14 (February 1949), 62–72. However, concerning festivals, a wider canvass would seem to be necessary; cf. Earl W. Count, *4000 Years of Christmas* (New York: Henry Schuman, 1948).

46. Concerning comparative sociological appraisal of the history of medical organization, see Joseph Ben-David, "Scientific Productivity and Academic Organization in Nineteenth Century Medicine," in this volume. Concerning social science development, an outstanding analysis may be found in Richard Hofstadter, *Social Darwinism in American Thought* (Philadelphia: University of Pennsylvania Press, 1944).

47. Two very different examples are Américo Castro, *The Structure of Spanish History* (Princeton: Princeton University Press, 1954) and Reinhard Bendix, *Work and Authority in Industry* (New York: John Wiley and Sons, 1956); excerpts from both works are reproduced in this volume.

48. Benjamin Nelson, *The Idea of Usury: From Tribal Otherhood to Universal Brotherhood* (Princeton: Princeton University Press, 1949); Leland Jenks, "Some Early Phases of the Management Movement," *Administrative Science Quarterly*, Vol. 5, No. 3 (December 1960), 421–447; Sigmund Diamond, *The Reputation of the American Businessman* (Cambridge: Harvard University Press, 1955).

49. Outstanding are the studies of Cochran and Miller. For example, Thomas C. Cochran and William Miller, *The Age of Enterprise: A Social History of Industrial America* (New York: Macmillan 1947); Thomas C. Cochran, *Railroad Leaders, 1845–1890: The Business Mind in Action* (Cambridge: Harvard University Press, 1953); Thomas C. Cochran, *The American Business System: A Historical Perspective, 1900–1955* (Cambridge: Harvard University Press, 1957); William Miller, *Men in Business, op. cit.;* compare also, Arthur H. Cole, *et al., Change and the Entrepreneur: Postulates and Patterns for Entrepreneurial History* (Cambridge: Harvard University Press, 1949); Louis M. Hacker, *The Triumph of American Capitalism: The Development of Forces in American History to the End of the Nineteenth Century* (New York: Columbia University Press, 1947); Oscar Handlin and Mary F. Handlin, "Origins of the American Business Corporation," *Journal of Economic History*, 5, 1945, 1–23; Irving G. Wyllie, *The Self-Made Man in America* (New Brunswick: Rutgers University Press, 1955); Richard B. Tennant, *The American Cigarette Industry* (New Haven: Yale University Press, 1950); Barry E. Supple, "A Business Elite: German-Jewish Financiers in Nineteenth-Century New York," *Business History Review*, XXXI, 2 (Summer 1957), 143–178; Bernard Bailyn, *The New England Merchants in the Seventeenth Century* (Cambridge: Harvard University Press, 1955).

50. Johan Huizinga, *Homo Ludens: A Study of the Play Element in Culture* (Boston: Beacon Press, 1950).

51. Kurt Mayer, "Developments in the Study of Population," *Social Research*, 29 (August 1962), 293–320; cf. Gerhard Mackenroth, *Bevölkerungslehre: Theorie, Soziologie und Statistik der Bevölkerung* (Berlin: Springer, 1953).

52. Julius Beloch, *Die Bevölkerung der Griechisch-römischen Welt* (Leipzig: Duncker & Humblot, 1886); J. C. Russell, "Demographic Pattern in History," *Population Studies*, 1, 4 (March 1948), 388–404, reprinted in Joseph J. Spengler and Otis Dudley Duncan, eds., *Demographic Analysis* (New York: The Free Press of Glencoe, 1956), pp. 147–161; J. C. Russell, "Late Ancient and Medieval Population," *Transactions of the American Philosophical Society*, 48, 3 (June 1958); J. C. Russell, *British Medieval Population* (Albuquerque: University of New Mexico Press, 1948); Sylvia L. Thrupp, "A Survey of the Alien Population in England in 1440," *Speculum*, Vol. XXXII, No. 2 (April 1957), 262–273; Arthur E. R. Boak, *Manpower Shortage and the Fall of the Roman Empire in the West* (Ann Arbor: University of Michigan Press, 1955); John M. Durand, "Mortality Estimates from Roman Tombstone Inscriptions," *American Journal of Sociology*, 65 (January 1960), 365–373; William Petersen, *Population* (New York: Macmillan, 1961), Chaps. 13, 14, and literature mentioned therein; John T. Krause, "Some Implications of Recent Work in Historical Demography," *Comparative Studies in Society and History*, 1 (1958–1959), 164–188; Kingsley Davis, "The Origin and Growth of Urbanization in the World," *American Journal of Sociology*, 60, 5, 429–437; David C. Marsh, *The Changing Social Structure of England and Wales, 1871–1955* (New York: Humanities Press, 1958); Ping-ti Ho, *Studies on the Population of China, 1386–1953* (Cambridge: Harvard University Press, 1959); Gonzalo Aguirre Beltran, *La Poblacion Negra de Mexico, 1519–1810* (Mexico, D. F.: Editiones Fuente Cultural, 1946).

53. Petersen, *op. cit.*, Chaps. 11, 13, 16; Rupert B. Vance, *All These People* (Chapel Hill: University of North Carolina Press, 1945), Part I.

54. The cycle theories of Robert E. Park, E. S. Bogardus, William O. Brown, and Clarence E. Glick are summarized in Brewton Berry, *Race and Ethnic Relations* (Boston: Houghton Mifflin, 1958), Chap. 6. Amazingly—considering the historical record—Berry's is the only race relations text that deals with "annihilation and expulsion" as likely consequences of contact and conflict, *op. cit.*, Chap. 7. The outstanding account of the most recent genocide is Raoul Hilberg's *The Destruction of the European Jews* (Chicago: Quadrangle Books, 1961).

55. This idea, which is clearly historical in nature, has been expressed in Herbert Blumer's "Reflections on the Theory of Race Relations," in Andrew W. Lind, ed., *Race Relations in World Perspective* (Honolulu: University of Hawaii Press, 1955), Chap. 1.

56. Stanley Lieberson, "Theory of Race and Ethnic Relations," *American Sociological Review*, 26 (December 1961), 902–909.

57. Two publications contain much of the literature prior to 1945, but not much of the newer literature: Edgar T. Thompson and Alma M. Thompson, *Race and Region: A Descriptive Bibliography Compiled with Special Reference to the Relations between Whites and Negroes in the United States* (Chapel Hill: University of North Carolina Press, 1949) and Edgar T. Thompson and Everett C. Hughes, *Race: Individual and Collective Behavior* (New York: The Free Press of Glencoe, 1958). Compare, however, Andrew W. Lind, *op. cit.* Concerning the historical and sociological approaches to race relations, see the papers by Michael Banton, H. S. Deighton, and Philipp Mason in *Race—The Journal of the Institute of*

Race Relations, London, Vol. 1, No. 1 (November 1959). Concerning structure and attitude, see Roy Harvey Pearce, *The Savages of America: A Study of the Indians and the Idea of Civilization* (Baltimore: Johns Hopkins Press, 1953); Rupert B. Vance, *Human Factors in Cotton Culture: A Study in the Human Geography of the American South* (Chapel Hill: University of North Carolina Press, 1929); Frank Tannenbaum, *Slave and Citizen: The Negro in the Americas* (New York: A. A. Knopf, 1947); Werner J. Cahnman, "Mediterranean and Caribbean Regions: A Comparison in Race and Culture Contacts," *Social Forces,* 22 (December 1943), 209–214; Donald Pierson, *Negroes in Brazil* (Chicago: The University of Chicago Press, 1942); G. William Skinner, *Chinese Society in Thailand: An Analytical History* (Ithaca: Cornell University Press, 1957); Raymond T. Smith, *British Guiana* (New York: Oxford University Press, 1962); Werner J. Cahnman, "France in Algeria," *The Review of Politics,* 7 (July 1945), 343–357; Theodore W. Sprague, "The Rivalry of Intolerances in Race Relations," *Social Forces,* 28 (October 1949), 68–76. Concerning structure and ideology, an indispensable base, although only for the study of one problem, is indicated in James Parkes, *The Conflict of the Church and the Synagogue: A Study of the Origin of Anti-Semitism* (London: Soncino Press, 1934) and James Parkes, *The Jew in the Medieval Community: A Study of His Political and Economic Situation* (London: Soncino Press, 1938). Compare further: Werner J. Cahnman, "Die wirtschaftlichen und gesellschaftlichen Ursachen der Judenfeindschaft," in Franz Boehm and Walter Dirks, eds., *Das Judentum in Geschichte und Gegenwart* (Wiesbaden: Franz Steiner Verlag, 1965), as well as the shorter version, "Socio-Economic Causes of Anti-Semitism," *Social Problems,* 5, 1 (July 1957), 21–29; Paul Massing, *Rehearsal for Destruction: A Study of Political Anti-Semitism in Imperial Germany* (New York: Harper & Bros., 1949); Eva Reichmann, *Hostages of Civilization: The Social Sources of National-Socialist Anti-Semitism* (Boston: The Beacon Press, 1951); John Higham, "Anti-Semitism in the Gilded Age," *The Mississippi Valley Historical Review,* XLIII, 4 (March 1957), 559–578; cf. Christen T. Jonassen, "Some Historical and Theoretical Bases of Racism in Northwestern Europe," *Social Forces,* 30 (December 1951), 155–161. The same problem, regarding the American Negro, is admirably summarized in C. Vann Woodward. *The Strange Career of Jim Crow* (New York: Oxford University Press, 1955); the preceding period is analyzed in W. E. B. Du Bois, *Black Reconstruction* (New York: Harcourt, Brace, 1935). For South Africa, see Leopold Marquand, *The Peoples and Policies of South Africa* (New York: Oxford University Press, 1952); for Brazil, Gilberto Freyre, *The Masters and the Slaves, op. cit.*

58. The classic source is Ludwig Gumplowicz, *Der Rassenkampf* (Innsbruck: Universitaetsverlag Wagner, 1883); cf. Ludwig Gumplowicz, *Outlines of Sociology,* transl. by Irving L. Horowitz (New York: Paine-Whitman, 1963); cf. also Franz Oppenheimer's more optimistic treatment of the same topic in *Der Staat* (Frankfurt: Rütten & Löning, 1907), English transl. by John M. Gitterman, *The State* (Indianapolis: Bobbs-Merrill, 1914). As against the stress on origin and development by Gumplowicz and Oppenheimer, compare the stress on purpose and function in M. L. Finley, "Was Greek Civilization Based on Slave Labour?" in *Historia,* VIII (Wiesbaden: Franz Steiner Verlag, April 1959), 145–164.

Author and Name Index

This index is constructed to serve also as a bibliography. Therefore, all full bibliographic page citations are followed by an *n*. Consequently, the Author and Name Index is more extensive than is usually the case. Quotations of a topical nature, however, are selective.

Subject Index

DATE DUE

MAR 10 '71			
MAR 12 '71			
JAN 22 '75			
DEC 20 '76			
GAYLORD			PRINTED IN U.S.A.